social
cognition

social cognition

SUSAN T. FISKE

Carnegie-Mellon University

SHELLEY E. TAYLOR

University of California at Los Angeles

ADDISON-WESLEY PUBLISHING COMPANY

Reading, Massachusetts
Menlo Park, California
London • Amsterdam • Don Mills, Ontario • Sydney

TOPICS IN SOCIAL PSYCHOLOGY

Charles A. Kiesler
Series Editor

Quotation on page 242 is published with the permission of the copyright owner of the Sir Arthur Conan Doyle literary estate.

Library of Congress Cataloging in Publication Data

Fiske, Susan T.
    Social cognition.

    Bibliography: p.
    Includes index.
    1. Social perception.   2. Cognition. I. Taylor,
Shelley E.   II. Title.
HM 132.F573   1984   302'.12   83-21458
ISBN 0-201-11501-8

38,794

ABCDEFGHIJ-AL-8987654

To Bob and Mervyn

The series *Topics in Social Psychology* is directed toward the student with no prior background in social psychology. Taken as a whole, the series covers the ever-expanding field of social psychology reasonably well, but

foreword

a major advantage of the series is that each individual book was written by well-known scholars in the area. The instructor can select a subset of the books to make up the course in social psychology, the particular subset depending on the instructor's own definition of our field. The original purpose of this series was to provide such freedom for the instructor while maintaining a thoughtful and expert treatment of each topic. In addition, the first editions of the series have been widely used in a variety of other ways: as supplementary reading in nonpsychology courses; to introduce more advanced courses in psychology; or for the sheer fun of peeking at recent developments in social psychology.

We have developed second editions that serve much the same purpose. Each book is somewhat longer and more open in design, uses updated materials, and in general takes advantage of constructive feedback from colleagues and students across the country. So many people found the first editions of the individual books useful that we have tried to make the second editions even more thorough and complete and therefore more easily separated from the rest of the series.

This volume is the first addition to the series since its original conception. During the last decade or so, the topic of social cognition has developed at a very rapid rate. In an interesting and informative volume, Fiske and Taylor describe both the sense of intellectual excitement and the burgeoning growth of research in this important area.

Charles A. Kiesler

preface

Not long ago, virtually every psychological convention had its requisite number of symposia on the decline and despair of social psychology. Lately, the crisis has passed, and two factors help account for it. First, many researchers have moved out of the laboratory and its experimental paradigms into field research on practical problems. Social psychology has a long tradition of applied research, but the latest trend has been especially useful in providing perspectives on theory and problems often initiated in the laboratory. What makes this current trend toward field research so important is the two-way street between field and laboratory. All too often, theory has gone in one direction, from lab to field, but now researchers increasingly recognize the power of field settings to refine theory, to suggest new parameters and hypotheses, and to qualify laboratory-based induction.

A second reason for the vanishing crisis, one that is not unrelated to the first, is the advent of social cognition. The recent cognitive approaches have contributed to every area of social psychology, including attitudes, small groups, impression formation, stereotypes, close relationships, and self-concept, to name a few. "Cognitive" is not just a name for the approach; cognitive ideas have transformed the methodology of social psychology. Techniques for the measurement and manipulation of cognitions are ubiquitous. In addition, there has been a corresponding change in metatheory. It is not just that social psychologists have imported specific theories from cognitive psychology; rather, the specification of mental organization and processes is seen as not only tractable but necessary.

This book is designed to provide a critical overview of the theories and methods in the newly emerging field of social cognition. The major theme of this book is that normal cognitive processes account for much of how people understand themselves and others. By itself, this may seem a dry abstraction, but the basic and applied research payoffs have been substantial. In basic research, social cognition theories of attribution, psychological control, social schemata, attention, person memory, and social inference have become central to the field. In a recent poll, social psychologists predicted that topics within a cognitive approach would be the most popular research area in the coming decade (Lewicki, 1982).

Colleagues outside of basic social psychology have quickly picked up social cognition theories and methods, applying them to research on health, law, marketing, education, organizations, politics, therapy, and more. For example, in health psychology, it is increasingly recognized that the perception of personal control is critical to coping with stress and medical treatment. In the psychology of law, many people now think that eyewitnesses' memory for a criminal's face is frequently biased. And in the psychology of marketing, it is now believed that the most vivid, eye-catching ads are not inherently more persuasive than pallid ones. Throughout this book, such applications of social cognition research are featured.

On a more personal note, writing this book has been an occasion for social affect as well as social cognitions. In reviewing a decade's research, we have felt intense pride and stunned admiration for the accomplishments of our colleagues. We also sometimes have felt frustrated and discouraged at the all-too-common pitfalls in the field. On balance, nevertheless, it has been exciting and edifying. We hope the book is as scholarly and entertaining as the field it reviews.

Pittsburgh, Pennsylvania   S. T. F.
Los Angeles, California   S. E. T.
December 1983

We are indeed grateful
to the many individuals   **_acknowledgments_**
who have participated
in this book's creation.
Our secretaries, Muriel

Fleishman, Alex Pinkston, and Garrett Gafford, have been full partners in the tedious process of translating scribble into manuscript; their patience and good humor were priceless. Charles Kiesler originally suggested the book, then generously encouraged, critiqued, and listened throughout its development. Our insightful colleagues who tirelessly reviewed the entire book improved it immeasurably: Douglas McCann, Thomas Ostrom, and Michael Ross. And the perceptive comments of numerous others have been a huge help; they are Robert Abelson, John Anderson, Gema Barkanic, Ann Beattie, Eugene Borgida, Nancy Brekke, John Cacioppo, Charles Carver, Margaret Clark, Shelly Chaiken, Preston Covey, Kay Deaux, Linda Dyer, Alice Eagly, Ralph Erber, Constance Hammen, Tory Higgins, Donald Homa, William Ickes, James Kulik, Richard Lau, John Lingle, Patricia Linville, James March, Karen Matthews, Leslie McArthur, Sandra Milberg, Richard Moreland, Mark Pavelchak, Richard Petty, Felicia Pratto, Barbara Ripley, Daniel Romer, Michael Scheier, Mark Snyder, William Swann, Suzanne Thompson, Bernard Weiner, Joanne Wood, Wendy Wood, and Mark Zanna. At the end, Priscilla Battis's rapid, painstaking work on the index was a godsend. Finally, the support of Barbara Fiske, Donald Fiske, Joseph Hinchcliffe, and Charles Taylor has meant more to us than words can tell. None of these people is liable for our errors and omissions; unfortunately, those are all our own. We hope they are minimal.

contents

1

part one:
elements of
social cognition

social schemata 139

part two:
processes in
social cognition

attention 184

person memory 213

social inference *246*

10

*designing research in
social cognition* *285*

*part three:
beyond cognition*

affect *310*

12

*attitudes: cognition
and persuasion 340*

13

behavior 369

14

conclusion 400

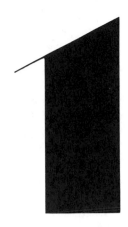

Try telling someone at a party that you are a psychologist or even that you are simply studying psychology. It does no good to say you do research and do not read minds. The inevitable

introduction

reaction is either that the person draws back in horror of being analyzed on the spot or that the person leans over to disclose all sorts of intimate secrets. One psychologist we know avoids these situations by claiming to be a computer programmer. We have hit upon a different strategy, which is to say calmly, "I study how people make first impressions on strangers." That is a real conversation stopper.

Suppose, however, that the conversation did not end right there. Suppose the person began to talk about what makes people tick, about his or her impressions of various friends, relatives, and strangers at the party. That would be the kind of raw data with which this book is concerned. Social cognition is the study of how people make sense of other people and themselves. It focuses on how ordinary people think about people and how they think they think about people.

People's understanding of the social world can be studied, first, by *asking* them how they make sense of others (Heider, 1958). This is the route of phenomenology: to describe systematically how ordinary people say they experience their world. If people are right, one can build formal theories by making their insights scientific, by pulling together patterns across many people's intuitions. Even if people are wrong, one can study people's common-sense theories in and of themselves; how people think, not their accuracy, is the phenomenon of interest. Social cognition research is concerned, second, with commonsense theory or "naive psychology" for its own sake. That is, people's everyday theories about each other are themselves interesting objects to study. Thus, if the person at the party has some ideas about how people form impressions of each other, the person's informal ideas are interesting in their own right. Hence, commonsense psychology is useful for two reasons.

Research on social cognition also goes beyond naive psychology. The study of social cognition entails a fine-grained analysis of how people think about themselves and others, and it leans heavily on the theory and methods of

1

cognitive psychology. The influx of fine-grained or detailed models from cognitive psychology is one of the hallmarks of the current approaches to social cognition. Cognitive psychology's models are important because they precisely describe mechanisms of learning and thinking that apply in a wide variety of areas, perhaps including social perception. Because these models are general and because cognitive processes presumably influence social behavior heavily, it makes sense to adapt cognitive theory to social settings.

Both the naive psychology viewpoint and the cognitive viewpoint are important themes in social cognition research. These two viewpoints also characterize the double appeal of social cognition: the entertaining part of studying how people think about others is its appeal to your intuitions; it resembles what is fun and absorbing about sitting around with a friend after midnight, speculating about human nature. The fine-grained part forces you to be accurate and precise; its appeal resembles that of a favorite intricate puzzle. Whether your taste runs to crosswords, math games, jigsaw puzzles, mystery novels, or Rubik's Cube, there is considerable pleasure in getting all the pieces to fit.

Approaches to Studying the Social Thinker

Two broad intellectual approaches to the study of social cognition—elemental and holistic—can be traced to psychology's origins in philosophy, and knowing something of social cognition's intellectual history will give perspective to its current efforts. The elemental approach is characterized by breaking scientific problems down into pieces and analyzing the pieces in separate detail before combining them. The holistic approach is characterized by analyzing the pieces in the context of other pieces and focusing on the entire configuration of relationships among them. The distinction will become clearer as the two approaches are described.

THE ELEMENTAL ORIGINS OF SOCIAL COGNITION RESEARCH

Until the beginning of this century, psychology was a branch of philosophy, and philosophers provided some basic principles of mind that still carry weight today (Boring, 1950). In the elemental tradition of the British philosophers, the mind is likened to chemistry, in which ideas are the elements. Any concept, whether concrete like "salt" or abstract like "shame," is a basic element. Any element can be associated with any other element. The bonds between concepts create mental chemistry (Locke, 1690/1979).

In the elemental view, ideas first come from our sensations and perceptions. Then they are associated by contiguity in space and time (Hume, 1739/1978). That is, if salt is next to pepper on the table, the two can become a unit through contiguity. Repetition is the key to moving from simple contiguity to a mental compound (Hartley, 1749/1966). If salt and pepper are on the table together every day of your life, then when you think of salt you will automatically think of pepper. Salt-and-pepper becomes a mental "compound." Similarly, if the concept "professor" often comes up (on television, for example) at the same time as the concept "absentminded," they are likely to be associated simply as a function of repeated pairings. People consciously use the principles of repetition and contiguity in daily life, too; think of the last time you attempted to memorize the seven contiguous digits of a phone number by repeating them until they became a unit. Frequency of repetition is a major factor that determines the strength of an association (J. Mill, 1869; J. S. Mill, 1843/1974).[1]

Around the turn of the century, psychology began to emerge as a discipline separate from philosophy, and at that time the notions of mental chemistry were first put to empirical test. The first laboratory psychologists, such as Wilhelm Wundt and Hermann Ebbinghaus, trained themselves and their graduate students to observe their own thought processes: to introspect on how they committed ideas to memory and on how they retrieved ideas from memory (Ebbinghaus, 1885/1964; Wundt, 1897). Their method was to analyze experience into its elements, to determine how they connect, and to determine the laws that govern the connections. These themes that started with the British philosophers continue to form the basis of modern experimental psychology. Shortly, we will see how the elemental approach is currently represented within the study of social cognition.

THE HOLISTIC ORIGINS OF SOCIAL COGNITION RESEARCH

In reaction to the elemental approach, the German philosopher Immanuel Kant (1781/1969) argued for an emphasis on tackling the whole mind at once. In his view of the mind, mental phenomena are inherently subjective. That is, the mind actively constructs a reality that goes beyond the original thing in and of itself. A bunch of grapes is perceived as a unit, but that perception is a construction of the mind. Perceiving a "bowl of grapes" differs from perceiving each individual grape separately. Similarly, if someone cuts off some grapes and the remaining ones topple out of the bowl, the two movements are perceived as linked in a cause-effect relationship. Again, that perception is furnished by the mind; it is not inherent in the stimulus. The intellect organizes the world, creating perceptual order from the properties of the surrounding field.

Gestalt psychology drew on these initial holistic insights (Koffka, 1935; Kohler, 1938/1976). In contrast to analysis into elements, psychologists who use Gestalt methods first describe the phenomenon of interest, the immediate experience of perception, without analysis. This method, called phenomenology, focuses on systematically describing people's experience of perceiving and thinking. It later became one of the major foundations of social cognition research: the reliance on asking people how they make sense of the world.

---

1. Other principles of association were proposed at various times and then dropped in favor of repeated contiguity. These included similarity and causality as creating associations, and vividness as strengthening associations (Boring, 1950).

Although both the elemental and holistic groups drew on introspections, Gestalt psychologists focused on people's experience of dynamic wholes, and elementalists focused on the expert's ability to break the whole into pieces. As an illustration of the difference between Gestalt and elemental approaches, think of a song in your mind. A song can be perceived as a series of individual notes (elemental) or as a melody that emerges from the relationships among the notes (Gestalt). The emergent structure is lost by analyzing it into its sensory elements, in the Gestalt view. Gestalt psychologists saw the mental chemistry metaphor of the elementalists as misguided because a chemical compound has properties not predictable from its isolated elements. Similarly, the perceptual whole has properties not discernible from the isolated parts. For example, the note middle C can seem high in the context of many lower notes or low in the context of many higher notes, but it would not stand out at all in the context of other notes close to it. Psychological meaning goes beyond raw sensory parts to include the organization people impose on the whole.

Kurt Lewin (1951) imported Gestalt ideas to social psychology and ultimately to social cognition research (Boring, 1950; Bronfenbrenner, 1977; Deutsch, 1968). Like other Gestalt psychologists, Lewin focused on the person's own subjective perceptions, not on "objective" analysis. He emphasized the influence of the social environment *as perceived by the individual*, which he called the "psychological field." A full understanding of a person's psychological field thus cannot result from an "objective" description by others of what surrounds the person. The crucial factor is the person's own interpretation. This is not to say that the person can necessarily verbalize his or her perceived environment, but that the person's own reports typically provide better clues than do the researcher's intuitions. For instance, a researcher may objectively report that Barb complimented Ann on her appearance. The researcher may even have strong hunches about why Barb did it. But Ann's reaction will depend on her own perception of Barb's intent: ingratiation, envy, reassurance, or innocent friendliness. A prime way to find that out is to ask Ann to describe what happened in her own terms. Just as in Gestalt psychology generally, then, Lewin emphasized the individual's phenomenology, the individual's construction of the situation.

Another theme imported from Gestalt psychology to social psychology was Lewin's insistence on describing the total situation, not its isolated elements. A person exists within a psychological field that is a *configuration of forces*. One must understand all the psychological forces operating on the person in any given situation in order to predict anything. For example, some forces might motivate one to study (an upcoming exam, the sight of one's roommate studying), but other forces might motivate one to spend the evening another way (a group of friends suggesting a movie). No one force predicts action, but the dynamic equilibrium among them—the everchanging balance of forces—does predict action.

The total psychological field (and hence behavior) is determined by two pairs of factors. The first pair consists of the *person* in the *situation*. Neither alone is sufficient to predict behavior. The person contributes needs, beliefs, perceptual abilities, and more. These act on the environment to constitute the psychological field. Thus, to know that a particular person is motivated to study does not predict whether or how much he or she will study. But a motivated person in a library is extremely likely to study a lot. Ever since Lewin, social psychologists have seen both the person and the situation as essential to predicting behavior. The study of social cognition focuses on perceiving, thinking, and remembering as a function of who and where one is.

A second pair of factors cut across the psychological field to determine what behavior will be; they are *cognition* and *motivation*. Both are joint functions of person and situation. Both are essential to predicting behavior. Cognition provides the perceiver's own interpretation of the world; without clear cognitions, behavior is not predictable. If a person has incomplete cognitions or confused cognition about a new setting, behavior will be unstable. For example, if you do not have the foggiest cognition about what an upcoming exam in music composition will be like, you may behave erratically and hence unpredictably; you may try several study strategies, none of them very systematically. Cognitions help determine *what* a person will do, which direction behavior will take. If a musician friend explains what composition exams typically contain, your cognitions and hence your studying will settle down along the lines laid out. But this assumes that you actually do study. The second feature of the psychological field is motivation; its strength predicts *whether* the behavior will occur at all and, if it does, how much of it will occur. Knowing what to do does not mean you will do it; cognition alone is not enough. Motivations provide the motor for behavior.

To summarize, Lewin focuses his analysis on psychological reality as perceived by the individual; on confronting a whole configuration of forces, not single elements; on the person and situation; and on cognition and motivation. These major themes that date back through Gestalt psychology to Kant are theoretical points that still survive in modern approaches to social cognition, as well as in psychology as a whole.

CONCLUSION

We have characterized the historical origin of current approaches to social cognition as a contrast between the elemental and the holistic viewpoints. The elemental approach aims to build up from the bottom, combining smaller pieces into larger ones until the whole puzzle is assembled. The piecemeal nature of this approach contrasts sharply with the holistic nature of the Gestalt alternative. To describe a person's active construction of reality, in the holistic view, it is necessary to tackle the entire configuration as seen by the perceiver. The tension between the elemental and configural or holistic approaches will surface again. The score, however, is perpetually tied. In direct confrontations, both sides often can account for the other's data.[2] It is ultimately more useful

---

2.   For examples of such controversies that can be interpreted essentially as a debate between

for each side to develop its own theories in as much detail as possible, attempting to assimilate evidence and criticism from the other side, and modifying the theory where it is proved wrong. An integration of the two approaches probably is superior to either one alone. There are no dominant solutions, then, merely different but complementary approaches to common continuing problems. The central issues of both elemental and Gestalt theories are how to understand structures and processes occurring inside the mind.

The Ebb and Flow of Cognition in Psychology

Psychologists have not always agreed that it is important to get inside the mind. The study of cognition has received both good and bad reviews over time. To prevent an overly myopic view of the importance of cognition, we will take a brief look at its place in experimental and social psychology. Early psychologists, whether elemental or holistic, relied heavily on introspection as a central tool for understanding human thought. As we will see, however, introspection developed a bad reputation, and with it cognition fell into disrepute. Experimental psychology rejected cognition for many years, while social psychology did not. The next two sections present the contrasting histories of cognition in the two subfields, experimental and social psychology.

COGNITION IN EXPERIMENTAL PSYCHOLOGY

Wundt's work at the dawn of empirical psychology, as already described, relied heavily on trained introspection.[3] The use of introspection was linked to the fact that Wundt's goal was emphatically cognitive: people's experience was the subject matter of interest. Wundt and others gathered data about mental events and constructed theories to account for those data. However, introspection was ultimately abandoned as a methodology in experimental psychology because it did not conform to the principles appropriate to scientific investigation. By usual scientific standards, both theory and data should be publicly reproduceable. Other scientists ought to be able to examine the data, and they should be able to decide how much the data fit the specific theory. In early experimental psychology, theories were required to account for introspections (i.e., self-observations), and therein lay the problem. If the criteria for a theory's success depended on private experience, the evidence could not be produced in public. The research could not be checked by others. The most absurd version of the problem would be this: if my theory accounts

---

holistic and elemental approaches, see Chapter 6, p. 142, and Ostrom, 1977, or Chapter 8, pp. 222-223, and J. R. Anderson, 1978.

3.   He also took measures that did not rely on people's own reports of their internal processes; for example, he also emphasized the measurement of reaction time, which is the time between stimulus and response. If you ask me how old I am, I can respond instantly. If you ask me how old my brother is, I have to calculate it, and that takes longer. Thus, from reaction time one could infer more or less intervening thought. Such measures supplemented introspective data.

for my introspections and your theory accounts for yours, how do we decide who is right?

When introspection was abandoned because of problems such as this, the study of cognition was neglected too. There was a shift away from studying internal (cognitive) processes and toward external, publicly observable events. The ultimate development of this approach was American behaviorist psychology in the early decades of this century. Behaviorists held that only overt, measurable acts are sufficiently valid objects for empirical scrutiny. One of the founders of this approach was Edward L. Thorndike. B. F. Skinner and others further developed Thorndike's work. For example, Thorndike's theory of instrumental learning (1940) held no place for cognition. According to the theory, behavior has certain rewarding and punishing effects, which cause the organism to repeat or avoid the behavior later. In short, "the effect becomes a cause." Both effect and cause are observable, and cognition is thought to be irrelevant (Skinner, 1963). One behaviorist even called the idea of cognition a superstition (Watson, 1930).

Behaviorists argue that specifying an observable stimulus (S) and response (R) for every part of one's theory is the strict scientific discipline necessary to the advancement of psychology, including social psychology (Berger & Lambert, 1968). For example, a behaviorist might approach the topic of racial and ethnic discrimination by noting that some children are punished for playing with children of certain other ethnic groups and rewarded for playing with children of the family's own ethnic group. A simplified model of this would include "the other ethnic group" as the stimulus and "not playing together" as the response. A behaviorist would not consider the possible role of stereotyping (cognition). In experimental psychology generally, one net effect of behaviorism was that the role of cognition fell into disrepute for about half a century and behaviorist theories dominated.

Several events caused experimental psychologists to take a fresh interest in cognition during the 1960s (J. R. Anderson, 1980a). First, linguists criticized the failure of the stimulus-response framework's attempts to account for language (cf. Chomsky, 1959, criticizing Skinner, 1957). It became clear that the complex, symbolic, and uniquely human phenomenon of language would not easily yield to behaviorist approaches.

Second, a new approach called information processing arose out of work on how people acquire knowledge and skills (Broadbent, 1958). Information processing refers to the idea that mental operations can be broken down into sequential stages. If you ask me when my niece was born, I think back to the circumstances surrounding the event and recall that it was August 1979. An information-processing theory might represent my cognitive operations as: understand the question's meaning → search for information on that topic → verify answer → state answer. The point of an information-processing theory is that one tries to specify the steps intervening *between* stimulus (question) and response (answer). From this point of view, the important feature is the sequential processing of information. Information-processing approaches entail the effort to specify cognitive processes, which behaviorists would not do.

New scientific tools have developed that allow cognitive psychologists to trace the nonobservable processes presumed to intervene between stimulus and response. The most important of these tools is the computer, which has become a methodological tool as well as a theoretical metaphor. It serves as a tool in that cognitive scientists actually use computers to simulate human cognitive processes; they write complex programs that play chess, learn geometry, and summarize the news (J. R. Anderson, 1976; Newell & Simon, 1972; Schank & Abelson, 1977). The computer is also a metaphor in that it provides a framework and a jargon for characterizing mental processes; psychologists talk about input-output operations or memory storage and retrieval, with respect to human cognition. More important, most current theory builds on the idea that human cognition resembles computer information processing in important ways. So far, the metaphoric impact of computers has probably been greater than its actual use as a simulation tool in psychology generally.

To summarize, experimental psychology began with introspection as a legitimate method for gaining insight into thinking and cognition as a legitimate focus for theory. Behaviorists virtually eliminated such techniques and concerns for decades, and cognition fell into disrepute. Recently, cognitive psychology has re-emerged as a scientifically legitimate pursuit (J. R. Anderson, 1980a; Neisser, 1967; D. A. Norman, 1976).

COGNITION IN SOCIAL PSYCHOLOGY

In contrast to experimental psychology, social psychology has consistently leaned on cognitive concepts, even when most psychology was behaviorist. Social psychology has always been cognitive in at least three ways. First, since Lewin, social psychologists have decided that social behavior is more usefully understood as a function of people's perceptions of their world, rather than as a function of objective descriptions of their stimulus environment (Manis, 1977; Zajonc, 1980a). For example, an objective reward like money or praise that people perceive as a bribe or as flattery will influence them differently than a reward they perceive as without manipulative intent. What predicts their reaction, then, is their perception, not simply the giver's actions.

Other people can influence a person's actions without even being present, which is the ultimate reliance on perceptions to the exclusion of objective stimuli. Thus someone may react to a proffered bribe or to flattery by imagining the reactions of others ("What would my mother say?" "What will my friends think?"). Of course, such thoughts are totally the person's own fantasies, having perhaps tenuous connection to objective reality. Thus the *causes* of social behavior are doubly cognitive; our perceptions of others actually present and our imagination of their presence both predict behavior (cf. G. W. Allport, 1954).[4]

---

4. One might well ask, what is the logical alternative to this approach? Who does research on reactions to the objective as opposed to cognized world? The answer is behaviorists, as described, and some perceptual theorists (Gibson, 1966; see Chapter 7).

Social psychologists view not only causes, but also the end *result* of social perception and interaction in heavily cognitive terms, and this is a second way in which social psychology has always been cognitive. Thought often comes before feeling and behaving as the main reaction that social researchers measure. A person may worry about a bribe (thought), hate the idea (feeling), and reject it (behavior), but social psychologists often mainly ask: "What do you think about it?" Even when they focus on behavior and feelings, their questions are often "What do you intend to do?" and "How would you label your feeling?" These arguably are not behavior and feelings but cognitions about them. Thus social psychological causes are largely cognitive, and the results are largely cognitive.

A third way in which social psychology has always been cognitive is that the person in between the presumed cause and the result is viewed as a *thinking organism*; this view contrasts with viewing the person as an emotional organism or a mindless automaton (Manis, 1977). Many social psychological theories paint a portrait of the typical person as reasoning (perhaps badly) before acting. In attempting to deal with complex human problems, as social psychology always has, complex mental processes seem essential. How else can one account for stereotyping and prejudice, propaganda and persuasion, altruism and aggression, and more? It is hard to imagine where a narrowly behaviorist theory would even begin. A strict stimulus-response (S-R) theory does not include the thinking organism that seems essential to account for such problems. In several senses, then, social psychology contrasts with strict S-R theories in its reliance on S-O-R theories that include stimulus, organism, and response. Consequently, the thinker, who comes in between stimulus and response, has always been paramount in social psychology.

The social thinker has taken many guises in recent decades of research. These guises describe the various roles of cognition in social psychology. Besides the varied roles of cognition, motivation has played different roles in the view of the social thinker. Keeping in mind these two components, cognition and motivation, we can identify three general views of the thinker in social psychology (S. E. Taylor, 1981): consistency seeker, naive scientist, and cognitive miser.

The first view emerged from the massive quantities of work on attitude change after World War II. In the late 1950s, several theories were proposed, and they shared some crucial basic assumptions. The consistency theories, as they were called, viewed people as consistency seekers motivated by perceived discrepancies among their cognitions (e.g., Festinger, 1957; Heider, 1958; see Abelson *et al.*, 1968, for an overview). For example, if David knows he is on a diet and knows that he has just eaten a hot fudge sundae, he must do some thinking to bring those two cognitions into line.

Chapter 12 ("Attitudes") will deal more thoroughly with consistency theories, but for the moment two points are crucial. First, these theories relied on perceived inconsistency, which places cognitive activity in a central role. For example, if would-be dieters can convince themselves that one splurge will not matter, eating a sundae is not inconsistent for them. Objective inconsistency, then, is not important. Subjective inconsistency—among various cognitions or among feelings and cognitions—is central to these theories. Actual inconsistency that is not perceived as such does not yield psychological inconsistency.

Second, once inconsistency *is* perceived, the person is presumed to feel uncomfortable (a negative drive state) and to be motivated to reduce the inconsistency. Reducing the aversive drive state is a pleasant relief, rewarding in itself. This sort of motivational model is called a drive reduction model. Less formally, the sundae-consuming dieter will not be free from anxiety until he manufactures some excuse. Hence consistency theories posit that people change their attitudes and beliefs for motivational reasons, because of unmet needs for consistency. In sum, motivation and cognition both were central to the consistency theories.

Consistency theories ceased to dominate the field, ironically, as they proliferated, partly because the variants on a theme became indistinguishable. Moreover, it was difficult to predict what a person would perceive as inconsistent and to what degree, and which route to resolving inconsistency a person would take. Finally, people do in fact tolerate a fair amount of inconsistency, so the motivation to avoid it—as an overriding principle—was called into doubt (cf. Kiesler, Collins, & Miller, 1969).

Research in social cognition began in the early 1970s, and with it two new models of the thinker emerged. Cognition and motivation played rather different roles in these two models, compared to the roles they played in the consistency seeker model. In both new cases, motivation is secondary in importance to cognition. Both views are central to social cognition research, and they will be covered in more detail throughout the book. At present, however, a brief look is useful.

The first new model within the framework of social cognition research is the *naive scientist*, who works to uncover the causes of people's behavior. Attribution theories concern how people explain their own and other people's behavior; they came to the forefront of research in the early 1970s (see Chapters 2-4). Attribution theories describe people's causal analyses of or attributions about the social world. For example, an attribution can address whether someone's behavior seems to be caused by the external situation or by the person's internal disposition. If you want to know why your acquaintance Bruce snapped at you one morning, it would be important to decide if there were mitigating circumstances (his girlfriend left him; you just backed into his car) or if he has an irritable disposition (he always behaves this way and to everyone).

Attribution theorists at first assumed that people are fairly rational in distinguishing among various potential causes, as we will see in subsequent chapters. In part, this was a purposeful theoretical strategy designed to push a rational view of people as far as possible, in order to discover its shortcomings. The theories started with the working hypothesis that, given enough time, people resemble naive scientists, who will gather all the relevant data and arrive at the most logical conclusion. In this view, you would think about your friend's behavior in a variety of settings and carefully weigh the evidence for a situational cause or a dispositional cause of his behavior. Thus the role of cognition in the naive scientist model is as an outcome of fairly rational analysis.

If you are wrong about why Bruce was irritable, the early theories would have viewed your error as an emotion-based departure from the normal process or as a simple error in available information. For example, if you attribute Bruce's unpleasant behavior to his irritable disposition, it may be because you are motivated to avoid the idea that he is angry at you. Hence errors arise, mainly as interference from nonrational motivations. In the early attribution theories, motivation enters mainly as a potential qualification on the usual process.

Recall that in consistency theories, in contrast, motivation drives the whole system. The role of motivation in consistency theories is quite central; it acts as an aversive drive state that persists until inconsistencies are resolved. Attribution theorists traditionally have not viewed unresolved attributions as causing an aversive drive state. Motivations for predicting and controlling one's social world (see Chapter 5, "Psychological Control") presumably set attributions in motion; in that sense, motivation does help to catalyze the attribution process, just as it catalyzes the entire consistency-seeking process. Nevertheless, motivation is far more explicit in consistency theories than in attribution theories.

The usual attributional process, then, is viewed as a quasi-scientific cognitive analysis of causes, with an occasional motivation-based departure. As such, attribution theories at first set forth a prescriptive or *normative* model: what sensible people ought to do, given complete data and full leisure. Under some circumstances, people clearly do proceed as attribution theories suggest, and the theories have led to quantities of research, as will be seen in Chapters 2-4. Much of this research views the person as a naive scientist in careful pursuit of truth.

Unfortunately, people are not always so careful. On an everyday basis, people often make attributions in a relatively thoughtless fashion (see Chapter 4). The cognitive system is limited in capacity, so people take shortcuts. The limitations of the cognitive system can be illustrated by such trivial problems as trying to keep a credit card number, an area code, and a telephone number in your head as you dial, or by more serious problems such as driving badly when you are distracted. The impact of cognitive limitations shows up in social inferences, too. To illustrate, in deciding why Bruce was irritable, you may seize on the easiest explanation rather than the most accurate one. Rather than asking Bruce whether there is something disturbing him, you may simply label him as unpleasant, without giving it much thought. Quite often, people simply are not very thorough. Under some circumstances, of course, people may be thorough.

Hence the third general view of the thinker (and the second major type of model in social cognition research), comes under the rubric of a *descriptive* model: what people actually do, rather than what they should do. One name for this is the *cognitive miser* model. The idea is that people are limited in their capacity to process information, so they take shortcuts whenever they can (see especially Chapters 6-9). People adopt strategies that simplify complex problems; the strategies may not be normatively correct or produce normatively correct answers, but they emphasize efficiency. The capacity-limited thinker searches for rapid adequate solutions, rather than slow accurate solutions. Consequently, errors and biases stem from inherent features of the cognitive system, not necessarily from motivations. Indeed, the cognitive miser model is silent on the issue of motivations or feelings of any sort. That may prove to be the model's fatal flaw, but that remains to be seen. In any event, the role of cognition is central to the cognitive miser view, and the role of motivation has vanished almost entirely, with isolated exceptions.

In summary, social psychology has always been cognitive, in the broad sense of positing important steps that intervene between observable stimulus and observable response. One early major set of theories viewed people as consistency seekers, and motivation played a central role in driving the whole system. With the rise of social cognition research, two new views have emerged. In one major wave of research, psychologists view people as naive scientists. These psychologists see motivation mainly as a source of error. In another recent view, psychologists see people as cognitive misers and locate errors in the inherent limitations of the cognitive system, saying almost nothing about motivation.

What Is Social Cognition?

The study of social cognition does not rely on any one theory. The object of study concerns how people make sense of other people and themselves. As a topic, it is relevant to the study of attitudes (Zimbardo, Ebbesen, & Maslach, 1977), person perception (Schneider, Hastorf, & Ellsworth, 1979), stereotyping (D. L. Hamilton, 1981a; Jones, 1972), small groups, and much more. Social cognition research on all these topics shares some basic features: unabashed mentalism, orientation toward process, cross-fertilization between cognitive and social psychologies, and at least some concern with real-world social issues (cf. Hastie & Carlston, 1980; S. E. Taylor, 1981).

MENTALISM: A COMMITMENT TO COGNITIVE ELEMENTS

The first of these assumptions, an unabashed commitment to mentalism (cognition), has just been discussed at some length. The cognitive elements people naturally use to make sense of other people constitute the first third of this book, the "what" of social cognition. Attributions, as defined above, are people's causal explanations for events in the social world. Chapter 2 presents the fundamentals of various central attribution theories. Chapter 3 presents the applications of attribution theories to achievement settings, to sex stereotyping, to the potentially subversive effects of rewards, to people helping the needy, to depression, and more. Chapter 4 describes the ways social perceivers fail to fit the normative models posited by early attribution theories and addresses shortcomings in attribution theories themselves.

Attributions result from people's need for understanding, prediction, and control over their environment. People's sense of control is fundamental to judgments they make about themselves and others. A sense of control means that one feels responsible and potentially able to cause specific outcomes, especially positive ones. Chapter 5 describes people's needs for control, their reactions to a loss of control, and various interventions designed to offset the stress produced by the loss of control.

Another basic cognitive element in people's understanding of themselves and others is the social *schema*. A schema may be defined as a cognitive structure that represents one's general knowledge about a given concept or stimulus domain. For example, your knowledge about yourself may be organized into a schema that includes your view of yourself as independent but not a loner, friendly but not saccharine, and athletic but not a star. A schema for a concept (e.g., the self) includes both relevant attributes (e.g., independent, friendly, athletic), and the relationships among the attributes (e.g., what your independence has to do with your friendliness). General knowledge about ourselves and others provides us with the expectations that enable us to function in the world. Chapter 6 describes research on social schemata for oneself and others, as well as for social events; it also discusses how schemata seem to operate: how they develop and change, and how they guide perception, memory, and inference in social settings. With the schema concept, the book crosses the fuzzy line from the elements to the processes of social cognition.

COGNITIVE PROCESSES IN SOCIAL SETTINGS

The second basic assumption in research on social cognition concerns cognitive process, that is, how cognitive elements are formed, used, and changed over time. A process orientation follows from the fundamental commitment to cognition. That is, concern with cognitive elements that intervene between observable stimulus and observable response requires an explanation of *how* one gets from S to R. Recall that, in their theories, behaviorists explicitly avoided discussion of internal processes, because behaviorists were concerned with predicting a publicly observable response from a publicly observable stimulus. In that sense, they were response or outcome oriented, rather than process oriented.

But outcome orientations arose elsewhere, too. The early methodology of research on consistency theories, for example, used to be more outcome oriented than process oriented. Although the researchers originally theorized and made assumptions about process, they focused empirically on predicting outcomes from stimuli. For example, inconsistency was manipulated (stimulus) and the resulting attitude change measured (outcome). Later psychologists doing consistency research did attempt to measure the intervening process, but the initial thrust of the research methods were outcome oriented. One of the recent shifts in attitude research and in social psychology generally has been away from outcome-oriented approaches and toward examinations of process.

In social cognition research, some theories are now available to describe and some tools to measure various implicit but hitherto unexamined assumptions about process. Social cognition research attempts to measure the stages of social information processing. That is, when one is confronted with a social stimulus, there are several steps posited to occur before one makes a response.

First, one must attend to the stimulus and encode it as an internal representation of external reality. Chapter 7 discusses which social stimuli typically capture attention and the ways this fact might be explained by their salience or vividness. The chapter also looks at the consequences of focusing attention on oneself or on the environment.

After attending to the stimulus and encoding it, one can store it away in memory. Chapter 8 describes current theories of how one organizes memory for information about other people, as well as the effects of various tasks on how one remembers such information. For example, forming an impression of someone can create a different set of memories than does memorizing the person's actions.

Finally, the third chapter in the process section addresses how people make inferences about social events. Chapter 9 is concerned with how the social perceiver makes inferences by specifying relevant information, sampling that information, and combining it into some judgment, such as a decision, a probability estimate, or a judgment of covariation.

CROSS-FERTILIZATION: STUDYING SOCIAL COGNITIVE PROCESSES

So far, we have described two themes in social cognition research and in this book: a commitment to cognition or mentalism and a commitment to process analysis. The third theme, cross-fertilization between cognitive and social psychology, is another feature of social cognition research that we address. Borrowing relatively fine-grained cognitive theory and methods has proved fruitful for social psychological research. Not only do researchers specify the steps in a presumed process model, but researchers attempt to measure the steps in some detail. Chapter 10 presents some of the research strategies that have been adopted from cognitive psychology for use in social settings. Various traditional and newer experimental methods allow researchers to support differing aspects of process models. Various research strategies attempt to trace the processes of attention, memory, and inference. We also discuss some of the pitfalls of the process techniques borrowed from cognitive psychology.

BEYOND COGNITION: REAL-WORLD SOCIAL ISSUES

The fourth theme of social cognition research is application to the real world. Social psychologists have a long tradition of addressing important contemporary issues. Early research provided insights into crowd behavior, propaganda, anti-Semitism, military morale, and other social issues. In keeping with this tradition, research in social cognition informs us about important issues. It applies the often heavily cognitive theory and method to real-world social problems. Throughout this book, we illustrate the ways social cognition can guide work in areas such as psychotherapy, health care, the legal system, stereotyping, advertising, political campaigns, strangers helping strangers, and romantic involvements. All these applications illustrate the flexibility of social cognition research. They also demonstrate how some otherwise highly technical or abstract ideas generalize outside the laboratory.

Social cognition applications to real-world issues define some boundary conditions for cognitive processes. That is, the research reveals phenomena that do not lend themselves to a purely cognitive analysis; other factors must be considered in many interpersonal settings of consequence. For example, what happens when the cognitive miser encounters feelings? What relationship does social information-processing have to situations of intense personal involvement? How do social cognitions get translated into behavior?

Part Three of the book, "Beyond Cognition," focuses more explicitly on the issues neglected by an overly narrow cognitive approach to social settings. Chapter 11 describes the links between cognitions and affect (feelings or emotions). In the study of how people think about people, affect is a crucial feature, but it has been for the most part neglected by cognitive psychology. As social psychologists became more cognitively oriented, they imported the study of affect into studies of social information processing.

Chapter 12 takes a central area of social psychology, attitudes, and shows the impact of recent cognitive approaches. Attitudes are affect-laden reactions to people, issues, or events, with important links to cognitions and behavior. Personal involvement emerges as a central issue in attitude research. The application of cognitively oriented theory and method to this well-established area focuses on old variables in new ways and makes a case for social cognition research on attitudes.

Chapter 13 tackles the question of the ways that behaviors (overt actions) influence and are influenced by cognitions, and Chapter 14, the final chapter, comments on the field as a whole and points toward future directions for research in social cognition.

To summarize, the book addresses the four major themes of social cognition research: unabashed mentalism in the study of cognitive representations of people, a commitment to fine-grained analyses of cognitive process, cross-fertilization between cognitive and social theory and methods, and a commitment to real-world social issues.

People Are Not Things

As one reviews research on social cognition, the analogy between the perception of things and the perception of people becomes increasingly clear. The argument is made repeatedly: the principles that describe how people think in general also describe how people think about people. Many theories of social cognition have developed in ways that undeniably build on fundamental cognitive principles, as we will see. Nevertheless, in borrowing such principles, we must consider fundamental differences when applying them to cognition about people. After all, cognitive psychology is relatively more concerned with the processing of information about inanimate objects and abstract concepts, whereas social psychology is more concerned with the processing of information about people and social experience.

At this point, the reader new to social cognition research already may be saying, "Wait, you can't tell me that the way I think about mental arithmetic or about my coffee cup has anything to do with the way I think about my friends." The wisdom or folly of applying the principles of object perception to the perception of people has been debated for some time (Heider, 1958; Higgins, Kuiper, & Olson, 1981; Krauss, 1981; Schneider *et al.*, 1979; Tagiuri & Petrullo, 1958). Some of the important differences between people and things include the following:

- People intentionally influence the environment; they attempt to control it for their own purposes. Objects, of course, are not intentional causal agents.
- People perceive back; as you are busy forming impressions of them, they are doing the same to you. Social cognition is mutual cognition.
- Social cognition implicates the self, because the target is judging you, because the target may provide you with information about yourself, and because the target is more similar to you than any object could be.
- A social stimulus may change upon being the target of cognition. People worry about how they come across and may adjust their appearance or behavior accordingly; coffee cups obviously do not.
- People's traits are nonobservable attributes that are vital to thinking about them. An object's nonobservable attributes are somewhat less crucial. Both a person and a cup can be fragile, but that inferred characteristic is both less important and more directly seen in the cup.
- People change over time and circumstance more than objects typically do. This can make cognitions rapidly obsolete or unreliable.
- The accuracy of one's cognitions about people is harder to check than the accuracy of one's cognitions about objects. Even psychologists have a hard time agreeing on whether a given person is extraverted, sensitive, or honest, but most ordinary people easily could test whether a given cup is heat resistant, fragile, or leaky.
- People are unavoidably complex. One cannot study cognitions about people without making numerous choices to simplify. The researcher has to simplify in object cognition, too, but it is less of a distortion. One cannot simplify a social stimulus without eliminating much of the inherent richness of the target.
- Because people are so complex, and because they have traits and intents hidden from view, and because they affect us in ways objects do not, social

cognition automatically involves social explanation. It is more important for an ordinary person to explain why a person is fragile than to explain why a cup is.

For these reasons, social cognitive psychology will never be a literal translation of cognitive psychology. It profits from theories and methods adapted to new uses, but the social world provides perspectives and challenges that are dramatic, if not unique, features of thinking about other people and oneself.

Summary

The study of social cognition concerns how people make sense of other people and themselves. It focuses on people's everyday understanding both as the phenomenon of interest and as a basis for theory about people's everyday understanding. Thus it concerns both how people think about the social world and how they think they think about the social world. It also draws heavily on fine-grained analyses provided by cognitive theory and method.

Two general approaches to social cognition date back to early modern philosophy. The elemental approach begins with ideas as elements that become linked into increasingly complex compounds. People form associations between ideas by the ideas' repeated contiguity in space or time. Early psychologists used introspective analysis as a method to break down their memory processes into those basic elements.

Gestalt psychologists had a holistic approach. They focused on the mind's active construction of reality, rather than on objective descriptions of the stimulus field. They also focused on the person's experience of dynamic wholes, rather than elements. Lewin imported such ideas to social psychology, emphasizing that the perceived environment — the psychological field — predicts behavior, and that one must consider the entire dynamic equilibrium of forces acting on an individual. The psychological field is the joint product of person and situation, and of motivation and cognition.

Cognition has not always been prominent in experimental psychology. After introspection proved to be a weak basis for an empirical science, every sort of cognition fell into disfavor with psychologists. Behaviorists dominated psychology for decades, insisting on an observable stimulus, an observable response, and no intervening cognitions. Later, behaviorist approaches seemed inadequate to explain language, and, at the same time, information-processing theories and computer-aided theory and technology paved the way for the reemergence of cognition in experimental psychology.

In social psychology, however, cognition has always been a respectable idea. The causes of social interaction predominantly lie in the perceived world, and the results of social interaction are thoughts, as well as feelings and behavior. In addition, social psychologists have always been cognitive in their view of the thinker who reacts to the perceived stimulus and generates a substantially cognitive response. They have viewed the social thinker at some times as a consistency seeker, motivated to reduce perceived discrepancies; at other times, they have seen the social thinker as a naive scientist who makes every effort thoroughly to ferret out the truth, with motivation contributing mainly error. But now social psychologists tend to see the social thinker as a cognitive miser, one who attempts to increase or maintain the efficiency of a capacity-limited cognitive apparatus, and they currently have little to say about motivation.

Social cognition, as an area of study, cuts across various topics. Those who study it focus on various cognitive elements such as attributions, feelings of control, and schemata. They analyze the processes of social cognition: attention, memory, and inference. The methods they use are borrowed from cognitive psychology and adapted to social settings. Social cognition research also can be informative about a number of important real-world social issues.

Social cognition of course differs from the general principles of cognition in some ways. Compared to objects, people are more likely to be causal agents, to perceive as well as being perceived, and intimately to involve the observer's self. They are difficult targets of cognition; because they adjust themselves upon being perceived, many of their important attributes (e.g., traits) must be inferred, and the accuracy of observations is hard to determine. People frequently change and are unavoidably complex as targets of cognition. Hence those who study social cognition must adapt the ideas of cognitive psychology to suit the specific features of cognitions about people.

part one

elements of
social cognition

attribution theory

If one were to flip through the pages of social psychology's leading journals, a task not recommended for bedside reading, one would quickly conclude on the basis of quantity alone that attribution theory is the leading theoretical concern and dominant empirical topic of the field. Yet, were one to read a sample of the available articles, it would be hard indeed to come up with any clear idea of what attribution theory is or what topics it covers. Several qualitatively different theoretical positions all pass for theories of attribution. There are attributional analyses of attraction, achievement, depression, and reactions to sports events, among many other phenomena. What all these individual contributions have in common, at the very minimum, is a focus on perceived causality: people's ideas about what causes things to occur, and why things happen as they do (see Harvey & Weary, 1981; Kelley & Michela, 1980; and M. Ross & Fletcher, in press; for extensive reviews of the attribution field).

The emphasis on causal analysis is central to social cognition because even the most trivial of observations often contains an implicit causal analysis. When one of the authors was in high school, more years ago than she cares to remember, a new boy came to school wearing a suit and carrying an umbrella. The other students immediately decided that he was odd. Why? Since no one else wore a suit, they assumed that something about the new student caused him to behave this way. Because it was not raining, he was obviously carrying an umbrella for some peculiar reason of his own. The students, then, made causal inferences about him by comparing his behavior with that of other students and to the social norms regarding the expected attire of high school students. Their impression, though quickly formed, was the consequence of causal analysis.

There are many circumstances in which causal analyses are more intentional, deliberate, and time-consuming. Unexpected events, for example, often produce extensive causal search. Receiving a low grade on a test when one thought one had done well will produce considerably more analysis (Did I study hard enough? Did the teacher grade especially hard? Did I misunderstand the questions?) than will receiving the grade one expected. Similarly, being snubbed by a close friend will produce more consideration of possible reasons for this occurrence than will being snubbed by a stranger. In sum, although people usually casually analyze the social world, causal analysis becomes especially important when people are surprised or threatened by events that undermine their beliefs and expectations (e.g., T. S. Pittman & Pittman, 1980; Pyszczynski & Greenberg, 1981; Wong & Weiner, 1981).

Research on causal attribution has been directed toward both the development of theory and the application of theory to specific content domains. On the theoretical level, psychologists involved in attribution research have attempted to discover the general rules people follow in ascribing causality for events. These rules are thought to be relatively stable generalizations of causal logic that are not restricted to particular content domains. We will discuss such theoretical work in this chapter. In Chapter 3 we will examine how these ideas have been applied to particular content domains such as achievement behavior, helping, and depression. In Chapter 4 we will examine biases in the attribution process and critiques of attribution theory.

WHAT IS ATTRIBUTION THEORY?

Attribution theory is a collection of diverse theoretical and empirical contributions that share several common concerns. First, attribution research deals with how the social perceiver uses information in the social environment to yield causal explanations for events. It examines what information is gathered and how it is combined to form an attribution. Second, work on causal attribution has generally assumed, either implicitly or explicitly, that motivational factors are, or can be, the impetus for causal analysis. People's needs to predict the future and to control events or other people are thought to be important in initiating causal analysis. However, once in operation, causal analysis is thought to continue largely according to cognitive principles.

A third characteristic of much attribution theorizing has been the tendency to view the social perceiver as a naive scientist who accomplishes many of the same tasks that the formal scientist conducts using not dissimilar methods. Although it is acknowledged that there are some biases in the attribution process, generally researchers feel that the social perceiver does a fairly good job of assembling relevant information, sifting through it in a logical, correct manner, and combining it to reach good and accurate conclusions. If the social perceiver departs from a rational analysis, researchers assume that motivational factors or emotions interfered with otherwise rational thought. Finally, an often implicit but perhaps the most fundamental assumption of attribution researchers is that attributions are important. Presumably, the social perceiver is not merely entertaining himself or herself by constructing causal analyses of the social world. Psychologists assume that these analyses are the bases of behavior, other cognitions, and feelings (see E. E. Jones *et al.*, 1972). Although there is reason to question some of these assumptions, they nonetheless form the underpinnings of the attribution theories we will consider.

Six different theoretical traditions form the backbone of what is now called attribution theory. The first is Heider's analysis of commonsense psychology (1958). His work strongly influenced both E. E. Jones and Davis's analysis of correspondent inference (1965), a theory of how people form inferences about other people's attributes, and Kelley's work on covariation and causal schemata (1967), which are general models of causal inference. Schachter's theory of emotional lability (1964) and D. J. Bem's self-perception theory (1967, 1972) extended attribution ideas into the arena of self-perception. Rotter's work on locus of control (1966) examined the effect of the perceiver's own attributes on causal inference. We will consider each in turn.

Heider's Theory of Naive Psychology

The work of Fritz Heider (1944, 1958) spearheaded the field of attribution theory. Heider maintained that a systematic understanding of how people comprehend their social world can be greatly enlightened by commonsense psychology: the ways in which people usually think about and infer meaning from what occurs around them. This commonsense psychology, or, as some call it, naive epistemology, can best be learned through the natural language that people employ for describing their experience. To oversimplify, if I listen to you talk for a while about other people, I should gain some insight into how you think about what causes people to behave as they do; and if I listen to enough people talk, the common elements in how they understand others should help me construct a theory of causal inference. Heider believed that what motivated this inference process was people's need to predict and control the environment. People, he maintained, have a need to anticipate and influence what will happen to themselves and to others around them, and the best way of so doing is through understanding the causes of behavior.

Heider based his theory on the "lens" model of perception originally developed by Brunswik (1956) to explain how people perceive objects. According to Brunswik, objects are never directly perceived; instead, how they are perceived by an individual depends on the attributes of the object itself, on the context in which the object is perceived, on the manner in which it is perceived (e.g., through a fog, a tunnel, or a prism), and on characteristics of the perceiver. The final perception, then, is based on all these components—object, context, mediation, and perceiver.

Heider believed that object perception and person perception have much in common and maintained that person perception processes involve many of the same inferential tasks and problems as exist with object perception. As in object perception, perception of another individual (e.g., your reaction to a blind date) will be a function of the person's behavior (how smooth or oafish your date was), the context in which it was enacted (whether your date was oafish at a party or in private), the manner in which the perceiver experienced it (overhearing your date interact with others or deciding about him or her based on your mutual interactions), and the perceiver's own characteristics and preconceptions about how and why others behave as they do (whether or not this type of person generally appeals to you and whether or not you see his or her behavior as redeemable). However, as we noted before, people also differ from objects in important ways: people cause actions; they have intentions, and they have abilities, desires, and sentiments; they are aware of being perceived and are, in turn, perceivers themselves. As a consequence of these factors, their status as causal beings is particularly central in the attribution process.

Fundamental to the question of why someone behaves as he or she does, according to Heider, is whether the locus of causality for that behavior is in the person, in the environment, or both. Internal locus or personal factors consist of *motivation* (trying) and the *ability* to accomplish that action. For example, I may be able to help my sister with her homework, but without any motivation to do so, I will not help her. Alternatively, I may want to help her, but I may lack the skill to do so. Moreover, motivation and ability are not necessarily enough; to these factors must be added or subtracted situational forces that favor or oppose the outcome. For example, if my sister's homework is easy, my motivation and ability may be sufficient to do the work; if it is hard, they may not be. Whether one can succeed at a task, then, is a joint feature of task difficulty and ability; whether one does succeed is additionally determined by the motivational factors of intention and effort. The social perceiver uses what information he or she has about motivational factors, ability, and situational factors to infer the cause of the event. If I successfully help my sister to do her homework, then my ability, motivation, and situational forces have obviously been adequate for the task.

Heider was also concerned with perceptions of responsibility for outcomes. Under many circumstances, it matters less what caused an event to happen than who is responsible for it. If someone tells you that I shot my neighbor, the causality question of "who" has been answered but not the responsibility question. Did I shoot him literally or only in a metaphorical sense? Did I shoot him by accident or on purpose? Heider hypothesized that there are varying levels of responsibility that determine how accountable one is for one's actions. The most removed level of responsibility is *association*, whereby a person is held accountable for an action with which he or she is not causally involved. If my neighbor shot himself, but his son tells me I "shot" him for not having noticed his darkening mood or erratic behavior, then I have been labeled responsible by association. *Causal responsibility*, the next level of responsibility, occurs when a person, in fact, does an action, but neither intended nor foresaw it. If I shoot at a coyote in the brush, and my neighbor, who happens to be walking there unbeknownst to me, is hit, then I am causally responsible for the shooting. If I knew he was in the brush, but fired anyway, expecting to hit the coyote instead, then I bear a greater amount of responsibility because I should have anticipated the possible outcome (*foreseeability*). If I intended to shoot my neighbor and used the coyote as an excuse, then my behavior is *intentional*, and I bear a great deal of responsibility for the outcome. Finally, if I shoot at my neighbor because he shot at me first, then my behavior would be thought by most people to be *justifiable*; although I would be held responsible for my behavior, the behavior would be considered justified by the situation.

It is important to note the obvious parallels between naive judgments of responsibility and legal categories for the dispensation of justice. Such terms as *criminal negligence, involuntary manslaughter,* and *first degree murder* reflect in their definitions many of the same distinctions contained in the different levels of responsibility outlined by Heider. This is one example demonstrating that attributions are made not merely because they are personally enlightening, but also because they reflect distinctions that societies find meaningful as a basis for collectively interpreting and acting upon experience.

Heider's thinking on causality and responsibility did not itself prompt much research; indeed, many readers could not decide what to do with it. However, it did give rise to subsequent theoretical work by E. E. Jones and Davis (1965) and Kelley (1967), among others, that was more amenable to empirical scrutiny. Thus Heider's major contribution to attribution theory was defining many of the basic issues that would later be explored more systematically in further theoretical ventures.

Jones and Davis's Correspondent Inference Theory

One model of attributional processes that was heavily influenced by Heider concerns how the social perceiver makes attributions about the causes of other people's behavior. This model is termed *correspondent inference theory* (E. E. Jones & Davis, 1965). Other people, unlike objects, have intentions and the capacity to act on them; because of this, their actions are meaningful and are most likely to be the objects of our attributional interest.

Jones and Davis began with the assumptions that we search for meaningful explanations for others' behavior that are both stable and informative. According to Jones and Davis, the behavior of another person will be most informative when it is judged to be intentional, and further, to have been produced by a consistent underlying intention, not one that changes from situation to situation. In short, whims tell you less about a person than do regularities in intentions. The goal of the attribution process, according to Jones and Davis, is the ability to make *correspondent inferences* about another person: to reach the conclusion that the behavior and the intention that produced it correspond to some underlying stable quality in the person, that is, a disposition. Knowing the dispositional attributes of others presumably enables one both to understand and to predict their behavior.

Jones and Davis maintained, as did Heider, that the ability to impute intentions depends on knowing whether or not the person committing the behavior (actor) knew the effects that the behavior would produce and had the ability to produce the behavior. One would not, for example, infer an intention if a three-year-old child shut off the house lights during a concert, but one would certainly infer an intention if the chief custodian did so. Hence the imputation of intention requires the minimum assumptions of knowledge and ability on the part of the actor.

THE ANALYSIS OF NONCOMMON EFFECTS

To infer that an intention is based on an individual's underlying disposition or preference requires further analysis. According to Jones and Davis, a main tool by which this task is accomplished is the *analysis of noncommon effects*. That is, when more than one course of action is available to an individual, one can ask: What did the chosen behavior produce that some other behavior would not have produced? By comparing the consequences of the action that is actually taken with the consequences of actions that are not taken, one can often infer the strength of the underlying intention by looking for distinctive consequences. For example, if I am accepted to two graduate psychology programs that are identical in format except that one has a clinical program, and I choose that one, then you may infer that clinical training is important to me. Furthermore, if many relatively negative elements are incorporated into the chosen alternative, relative to the unchosen ones, you may infer that the positive elements are especially important to me. Thus, if I choose the school with the clinical program, despite the fact that it is at a less prestigious university and in an undesirable part of the country, you can infer that clinical training is very important to me indeed. Figure 2.1 illustrates how the analysis of noncommon effects is used to reach conclusions about an individual's intentions.

One can also infer dispositions more confidently when there are fewer noncommon effects between the chosen and unchosen alternative (Ajzen & Holmes, 1976). If the only thing that distinguishes the two graduate psychology programs is that one has a clinical program, then you can more confidently infer my interest in clinical training than if the two programs differ in several ways.

In conclusion, then, the analysis of noncommon effects leads to correspondent inferences by identifying the distinctive consequences of an actor's chosen course of action. The fewer the distinctive consequences, the more confident the inference. The more negative the elements incorporated into the chosen alternative, the more one can infer the importance of the distinctive consequence. Of course, alternative courses of action, as well as their consequences and their noncommon effects, may be very difficult to ascertain. Hence the analysis of noncommon effects can be fraught with ambiguity.

OTHER BASES FOR FORMING CORRESPONDENT INFERENCES

Because the analysis of noncommon effects can produce ambiguous conclusions concerning an actor's dispositional qualities, the social perceiver must draw on other cues as well. These include choice, social desirability, social role, and prior expectations. We will consider each in turn.

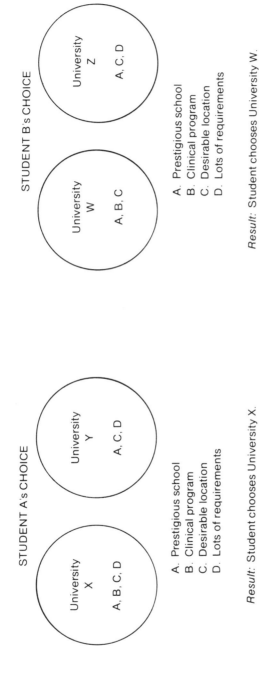

STUDENT A's CHOICE

University
X

A, B, C, D

University
Y

A, C, D

A. Prestigious school
B. Clinical program
C. Desirable location
D. Lots of requirements

Result: Student chooses University X.

Conclusion: University X has the noncommon effect of a clinical program.

Inference: The student wants clinical training.

STUDENT B's CHOICE

University
W

A, B, C

University
Z

A, C, D

A. Prestigious school
B. Clinical program
C. Desirable location
D. Lots of requirements

Result: Student chooses University W.

Conclusion: Either the student wants clinical training or he does not want to do a lot of work.

Inference: Inference unclear due to absence of noncommon effects.

Fig. 2.1 The analysis of noncommon effects: choosing a graduate school. (After E. E. Jones and Davis, 1965)

One basis for inferring an actor's dispositions is whether the behavior of the actor is situationally constrained or whether it occurs from the actor's *choice*. For example, it would be unwise of you to infer that I am altruistic because I gave money to a man who held a gun to my head. My behavior, under the circumstances, would be situationally constrained and could not be judged to be dispositionally based. The incident would give you little meaningful information about me. On the other hand, if you observed me on several occasions giving five dollars to panhandlers apparently of my own free will, you could more accurately infer that there is an underlying intention that can explain my behavior across the several situations.

A second condition that helps resolve the ambiguity of action is the *social desirability* of the behavior. With the decreasing social desirability of the action, one is able to infer more confidently an underlying disposition. For example, though it is usually appropriate for someone to enliven a party with jokes and stories, at a funeral such behavior would be in doubtful taste. In this case, one might conclude that the actor is an uncontrollable extravert with little understanding of social conventions (see E. E. Jones & McGillis, 1976). Social desirability is an important criterion for determining causality, because so often behavior is constrained by social propriety. When people are willing to break with norms or conventions to act a certain way, one can be reasonably certain that it reflects their true beliefs because by so doing they are risking socially aversive consequences, such as rejection.

In a classic study demonstrating the importance of social desirability in drawing correspondent inference, E. E. Jones, Davis, and Gergen (1961) had subjects listen to a tape of a job interview in which the applicant was supposedly interviewing to be either an astronaut or a submariner. Prior to hearing the tape, subjects were told the ideal qualifications for the job. They learned that astronauts are ideally inner-directed (autonomous, able to exist without social interaction), whereas the ideal submariner is other-directed (gregarious). Subjects believed that the job candidates also understood these ideal qualifications. The tape then represented the job candidate as behaving either in accord with the ideal job qualifications or opposite to what would be expected on the basis of the job qualifications. When subjects were then asked to give their impressions of the job candidate, those who heard the candidate behave in a manner opposite to the job qualifications (e.g., extraverted for the astronaut job or introverted for the submariner job) more confidently rated the candidate as actually being the way he had presented himself, compared with subjects who had heard the candidate present himself in the manner that was desirable for that particular job.

A third condition that helps to resolve the ambiguity of an action's meaning is whether the behavior is part of a *social role*. Role-related behaviors are not necessarily informative about underlying behavior. For example, if firefighters put out a fire, we would not infer that they are helpful; they are just doing their job. But when people in well-defined social roles display out-of-role behavior, their actions can be used to infer underlying dispositions, since role-related explanations are effectively ruled out as explanations for their behavior. For example, if the owner of a football team sides with the players in a strike, this out-of-role behavior would lead us to conclude that the owner must really believe in the players' demands (see E. E. Jones *et al.*, 1961).

Prior expectations about an actor can help identify his or her dispositional qualities (E. E. Jones & McGillis, 1976). Expectations are particularly likely to develop when people have multiple experiences with the same actor. For example, background knowledge about an individual, information about his or her prior behavior, or consistency in his or her behavior or intention over time can prompt dispositional attributions. Deviations from expected patterns of behavior or intention may also help the social perceiver refine prior dispositional attributions. If Sue knows one of her colleagues is a highly conscientious worker but observes that he stays home when one of his children is sick, she can make more precise inferences about his priorities. People can also use expectations to dismiss the significance of information: when information is too discrepant with prior expectations, people will downplay its veracity or significance (E. E. Jones & McGillis, 1976).

In summary, then, correspondent inferences can be drawn or further refined by determining whether or not a given behavior is freely chosen, socially desirable, or consistent with social roles or prior expectations.

BIASES IN THE CORRESPONDENT INFERENCE PROCESS

The perceiver does not always infer an actor's intentions and dispositions in an unbiased way. E. E. Jones and Davis (1965) discuss two perceiver biases that may have motivational origins and interfere with an accurate assessment of another person's motives. These biases are hedonic relevance and personalism.

Hedonic relevance refers to the impact that an actor's behavior has on the perceiver, that is, whether the action obstructs or promotes the perceiver's goals or interests. Generally, perceptions of correspondence increase with hedonic relevance. The reason is that hedonic relevance provides a potential explanation for viewing the other's actions. For example, if your car rolls down a hill and strikes mine, I am more likely to infer that you are careless than if your car strikes someone else's car. Neutral actions may then also be assimilated to the hedonic value of the primary action, strengthening the inference. Thus I may also see other of your actions, such as your chronic lateness, as further evidence for this disposition of carelessness.

Personalism is the perceiver's perception that the actor intended to benefit or harm the perceiver. In this case, not only is the actor's action hedonically relevant for the perceiver, but it is seen by the perceiver as intending to be so. If my roommate not only fails to take out the trash, but leaves a note saying, "Take it out yourself," I will be angrier than if I believe he simply did not have time to do it. The perception of personalism increases correspondent inference not only because the outcome is hedonically relevant, but also because it leaves no doubt in the perceiver's mind that the action was intended. The perception of personalism can also lead one to discount another's behavior, as when it is seen as manipulatively ingratiating. If I believe that a student's compliments on my recent article reflect angling for a better grade, I will be less favorably inclined toward him or her than if I believe his or her compliments were not intentionally manipulative.

To summarize, then, Jones and Davis's theory concerns the perception of people's actions and the problem of inferring intentions from ambiguous information. Assuming an actor has both the ability to complete an action and knowledge of its consequences, his or her action is most likely to be perceived as intentional if any of the following is true: the action has produced an outcome that is distinctive, it is judged to have occurred from choice, it is either socially undesirable or out of role, or it violates prior expectations. The specific intention can be inferred from the noncommon effect the action produced that other possible actions would not have produced. However, the perceiver's attributions are not always unbiased, and two factors that can enter into the attributional process are the hedonic relevance of the action for the perceiver and the judgment that the action was intended to benefit or harm the perceiver (personalism).

Kelley's Attribution Contributions

Kelley developed two formulations of the attribution process that we will consider in this section. For cases in which people have access to multiple instances of the same or similar events, he formulated the covariation model (1967); for cases in which information is limited to a single event, he formulated the concept of causal schemata (Kelley, 1972a). Kelley's attribution formulations differ from that of Jones and Davis in several important ways. First, as just noted, Kelley's models cover both multiple events and single events. Second, his models detail the processes for making attributions of causality not only to other people but to environmental factors and to the self as well.[1]

Kelley began with the observation that knowledge about the world, especially the social world, is never complete. The meaning of others' behavior is often elusive or ambiguous. Although people usually have enough information to function effectively on a social level (see Thibaut & Kelley, 1959), under some circumstances, the information level is not adequate. This situation can occur when one's beliefs or opinions receive little support from others, when problems exist that are beyond one's capabilities, when information about an issue is poor or ambiguous, when one's views have been labeled as untrue or inappropriate, or when one encounters some other experience that produces low self-confidence. When any of these conditions occurs, attributional instability results (Kelley, 1967). Under these circumstances, people are especially susceptible to social influence, and they are likely to seek out additional

---

1. The E. E. Jones and McGillis (1976) update of E. E. Jones and Davis (1965), and Kelley's later work (1972a) make the theories now much more similar in their predictions and in the phenomena they encompass than was originally true.

information to validate a tentative impression of what is occurring or to develop an explanation of what is occurring. In short, uncertainty prompts causal analysis.

THE COVARIATION MODEL

Under many circumstances, an individual will have access to multiple instances of the same or similar events. For example, we see our friends interacting with many different people or we observe our own repeated interactions with others. Generally, experience replicates itself, if not exactly, at least in very similar ways. With information about multiple events, we can employ a covariation principle to infer the causes of events. Covariation is the observed co-occurrence of two events. If my dog sneezes every time I put on my fur coat, that is a high covariation. If he sneezes only sometimes when I put on my coat and also at other times, that is a low covariation. In trying to understand the cause of some effect (e.g., sneezing), we observe its covariation with various potential causes and attribute the effect to the cause with which it most closely covaries. If my dog's sneezing covaries closely with my putting on my fur coat, I can conclude that he is allergic to it.

According to Kelley, people assess covariation information across three dimensions relevant to the entity whose behavior they are trying to explain. An entity may be another person or a thing. As an example, consider a young man who goes with a young woman (entity) to a party only to find himself ignored while she flirts with several other men. He is likely to wonder why she bothered to go out with him in the first place and to be curious about why this has happened. The three dimensions along which he will test his attributions, according to Kelley, are:

- *Distinctiveness*—Does the effect occur when the entity (the young woman) is there and not when it is not? (For example, is she the only woman to have behaved this way toward him in the past, or have other women done the same thing?)
- *Consistency over time/modality*—Does the effect occur each time the entity is present and regardless of the form of the interactions? (For example, has she done this to him before and at other events as well as at parties?)
- *Consensus*—Do other people experience the same effect with respect to this entity? (For example, has she done this to other people?)

According to Kelley, one is able to make a confident entity attribution with the combination of high distinctiveness, high consistency, and high consensus information. In this case, one may conclude that this entity, the young woman, is an impossible hussy if she is the only person who treats the wretched young man this way (high distinctiveness), if she has always done this in the past, assuming he has been foolish enough to take her out before (high consistency), and if others have had a similar experience with her (high consensus).

Other combinations of information can also yield meaningful causal inferences. For example, suppose we learned that the young lady has never ignored other dates before (low consensus), she has always ignored this date in the past (high consistency), and most other women have also ignored this young man (low distinctiveness). One might be inclined to think there is something rather offensive, such as rude manners or bad breath, about the young man. The combination of low distinctiveness, high consistency, and low consensus reliably produces this kind of person attribution (McArthur, 1972).

Covariation principles can also be employed to form joint attributions of causality. Suppose we learned that the young man has never been ignored by another date (high distinctiveness), the young lady has never ignored any other date (low consensus), but she has always ignored this fellow every time they have gone out together (high consistency). Under the circumstances, we would be inclined to attribute responsibility to them jointly, concluding that they are a fatal combination as well as gluttons for punishment (McArthur, 1972). Table 2.1 shows how the covariation model can be used to reach different causal attributions.

Attributions can also provide guidelines for future behavior (McArthur, 1972). Specifically, entity attributions produce *response generalization*. For example, if the young man decides that the young lady is at fault for the unpleasant evening, then several responses will follow: he will be unlikely to date her again, call her, or even speak to her if he can help it. The attribution to her (i.e., to the entity) suggests numerous responses for dealing with her in the future. Person attributions, in contrast, provoke *stimulus generalization*. For example, if the young man decides that he is at fault for being ignored, then he can infer that not only this young lady, but other "stimuli," namely, other women, will behave in the same way. Kelley's model, then, is highly flexible: the information obtained in a causal search can yield any of multiple meaningful patterns that in turn define guidelines for behavior.

Empirical investigations have generally supported the covariation model or at least aspects of it (e.g., D. J. Pruitt & Insko, 1980; Ferguson & Wells, 1980; McArthur, 1972; Orvis, Cunningham, & Kelley, 1975; Zuckerman, 1978). Researchers have found distinctiveness, consistency, and consensus to be relevant dimensions on which people base attributions. However, some studies using either hypothetical or real-world attributional dilemmas have revealed qualifications (Stevens & Jones, 1976; Tillman & Carver, 1980). For example, studies that have let subjects select their own information when faced with an attributional dilemma have found mixed support for the model; although subjects examine consensus, distinctiveness and consistency information, the search is neither thorough nor systematic in the ways the covariation model would suggest. Consistency information is preferred over distinctiveness (e.g., Kruglanski, 1977), and consensus is least utilized (e.g., Kruglanski, Hamel, Maides, & Schwartz, 1978; Major, 1980; see also Chapter 4). Furthermore, when given the opportunity, people choose to acquire additional information about the actor (such as information about his or her personality) or informa-

TABLE 2.1
Using Kelley's Covariation Model to Answer the Question:
Why Does Ralph (Person) Trip over Joan's (Entity) Feet while Dancing?
(After McArthur, 1972)

	High distinctiveness				Low distinctiveness			
Distinctiveness	Ralph does not trip over almost any other partner's feet.				Ralph trips over lots of partners' feet.			
	High consistency		Low consistency		High consistency		Low consistency	
Consistency	In the past, Ralph has almost always tripped over Joan's feet.		In the past, Ralph has almost never tripped over Joan's feet.		In the past, Ralph has almost always tripped over Joan's feet.		In the past, Ralph has almost never tripped over Joan's feet.	
	High consensus	*Low consensus*	*High consensus*	*Low consensus*	*High consensus*	*Low consensus*	*High consensus*	*Low consensus*
Consensus	Almost everyone else who dances with Joan trips over her feet.	Hardly anyone else who dances with Joan trips over her feet.	Almost everyone else who dances with Joan trips over her feet.	Hardly anyone else who dances with Joan trips over her feet.	Almost everyone else who dances with Joan trips over her feet.	Hardly anyone else who dances with Joan trips over her feet.	Almost everyone else who dances with Joan trips over her feet.	Hardly anyone else who dances with Joan trips over her feet.
Attribution	Joan is not coordinated. She is at fault. An *entity* attribution should be made.	Ralph and Joan are jointly responsible. Both are *necessary* to produce the outcome. A *person-entity* attribution is warranted.	Usually Ralph is able to overcome Joan's uncoordination, but not today. A *circumstance* attribution is warranted.	It's a bad day. A *circumstance* attribution is warranted.	Ralph and Joan are jointly responsible. Either is *sufficient* to cause the outcome. A *person-entity* attribution is warranted.	Ralph is uncoordinated and is at fault. A *person* attribution should be made.	Ralph and Joan are both uncoordinated. Usually they overcome it. But not today. Attribution is ambiguous.	Ralph is uncoordinated. Joan is usually able to overcome it. But not today. Attribution is ambiguous.

tion about the situation in which the act occurred (e.g., various situational constraints) rather than the types of information suggested by the covariation model (Garland, Hardy, & Stephenson, 1975). Moreover, the covariation model obviously relies on people's ability to assess covariation, a task that is by no means error free (see Crocker, 1981; Abramson & Alloy, 1980; Chapter 9). These studies, in total, do not suggest that the covariation model of attribution is wrong, but merely that its generalizability may be limited by various constraints, not yet completely understood.

To summarize, Kelley's covariation model posits that the social perceiver identifies an effect and then observes its occurrence across entities (distinctiveness), across time and modality (consistency), and across persons (consensus). Once this information is gathered, it can be used to validate a tentative attribution or to form a new one.

The procedures for inferring causality outlined by Kelley may seem quite rational and time-consuming. Indeed, Kelley likens this view of the social perceiver to a naive scientist who is trying to draw inferences in much the same way a formal scientist draws conclusions from data. However, this process is not thought to be engaged any time some mildly curious event transpires; rather, as noted earlier, it is reserved for those occasions when one's beliefs and impressions have been seriously challenged by environmental events. Finally, psychologists usually interpret Kelley's covariation model as a normative model, and not necessarily a descriptive one. In other words, it describes an idealized way of drawing inferences, but the actual procedures that people use to infer causality may differ somewhat from this model. The covariation model is useful for inferring causality when considerable information about an event is available. Other principles, such as those that are about to be described, must be used when less information is available.

THE DISCOUNTING AND AUGMENTING PRINCIPLES

Often when a person is trying to understand the causes of an event, evidence is not available about its consistency over time, its distinctiveness, and other people's experiences with it. Rather, the only information is a single occurrence of the event. In such cases, the social perceiver must fall back on other strategies or rules of causal inference than covariation. One such rule noted by Kelley (1972b) is the *discounting principle*. The discounting principle maintains that a social perceiver discounts any one candidate as a potential cause for an event to the extent that other potential causal candidates are available. For example, if I wreck my car at 2:00 a.m., you may be less inclined to conclude that I was tired and not paying careful enough attention if you learn that it was raining. If you then find out that my brakes malfunctioned, you may be less likely to blame the rain.

In addition, any cause can facilitate or inhibit a particular effect. An *inhibitory cause* interferes with the occurrence of a given event, whereas a *facilitative cause* increases the likelihood of its occurrence. When an effect occurs in the presence of both a facilitative cause and an inhibitory cause, people give the facilitative cause more weight in producing the outcome, because it had to be strong enough to overcome the inhibitory cause; this generalization is termed the *augmenting principle*. For example, if you learn that Sam was the winner of the Frisbee contest, you infer that he must be a good Frisbee player. If I then explain that Sam is 53 years old (inhibitory cause), you will probably infer that he is especially good to have successfully eliminated a field of younger contestants.

The social perceiver, then, uses whatever information is available about potential facilitative or inhibitory causes and discounts or augments the importance of particular causes accordingly when trying to infer causality for a single event.

CAUSAL SCHEMATA

Another method a person may use to infer causality for events involves the application of *causal schemata*. "A causal schema is a general conception the person has about how certain kinds of causes interact to produce a specific kind of effect" (Kelley, 1972a, p. 151). Each of us, in our experiences with cause-effect relations in the world, develops certain abstract conceptions about how causes work together to yield effects; we can use these so-called schemata when we wish to explain effects for which causal information is ambiguous and unclear.

Kelley described two types of causal schemata in particular: the multiple necessary causes schema and the multiple sufficient causes schema. We may know, for example, that when a particularly difficult or extreme effect is involved (such as winning a marathon), multiple causes will be needed to produce the outcome (such as ability, effort, good training and favorable course conditions). We term this the *multiple necessary causes schema*. To fail such a task would not be very informative, because any one of the necessary conditions could be absent and the effect would not occur. To succeed in performing a difficult task is informative about the presence of several causes.

On the other hand, a *multiple sufficient causes schema* accounts for less extreme outcomes and assumes that any one of several causes could be sufficient to produce the effect. If I beat my four-year-old niece at checkers, you can attribute my victory to my ability, my effort, the fact that the task is familiar to me, or the fact that I can cheat and she does not know enough to catch me. Any one of the causes will do equally well, and to the extent that any one is present, the social perceiver will employ the discounting principle to downplay the significance of any of the others (Cunningham & Kelley, 1975). For outcomes that are not extreme or difficult, then, success is not surprising or informative: any of a number of factors could have produced it. On the other hand, failure is somewhat informative, since failure on an easy task suggests that a variety of factors must not have been present.

The presence or absence of potential causes is not the only information that people can use to judge causal relations. Perceivers can also use information about the relative *strength of causes* to judge cause-effect relationships.

For example, if you know that I had a lot of money riding on the outcome of the checkers game with my niece and you also know that I tried hard, you may infer that I probably won by a handy margin. *Strength of effect* also provides information about cause-effect relationships. For example, if I beat my niece at checkers but just barely, you may infer that my ability is low, my effort was weak, the task may be novel, and I did not cheat very much.

Research on causal schemata has been plentiful (Cunningham & Kelley, 1975; DiVitto & McArthur, 1978; Karniol & Ross, 1976; Kun & Weiner, 1973; M. C. Smith, 1975), although the adequacy of this research has been challenged conceptually (Fiedler, 1982) and empirically (Surber, 1981). Nonetheless, causal schemata are thought to be important aspects of causal inference for several reasons. First, causal schemata help people to make causal inferences when information is incomplete, sketchy, or derived from only one incident or observation. Second, they represent general conceptions about patterns of cause-effect relationships that may apply across a wide range of specific content areas. Causal schemata, in essence, give the social perceiver a causal shorthand for accomplishing complex inferential tasks quickly and easily. Based on our knowledge of causal schemata, we are able to use information about presence, absence, or strength of causes to infer effects when information is less then complete. And we are also able to use presence, absence, or strength of effects to infer causes and their relative strength.

Attribution Theory: A Note

The ideas of Heider, Jones and Davis, and Kelley constitute the critical theoretical contributions to attribution theory, and accordingly, form the groundwork for defining it. The reader accustomed to viewing theories competitively may wish to know which one is right. The answer is that all of them are probably "right," but under different circumstances and for different phenomena. The theories cannot be pitted against each other in the usual scientific manner. Rather, each outlines a series of processes that can be used to infer attributions if the appropriate circumstances are present. For example, if one has the opportunity to view an individual's behavior over time, then one can employ Kelley's covariation model to infer another person's dispositional qualities. If not, then one may have to infer the person's dispositions from knowledge of the social desirability of the act and/or whether or not the person chose it. Despite the best efforts to compare and contrast the theories (e.g., E. E. Jones & McGillis, 1976; K. G. Shaver, 1975), relatively little has emerged in the way of theoretical refinement. The theories adopt different slants rather than differing hypotheses or stands on fundamental issues.

In addition to the very central contributions of Heider, Jones and Davis, and Kelley, three other lines of work contributed significantly to the theoretical and empirical tradition of attribution research.

Schachter's Theory of Emotional Lability

One such contribution is Schachter's theory of emotional functioning (Schachter, 1964, 1971; Schachter & Singer, 1962). In particular, Schachter's work extended attribution ideas to self-perception, especially the self-perception of emotions.

In his early work on affiliation, Schachter (1959) had observed that when people expect to undergo a stressful experience, they often choose to affiliate with others who will also be undergoing similar stressful experiences. After ruling out several possible explanations for this effect, he concluded that people have a need to compare their emotional state with that of similar others so as better to understand and to label their own reactions. If this is true, Schachter reasoned, then the internal physiological cues on which people normally draw to help interpret their emotions must be relatively ambiguous and subject to multiple interpretations. Consequently, people's perceptions of their emotions are indirect and relatively labile (unstable). If people have direct access to their emotions, why would they need to compare them with others?

These and other observations led Schachter to posit that there are two necessary conditions for emotion: a state of physiological *arousal*, thought not to be specific with respect to a particular emotion, and *cognitions*, which label the arousal and determine what emotion is experienced. Under some circumstances, cognitions precede arousal (for example, knowing that one must beware of bears and then becoming aroused when one encounters one in the woods). Under other circumstances, a state of arousal may occur first, which then prompts a cognitive search for a causal explanation of that aroused state. Under these circumstances, cues from the immediate environment then become likely candidates for labeling arousal as a particular emotion.

To see if the interpretation of arousal is indeed malleable, Schachter and Singer (1962) conducted a now-classic experiment. One group of undergraduate students was injected with epinephrine: half were told its true side effects (e.g., rapid breathing, flushing, increased heart rate), and half were told to expect effects that are not, in fact, produced by epinephrine (e.g., dizziness, slight headache). A control group of subjects was given no drug. Subjects were then placed in a room with a confederate of the experimenter and were instructed to fill out some papers. After a brief time (during which the epinephrine took effect in those who had received it), the confederate began to act in either a euphoric manner (engaging in silly antics and making paper airplanes) or in an angry manner (ripping up the papers and stomping around the room).

Schachter and Singer reasoned that if physiological experience is indeed subject to multiple interpretations, then those subjects who had been misinformed about the side effects of epinephrine and who later found themselves in a state of arousal would be searching for an explanation of their state. For these subjects, the behavior of the confederate could act as a salient cue for explaining their own arousal, suggesting to those subjects in the euphoric condition that they also were euphoric and to those in the angry condition that they were angry. Subjects who had been informed about the side effects of epinephrine, in contrast, already had an adequate explanation for their arousal state and could remain amused or annoyed by the confederate without acquiring his mood. Subjects in the control condition would have no arousal state to explain and also should not catch the mood of the confederate. Generally speaking, this is what Schachter and Singer found; the results of their experiment are presented in Table 2.2.

Schachter's ideas and the results of this experiment extensively influenced both the study of emotion and the understanding of causal attribution. As our present concern is with attributions, we will not cover the work on emotions until Chapter 11.

One of the most important aspects of Schachter's work is the point that attributions for arousal are malleable. This point is important in part because it suggests that emotional reactions induced by a threatening experience can be reattributed to a neutral or less threatening source. This idea has profound clinical implications, because it provides a potential general model for the treatment of emotional disorders (Valins & Nisbett, 1972). Consider the fact that there are a great many people who are anxious over real or imagined faults. An adolescent boy may believe he is unable to talk to girls and so avoids them. A middle-aged woman returning to work after years of child rearing may doubt her ability to convey a good impression and thus avoid tackling the job market. In such situations, a cycle of emotional exacerbation may occur (Storms & McCaul, 1976). The adolescent, fearful that he will ruin his chance with a girl, becomes so anxious that his hands get sweaty and he stutters just saying "hello." Or the middle-aged woman may think of so many things that could go wrong in a job interview that she cannot even get up the courage to check the newspaper listings.

The misattribution paradigm suggests that by inducing people to reattribute their arousal to some nonthreatening source, the exacerbation cycle can be

TABLE 2.2
The Misattribution of Arousal
(After Schachter and Singer, 1962)

	Subject informed of true side effects of epinephrine	Subject misinformed of side effects of epinephrine	No arousal
Exposure to angry confederate	Subject correctly labels arousal; does not infer that he is angry	Subject interprets own arousal as anger	Subject has no arousal and infers no emotion for the self
Exposure to euphoric confederate	Subject correctly labels arousal; does not infer that he is euphoric	Subject interprets own arousal as euphoria	Subject has no arousal and infers no emotion for the self

broken. Consequently, they will function more effectively in the settings that currently make them anxious. The woman contemplating a return to work might be told that changes in schedule, strange settings, and trying to get to new places on time all produce some change in heart rate and breathing, and therefore, if she finds herself experiencing these changes she should realize that they are normal physiological responses to changes in one's daily activities. Now having a safe, external stimulus to account for her arousal, the woman should calm down enough to schedule an interview and follow through on it. A number of experiments using this kind of intervention have yielded support for the reattribution approach (e.g., Brodt & Zimbardo, 1981; G. C. Davison & Valins, 1969; Nisbett & Schachter, 1966; L. Ross, Rodin, & Zimbardo, 1969; Storms & McCaul, 1976; Storms & Nisbett, 1970; Valins & Ray, 1967).

After the early work supporting Schachter's ideas, some researchers criticized both the theory and its potential clinical applications. One criticism concerns whether environmental cues are easily accepted as a basis for inferring one's own emotions, as Schachter implies (e.g., Maslach, 1979; Marshall & Zimbardo, 1979; Plutchik & Ax, 1967). Using the original Schachter and Singer (1962) paradigm, Maslach (1979) found evidence that subjects' efforts to understand an unexplained state of arousal are more extensive than a quick examination of salient cues in the surrounding environment. Others have questioned whether unexplained arousal is equally likely to be interpreted positively or negatively. Both Maslach (1979) and Marshall and Zimbardo (1979) reported that people are more likely to interpret unexplained arousal negatively, for example, as feelings of unease or nervousness, rather than positively. These results question the extent of emotional lability (see also Schachter & Singer, 1979).

Researchers have also criticized the misattribution effect. They point out that it is not completely reliable (e.g., J. Duncan & Laird, 1980; M. Ross & Olson, 1981), that it may be rather short-lived (Nisbett & Valins, 1972), and that some attempts to demonstrate it have failed (e.g., Conger, Conger, & Brehm, 1976; Kellogg & Baron, 1975; Singerman, Borkovec, & Baron, 1976; see Reisenzein, 1983, for a review). Even when people have successfully been induced to reattribute their arousal to a nonthreatening source and accordingly experience reduced symptoms or anxiety, it is not clear that attributions per se mediate these effects (Girodo, 1973; Thompson, 1981).

Unfortunately, too, laboratory investigations of the misattribution effect seem to be more successful than actual clinical investigations (e.g., Nisbett, Borgida, Crandall, & Reed, 1976). It may be that a person with a real problem already has a stable explanation for his or her arousal and does not search for alternative explanations; hence he or she may not be vulnerable to misattribution efforts. Or perhaps people with real problems test out the misattributions they are given for their problems more fully than do people with laboratory-induced or short-term problems. In so doing, they may learn that the misattribution feedback is not true or at least not completely true. Suppose, for example, that our anxious job hunter has been told that her anxiety is due to the newness of the experience. She then decides to have several dress rehearsals for her job interview to rid herself of the anxiety. She rises in the morning, dresses, drives to the spot where the interview will be held, and takes the elevator up to the office so that she is completely comfortable with the route. On the morning of the job interview itself, however, she is still terrified, because it is in fact the job situation that makes her nervous, not the unfamiliarity of the experience at all.

To summarize, although Schachter and Singer's emotional lability hypothesis has had a substantial impact on the development of attribution theory, twenty years of research suggest that its ability to explain or modify emotional experience has limitations. One can conclude that, within limits, people can be induced to reattribute arousal from one stimulus to another, particularly when the circumstances are short term and relatively uninvolving. However, people have multiple methods for understanding their own emotional experiences, and when they are motivated to use them, misattribution effects may be weak.

Bem's Self-Perception Theory

Another important contribution to attribution theory was Daryl Bem's work on self-perception (1967, 1972). Bem was concerned, as Schachter was, with how people infer their own reactions, emotions, and attitudes. And he argued, as Schachter did, that people's internal cues to their reactions are neither as directly accessible nor as unambiguous as they usually think they are. Instead, as Schachter posited, Bem argued that people often infer their internal reactions from environmental factors that provide cues about their beliefs.

Specifically, Bem's theory of self-perception posits that the processes people use to infer their own attitudes are not substantially different from those they apply in trying to infer other people's attitudes. "Individuals come to 'know' their own attitudes, emotions, and other internal states partially by inferring them from the observation of their own overt behavior and/or the circumstances in which this behavior occurs" (Bem, 1972, p. 2).

Suppose someone asks me if my roommate likes jazz. I may have never heard him state a preference, but I will likely think over what tapes or records he chooses to play and what radio stations he selects. If he plays Mozart and Brahms all day, I am likely to conclude that he does not like jazz much. If he never turns the jazz station off the radio, I am likely to conclude that he does. Bem's point is that we often infer our own attitudes in the same way that we infer those of others, namely, by observing behavior. If someone asks me if I like jazz, according to Bem, I may well employ the same process I would apply to others. I think over how often I choose to listen to jazz and decide on that basis if I like it.

Bem added several qualifications to this process. Choice is an important variable in the model. Obviously I would not infer that I like jazz if the reason I hear it all the time is that my culturally myopic roommate will not listen to anything else. Bem maintained that we observe whether our behavior is "manded" (under external control) or "tacted" (under our own discretion), and infer our attitudes from our behavior only under conditions of choice. As a further caveat, Bem (1972) maintained that self-perception processes are more likely to be used as a basis for one's own attitudes when two other conditions exist: when internal cues that represent alternative bases for inferring attitudes are ambiguous or weak (Chaiken & Baldwin, 1981; Wood, 1982), and when external sources of feedback about one's attitude are absent (Valins, 1966). For example, if I am president of the local jazz club, I will not have to think over how often I listen to jazz to infer my attitude. I have an unambiguous cue that renders my attitude unambiguous. Finally, others have shown that one must perceive the behavior to be relevant to the attitude for self-perception effects to occur (Kiesler, Nisbett, & Zanna, 1969).

Bem's theory, is, of course, very different from those of Jones and Davis and of Kelley, especially in the amount of mental effort the perceiver is hypothesized to undertake. Whereas the previous theories make fairly detailed assumptions about the amount and kind of cognitive work the social perceiver engages in, Bem's theory posits very little cognitive work at all. Indeed, Bem is not considered so much a cognitive theorist as a radical behaviorist in the tradition of B. F. Skinner (see Chapter 1). Why, then, did his work contribute substantially to the development of attribution theory?

One answer lies in the fact that Bem's theory mounted a substantial challenge to the cornerstone of the cognitive consistency framework: cognitive dissonance theory (Festinger, 1957). Although a number of alternative explanations for dissonance effects had been proposed, Bem's theory provided the first nonmotivational theoretical position that could explain most of the results of dissonance theory without positing an intervening state of arousal. To take a specific example, consider an experiment conducted by Aronson and Mills (1959). Female subjects were invited to participate in a sex discussion group. Some of the subjects were told that they would first have to go through an initiation process to be certain that they could participate in the group without embarrassment. One group of subjects was given a list of dirty words to say in front of a male experimenter (severe initiation). Another group was given a list of mildly dirty words (mild initiation), and a third group received no initiation. All subjects, then, heard a boring discussion of animal sex, and at its close, they were asked to evaluate it. Those in the more severe initiation condition evaluated the discussion group more favorably than those in the mild initiation condition or the control condition.

Dissonance theory and Bem's self-perception theory offer very different explanations for the results. Dissonance theory, which will be further discussed in Chapter 12, maintains that holding two conflicting cognitions simultaneously —"I underwent a severe test to get into this group," and "This group is boring"—generates a motivational state of dissonance that can be resolved by changing one of the two cognitions. Since subjects cannot deny that they underwent the initiation, they reevaluate the group discussion more positively. Bem's theory, in contrast, maintains that the subject looks at her behavior as an observer would and infers that, if she was willing to undergo the initiation to be in the group, she must like the group quite a bit. According to self-perception theory, then, no aversive motivational state need exist. One's stated attitude is simply a function of the available evidence that is observable to all.

The value of Bem's work for attribution researchers goes well beyond its role as an alternative explanation for dissonance phenomena. The theory predicts that by manipulating the circumstances within which people express their attitudes or by giving people (false) feedback relevant to their beliefs, one can actually affect their self-perceptions and expressions of belief. One of many experiments that is consistent with these predictions was conducted by Freedman and Fraser (1966); it demonstrated what is known as the "foot-in-the-door" phenomenon. Suburban housewives were first approached by an experimenter at their homes and asked to comply with a small request. They were asked either to place a small sign in their window or to sign a petition. The action promoted either auto safety or keeping California beautiful. Two weeks later, the same people were asked to comply with a larger request, to place a large unattractive billboard promoting auto safety on their front lawn. A control group was asked only the second request. Results indicated that those who had initially agreed to the small request were more likely to comply with the large request; this was true regardless of which initial small request had been made. The self-perception explanation for this effect, which continues to be supported (e.g., Tybout & Scott, 1983), is that people's attitudes about themselves change when they agree to the first request. They come to think of themselves as the sort of person who does these things (i.e., cooperates, supports good causes), and so, when the second request comes, it is now consistent with this new attitude.

Self-perception processes may, however, apply in only a limited number of settings. Imagine that you are asked what television program you would like to watch tonight. You may think about what show you watch most often and answer, "Star Trek," overlooking the fact that "Star Trek" reruns always come on after the news (which you always watch with dinner) and that you usually have not finished eating when "Star Trek" comes on. Now imagine that a newly incarcerated convict who will have limited viewing time is asked the same question. The convict is unlikely to make the same mistake. He or she may think over the merits of different shows more carefully and decide on the basis of something other than chance factors (what comes on after the news), since his or her choice of shows involves higher stakes.

A study by S. E. Taylor (1975) suggests that the consequences of one's attitudes do indeed affect whether or not people base their attitudes on self-perception processes. Taylor presented female subjects with erroneous physiological feedback implying that they were physically attracted to particular men whose photographs they observed. One group of subjects received feedback indicating that they were attracted to men whose photographs they had previously judged as highly attractive, whereas another group received feedback indicating that they were attracted to men whose photographs they had originally found to be only moderately attractive. In addition, half the subjects expected to interact with the men later on, whereas the other half had no such expectations. When attitudes toward the pictured men were reassessed some time later, those who had no expectations of meeting the men in the future expressed attitudes that were relatively consistent with the false feedback they had received. In contrast, those who did expect future interactions used their own internal reactions as a basis for their attitudes. In particular, the women receiving feedback indicating that they had responded to photographs other than those they had actually preferred rejected the feedback and based their final judgments on their initial preferences. These results imply that people may indeed make use of external cues that imply particular attitudes when the consequences of those attitudes are minimal; however, when the consequences are greater, more time and information is brought to bear on one's attitudes, and so use of such external cues may be limited.

In summary, Bem's self-perception approach has been important in the development of attribution theory for several reasons. First, it posited a very simple model of self-perception, which, although not the whole picture, is certainly an important mechanism in understanding how people perceive and understand their own beliefs. Second, it provided a viable, nonmotivational alternative to dissonance theory. Finally, the simplicity of Bem's model and lack of complex assumptions regarding the thought processes of the social perceiver foreshadows the cognitive miser perspective that currently dominates much thinking within social cognition; emphasis on the capacity limitations of the social perceiver and the need to use shortcuts to solve problems quickly and efficiently are implicit in Bem's work.

Rotter's Locus of Control Theory

A final line of theory and research that influenced the development of attribution theory was Rotter's work on locus of control (1966). Rotter's formulation is very different from the theoretical positions just reviewed. The other theories have detailed the conditions that prompt attributions and have outlined methods for making causal inferences, both of which are presumably followed by most individuals. In contrast, work on locus of control posits that stable individual differences among perceivers influence causal inference.

Rotter argued that people differ in the expectations they hold about the sources of positive and negative reinforcements for their behavior. Some people, termed *internals*, credit themselves with the ability to control the occurrence of reinforcing events. Others, termed *externals*, perceive reinforcing events as under the control of luck, chance, or powerful other individuals—factors external to themselves. Each of us no doubt knows people who embody the extremes of this dimension. Some people's sense of control is so great that they almost seem to believe they make the sun come up in the morning and set at night, whereas other people seem never to see a connection between their own behavior and what happens to them.

Although Rotter does not suggest that one's locus of control will operate equally strongly in all situations, he regards it as a general, relatively stable propensity to view the world in a particular way. Locus of control is assessed using a 29-item scale that includes items like those in Table 2.3. If you answer option *a* for all or most items, then you would be well on your way to a high internal locus of control score, whereas more option *b* answers would push you toward the external extreme.

The locus of control concept has been widely researched (see Lefcourt, 1976; Phares, 1976, for general reviews), and studies demonstrate that locus of control influences both how one perceives events that befall the self and how one interprets the experience of others. For example, in one study (Phares, Wilson, & Klyver, 1971), college student subjects were made to fail on an intellectual task that they had performed under either distracting or non-distracting conditions. Under the distracting conditions, both internals and externals blamed the distraction for their failure. However, when there was no distraction and accordingly no obvious existing attribution for failure, internals blamed themselves for their poor performance, whereas externals were more likely to blame external factors. Thus locus of control represents a chronic way of explaining one's own successes, failures, or other experiences when environmental conditions do not provide any obvious explanation.

In a second study (Phares & Wilson, 1972), college students read an account of an automobile accident and then attributed responsibility for it. Generally, internals attributed more responsibility to the driver than externals did. These results indicate that locus of control is a general propensity to view people either as the masters of their own fate or as pawns in the hands of others; it is not merely self-descriptive. Studies have shown that locus of control influences perceptions of experiences as diverse as political beliefs (e.g., Gurin, Gurin, Lao, & Beattie, 1969), achievement behavior (e.g., Crandall,

TABLE 2.3
The Assessment of Locus of Control
(From Rotter, J. B. External control and internal control. *Psychology Today*, 1971, 5, 37-42, 58-59. Reprinted from *Psychology Today* magazine. Copyright © 1971 American Psychological Association.)

(Choose one option for each question)

1. a. Promotions are earned through hard work and persistence.
   b. Making a lot of money is largely a matter of getting the right breaks.
2. a. In my experience, I have noticed that there is usually a direct connection between how hard I study and the grades I get.
   b. Many times the reactions of teachers seem haphazard to me.
3. a. When I am right I can convince others.
   b. It is silly to think that one can really change another person's basic attitudes.
4. a. In our society, a man's future earning power is dependent upon his ability.
   b. Getting promoted is really a matter of being a little luckier than the next guy.
5. a. If one knows how to deal with people, they are really quite easily led.
   b. I have little influence over the way other people behave.

Katkovsky, & Crandall, 1965), reactions to illness and hospitalization (Seeman & Evans, 1962), and learning (Wolk & DuCette, 1974), among others.

The locus of control concept has not been without its critics. Perhaps the most vociferous ones have focused on the fact that the scale is not composed of a single dimension, as Rotter had originally proposed, but rather may well consist of a number of control-related beliefs. Belief that the world is just, for example, need not predict belief in a politically responsive world, which in turn may be independent of a belief that the world is difficult or merely unpredictable (B. E. Collins, 1974). Yet each of these factors speaks to some aspect of perceived controllability in the world. Another criticism hinges on the fact that the scale may be more suited to white middle-class norms and values than to the values of minority-group members or lower social classes (Gurin *et al.*, 1969; Phares, 1976).

Despite these criticisms, work on locus of control has been both prevalent and fruitful within attribution research. It is one of the few systematic efforts to examine how the perceiver's own personality or style influences social perception, a factor Heider (1958) considered essential in understanding the attribution process. Moreover, the effects of locus of control are quite widespread, suggesting that internality-externality is a basic dimension of causal inference. As we will see in Chapters 3 and 4, locus (internality, externality) does indeed play a prominent role in the ascription of causal responsibility when attributional concepts are applied to social issues and problems.

Summary

Attribution theory is a collection of ideas about when and how people form causal inferences. It examines how individuals combine and use information in a quasi-scientific manner to reach causal judgments. Although the impetus for the attribution process is thought to be motivational, causal analysis itself is believed to proceed cognitively in a relatively unbiased fashion; faulty processing is generally believed to be due to motivational factors and emotions. Psychologists consider attributions important because attributions are the underpinnings of further judgments, emotional reactions, and future behavior.

Attribution theory began with Heider's work on naive psychology, which maintained that the natural language people use to characterize causal action can form a basis for a theory of causal inference. Drawing on Brunswik's lens model of perception, Heider maintained that social perception is much like object perception in the need to consider attributes of the target person, attributes of the perceiver, and the context and manner in which the perception occurs. Heider thought causal inference depends on perceptions of an actor's motivation and ability and on situational factors that impede or promote an action. In addition to his work on causal inference, Heider heavily influenced theoretical and empirical research on attributions of responsibility.

Jones and Davis's theory of correspondent inference, a second cornerstone of attribution theory, maintains that the goal of the causal inference process is to locate the stable underlying attributes of individuals that explain their behavior across situations. Behaviors that are believed to be unconstrained and freely chosen, those that are out of role, actions that are not socially desirable, actions that violate prior expectations, and actions that produce distinctive consequences are all believed to reveal underlying attributes. The perceiver's needs also influence the interpretation of action; actions that are hedonically relevant for the perceiver and those perceived as produced for the perceiver's benefit (personalism) will be regarded as more correspondent than actions that do not directly affect the perceiver.

Kelley, the third major early contributor to attribution theory, developed the covariation model of how individuals form causal inferences when they have access to multiple instances of similar events. According to the model, individuals employ a covariation principle to determine how the outcome in question varies across entities (distinctiveness), across time and modality (consistency), and across people (consensus). The goal of this process is to attribute the outcome to a stable cause or pattern of causes. When only a single occurrence of an event is known to a perceiver, the covariation principle cannot be used, and other rules or strategies of causal inference must be employed. One such rule is the discounting principle, which maintains that the role of any one potential cause of an event is discounted to the extent that other causal candidates are available. The perceiver may also employ complex causal schemata that tie patterns of causes to patterns of effects, including the multiple necessary causes schema for difficult or extreme events and the multiple sufficient causes schema for easy or more common events.

Three other lines of work also heavily influenced early attribution formulations. Schachter's theory of emotional lability examines attributions for emotional states. He argued that internal physiological cues are often ambiguous and thus may be labeled as consistent with any of several emotions or sources of arousal. This emotional lability makes arousal subject to misattribution, a finding that has prompted therapeutic work inducing people to reattribute their arousal from threatening internal sources to nonthreatening external sources. Support for the emotional lability argument, however, is mixed. In a formulation similar to Schachter's, Bem's theory of self-perception argues that people infer their own attitudes using substantially the same processes as they employ to infer others' attitudes, that is, the observation of behavior. When asked one's attitude, one considers one's previous behavior, determines whether or not it was freely chosen, and infers one's attitude accordingly. With this line of work, Bem extended attribution ideas to include causal inferences about the self. Finally, research by Rotter and his associates provides a basis for integrating individual differences with attribution theory. In the locus of control formulation, individuals are judged to be primarily oriented toward the environment (externals) or toward the self (internals) as a source of reinforcement.

In the next chapter, we will examine how ideas about the causal inference process have influenced social psychological theorizing about a variety of social issues and problems.

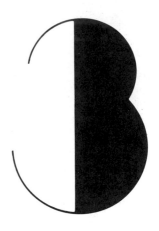

applications
of
attribution
theory

Every theory develops around some specific set of phenomena. Cognitive dissonance theory, for example, developed to explain how people resolve discrepancies among their beliefs or between their beliefs and their behavior. Attribution theory originally focused on how people perceive the causes of others' behavior. One mark of a successful theory is its ability to move beyond its initial boundaries to provide perspectives on issues not initially encompassed by the theory and, in so doing, to provide fresh insights into those issues. According to this criterion, attribution theory has been highly successful. It is one of the most widely exported sets of ideas ever developed by social psychologists, and its impact can be felt in fields as diverse as education, law, and medicine.

Successfully applying a theory often involves more than simply borrowing ideas to shed light on a new issue. In the ideal case, the issue itself causes difficulties for the theory, forcing the theory to expand or otherwise accommodate these unforeseen contingencies. The successful application, then, is a two-way street: the theory sheds light on the issue, and the issue, in turn, points out gaps, flaws, and possible new directions for the theory. Such has been the case with several of the applications of attribution theory that have arisen in the wake of the seminal contributions covered in Chapter 2.

It is impossible to cover every application of attribution theory in one chapter. We have mentioned some briefly, such as the applications of Schachter's misattribution paradigm to therapy (e.g., Storms & McCaul, 1976). Other applications can be found in collections by Frieze, Bar-tal, and Carroll (1979) and in Harvey, Ickes, and Kidd (1976, 1978, 1981). In this chapter, we highlight a few applications of attribution theory with several purposes in mind: to feature those contributions that have attracted the largest number of researchers, to give particular attention to contributions that have yielded results of theoretical significance to attribution theory, and to provide a sense of the diversity of the problems that have been handled by an attribution perspective.

The application of attribution theories to social issues has made one especially substantial contribution to answering the basic question of how people infer causality: it helps define the structure of perceived causality and the dimensions that underlie it.

The Structure of Causal Experience

As we saw in Chapter 2, whether a cause is internal (generated by the person) or external (caused by the situation) is an important dimension of causality in many of the early attribution formulations (Heider, 1958; Rotter, 1966). For example, if you observe your boss yelling at one of your co-workers, it is important to you to know if your co-worker made an error or if your boss did not control his or her temper. But knowing the *locus* of a cause (i.e., whether it is internal or external) is not enough. Even if you decide your boss caused the incident in question, it makes a big difference to you whether he or she is like this frequently or rarely. Thus the *stability* of the behavior is also important, for it helps you further to refine what you think of your boss and how you should regard his or her behavior. As the contributions of Kelley (1967) and E. E. Jones and Davis (1965) make clear, causal analysis is most informative when stable causes are uncovered, such as dispositional qualities that do not change from situation to situation. Thus, at the very least, two dimensions of causality seem to be important: locus (internal, external) and stability (stable, unstable).

But recall that people do not make causal attributions solely to understand why something happened. People also make causal attributions to gain a sense of control over future events (Heider, 1958; Kelley, 1967). Thus a third dimension, *controllability*, may also be important for understanding the implications of causal analysis. If the cause of your boss's behavior is something you can control, its implications for your work life are very different than if the cause of his or her behavior is beyond your control.

Drawing upon these observations and assumptions, Weiner and his associates have integrated the three dimensions of locus, stability (Weiner, Frieze, Kukla, Reed, Rest, & Rosenbaum, 1972), and controllability (Weiner, 1979) into a model of causal attributions that they have explored in the context of achievement behavior. The model maintains that in an achievement situation, a person assesses whether he or she has failed or succeeded and reacts in a general emotional way (positively or negatively) to that judgment. These general emotions prompt a search for the cause of the outcome along the three dimensions of locus, stability, and controllability. The outcome of the causal search, that is, the causal attribution, then dictates future achievement expectations and more specific emotional reactions, such as pride or shame. Expectations and emotions, then, jointly determine subsequent achievement-related performance. This model is depicted in Fig. 3.1 and is described in more detail in the sections that follow.

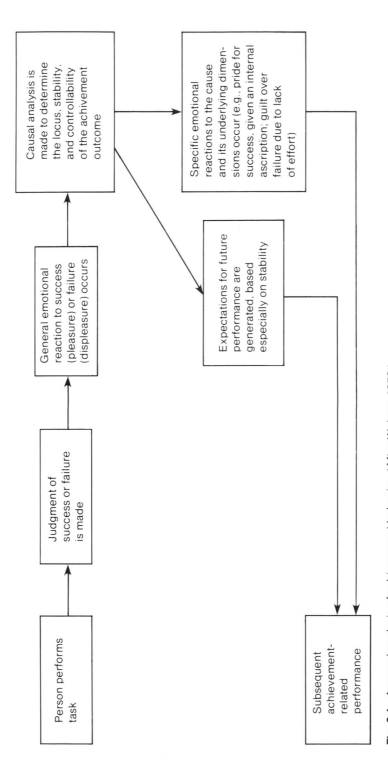

Fig. 3.1 A causal analysis of achievement behavior. (After Weiner, 1979)

Causal Attribution and Achievement Behavior

One Saturday morning many years ago, one of the authors was at her high school taking her college entrance examinations (SATs) in a large gymnasium full of other petrified students. Just as the test was about to start, a snake slithered out of the pocket of the boy in front of her, crawled along the floor, and disappeared into the bleachers. Many surrounding students screamed and stood on their chairs. Later, when the test scores came back, they were lower, on the average, than expected. The school administrators, upset by the low scores, investigated the matter and discovered that the low scores were concentrated in the particular part of the gym where the snake had been. The affected students were accordingly urged to take the examination again without prejudice.

This example, though unusual, illustrates an attributional analysis of achievement behavior and makes several important points. First, emotional reactions prompt causal analysis. If test scores had been as expected, no one would have asked the students to retake the exam. The administrators' displeasure over the low scores prompted a search into why they occurred. Second, people use the dimensions of locus, stability, and controllability in searching for the cause of behavior. The school administrators inferred that a test that normally taps stable, internal, uncontrollable qualities such as student ability had instead tapped quite unstable, external but potentially controllable factors, namely the effect of the presence of a snake on test performance. Third, some outcomes produce more causal search than others. Expected outcomes may produce little causal analysis. No one asked why the students in the parts of the gym away from the snake received the scores they did. Unexpected outcomes, especially if they are negative, result in more causal analysis. When a group of students performs lower than expected on a test, there must be a reason. Fourth, causal attributions have implications for the future. Expectations for future behavior, actual performance, and affective reactions may all be determined by causal analysis. Thus, attributing poor performance to an external, unstable, controllable cause (i.e., the snake) implies that, upon retaking the test, the students will do well, and the students are not faulted for their poor performance.

Table 3.1 presents the three dimensions of achievement behavior and examples of each kind of cause. Let us first consider the four internal causes. Ability is both stable and uncontrollable, presumably because it is determined by raw intelligence. Mood is also uncontrollable, but it is unstable: one's mood varies from situation to situation, but generally not as a function of one's own attempts to control it. Effort is controllable, but it may be either stable or unstable. The typical effort one puts into a task (e.g., studying three hours each night) is stable, but the effort exerted for a particular task (e.g., studying extra hard for this test) is unstable.

When we consider external causes, task difficulty is similar to ability in that it is stable and uncontrollable: the task cannot be changed. Luck bears

TABLE 3.1
**Possible Causes of Achievement Outcomes According to
Locus, Stability, and Controllability**
(After Rosenbaum, 1972, p. 21; Weiner, 1979)

Controllability	Internal		External	
	Stable	*Unstable*	*Stable*	*Unstable*
Controllable	Typical effort exerted	Temporary effort exerted (for this particular task)	Some forms of teacher bias	Unusual help from others
Uncontrollable	Ability	Mood	Task difficulty	Luck

some similarity to mood by being both unstable and uncontrollable. Some external factors are controllable, however. A teacher bias, such as a particular teacher's belief that you are the best student she has had in ten years, may be stable, but under control: there are things you could do to undermine her faith in you. And finally, unusual help from another person is typically controllable, but unstable. For example, if you enlist your best friend's help in studying for one test, presumably you will not need to do so for every test you take.

Much of Weiner's analysis has focused on how causal attributions influence future expectations, emotions, and performance. Thus the model is a dynamic one; that is, it focuses on change over time. Weiner maintained that expectations about the future are determined primarily by the stability of one's causal attributions. For example, if I expect to succeed but actually fail on a test, my expectations should shift little in response to the failure if I attribute the failure to unstable factors such as effort or luck; I would expect the unstable factors not to be present again, so I shall simply try again, expecting to succeed. On the other hand, if I expected to succeed and failed, but attribute the failure to my lack of ability or to task difficulty (stable factors), my expectations should now shift in response to the failure; neither the task's difficulty nor my ability are going to change the next time I try the task.

Specific emotional reactions to an attribution are influenced by such factors as its locus, its controllability, and who the recipient of the outcome is. Some emotions depend upon locus. For example, one might feel pride if one performed a positive act (internal locus), and gratitude if another person did the same thing (external locus). Shame over one's own irresponsible behavior (internal locus) might turn to anger if another person did the same thing (external locus). Thus some emotions are only felt toward other people, and other emotions are only experienced as a consequence of one's own actions.

The controllability of the outcome is also important for understanding emotions. If a negative outcome hurts either oneself or another person, and that outcome is under the control of another person, one is likely to be angry. For example, a careless camper who strews food around the campsite will invoke the ire of all in the area when a skunk arrives to investigate. Guilt is the emotion probably experienced by one who brings about negative outcomes for others, when those factors are within his or her control; this is the emotion the careless camper should experience the next day when facing the wrath of other campers. Finally, pity may be felt for those who experience negative outcomes beyond their control; for example, everyone will likely pity the unsuspecting dog who approaches the investigating skunk. Finally, if one is benefited by another's actions for reasons under that other's control, the dominant emotion will be gratitude. For example, everyone will appreciate the person who cleans up after the careless camper. Thus Weiner maintained that locus and controllability primarily determine the emotional consequences of attributions. Stability seems to intensify affect. If a cause is seen as stable, the resulting affect will be more pronounced than if the cause is unstable (Weiner, 1979). The preceding examples do not, of course, exhaust the range of emotional responses to different outcomes, but do illustrate the point: attributions lead to emotions that then help determine future performance (Weiner, Russell, & Lerman, 1978).

Performance, in turn, typically parallels expectations and affect, being jointly determined by them. For example, one may try harder when one attributes one's prior failing performance to unstable rather than stable factors, and these effects may be enhanced by feelings such as embarrassment or shame over one's prior performance. Alternatively, one may cease trying if expectations of future success are low and feelings of hopelessness are high.

So far, we have focused primarily on people's self-attributions for behavior and their implications for future expectations and performance. Attributions are also important in determining how one responds to another person. For example, an individual must often react to another person, for instance deciding whether or not to offer the person help or how to evaluate the person. Weiner (1979, 1980b) argues that the controllability dimension carries special weight in making such decisions. For example, teachers are often especially hard on students who are clearly able but perform badly. Presumably a teacher sees the student's behavior as under the student's control, and thus the teacher believes that the able student who performs poorly has failed to make the necessary effort. On the other hand, a teacher may be inclined to help students whose difficulties are beyond their control (Brophy & Rohrkemper, 1981).

To summarize Weiner's model briefly, three dimensions underlie the causal attributions that are made for the achievement outcomes of success and failure. The stability dimension indicates whether the cause will change or not and is strongly associated with subsequent expectations of success or failure. The locus dimension concerns whether an individual attributes performance to internal or external factors and is thought to be strongly tied to particular affective or emotional changes. The controllability dimension relates to whether or not a person has control over the outcome; people often use it as a basis for evaluating someone or offering a person help. In the typical achievement situation, people first assess whether or not they succeeded or failed and feel happiness or unhappiness accordingly. They then make a causal attribution for that outcome, which leads to more specific emotional responses, for example, guilt over an effort attribution for failure or pride over an ability attribution for success. People then generate expectations of the probability of subsequent success, and these expectations are again followed by predictable emotional responses; for example, an attribution of failure to low ability produces low expectations of subsequent success as well as feelings of hopelessness. Expectations and emotional reactions jointly determine subsequent performance.

A Critique of Weiner's Model

As we will see in subsequent sections, Weiner's model has been popular and widely supported. That success has not precluded criticism, however. Although researchers have generally agreed that locus is an important dimension of causal experience, and many concur that stability is also important, some question whether controllability contributes much to the model (Abramson, Seligman, & Teasdale, 1978; Ickes & Kidd, 1976; Passer, 1977; Phares, 1976). It may be that controllability is an important dimension for understanding achievement behavior (Meyer, 1980), but it may not be as important for other domains of attribution. We will return to this issue later in this chapter, as well as in Chapter 4.

Critics have also focused on Weiner's hypothesized temporal sequence of events (see Fig. 3.1). Some research suggests that performance changes or changes in expectations may precede or be independent of causal attributions (see, for example, Covington & Omelich, 1979). Other researchers suggest that general affective changes may be caused by attributions rather than by the outcomes of success or failure (McFarland & Ross, 1982). Thus critics have questioned both the temporal sequence itself and the place of attributions in it.

Some of the evidence for Weiner's model comes from studies using role playing or scenario methodologies. Researchers ask subjects how they think they or others would behave in particular situations such as failing a test. Because Weiner's model makes sense intuitively, the danger exists that subjects merely report what makes sense to them, rather than reporting how they would actually behave in the situation, thus providing only apparent support for the model.

In the net evaluation, however, Weiner's model fares quite well. Overall, the model is admirably specific in its hypotheses and hence easily subject to empirical validation. Although not all studies have supported all contentions of the theory, that may in part be due to measurement problems (e.g., Elig & Frieze, 1979; D. Russell, 1982). Moreover, most of its basic elements have a substantial amount of support.

Weiner's model was originally developed to encompass attributions about achievement-relevant behaviors and to predict changes in subsequent motivation, emotions, expectations, and performance. It is a mark of the theory's success that aspects of it have now been applied in other domains as well, including sex stereotyping (Deaux, 1976a), helping (Ickes & Kidd, 1976), loneliness (Michela, Peplau, & Weeks, 1983), parole decision making (Carroll & Payne, 1976a), reactions to hypertension medication (e.g., Henker & Whalen, 1980), and reactions to perceived lack of control (Abramson *et al.*, 1978). As we explore some of these other areas, the influence of Weiner on these other formulations will be apparent.

Sex Stereotyping and Attributions

An admiring graduate student recently remarked to a female professor, "Gee, you've published so much. You must work really hard." "No," snapped the professor in response. "I don't work especially hard. I'm just smart." Why was the professor annoyed by the student's seemingly flattering remarks?

Not only do attributions constitute the endpoint of a causal search for meaning, but they may also represent an enduring explanation for some domain of behavior. Often these explanations are incorrect or biased, and when a substantial number of people share an incorrect or biased explanation, stereotyping is one possible result. Deaux (1976a, 1976b) has suggested that precisely this problem exists in the characteristic explanations people offer for the behavior of men and women. She argues that stereotypes generally favor men over women and that causal attributions made for the success or failure of a man or woman help perpetuate these stereotypes by offering different explanations for the same behavior, depending on whether a man or woman did it (see also Hansen & O'Leary, 1983).

That stereotypes of men are more positive than those of women is unquestionably true (e.g., Broverman, Vogel, Broverman, Clarkson, & Rosenkrantz, 1972). Stereotypically, men are active, independent, competitive, and ambitious, while women are passive, dependent, intuitive, and uncompetitive (descriptive terms that are usually regarded less positively). Expectations that men will succeed at tasks are stronger than expectations for the success of women. When a man and a woman perform exactly the same behavior, a man's performance may be evaluated more favorably than a woman's (e.g., P. A. Goldberg, 1968). This differential evaluation is particularly likely to be true at low or moderate levels of performance; at exceptionally high levels of performance, men and women are more likely to be evaluated similarly (e.g., Pheterson, Kiesler, & Goldberg, 1971).

Also important are the causal attributions made for performance. When people behave according to expectations, their behavior is attributed to stable causes. When people behave inconsistently with prior expectations, their behavior is attributed to unstable causes (e.g., Feather & Simon, 1975; Gilmor & Minton, 1974). Based on these assumptions and the fact that sex stereotypes favor men, one can predict that when a male succeeds on a task, his behavior will be attributed to a stable quality, namely his ability, but when a woman succeeds, her behavior will more likely be attributed to an unstable factor, either luck or effort (Deaux, 1976a, 1976b).

Perhaps this is why the female professor was so sensitive when her publishing exploits yielded the dubiously flattering comment, "You work so hard." "You were at the right place at the right time." "Slow down!" Men, who may in fact be working harder, are thought to be brighter, so their greater effort and occasional spots of luck may go unnoticed. In contrast, when a man fails, others may blame some temporary factor such as not trying hard enough or bad luck. When a woman fails, people more likely attribute it to lack of ability. These predicted attributions for success and failure as a function of sex are illustrated in Table 3.2. It should be noted that these effects are not always found in studies of attributions for men's and women's performance; however, when differences are found, they tend to be in this direction (Deaux, 1976a, 1976b; M. Ross & Fletcher, in press).

Stereotypes can carry over into task evaluations. Tasks that are seen as appropriate for males are evaluated more favorably and are perceived as more difficult and important than tasks that are designated as feminine. Baseball, building model airplanes, and taking out the trash are thought to involve more importance and difficulty than figure skating, needlepoint, or cooking. Furthermore, a task need only to be labeled as masculine to be seen as more difficult or as feminine to be seen as easier. For example, students are sometimes told (falsely) that a particular task is one at which men (or women) excel, for example, forming anagrams; their rating of the task's difficulty changes accordingly (Deaux, 1976a).

How are males' and females' performance evaluated when sex appropriateness of the task is taken into account? On masculine tasks, men's ability is again regarded as a more important determinant of their success than is ability for women performing a masculine task. On feminine tasks, surprisingly, men and women are rated about the same. Apparently, the belief that men are just better at everything can cancel out any advantage that women might be thought to have on a feminine task (Deaux & Emswiller, 1974; Deaux & Farris, 1977; Etaugh & Brown, 1975; Feldman-Summers & Kiesler, 1974).

Perhaps the saddest aspect of these biases in perceived causes of success and failure is that not only do men and women believe these generalizations about others' behavior, but they also sometimes believe them about themselves. Females expect to do less well than males as early as elementary school (Crandall, 1969),[1] and when they do succeed they may attribute it to an external factor such as luck; females' expectations for their own performance are somewhat elevated when the task is labeled as feminine, rather than masculine (Deaux & Farris, 1977; Huston-Stein, Pohly, & Mueller, 1971). Men, on the other hand, show a tendency to attribute their success more to ability.

---

1. See Dweck, Davidson, Nelson, and Enna (1978) for an intriguing analysis of some teacher behaviors that may produce such biases.

TABLE 3.2
Attributions for Success and Failure as a Function of Sex of Target
(After Deaux, 1976a)

	Success	Failure
Men	High ability	Lack of effort or bad luck
Women	High effort or good luck	Low ability

However, it should be noted that men's and women's self-attributions do not always follow these patterns, e.g., Frieze, Whitley, Hanusa, & McHugh, 1982; McHugh, Frieze, & Hanusa, 1982.

Someone, of course, is wrong. Men and women simply do not perform all that differently on most tasks (e.g., Maccoby & Jacklin, 1974). Do women underestimate their performance or do men overestimate theirs? It appears that some of both is responsible; however, generally men seem to have a substantially inflated assessment of their performance, whereas women are only slightly more modest than they should be (Deaux, 1979; Deaux & Farris, 1977).

Causal attributions, then, can reinforce pernicious stereotypes by offering explanations for both stereotypic and counterstereotypic behaviors. What this fact suggests, of course, is that behavior that violates a stereotype will never be sufficient to undo the stereotype; it can simply be explained away by causal attributions.

These issues have been discussed solely in the context of sex stereotyping, since that is the area in which they have usually been investigated. However, it is entirely likely that similar processes underlie the maintenance of stereotypes about other groups such as blacks or Hispanics (see, for example, Yarkin, Town, & Wallston, 1982). Thus, although causal attributions serve important functions in understanding reality, they can also mislead by constructing a pseudo-reality.

Attributions and Helping

A number of years ago, a young woman, Kitty Genovese, was attacked and eventually murdered by a man. Although 38 of her neighbors witnessed the half-hour long event, no one intervened to help. No one even called the police. Why? Attribution theories provide some suggestions about when people will and will not help other people.

Drawing on Weiner's dimensional formulation of attributions, Ickes and Kidd (1976) proposed an attributional model of helping. They argued that when one encounters an individual in need of help, one attempts to infer why the person needs help. One determines whether or not the need was occasioned by the person or by someone else (locus) and whether the need for help was a consequence of that individual's intention. Ickes and Kidd refer to this last dimension as intentionality (cf. Rosenbaum, 1972), but in fact it is very close in meaning to Weiner's controllability dimension.

Previous research on helping (e.g., Berkowitz, 1969) had suggested that people will help another if they believe the other's need comes from an environmental barrier or other external factor, but they are not as likely to help if they believe the problem was caused by the person (i.e., an internal factor). Ickes and Kidd maintained that such an interpretation confuses the importance of locus (internal versus external) and intentionality and that it is intentionality that determines whether one person gives another aid. Consistent with this point is a study by Piliavin, Rodin, and Piliavin (1969). They staged an accident in a New York subway, leading passengers to believe either that a fallen person was drunk or crippled. They found that bystanders were more likely to help the cripple than the drunk. Both drunkenness and being crippled are internal factors, but whereas drunkenness is presumably intentional, being crippled is not. Following this logic, why did no one help Kitty Genovese? When her neighbors were interviewed after the event, many of them indicated they thought she was being beaten up by her boyfriend and had some role in bringing on the attack. Intentional need, then, does not inspire help; unintentional need does.

Recently, researchers have investigated whether giving or withholding help depends on the emotional changes that are thought to occur in response to particular attributions. In Weiner's model (1979, 1982) attributions of others' unfortunate circumstances to controllable factors should produce anger, which discourages helping, whereas attributions to uncontrollable factors should produce pity and subsequent helping. Recent studies have supported this reasoning (Meyer & Mulherin, 1980; Weiner, 1980a) (although the studies have involved role-played helping only).

To summarize, research in the area of helping behavior suggests that perceived intentionality (or controllability) of the need for help is an important determinant of whether or not others will give help. People help those who are in predicaments due to uncontrollable or unintentional circumstances, whereas they are less likely to help people who have brought on their problems themselves. This work also provides some very basic support for Weiner's underlying dimensions of attributions and for the idea that attributions produce emotional reactions that, in turn, produce behavior. We will return to these issues in Chapters 12 and 13.

The Overjustification Effect: An Attributional Analysis

One of psychology's most basic principles, derived from learning theory, is that rewards enhance behavior. If you give a carrot to a donkey, it will pull the cart harder. If you give a child a gold star for making his or her bed, the child will do it again tomorrow. If prisoners can acquire reward tokens by doing chores or good works, they will be rehabilitated more quickly. Unfortunately, this relationship does not always hold.

Recently, psychologists have discovered that interest in an activity and subsequent performance can actually be undermined by the presence of rewards. The overjustification hypothesis maintains that if a person receives an *extrinsic* (external) reward for a task that he or she initially found *intrinsically* interesting, the person's interest in the task will subsequently decline. The reason for this effect derives from Kelley's discounting principle, discussed in Chapter 2. When one initially performs a task that is intrinsically interesting, one does it for personal pleasure. However, if one is then given external rewards for accomplishing the same task, one now defines the task as externally constrained, discounting intrinsic interest as a reason for one's performance. These predictions can also be drawn from Bem's self-perception theory (Chapter 2), which maintains that people observe their behavior, decide if it is tacted (freely chosen) or manded (under external constraint), and infer their attitude from these constraints (or lack of them). Table 3.3 presents an analysis of the overjustification effect.

Let us take a specific example. Suppose Marlene is running her friend Sylvia's roadside lemonade stand largely because she enjoys chatting with people as they stop to drink. Suppose Sylvia then comes along and tells Marlene that she will pay her five dollars an hour to continue to run the lemonade stand. Marlene may now question why she is selling lemonade. Instead of chatting easily with customers, she may feel she has to sell more lemonade. In turn, Marlene might change the way she runs the business. Before long, she may lobby for paid vacations and early retirement. Sylvia's inducement to Marlene actually undercuts Marlene's own interest and possibly even her behavior. If Sylvia them comes back and explains that times are hard, and she is going to have to take away the five dollars an hour, but she hopes that Marlene will continue to run the lemonade stand anyway, Marlene will not likely continue. Why should she do something for free that she used to get paid for doing? This is the essence of the overjustification problem.

Early research demonstrating the overjustification effect (e.g., Deci, 1971, 1972; Lepper, Greene, & Nisbett, 1973) used precisely this kind of procedure. Lepper, Greene, and Nisbett (1973) began by observing nursery school children playing with felt-tip pens, an activity that was intrinsically interesting to them. Once a baseline level of play was established, children were taken individually from the room and asked if they would "help the experimenter out" by drawing some pictures. Children in the "expected award" condition were shown a good player award consisting of a gold star and ribbon on an index card which they were to receive for their efforts. Children in the unexpected award and no award condition were told nothing. All children then drew pictures for several minutes. At the end of this time, unexpected award children were told that since they had done such a good job, they would

TABLE 3.3
An Analysis of the Overjustification Effect:
Rewards Undermine Intrinsic Interest

Reason for performing a task	Example	Will be the dominant reason for performing the task if:	Consequences
Intrinsic interest	Working at one's job because one loves it	Intrinsic interest is salient; extrinsic reasons for not performing the task are salient; rewards signify competence, rather than efforts at control; rewards are contingent upon good performance	Take more pleasure in the task; show more efficient and logical problem solving; maintain task performance in the absence of rewards; select more challenging subsequent problems; solve problems with fewer errors and more creativity
Extrinsic rewards	Working at one's job because it pays well	Rewards are salient or undesirable; rewards constitute efforts at control; rewards are not contingent on a high level of performance; rewards are not seen as given to reward competence	Work hard; generate more activity; show less enjoyment of task; show reduction in performance if rewards are withdrawn; choose easier subsequent tasks; solve problems less efficiently and less logically; be less creative, more error prone, more stereotyped in performance; quality will be lower

receive an award, and the good player award was presented with great flourish. The expected award children received the award, as they had anticipated, and the no award children received no award.

One to two weeks later, all children were again observed playing, and among the toys and games available to them were the felt-tip pens and paper. As predicted, expected award children spent half as much time drawing as did children in the other two groups, presumably because their intrinsic interest in the task had now diminished. Moreover, unexpected award and no award children played with the pens for similar lengths of time; this result means that rewards per se do not undermine intrinsic motivation, only rewards that are seen as extrinsic reasons for performing a behavior.

Subsequent to the original studies that sparked work on the overjustification effect, empirical investigations with both children and adults have confirmed the effect's existence (for reviews, see Condry, 1977; Lepper & Greene, 1978; M. Ross, 1976). People given an external reward for performing an intrinsically interesting task

> choose easier tasks, are less efficient in using the information available to solve problems, and tend to be answer-oriented and more illogical in their problem-solving strategies. They seem to work harder and produce more

activity, but the activity is of a lower quality, contains more errors, and is more stereotyped and less creative than the work of comparable non-rewarded subjects working on the same problem. Finally . . . subjects are less likely to return to a task they at one time considered interesting after being rewarded to do it. These facts appear true of a wide range of subjects doing a wide range of tasks. (Condry, 1977, p. 472; see also T. S. Pittman, Emery, & Boggiano, 1982)

The implications of the overjustification effect are, of course, staggering. Our entire economy runs on the assumption that rewards improve the quality and quantity of subsequent performance, assumptions that must now be questioned, at least under some circumstances. Much socialization of children rests on granting candy, toys, and other rewards for good behavior in the belief that the behavior will remain after the rewards leave. Token economies instituted at mental hospitals and prisons operate on a similar expectation that prosocial behavior will remain after extrinsic rewards are withdrawn. However, reviews of the success of these token economies now suggest that such expectations are wrong, behavior often returns to the same level or below once reinforcements are withdrawn (Kazdin & Bootzin, 1972). The overjustification effect has seemingly quite robust and widespread implications.

There is a problem with the overjustification effect, however. It is easy to think of cases in which it simply is not so. It is difficult to believe that Kenny Rogers likes singing less because he gets so much money for doing it, or that Moses Malone's enthusiasm for basketball declined as his salary went up. Cannot rewards actually enhance intrinsic motivation? No doubt many gleeful individuals are doing exactly what they want and relish that they are paid a great deal for what they would willingly do for far less. These kinds of salient counterexamples have forced researchers to question the pervasiveness of the overjustification effect.

As these observations suggest, rewards do not always undermine intrinsic motivation; sometimes they enhance it. Accordingly, psychologists doing research on the overjustification effect in recent years have attempted to separate out when intrinsic motivation increases or decreases under external reinforcement. One condition is the salience of rewards versus intrinsic interest. Intrinsic interest is undermined to the extent that external rewards are made salient (M. Ross, 1975); for example, constantly being reminded how much money you are making (or not making) may undercut interest. However, when initial interest is made salient (you are doing exactly the job you want) (Fazio, 1981) or when extrinsic reasons *not* to perform the activity are made salient (e.g., you could make more money elsewhere) (T. D. Wilson & Lassiter, 1982), initial interest is maintained. Thus relative salience of intrinsic versus extrinsic reasons for performing an activity respectively increase or decrease interest in the task.

A second, more hypothetical basis for predicting when rewards undermine performance is based on reward-performance contingency. Rewards that are not contingent on performance level may undermine motivation, but rewards that are contingent on performance level may not undermine performance. In

other words, if you give me money for doing a task, I may not like it so much anymore, but if you give me money for doing it well, I may maintain my level of interest. Research on this hypothesis is mixed. Although noncontingent rewards do seem to undermine performance consistently, the effects of contingent rewards are mixed (Calder & Staw, 1975; Enzle & Ross, 1978; Harackiewicz, 1979; Lepper et al., 1973; Rosenfield, Folger, & Adelman, 1980). We will return to this point in a moment.

A third hypothesis concerns whether the reward contains implications of accomplishment or of constraint. Deci's cognitive evaluation theory (1975) maintains that when the controlling aspects of rewards are salient, intrinsic motivation will be undermined, but when rewards communicate to an individual that he or she is competent, motivation will not be undercut. To return to the lemonade stand for a moment, Sylvia can conceivably pay Marlene five dollars an hour for either of two reasons: (1) because Sylvia thinks Marlene is doing a good job and wants to reward her, or (2) because Sylvia wants to be certain that Marlene does not lessen her efforts in the future, and the monetary reward gives Sylvia a certain amount of control over Marlene. Under the former circumstance, Marlene's intrinsic motivation may increase, whereas under the latter circumstances, her intrinsic motivation should decline. The most recent research evidence on overjustification supports the usefulness of this distinction (Boggiano & Ruble, 1979; Karniol & Ross, 1977; Rosenfield, Folger, & Adelman, 1980; Ryan, 1982; see also Fazio, 1981): rewards for competence enhance instrinsic motivation, rewards to control do not. This resolution also helps unravel the equivocal effects of contingent rewards on performance. If a contingent reward is seen as a sign of competence or effectiveness, it may enhance motivation; but if the contingent reward is seen as a controlling effort, it may reduce motivation (Rosenfield et al., 1980).

It should be clear that the overjustification effect has been viewed as cognitively mediated; that is, the attributions people make for why they are doing a task are thought to determine their performance and enjoyment. However, evidence that attributions are actually made and that they predict performance and enjoyment is weak (e.g., Morgan, 1981). Moreover, some aspects of overjustification can be explained comfortably by learning theory, which does not require any intervening cognitive interpretations. For example, performance is poorer following massed rather than distributed practice, and this fact can explain why extrinsic rewards (which yield more vigorous performance) can produce poorer performance. According to learning theory, some rewards may distract people from a task and thus undermine their performance. And, finally, learning theorists maintain that the distinction between rewards (for doing a task) and incentives (inducements to do a task) is an important basis for predicting what the effect of the reward or incentive will be.

Nonetheless, some aspects of the overjustification effect cannot be satisfactorily explained by traditional learning theory (see, for example, Lepper, Sagotsky, Dafoe, & Greene, 1982; M. Ross, 1976; T. W. Smith & Pittman, 1978). Such aspects include the importance of controlling versus competence-enhancing rewards: cognitive interpretation of the reward would seem to be essential in understanding this difference. Hence it seems likely that the attributional analysis of the overjustification effect will persist at least for the present, despite problems with demonstrating the mediating cognitive processes.

In summary, research on the overjustification effect demonstrates conclusively that the presence of extrinsic rewards can undermine motivation to perform an intrinsically interesting task. The overjustification effect is most likely to occur if (1) rewards are seen as an effort to control one's behavior, (2) the rewards are not contingent on obtaining a competent or designated level of performance, (3) the rewards are seen as contingent on obtaining a competent or designated level of performance, but that contingency is interpreted as an effort to control, and (4) the rewards are not very desirable. Rewards can help increase intrinsic motivation if they signal that one has behaved in a competent or successful manner.

The fact that overjustification can occur makes clear that reinforcements in educational, institutional, and economic settings must be used carefully and with an understanding of how recipients are likely to interpret the meaning of those reinforcements. Apropos of this fact, students can take grim satisfaction from the words of Albert Einstein concerning his final exams: "This coercion had such a deterring effect that, after I had passed the final examination, I found the consideration of any scientific problems distasteful to me for an entire year" (Bernstein, 1973, p. 88, cited in Condry, 1977).

An Attributional Analysis of Depression

Depression is now one of the major mental health problems in our country. Approximately 325,000 people a year are treated for it, and at any given time approximately 15 percent of the population show some depressive symptoms such as loss of appetite, sleep disturbances, exhaustion, or an inability to function at their usual level of energy and enjoyment (Rehm & O'Hara, 1979). For many people, depression is a chronic, recurring, severe problem. Depression is diagnosed between two and five times more frequently in women than in men, and it is especially common among working-class women with young children.

Not surprisingly, a massive research effort has been launched to try to understand the causes of depression, what maintains it, and how it can be overcome. Among the many approaches to emerge is an attributional analysis, which maintains that how people interpret the causes of the positive and negative events they experience is an essential element in the development and maintenance of depression. Several theories of depression have incorporated attributional elements (Beck, 1974; Rehm, 1977). We will consider the approach of Seligman and his associates here because it is the most widely adopted model that gives attributions a central status (Rehm & O'Hara, 1979).

The attributional analysis of depression comes directly out of Seligman's theory of learned helplessness (1975); therefore it is useful to begin with an outline of that theory. Everyone has had the experience of trying to bring about some event and not succeeding. One calls up an acquaintance for a date and is turned down, or one tries to explain an idea to a teacher and is misunderstood. For some people, these kinds of experiences are perceived as chronic, at least in certain areas of their life. The crux of learned helplessness is that when one's efforts at control repeatedly fail, not only does one cease trying to cause that particular outcome (helplessness), but one may also actually fail to exert control in some new situation in which control is possible. In other words, people can learn to be helpless by experiencing repeated instances of lack of control (Seligman, 1975).

In one experiment designed to test this theory (Hiroto & Seligman, 1975), students were assigned to one of three initial training groups. One group was subjected to loud noise that could be terminated by pressing a button. The second group was subjected to loud noise but had no control over its termination. The third group experienced no noise. In the second session of the experiment, all subjects were then exposed to noise that, unbeknownst to them, could be terminated by moving a shuttle in front of them. Although the "controllable noise" and the "no noise" groups quickly learned this fact, subjects in the initial uncontrollable noise condition failed to discover it, and instead listened passively to the noise. They had learned erroneously that the noise situation was something they could not control.

Seligman and his colleagues (e.g., Maier & Seligman, 1976) maintained that learned helplessness creates three deficits. The first is *motivational:* the helpless person makes no effort to take the steps necessary to change the outcome. The second is *cognitive* in that helpless people fail to learn the responses that could help them avoid the aversive outcomes. The third is *emotional:* learned helplessness can produce mild or severe depression. Early experiments on learned helplessness were conducted with animals, and so the research emphasis was on learning deficits produced by learned helplessness. However, as work with people has progressed, the emphasis has shifted somewhat to examine more closely the motivational and emotional concomitants of helplessness. In particular, Abramson, Seligman, and Teasdale (1978) have focused on depressed affect and how it may be caused and maintained by learned helplessness.

The underlying principle of the attributional model of learned helplessness is that when people feel they lack control, they want to know why (Tennen & Eller, 1977). Ultimately, what attribution one makes for lack of control determines whether one becomes depressed and to what degree (see also Weiner & Litman-Adizes, 1980). Three attributional dimensions are important in this determination, according to Abramson *et al.* (1978). The first is *internality-externality.* One can attribute helplessness externally ("No one could have done anything") or internally ("I couldn't do anything"). For example, if Patricia asks Bill out, and he turns her down, and she finds out later that he never accepts dates from women, Patricia will attribute his behavior externally to him, and her pride should not be wounded. However, if Patricia learns Bill frequently accepts dates from other women, she will more likely attribute his behavior to personal factors about herself and feel hurt. Whether one attributes a negative event internally or externally, then, determines its effect on self-esteem.

However, whether or not a loss in self-esteem will be serious and possibly lead to pervasive depression depends upon two other factors about the attribution: how *global* it is and how *stable* it is. In making attributions for Patricia's failure to snare Bill, Patricia can blame either a specific factor such as "Bill doesn't like short women" or a global factor, such as "men just don't like short women." Global attributions usually produce more helplessness than specific attributions. That is, Patricia's global attribution to men would prompt her to avoid all men, whereas a specific attribution would lead her to avoid just this man, Bill.

Finally, an attribution can be stable or unstable. If Patricia is eleven years old and has blamed her failures with men on being short, there is hope, since she may grow (unstable attribution). On the other hand, if Patricia is thirty-five and attributes her difficulties to being short, she is out of luck (stable attribution). Whether one makes a stable or unstable attribution influences how long helplessness may persist. Stable attributions lead to persistent helplessness, whereas unstable ones do not (cf. Weiner, 1979).

In summary, then, the internal-external dimension of attributions determines the effect of helplessness on self-esteem; the global-specific dimension determines how general or pervasive the helplessness will be; and the stable-unstable dimension determines how long it will persist over time. In their formulation, Abramson *et al.* report some experimental evidence that is consistent with the predictions generated by these dimensions. The dimensions and their implications for depression are presented in Table 3.4.

Given these dimensions and the learned helplessness model, exactly where does depression fit in? When one believes that desirable outcomes are unlikely, expects undesirable outcomes to occur, and sees no way to change this situation, helplessness and depression will occur. Like the helpless individual, the depressed person experiences both cognitive and motivational deficits as a consequence of the perceived uncontrollability of outcomes. How severe the depression is and how much of a toll it takes on self-esteem depend on the attributions for the uncontrollable events. Internal atributions will lead to greater loss in self-esteem; global attributions will produce more pervasive depression; and stable attributions will produce longer depression. Global, stable, internal attributions, then, produce the most far-reaching depression. Finally, the intensity of these deficits depends on how certain one is that one cannot control one's outcomes. The degree to which this prompts negative affect and lowered self-esteem depends on how important the outcomes are that one wants to control.

As the preceding analysis implies, there are several different types of depression. For example, reactive depression, which is usually associated with a specific event, such as the death of a close friend, may yield specific, external

TABLE 3.4
Perceived Causes of Lack of Control and Their Emotional Consequences
(After Abramson, Seligman, and Teasdale, 1978)

	Global		Nonglobal	
	Stable	Unstable	Stable	Unstable
Internal	Pervasive, stable, low self-esteem; potentially serious depression (e.g., I am unlovable)	Temporary, but pervasive loss of self-esteem (e.g., 1983 was a really bad year for me)	Loss of self-esteem but confined to limited aspect of one's life (e.g., I cannot do athletics to save my life)	Some short-lived loss of self-esteem (e.g., I look terrible today)
External	Pervasive and long-term ennui or displeasure but no loss of self-esteem (e.g., The economy is lousy, and there are no jobs)	Temporary, but pervasive ennui with no loss of self-esteem (e.g., It's a wretched day, the electricity is out, and there's nothing to do)	Long-term ennui or displeasure confined to limited aspect of one's life (e.g., My tennis partner has moved out of town and now I have no one to play with)	No depression, little emotional disruption (e.g., He's in a bad mood today. Better wait until tomorrow)

attributions; such depression is normal and often goes away after a normal mourning period is over. Other forms of depression, which are external, global, and stable, may produce ennui and last for long periods of time without yielding the self-deprecation that is usually thought to be associated with depression (e.g., the person who assumes that his or her future plans have been stymied indefinitely by the chronically poor economy). The most severe depression has been thought to be marked by internal, global, stable attributions for failure and external, specific, unstable attributions for success (see, for example, Metalsky, Abramson, Seligman, Semmel, & Peterson, 1982). Recently, there has been speculation that this attributional pattern constitutes a risk factor for depression. That is, there may be people who chronically see success as external, unstable, and specific and failure as internal, stable, and global; when they are exposed to lack of control or perceive that they have no control, their chronic attributional style or way of interpreting events makes them vulnerable to depression. Evidence is still mixed on this conjecture (see, for example, C. A. Anderson, Horowitz, & French, 1983; Hammen, 1981; Klein, Fencil-Morse, & Seligman, 1976; Kuiper, 1978; Metalsky & Abramson, 1981; Seligman, Abramson, Semmel, & Von Baeyer, 1979).

An illustration may make the intricacies of the learned helplessness model clear. Suppose Denise is a college student who wants to go to medical school but does poorly on the MCATs (medical entrance exams). Depression will occur if she believes no amount of effort on her part can change the outcome. This belief in uncontrollability will, in turn, lead to unhappiness (affective deficit), no effort to study the relevant material (motivational deficit), and no success at learning it (cognitive deficit). If Denise blames the failure on herself, her self-esteem will also decline, and if she blames it on a global factor such as her own incompetence, her helplessness will generalize, perhaps preventing her from applying to law school, psychology graduate school, or any other training program as well. If her attribution is also stable, such as blaming lack of ability, it will persist; taking a year off from school, for example, will not make the situation better. To the extent that Denise is convinced that nothing can change the situation, her ability or motivation to do anything will be worse, and if the outcome is important—she has wanted to be a doctor all her life like her mother before her, and grandmother before that—her negative affect and low self-esteem will worsen (C. Peterson, Schwartz, & Seligman, 1981).

But there is hope. The attributional analysis of depression outlines, albeit briefly, four possible strategies for intervening with the depressed person using cognitive reappraisal strategies. First, a person can be induced to change his or her estimation of the outcome. Our would-be medical student could be encouraged to see ways in which her own behavior could lead to future success. Spending a year in a foreign medical school and then transferring back to the States is a possibility. Second, a person's evaluation of the outcome can be altered. For Denise, stressing the benefits of alternative careers and pointing out the negative side of being a physician would be one way of achieving this objective. Third, one could change the person's expectations from uncontrollable to controllable, assuming that medical school is, in fact, a realistic possibility. Retraining Denise to use her knowledge to the best of her ability, to focus her attention on the test, or to practice taking past MCATs, for example, might begin to help alter this cognition. Finally, one could alter the person's attributions for failure from internal, global, stable factors ("I am dumb") to external, specific, unstable ones ("That was an unusually hard MCAT"). Changing attributions should help break down some of the factors maintaining the dysfunctional behavior and depression.

The attribution/learned helplessness model of depression has enjoyed wide attention and mustered considerable empirical support (see Garber & Seligman, 1980, for a review). However, it has also had its critics (see especially Hammen, 1981; Wortman & Dintzer, 1978). Some have questioned whether attributions are as central to depression as the model maintains; others have suggested that learned helplessness per se may be a poor model for depression; and a third group points out that the model ignores important clinical aspects of depression.

To criticize the model fully would go well beyond the purpose of this chapter; thus we will focus chiefly on the criticisms that center around the central status accorded attributions. There is little empirical justification for the centrality of attributions in depression. Evidence is scanty that people make attributions for lack of control, and that these attributions are stable and prompt the predicted changes in mood, behavior, and cognitions (see, for example, Hanusa & Schulz, 1977; Wortman & Dintzer, 1978). Many other cognitions associated with depression—such as beliefs about whether one can cope with lack of control—may be more central to depression than are attributions (e.g., Wortman & Dintzer, 1978). Attributions may be a symptom of depression, rather than an instigating or maintaining condition (Hammen, 1981).

In conclusion, the attribution/learned helplessness model of depression is an intriguing analysis that has generated a lot of interest and research. Critics of the model, however, maintain that it ignores important features of the attribution process as well as important qualities of depression. These critics, for the most part, however, have come armed with persuasive arguments, but not much counterevidence. It will be on the research they generate that the attributional model of depression will ultimately stand or fall.

Attribution Therapy

Many problems that people have are clearly based on their interpretations of negative events, rather than on negative events themselves. Being fired from a job, for example, may lead one person to hunt cheerfully for a new one, whereas another person may suffer extreme loss of self-esteem and be unable to bring himself or herself to look for work. In the former case, the cheerful job seeker may attribute his or her firing to problems in the company and be glad to have a shot at something new. In the latter case, the upset individual may conclude that he or she is incompetent, and that no one will want him or her. To the extent that problems are rooted in attributions, attribution retraining or attribution therapy holds out a promise for improving the situation.

We have already examined two efforts at attribution therapy in previous sections. The misattribution paradigm (see Chapter 2) has been used as a basis for getting people to reattribute arousal from a threatening to a nonthreatening external source. Likewise, Abramson et al.'s suggestions regarding attribution therapy for depression (1978) maintain that inducing the depressive to change causal perceptions of failure from stable, internal causes to external, unstable ones should improve self-perceptions. Note that the focus of all these efforts, and indeed, of reattribution therapies generally (Valins & Nisbett, 1972) has been to induce people to shift their causal attributions from internal to external sources. The rationale for this assumption has been that internal attributions for negative events lower self-esteem, but external ones, in placing the cause outside the person, do not adversely affect self-esteem.

Recent efforts in attribution therapy question this assumption (e.g., R. Miller, Brickman, & Bolen, 1975). Some have argued that behavior changes attributed to *external* factors may be more enduring than those attributed to *internal* factors (G. C. Davison, Tsujimoto, & Glaros, 1973; G. C. Davison & Valins, 1969); when people attribute arousal externally, they may feel less threatened, but also feel they lack the ability to alter the situation. In this vein, Dweck (1975; Dweck & Goetz, 1978; Dweck & Reppucci, 1973), T. D. Wilson and Linville (1982), and others have suggested that the dimensions of stability and/or controllability may be more important to successful behavior change and recovery than is the internal-external dimension. That is, whereas externalizing a problem may reduce threat, it may not ameliorate the problem. In contrast, shifting one's attributions from stable, uncontrollable to unstable and/or controllable factors may not only reduce the threat, but may also provide a basis for changing the circumstances that produced the problem. By this logic, then, one might not want to induce an individual to externalize his or her problem, but rather to attribute it to controllable, unstable, internal factors such as effort.

Based on this reasoning, T. D. Wilson and Linville (1982) intervened with college freshmen who were worried about their academic performance. Students were told that grades in college are actually quite unstable and typically improve substantially over the four years. Subjects then were shown videotapes of older students testifying to their own dramatic improvement. Subjects who received this information (compared to those who did not) were less likely to leave college, improved their performance on Graduate Record Examination items, and actually increased their grade point average by their sophomore year. Presumably, then, knowing that grades are unstable and that improvement is very likely made these students realize that a poor first year was not a death blow for their future; they were, accordingly, more likely to stick it out than were their uninformed peers.

In contrast to Wilson and Linville's emphasis on the stability dimension, Dweck's attribution retraining approach (Dweck & Goetz, 1978) features the importance of controllability. Dweck (1975) chose as her subjects children who exhibited chronic extreme responses to failure. All of the children were given math problems for a number of treatment sessions. Half the children received only success feedback, which they were encouraged to attribute to internal factors. The other half received both success and failure experiences; these children were particularly encouraged to attribute their failures to low effort, an internal, controllable, and unstable factor. In a follow-up session, when both groups of children were exposed to failure, only the children who had been taught to attribute failure to lack of effort persevered; in contrast, the children who had received only success experiences in the training session showed worsened performance following failure.

Note, however, that both the studies by Dweck and by Wilson and Linville may be manipulating beliefs about stability and uncontrollability simultaneously by showing that, with effort, academic performance can improve. Hence there is likely to be no contradiction between the two sets of results, and both may support Weiner's predictions.

It is important to note that attribution theory is only one of a number of therapeutic approaches that emphasize how cognitive processes can bring about, maintain, exacerbate, or solve clinically significant problems (see, for example, Bandura, 1977). Self-control, self-efficacy, self-schemata, and self-calming talk are among the other cognitive mechanisms that have been proposed as intervention points for ameliorating dysfunctional behavior (Beck, 1976; Kendall & Hollon, 1979; Mahoney, 1974; Meichenbaum, 1977). Accordingly, it is useful to echo some of the cautions raised by the attributional model of depression as criticisms of attribution therapies more generally. Attributions are only one kind of cognition; they may not be made in all kinds of circumstances; and they may not be particularly modifiable when they are made. We already know that one version of attribution therapy, namely, that based on the misattribution paradigm of Schachter (see Chapter 2), has somewhat limited success in dealing with clinical problems. Whether the attribution retraining procedures described in this section will fare any better remains to be seen. An effort toward identifying which dimensions of attributions are associated with positive changes is certainly one promising direction.

Love, Sex, or Aggression?
An Attributional Analysis of Arousal

Most of us would like to think that we are attracted to people because they possess particular attributes that happen to appeal to us. We tend to downplay the importance of seemingly incidental factors such as proximity ("She works in the same building"), timing ("He's been divorced for a while and is ready for a new relationship"), or convenience ("We're on the same bus line"). Yet all these factors matter in determining whether or not two people actually establish a relationship. Another seemingly incidental factor that can influence whether or not one is attracted to another person is one's emotional state at the time of the initial meeting.

Several psychologists (Dutton & Aron, 1974; Walster, 1971; Zillmann, 1978) suggest that when we experience an intense emotion, the residue of that emotional experience will spill over into another emotion such as feelings of sexual or romantic attraction, or even aggression. Zillmann's excitation transfer theory (1978) provides the theoretical context for much of this work. Zillmann maintains that emotional experience depends on three factors: (1) a *dispositional* component that consists of an uninterpreted, immediate motor reaction (e.g., a startle response), (2) an *excitatory* component that energizes the organism (e.g., arousal), and (3) an *experiential* aspect in which the preceding reactions reach awareness and are interpreted (e.g., inferring that one is afraid). Because interpretation occurs only at this third stage, Zillmann argues, excitation can transfer from one source of emotion to another. Moreover, people usually cannot divide up excitation among several potential sources of stimulation, and so excitation caused by one source can be mistaken for another. This idea is not without practical significance. Although plying one's date with alcohol has always been a traditional mode of seduction, in theory, getting her to yell and cheer at a football game could conceivably have the same effect. Dancing, too, has its proponents.

One study by Dutton and Aron (1974) shows how excitation can transfer. They had an attractive woman interview men as they were venturing across a scary suspension bridge or as they were crossing a relatively sturdy wood bridge nearby. Each man was asked to tell a story to an intentionally ambiguous picture of a young woman. As Dutton and Aron predicted, the men who were crossing the scary bridge and were presumably fearful had more sexual content in their stories than did the men who crossed the safe bridge. Moreover, they were more likely to telephone the attractive woman experimenter later than were the men on the safe bridge. Additional studies have replicated this effect (Jacobs, Berscheid, & Walster, 1971; Stephan, Berscheid, & Walster, 1971). Thus, in this case, arousal initially instigated by fear transferred to romantic or sexual attraction.[2]

Fear and romantic attraction are not the only emotions that can function in this way. Residual excitement from physical exertion can intensify anger or aggression (Zillmann & Bryant, 1974; Zillmann, Katcher, & Milavsky, 1972). When one has been angered and is then exposed to erotic material such as stories, pictures of nudes, or an attractive opposite-sex confederate, reports of heightened sexual arousal are often found (e.g., Barclay, 1970; Barclay & Haber, 1970). Prior sexual arousal increases the likelihood of aggression (e.g., Zillmann, 1971). Disgust can facilitate the enjoyment of music (J. R. Cantor & Zillmann, 1973) or humor (J. R. Cantor, Bryant, & Zillmann, 1974).

Zillmann's theoretical position is, of course, very similar to that of Schachter and Singer (1962), described in Chapter 2. Indeed, a number of researchers who have explored the phenomenon of excitation transfer have interpreted their results in terms of Schachter and Singer's theory. However, as Kenrick and Cialdini (1977) point out, Schachter and Singer's original theory maintained that misattribution effects occur only under conditions when the source of the original arousal is ambiguous. Since, in studies of excitation transfer, the initial source of arousal is usually clear-cut, no misattribution effects should theoretically occur. Kenrick and Cialdini's points are well taken. In positing that the excitation stage of emotional experience is unlabeled, Zillmann avoids this interpretational problem.

So far, we have focused primarily on the transfer of an initial source of arousal. There is ambiguity also in the reattribution of arousal. That is, one aroused individual may interpret that arousal as sexual attraction (Dutton & Aron, 1974), whereas another may label it love at first sight (Berscheid & Walster, 1978). Such misunderstandings have, no doubt, been the cause of much personal tragedy. These differences simply illustrate, again, how modi-

---

2. Early studies of this phenomenon frequently refer to it as the attributional analysis of heterosexual behavior. There is no reason to think that homosexual erotic attraction would be any different.

fiable a person's emotional experience often can be. Diffuse internal cues may mean sex to one person and love to another, depending upon their previous experience, how they have been socialized, and the context in which they experience the arousal (cf. Schachter & Singer, 1962, and Chapter 11).

The attributional analysis of the so-called transfer of emotional states has not been without its critics. Kenrick and Cialdini (1977), for example, have argued that reinforcement, not misattribution, is the psychological phenomenon underlying these effects. They maintain, for example, that when one encounters an attractive potential partner after having experienced an intense aversive emotion like fear, the attractive person is reinforcing because he or she is soothing and lowers the emotional arousal level, making one feel good again. Thus it is not the arousal itself that leads to attraction, but its reduction. However, it is difficult to apply their analysis when positive arousal is reattributed as attraction (e.g., White, Fishbein, & Rutstein, 1981).

To summarize, it seems likely that, under some circumstances, arousal due to one source can be transferred to another. We have yet to learn how extensive a phenomenon it is, and whether it applies equally to negative and positive emotions.

Summary

In this chapter, we have examined the application of attribution theory to the diverse problems of achievement, sex stereotyping, the impact of rewards on behavior (overjustification), helping, depression, therapy, and romantic attraction. In each case, it is maintained that, when people are confronted with some ambiguous situation, how they make sense of that situation through their causal analyses determines both their subsequent emotional responses to that situation and their subsequent behavior.

Taken together, what have these attributional theories contributed to our understanding of the attribution process? Their major contribution has been to analyze the dimensions underlying causal analysis. The seminal work in this area was conducted by Weiner, who proposed three underlying dimensions: locus (internal-external), which is associated with changes in self-esteem and other affects; stability (stable-unstable), which is associated with changes in expectations and performance; and controllability (controllable-uncontrollable), which is associated with decisions to intervene in one's own or another's plight.

Although Weiner's work initially developed to explain achievement behavior, several other attributional theories have made use of one or more of the dimensions in their analyses of very different situations. Deaux's sex stereotyping work has utilized the locus and stability dimensions to generate predictions regarding how an identical successful action will be attributed to ability if a male performs it, but to effort or luck if a female performs it; the reverse is often true for unsuccessful actions. Ickes and Kidd's helping model has utilized two dimensions, locus and intentionality (which is very similar to

Weiner's controllability dimension). They find that when another person's need for aid is seen as arising from factors beyond that person's control, other people often help. When other people see a person as responsible for his or her problems, they are less likely to help. Overjustification research by Lepper, Deci, and others maintains that locus of a perceived reinforcement is an important determinant of its effect on performance; when intrinsically rewarding activities are subsequently accompanied by extrinsic rewards, interest in the task can be undermined. Abramson, Seligman, and Teasdale developed an attributional model of depression which posited that three dimensions of perceived lack of control are important for predicting whether or not depression will result: locus, stability, and globality (a substitution for Weiner's controllability dimension). The pervasiveness and length of depression as well as its toll on self-esteem can be predicted from knowledge of an individual's interpretation of events according to the three dimensions. However, in therapeutic applications of attributional ideas, it is unclear whether the locus dimension (e.g., Storms & McCaul, 1976), the stability dimension (e.g., Weiner, 1979; T. D. Wilson & Linville, 1982) or the controllability dimension (e.g., Dweck, 1975; Dweck & Goetz, 1978) is most associated with successful behavior change.

No one set of attributional dimensions is likely to be appropriate for and generate the same behavioral responses in all kinds of situations. Depression may be one situation in which globality is a critical dimension, but globality may not matter so much in predicting achievement behavior. Likewise, for some people's behavioral dysfunctions, changing perceptions of stability may improve adjustment, whereas for others, changing beliefs about controllability may be more successful. It is important not to let one's understanding of a problem area be limited by the use of an a priori set of dimensions. Instead, successfully applying theory to a problem area requires the intelligent interplay of theoretical ideas and of demands and contingencies imposed by the problem itself.

Problems clearly remain in applying attribution theory to social issues. We do not know how robust attributions are and whether or not they truly mediate the affective and behavioral changes that people make in response to ambiguous situations. We will consider this and other more general problems with attribution theory in the next chapter.

Nonetheless, attribution theory has been successfully applied well beyond its original boundaries. Moreover, application to problem areas has yielded a set of empirically and conceptually useful dimensions that may well have general theoretical applicability. As a consequence, our understanding of both the problem areas themselves as well as the texture of causal analysis has been enriched.

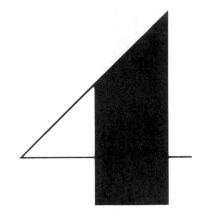

Attribution theory has generated an enormous number of empirical studies, some of which were designed to establish theoretical points (Chapter 2), others of which extended attribution ideas to the analysis of social phenomena (Chapter 3). However, precisely because of this substantial interest, research soon uncovered important qualifications to attributional theorizing. Some of these qualifications constitute biases or errors that social perceivers make when they attempt to apply attribution principles in social situations; these errors and biases will be discussed in the first section of the chapter. Others constitute more fundamental threats or questions about attribution theory itself, and these will be discussed in the second part of the chapter.

attribution theory: biases, errors, and criticisms

Errors and Biases in the Attribution Process

The attribution theories outlined by Kelley (1967, 1972a), and to some extent, the theories of Heider (1958), E. E. Jones and Davis (1965), and Weiner (1979) detail the "correct" manner in which the social perceiver should make attributions. Psychologists call such theories normative, because they detail the appropriate norms or guidelines for how a process should proceed. But research in attribution theory soon revealed that the social perceiver does not always follow these normative guidelines. Rather, the attribution process is marked by a number of persistent errors and biases. Deviations from normative processes are called "errors" if what the social perceiver does is wrong. These deviations are termed "biases" if the social perceiver systematically distorts (e.g., overuses or underuses) some otherwise correct procedure. Some of these errors and biases derive from limitations on cognitive processes, others stem from individual motivations, and a few may come from both motivational and cognitive factors. These biases and errors are important in their own right, not merely because they indicate where the social perceiver is most likely to go wrong in the causal inference process, but also because, taken together, they provide a better descriptive analysis of causal attributions than the normative models against which the perceiver's processing is usually compared.

THE FUNDAMENTAL ATTRIBUTION ERROR

Under most circumstances, behavior stems from a mixture of an individual's personal characteristics and situational factors. Certainly, situational pressures can be very powerful. For example, at a wedding everyone sits rather still, and then rises, turns, and smiles at the right moment. But individual differences are important too. Several people at the wedding are probably bored, one or two may be resentful, still others are tearful, and yet a fourth group is desperately trying to figure out when to stand up, sit down, or kneel. Despite the importance of the interplay of individual and situational factors in determining behavior, the social perceiver often does not see things this way. Perhaps the most ubiquitous error the social perceiver makes, one that psychologists have accordingly called the fundamental attribution error, is to attribute another person's behavior to his or her own dispositional qualities, rather than to situational factors (Heider, 1958; see also L. Ross, 1977). Instead of seeing that there are situational forces such as social norms or roles that lead to particular behavior, people generally see behavior as freely chosen by an individual and furthermore as representing the person's stable qualities. A Hollywood star with a macho image reports that his fans expect to see him in ordinary life busting up furniture and riding off after villains, firing his gun indiscriminately.

A number of studies testify to the strength of the fundamental attribution error. Recall that E. E. Jones and Davis (1965) hypothesized that a perceiver will infer that an actor's attitude is the cause of a behavior when the behavior is freely chosen, but not when it is constrained. In fact, although research testing this hypothesis is generally supportive, what is more striking is the fact that even when a person has been assigned or otherwise coerced into behaving in a particular way, the person's behavior is still seen as indicative of his or her underlying attitude. For example, in one study (E. E. Jones & Harris, 1967), subjects evaluated essays that either favored or opposed Castro's programs in Cuba; they further learned either that the essay writers had freely chosen their position or that the essay position (pro or anti) had been assigned to the writers by the experimenter. Despite subjects' knowledge of the external constraints under which the essays were written, they judged the assigned pro-Castro writers to be more pro-Castro than the assigned anti-Castro essay writers (see also E. E. Jones, Worchel, Goethals, & Grumet, 1971; A. G. Miller, Jones, & Hinkle, 1981; M. L. Snyder & Jones, 1974; Yandrell & Insko, 1977). The tendency to attribute behavior to enduring dispositions such as attitudes is, then, strong, even when situational factors can or do fully account for the behavior.

Conferred role is another situational factor that may be overlooked when attributing the causes for behavior. L. Ross, Amabile, and Steinmetz (1977) demonstrated this point particularly well in a study that simulated a television quiz show. College student subjects were randomly assigned to the role of questioner or contestant. The questioner was told to compose a set of general knowledge questions of some difficulty (e.g., "What do the letters *D. H.* stand for in D. H. Lawrence?") that would be posed to the contestant and could be scored as correct or incorrect. The contestant was merely supposed to answer as many of the questions as he or she could. Of course, the questioner was at a decided advantage in displaying his or her range of knowledge, whereas the contestant was at a distinct disadvantage, at the mercy of whatever questions the questioner posed. Needless to say, contestants were able to answer relatively few of the questions posed to them. Despite the clear advantage of the questioner role conferred by the task, however, both the questioner and the contestant rated the questioner as more generally knowledgeable than the contestant; the effect was strongest for the contestant's beliefs about the questioner.

There are many unfortunate implications of the fundamental attribution error. Victims of situational forces may be held more accountable for their situation than they should be. For example, a welfare mother with three preschoolers may be branded as lazy for not working, while such objective barriers as the absence of day-care facilities or inadequate job training may be ignored. Moreover, since behavior is likely to be attributed to a person's enduring qualities, other people are likely to try neither to modify the person's situation nor to get the person to change his or her behavior. Having branded the welfare mother as lazy, others may fail to institute day-care or to develop training programs so the woman could learn skills that would lead to a job.

What leads to the fundamental attribution error? Its primary cause seems to be the fact that behavior engulfs the field (Heider, 1958). That is, what is dominant when one observes another person is that person behaving: the person moves, talks, and engages in other actions that attract attention. Background factors, social context, roles, or situational pressures that may have given rise to the behavior are, by contrast, relatively pallid and dull and unlikely to be noticed when compared with the dynamic behavior of the actor. Accordingly, the social perceiver may simply underrate or not notice these less salient factors when trying to comprehend the meaning of behavior. Because the person is dominant in the perceiver's thinking, aspects of that person come to be overrated as causally important.

How do we know the fundamental attribution error is an error? Perhaps people's behavior is in fact primarily motivated by enduring predispositions. As evidence that the fundamental attribution error *is* an error, L. Ross (1977) and others (e.g., E. E. Jones & Nisbett, 1972) draw on literature from personality researchers (e.g., Mischel, 1968), showing that individual people's cross-situational consistencies in behavior are relatively weak. If there is in fact little cross-situational consistency in behavior, then the idea that people have stable dispositions is questionable. If people do not have stable dispositions, then attributing behavior generally to such dispositions would clearly be in error.

However, recent analyses have suggested that the fundamental attribution error may not be an error. First, our methods for detecting the actual causes of behavior are quite poor. Possibly, people's dispositional qualities *are* the causes of their behavior, and psychologists have not yet found the appropriate ways either to measure those dispositions or to demonstrate that those dispositions cause behavior. Until such methods are developed, it will be hard to know for certain whether or to what degree the fundamental attribution error is an error (Epstein, 1979; Harvey, Town, & Yarkin, 1981; Monson & Snyder, 1977).

A second reason why the fundamental attribution error may not be an error is that subjects in experiments may be answering a different question than the researcher believes is being asked. When researchers ask, "Did this behavior occur for situational (external) reasons, or for dispositional (internal) reasons?" the researcher means, "Did the actor's stable qualities cause the action or not?" In essence, the researcher may be asking, "What are this actor's stable qualities?" Subjects in experiments, however, may be answering the question, "Should the actor be held responsible for the action?" (e.g., blamed or credited for it). It is entirely possible to blame or credit an actor for an action without believing that the actor's underlying personality has been exposed. One may, for example, appropriately blame a shopper for knocking over the catsup display, but one need not infer a general disposition of clumsiness. Thus, until there is reason to believe that subjects and researchers mean the same thing by *cause* and *disposition*, the extent of the fundamental attribution error will remain unknown (V. L. Hamilton, 1980; Harvey & McGlynn, 1982; Harvey et al., 1981; Reeder & Brewer, 1979).

Belief that the fundamental attribution error is pervasive must be further qualified by the fact that under some circumstances, people overattribute another's behavior to situational factors. Kulik (1983), for example, found that when an actor's behavior was inconsistent with prior expectations about that actor's dispositions, the behavior was attributed to situational factors; moreover, this effect occurred even when the situational factors would be expected to inhibit the behavior, not facilitate it. Quattrone (1982) found that under certain circumstances, "behavior engulfs the person" (p. 593). Specifically, when people's attention is focused on the situational factors that could have produced a person's behavior, they may underestimate the role of dispositional factors. Thus, for example, if I believe someone pressured you to make statements favoring the legalization of marijuana, I may consider the pressure the reason for your statements, overlooking that you actually are in favor of legalizing marijuana (Quattrone, 1982).

The fact that there may be a bias toward situational explanations under some circumstances does not invalidate the fundamental attribution error;

dispositional attributions may still be more common than situational attributions. At the very least, however, it suggests that the bias is far from universal (see also Wetzel, 1982).

Overall, it appears that the term *error* for the fundamental attribution error is a misnomer. Few would claim that people's underlying dispositions have no effect on behavior. Thus, if it exists, the fundamental attribution error deserves to be called a *bias*, in that it may represent a customary overemphasis on personal rather than situational causes for behavior.

THE ACTOR-OBSERVER EFFECT

Before reading any further, try the experiment in Table 4.1. First, rate a friend on the adjectives listed using the indicated scale. Then do the same for yourself. Now go back, ignore the pluses and minuses, and total up the two columns. If you are like numerous students in social psychology classes, your friend's score will exceed your own. If this is true, it means that you see your own behavior as quite variable, but you see others' behavior as quite cross-situationally stable. This is called the actor-observer effect (E. E. Jones & Nisbett, 1972).

The actor-observer effect is a close relative of the fundamental attribution error. It suggests that although we see other people's behavior as caused by relatively enduring dispositional factors, we tend to attribute our own behavior to external factors and see it as more variable from situation to situation. Accordingly, in the previous exercise, most people perceive the behavior of a friend as more stable than their own, and hence give more extreme (positive or negative) ratings to the friend than to themselves.

Why does this difference exist in how we see ourselves versus others? One possible explanation follows the behavior engulfing the field explanation for the fundamental attribution error. When one is an actor, one literally cannot see oneself behaving, so one's own behavior or activity is not particularly salient. Rather, the situational forces impinging on one's behavior are most salient, so they are perceived as exerting a causal influence. In contrast, when one is observing another person, that person's behavior is figural or dynamic against a more pallid and dull situational background, so causality is attributed to the person. Obviously, this explanation draws on the perceptual experience of the social perceiver, a topic that we will cover in more detail in Chapter 7 (see S. E. Taylor & Fiske, 1975, 1978).

Support for the perceptual explanation of the actor-observer effect was provided in a study by Storms (1973), the procedure for which is outlined in Fig. 4.1. In the first part of the study, two actors (A and B) had a conversation while two observers, one assigned to each actor, looked on. At the close of the conversation, all four rated the actors as to whether their behavior had been dispositionally or situationally determined. All four next observed a videotape of actor A during the conversation and then re-rated the participants.

Consider the change in experience that is produced by viewing the videotape of actor A. For actor A, seeing himself behave is a new experience that makes his own behavior salient, and accordingly his self-attributions should

TABLE 4.1
Who Has the More Stable Personality?

First, rate a friend of yours on the following characteristics using the scale that follows. Then go back and do the same for yourself.

Rating Scale

−2	Definitely does not describe
−1	Usually does not describe
0	Sometimes describes, sometimes not
+1	Usually describes
+2	Definitely describes

	Friend	*Self*
Aggressive	_____	_____
Introverted	_____	_____
Thoughtful	_____	_____
Warm	_____	_____
Outgoing	_____	_____
Hard driving	_____	_____
Ambitious	_____	_____
Friendly	_____	_____
Total	_____	Total _____

Now, go back, ignore the pluses and minuses, and total up the two columns.

become more dispositional. For the observer assigned to B, viewing actor A is also a new experience, and his ratings of actor B should become more situational. For the remaining two people, namely actor B and observer A, seeing actor A repeats their prior experience and hence, their attributions should remain unchanged. This is generally what Storms found.

Another explanation for the actor-observer effect relies on the differing information that the actor and the observer have regarding the event for which they are attributing causality (E. E. Jones & Nisbett, 1972). Actors know their feelings with respect to an event, what their intentions were, and what factors gave rise to those intentions, including temporary ones. Thus they may properly attribute their behavior to short-term factors of which observers may be unaware. Actors also have direct access to their own history and know that sometimes they have behaved similarly in the past and sometimes not. An understanding of variability in one's own behavior may discourage disposi-

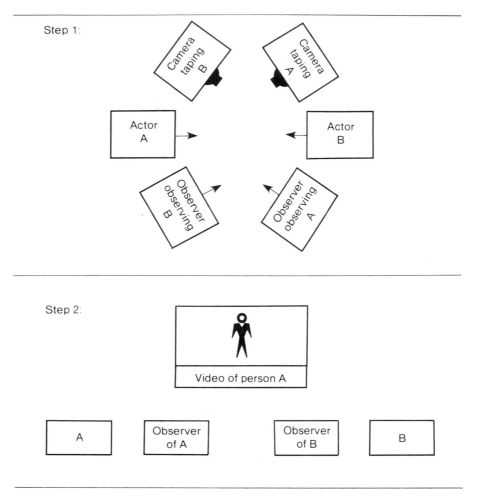

Fig. 4.1 Testing the perceptual explanation for the actor-observer effect. (After Storms, 1973.)

tional attributions. Observers, in contrast, have little information available to them about an actor and must infer what they can from the immediate event. Hence they may be in a poor position to appreciate the many subtle contextual factors that influence the actor's behavior and instead infer that the actor always or usually behaves in this way. Empirical support currently exists for both the perceptual explanation (e.g., Storms, 1973; see also Wyer, Henninger, & Hinkle, 1977) and the informational explanation (e.g., Eisen, 1979), and it seems likely that both sets of factors can contribute to the effect.

Evidence for the actor-observer effect is plentiful (e.g., L. R. Goldberg, 1978; E. E. Jones & Nisbett, 1972; Nisbett, Caputo, Legant, & Maracek, 1973; see E. E. Jones, 1976; Kelley & Michela, 1980; Monson & Snyder, 1977; and L.

Ross, 1977, for reviews), but further research has highlighted some limitations and extensions. First, the actor-observer effect is weakened when positive or negative, as opposed to neutral, outcomes are involved. Positively valued outcomes (such as doing something nice for someone) are more often attributed to people ("She's a nice person"), whereas negatively valued outcomes (such as being very late for a social occasion) are more often attributed to situational factors (e.g., "He got delayed"), regardless of who committed them, the self or another person (S. E. Taylor & Koivumaki, 1976; Tillman & Carver, 1980). When either the self or someone involved with the self has committed the action, credit for positive events and denial of blame for negative events is even stronger (S. E. Taylor & Koivumaki, 1976; see Monson & Snyder, 1977). We will review this self-serving bias shortly.

A second qualification to the actor-observer effect suggests that there are circumstances under which an actor might make more dispositional attributions for his or her own behavior than an observer would (Quattrone, 1982). For example, such a reversal is likely to occur when the actor's behavior actually is dispositionally based; this might happen because the actor knows he or she has always behaved this way in the past and intends to do so in the future (Monson & Snyder, 1977). If George has been lying in wait to trap Smedley for two years and finally gets his chance to make him look like an idiot, George will likely see his own behavior as even more intentionally based than will a neutral onlooker (see also Monson & Hesley, 1982).

A third qualification concerns how the actor-observer effect is measured. The category "situational attributions" is ambiguous, and people may use it when they are not sure what caused behavior. When situational factors *are* clearly specified in the question wording, and uncertain, neutral, or ambiguous attributions are assessed separately, the actor-observer effect largely disappears (L. R. Goldberg, 1981).

Perhaps the most intriguing qualification of the actor-observer effect is that it can be reversed with *empathy set instructions*. For example, being told to pretend that one is observing oneself as another person might or being induced to take the role of another person changes attributions for behavior: actors induced to "see" their own behavior as observers might become more dispositional in their attributions, and observers induced to empathize with actors become more situational in their explanations (Gould & Sigall, 1977; Regan & Totten, 1975; Wegner & Finstuen, 1977).

Researchers have also compared the attributions of active observers, namely people who are simultaneously interacting with the actor, with those of passive observers, those who are uninvolved onlookers. D. T. Miller and Norman (1975) suggest that active onlookers would be even more inclined than passive observers to attribute an actor's behavior to dispositional factors. The reason is that since active observers are involved in the action, they have greater needs to predict and control the situation, especially the actions of others; dispositional attributions produce more stable inferences and hence produce a greater sense of control. According to this reasoning, then, if Joan misses a shot in a volleyball game, Carol is more likely to think Joan is uncoordinated if Carol is also playing than if she is watching the game from the sidelines.

Although studies have supported this hypothesis (D. T. Miller & Norman, 1975; D. T. Miller, Norman, & Wright, 1978; M. L. Snyder, Stephan, & Rosenfield, 1976; Stephan, Rosenfield, & Stephan, 1976), there are some qualifications to the finding. Although active observers usually may be more likely to attribute an actor's behavior dispositionally than passive observers, this will not occur if the behavior in question is neutral (i.e., without any hedonic relevance for the active observer). Thus, for example, if Joan stubs her toe during the game but it has no impact on the play, Carol's inferences about Joan's clumsiness will not differ whether Carol is a player or a spectator. Moreover, active observers may actually be less likely than passive observers to make dispositional attributions for an actor's behavior if they empathize with him or her (Wolfson & Salancik, 1977). If Carol has just missed a shot and Joan does the same, Carol may empathize with Joan's situation and see her error as more due to situational factors than would an onlooker.

Overall, the actor-observer effect is modest in size (L. R. Goldberg, 1981), and, as just noted, can be undone or reversed depending upon the orientation of the observer or the type of behavior for which attributions are made. Nonetheless, the actor-observer effect has been heavily researched, and, as a consequence, knowledge of self-attribution, attributions about others, and how the two differ in some important ways has been enlarged.

THE UNDERUTILIZATION OF CONSENSUS INFORMATION

One of the ways the social perceiver can assess the accuracy of his or her causal perceptions is by comparing them with those of others (Festinger, 1954; Kelley, 1967). Indeed, Kelley argues that consensus information is one of the three determinants for resolving attributional instability. However, research that built on Kelley's model (McArthur, 1972; see Nisbett & Ross, 1980, for a review) quickly uncovered the fact that of the three dimensions (distinctiveness, consistency, and consensus), consensus exerted the weakest effect on attributions.

Several years ago, one of the authors, a lowly assistant professor of exactly one month, received a letter informing her that if she was feeling rotten about herself, her research, and her job, not to worry because every new assistant professor felt exactly the same way. The letter went on to say that moving to a new city where one has few friends and undertaking a new job where one has little opportunity for research because course preparation is so time-consuming takes its toll on all new Ph.D.'s. Somewhat comforted by this information, the professor went back to preparing her umpteenth lecture of the semester. Several weeks later, a questionnaire arrived asking her how she was faring as a new Ph.D., how the year was going, and generally how depressed she was about it. Flattered by this interest, she filled it out, answering that the year was simply wretched. In so doing, she had inadvertently contributed to one of Richard Nisbett's ingenious but unsuccessful consensus experiments.

Nisbett's interest in consensus had been sparked by Kelley's covariation model suggesting that consensus is one basis on which we infer the causes of behavior. Nisbett reasoned that new Ph.D.'s who were informed that their peers were having exactly the same awful experience would be less likely to attribute their problems to themselves, see the problem as a function of the environment, and thereby be less depressed than new Ph.D.'s who did not receive the original letter. However, both groups of Ph.D.'s were equally depressed (Nisbett, Borgida, Crandall, & Reed, 1976). This apparent failure of consensus information to have an impact on attributions and other inferences has been found in many other studies (see Kassin, 1979b, for a review). Why is this true?

One possible explanation for the findings of the "new Ph.D." study is that, whereas consensus information may change one's perceptions of how common an experience is, it does not change the experience itself. Knowing that others felt as awful as I did made me glad I was not alone, but it did not make the year any better. Another possibility is that consensus information may not seem to be as inherently trustworthy as other kinds of experience. If told that a particular group of people has a particular reaction or opinion, one may be inclined to ask: What people? Are they similar to me? How trustworthy are their opinions? If their reactions or opinions turn out to be at odds with one's own, one is likely to reject the consensus information, rather than question one's own conclusions. In short, unlike the direct experience of one's own senses or impressions, information about the reactions of others requires additional tests of its value or relevance.

Consistent with this point, some have argued (e.g., Hansen & Donoghue, 1977) that consensus information is often overruled by what might be termed self-based consensus. That is, people often decide how they feel or what they would do in a situation and then assume others would do or feel the same (self-based consensus); the others' actual opinions or behavior (sample-based consensus) may be ignored. Thus, for example, if I consider a particular comedian to be funny, then, in my mind, he *is* funny. I may ignore the fact that other people do not think he is. The self-based or false consensus effect is discussed in the next section, and it does, in fact, seem to explain some rejection of consensus information.

Information provided by others (sample-based consensus) is by no means always overruled by self-based consensus (e.g., Kulik & Taylor, 1980). Sample-based consensus may be used when one has no expectations about how others would behave, when it is presented in a particularly strong manner, or when it is perceived as clearly relevant to the judgments the social perceiver is making (see Kassin, 1979b, for a review). However, when an individual has strong prior beliefs about what is normative (i.e., what others would think or do), he or she is likely to ignore discrepant opinions offered by others (sample-based consensus).

THE SELF-BASED (FALSE) CONSENSUS EFFECT

As we just noted, the social perceiver does not draw on the opinions or behaviors of others as much as one might expect when making causal judgments. Rather, the consensus information the perceiver prefers is often self-generated, representing what the social perceiver believes others think or would do when faced with a particular situation. Self-based or false consensus is the tendency to see one's own behavior as typical, to assume that under the same circumstances, others would have reacted the same way as oneself.

For example, in one study (L. Ross, Greene, & House, 1977) college students were asked if they would walk around their college campus for thirty minutes wearing a large sandwich board with the message, "Eat at Joe's." Some of the students agreed, others politely demurred. The students were then asked to estimate the percentage of students who would make the same choice they made. Those who agreed estimated that 62 percent of their peers would also have agreed, whereas those who refused estimated that 67 percent of their peers would also have refused. Several additional studies yield similar conclusions, and so the question that arises is, why does this effect occur?

One possible explanation is that we often seek out the company of people who are similar to us (*selective exposure*) and who may in fact behave as we do. Thus our estimate of how others would behave reflects the biased sample of people we have available to us as a basis for our inferences.

Another possibility is that in trying to predict how we would respond in a situation, we must resolve ambiguous details in our minds; those details in their own right may favor or discourage one course of action over another and thus make the selected course of action seem like the obvious choice. For example, a person who imagines others pointing and laughing when he or she appears in the sandwich board will likely decline and estimate that others, anticipating the same harassment, would do the same. In contrast, someone who sees the sandwich board caper as a lark that others will find funny too will likely accept and expect that others would as well.

A third possible explanation is that people have a need to see their own beliefs and behaviors as good, appropriate, and typical, and so attribute them to others defensively to preserve their self-esteem (L. Ross, Greene, & House, 1977). It is not currently possible to distinguish which of these factors causes the false consensus effect, and indeed, they may all contribute to it (see also Zuckerman, Mann, & Bernieri, 1982).

The self-based (or false) consensus effect is an important bias in the inference process. Not only do people overestimate how typical their own behavior is, they also overestimate the typicality of their own feelings, beliefs, and opinions. The false consensus effect is a chief vehicle by which people maintain that their own beliefs or opinions are right. It may, for example, lead one to assume that there are a lot of other people "out there" who feel the same way as oneself, when, in fact, there may not be (e.g., Judd & Johnson, 1981). It can accordingly function as a justification for the imposition of one's own beliefs on others, and has likely been a basis for religious and political oppression. More commonly, the false consensus effect no doubt prompts many errors of inference and exaggeration of one's own opinions in daily interactions with others (Fields & Schuman, 1976; Harvey, Wells, & Alvarez, 1978; Holmes, 1968).

DEFENSIVE ATTRIBUTIONS

Suppose you observe a clumsy friend, Debra, bump into a table, knocking its contents everywhere. Obviously, she did not mean to do it, and so you should not blame her too much for any damage that was done. But suppose there was a Ming vase on the table that is now in a hundred pieces. Might your attributions for her behavior not change a little? She is no longer simply clumsy, she is now a truly careless and perhaps even inconsiderate person. Shouldn't she have known better than to be clumsy around such a valuable treasure?

This example illustrates what has been termed the defensive attribution hypothesis: the hypothesis that observers attribute more responsibility for an accident that produces severe, rather than mild, consequences (K. G. Shaver, 1970a, 1970b; Waltster, 1966). The original study of this phenomenon conducted by Walster had subjects respond to a hypothetical scenario in which a parked car rolled down the hill, either landing harmlessly or doing considerable damage. Walster found that more responsibility was attributed to the car's owner in the scenario depicting severe consequences. As an explanation, she suggested that as consequences become more severe, they become more unpleasant, and the notion that they might be accidental becomes less tolerable: the fear that the same thing might befall the self becomes a realistic possibility. Seeing the accident as avoidable and blaming someone for its occurrence makes the action more predictable and hence avoidable by the self.

Empirical evidence for the defensive attribution hypothesis has been equivocal (see Burger, 1981, for a review). By way of reconciliation, K. G. Shaver (1970a, 1970b) hypothesized that situational and personal similarities account for its occurrence. Specifically, he argued that if you, as an observer, are never going to find yourself in a situation like that of the accident perpetrator (e.g., low situational similarity: you do not drive, so you will never have a car that rolls down the hill), the accident may not arouse a great deal of defensiveness in you. But, if you are likely to be in a similar situation (e.g., high situational similarity: you drive a lot and park in the hills of San Francisco), your defensiveness will be aroused and you may attempt to deny personal similarity to the perpetrator. However, if personal similarity is high, denying personal similarity may be difficult. When personal similarity is high, Shaver predicts, you will attribute the accident to chance or bad luck to minimize implications for similar future outcomes befalling you.

Recently, Burger (1981) examined 22 studies that tested the defensive attribution hypothesis and found support for Shaver's predictions. When subjects were personally and situationally similar to the accident perpetrator, they attributed less responsibility to the perpetrator as severity of the consequences increased; presumably these defensive attributions served to avoid the threatening implications for the subjects. When subjects were situationally or personally dissimilar to the perpetrator, they attributed more responsibility as accident severity increased. More involving manipulations (e.g., having subjects hear about the accident from the perpetrator versus reading about it) also tended to increase the likelihood of defensive attributions.

In short, then, the attribution process may be biased when the events for which attributions are made have implications for one's own future circumstances. High similarity to a severe accident perpetrator leads to perceiving the outcome as random; low similarity produces increased responsibility attributions to the perpetrator as severity increases. Both patterns successfully minimize any negative implications that the accident might have for one's own circumstances.

We should note that the defensive attribution hypothesis is very similar to another line of work known as the just world hypothesis (Lerner, 1970). We will cover that work in the next chapter.

SELF-SERVING ATTRIBUTIONAL BIASES

After you have soundly beaten an opponent, Henry, on the tennis court, how often do you hear from him a gratifying, "Gee, you're much better than I am, aren't you?" Usually you hear that it was a bad day, his serve was off, he is still working on his backhand, or the light was in his eyes. On the other hand, when you have just been badly beaten, the smug look and condescending "Bad luck" from the opponent are particularly grating, because you know he does not believe it was "bad luck" for a moment; he simply thinks he is better. This tendency to take credit for success and deny responsibility for failure is appropriately known as the self-serving attributional bias, and psychologists have researched it at length (see, for example, Bradley, 1978; D. T. Miller & Ross, 1975; M. L. Snyder et al., 1978; Zuckerman, 1979; cf. Knight & Vallacher, 1981).

Overall, there is considerably more evidence that people take credit for success—the self-enhancing bias—than that they deny responsibility for failure—the self-protecting bias (D. T. Miller & Ross, 1975). Rather, people are sometimes willing to accept responsibility for failure, particularly if they can attribute it to some factor over which they have future control, such as effort. For example, if I lose badly at tennis and blame it on the condition of the clay, that will not do much to help me improve my game. But if I realize I faulted on nearly every one of my first serves, I have something to work on at my next lesson (see Weiner, Frieze, Kukla, Reed, Rest, & Rosenbaum, 1972).

Much of the work on self-serving biases has assumed that the biases stem from a need to protect the ego from assault (e.g. M. L. Snyder et al., 1978). Presumably, one feels better about oneself if one causes good things to happen and not bad ones. However, ego-enhancing needs would seem to be more threatened by accepting blame for failure than by denying credit for success; given that accepting blame for failure is relatively common, researchers began to question whether ego-relevant needs could adequately explain the bias.

D. T. Miller and Ross (1975) argue that in the absence of a clear self-protective bias (i.e., denying blame for failure), the self-enhancing bias (i.e., accepting credit for success) can be explained by cognitive factors. First, people expect to succeed and may accordingly accept responsibility for success because it fits their expectations. Second, people strive to succeed, and when they do, their apparent self-enhancing explanation for it may reflect nothing more than the perceived covariation between their effort and the outcome. Finally, when people estimate the amount of control they have in a situation, they utilize instances in which they have been successful more often than ones in which they have been unsuccessful and hence overestimate the amount of control they have exerted (e.g., H. M. Jenkins & Ward, 1965). All of these factors can, then, explain the self-enhancing bias (D. T. Miller & Ross, 1975).

Scientifically compelling as these cognitive explanations are, they are not very intuitively compelling. The idea that ego-defensive needs underlie self-serving biases is too appealing to be dismissed so easily. Indeed, the adequacy of these cognitive explanations has been challenged and rebutted several times (e.g., Bradley, 1978; D. T. Miller, 1978; Sicoly & Ross, 1977; Zuckerman, 1979). Weary (formerly Bradley, 1978) has pointed out that, although ego needs are sometimes met by one's taking responsibility for success and denying responsibility for failure, sometimes the opposite is true. For example, when one's success is too obvious to be denied, as in the case of a publicly heroic act, a strategy of modesty may be more self-serving. One may also back off from taking too much credit for success if others will know that one is being self-serving or if one's future performance will be scrutinized by others (Reiss, Rosenfeld, Melburg, & Tedeschi, 1981; Weary, Harvey, Schweiger, Olson, Perloff, & Pritchard, 1982). Given that public scrutiny or other contextual factors (see also Arkin, Appelman, & Burger, 1980) can reverse the expected self-serving biases, pinning down self-serving biases has been somewhat difficult (see, for example, Hull & Levy, 1979).

In response to D. T. Miller and Ross's critique, several tests of the self-serving bias were conducted in which possible cognitive explanations for self-serving effects were, for the most part, ruled out. For example, if one can arouse subjects' ego involvement in a task *after* a task has been performed, then certain of the nonmotivational explanations (centering on expectations of success and observed covariation between one's efforts and outcomes) can be ruled out (D. T. Miller, 1976); only motivational factors are left to explain any differential attribution of success to the self. (See also Federoff & Harvey, 1976; D. T. Miller, 1976; Sicoly & Ross, 1977; M. L. Snyder et al., 1976; Weary, 1980.) In all these tests, subjects took more credit for successful than unsuccessful outcomes.

Before we conclude that the motivational basis of self-serving attributions has been confirmed, it is useful to point out one caveat about experimentation. Whose position is supported empirically is sometimes more a question of who has designed the more clever experiment, rather than who is actually correct. It seems likely that both cognitive and motivational factors contribute to self-serving biases, and the effort to rule out one or the other set of factors may be misplaced (see also Tetlock & Levi, 1982).

Self-serving biases can extend beyond explanations of one's own behavior to include perceptions of one's intimates, close friends, and other groups with which one is allied, even temporary ones (e.g., Burger, 1981; Lau & Russell, 1980; Schlenker & Miller, 1977). For example, when asked to provide explanations for their spouse's positive or negative behaviors, people are even more likely to credit the spouse's positive behaviors to personal factors and negative behaviors to external factors than they are to do the same for themselves (e.g., Hall & Taylor, 1976). Such biased interpretations also extend to the sports teams a person follows or the political candidate a person favors. When asked to explain why their candidate did so poorly in the presidential debate, advocates may attribute the problem to a bad day and assume that their candidate would win in a rematch, whereas opponents are likely to point out that their candidate is simply better (Winkler & Taylor, 1979). It is important to recognize these social concomitants of attribution. All too often, attribution research has focused on the single individual, ignoring the fact that the individual lives in a larger social context which both affects and is affected by the causal explanations the individual makes.

To summarize, people generally assume more credit for success than responsibility for failure, although researchers find accepting credit for success is more common than denying responsibility for failure. Some of the findings can be explained by cognitive factors, such as expecting success; however, motivational needs both to preserve one's ego and to present oneself in the best light to others seem to be important too (Reiss et al., 1981). Furthermore, self-serving biases extend beyond explanations for one's own behavior to include the people and institutions with which one is allied. However, the self-serving bias is by no means inevitable, as its expression may be influenced by such factors as public scrutiny of the outcome or of the actor's behavior, ambiguity of the outcome, or competing motives such as the desire to appear modest (see also Wetzel, 1982).

THE SELF-CENTERED BIAS

If two roommates are asked to estimate how much of the housework each does, each may well see his or her share as larger than the other's. Or if two collaborators are asked who should be the first author listed on a paper, each may say, "I should." The *self-centered bias* consists of taking more than one's share of responsibility for a jointly produced outcome. It is useful to distinguish the self-centered bias from the self-serving bias. The self-serving bias is taking credit for success, but not for failure. The self-centered bias consists of taking more responsibility for a joint outcome than is one's due, regardless of whether the outcome is successful or unsuccessful.

In one study (M. Ross & Sicoly, 1979) researchers asked married couples to indicate the extent to which they or their spouses had responsibility for each of twenty household chores. The subjects were then asked to provide some examples of their own or their spouse's contributions for each of the chores listed. When the researchers added the responsibility scores of each member of the couple, in most cases the total exceeded 100 percent; each thought he or she had contributed more than the other thought he or she had. Furthermore, each person provided more examples of his or her own contributions than of the spouse's. A similar pattern has been found across a variety of joint experiences (see M. Ross & Sicoly, 1979; Thompson & Kelley, 1981). Why does this bias occur?

M. Ross and Sicoly (1979) suggest several possibilities, some of which are cognitively based, others of which are motivational. First, it is easier to notice one's own contributions than those of another person. That is, one may be distracted from another's contributions by one's own thoughts; one may spend more time attending to one's own contributions than those of another; and one's own contributions fit with one's conception of the project or one's past values or experience better than do another's contributions. Second, it may be easier to recall one's own contributions than those of another person. Recalling more of one's own contributions can lead to the inference that one did more. Third, there may be informational disparities that favor one's own contributions over another's. For example, if I am not in the house when my roommate does his share of the housework, I may underestimate how much he actually did. Fourth, there may be motivational factors involved in the self-centered bias. For example, thinking about how much I have contributed can increase my self-esteem. Finally, each individual may think of the self as the kind of person who does a given activity and infer greater responsibility from the match of the task to his or her dispositions (Thompson & Kelley, 1981).

Which of these explanations is correct? Clearly, not all of them apply in all instances. For example, I may take more credit for messing up the house than my roommate, but dwelling on the fact is unlikely to raise my self-esteem. Indeed, the fact that people often take as much credit for negative as positive outcomes argues generally against the motivational explanation (M. Ross & Sicoly 1979). Likewise, in an effort to rule out differential attention, you could force me to list every single thing my roommate does to help around the house, but I would still believe that I do more (Thompson & Kelley, 1981). Moreover, highly visible, desirable, or stressful activities do not contribute disproportionately to overestimating responsibility, thus also questioning the attention explanation (Thompson & Kelley, 1981). Even under conditions of information equivalency, the self-centered bias thrives (M. Ross & Sicoly, 1979). Overall, differential recall (i.e., the fact that one can bring to mind instances of one's own contributions more easily than those of another person) and match to prior dispositions (i.e., the self-perception that one is the kind of person who does this kind of task) appear to be the strongest among the contenders for producing the self-centered bias (M. Ross & Sicoly, 1979; Thompson & Kelley, 1981).

BIASES IN THE ATTRIBUTION PROCESS: A COMMENT

Although the preceding examples are probably not the only ways in which the attribution process is biased, they represent the major sources of error and bias that have been studied to date. It is useful at this point to ask what kind of picture of the social perceiver they paint. Recall that the attribution models sketched out by Kelley (1967) and by E. E. Jones and Davis (1965) and to a lesser extent, those of Heider (1958) and Weiner (1979), are normative models in that they offer an account of how causal attributions could be inferred correctly, were information gathered and utilized according to the processes outlined. The errors and biases presented in this section portray what social perceivers actually *do* when they fall short of being efficient naive scientists (Hansen, 1980).

When contrasted with the normative models, what portrait of the social perceiver do these actual inferential processes, errors, and biases create? There are at least two striking commonalities in the pattern of differences that have been identified. The first is that, unlike the formal scientist whose role in gathering data is merely that of an observer, the social perceiver adopts the self as a central point of reference. For example, the self's perceptual experience is dominant in the fundamental attribution error and the actor-observer effect. That is, rather than obtaining an unbiased picture of action, the social perceiver sees as causally significant the information that dominates his or her own perceptual field. The self's recollections or impressions are determinants of the self-centered bias and the false consensus effect. It seems to matter little if there is contradictory information such as differing consensus from others; the social perceiver's own needs and motives intrude into a dispassionate causal analysis, leading him or her to see things in a way that is advantageous to the ego (defensive attributions, self-serving bias) (Greenwald, 1980a, 1980b).

The second commonality among the biases is that they produce an underlying conservatism: a willingness to form stable attributions, especially about others (fundamental attribution error, actor-observer effect) and an unwillingness to amend or change one's beliefs, whether about others or the self, in the face of discrepant evidence (e.g., self-centered bias, consensus bias).

What, then, does the social perceiver look like? Instead of a naive scientist entering the environment in search of the truth, we find the rather unflattering picture of a charlatan trying to make the data come out in a manner most advantageous to his or her own already held theories. Perhaps this portrait seems too harsh. Indeed, since few charlatans survive for long within the scientific marketplace, can the social perceiver survive in the real world using the same bag of tricks? Apparently he or she does, and how this occurs will constitute much of the focus of the remainder of the book. Before turning to it, it is important to take a few steps backward to look at attribution theory more dispassionately. Its successes are evident. Where has it failed?

A Critique of Attribution Theory

The errors and biases that the social perceiver characteristically makes constitute important qualifications to attribution theory, but they are not difficult for the theories to handle. A function of normative theories is to provide formal guidelines with which actual behavior can be compared, so that discrepancies can be observed and studied. Researchers who have examined errors and biases in the attribution process have made a successful beginning on this task. However, some of these errors and biases, as well as consistencies across them, suggest that some of the underlying assumptions of attribution theory may themselves be questionable. Likewise, the voluminous empirical literature generated by attribution theory now puts researchers in a position to assess how successful it has been as a central research focus. Is attribution theory a theory? If so, how good a theory is it? Are the currently utilized methods and causal dimensions adequate for investigating attribution theory? Is naive psychology a sufficient basis for constructing a theory? What are the roles of cognition and of complex causal analysis in real-world attributions? What is the scope of attribution theory? It is to these questions that we now turn.

IS ATTRIBUTION THEORY A THEORY?

The famous psychologist Kurt Lewin reputedly said, "There is nothing so practical as a good theory." There are several reasons why Lewin's point is a valid one. First, a good theory is a set of internally consistent and linked propositions. Internal consistency and interconnectedness means that one does not have to discover each proposition individually; rather, knowing some of the propositions of a theory enables you to infer others. To take a simple analogy, it is a little like the difference between trying to remember that a friend's phone number is 435-7385 and knowing that his number forms the word H-E-L-P-F-U-L. In the latter case, the coherence of the pattern enables you to remember and use the number more easily, rather than having to remember each of its digits.

A good theory is also falsifiable. That is, it generates clear predictions that can be tested and found to be true or false. Thus it gives one a way to make the world less ambiguous both by providing the general hypotheses and by enabling one to test them. For example, if someone tells you another person is two-faced, this knowledge gives you a way to interpret the person's nice behavior toward you. It also provides you with a hypothesis that you can test for yourself, as by asking the person what he or she thinks about a mutual acquaintance both in and out of the acquaintance's presence.

A good theory also explains a body of data satisfactorily; one should not have to revise the theory each time a new fact is learned. Rather, a theory should anticipate and accommodate new facts. For example, one would not have a very good theory about one's friend Stan, if one believed that Stan is an extravert except at hayrides or weddings; a better theory would predict and find cross-situational consistency in Stan's extraversion.

At a minimum, then, a good theory should consist of a set of propositions that are internally consistent, coherent, and falsifiable. From the propositions, it should then be possible to generate testable hypotheses to see if the theory's predictions are true or false. A good theory's predictions are true, rather than false, and explain a large body of specific facts (see Deutsch & Krauss, 1965, for a discussion of the criteria of a good theory). Using these criteria, is attribution theory a good theory?

Perhaps the biggest problem facing the field of attribution is the fact that attribution theory is not an internally consistent, coherent, and falsifiable set of propositions and empirical findings. In short, it simply does not contain the features of a good theory. It is rather a collection of knowledge that shares basic but minimal commonalities. It is true that some of the specific theoretical contributions to the area such as E. E. Jones and Davis's correspondent inference theory (1965) or Kelley's covariation model (1967) do meet many of the criteria necessary for a good theory. But boundaries around each of these contributions defining when the theory applies and when it does not are weak, and each speaks only to a portion of the question, "How do people infer causality?"

It is not essential that every test of attribution theory draw on a common set of theoretical propositions. Conceivably, a catalogue of empirical findings would eventually produce a common set of rules about causal inference: theoretical advancement can conceivably come from empirical generalities. However, without a common theoretical focus, certain problems can arise.

A first problem stems from the lack of shared concepts and hypotheses. A theoretical focus helps to pinpoint critical concepts, and it usually produces convergent evidence on these concepts. For example, if a theory makes a particular concept like "choice" central to its predictions, then many different studies will be conducted that examine the effects of choice. Since one successful test of a prediction never proves a prediction, these multiple converging studies together more fairly test the predicted effects of choice and help refine its place in the theory. With the absence of a central theoretical focus, these advantages of multiple tests using similar concepts often do not develop. Hence theoretical propositions and concepts are not as closely examined as they would be if a formal theory were guiding the research endeavor. Thus one researcher may feel that "choice" is an important variable, but if no one else tests out his or her ideas under different circumstances, the full importance of the variable "choice" will never be known.

Another problem that can result from the lack of an overall guiding theoretical perspective concerns the likelihood of generating theoretical inconsistencies. When many individual researchers advance theoretical propositions without reference to some already existing, agreed-upon body of statements, the possibility is great of generating inconsistent statements under what is ostensibly the same general topic. Consider again the example of "choice." If there is no formal theory from which to derive hypotheses about choice, two different researchers could manipulate what they called "choice" and come up with opposite conclusions.

How could this happen? First, each researcher would mean something slightly different by "choice," and so the two uses of the concept would be different. Each researcher might then manipulate "choice" in a way different from the other researcher, and so the operationalizations would also vary. And because each researcher would be interested in slightly different aspects of choice, they would probably examine it in contexts that varied unsystematically from each other. It would then take a great deal of time and energy to understand precisely why the contradictory results emerged. An a priori theory that defined the concept, suggested limits in its operationalizations (i.e., manipulation), and specified relevant contextual factors would avoid such problems.

In summary, then, a major problem with attribution theory is its theoretical diversity; without a common theoretical core, a multitude of empirical findings can develop that bear little more than surface similarities to each other.

THE METHODOLOGY OF ATTRIBUTION THEORY

Methodological problems are another source of difficulty in attribution theory. Attribution theory is essentially a collection of theories about the processes people go through in forming causal attributions. That is, attribution theories all posit process models that make assumptions about how information is gathered and put together over some period of time. Unfortunately, these process models usually look only at the outcomes of the causal inference process, that is, attributions themselves. Researchers then infer support for the underlying process because the outcome occurred as expected. For example, consider a hypothetical use of Kelley's covariation model in which subjects meet a fellow subject, Mike, and get the following information about him in an attempt to induce a dispositional attribution of likability: Andy likes Mike, he has always liked Mike in the past (high consistency), Andy does not like a lot of people (high distinctiveness), and other people like Mike too (high consensus). Subjects are then asked, "Will Teresa like Mike?" If subjects answer yes, the researcher will assume that they used the consistency, consensus, and distinctiveness information to reach that conclusion.

However, closer examination of subjects' inference process may reveal that subjects found Mike to be attractive and personable and believe that attractive, personable guys usually attract girls. Thus Kelley's prediction would be borne out, but not for the right reason. Methodological techniques now exist that permit more direct examination of the underlying cognitive processes themselves (see Chapter 10), and much of the theory underlying attribution processes could be bolstered by use of such procedures (cf. E. R. Smith & Miller, 1983).

THE STRUCTURE OF CAUSALITY

What is the structure of causal perception? As must be readily apparent, attribution researchers have drawn heavily on the internal-external dimension as a way of analyzing causal explanation; an internal cause is located within the person, whereas an external attribution locates causality in the environment. Person (internal) versus situation (external) attributions are important in both Kelley's (1967) and E. E. Jones and Davis's (1965) theories; internal versus external locus of control is the central dimension of Rotter's theory (1966); and Weiner's achievement theory (1979) posits locus (internal, external) as one of its central dimensions. Empirical justification for the theoretical centrality of this dimension is, frankly, weak. There is some evidence that the distinction does not make particularly good sense to people; subjects in attribution experiments often ask for clarification of the dimension and items measuring it (S. E. Taylor & Koivumaki, 1976). This criticism, however, is by no means devastating, since resonance with common sense is only one of many possible reasons for the importance of the internal-external distinction.

Nonetheless, conceptually and methodologically, it is often hard to distinguish between internal and external causes. if Beth is a mean, aggressive person to others because her sister beat her up as a kid, is the cause of her current behavior internal or external? It is possible to imagine a regress of causes for any particular event, some of which would be thought of as internal and others as external (Brickman, Ryan, & Wortman, 1975; see also Vinokur & Ajzen, 1982). Conceptually, internal and external causes have been treated as mutually exclusive categories of causality, and yet when ratings of internal and external causes for an event are made, they are often somewhat positively correlated (F. D. Miller, Smith, & Uleman, 1981; S. E. Taylor & Koivumaki, 1976).

The fact that there are conceptual problems underlying the internal-external distinction has not prompted its abandonment, largely because convincing arguments for substitute dimensions have yet to be made. One strong effort was made by Kruglanski (1975). He proposed a distinction between *occurrences* (which are not completely voluntary) and *actions* (which are voluntary). He argued that, although occurrences can be caused by either internal (person) or external (situational) factors, actions cannot; actions are always internally caused. He further maintained that actions consist of two subtypes: *endogenous acts* (acts that are committed as ends in themselves) and *exogenous acts* (acts that are committed in service of other goals). For example, if I read through a paper you have written because I am interested in the topic, my action would be endogenously based, whereas if I read through it for you because you will appreciate the gesture, then my action is exogenously based. Figure 4.2 illustrates the distinction.

In fact, the endogenous-exogenous distinction often matters. Recall the studies on overjustification, described in Chapter 3, indicating that intrinsic motivation can sometimes be undercut by extrinsic rewards. One could argue, according to Kruglanski's model, that what extrinsic rewards do is change one's perception of one's action from endogenous (i.e., done for its own sake) to exogenous (e.g., done for some external reward). Kruglanski's theory predicts that exogenously attributed acts are seen as less freely chosen and yield less pleasure. These predictions, in fact, correspond to the results of studies on overjustification (see Calder, 1977, and Zuckerman, 1977, for critiques of Kruglanski's position).

Kruglanski's fundamental point (1975, 1977) is that one must distinguish between causal explanations (which account for what caused an act to happen) and teleological explanations (why was the action accomplished, i.e., to what end). Attribution theory has been heavily concerned with "what" questions, sometimes to the exclusion of "why" questions. Although one can sometimes

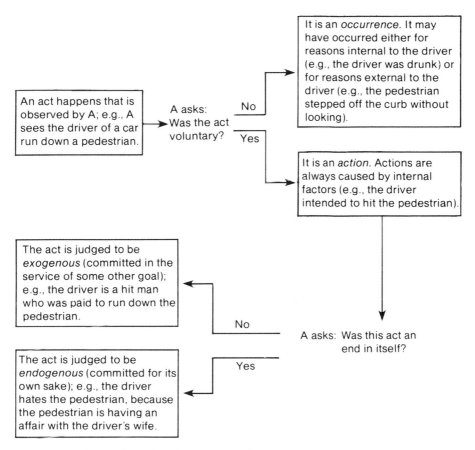

Fig. 4.2 The layman's explanation of action. (After Kruglanski, 1975)

infer why a person committed an action from the context in which it occurs, attribution theory is largely lacking formal statements about teleological explanation (see A. R. Buss, 1978, 1979; Harvey & Tucker, 1979; Kruglanski, 1979; D. Locke & Pennington, 1982). This is an important oversight of both theory and research.

Are there necessarily fundamental dimensions of causal explanation that are relevant to all situations? Rather than a single set of questions or dimensions that are important for most attributional quandaries, it may be that each specific domain defines a set of questions or dimensions that may or may not apply across other domains. Recall, for example, that Weiner's analysis of achievement behavior yielded a different set of causal dimensions than Seligman's analysis of depression. Different issues prompt different questions, and it is entirely likely that our search for generic causal questions or dimensions is misplaced.

What has emerged from the preceding debate are the shortcomings of our understanding of explanation, rather than any definitive answers. The dimension of internality-externality enjoys wide use, but may contain some logical and empirical problems (see also Reeder & Brewer, 1979). Clearly, psychologists are interested in alternative modes of explanation, but what those modes might be, how domain-specific they are, and how they might be incorporated into attribution theory has yet to emerge.

THE ROLE OF NAIVE EPISTEMOLOGY IN THEORY

Another problem that has plagued attribution research is the relationship between naive epistemology and formal theory (Calder, 1977). As we noted in Chapter 2, Heider believed that naive conceptions of causality can form the underpinnings of a scientific theory of causal perception. However, by this point, Heider did not mean that naive epistemology *is* a formal theory. People's phenomenological explanations for events may be rich and intrinsically interesting, but they may not contain the elements or distinctions that provide a good theoretical representation of reality.

Suppose, for example, that one wanted to understand the problem of procrastination. One could conceivably construct an elaborate model of the phenomenon from procrastinators' own excuses, but it might not be a very good representation of the problem of procrastination. Unlike scientific explanations, people's everyday explanations are full of inconsistencies (e.g., the procrastinator may claim that he has not gotten to a project because he wants to do a thorough and careful job while simultaneously claiming that he can knock it off quickly once he gets going). Everyday explanations may also be specific to particular situations and thus have little generalizability (e.g., the procrastinator's claim that this particular piece of work is a problem). And everyday explanations can be affected by motivational needs such as the desire to save face or look good (e.g., the procrastinator's claim that the delay is due to an abundance of good ideas). In contrast, scientific explanations must be internally consistent, consistent with empirical observation, more powerful than everyday explanation, and subject to rigorous investigation (Calder, 1977).

Calder suggests that attribution theorists have sometimes confused scientific and everyday explanations. For example, he points out that researchers who have urged abandonment of the internal-external distinction in attribution research have sometimes done so on the grounds that the distinction does not make sense to people; researchers have, in turn, attempted to substitute dimensions that do make common sense. However, the problem with common-sense distinctions is that they may not reflect empirically valid dimensions, and the distinctions may have little cross-situational usefulness or consistency. By confusing common sense and theoretical sense, Calder maintains that we have neither an adequate descriptive analysis of naive understanding of causality nor a formal body of knowledge that stands up to the criteria of a good theory. Until the two are adequately distinguished, attribution theory will remain a somewhat haphazard blend of naive concepts and scientific propositions.

IS ATTRIBUTION THEORY'S EMPHASIS ON COGNITIONS WELL PLACED?

Another general criticism of attribution theory is that much of it contains a high degree of cognitive naiveté. Although cognitive psychologists originally posited that inferences are made according to normative processes, they were quickly disabused of the idealistic notion that cognitive processes produce thorough, logical, or rational outcomes. However, attribution theorists clung to these notions longer, as if their normative models of causal inferences were actually descriptive (Fischhoff, 1975). In fact, as the well-documented errors and biases in the attribution process testify, the social perceiver falls far short of normative procedures. A comprehensive descriptive model of the causal attribution process would contribute much to the field.

An even more basic question concerns the trust researchers put in cognition. Some have maintained (e.g., Nisbett & Wilson, 1977a; see also Chapter 9) that direct access to our own cognitive processes is limited. To the extent that this is true, it may be problematic to give cognitions such a central status in a theoretical model. That is, how useful is the social perceiver's phenomenology as a theoretical base if it is partly an illusion?

Another problem with cognitions concerns how ephemeral they are. Imagine all the thinking that can be accomplished in the time it takes to *do* anything. The average social perceiver thinks a few profound thoughts, more commonplace ones, and a great many silly or very fleeting ones. Which thoughts are to be trusted? More precisely, most of the problems that require attributional analysis by the social perceiver are both complex and at least somewhat ambiguous. Accordingly, even a meager amount of thought can undoubtedly generate four or five possible answers to any problem. On which does the social perceiver base future action?

HOW MUCH AND WHAT KIND OF CAUSAL WORK DO PEOPLE REALLY DO?

The many available theories of attributional processing differ widely in how much and what kind of causal work they posit. Kelley (1967), Weiner (1979), and E. E. Jones and Davis (1965), for example, derive some fairly complex assumptions about the type of information a social perceiver must generate and/or sift through before reaching a causal inference. In contrast, D. J. Bem (1972) and Schachter (1964) suggest that causal inferences are generated from a fairly rapid perusal of a few salient cues. Who is right? There are several ways to answer this question.

Every attribution theory has its supportive empirical base, and so in some sense, each is correct. On the other hand, every theory has had its share of disconfirmations, and so none is always right. The degree of empirical support for a theory is often more a matter of ingenuity than truth. If the right situation is picked and the information is presented to the subject in just the right way, then causal analysis may proceed according to the theory's hypotheses.

Although these situational and presentational factors could themselves be used to define the boundaries of the theory, unfortunately, they are rarely systematized for use in this fashion. Rather, they usually constitute the researcher's informal guesses and hunches about when the theory is likely to work, and hence are rarely stated formally as limits to the theory. Until theoretical boundaries are more carefully noted, it will be difficult to know when each theory applies.

A secondary question concerns whether the social perceiver does the kind of detailed causal work some of the theories posit or whether causal analysis is, in fact, a rapid process that utilizes few cues (cf. Hansen, 1980). There is some evidence that causal processing becomes more detailed and thoughtful as the issues themselves become more consequential (e.g., Chaiken, 1980; S. E. Taylor, 1975; see also Chapter 12). On the whole, however, psychological opinion is shifting away from those models that posit a quasi-scientific account of the causal inference process toward those that emphasize the rapid utilization of shortcuts to make inferences. Preference for these latter kinds of theoretical models stems in a large part from research in cognitive psychology that emphasizes the limited capacity of the perceiver: it is simply very difficult and time-consuming to go through a lot of information to reach an inference, particularly as the world continues its blooming, buzzing confusion while one is trying to think. Accordingly, it is often more functional to make inferences quickly, so that we can continue to monitor what is going on. We will see that this theme is echoed throughout current work in social cognition in later chapters of this book (see especially Chapters 6-9). To summarize, then, evidence that people go through the kinds of complex causal analyses that attribution researchers impute to them is rare, raising doubts about the customary depth of causal analysis.

WHAT IS THE SCOPE OF ATTRIBUTION THEORY?

Another general issue of attribution theory is its scope. One part of this problem concerns the relationships among attributions, information, and other cognitions. The causal attribution itself has been the target of a remarkably large amount of theoretical and empirical effort. As a recent graduate student so bluntly put it, "Why has so much attention been paid to that one crummy little cognition?" We make other inferences such as predictions, evaluations, or explanations, and no voluminous literature has developed to explain these.

The common answer to the graduate student's question is that causal attributions are our most basic or fundamental cognitions, the first ones formed from raw information and the ones on which other inferences are subsequently based. For example, if I know what caused my dog to bark, I can predict whether or not he will bark again, decide whether or not to punish him, and explain his behavior to my angry neighbor. However, the primacy of the causal attribution has recently been questioned. For example, a study by Zuckerman and Mann (1979) reversed the usual pattern of causal implication in attribution studies: instead of showing that information such as consistency, consensus, and distinctiveness can cause attributions, they showed that attributions formed through other means themselves influence beliefs about those informational bases. Hence the idea of a fixed unidirectional causal relationship between information and attributions is doubtful. One may be able to start at any point in the inference process and infer other judgments from existing ones (see also E. R. Smith, 1982).

Although much attention has been devoted to how attributions are made and what attributions are made, relatively less attention has been paid to the consequences of attributions. Of particular concern is the relationship between attributions and behavior. Researchers learned a bitter lesson from attitude change researchers who examined the attitude-behavior relationship; it proved to be less than direct and weaker than expected (e.g., Schuman & Johnson, 1976). It is difficult to know whether or not the same will be true of attribution research, but some work suggests that it may be (e.g., Nisbett & Wilson, 1977a). As in the case of much attitude research, attribution researchers rarely include behavioral measures. There are, of course, exceptions. But one would like to know, for example, if skiers who believe they are inherently clumsy try less hard than those who believe they simply lack practice. One of the few efforts to examine systematically the attribution-behavior relationship within a defined domain revealed surprisingly low correspondence (see Nisbett & Valins's 1972 consideration of false feedback studies), although there is no reason to conclude that a similar relationship would necessarily emerge within other areas of attribution research. More consistent efforts to examine the consequences of attributions, not merely their antecedents and content, are necessary, and behavioral consequences would seem to be one of the highest priorities.

Finally, one can legitimately ask of attribution theory what phenomena it encompasses. For many events, the causes are obvious. If I hit a car, and the driver yells at me, I need not wonder for long why he is yelling. For other events, the causes do not matter or causal attributions may not be made (e.g., Hanusa & Schulz, 1977). If a dog bites me, I frankly do not care if he bites many people, or if he has merely singled me out for special attention. I will avoid him in the future, regardless. For a third group of events, one can easily discern the cause through social communication. If my best friend does not telephone me for three weeks, I can telephone her and find out what is wrong. And for a fourth group of events, the causes are ultimately unknowable. Who can say why one of my closest friends has cancer? She and I can ponder that question for years, and we will never have a satisfactory answer. What is left to be compassed by attribution theory? It would seem that all that remains is a narrow band of events for which the causes are knowable but temporarily elusive. Is so much theory needed for so small a domain?

It is true that much potential attribution work may not be done, because the causes are obvious or irrelevant or unknowable; some causal analysis is done quickly; and a lot is accomplished through social communication. Nonetheless, attributions are clearly important and may well be basic to other inferences, behaviors, or emotions (R. D. Sherman & Titus, 1982). Even obvious causes are inferred using the types of inference processes outlined by attribution theory. Even when causal attributions do not matter in terms of the consequences they produce, they may well be made for the personal satisfaction of understanding what has happened. Attributions that are made through social communication undoubtedly have most of the same consequences as those made through cognitive inference processes. And even if causes are ultimately unknowable, as in the case of cancer, the process of thinking through possible causes may itself be important for understanding and coping with the event (S. E. Taylor, Lichtman, & Wood, in press).

Summary

Research testing attribution theory and applying an attributional approach to social issues has pinpointed a number of persistent errors and biases that people consistently employ in the attribution process. Foremost among these is the fundamental attribution error, which maintains that people overattribute the behavior of others to dispositional causes, ignoring contributing situational factors such as context or role.

The actor-observer effect, a related phenomenon, reveals that whereas people's explanations for others' behavior are heavily dispositional, explanations for one's own behavior are more situational. The actor-observer effect appears to be due both to perceptual factors (i.e., what is relatively salient when offering causes for one's own or another's behavior) and to differences in information one has about one's own versus another's behavior. However, when perceptual experience is equated, when valenced actions are involved, when information is equivalent, or when an empathy set is engaged, actor-observer effects are weakened or reversed; active observers also make different attributions than passive observers.

Another pair of biases centers on the use of consensus information. Researchers consistently find that consensus information (i.e., the opinions or experience of others) is relatively underutilized in the judgment process. One reason may be that the adequacy of consensus information (e.g., who the people are or how relevant their beliefs are) is questioned by the social perceiver. Instead of using real consensus information, people often use self-based consensus information, that is, what they think others might or ought to believe or do in a given situation. In so doing, they are likely to exaggerate the extent to which others share their own beliefs.

The self-serving attributional bias refers to the fact that people are more likely to take credit for good outcomes than bad ones. However, accepting credit for success is more common than denying responsibility for failure. Reasons for this bias are both cognitive (e.g., it is easier to perceive a covariation between an intended outcome such as success and its occurrence) as well as motivational (e.g., a need to preserve self-esteem). Self-serving biases can also be seen in the explanations offered for the behavior of one's close associates and social groups. The bias can be moderated or eliminated by such factors as competing motives or public scrutiny of one's explanations.

A related bias, the self-centered bias, suggests that people take more credit for a joint outcome than is their due; this bias occurs for both favorable and unfavorable outcomes. Reasons for its existence are several and include the fact that it is easier to notice, store, and recall one's own contributions than those of another; one often has more information about one's own than another's contributions; and the belief that one did more than another person can be ego enhancing. Overall, these biases in the attribution process suggest that, rather than being a naive scientist, the social perceiver can be a self-centered, conservative charlatan who distorts reality in a personally advantageous manner.

The research on attribution theory and its applications to social phenomena has also highlighted a series of problems with and gaps in the existing formulations. Chief among these is the absence of a strong conceptual superstructure within which to test hypotheses about causal relationships and causal search. Although individual theoretical contributions to the area possess some of the criteria of a good theory, attribution theory per se is not a theory. Second, methodological tests of attribution theory are often insufficient to tap the complex process models thought to underlie causal processing. Third, the central dimension of attribution theory, namely the internal-external dimension, has little empirical justification, but efforts to substitute alternatives have met with mixed success. Fourth, naive psychology has sometimes been a substitute for, rather than a basis for, formal theory; the two are not clearly distinguished in some research. Fifth, cognitions are ephemeral, and people may be very limited in the extent to which they can access their cognitive processes; hence more justification is warranted for the centrality of cognitions in attribution theory. Finally, the scope of causal attributions is questionable: are they the driving force behind other cognitive, behavioral, and affective changes? Do they really predict behavior?

To summarize, some of the problems with attribution theory have to do with the intrinsic validity of a cognitive model; others are methodological, concerning how one best tests a process model; others are theoretical, deriving from the absence of a central theoretical framework in the field; and still others stem from the failure to refine and extend the theory's domain. Despite the presence of these problems, attribution theory has had an important impact, not only on social cognition research, but on the many social issues to which it has been applied. It suggests the centrality of the causal attribution to other inferences, emotions, and behavior. It has unearthed the processes people use in inferring causality and has simultaneously uncovered many of the errors and biases in so doing. Moreover, the problems encountered by attribution theory foreshadowed and gave rise to subsequent theoretical and empirical directions within social cognition research. As a consequence, attribution theory remains the cornerstone of the field.

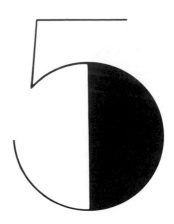

The topic of attributions leads logically into the issue of psychological control for several reasons. First, attributions of control are basic to perceived causality. One will not make a dispositional attribution either for one's own or

psychological control

for another person's behavior unless one believes that the behavior was under personal control. Second, virtually every theory of attribution assumes that causal attributions are made so that individuals feel they can gain some sense of predictability and control over their environment (e.g., Heider, 1958; Kelley, 1967). In fact, empirical tests of these hypothesized underlying needs suggest that a need for control and the process of making attributions are intertwined (Janoff-Bulman, 1979; T. S. Pittman & Pittman, 1980; Swann, Stephenson, & Pittman, 1981; Wortman, 1976). Why is a sense of control so basic? Attribution theorists maintain that without a sense of both our own and others' predictability and control, the world would seem random. We would be unable to understand the responses of others or to plan our own reactions. Thus people's cognitions that they can predict and control their environment are, in a very important sense, fundamental to the causal inference process.

But a sense of personal control has implications far beyond its centrality to the attribution process. Some have argued that personal control is integral to self-concept and self-esteem, constituting a fundamental psychological need (Bandura, 1977; de Charms, 1968; Fenichel, 1945; Hendrick, 1942; R. W. White, 1959). Moreover, psychological control appears to be especially important under stressful or aversive circumstances. Feelings of control can reduce the experience of stress, help people cope with unavoidable unpleasant events, and perhaps even enable them to live longer.

We begin this chapter with a discussion of attributed control, freedom, and responsibility. We consider such questions as: How and when do people ascribe control to others? What factors lead people to believe that actions are freely chosen or unconstrained? What are the consequences of attributions of control, freedom, and responsibility? We then turn to the need for personal control itself. We consider the consequences of loss of personal control. When do people become angry, and when do they become helpless due to loss of control? When do people voluntarily yield control, and what are the consequences of yielding control? We next examine the effects of control-based interventions designed to offset feelings of loss of control. Following that discussion, we consider the questions, Can control be a double-edged sword? Is it beneficial under some circumstances and not under others? Is it beneficial for some people and not for others? Finally, we conclude by considering why feelings of control are so important and what functions they serve.

Attributed Causality, Control, Freedom, and Responsibility

Suppose we see the aftermath of an accident in which a car is badly damaged, its male driver surveying the damage ruefully. What are we to surmise? Did the car go out of control due to a steering defect or malfunctioning brakes? Or was the driver in control? Did the driver cause the accident? Was the driver free to drive as he wished or was he forced off the road by an oncoming car in his lane? Should we consider him responsible for the accident and blame him or should we credit him with the ability to avoid a potentially fatal head-on collision? The questions arising from this ambiguous picture involve manifold attributions: *control*, *causality*, *freedom*, and *responsibility*. How are we to distinguish among them and how are they related to each other?

Causal attribution, the topic of the previous three chapters, is concerned with the question, Did an individual cause a given action or not? Attributed control is related to causal analysis in that it is a precondition for attributed causality. We must assume that an individual has the ability to perform (i.e., is able to control) an action before we can attribute causality to that person. Thus, in the previous example, we could not attribute causality to the driver if the steering wheel locked, because he no longer had the ability to control his car.

Attributed freedom enters the picture by helping to define the type of causal attribution that is made. One usually infers that an individual was free to perform a given action by examining the context in which the action was performed. The more freedom one infers, the more one is likely to attribute the person's behavior to dispositional factors. Thus, if the driver had lots of space, high visibility, and no oncoming traffic, we assume that he was free to drive as he wished, and we may thereby form a strongly negative opinion about his driving.

Finally, the greater the attributed control and freedom, the more responsibility for an action increases. Thus, if the driver could have controlled the car (e.g., if the steering wheel did not lock) and if he was free to drive as he chose, then we must blame him for the accident that occurred. These relationships among causality, control, freedom, and responsibility are illustrated in Fig. 5.1 and are discussed in more detail below.

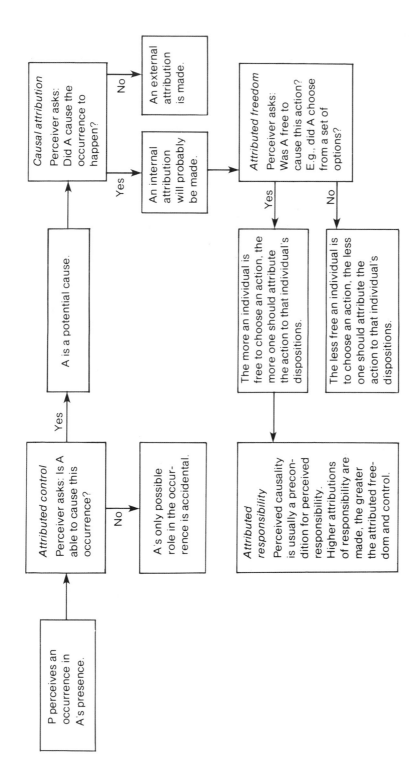

Fig. 5.1 Relationships among causality, control, freedom, and responsibility.

ATTRIBUTED CONTROL

As we just noted, attributions of control are fundamental to the causal attribution process. To infer that an individual has caused an action, one must first assume that the person has the ability to perform the action (Heider, 1958). Ability implies that the capacity to do something exists, and so if that action occurs, the individual is likely to have controlled it. Indeed, as noted in Chapter 2 ("Attribution Theory"), Heider (1958), Kelley (1967), and E. E. Jones and Davis (1965) all argue that one must perceive that another has the ability to perform a particular action before attributing him or her with causal credit for that action.

The perception of ability is a precondition to a sense of one's own control as well. One does not attribute causality to the self for an action one believes one cannot do. Hence control is an implicit attribution in analyzing the meaning of both one's own and others' behavior (see also E. E. Jones & Davis, 1965).

ATTRIBUTED FREEDOM

Attributed freedom is closely related to attributed control. One may assume control (or the potential to exert it) exists whenever one knows that an individual is able to do something. But ability alone does not imply the freedom to do it. Rather, perceived freedom depends on the context within which control is exerted. For example, the fact that you completed a 25-yard pass in a football game tells me that you can control a football, at least under some circumstances. It does not tell me whether you chose to throw it (high freedom) or whether you were pressured to because you were rushed by three linemen (low freedom). As this example illustrates, an important precondition of attributed freedom is the perception that an action was chosen from a set of available options and not merely forced upon one by circumstances (Harvey, 1976; Harvey, Harris, & Lightner, 1979). Thus, relative to attributed control, attributed freedom leads to even stronger dispositional attributions for behavior: one assumes the actor has not only the ability to do an action but also the motivation to do so. The reverse is also true: behavior one believes to be caused by an actor's dispositions is also usually perceived to be more free than behavior that one thinks is prompted by situational factors or normative pressures (Trope & Burnstein, 1977).

What contextual factors enhance attributions of freedom? First, self-attributions of freedom are increased when (1) one is choosing among a set of similar, rather than dissimilar options (Harvey & Johnston, 1973); (2) the options are all positive (e.g., Harvey & Harris, 1975); (3) there is a moderate number of options (e.g., Harvey & Jellison, 1974), rather than too few or too many; (4) one knows what one wants to do and brings it about (Wortman, 1975); and (5) the outcome of the ultimately chosen option is positive (Harvey, Harris, & Barnes, 1975). One should, for example, feel freedom when one chooses to go to one of four favorably reviewed movies, and the chosen movie turns out to be a good one. If one chooses between a not so highly rated movie and the dean's student tea, and the chosen alternative turns out to be boring, perceived freedom should be low.

Similar criteria are employed when one attributes freedom to another person (Steiner, 1970, 1979). For example, one attributes high freedom to another person when he or she has (1) good options to choose from, (2) a clear best choice among the alternatives, and (3) a relatively similar set of options. Variability in choice also implies personal freedom. If a person chooses to go dancing one night, to a movie the next night, and to a lecture the third night, one should perceive that person as more free than the person who goes to movies three nights in a row (Davidson & Steiner, 1971).

In short, then, one attributes freedom on the basis of the contextual factors associated with an action. Conditions favorable to making a satisfying choice imply considerable freedom, whereas the absence of attractive options generally implies little freedom. Attributed freedom enables one to refine one's causal attributions more precisely; with a high degree of freedom, a dispositional attribution is more likely, and with low perceived freedom, a dispositional attribution is less likely.

ATTRIBUTIONS OF RESPONSIBILITY

Attributions of responsibility involve assigning credit or blame for an action. Most commonly, perceived causality is a precondition for attributed responsibility. We do not usually blame or credit people for things they did not do. However, this relationship between causality and responsibility is by no means necessary. For example, if your dog digs up the neighbor's garden, you will most certainly be blamed for it, even though you did not cause it. Accordingly, attributed control is also important in responsibility attributions. One will be perceived as responsible for events that one controls as well as those that one ought to be able to control. The greater the perceived control over an occurrence, the greater responsibility one bears for it in the eyes of others.

Perceived freedom is also fundamental to attributed responsibility. With increasing freedom, one bears increasing responsibility for an action. For example, if you decided to let your dog run free, you bear more responsibility for his rampant destruction than if he chewed through his rope and got loose.

Attributed responsibility is not always a simple issue, however. In making attributions of responsibility, one must at a minimum distinguish between responsibility for the cause of the problem and responsibility for its solution. Although frequently people are expected to solve the problems they create, it does not follow that this will always be so. A recent theoretical analysis of responsibility attributions distinguishes between those two factors, and creates four models of perceived responsibility based on the combination of perceived responsibility for the cause versus the solution of an event (Brickman, Rabinowitz, Karuza, Coates, Cohn, & Kidder, 1982). The analysis further posits that knowledge of these two factors helps predict what kind of help one person will likely give another when the other is perceived as needing aid. These models are presented in Fig. 5.2.

Responsibility for the solution

		Yes	No
Responsibility for the cause	Yes	Moral model (e.g., self-help groups like est)	Enlightenment model (e.g., Alcoholics Anonymous)
	No	Compensatory model (e.g., Headstart)	Medical model (e.g., treatment for illness)

Fig. 5.2 Attributions of responsibility for the causes and solutions of a problem. (After Brickman, Rabinowitz, Karuza, Coates, Cohn, & Kidder, 1982)

The first is the *moral model* in which others see a person as responsible for both the cause of a problem and its solution. The coach who urges his star athlete to pull out of a slump, and the self-help manual that exhorts people to change their self-destructive behaviors in favor of a new life-style are both subscribers to this model. Belief in the moral model does not lead to helping; rather, those who subscribe to the model perceive the needy other person as requiring more motivation and may well urge him or her to get on with solving the problem.

Under the *compensatory model*, a person in need is seen as not responsible for the problem, but as responsible for the solution. As Jesse Jackson has said to black audiences, "You are not responsible for being down, but you are responsible for getting up" (Brickman *et al.*, 1982, p. 14). Under this model, it is again the people in need who are regarded as the agents for solving the problem, but they can do so free of the burden of responsibility for its cause.

The *enlightenment model* blames people for their problems while absolving them of responsibility for the solution. Alcoholics Anonymous, for example, urges new members to take responsibility for their drinking problem, while simultaneously acknowledging that they are unable to solve it alone; rather, they need the help of an organized group of ex-alcoholics in order to end the problem. Under this model, then, those with problems do receive aid from outsiders, but continue to bear the guilt of having brought on the problem.

Under the *medical model*, a person in need of help is seen as responsible for neither the problem nor its solution. The model obviously gets its name from the illness situation in which people contract a disease through no apparent fault of their own and are incapable of curing themselves due to inadequate resources or training. Under these circumstances, the person in need of aid is not faulted for the problem and is given aid by an outside agent.

Each of these models has implications both for whether or not an individual in need of help will receive it and what the impact of the help will be on the recipient. The compensatory and moral models (i.e., those in which a person is held responsible for a solution) may well enhance competence by encouraging the person to find solutions to a problem. The enlightenment and moral models (those in which a person is held responsible for the problem) can have the effect of lowering self-esteem. Particularly problematic are those models in which the individual is judged to be incapable of solving the problem (the medical model and the enlightenment model). This situation creates what Brickman *et al.* (1982) term the *dilemma of helping*. Although the needed help may be provided, it may undermine the recipient's competence and sense of control.

Brickman and his colleagues argue that different models characterize different help-giving and help-receiving agents in the society. Problems clearly arise when providers and recipients of help hold different models. For example, if a particular female unemployment interviewer subscribes to a moral model toward her cases, while a given male unemployment recipient subscribes to a medical model of the same situation, misunderstandings would abound: the counselor, believing that the client had brought his unemployment on himself and could solve it merely by trying to find a job, would exhort him to get out there and look for work; the unemployed man himself, believing that he lost his job through no fault of his own and had little chance of finding another, would likely consider it his counselor's responsibility to get him some benefits. Models of responsibility are, then, fundamentally perceptions of the distribution of social power, as well as perceptions of what constitutes correct or sufficient help when another is in distress.

To summarize, attributions of causality, control, freedom, and responsibility are intertwined. It is important to note that the social perceiver need not make all four types of attributions in all situations. One can attribute causality for an event without attributing responsibility; for example, I may hear a large bang and note that my daughter knocked her ball down the stairs, but I need not infer that she is clever or clumsy for doing so. Similarly, I may blame myself for being late to the office without deciding whether I was free to be late or forced to be late. Thus the relationships pictured in Fig. 5.1 by no means represent a fixed chain of inferences that necessarily depend upon each other. Rather, Fig. 5.1 represents how these cognitions fit together when they all do arise in the inference process.

In the next section we shift our concern from attributions of control to the sense of personal control itself. Although it is important to know what leads us to infer control for both our own and others' behavior, by far the more significant question is, Why is a sense of control so important? Why are people so threatened when their sense of control is undermined?

Reactions to Loss of Control

Each of us has no doubt experienced a personal blow that left us feeling devastated and out of control: the death of a family member, the end of a personal relationship, a failure to achieve some important goal, or the experience of some external threatening event such as a burglary or a rape. Often people will feel the repercussions of such an event for weeks or even months. Occasionally, one such event will affect a person for life.

Control needs become particularly important whenever an individual faces a threatening situation for which there is no apparent adaptive response. Loss of control may occur either because existing freedoms are threatened by some outside force, or because some new situation presents a threat in the form of an uncontrollable aversive outcome. When people experience loss of control in their environment, they may react in any of several ways. These include information seeking, increased reactions to stress, reactance, and helplessness.

SEEKING INFORMATION

Perhaps the earliest response to a loss of control is the desire to gain more information. As we noted in Chapter 2 ("Attribution Theory"), whenever one's beliefs or opinions are undermined and attributions become unstable, one's sense of control is threatened (Kelley, 1967; T. S. Pittman & Pittman, 1980), and one initiates attributional search. People gather information in an effort to establish what impressions are appropriate for the situation. A logical consequence of this increased need for information is an increased susceptibility to social influence (Kelley, 1967). Another consequence is less careful processing of the information that is obtained (Janis & Mann, 1977).

Consider, for example, the situation of a medical patient who suddenly finds he is ill with a disease he does not understand and whose physician has not told him the details of treatment. Patients who are kept in a low state of information about their illness will often go to great lengths to extract information from available medical personnel or to trap a physician into acknowledging a fact about their case (Tagliacozzo & Mauksch, 1972). Other patients will amass an array of incomplete or erroneous conceptions from their own reading or from conversations with friends and relatives or will misapply information from other medical cases they have heard about (Klagsbrun, 1971; McIntosh, 1974). Some desperate seekers will use any chance opportunity to try to read their own charts. Such information may then be used to take active, sometimes faulty steps in their own cases, such as rejecting treatment or seeking discharge against medical advice (S. E. Taylor, 1979). Thus, seeking information after loss of control can lead to a vigilant, useful search, or it can produce a hypervigilant, nondiscriminating information search (Janis & Mann, 1977).

INCREASED REACTIVITY TO STRESS

When loss of control occurs in response to the anticipation of some aversive event, people often react more negatively to that event. Laboratory studies in which subjects face shock, loud noise, a major test, or other stressors show that when people have no information about the timing or onset of those events or have no action they can take to alter the event, they react more negatively. They often show high physiological reactivity, such as increases in adrenalin and its accompanying side effects (e.g., heart pounding, jitters); they also show reduced concentration for other tasks; and self-reports of pain or discomfort increase (e.g., Bowers, 1968; Corah & Boffa, 1970; Geer, Davison, & Gatchel, 1970; Holmes & Houston, 1974; Kanfer & Seidner, 1973; Staub & Kellet, 1972; Staub, Tursky, & Schwartz, 1971).

An example of the deleterious effects of loss of control is provided by Glass and Singer (1972), who systematically explored the effects of noise on people's performance of tasks both in the laboratory and in field settings. In one study, subjects were given a task to perform during which they experienced no noise, uncontrollable bursts of noise, or controllable bursts of noise. Their performance on both the experimental task and on later tasks (after the noise had ended) was measured. Results indicated that uncontrollable bursts of noise not only interfered with performance during the noise itself but that it carried over, leading to lower tolerance for frustration generally and reduced persistence in later tasks. Predictable bursts of noise, though unpleasant, did not have these carry-over effects.

Not only is one's performance affected by uncontrollable stressors, but one can actually experience more symptoms. Uncontrollable noise or shock can lead to a heightened experience of sensations associated with the stressors (e.g., ringing in ears, sweating), relative to controllable aversive experiences (Pennebaker, Burnam, Schaeffer, & Harper, 1977; Weidner & Matthews, 1978).

REACTANCE

Reactance is a response to loss of control that is most likely to occur when existing or expected control is arbitrarily threatened or withdrawn (J. W. Brehm, 1966; S. S. Brehm & Brehm, 1981; Wortman & Brehm, 1975). Critical to the arousal of reactance is a sense that personal freedom over one's outcomes has been challenged (Wicklund, 1974). Emotionally, reactance can lead to anger or hostility. It may develop when outside agents restrict one's alternatives or when outside agents exert pressure when one is about to make a choice.

Consider, for example, what your response would be if a course instructor had indicated you could choose between an objective test or an essay exam as the final exam, and then at the last minute announced that everyone would take the objective test. Reactance will be greater the stronger one's expectation of freedom (the instructor had promised the option several times), the greater the threat (the objective test will clearly be harder), the greater the importance of the event (it is a final, not a midterm), and the stronger the implications for other freedoms (if you fail this test, you may not get into law school) (J. W. Brehm, 1966; Wicklund, 1974).

Reactance leads to several responses. One is hostility or aggressive feelings; for example, you will likely be angry at the teacher. Another response is direct efforts to restore the lost freedoms; you and other class members may firmly remind the instructor of the promised option. A third response is changes in perceptions of the outcomes: threatened or arbitrarily eliminated outcomes become more attractive, whereas outcomes that remain available lose some of their attraction; you may, for example, decide that you absolutely wanted to take the essay exam, now that it is no longer available, even though until you entered the classroom, you had actually not decided which exam to take. And finally, freedom may be restored by implication; for example, you might write a brief essay at the end of the objective test as a symbolic gesture of defiance. A large number of studies (see S. S. Brehm & Brehm, 1981; Wicklund, 1974) document the pervasiveness of the reactance response when the perception of freedom has been undermined. Although some studies question whether reactance is primarily an act of impression management (e.g., appearing to be angry following a threat to freedom) (Baer, Hinkle, Smith, & Fenton, 1980), most researchers accept that it is a reliable psychological reaction to loss of freedom that is manifested both emotionally and behaviorally (see Wright & Brehm, 1982).

Reactance is often accompanied by heightened physiological reactions (such as the release of adrenalin), and it may remain with an individual for long periods of time. When these responses occur, health risks may be sustained. Studies of hospital patients, for example, suggest that certain so-called bad patients (so labeled by hospital staff for their difficult, complaining behavior) may actually be suffering reactance due to the restrictions the hospital imposes on individual freedoms (Lorber, 1975; S. E. Taylor, 1979). The adrenalin increase that can accompany such reactance may aggravate a number of medical conditions such as hypertension or angina.

HELPLESSNESS

As a reaction to loss of control, *helplessness* is in many ways the exact opposite of reactance. Instead of responding with anger and efforts to restore lost freedoms, the person, in essence, gives in and fails to make even the most minimal efforts to change the situation. One will occasionally see newspaper accounts of extreme helplessness in which, for example, a widower, upset by the sudden death of his wife, is unable to take any action on his own behalf such as feeding or dressing himself (Engel, 1968). Most of us experiencing a sudden shock may have a brief period in which we are too stunned to take any action to combat the situation. This period of anxiety, uncertainty, and passivity gives us a brief glimpse into the phenomenology of people who experience helplessness as part of their daily life.

Helplessness can also result when an individual makes some efforts to change the aversive environment, which then prove to be unsuccessful. If control-restoring efforts go unrewarded, the individual capitulates and ceases trying. A particular danger of helplessness is that it can lead to learned helplessness (Abramson, Seligman, & Teasdale, 1978; Seligman, 1975). We discussed the learned helplessness model extensively in Chapter 3 ("Applications of Attribution Theory"), so we will only briefly recapitulate it here. According to the model, the discovery that one's responses are failing to change the uncontrollable environment can generalize to new environments in which control is actually possible. However, the helpless individual may never learn that the new environments are controllable, because he or she never makes an effort at control.

Helplessness may have other debilitating concomitants. Some experiments, done largely with rats, have demonstrated that depletion of physiological reserves such as adrenalin accompanies exposure to uncontrollable, stressful environments; it may be this depletion of physiological reserves that interferes with the ability to take aggressive action (Weiss, Stone, & Harrell, 1970; Weiss, Glazer, & Pohorecky, 1974, 1976). Another deleterious concomitant is that helpless people may develop chronic anxiety or depressive disorders (see Chapter 3).

HELPLESSNESS VERSUS REACTANCE

Helplessness and reactance are both thought to result from loss of control, but they are different in almost every conceivable way. Hence it is useful to try to understand when one or the other response will occur. Wortman and Brehm (1975) have outlined several conditions that determine which reaction will result. They predict that strong initial expectations for control will first produce reactance, rather than helplessness, whereas weak initial expectations for control will produce helplessness (see N. L. Pittman & Pittman, 1979; T. S. Pittman & Pittman, 1980).

For example, if one tackles a bureaucracy over some foul-up and fully expects to solve the problem, one will likely be angrier and try harder than if one tackles the bureaucracy knowing that one's efforts will probably be for naught. Either response (reactance or helplessness) should be more intense if the foul-up involves something important (such as financial aid) than if it involves some minor inconvenience (such as the scheduling of a class during lunch). Wortman and Brehm also suggest that small amounts of experience with lack of control will produce reactance and enhanced striving, whereas large amounts of experience with loss of control will produce helplessness. For example, failing to do well on an electronic game when one has always done well in the past should lead to enhanced striving, whereas if one's current poor performance is as dismal as one's past performance, the likely reaction will be to give up. Finally, Wortman and Brehm hypothesize a temporal sequence to loss of control whereby individuals initially respond with reactance which eventually gives way to helplessness when efforts to restore control fail.

Certain individual difference factors may also predict whether helplessness or reactance will occur when one loses control (S. E. Taylor, 1979). Highly controlling individuals might have chronically higher expectations for control than less controlling individuals, and hence might be expected to show reactance (N. L. Pittman & Pittman, 1979). Individuals who are used to having control (such as middle-aged, high-status males) may be more likely to show reactance than individuals not so accustomed to control (such as children, the elderly, women, or lower-status people); these latter groups might be more likely to respond to loss of control with helplessness. The adverse consequences of loss of control and of its two manifestations, reactance and helplessness, are summarized in Table 5.1.

Self-Induced Loss of Control: The Effects of Mindlessness

We now turn our attention to a different type of loss of control. Whereas the previous discussion of loss of control centered on what happens when external events threaten one's ability to determine one's outcomes, the present discussion will focus on self-induced loss of control: What happens when people are unable to exert control over some task or activity that they were once able to control?

One condition that facilitates self-induced loss of control has been termed *mindlessness* (Chanowitz & Langer, 1981; Langer, 1975). Mindlessness refers to the fact that when one has "overlearned" a task and knows it very well (e.g., driving a car), one often performs it without thinking about it at all, in a routine, automatic fashion. The routinization process, according to Langer, leads one to relinquish conscious control over the task and leaves one vulnerable to certain problems or errors. Although one is still able to perform the task, if the task parameters change suddenly, it may be hard to change so as to deal mindfully with the new contingencies. Thus, to continue the driving example, mindless processing may leave one vulnerable to an accident if another car suddenly darts into the street. Presumably, more mindful or conscious driving might enable one to avert the accident. In this section, we will consider mindlessness and two of its manifestations: self-induced dependence and premature cognitive commitment.

AN EXAMINATION OF MINDLESSNESS

Several studies have demonstrated that mindless processing does indeed lead to the failure to monitor task contingencies effectively. In one study, for example (Langer, Blank & Chanowitz, 1978), a person about to use a photocopy machine was interrupted by an experimental confederate who asked either, "Excuse me, may I use the Xerox machine," "Excuse me, may I use the Xerox machine, because I want to make copies," or "Excuse me, may I use the Xerox machine, because I'm in a rush." Were subjects paying adequate attention to the confederate's behavior, they would realize that only the last explanation—being in a rush—is a legitimate reason for asking to go ahead of someone else in a photocopy line. However, consider the statement, "Excuse me, may I use the Xerox machine, because I want to make copies." Although "because I want to make copies" provides no legitimate reason for going ahead of the subject—indeed, everyone is using the copier because they want to make copies—it is semantically similar to the legitimate request in that it seems to provide a reason. If subjects are processing information mindlessly, as they well might in such an uninvolving situation, they might fail to distinguish between the *content* of the legitimate and illegitimate requests, processing only

TABLE 5.1
Some Possible Consequences of Loss of Control, Reactance, and Helplessness
(After S. E. Taylor, 1979)

State	Behaviors	Cognitions	Affect	Physical state
Loss of control	Indiscriminant information seeking and use; increased reactions to perceived stress; performance deficits	Inadequate expectations	Anxiety	Heightened physiological reactions
Reactance	Efforts to restore lost freedoms	Lost freedoms become even more desirable	Anger or hostility	Heightened adrenalin secretion; possible aggravation of some health problems; eventual adrenalin depletion
Helplessness	Passivity; learned helplessness; inability to take in information	Feelings of helplessness; powerlessness	Anxiety or depression	Possible adrenalin depletion; helplessness also related to health problems

the *form* of the request. Hence both conditions, in appearing to offer reasons for going ahead of the subject, might lead the subject to yield the copier. In fact, when the number of copies the confederate wanted to make was small, both the legitimate and illegitimate reason conditions produced more yielding of the copy machine than did the request without a reason ("Excuse me, may I use the Xerox machine"). However, when the number of copies the confederate needed to make was large, subjects presumably snapped out of their mindless state and let the confederate go ahead of them only in the legitimate request condition.

What does this study imply about control? It suggests that when one knows a task too well (i.e., one has overlearned it), one no longer pays attention to individual components of the task; as a consequence, one may at least partially lose the ability to do so. Rather, a routine for the activity substitutes for more conscious or mindful processing. Any task component that seems to satisfy the form of the routine will be accepted, perhaps wrongfully. Langer (1978) has further hypothesized that when a person has overlearned a task (and thereby loses control over it) the person will perform less creatively and be less able to modify performance when external interruptions or novel task elements are suddenly introduced into the task environment. In contrast, when a task is new, attention is concentrated on the task, leading to effective learning, better learning of the task environment, and high accuracy (e.g., Langer & Imber, 1979).

SELF-INDUCED DEPENDENCE

Another condition under which mindlessness induces loss of control and reduces the efficacy of performance is termed *self-induced dependence* (Langer & Benevento, 1978). This situation occurs when a person who was previously able to perform a task quite successfully and mindlessly comes to doubt his or her ability to do so because of external situational factors that promote passivity, dependence, or a general feeling of inferiority. Consider, for example, a woman who has always balanced her checkbook, managed her money, and stayed within her monthly budget. No doubt practice has made it possible for her to accomplish these tasks virtually automatically. Suppose she marries and, as is often customary, turns these activities over to her husband on the grounds that money management is a man's job. Later, if she is divorced and has to resume the functions she previously performed quite successfully, she may find her competence in doing so has been undermined by the interim period in which both she and her husband decided she should not manage money. She may doubt her ability because she has learned to be passive and dependent or because the fact of her husband's taking over the job suggests she is incompetent at it. Moreover, because she used to perform the tasks mindlessly, the task components are no longer easily accessible to her. She may find it hard to remember her routine exactly. As a result, her new level of performance is likely not to reach her previous demonstrated capabilities, at least for a while.

Several studies have mirrored this format in which subjects are initially successful on a routine task, their ability is subsequently questioned during some interim task, and performance on the initial task is reassessed. Under these circumstances, retested performance is undermined. Moreover, this is true even when the interim period of being labeled as incompetent bears no relationship to the task being evaluated (Langer & Benevento, 1978). For example, subjects in the first part of one study performed a word puzzle task and were led to believe that they had done quite well. In the second part of the study, subjects either worked under another person performing a menial clerical task or they performed the task without being under another person's supervision. In the third part of the study, subjects again performed a word puzzle task, and those who had worked under a supervisor in the second part of the study performed more poorly in the puzzle task than those who had worked on their own.

Interestingly enough, it is overlearned tasks (i.e., those performed mindlessly) and completely new tasks that are most likely to show performance decrements following negative labeling. For moderately well-learned tasks, the task components remain more accessible to consciousness and hence are undermined less by negative labeling or irrelevant failure experiences (Langer & Imber, 1979; cf. Fiske & Dyer, 1983; Hayes-Roth, 1977; and Chapter 6).

PREMATURE COGNITIVE COMMITMENT

A third circumstance in which mindlessness can adversely affect performance is termed *premature cognitive commitment* (Chanowitz & Langer, 1981). Premature cognitive commitment refers to the fact that when one learns information for one purpose and then is called upon to use it for a different purpose, it may be hard to reorganize or restructure the information for the second purpose. Suppose, for example, that an instructor gave you a short article to read and then, to your surprise, asked you to critique it for the class. It would probably be hard to do, because you may have not read the article in that way. You may have learned the contents, but rather casually; had you known you would have to criticize it, you would have read it much more carefully and counterargued its contents as you read.

In a study demonstrating this effect, Chanowitz and Langer gave subjects fictitious information about a perceptual deficit called field dependence, having led them first to believe that the deficit was either very common (80 percent of people) or very rare (10 percent of people). Those subjects who believed the deficit was common presumably feared it might have consequences for themselves, so they read the communication quite carefully. Those who believed the deficit was rare, however, presumably processed the information quite mindlessly, in an uncritical and cursory fashion. In addition to the information about the prevalence of field dependence, half the subjects were instructed to think of strategies that might be used by people who have field dependence to compensate for the disorder; the other half were given no such instructions. All subjects then completed perceptual assessment tasks which indicated that they, in fact, were field dependent.

Following the feedback, subjects were then tested on a field dependence task. Presumably, subjects should now have trouble on the task, since they believe they have a deficit that makes it hard to perform effectively. However, subjects who had been instructed to think up compensating strategies evidenced no difficulty on the task. More interestingly, subjects who had believed that the information about the deficit was relevant to them (i.e., the 80 percent group) behaved like the subjects who had thought up compensating strategies and also performed well. Presumably, they had read the initial information carefully and counterargued it, perhaps also thinking up some of their own compensating strategies for field dependence. However, subjects who had originally thought the information was irrelevant to them and who presumably read it without challenging its implications, performed quite badly.

The implication of the preceding discussion of mindlessness is that mindlessness is bad, and this is far from true. The ability to process information in a mindless fashion can be a valuable asset, freeing capacity for other, more important problems. However, mindlessness is not without its liabilities; under some circumstances it can lead to ineffective learning, the inability to deal with novel or interrupting conditions, and vulnerability to negative labels or failure experiences. The characteristics of mindlessness and two of its potential consequences, self-induced dependence and premature cognitive commitment, are presented in Table 5.2.

Control-Based Interventions to Offset Stress

As noted, loss of control can produce heightened reactivity to stressful experiences, reactance, helplessness, or an increased and often hypervigilant search for information. When loss of control results from overlearning, performance can be undermined through the inability to deal mindfully with performance contingencies. How can the deleterious effects of loss of control be offset?

Perhaps the most intriguing use of the idea of psychological control is the development of control-based interventions to offset stress. There are many unavoidably stressful events that one encounters in one's normal life, including going to the dentist, trying out for an athletic team, being interviewed for a job, or taking a test. Under such circumstances, one may begin to feel an anticipatory loss of control, especially if one knows little about the forthcoming aversive event and has few ways to regulate or change it. A wide variety of efforts to restore control examined in both laboratory and field settings suggest that the aversiveness of such stressful events can be reduced by control-inducing interventions (see Averill, 1973; S. M. Miller, 1979; and Thompson, 1981, for reviews). These efforts include behavior control, cognitive control, information control, decision control, retrospective control, and

TABLE 5.2
The Effects of Mindlessness and Potential Consequences of Self-Induced Dependence and Premature Cognitive Commitment

Term	Definition	Conditions that lead to it	Effects
Mindlessness	Performing a task in a routine, uncritical way	Overlearning, practice, familiarity, prior expectations	Failure to attend to individual task components; inability to adjust to changes in expected task parameters; low creativity in task enactment
Self-induced dependence	Self-generated inability to perform a task one was previously able to perform mindlessly	Failure experience, negative self-labeling, subordination to another person	Inability to identify individual task components; difficulty in performing previously performed task; low self-esteem
Premature cognitive commitment	Limitation of information use as a consequence of the context of initial exposure; especially likely to occur when information is initially processed mindlessly	Any factor that suggests that new information will have only a limited usefulness	Failure to attend to information closely or to evaluate it critically; later inability to use the information in a new or critical way

secondary control (Averill, 1973; Rothbaum, Weisz, & Snyder, 1982; Thompson, 1981); they are illustrated in Table 5.3.

BEHAVIOR CONTROL

I'm saving that (call) button. When I push that thing you'll know I need help.

—Hospital patient
(Tagliacozzo & Mauksch, 1972, p. 171)

One way of alleviating the stress of an aversive situation is through *behavior control*. Behavior control is the ability to take some step to end the event, make it less likely, reduce its intensity, or alter its timing or duration. Behavior control can include any active response that a person commits to influence the event such as pressing a button to terminate an aversive stimulus, self-administering a noxious stimulus (instead of having someone else do it), or reducing the unpleasantness of an event by performing successfully on some other task. Under such circumstances, the stressfulness of an event can be reduced.

Much of the research that has provided people with a sense of behavior control actually gives people only the impression that they have behavior control, not the reality. For example, a subject in an experiment may be told that she need only press a button, and the intensity of the shock she will receive will be cut in half. In fact, she may receive shocks of the same intensity as subjects not given the button. Even when subjects receive the same shocks, those with apparent behavior control will often adjust better than those without behavior control. To be effective, then, behavior control need not be real; the belief that one can take steps to reduce the aversiveness of an event can itself reduce stress.

Behavior control appears to have a strong impact on anticipatory anxiety, that is, anxiety that occurs prior to the occurrence of the event (Gatchel & Proctor, 1976; Geer *et al.*, 1970; Geer & Maisel, 1972; Glass, Reim, & Singer, 1971; Stotland & Blumenthal, 1964; Szpiler & Epstein, 1976). This ability to reduce anticipatory distress applies across a wide variety of aversive events including shock, loud noise, or even waiting to take an intelligence test. Behavior control also seems to increase tolerance of the aversive events themselves: subjects in experiments who have some potentially stress-reducing technique available to them can take more shock or more loud noise than those without such control. However, the impact of behavior control on felt distress or emotionality during the actual event is equivocal. There is no clear evidence that the distress experienced during the event is lessened by available, but unutilized behavioral control (Thompson, 1981).

Nonetheless, postevent distress may well be lower when one feels one had control. Those without control often experience disruptive effects on their performance following an aversive event, compared with those who had control (Gatchel & Proctor, 1976; Glass *et al.*, 1971; R. T. Mills & Krantz,

TABLE 5.3
Types of Control and Their Effects on Adjustment to Aversive Events

Type of control	Definition	Example	Effects
Behavior control	Taking some concrete step to reduce the aversiveness of a negative event	Pressing a button that will reduce the intensity of electric shock	Actual or perceived behavior control helps to reduce anxiety prior to the negative event; increases tolerance of aversive event; may not reduce distress of aversive event; may reduce post-event distress
Cognitive control	Thinking about the aversive event differently or refocusing attention on nonnoxious aspects of aversive situation	Focusing on the benefits of a noxious medical procedure while it is occurring	Appears to improve adjustment at all phases of an aversive event
Decision control	Ability to make decisions regarding the onset, timing, occurrence, or type of aversive event	Choosing between two types of surgery	Appears to be beneficial if outcome of decision is beneficial; effect if outcome is unfavorable remains equivocal
Information control	Obtaining or seeking information about the nature of the aversive event (e.g., sensations, duration, timing, cause)	Learning the side effects associated with surgery	Warning sign and causal information have equivocal effects; sensation information and procedure information reliably reduce stress of an aversive event
Retrospective control	Beliefs that one can control an event that has already occurred	Believing that one could have forestalled the accident that has left one crippled	Effects are as yet unknown—may improve adjustment to some noxious events but not others
Secondary control	Bringing one's thoughts and behaviors in line with environmental forces	Putting oneself in expert hands and "going with the flow"	May help to improve adjustment to aversive events when control is not possible

1979). For example, if you are taking a test and a radio is blasting outside, even after the noise stops it is often hard to return to work. However, if the radio is yours, or you can control its volume, you can likely return to work more easily. In balance, then, behavior control does seem to reduce the stressfulness of an aversive event, although its effects may vary, depending upon which time period—pre-event, during the event, or postevent—is being evaluated.

COGNITIVE CONTROL

It was kind of a game with me, depending on my mood. If I was peaceful and wanted to be peaceful, I would image a beautiful scene, or if I wanted to do battle with the enemy, I would mock up a battle and have my defenses ready.

—Cancer patient coping with
chemotherapy through imagery

Cognitive control is the availability of some cognitive strategy that either leads one to think about an aversive event differently or focuses one's attention on non-noxious aspects of the aversive situation. For example, a hospital patient about to undergo an unpleasant diagnostic medical procedure may be instructed to focus on the benefits the procedure will provide, rather than on the current discomfort it will produce. Or a woman about to skydive for the first time will focus on the technical details of the parachute and the jump point, instead of on the reality of leaping from a plane.

Most of us practice some form of cognitive control in our own lives. A student may decide to put himself through four grueling years of medical school because he has a vision of himself as a future physician. During an awkward encounter with an ex-girlfriend or ex-boyfriend in a restaurant, one may become intensely aware of how the napkin holder operates. One of us still knows her childhood dentist's degree certificate by heart, because that was the only thing to concentrate on while the dentist was drilling.

What research there is on cognitive control suggests that our intuitive reactions of how to reduce stress are well placed. Cognitive control seems to ameliorate stress during the anticipatory period (Holmes & Houston, 1974; Houston, 1977; Langer, Janis, & Wolfer, 1975), during the occurrence of the event itself (e.g., Chaves & Barber, 1974; Girodo & Wood, 1979; Houston, 1977; Kanfer & Goldfoot, 1966; Spanos, Horton, & Chaves, 1975), and during the postevent period (F. Cohen & Lazarus, 1973; Egbert, Battit, Welch, & Bartlett, 1964; Langer et al., 1975).

There is, of course, a variety of cognitive control strategies available to an individual. For example, in natural childbirth, one can direct attention away from pain by focusing on the process (e.g., the baby's movements), the outcome of the experience (e.g., the birth of a person), or the meaning of the experience (e.g., becoming part of the stream of life). What differentiates all these strategies from behavior control or, more important, a belief in behavior control, is the fact that it is the cognitive effort and/or the restructuring of the stressful event that reduces stress, rather than the availability of some concrete behavioral action.

Some cognitive control strategies involve merely avoiding dealing with an aversive event (such as thinking about something else during a fight with a romantic partner); others are nonavoidant (such as focusing on the potential beneficial changes in the relationship that may result from the fight). In comparing the results of the two types of strategies, Thompson (1981) suggests that avoidant strategies may improve coping before or even during an event, but not necessarily afterwards, whereas nonavoidant strategies may lead to increased stress prior to the event, but reduced stress afterward. For example, a study of patients awaiting surgery found that those who minimized the significance of the surgery were more calm ahead of time, but became highly stressed after surgery; because they had failed to appreciate the seriousness of the event, they were ill prepared for its side effects. In contrast, those who were moderately distressed ahead of time were vigilant in seeking information about the consequences of surgery, and accordingly coped better postsurgically (Janis, 1958).

Which, then, is better: avoidant or nonavoidant strategies? There is no clear answer. For some events, avoidant strategies will be preferable on balance, whereas for others, nonavoidant strategies may be preferable. Thompson (1981) concludes that, if a nonavoidant strategy can be successful, it may be useful, but if not, it may arouse anxiety (see also Averill, O'Brien, & DeWitt, 1977). Perhaps, then, the best strategy is to focus on what one can do to alleviate the aversive event, and when one has done all one can do, to put it out of mind.

DECISION CONTROL

Decision control is the ability to make a decision or decisions with respect to the forthcoming aversive event: it may involve the decision to engage in the event itself, the ability to choose from among a set of more or less aversive alternatives, or the ability to decide on some other aspect of the event such as its timing or duration. As in the case of behavior control, decision control may be illusory; one may be given the appearance of choice, when, in fact, the situation is structured so as to virtually ensure compliance with a particular option. Alternatively, decision control can be real (Averill, 1973). There are often circumstances in which we, or someone else, must make decisions about aversive or potentially aversive events that have profound consequences for our lives. Treatments for many diseases now often include a variety of options from which a patient may select; alternatively, the patient may leave it up to the physician. Undergraduate students may select a variety of electives or they may ask their adviser what will fit in best with their major. Having been arrested for a traffic violation, one may choose driver improvement school or let the conviction stand on one's license.

There is some evidence that choice can improve adjustment to later deleterious effects of that choice. There is much literature from dissonance research showing that when people have committed themselves to a course of action that has aversive consequences, they reduce postdecisional conflict by reappraising their situation in a more positive light (see, for example, Kiesler, Collins, & Miller, 1969, for a review). People induced to choose to undergo thirst deprivation, for example, report being less thirsty than subjects not provided with choice. People who choose to forego food when they are hungry have been found not only to report less hunger, but to show fewer stomach contractions (an indication of hunger) than those not given choice (Zimbardo, 1969). Schulz and Brenner (1977) found that elderly people who had chosen to relocate to a nursing home showed better physical and emotional adjustment than those who had been sent to a nursing home by relatives or the state.

But how far can one generalize these preliminary results of decision control? Does it follow that a cancer patient who chooses minimum surgery and then develops a new cancer lesion will be better adjusted to the consequences of a recurrence than will someone who received the same surgery but did not choose it? Is it better to be able to blame the doctor or better to take on the responsibility oneself? These are the kinds of situations one would want to understand, but for which the evidence is still too sparse to reach strong conclusions.

INFORMATION CONTROL

> *What's up? I don't know what's up. It's driving me crazy . . . I have to have an explanation . . . I can live with anything I can understand.*
>
> —Hospital patient
> (Skipper, Tagliacozzo, & Mauksch, 1964, p. 38)

Information control is the sense of control that is achieved when one obtains or is provided with information about a noxious event itself. Such information may include what sensations the event will produce, when it will occur, what causes it, what the procedures involved are, or how long it will last. A patient awaiting surgery, for example, may have all of the postoperative side effects carefully explained (e.g., stretching, pain, gas) so that when they do occur, they will not be so distressing.

Not all forms of information control are equally effective. Subjects who are given a warning signal prior to the onset of a noxious event sometimes adjust to the event more successfully and sometimes less successfully (Thompson, 1981). The bulk of the research, however, examines the impact of information about sensations or procedures associated with noxious events, and here the results are more successful.

Information about the sensations that will be experienced during a noxious event has been provided to subjects in both the laboratory (Staub & Kellet, 1972) and field settings involving unpleasant medical procedures such as surgery (see J. E. Johnson, in press, for a review). Although sensation information does not affect every indicator of adjustment equally, the research evidence strongly shows that having sensation information improves adjustment to these aversive events (J. E. Johnson, in press). Information about the specific procedures one will go through during aversive events also improves adjustment to those events (J. E. Johnson, in press). However, the effects are not quite as strong as for interventions involving sensation information. Qualifications notwithstanding, information control generally appears to have positive effects on adjustment to noxious events.

Why do psychologists consider information to be a form of psychological control? Unlike other forms of control considered so far, the person with so-called information control cannot actually influence the noxious event. In fact, an illusion of control is not even provided. Why, then, would we expect information to reduce discomfort in a stressful situation? One possible explanation is that information control provides a schema for the event, that is, a general understanding of what will happen and why. Accordingly, when people face the event, they can make sense of each individual step, and they know when something signals a potential problem. Another possible explanation is that having basic information about an aversive event enables people to employ their own coping styles more effectively by seeing how their efforts will mesh with forthcoming procedures and sensations.

The fact that information control does have positive effects on coping has both theoretical and practical significance. Theoretically, it implies that an individual need not be actively involved in an event to adjust to it, but that, at least in some cases, understanding is sufficient. The practical significance of information control lies in the fact that such interventions are simple to implement in field settings where more active involvement of a subject or patient may be difficult or impossible.

RETROSPECTIVE CONTROL

I was really dumb. If I had just put locks on the windows, it wouldn't have happened.

—Rape victim

Retrospective control, a term coined by Thompson (1981), refers to beliefs about an event that has already occurred, beliefs that may restore or enhance the feeling that one can influence or forestall the event's recurrence. For example, victims of misfortune will sometimes construe a past event as something they brought on themselves, in a possible effort to enhance their feelings of control (Bulman & Wortman, 1977; Taylor, Lichtman, & Wood, in press; Wortman, 1976). For example, victims of rape will sometimes blame themselves for walking alone at night, not having adequate locks on their doors, or just being in the wrong place at the wrong time; through self-blame, these victims may well be attempting to reassert control by identifying things they can do to prevent a repetition of the event (Janoff-Bulman, 1979).

Although previous discussions of retrospective control confine themselves largely to attributions for the cause of the event (Thompson, 1981), it seems reasonable to include a somewhat larger set of beliefs within the term. For example, a recent study of cancer patients revealed that, although few of the patients believed they had caused their initial cancer, most believed they could forestall a recurrence by maintaining a positive attitude, changing their diet, or lowering their level of stress (S. E. Taylor, 1981). Similarly, in a study of attributions for the 1976 Super Bowl, both Dallas and Pittsburgh fans agreed that the cause of the Pittsburgh's victory was their superior playing. However, Pittsburgh fans believed that in a hypothetical rematch, Pittsburgh would win again, whereas Dallas fans believed Dallas would win (Winkler & Taylor, 1979). Hence retrospective control need not refer solely to perceptions of the cause of an event; it can also refer to perceptions that an event is (un)replicable or (un)modifiable.

Relatively few studies have examined retrospective control, with the exception of those just noted. Although a few additional studies have noted that victims often do blame themselves for events an outsider would attribute to external factors or chance (Abrams & Finesinger, 1953; Chodoff, Friedman, & Hamburg, 1964), most have not gone on to demonstrate that the function of such self-blame is to restore feelings of control and enhance coping (see Bulman & Wortman, 1977, for an exception). The idea that enhanced feelings of control result from self-blame is merely an interpretation. In fact, self-blame may be an effort to find meaning in an aversive event, rather than an effort at regaining control (Thompson, 1981). Furthermore, it is important to remember that self-blame is not the only means of restoring a sense of control after the fact. Accordingly, then, what constitutes retrospective control is still conceptually unclear, and adequate demonstrations that it exists are still needed. It is, however, an intriguing idea that may take the control concept beyond understanding merely how people achieve control over events while they occur, to understanding how people achieve a sense of control retrospectively with events once they have occurred.

SECONDARY CONTROL

I wasn't doing very well, and I didn't see any point in sticking around and letting it drive me nuts.

> —Twenty-one-year-old
> college dropout

Secondary control, a term coined by Rothbaum, Weisz, and Snyder (1982), is a very different type of control-restoring measure than the types of control we have considered to this point. Whereas behavior control, cognitive control, decision control, information control, and retrospective control all involve attempts to bring the environment (e.g., the aversive event) in line with one's wishes (primary control), secondary control involves relinquishing primary control and bringing one's self into line with environmental forces. It is perhaps best embodied by the phrase "going with the flow." Consider, as an example, the learned helplessness phenomenon (discussed in Chapter 4, "Applications of Attribution Theory"), in which one experiences repeated instances of lack of control. If one then does no attempt to exert control in a new environment where control is possible, the lack of response is interpreted as learned helplessness. By contrast, the secondary control model would maintain that one has decided that it is not worth trying—the game cannot be won, one may just perform the task poorly—and thus sees no point in becoming more frustrated.

Why is this kind of response believed to be an effort at control, rather than giving up, giving in, or becoming helpless? Secondary control is thought to be the second step in a two-process effort at control. First, an individual makes attempts at primary control. If those attempts fail or are perceived as likely to fail, then the person may respond with secondary control. Secondary control enables the individual to avoid the frustration of a situation he or she cannot remedy. In essence, the individual says, "I may not be able to control it, but I'm not going to let it control me."

Secondary control can assume any of several forms. One may attempt to predict events so as to avoid disappointment (*predictive secondary control*). For example, if one decides that one is simply incompetent at a task and that one will surely fail it if one tries, one will avoid the disappointment of actually failing. *Illusory secondary control* involves allying one's outcomes with chance. Going to a fortune-teller to decide whether or not to accept a new job is an example. *Vicarious secondary control* results when one allies one's outcomes with powerful others; presumably one can sit back and relax while others achieve the desired outcomes. *Interpretive secondary control* involves thinking about events so as to extract meaning from them and to accept them. Deciding that a conspicuous failure is a growth experience is an example. In sum, then, passive behavior, withdrawal, and attributions of one's behavior to external forces like chance or powerful others need not mean that an individual has relinquished control altogether. Rather, it may simply mean that primary control has been exchanged for secondary control.

What is the evidence that secondary control actually exists and that it is adaptive when it does? Rothbaum *et al.* present an impressive and diverse array of evidence suggesting that behaviors like withdrawal or passivity can function as control-restoring efforts. However, the further question, namely whether or not secondary control enables people to adjust successfully to aversive events, remains largely unanswered. One study of cancer patients reported that those who found meaning in their experience (interpretive secondary control) were better adjusted than those who did not (S. E. Taylor, Lichtman, & Wood, in press). The same study also found that patients who believed that others (e.g., physicians) could control their cancer (vicarious secondary control) were better adjusted than those who did not. However, whether these relationships would hold in other situations and for other types of secondary control remains unknown. Indeed, the question, is secondary control adaptive, is likely to have a complex answer. Parameters of the event (whether it can be controlled or not, how long it will last), the balance between primary and secondary control efforts, and the type of event all may be important (Rothbaum *et al.*, 1982).

TYPES OF CONTROL: A COMMENT

The six types of control described—behavior, cognitive, decision, information, retrospective, and secondary—constitute procedurally distinct ways of providing an individual with a sense of control. However, the mechanisms by which they alleviate stress may actually reduce to two techniques: taking some action with respect to an aversive situation and thinking about that situation differently. For example, behavior control provides people with an action or potential action that can reduce the aversiveness of a situation, and it may also alter cognitions about that situation. Cognitive control obviously achieves its effect by directly leading people to rethink a situation or refocus their attention. Information control may achieve beneficial effects when it enables people to take action or reappraise the situation. Decision control clearly achieves its effect by allowing people to think about the situation differently (cf. Averill, 1973), and both retrospective and secondary control likewise involve rethinking the meaning or contingencies of a situation. To summarize, then, the beneficial effects of control appear to reside in the cognitive and behavioral changes that an individual can make in reacting to an aversive event; the means for instilling feelings of control are themselves, however, quite varied.

Feelings of Control and Short-Term Stress

The laboratory studies that have examined the effects of control on the experience of stress implicitly adopt a short-term model of stress; that is, the stressors are brief, and the control techniques suggested are tailored specifically to those short-term experiences. The relevance of such an approach to real-life stressors should be clear. Many of the stressors people experience are short-term, such as waiting to take a test, facing a medical examination, having a tooth filled at the dentist's office, or attempting to negotiate the New York subway system. Potentially, then, these results can be generalized to a wealth of situations. Many of them, as we have implied throughout the chapter, are medical ones, since the health arena is often one in which short-term stress must be exchanged for long-term benefit. However, the approach is obviously applicable to other stressors as well; crowding is one example that has been extensively investigated (e.g., Baum, Aiello, & Calesnick, 1978; Baum & Gatchell, 1981; Rodin, 1976; Rodin, Solomon, & Metcalf, 1978).

CROWDING AND COGNITIVE CONTROL: AN EXAMPLE

It is Christmas Eve and you have still not bought anything for your mother. You enter Macy's at five in the afternoon and you face hundreds of other people who have also not yet bought presents for their mothers. Every likely counter—scarves, perfume, jewelry—is jammed with people waving potential purchases, while a harried clerk tries to fix the broken register. Cursing Santa Claus under your breath, you begin to paw your way through the aisles, feeling your blood pressure rising and whatever thoughts you might have had for a present leave your head for good. So much for the Christmas spirit.

Although crowding is not always stressful, it often is. Temporary crowding can produce anxiety, antagonism toward other people, and the inability to perform simple, necessary tasks (Saegert, Mackintosh, & West, 1975). Crowding can make it difficult to size up the environment, predict it, and coordinate behavior with others; in short, it can produce cognitive and emotional overload (Saegert, 1973).

A study by Langer and Saegert (1977) demonstrated how feelings of control can offset some of the aversive effects of crowding. Subjects in the study were women attempting to shop for groceries during a time when the store was either heavily crowded or not. All of the women were given a shopping list of 50 items and told to note which brand and size would cost the least. Half the women were given an additional information control manipulation explaining that crowding often makes people feel aroused or anxious and so if such feelings did occur, the women would know why. Thirty minutes later, the number of correct and incorrect items found by each woman was tallied, and a questionnaire assessing perceptions of the store, difficulty finding products, and feelings of discomfort was administered.

Crowding had a marked effect on the shoppers. Crowded shoppers found fewer of the items on the list and had more negative perceptions of the experience. However, information about the effects of crowding successfully ameliorated some of these feelings. Those who had received the information finished more of the problems on the list, their solutions were more often correct, and they found the experience less aversive. Interestingly enough, these beneficial effects occurred in both the crowded and the uncrowded situation, suggesting that control may be important even in situations of relatively low stress. Apparently, then, as these women were shopping, and their arousal increased, they were able to think back to the information they had been given and thus could interpret their arousal as normal consequences of shopping and crowding, rather than as anxiety or stress. The information control manipulation, then, may have enabled them to think about the situation differently (cognitive control).

Feelings of Control and Long-Term Stress

Feelings of control are clearly beneficial in reducing stress in short-term aversive situations, but can feelings of control aid adjustment to more long-term aversive situations, ones that go on for days, months, or even years? There are many long-term situations in which an individual's control can be undermined. Living with an authoritarian father or a domineering mother can undermine one's sense of control. Having a chronic disease that requires daily care or limits physical activity reduces control. Residential environments such as prisons, schools, hospitals, or nursing homes often, wittingly or unwittingly, rob individuals of their freedom to behave, dress, or eat as they might like. Even nonresidential but highly regimented institutions, such as the welfare system, can make extreme demands on individual freedoms. These, then, are situations in which loss of control is not temporary, but more long-term, forcing the individual to make increasing accommodation to a set of standardized regulations and procedures. Can feelings of control enhance coping under these circumstances?

THE NURSING HOME STUDY

Most of us have, at one time or another, visited a nursing home. We may have gone caroling at Christmas, done a Scout's good deed by teaching older people how to make lanyards or baskets, or visited an institutionalized relative. Very likely a reaction to the first visit was shock. Here were once hearty, active individuals now sitting in rockers, with virtually no conversation, and little but television and rather silly crafts programs to occupy their attention. A common thought is, "This will never happen to me, and I will never let it happen to my parents, no matter how old or feeble they become." The fact is that our society makes relatively few safe, comfortable provisions for older people, and a nursing home is one of the better options available.

The nursing home is a good example of an environment in which often limited financial resources preclude variety, individualized activity programs, and much individual freedom. A study by Langer and Rodin (1976) demonstrated that by introducing even very small amounts of control, one could alter the morale and health of the institutionalized aged. Patients on one floor of a nursing home were given small plants that they were to tend (behavior control) and were also asked to choose when they wished to participate in some of the nursing home activities (decision control). Patients on a comparison floor were also given plants, but were told that the staff would tend them; they also participated in the same activities as the first group of patients, but were assigned to times, rather than being able to choose them. At the close of the study, nurses' ratings, patient self-reports, and behavioral measures indicated that the patients provided with control were more active and had a greater sense of well-being than those on the comparison floor. A year later, patients who had initially received control were psychologically and physically better off than patients who had not received control (Rodin & Langer, 1977).

This study was in some ways very simple, but it has profound implications. It demonstrates first that control can have an impact in an environment marked by long-term lack of control. Further, it shows how very little control is needed to achieve the impact; the steps introduced on the target floor were inexpensive and easy to implement, yet their effect was substantial. Hence the study provides a good model of a cost-effective intervention.

However, it is critically important to consider the constraints of the environment itself in determining how to implement control. In another nursing home study (Schulz, 1976), elderly people were matched up with college student volunteers in a visiting program such that the elderly people could control the duration and frequency of visits from the volunteer (control); or they were told in advance when their volunteer would be visiting and for how long (prediction); or they were not warned when the volunteer was coming or for how long (random). A fourth group received no visitors. The short-term effects were much as those in the Langer and Rodin study: those who had control or predictability over the visiting schedule showed improved level of activity and morale. But when the program had to be disbanded at the end of the school year, the patients who had had control or predictability worsened both physically and emotionally, compared with patients who had not received visitors or who had not been able to predict or control the visiting schedule (Schulz & Hanusa, 1978).

What is the critical difference between these two nursing home studies? In the first (Langer & Rodin, 1976), patients were given control over areas of their life which then became self-sustaining; they could continue on their own without the help of the investigators. In contrast, the college student visitor program could not be maintained without the help of the investigator, and hence the environment returned to its previous level of (in)activity. The point, then, is that in situations of long-term stress or control, it is important to consider not only the potential effect of a control-inducing intervention itself, but also to assess what its long-term impact will be. Interventions that can be incorporated into the ongoing structure of a restrictive environment will likely have beneficial effects on both the long- and short-term, whereas those that cannot may sacrifice long-term benefits to temporary gains.

Potentially Negative Consequences of a Sense of Control

So far, we have discussed the beneficial effects of a sense of personal control. Although a sense of control is usually functional both for coping with daily events and for dealing with particularly stressful occurrences, there are some negative consequences of a sense of control.

ILLUSION OF CONTROL

Under some circumstances, people exaggerate the degree of control they have in situations that are actually controlled by chance. One usually inconsequential manifestation of this *illusion of control* is superstitions; the man who only plays golf in his lucky hat is one such example. However, an illusion of control may also underlie habitual gambling, as with the man who bets his paycheck on a "sure win" horse, only to lose again. In a series of studies that simulated the gambling situation, Langer (1975) demonstrated how robust this illusion of control can be and how vulnerable people are to it. Simple behaviors like betting against a nervous (versus a confident) opponent, choosing (versus not) one's own lottery ticket, or prior practice (versus no prior practice) on a game of chance led people to perceive that they had a better chance of winning than the odds would suggest; in fact, their chances of winning remained unaffected by these manipulations.

One possible reason why people are susceptible to an illusion of control is that certain cues suggesting that skill is involved may intrude into chance situations. For example, the maxim "practice makes perfect" illustrates the fact that people usually get better at something if they have rehearsed it; however, practicing a game of chance obviously does not have this effect. Likewise, choice usually implies control, but not if one is choosing between one versus another random lottery ticket. Gambling situations, then, can seduce a player into acting as if skill is involved, when the odds are in fact chance determined.

The illusion of control will be greater, the more skill-related cues (e.g., familiarity, choice, high involvement, thinking up strategies, competition) are present in a chance situation (Langer & Roth, 1975; Wortman, 1975). This intrusion of skill-related cues into chance situations may also underlie persistent beliefs in extrasensory perception. When the telepathic sender of some message picks that message, practices sending it in advance, or otherwise becomes involved in sending it to another person, he or she may well develop an exaggerated sense of his of her extrasensory talents (Ayeroff & Abelson, 1976).

BELIEF IN A JUST WORLD

People not only exaggerate their own sense of control, but they also exaggerate the extent to which control exists generally. Lerner (1970) suggested that people have a need to see the world as a controllable place in which good things happen to good people and bad things happen to bad people. Lerner suggested that the basis for this belief in a just world is a defensive need to ward off threats to the self. If you see another person experience a negative event such as being struck by a car or developing an incurable disease, it is psychologically more comforting to believe that person deserved it (e.g., "She walked right in front of the car" or "He burned himself out working too hard, so of course he got sick"), than to believe that the event could be chance determined; after all, if negative events are random, they could befall oneself as well. Hence, when observing another's misfortune, one will blame the other's actions for bringing on the event; if no faulty action can be found, one will blame the person's character, assuming that he or she is a bad person who simply deserved the misfortune (Lerner, 1970; see also K. G. Shaver, 1970b; Walster, 1966).

In a series of experimental studies, Lerner and his colleagues (Lerner, 1965, 1970; Lerner & Matthews, 1967; Simmons & Lerner, 1968) investigated the just world phenomenon. They found that unless people believed that the suffering of an innocent victim had ended or was about to end or unless they could compensate the victim for that suffering, they often derogated him or her. Lerner and others (e.g., Ryan, 1971) have suggested that this belief in a just world often provides a justification for the oppression of society's victims.

> As a nation, we have the money and technology to virtually eliminate poverty and to provide the kind of professional facilities and services which would dramatically enhance the life chances of a parentless child or the emotionally ill person. Yet . . . we seem not to care enough; possibly we do not care at all . . . we tend to assume that the other man's suffering is probably a result of his own failures. (Lerner, 1970, pp. 205-206)

Hence control can be harmful when it is attributed to another falsely. Believing another has control can interfere with an accurate appraisal of the situational and chance factors over which the other cannot, in fact, exert control, and can lead to a falsely negative portrait of the other's resources and abilities to help the self.

TOO MUCH CONTROL?

A third circumstance in which a sense of control may have negative effects is if an individual is provided with too much control over an impending aversive event. Until recently, researchers generally assumed that more control is better, and indeed some laboratory studies have supported this contention (Sherrod, Hage, Halpern, & Moore, 1977). However, evidence now exists that questions the generality of this finding. Some researchers have attempted to provide people with several control-inducing strategies simultaneously, such as both behavioral control and cognitive control; rarely is the combined procedure more effective than one alone (e.g., either behavioral control or cognitive control). In fact, sometimes the combined technique is worse than one technique alone, with people in the combined condition faring no better than people given no control-inducing strategy at all (J. E. Johnson & Leventhal, 1974; Langer *et al.*, 1975; R. T. Mills & Krantz, 1979).

Why would using several control-inducing strategies simultaneously fail when one seems to work well? In some cases, the control-restoring measures may themselves be so effortful that anxiety and physiological arousal are not successfully reduced (e.g., Solomon, Holmes, & McCaul, 1980). In other cases, researchers may be combining control techniques that are actually antagonistic, thus canceling out the effectiveness of each. For example, a cognitive reappraisal strategy of thinking about an event differently may be sabotaged by sensation information that leads individuals to attend closely to the stimuli as they are experiencing them (see Leventhal, Brown, Shacham, & Engquist, 1979, for a related point). A third possibility is that too much control creates cognitive overload (R. T. Mills & Krantz, 1979). When one is under stress, it is often difficult to concentrate attention and remember what one is supposed to do. With too much information, concentration breaks down, and no information is used successfully. However, a very simple message can be processed effectively under stress, and so seemingly minimal control-inducing techniques can actually be quite effective. Perhaps one cancer patient summarized it best: "If the occasion should occur when I need a doctor's assistance, I don't want him to fly the plane, and I'm not willing to say I could fly the plane by myself. But I sure would like to be a co-pilot."

THE WRONG KIND OF CONTROL?

An intriguing idea that has not yet been adequately examined is that certain kinds of control may be beneficial for some situations, whereas other types of control may be needed in other situations. Consistent with this point, Baum, Fisher, and Solomon (1980) investigated how people cope with crowding depending upon their familiarity with the situation. They found that situational information (e.g., a description of the setting and how crowding might affect people's efforts to complete a task) was more helpful in reducing the subsequent stress of crowding for those unfamiliar with the situation. However, for those familiar with the situation, both situational information and emotional information (e.g., a description of the anxiety and arousal that can accompany crowding) were helpful in alleviating the stress of crowding. One implication of this study is that logistical (situational) information may be needed before one can make use of information about feelings and reactions. Another implication is that there are variables, such as familiarity with the situation, that determine the effects of different kinds of control information. A concerted research effort toward identifying other such variables can help determine the mechanisms by which control-enhancing manipulations are effective.

DISCONFIRMATION OF CONTROL

A final circumstance in which psychological control may have negative effects is when an individual believes he or she has control over an event, and that belief is disconfirmed (Wortman & Dunkel-Schetter, 1979). For example, what is the effect of a cancer recurrence on a patient who believed she could forestall a recurrence by taking vitamins, staying healthy, and stopping smoking? Might she not be worse off than a patient who sustains a recurrence but never believed she had any control over cancer?

Unfortunately, a definitive answer to this question is not yet available. J. M. Weiss (1971) found that rats who made more efforts at coping with aversive stimuli that they were unable to terminate were more stressed than rats who responded to those stimuli more passively. Would people necessarily show the same pattern? Possibly the greater cognitive capacity of the human enables him or her to respond more quickly or satisfactorily to an alteration in response-outcome contingencies than is true for the rat. Too, considerable research documents that people often draw self-protective inferences during times of threat (e.g., S. E. Taylor, 1982a; Wills, 1981), so, when the threat becomes real, people might rapidly abandon their prior feelings of control in favor of cognitions that are more adaptive for the now-changed reality (see, e.g., Koller & Kaplan, 1978). Nonetheless, the possibility that feelings of control may backfire when they are dramatically disconfirmed merits both research attention and caution regarding whether or not one should employ a control-enhancing intervention under conditions when control may ultimately fail.

Individual Differences and Control

Clearly, some people need or want control more than others. All of us know individuals who become distressed at the slightest threat to their plans: a stalled elevator, a temporarily dead telephone, a secretary who is ill on a day with lots of work. Other, more mellow people seem to glide through such minor distresses, but may also fail to assert control when their own freedom is seriously threatened by the actions of others. So far, there is no single individual difference test that measures a need for control, but there are several that approximate it.

TYPE A BEHAVIOR SYNDROME

Research on coronary artery disease has indicated that one risk factor is a particular kind of behavior pattern termed Type A behavior. The Type A individual is marked by three major characteristics: competitive achievement striving, a sense of time urgency, and aggressiveness. Accordingly, this person is often a hard-driving, over-achiever who works harder than his or her peers, becomes hostile and aggressive when thwarted, and has a high need for control (e.g., Glass, 1979; Carver & Glass, 1978). Type A behavior can be measured by responses on a questionnaire, the Jenkins Activity Survey for Health Prediction (C. D. Jenkins, Rosenman, & Friedman, 1968), which poses such questions as, "Has your spouse or friend ever told you that you eat too fast?" and "Do you ever set deadlines or quotas for yourself at work or at home?" A more valid measure is a clinical interview (Friedman & Rosenman, 1974; Rosenman et al., 1964), in which the interviewer tries to elicit Type A behavior by challenging the interviewee or stalling on a question to see if the interviewee completes the sentence or interrupts with an answer.

Type A behavior is obviously useful in many environments. People who react with Type A behavior to high-pressure environments, such as business or pretenure academia, may well do better and be perceived as performing better than those individuals (termed Type B's) who maintain a more relaxed style.

Though the need for control is only one aspect of Type A behavior, it is an important one. Type A's try harder to succeed than Type B's, and in so doing, suppress fatigue and other states that might interfere with completion of a task. When confronted by a threat, they increase their control efforts even more. However, if controlling efforts meet with repeated failure, they may be more vulnerable than Type B's to helplessness. This cyclical pattern of responses has been characterized as *hyper*responsiveness followed by *hypo*responsiveness. Physiological parallels to these behaviors include increased sympathetic activity (e.g., adrenalin release) during the hyperresponsive phase and possible depletion of physiological reserves accompanying the hyporesponsiveness phase. Glass (1979) has suggested that wear and tear created by these repeated abrupt changes in physiological activity may be implicated in heart disease and sudden death (Engel, 1968; Glass, 1979; Matthews & Glass, 1981).

The research on Type A behavior is important not only because it elucidates one important contribution to premature death, but also because it balances out what we know about control. On the one hand, feelings of control can be beneficial when one must face an unavoidable, aversive event. On the other hand, an excessive need for control can interfere with the ability to withstand small setbacks, or it can force one to push oneself so hard that it interferes with good health (see Matthews, 1982, for a review).

LOCUS OF CONTROL

In Chapter 2 ("Attribution Theory"), we discussed locus of control as a chronic propensity to locate causality for events either in the self or in the external environment. We raise the concept again here because individual differences in locus of control may lead to differential effectiveness of control-based interventions. It seems very likely that people with an internal locus of control will profit from control-based interventions that provide the self with specific things to do to modify the aversive situation, such as behavioral or cognitive control techniques. People with an external locus of control, on the other hand, might profit from interventions that provide information, but do not actually require the self's intervention. Or, to put the hypothesis another way, what internals may need is control, whereas externals may only need predictability.

There is some evidence that locus of control predicts reactions to loss of control. Davis and Phares (1969), for example, found that internals were more likely than externals to seek out information on an issue on which they had relatively little information. Seeman and Evans (1962) found that internal tuberculosis patients were more likely to have acquired information about their illness than had externals. N. L. Pittman and Pittman (1979) experimentally investigated the combination of helplessness and locus of control. They exposed internal and external locus of control subjects to a series of concept formation puzzles and gave them either random feedback on their performance (high helplessness) or a low degree of contingent feedback (low helplessness). They found that internals performed poorly under high helplessness conditions, whereas externals performed poorly under low helplessness conditions.

In sum, locus of control would seem to be an important variable to take into account when gauging the effects of both loss of control and control-restoring interventions.

HEALTH LOCUS OF CONTROL

Although locus of control maintains that there are general propensities to view events as caused by internal or external factors, it may actually be the case that people perceive control differently in different aspects of their lives. It is perfectly possible to imagine a person who sees politics as something over which she has little influence, but her health as something on which she can have substantial impact.

Indeed, health is, so far, the only specifically researched area in the locus of control field. One health locus of control scale, developed by Wallston and Wallston (1978), contains three subscales measuring internal health locus of control (e.g., "I am in control of my health"), the extent to which powerful others control one's health (e.g., "Health professionals control my health"), and the degree to which chance affects health (e.g., "When I am sick, I just have to let nature run its course"). Another scale, developed by Lau and his associates (Lau, 1982; Lau & Ware, 1980), measures beliefs in self-care, provider control over health, chance health outcomes, and the general perception that one's health is threatened.

Health locus of control (HLOC) has been used both as an independent variable, to see which kinds of health interventions work with what kinds of people, and as a dependent variable, to see if health locus of control itself is altered by interventions; researchers have had at least some success in both cases. As an independent variable, for example, HLOC appears to predict behavior with respect to chronic illness better than it predicts preventive health behavior (Wallston & Wallston, 1978). However, this is a field that is still relatively young, and we can expect considerable theoretical and empirical advances over the coming years.

A more recent development in health-relevant control needs is the Krantz Health Opinion Survey (Krantz, Baum, & Wideman, 1980) which measures preference for, rather than locus of, control. On the assumption that different individuals have differing desires for control and for different types of control, the scale measures both preference for information and preference for self-care and/or active participation in one's own care. Through this and similar measures, it will be possible to see if those who desire certain types of control actually profit more from control-based interventions than those who do not desire control (see also Baum, Calesnick, Davis, & Gatchel, 1982).

How Does Control Achieve Its Effects?

Although occasionally feelings of control may be detrimental both for the self and for dealing with others, for the most part, the effects of at least moderate degrees of psychological control are beneficial. What, exactly, is the mechanism by which psychological control improves adjustment to negative events?

Is there, first of all, any basis for concluding that it is control that is lost, manipulated, or restored in the studies described in this chapter? The answer is no. Control has been treated largely as an explanatory construct, rather than as a specific psychological state that can be measured. Researchers assume that psychological control is the important variable, but, in some cases, the terms *coping* or *understanding* could be substituted for feelings of control, just as *stress, distress,* or *confusion* could, in some cases, be substituted for the term *loss of control.* What has been amassed, however, is a theory of how control works if not a conceptual understanding of why.

Some researchers have suggested that one of the primary benefits of control-restoring interventions is that individuals gain enough information to predict what will happen to them and when. Prediction can, in its own right, have powerful effects on coping with both positive and negative events. In the nursing home study by Schulz (1976), for example, older people who were merely told when their college student visitors were coming (prediction group) showed mood and activity level improvements comparable to the older people who were actually able to make the arrangements themselves (control group) (see also Burger & Arkin, 1980). Studies on the effects of noise reveal that unpredictable noise lowers performance on tasks requiring concentration and produces more physical symptoms (Weidner & Matthews, 1978) than do predictable bursts of noise (Glass & Singer, 1972; Glass, Singer, & Friedman, 1969).

How does predictability improve adjustment to aversive events? Seligman (1975) has advanced a "safety signal" hypothesis, which argues that unpredictable events are stressful because there is no safe period during which one can relax; knowing when an event will occur enables one to rest and not worry about it. Others (e.g., J. E. Johnson, 1973; Kimmel, 1965; Leventhal & Everhart, 1979; Mandler & Watson, 1966) have stressed that predictable stressors can be planned for and incorporated into ongoing behavior more readily than unpredictable ones, also enabling the individual to make preparatory efforts at coping. S. Cohen (1978) and Matthews, Scheier, Brunson, and Carducci (1980) have suggested that unpredictable events exert a negative effect on coping, because they draw off attention that could be better used to deal directly with aversive events. In support of this contention, Matthews *et al.* found that when people can be encouraged not to attend to unpredictable aversive events, those effects have no more disruptive effect than do predictable aversive events.

Certainly, then, one benefit of control is enhanced predictability. But is that all control is? The answer appears to be no. When facing an aversive situation, control may be more important than merely the ability to predict, particularly if control provides more than just an illusion of control. In fact, studies that have specifically pitted control against predictability have found that control has effects over and above predictability (e.g., Geer & Maisel, 1972; Geer et al., 1970). In summary, it is clear that predictability in and of itself can often have beneficial effects in reducing the impact of an aversive experience, but control adds something more.

What that "something more" is has been hotly debated. Some have maintained that loss of control threatens self-esteem and motivation. Such difficulties are resolved by control-enhancing endeavors (de Charms, 1968; M. L. Snyder, Smoller, Strenta, & Frankel, 1981); these changes may then enable an individual to mobilize his or her resources more effectively against threat. S. M. Miller (1979) has advanced a "minimax" theory of control, which maintains that people try to minimize the maximum possible danger they may experience from an event. "A person who has control over an aversive event insures having a lower maximum danger than a person without control. This is because a person with control attributes the cause of relief to a stable internal source—his own response—whereas a person without control attributes relief to a less stable, more external source" (p. 294). Miller's theory, then, stresses attributions for restoring control as a central explanatory factor in the efficacy of control; moreover, with control, people gain knowledge not only about present circumstances, but also about future ones. However, there are many circumstances in which control-restoring interventions succeed without locating the cause of that success within the individual. Hence Miller's explanation would apply to some, but not all of the control literature.

No single theory seems to account adequately for all of the empirical evidence on the beneficial effects of predictability and control (Thompson, 1981). Indeed, predictability and control seem to have multiple beneficial effects, and in many cases, it is likely that several factors are operating together. Future efforts in pinning down the control concept might more profitably focus on the wide range of cognitive, emotional, behavioral, and physiological changes that can accompany feelings of control and attempt to map specific operationalizations of control to control-based changes to produce a more integrated theoretical position.

Summary

Psychological control is a conceptual cornerstone of much psychological thinking. Psychologists believe it underlies and motivates the attribution process, and even more important, they feel it is integral to self-esteem.

The potential for control depends fundamentally upon the perception that one is able to perform a given action. Ability in turn is a precondition for causal attributions. One does not ascribe causality for an event to an agent if that agent cannot control it. Perceived freedom results from an analysis of the constraints or options that surround a given action. When an action appears to have been chosen from a set of alternatives, high perceived freedom will result; characteristics of the options themselves also influence the attribution of freedom. High perceived freedom leads to more confident dispositional attributions. Attributions of responsibility depend upon attributed freedom and control; the greater the perceived freeom and control over an action, the more blame or credit will be assigned. Recently, research has distinguished between attributions of responsibility for the cause versus the solution of an event; the combination of these two variables yields four models of helping. The type of help offered and the reaction to it depend on both which helping model the recipient and agent of help subscribe to and whether or not they share a common model.

Although people seem always to need to feel some element of control in their lives, control becomes especially important when it is challenged or lost. Under such circumstances, people may react more negatively to stress, showing poorer task performance and an increased number of physical symptoms. They also seek additional information, sometimes becoming hypervigilant to faulty or erroneous sources of information. Reactance (i.e., anger or hostility) when one's freedoms are arbitrarily restricted or withdrawn is one common response to loss of control that increases with the importance of the freedoms, the magnitude of threat, higher expectations of freedom, and greater anticipation of future restrictions. Attempts to restore freedom when reactance has been aroused can be direct or indirect. Helplessness, or facing the aversive environment passively, is another response to loss of control than can lead to learned helplessness and depression. Which response to loss of control occurs (reactance or helplessness) depends on the magnitude of threat, one's expectations of control, the duration of the aversive experience, and individual differences. Finally, individuals may yield control voluntarily by responding mindlessly to overlearned tasks; under such circumstances, people can become vulnerable to negative labels or failure experiences (self-induced dependence), they may be unable to deal with novel or interrupting conditions, and they may fail to learn information that will later become useful to them (premature cognitive commitment).

Research designed to enhance or restore control has generally explored six different types of control. *Behavior control*, which provides an individual with a possible response to an aversive event, generally lowers pre-event stress, but does not necessarily affect perceptions of the event itself. *Cognitive control*, which helps people to think about aversive events differently, appears to reduce both pre-event stress and stress during the event itself. When people are able to make decisions about an aversive event, *decision control*, they seem to be able to withstand the negative side effects of those decisions better. *Information control*, or providing people with knowledge of the onset, duration, or timing of an aversive event, has equivocal effects; whereas warning signals for a forthcoming aversive event have no clear effect, sensation information, and to a lesser extent, procedural information, both reliably help people cope with aversive events. *Retrospective control*, or coming to think about the causes or controllability of past aversive events differently, may help people adjust to the unpleasant outcomes of events that have already transpired. Finally, *secondary control* may occur when efforts at direct or primary control are unsuccessful; secondary control involves bringing one's self in line with environmental forces and deciding to let one's situation be determined by external forces.

Many studies have now utilized control interventions in field settings of both short-term stress, such as crowding or undergoing a noxious medical test, and long-term stress, such as being kept in a nursing home or being constrained by the demands of a chronic disease. Generally, the work shows these control-restoring efforts to be successful.

The effects of control are not always beneficial. When people exaggerate the degree of control they have, they may respond inappropriately to chance situations, manifesting an illusion of control. This illusion is thought to be implicated in the pathology of gambling. The belief that good things happen to good people and bad things to bad people (the belief in a just world) can lead to erroneously blaming others for unfortunate circumstances such as poverty or infirmity. Under stressful circumstances, too much control can be as problematic as too little; giving people too many steps they can take on their own behalf may overload their capabilities, leading to poor, rather than successful, coping. Control may also fail if it is the wrong kind of control for the situation. Finally, it is possible that controlling efforts can have negative effects, if subsequent events disconfirm their effectiveness: people who expect to control an aversive event but fail to do so may be worse off than people who never had any expectations of control. Individual difference variables, such as the Type A behavior syndrome, locus of control, health locus of control, and preference for control may further differentiate those who respond more strenuously to loss of control and those who respond more favorably to control-enhancing interventions.

A remaining issue in the control field is exactly how psychological control aids adjustment to stressful events. The ability to predict noxious events is one of the mechanisms, but control seems to add something more such as increased self-esteem or self-attributions of causal responsibility for the reduction of stress. It is likely, however, that no single mechanism is responsible for all the beneficial effects of psychological control.

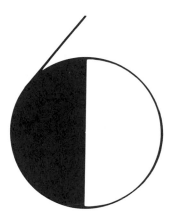

social schemata

A young woman, casually dressed, walked over to the campus bookstore's requisition desk. "I'd like to order the books for a course," she said. The older woman behind the desk said, "The books aren't in yet for the fall semester." "I know," the first woman replied. "I'd like to *order* the books for the course." "Oh, certainly. Well, what books does the professor want?" asked the other, helpfully. "I *am* the professor" was the frustrated reply.

Assumptions about other people enable all of us to function. Knowing or guessing that another person is a student, a secretary, or a professor allows us to observe and interpret, to remember and forget, to infer and judge, all in ways that fit our expectations about particular kinds of people. Accumulated general knowledge about categories of people does not do justice to the unique qualities of any given individual, but it makes possible a certain efficiency and adaptiveness in social cognition. In this chapter, we concentrate on the effects of such general expectations or social schemata. One of our primary messages in this chapter is that people do not easily change their interpersonal theories, assumptions, and expectations, even when the evidence contradicts them. Relying on one's own schemata provides the sense of prediction and control which, as noted in Chapter 5, is critical to one's well-being.

This chapter describes research on the functions of social schemata. We begin with a definition and example of schemata in action. Before detailing the research evidence on social schematic processes, it is useful to provide some background. The schema concept arose out of work in person perception, nonsocial memory, and categorization, all of which made the common point that perceivers actively construct their own reality. Then, the bulk of the chapter concerns the role of schemata in social information processing. In particular, psychologists posit that schemata guide the perception of new information, memory for old information, and inferences that go beyond both. Psychologists have studied schema-guided perception, memory, and inference under four major social cognition research paradigms; we will discuss each paradigm separately. Nonetheless, the message from each paradigm is the same: schemata serve the same functions in every case. After reviewing the converging evidence from different sources, we address unresolved issues concerning schema growth and change. We close by evaluating the schema concept as it is currently understood.

DEFINITION AND EXAMPLE OF SCHEMA-GUIDED PROCESSES

For our purposes, a *schema* is a cognitive structure that represents organized knowledge about a given concept or type of stimulus. A schema contains both the attributes of the concept and the relationships among the attributes (S. T. Fiske & Linville, 1980; Hastie, 1981; Rumelhart & Ortony, 1977; S. E. Taylor & Crocker, 1981). In the bookstore example which began this chapter, the clerk's schema for professor probably included at least the attributes older, male, orders books, and has female secretary. The last two attributes probably were linked: professors' secretaries were expected to do the actual book ordering.

The schema concept specifically maintains that information is stored in an abstract form, not simply as a collection of all the original encounters with examples of the general case. Thus a professor schema is stored in memory as a general case abstracted from specific professors. The schema then organizes incoming information thematically related to professors. In other words, people's general prior knowledge allows them to decide what information is relevant to a given theme or schema, and thus what is an important focus for information-processing. In sum, general prior knowledge about people and situations allows social perceivers to make sense of specific new encounters.

The schema concept reflects a concern with what are called "top-down," "conceptually based," or "theory-driven" cognitive processes, as opposed to "bottom-up" or "data-driven" ones (Abelson, 1981b; Bobrow & Norman, 1975; Rumelhart & Ortony, 1977). That is, researchers studying theory-driven processes focus on the ways that people's prior concepts and theories shape how they view data. Schemata are theories or concepts that guide how people take in, remember, and make inferences about raw data. The alternative would be to focus on data-driven processes, that is, how the data shape people's theories, or on how the data themselves shape the processes of attention, memory, and inference. Although both theory-driven and data-driven processes operate in tandem, social schema researchers focus on the former.

In this chapter we describe three types of processes guided by social schemata: perception, memory, and inference. A preliminary example will clarify how each functions. Suppose you read about a typical day in the life of a student, preceded by the following: "Nancy woke up feeling sick again and wondered if she really were pregnant. How could she tell the professor she had been seeing? And the money was another problem." At this point, most people have brought to bear their schema for unwanted pregnancies. In the story that follows, Nancy then visits the doctor, fidgets through a lecture, and attends a student-faculty cocktail party, where she cannot talk to the professor because he is totally surrounded by other students. As Nancy's day unfolds, the interpretation that the doctor's visit involves pregnancy tests and that she feels depressed at the party are obvious. Trying to have a word with the professor at the party takes on special significance, knowing what you know about her (and him). Your knowledge about people in such situations guides information processing; it clears up ambiguities in the information given (perception), helps you to remember otherwise trivial incidents (memory), and fills in where things are left unsaid (inference).

Suppose instead that the same day in an undergraduate life were prefaced by a description of an athlete, Jack, who is trying to gain weight and to pass chemistry in time for the football season. This brings to mind one's schema for athletes trying to make the team. Jack also visits the doctor, fidgets through a lecture, and attends a party. But now the same unspecified doctor's visit has a different meaning (whether he has gained those last few pounds). Suddenly, how many hors d'oeuvres the student ate is no longer a trivial point. Perception, memory, and inference can depend entirely on learning a person's goals, even if the events themselves stay the same. General prior knowledge or a schema (about unwanted pregnancies, college athletics, etc.) totally changes your understanding of what you read (Owens, Bower, & Black, 1979).

Schemata focus primarily on cognition: on how general information is represented in memory and on how new information is assimilated with existing knowledge. The most fundamental principle suggested by schema research is that people simplify reality; they do so in part by interpreting specific instances in light of the general case. Thus a typical schema for a politician, for example, contains a general belief that they are untrustworthy, self-serving, and ingratiating, but also sociable and outgoing. The schema contains knowledge about what information would be congruent (his smile is not to be trusted). By implication, it defines what would be incongruent (he avoids crowds) and what is irrelevant (whether or not he likes fried clams).

The Active Construction of Reality

The schema concept originated in response to long-standing issues running through research on person perception and object perception. The schema concept follows from a fundamental assumption: perceivers actively construct reality. People create meaning and add on to it the raw data of the objective world. This premise openly contradicts common sense. As ordinary people, we experience perception as instantaneous and direct, as if we simply took in an unchanged or literal copy of the data the environment presents. Notice, for example, that you are not aware of the ink on this printed page, which would be a literal copy of the raw data available to you. Rather, it seems as if you perceive the meanings of the words directly. In fact, your brain has constructed those meanings. In the commonsense view, the brain takes in a literal copy of the external world with no more active participation than a videotape camera.

Although ordinary people and philosophers alike held the literal copy view (Aristotle, 1931; J. Mill, 1869), the advent of Gestalt psychology encouraged a different view of perception (Brunswik, 1956; Koffka, 1935). Gestalt psychologists argued that perception is constructive and that perceptions are mediated by the interpretive faculties of nerves and brain. For example, what we "see" in any given objective stimulus depends on context; for example, the "1" in "1952" and in "life" objectively may be quite similar, but we interpret it differently in each case, in a way that reflects the context in which it occurs. The point may seem incidental, but it anticipates the schema concept's emphasis on the active construction of reality (cf. Bruner, 1957).

The schema concept is a direct descendant of Gestalt psychology in the following way. The schema concept builds on the constructive or interpretive view of perception by positing that organized prior knowledge shapes what is perceived and recorded in memory. The specific forebears of the schema concept are research in person perception, nonsocial memory, and object categorization, to which we now turn for some intellectual perspective.

ORIGINS OF THE SCHEMA CONCEPT IN PERSON PERCEPTION RESEARCH

In his pioneering work, Solomon Asch (1946) examined how people combine the components of another person's personality and come up with an integrated overall impression. In so doing, he built on Gestalt psychology and set the stage for much of person perception research (D. J. Schneider, Hastorf, & Ellsworth, 1979). Asch also specifically anticipated social schema research by his analysis of how people develop impressions of others. Asch's primary concern was the same as the Gestalt psychologists: how people make sense of incoming information. The actual task that confronted Asch's subjects was to form an impression of someone described by one or another trait list. For example, one group was told about someone who was "intelligent, skillful, industrious, warm, determined, practical, and cautious." Another group of subjects was told about someone who was "intelligent, skillful, industrious, cold, determined, practical, and cautious." The simple manipulation of the terms *warm* and *cold* created large differences in people's descriptions of the target person. For example, the cold, intelligent person was seen as calculating, and the warm, intelligent person was seen as wise.

Asch proposed two models to account for these results: the *configural model* and the *algebraic model*. To understand the configural model, suppose you value the individual trait of being intelligent. Now, would you always consider it good to be intelligent? That is, would you rather encounter a smart or a stupid con artist? The configuration as a whole alters the value of the individual trait of being intelligent. The critical assumption of the configural model is that it posits a change in the meaning of traits as a function of the other traits present in that context. An intelligent con artist is *sly*; an intelligent child is *clever*; an intelligent grandfather is *wise*. The evaluation and meaning of being intelligent, then, changes depending on context. To return to the previous example, subjects reading *intelligent* and *cold* together would perceive them as part of a unified whole, with each trait affecting the meaning of the other (see top of Fig. 6.1). Out of this configuration might come the inference that the cold, intelligent person is calculating, along with the corre-

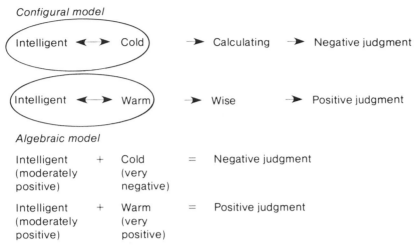

Fig. 6.1 Two models of impression formation.

sponding negative evaluation. The configural model suggests that an impression is made up of traits and the relationships between the traits, just as a schema would later be defined to consist of attributes and the relationships among attributes.

The alternative, the algebraic model, provides a direct contrast to the configural model and, by extension, to the schema models that echo the early configural approach. The algebraic model is an example of an elemental approach to social cognition, as described in Chapter 1. The algebraic model takes each individual trait, evaluates it in isolation from the others, and combines the evaluations into a summary judgment (see Fig. 6.1). It is as if, upon meeting someone new, you were simply to average together all the person's pros (e.g., intelligence) and cons (e.g., coldness) to form your impression. The algebraic model of information averaging boasts an impressive program of research (N. H. Anderson, 1974, 1981) that testifies to its conceptual value.

Both the algebraic and configural models encountered problems of two sorts: theoretical and methodological. Within the theoretical frameworks of their times, neither the algebraic model nor the configural model could be disproved. This was in part because neither was stated in a falsifiable form. Both were flexible enough to account for almost any result. Thus each model could be made consistent with the data generated by the other, so there was no way to prove either model right—or wrong (D. L. Hamilton & Zanna, 1974; Schumer, 1973; Wyer, 1974; Wyer & Watson, 1969; Zanna & Hamilton, 1977; versus N. H. Anderson, 1966; N. H. Anderson & Lampel, 1965; Kaplan, 1971, 1975). After much debate, the "futility of the adversarial approach" was declared (Ostrom, 1977), and there were pleas for fresh theory development.

Research on social schemata filled some of this theoretical gap, as we will see. It built—explicitly or implicitly—on Asch's configural model. Both Asch and schema theorists are concerned with the relationships among individual pieces of information that fit into an overall configuration. Just as knowledge of the trait cold affects the meaning of the trait intelligent, so knowledge of an unwanted pregnancy can affect the meaning of a cocktail party. General prior knowledge links isolated pieces of information in both cases, creating meaning out of the configuration. Understanding depends on cognitive organization, in both views. Thus there is theoretical continuity from early work on the configural model to recent work on schematic models. However, as we will see, the newer impression formation research is marked by its more elaborate cognitive models, especially by schematic models of cognitive structure. This cognitive specificity has been possible because of new methodological approaches that complement the newly emerging theories (D. L. Hamilton & Katz, 1975; Lingle, Geva, & Ostrom, 1975; Chapter 10; for an example of old problems being approached in new ways, see Woll, Weeks, Fraps, Pendergrass, & Vanderplas, 1980).

To summarize, research in person perception originally pitted a configural model against an algebraic model of impression formation. The configural model anticipated schema theories, but neither the configural nor the algebraic model could be decisively tested, for both theoretical and methodological reasons. Frustration with the stalemate in person perception research created a shift toward cognitive viewpoints. The cognitive reorientation of impression-formation researchers led them straight to the door of cognitive psychology's theories of representation and processing, and to cognitive schema theories in particular, as a more viable approach.

ORIGINS OF THE SCHEMA CONCEPT
IN NONSOCIAL MEMORY RESEARCH

Any time one encounters a new concept or theory, it is helpful to ask the question, "What is the alternative?" The configural model of person perception, which anticipated schematic models, was best understood in contrast to the algebraic model. In cognitive psychology, the schema concept is best understood in contrast to early traditional memory models. Traditional "associationist" models viewed memory as built up entirely from simple links or associations between pairs of impoverished stimuli such as nonsense syllables (Ebbinghaus, 1885/1964). Associations were strengthened by rehearsal (repetition), in this view (L. R. Peterson & Peterson, 1959). For example, cat and mouse would be elements linked by their frequent contiguity. Traditional memory models were a basic part of the elemental approach to psychology as we noted in Chapter 1.

Cognitive schema theories were born in reaction to the traditional associationist position (Hastie, 1981). In particular, cognitive schema theories developed to explain the following basic observation: it is difficult to understand and remember things without drawing on abstracted general knowledge about how the world works and filling in where information is missing or ambiguous. The role of generic prior knowledge was difficult for traditional associationist theorists to explain, because their theories had no mechanisms for going beyond the information given. Generalizations, inferences, and expectations are difficult to describe in the simplest of traditional associationist terms. They are easier to describe in terms of guiding themes, frameworks, schemata, or prior knowledge.

For an example of how mysterious ordinary events can be without the proper schema or guiding theme, consider the following stimulus materials from an early experiment in the tradition of cognitive schema theories. Try to learn these sentences by memory by simply associating each with the next:

> The procedure is actually quite simple. First, you arrange things into different groups. Of course, one pile may be sufficient depending on how much there is to do. . . . It is important not to overdo things. That is, it is better to do too few things at once than too many. In the short run this may not seem important, but complications can easily arise. A mistake can be expensive as well. At first the whole procedure will seem complicated. Soon, however, it will become just another facet of life. (Bransford & Johnson, 1972, p. 722)

When people are given an appropriate title beforehand, they have a guiding theme, so they are better able to recall the passage than those given no title or given the title afterwards. "Washing Clothes" is the proper title. (For a readable review of this and his related research, see Bransford, 1979.)

How do cognitive psychologists demonstrate the impact of schemata on understanding? They have used several approaches, that is, the amount, accuracy, speed, and focus of memory. In the laundry example, one can demonstrate that people simply remember *more* when they can use the title as an organizing theme. Alternatively, one might find that people *falsely* remember information related to the guiding theme—information that was never actually presented. That is, they might report that the passage contained a description of putting soap into the machine when, in fact, it did not (e.g., Bransford & Franks, 1971). Alternatively, one might show that the story details are remembered *faster* when they have a unifying theme than when they do not (e.g., E. E. Smith, Adams, & Schorr, 1978). Another possibility is to show that people remember *different* things depending on which of two themes they are given. The same story attributed to pregnant Nancy or athletic Jack at the beginning of the chapter is one example of this approach.

To summarize, cognitive research on the role of generic prior knowledge has demonstrated the importance of schemata in basic processes of understanding and memory. The schema concept emphasizes generalizations, inferences, and complex expectations that are difficult to explain from a traditional associationist perspective. Newer associationist models are far more complex (e.g., J. R. Anderson & Bower, 1973; A. M. Collins & Quillian, 1972; Rumelhart, Lindsay, & Norman, 1972), in part so that they can account for many of the findings of schema theories (J. R. Anderson, 1982; Alba & Hasher, 1983; Reder & Anderson, 1980). Thus, in cognitive psychology, the schema concept arose in reaction to early research on memory, and its configural viewpoint has enriched that field, as well as being useful to social psychologists looking for explicit models of cognitive structure in impression formation.

ORIGINS OF THE SCHEMA CONCEPT IN CATEGORIZATION RESEARCH

Our overview of the origins of schema research would be incomplete without one final excursion. Besides drawing on discontents among person perception researchers and on theoretical developments in nonsocial memory, schema research emerged from a parallel theoretical development in research on how people categorize objects. That research is concerned with situations such as this: given a small winged creature, how does one decide that it is an instance of the category bird and not a very large instance of the category insect? Categorization researchers independently developed theories that echo the configural aspects of nonsocial schema research, and these have proved useful in social cognition research as well.

Several views of categorization depend on the concept of central tendencies or prototypes. In this approach, knowledge about a category is composed of a typical or ideal instance, which is called a *prototype*, accompanied by the full range of peripheral or less good examples. So, for example, a robin (prototype) is a better instance of the category bird than a turkey (peripheral example) is. People decide if a new instance is a member of the category by assessing its similarity to the prototype. The more similar it is, the more certain they are that it belongs in the category.

People base judgments of similarity to a prototype on the *family resemblance* criterion. This means that no single set of features defines the category bird or chair or fruit. Rather, any of several features contribute to the judgment that an object resembles the category prototype. Consider the category of one's family and how an observer could decide, on the basis of appearance, who belonged to the family and who did not; people resemble their siblings and parents in various respects that are not necessarily all the same ones. For example, you might have your father's hair and your mother's eyes, while both your brother and you have your grandfather's nose. Similarly, there is supposed to be a family resemblance that identifies objects as category members, but not all category members necessarily share the same rigid set of features (Wittgenstein, 1953). The more features an instance shares with other category members, the more consistently, consensually, and quickly it is identified as a typical category member (McCloskey & Glucksberg, 1978; Rosch, 1978). This conception of categories refers to them as fuzzy sets, rather than as fixed, well-defined, formal categories. The notion of fuzzy sets is particularly useful in complex areas of knowledge, such as social information processing, as we will soon see.

The concept of a category as composed of a fuzzy set including a prototype and peripheral instances has been supported by research on category formation. People derive the average or central tendency of a category through exposure to instances, even if they never actually see the single best example or prototype (Hayes-Roth & Hayes-Roth, 1977; Posner & Keele, 1968, 1970; Reed, 1972). Hence, if a little girl sees many examples of sports cars, eventually she distills an impression of their most usual size, color, and shape. If she later encounters the prototypic sports car, say a small, red Porsche, for the first time, she will reliably identify it as a category member even though she has never before seen the prototype itself. Moreover, the more clearly prototypic it is, the faster she will categorize it.

Categories are organized hierarchically, at varying levels of inclusion. That is, a chair is an instance of the larger category furniture and includes instances of its own, such as rocking chair, desk chair, and arm chair (see Fig. 6.2). Different levels of categorization are useful for different purposes (Rosch, Mervis, Gray, Johnson, & Boyes-Braem, 1976).

To summarize, categorization researchers established the notion that people identify category members by assessing their similarity to the category prototype. Categorization operates by family resemblance within a fuzzy set, not by a rigid set of rules. Categories are organized in a hierarchy of varying levels of abstraction.

Categorization processes tie into schematic processes by explaining how a given schema might be applied to a particular instance. For example, categorization research tells you how to decide that a very large beanbag might be a chair, and schematic processes describe the effects of the label chair on subsequent perceptions, memory, and inferences. That is, categorization explains how the label chair is applied in the first place, and schematic processes explain what effects the label chair has, once it has been applied. As we will see, social cognition research has borrowed directly from research on categorization, as well as from memory research.

A note on prototypes versus schemata   The notions of prototypes and schemata often are used by social cognition researchers as if the terms were interchangeable. For some purposes, they may be, but it is useful to define the differences. Prototypes resemble instances, in that all their known attributes are filled in, even if all the attributes are not directly relevant to category membership (J. R. Anderson, 1980a, 1980b). The prototypic sports car comes

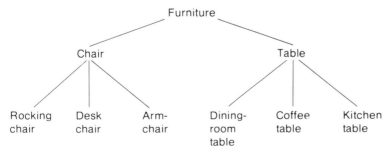

Fig. 6.2 Hierarchy of object categories.

in a particular size and color (small, red), even if actual category members vary so much on these dimensions that they become meaningless for identifying them, for example, some have stripes, some are silver, others blue, black, or white; some are tiny, others relatively large. Nonetheless, the prototype has a typical color and size.

As an alternative to the prototype view of categorical knowledge, the schema concept raises the possibility that particular attributes may be ignored. Although one *could* generate a "typical" color for a sports car, the schema concept implies that perhaps it is not a usual feature stored with knowledge about the category. In contrast to prototypes, a schema permits some features to be unspecified. Because of this flexibility, a schema could be a more efficient representation than is a prototype because it has fewer details and is more focused on the essentials of category membership (J. R. Anderson, 1980a; for another view of the differences between categorical and schematic memory, see J. Mandler, 1979).

We will use the terms *category*, *prototype*, and *schema* in this chapter. Our usage follows the particular focus of the literature under discussion at any given point. For the present purposes, the important common point in the term *schema* and related terms is this: general expectations guide processing of specific data. In other words, the ideas of a schema, prototype, and category each reflect a theoretical concern with what we called "top-down" processes. Each is concerned with the ways that abstracted prior knowledge shapes the understanding of new information. The abstracted knowledge is composed of the prototype's or schema's attributes and the relationships among the attributes. Each is a configuration of old general information that guides the processing of new information.

SUMMARY

The schema concept emerged from several sources. First, there was social psychologists' frustration with an unresolvable conflict between impression formation models that focused on a holistic, configural approach or on an elemental, algebraic approach. The configural approach is a direct theoretical ancestor of the schema concept. Cognitive theories and methods provided the framework that would allow fine-grained analyses of person perception and social cognition. Cognitive research on schemata specified the role of generic prior knowledge in perception, memory, and inference. Cognitive research on categorization focused on how general knowledge about a category could be stored as a prototype and on the hierarchical relationships among categories.

Schemata in Social Cognition

Social schema research goes well beyond its origins in research on person perception, cognitive schemata, and categorization, as we will see. But the basic message of this research is similar to that of the cognitive research:

organized generic prior knowledge enables us to function in a social world that otherwise would be of paralyzing complexity.

Social schema research falls into essentially four groups (see Table 6.1 and S. E. Taylor & Crocker, 1981). Research on *person schemata* focuses on knowledge about the traits and goals that shape other people's behavior. Person schemata capture the perceiver's complex understanding of the psychology of typical or specific individuals; for example, person schemata might include abstract schemata such as what a typical introvert is like or specific ones such as what your best friend is like. A second kind of schema that has generated much research of its own is the *self-schema*. A self-schema contains information about one's own personality, appearance, and behavior. For example, you might know that you are introverted or overweight or chronically late and what that means. Researchers also study *role schemata*, which focus on knowledge about broad social categories, such as age, race, sex, or occupation. Role schemata include information that places the individual in society. For example, you know a great deal about the role of professor, what professors can (and cannot) ask of students, what kind of clothes they wear to class, and how they typically lecture. Finally, researchers study *event schemata*, which include shared understandings of what typically happens on certain occasions, such as birthday parties, restaurant visits, or even political

TABLE 6.1
Types of Schemata in Social Cognition

A schema is a cognitive structure that contains knowledge about the attributes of a concept and the relationships among those attributes. All types of schemata guide perception, memory, and inference in similar ways, toward schema-relevant information, and often toward schema-consistent information. Disconfirming or incongruent information requires more effort to process than congruent information; if that effort is made, it may be well remembered.

Person schemata: People's understanding of the psychology of typical or specific individuals, composed of traits and goals, helps them to categorize others and to remember schema-relevant behavior.

Self-schemata: General information about one's own psychology makes up a complex, easily accessible verbal self-concept that guides information processing about the self.

Role schemata: Intergroup perception and stereotyping are affected by role schemata that describe the appropriate norms and behavior for broad social categories, based on age, race, sex, and occupation.

Event schemata: People's prior knowledge of the typical sequence of events on standard social occasions helps them to understand ambiguous information, to remember relevant information, and to infer consistent information where it is missing.

Content-free or procedural social schemata: A rather different kind of social schema consists entirely of rules for linking content but not much content; it guides information processing toward schema-relevant information.

---

coups. Other types of social schemata may exist in addition to these four, but they capture the essential research areas.

The research on social schemata—whether focused on person, self, role, or event schemata—shows that they all have similar effects on information processing. All four areas of research demonstrate parallel functions of social schemata in the perception of incoming information, the retrieval of stored information, and inferences based on that information. Nevertheless, we will cover each type of schema separately because the research paradigms differ. It is important to remember that, in the final analysis, findings from each paradigm make many of the same points.

PERSON SCHEMATA

The types of person schemata that researchers usually study are personality traits and goals. Both traits and goals determine what information is relevant to and consistent with a given person or type of people. For example, a schema for the trait "curious" might include what curious people do, examples of curious people, and what subcategories of curious people there are (intellectually questioning, personally prying, innocently inquiring, etc.).

Person schemata also include schemata for people's goals as well as traits; goals are people's situation-specific intents, so they may alternatively be thought of as a person-in-situation category. For example, the goal of burglary is meaningless in some situations (e.g., on a deserted island where there is nothing to steal) and the goal of burglary is unlikely for some people (e.g., a rich person or a moral person). Goals or person-in-situation schemata are a joint function of the goals the situation suggests and how those possible goals fit the particular people who happen to be in the situation. A person-in-situation category is highly accessible to memory (Cantor, 1980), that is, the prototypic burglar (trait category) at a prototypic burglary-prone house (situation category) is especially easy to imagine. This appears to be because a person-in-situation category suggests certain very specific behavior (e.g., break in without being caught, find many valuables), and as such a person-in-situation schema is rich in content and easily accessible. Hence a goal or person-in-situation schema is often useful for accurately predicting a particular person's behavior in a particular setting.

To see the impact of goals on understanding, take a mental tour of a friend's house, with burglary in mind. What details are important? You know that burglary includes looking for expensive, easily disposable items such as color televisions, silver, and stereos, so that is what you will focus on most. To get an idea of the schema's impact, think again of the friend's house with the goal of possible purchase. Suddenly, the leaky basement matters; you remember the sagging stairs and forget the stereo. It has been demonstrated that just such a shift in a goal schema allows one to recall details not easily recalled from the other perspective (R. C. Anderson & Pichert, 1978).

Thus the goal schema one brings to mind determines what information is relevant and consistent. The same is true for trait schemata. This central function of every type of schema shows up in a variety of research on person schemata, and in particular, research on their role in perception, memory, and inference.

Perception   Placing another person's behavior into the proper trait category operates on many of the same principles as does categorizing an object, which we just covered. In the same way that our perception of a beanbag chair is shaped by our knowledge that it is an instance of chair, not a deflated punching bag, so our perception of a person who interrupts us is shaped by our categorizing him by the trait excitable, rather than the trait insensitive.

How exactly does social categorization operate? People have in mind the prototypic extravert, or cheater, or paranoid schizophrenic, just as they do the prototypic bird, or vegetable, or chair. Just as with objects, a social prototype allows people to categorize instances by the family resemblance criterion (Cantor & Mischel, 1977, 1979; Cantor, Mischel, & Schwartz, 1982). Recall that this means that while no one extravert may possess all the same extraverted qualities, having several of them nonetheless identifies the person as an example of an extravert. The family resemblance criterion suggests the processes by which particular traits are fit to a given person's behavior.

A related issue is the *level* at which the categorization occurs (Cantor & Mischel, 1979; Rosch *et al.*, 1976). That is, categories for people, like categories for objects, are organized hierarchically: a gourmet is a special case of a sophisticate, and a sophisticate is a special case of a cultured person (see Fig. 6.3). Higher and lower levels of categorization differ on two features: amount of detail within each category and amount of overlap between categories. To begin with detail *within* category, the farther down one goes in the hierarchy, the more specific detail there is. Imagine all you could say about a gourmet, who is at the lowest and most detailed level of categorization. Now imagine how few specific things you could say about the higher level category of a cultured person, who could be cultured with respect to food, travel, theater, or music but not necessarily any of them in particular. Higher levels in the hierarchy have fewer details that are necessarily characteristics within that category.

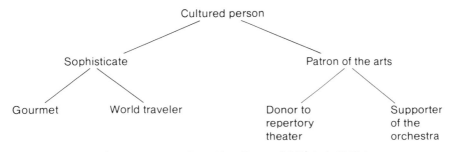

Fig. 6.3   Hierarchy of person categories. (After Cantor & Mischel, 1979.)

Nevertheless, higher levels contain less overlap *between* categories compared to lower levels. That is, higher levels have little in common—little overlap—with other categories at their own level. A cultured person is quite different from an uncultured person. At the lower levels, there is far more overlap between categories. A world traveler has a lot in common with a gourmet. Hence lower level categories are a less accurate basis for distinguishing one person from another, precisely because there is relatively more between-category overlap. To summarize, lower levels contain more between-category overlap and more within-category detail. Higher levels contain less between-category overlap and less within-category detail.

Memory   Once a perceiver places a person into a particular category, the perceiver is likely to misremember the presence of category-consistent but never-seen attributes. Cantor and Mischel (1977) tested this idea by having subjects read lists of adjectives that described, for example, an extravert. The lists contained words that were moderately related to extraversion (e.g., energetic, entertaining). On a later recognition test, people falsely recognized highly prototypic words that were never in the original list. That is, highly related traits such as spirited and outgoing were misremembered as being part of the original stimuli. Thus people can falsely recognize traits that are prototypically related to a category but in fact not contained in a specific instance they encountered. This effect occurs regardless of whether the schema is implicit or explicit (cf. Tsujimoto, 1978).

Person schemata include goals as well as traits, as we noted above. Thus, knowing a person's goals also can bias memory in the direction of goal-consistent information, just as knowing the person's traits can bias memory toward trait-consistent information. As an illustration of the impact of goals on memory, consider the following scenario that was used in one study. Subjects were shown a skit in which a student had the goal of enrolling in classes to complete his major area requirements. Some subjects were told his major was chemistry; others were told his major was music; still others were told his major was psychology. The student dropped his books and papers upon entering the room, and then tried to register for several specific classes. When told that the student's goal was to complete a major in music, subjects recalled more music-related items, such as the Beethoven sheet music he had dropped and the music classes he wanted. When subjects thought his major was psychology, they recalled psychology-related items, and when they thought it was chemistry, they remembered chemistry-related items (Zadny & Gerard, 1974). That is, people tended to recall goal-consistent information better than inconsistent information. Several studies show the impact of goals on recall for otherwise ambiguous situations (R. C. Anderson & Pichert, 1978; Owens *et al.*, 1979).

In sum, schemata for people's traits and goals typically help the perceiver to remember schema-consistent information in more detail than would be possible without the schema. What is most interesting about the effects of

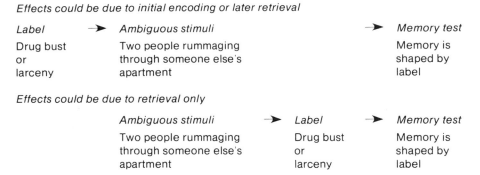

Effects could be due to initial encoding or later retrieval

Label	$\rightarrow$	*Ambiguous stimuli*		$\rightarrow$	*Memory test*
Drug bust or larceny		Two people rummaging through someone else's apartment			Memory is shaped by label

Effects could be due to retrieval only

	Ambiguous stimuli	$\rightarrow$	*Label*	$\rightarrow$	*Memory test*
	Two people rummaging through someone else's apartment		Drug bust or larceny		Memory is shaped by label

Fig. 6.4 Two sequences that show schematic effects.

schemata on memory is that even when consistent, inconsistent, and irrelevant information all are equally available at the time that the information is first encountered, the schema still determines what is most easily remembered.

One question arises in examining the effects of prototypes and person schemata on memory: Exactly when do the effects occur in the information processing sequence, at perception or at memory? Some research locates most schematic effects at the initial perception of the information and some at later memory retrieval. To resolve this contradiction, other research has explicitly pitted initial perception and memory retrieval against each other. It does this by providing schematic structure either before or after subjects encounter a set of ambiguous stimuli (see Fig. 6.4). For example, one set of subjects might be told beforehand that a film was called *Drug Bust* and then watch the person's relevant and irrelevant activities. And another set of subjects might watch the film and only learn its title afterward. The title provides a relevant schema at encoding (beforehand) or at retrieval (afterward). Effects of providing schematic structure beforehand are typically stronger (Howard & Rothbart, 1980; Rothbart, Evans, & Fulero, 1979; Wyer, Srull, Gordon, & Hartwick, 1982; Zadny & Gerard, 1974), but that is not surprising. The prior framework allows schematic effects at both initial perception (encoding) and at later retrieval. In contrast, a post hoc framework allows only retrieval effects. Nonetheless, schematic effects clearly can occur at retrieval; people are perfectly capable of reinterpreting information they already know, in light of a new social schema (R. C. Anderson & Pichert, 1978; M. Snyder & Uranowitz, 1978). Accordingly, this research suggests that schematic effects are greatest when available at both initial perception and retrieval, but can operate independently at the retrieval stage.

Inference In addition to their effects on initial perceptions and later memory, person schemata and prototypes affect subsequent inferences. For example, if you know someone who does one typically extraverted thing such as planning lots of parties, you are likely to infer that the person also has other extraverted attributes, such as liking to talk (Semin & Rosch, 1981). Even psychiatrists, who are trained in judging people, are influenced by the vagaries of prototypes. When a patient has the prototypic symptoms of a particular illness such as schizophrenia, therapists are more reliable, confident, and accurate in their diagnoses (Cantor *et al.*, 1982). Perhaps prospective patients should be facetiously advised that if they intend to have a mental problem, they should make sure it fits the prototype in the case book so that the psychiatrist can make an accurate diagnosis. The better a person's fit to a social category, the more powerful the effects on inferences.

Prototypes and schemata provide people with information about what attributes generally go together in other people's personalities. This aspect of prototypes was anticipated by earlier research on people's implicit personality theories, which are people's naive notions of the typical links between traits (D. J. Schneider, 1973; D. J. Schneider *et al.*, 1979). An important feature of schema-driven inference is that people may categorize someone on the basis of some attributes (e.g., "This man looks like my high school math teacher") and infer similarity on other objectively unrelated attributes (e.g., "Therefore he has a weird sense of humor") (S. T. Fiske, 1982; Gilovich, 1981).

Summary   Person schemata include prototypic representations of traits such as extraversion and introversion, as well as notions of what behavior is consistent with a given goal. Person schemata of all sorts shape the processes of perception, memory, and inference to conform to our general assumptions about other people. The effects of schemata on perception, memory, and inference are not necessarily well suited to accuracy in identifying individual instances. Schemata are used by the mind to manage such processes economically, if not always accurately.

SELF-SCHEMATA

What is your personality like? How outgoing do you consider yourself to be? How hard working are you? How honest? How dependent? Most people have clear conceptions of themselves on some attributes and less clear self-conceptions on others. Connie may feel she is hard working and full of integrity, but when asked if she is shy or dependent, she may hedge, not knowing how to answer. Daniel may be certain about his shyness and dependency, but uncertain about his hard work and integrity.

There are several criteria for deciding if someone has a schema (is *schematic*) or has no schema (is *aschematic*) on particular dimensions of his or her self-concept. People are self-schematic on dimensions that are important to them, on which they think of themselves as extreme, and on which they are certain the opposite does not hold (Markus, 1977). Thus, if independence is important to you, and if you think of yourself as extremely independent and as not at all dependent, that implies that you have accumulated considerable knowledge about yourself on that dimension. For example, you should be certain that you would never ask for help setting up your stereo, even at the potential cost of damage to it or harm to yourself.

In contrast to schematics, aschematic individuals rate themselves as low to moderate on the given trait and rate the trait as low to moderate in importance. Of course, people who are aschematic on one trait may well be schematic on others; everyone has some dimensions of self-concept that are idiosyncratically salient. I may think about myself predominantly in terms of independence, you may think about yourself in terms of extraversion, and a third person might be obsessed with weight. Regardless of the content of a person's self-schema, it has critical effects on perception, memory, and inference.

Perception   Being schematic on a particular dimension allows a person to filter incoming information about that dimension in much the same way that having a schema for other people guides information processing about them. Hence we categorize ourselves much as we categorize others, with similar effects (see Markus & Sentis, 1982, for a review). Both the content and the speed of judgments about oneself show the advantages of being schematic. For example, people who are schematic on independence (called independence schematics) consistently and quickly respond "that's me" to traits related to independence; they do not show this pattern with respect to dependent traits. Aschematics on independence do not differ in the speed of their response to dependent and independent adjectives, as would be predicted. So, being schematic for a given trait means that one is a rapid judge of oneself on that trait. If independence is important to me, it is likely that I will make many judgments about my independence in a variety of circumstances, so it is useful to be able to make those judgments rapidly and efficiently (Bargh, 1982).

People who are self-schematics on a given attribute also notice it in other people. We all have friends who think only about their weight and consequently inform you the instant *you* gain or lose an ounce. Noticing self-schematic traits in others seems to depend on an ability to group scattered clues into an overall pattern. A weight schematic (i.e., a person self-schematic on weight) will notice a friend eating dry toast and grapefruit for breakfast, plain yogurt for lunch, and conclude that he is dieting. Someone aschematic on weight might not associate those bits of behavior (Fong & Markus, 1982; Hamill, 1980; Markus & Fong, 1979; Markus & Smith, 1981; Markus, Smith, & Moreland, in press; Sentis & Markus, 1979).

Finally, people's self-schemata make them think harder about all kinds of schema-relevant information that comes their way. For example, people who consider themselves religious respond in more detail to religious (rather than, say, legalistic) arguments on any given topic (Cacioppo, Petty, & Sidera, 1982).

Memory   Self-schemata help people to remember schema-relevant information. This fact enables schematics easily to muster evidence in support of their self-concept. Independence schematics can remember many examples of independent behavior, expect to behave independently in the future, and resist people telling them that they are not independent. These self-schema effects replicate across such areas of self-knowledge as social sensitivity (Sweeney & Moreland, 1980), sex-role self-concept (Markus, Crane, Bernstein, & Siladi, 1982; Tunnell, 1981), and body weight (Markus, Hamill, & Sentis, 1979).

Like many knowledge structures, self-schemata are difficult to change. Of course, this makes sense; if you changed your mind about your integrity every time you let a parking meter run out, you would never be sure of exactly who you were. People consistently seek and recall information that confirms their self-concepts (Swann & Read, 1981a, 1981b). For most people, the bias is in a self-enhancing direction (Greenwald, 1980b); that is, people especially seek information related to the positive aspects of their self-concepts. However, chronically depressed people are a possible exception to this. They appear to accentuate the negative in everything that pertains to themselves, assuming personal responsibility for disaster and often remembering things they do badly (Kuiper, 1978; Kuiper & Derry, 1981; Kuiper, MacDonald, & Derry, 1983). Their negative self-image thus resists change.

In general, self-schemata appear to be stored in memory and to function much as do schemata assigned to other people. Nevertheless, knowledge about oneself and others differs in several ways. First, knowledge about oneself seems to be more accessible in memory than knowledge about others. Imagine the difference between trying to decide whether or not you are extraverted and whether or not someone else is. Deciding about yourself should be faster, especially if you are certain that you definitely are (or are not) an extravert. Having judged yourself and someone else, the self-judgment is far more memorable (Kuiper & Rogers, 1979; Rogers, 1981; Rogers, Kuiper, & Kirker, 1977).

The relative memorability of self-judgments decreases, the more familiar the other person being judged (G. H. Bower & Gilligan, 1979; Ferguson, Rule, & Carlson, 1983; Keenan & Baillet, 1980). One difference between judgments about the self and about most others is sheer familiarity of the knowledge on which they are based. Moreover, since we usually spend a lot of time in our own company, our self-schemata are bound to be more complex than our schemata for others (Linville, 1982a).

Schemata for oneself and others may differ in another way; self-knowledge may be stored in verbal rather than visual form (Lord, 1980). Given the rather considerable difficulty of keeping an eye on yourself, perhaps it is not surprising that we store limited visual information about ourselves. In contrast, we tend to store knowledge about other people in visual form.

Finally, knowledge about the self is more affect laden than is knowledge about others, especially unfamiliar others. Several theorists have suggested that the advantage of self-relevant information in perception and memory accrues in large part from its emotional importance to people (Bargh, 1982; Ferguson et al., 1983; Greenwald & Pratkanis, in press; Rogers, 1981). In sum, a self-schema is a familiar, affective, robust, complex, verbal self-portrait. Our schemata for others are less familiar, less accessible in memory, less affective, simpler, and more likely to be stored in image form.

Inference When people are asked to predict their own behavior, they usually make predictions consistent with their self-schema, for example, that they are independent now and always will be (Markus, 1977). In addition, people usually make self-schematic judgments rapidly (Markus, 1977; Markus *et al.*, 1982). However, it is not entirely clear that schemata invariably shorten the time it takes to make judgments and remember things. Under some circumstances, self-relevant judgments take *longer* for schematics than for aschematics (Kuiper, 1981; Markus, Hamill, & Sentis, 1979). Since the circumstances of faster and slower self-schematic judgments have not yet been specified, one can only speculate about what they are.

One speculation centers around the novelty of the judgment required. To take a concrete example, if you ask a self-schematic on diligence whether he is working hard, you will get an immediate answer because the answer is an integral part of his self-image; it is relevant to his self-schema, and it is not a novel question. Of course, if you ask an aschematic on diligence, you will get a slower answer because it is not relevant to the central (i.e., schematic) part of his self-image. This is simply the standard difference between schematics and aschematics. However, if you ask the diligence schematic a novel schema-relevant question he has not answered before, the answer to this novel question may not be stored as part of his self-schema. For example, the diligence schematic may not yet have thought about the best study strategy for the Graduate Record Exam (GRE). However, study strategies and exams are relevant to the diligence self-schematic, so presumably he knows a lot that could be related to it. Because he is a diligence schematic, he has a lot of information on the subject, so he will take a long time to answer the novel question about GRE strategies. Someone who is not a diligence self-schematic would have a lot less information on the subject and presumably take a shorter time to answer the same novel question. Accordingly, self-schemata may shorten processing time for familiar schema-relevant questions and lengthen processing time for novel schema-relevant questions. Conversely, aschematics may be slower than schematics for familiar schema-relevant questions and faster for novel schema-relevant questions.

There is some support for this resolution of the discrepancy between the efficiency of self-schemata on familiar judgments and the apparently enormous quantities of knowledge self-schemata contain. This support comes from work on the more general problem of expertise. In that area of research, the same discrepancy between efficiency and unwieldy amounts of knowledge has been called the paradox of the expert (E. E. Smith *et al.*, 1978): if you know many facts about a given topic, why doesn't that make you slower to retrieve any one of them? Experts resemble self-schematics in several respects (S. T. Fiske, Kinder, & Larter, 1983; Markus, Smith, & Moreland, in press). Experts usually remember schema-relevant things faster. And yet experts, like self-schematics, have more material to sort through than do novices and aschematics.

Research on expertise indicates that experts' schemata subsume large, well-integrated chunks of information, so ordinarily efficiency should be increased—for familiar judgments (e.g., Chase & Simon, 1973). Instead of handling several discrete items of information, an expert schema combines several items into one. For example, as noted above, the diligence schematic can subsume all his study habits under the single familiar judgment that he is hard working. This integration of separate bits of information speeds access (e.g., Sentis & Burnstein, 1979; E. R. Smith *et al.*, 1978), minimizes confusion (e.g., Hayes-Roth, 1977; S. T. Fiske & Dyer, 1983), and creates larger perceptual units (e.g., Chase & Simon, 1973; Markus & Smith, 1981). With experts as with schematics, it seems likely that when a judgment is novel and requires integrating old evidence in new ways, experts and self-schematics may take longer. When the judgment draws on previously integrated judgments, experts and self-schematics should be faster. Thus, experts and self-schematics both excel at retrieving information and making judgments that are routine. A novice or an aschematic may know the same answer but may reach it more slowly and have less information to back it up.

One implication of this speculation is that extreme and familiar judgments will be processed more efficiently than moderate and familiar judgments. The reasoning on this follows from the definition of self-schemata. Recall that people are defined as self-schematic on dimensions that are important, on which they think they are extreme, and on which they are certain the opposite does not hold. That means that extreme and familiar judgments are more likely to be schematic dimensions, by definition. Thus such (self-schematic) self-judgments will elicit rapid responses. This speculation is consistent with the data on self-relevant judgments: reasonably familiar adjectives that are extremely like or extremely unlike the self are judged quickly, compared to moderately self-descriptive adjectives (Kuiper & Rogers, 1979). The principle may generalize to extreme judgments in other domains (Judd & Kulik, 1980).

Summary Self-schemata sensitize people to perceiving schema-relevant information in themselves and others. Self-schemata enable people efficiently to remember and to judge schema-relevant information. However, sometimes self-schemata lengthen processing time; this is apparently most likely when the judgment is novel.

A comment on the cuing and development of self-schemata Given the pervasive effects of self-schemata, it is interesting to consider how self-schemata are cued in any given context. That is, we all presumably are self-schematic on several dimensions. But what determines which of one's self-schemata will apply at any given time? If you think of yourself as both hard working and sociable, which will affect how you process information at any given time? Context is clearly a major factor in activating one self-schema rather than another. If everyone around you is lazy, you may think of yourself as the hard working one. Evidence for the impact of context on cuing of self-schemata comes from research on self-descriptions. Although self-knowledge is remarkably resistant to change, people are sensitive to short-term context in their self-descriptions. People will most likely mention whatever attributes make them distinctive in a given context when they describe themselves (McGuire, McGuire, Child, & Fujioka, 1978; McGuire & Padawer-Singer, 1976). That is, if you are in a room full of white Anglo-Saxon Protestant students, you may not mention that you are a student but you may mention that you are Jewish.

Of course, context-based changes in self-descriptions do not necessarily mean comparable changes in fundamental self-concept, but over time one's most usual context might shape self-concept (cf. Higgins & King, 1981). Consistent short-term contexts add up to long-term context over time. A child who grows up as the smartest child on the block should be acutely aware of being smart in most day-to-day contexts. Over time that child is more likely to be self-schematic about intelligence than is a child who grows up in an intellectual neighborhood. The second child would not be so aware of being smart because it is not a distinctive attribute in most of that child's daily contexts.

The changes in self-description that depend on context have another implication for self-schemata. If people are most likely to be schematic on those traits that distinguish them from others, then people are most likely to be schematic on traits where they fall at one extreme or the other. Consequently, the definition of self-schematic dimensions as inherently extreme would seem to follow directly from the effects of context on self-concept. We will return to the issue of other contextual factors that cue schemata more generally.

Note, however, that the dependence of self-schemata on context has implications for the difficulty of determining their accuracy as self-descriptors. That is, if self-schemata arise largely as a function of context, they are necessarily not a sole function of one's actual personality. One can be aschematic on traits that are just as true of oneself as are traits on which one is schematic. There is no necessary correlation between being schematic on a trait and it being true of oneself, nor is there any correlation between being aschematic on a trait and it not being true of oneself. Self-schematic dimensions are subjective perceptions determined in part by context. Consistent short-term contexts create dimensions on which one is usually distinctive and therefore more probably self-schematic.

ROLE SCHEMATA

We have now discussed two types of schema: person schemata and self-schemata (see Table 6.1). The third area of research on social schemata concerns role schemata. A social role is the set of norms and behaviors attached to a social position, so a role schema is the cognitive structure that organizes one's knowledge about those appropriate norms and behaviors. For example, a doctor is someone whose role in society is to diagnose and treat disease; as such, a doctor asks you in detail about your symptoms, conducts tests, and prescribes drugs. A doctor is supposed to behave in a warm but professional manner. A doctor has about the only role (except for a movie producer) that allows him or her to ask strangers to disrobe on demand. Characteristics one acquires by effort and intent determine one's job and other *achieved* roles (e.g., training, experience, etc.); characteristics one acquires at birth or automatically determine one's *ascribed* roles (e.g., sex, age, race). Each of these characteristics carries with it role-based expectations for appropriate standards and behavior; these expectations may be organized in other people's minds as schemata (e.g., Kinder, Peters, Abelson, & Fiske, 1980).

Role schemata serve many of the same functions that other social schemata do; they are aids to information processing. But role schemata do more than help perception, memory, and inference. Role schemata are one plausible way to account for stereotyping. As we will see, stereotypes are "nouns that cut slices"; they are the cognitive culprits in prejudice and discrimination (G. W. Allport, 1954; Pettigrew, 1979). One way to think about stereotypes is as a particular type of role schema that organizes one's prior knowledge and expectations about other people who fall into certain socially defined categories. For example, certain behaviors and standards are expected of people on the basis of their age, race, sex, religion, education, and so on. Thus stereotypes may be seen as an important kind of role schema.

In linking role schemata to stereotyping, it becomes clear that schemata can have clear affective and behavioral consequences. Note that with the other types of social schemata addressed so far, person and self-schemata, the research mainly demonstrates their roles in guiding perception, memory, and "cold" cognitive judgments. As such, that research builds closely on cognitive psychology. A separate line of research on role schemata for social groups closely builds on stereotyping research in social psychology. Because of the perspectives raised by stereotyping research, work on role schemata goes beyond the point that social schemata can be aids to information processing, and it tends to incorporate affect and behavior. To put it another way, deciding that some people have adopted the role of gang members does more than help you to notice and remember that they wear black leather jackets and drive motorcycles. It helps you decide how you feel about them and whether you would want to go out on the town together. The pervasive effects of one's role schemata are easiest to see if the separate processes are again considered in turn: perception, memory, and evaluation.

Perception   Since stereotypes are often based on visually prominent features such as age, race, sex, and ethnicity, perceptual processes are important to this kind of schema (McArthur, 1982). One issue is the effects of categorization on perception. Once a person is categorized as black or white, young or old, male or female, the stereotypic content of the schema is likely to apply regardless of how much or how little the person looks like the typical category member (Secord, 1959; Secord, Bevan, & Katz, 1956).

Why should this be so? One might expect, for example, that paler black people are less subject to whites' prejudice than are darker blacks. It might seem reasonable that racism would depend on how physically typical people are of their category. However, this is not the case. The act of categorizing someone makes that person seem even more like other category members than would otherwise be true. When a bigot says "Oh them. They're all alike," the person is minimizing the amount of *variability* in that group. Minimizing within-group variability leads to mistakes. The bigot is also likely to add, "And I can't tell them apart anyway" (Malpass & Kravitz, 1969; Malpass, Lavingueur, & Weldon, 1973).

It does not take a bigot to misperceive members of a given group as all alike. Any group of outsiders (an out-group) appears less variable than one's own group (in-group), whether the out-group is students at a neighboring college or members of another profession (Gerard & Hoyt, 1974; Goethals, Allison, & Frost, 1979; Park & Rothbart, 1982; Quattrone & Jones, 1980; Tajfel, Sheikh, & Gardner, 1964; Tajfel & Wilkes, 1963; Wilder, 1981). Because people see out-groups as less variable than in-groups, they are willing to make inferences when they have less information about them. People may make rash predictions about a whole group of outsiders on the basis of meeting only one.

People not only see out-group members as less variable than in-group members, they also have less *complex* conceptions of them. For example, young people think about old people along fewer dimensions than they do other young people, and the same is true across racial groupings (Linville & Jones, 1980). Once a person is categorized, the person becomes just another example of the relevant schema and so is seen as very much like everyone else who fits that schema. If the person fits an out-group schema, the fit is seen as particularly tight, since out-group schemata are less variable and less complex than in-group schemata.

In addition to variability and complexity, categorizing someone as an instance of a schema slants perception of the *content* of what the person does. One child taking an eraser from another may be seen as aggressive if he is black but only as assertive if he is white (Duncan, 1976; Sagar & Schofield, 1980). A colleague being sarcastic may be seen as spiteful if female but cynical if male (S. E. Taylor, Fiske, Etcoff, & Ruderman, 1978). A normal person may seem maladjusted simply by virtue of the label "mental patient" (e.g., Langer & Abelson, 1974). Numerous studies attest to the stereotypic content of perception, even when the very same behavior is performed by people from two different categories (Brigham, 1971; Tavris & Offir, 1977). Role schemata suggest that stereotypic interpretations shape the earliest moments of perception (Klatzky, Martin, & Kane, 1982), and often do so negatively.

Memory Role schemata shape memory in a schema-consistent fashion, just as was true for self-schemata and person schemata. Occupations, which can cue one kind of role schema, appear to bias memory toward consistent attributes. For example, in one study, subjects observed a videotape of a woman having a birthday dinner with her husband. If told that she worked as a waitress, subjects remembered her drinking beer and owning a television. Other subjects watching the same videotape were told she worked as a librarian; they remembered her wearing glasses and owning classical records (Cohen, 1981b). Thus memory is guided by the role schema applied to the person. In another study, discovering that someone was gay shaped people's recollection of the person's past behavior and background; when the person became openly known as a homosexual, people found retrospectively "obvious" all the factors leading up to the person's life-style choice, even if those factors were never obvious before (M. Snyder & Uranowitz, 1978). In general, people remember individual behavior when it confirms a group stereotype (Rothbart et al., 1979).

The main principle of schematic memory is that the usual case overrides details of the specific instance. That is, memory for categorical information appears to be so central that perceivers will remember a person's role even if they remember nothing else about the person. The net effect is that people often remember the other person's category and forget the individual. At a meeting, people may remember that a woman made a certain comment, but not which woman made it (S. E. Taylor et al., 1978). People in categories such as redhead, black, female, or even child (in a large family) may find themselves called by another's name, responsible for another's comment, or simply not remembered apart from other members of their category.

As noted earlier, perceptions of out-group members are less variable, simpler, and more negative than perceptions of the in-group. From this, one might predict that people will always distinguish among members of their own group better than another group. Nevertheless, when asked to remember other people's comments, people do not necessarily keep in-group members separate better than out-group members. For example, males recalling a meeting are no more likely to distinguish among comments made by males than by females, and the same is true for females (S. E. Taylor et al., 1978).

Even if they cannot always tell them apart, people do tend to remember the ways that in-group members are similar to themselves and to forget the negative behavior of their own group. Conversely, people remember the ways the out-group differs from themselves, particularly the negative behavior of the out-group (Dutta, Kanungo, & Freibergs, 1972; Howard & Rothbart, 1980; Kanungo & Dutta, 1966; Wilder, 1981).

A note on memory, encoding, and schema-relevant information A common theme running through all the schema research is that people remember information that confirms their schema and forget information that disconfirms it. However, nothing is as simple as it seems. Memory advantages can accrue to both consistent *and* inconsistent information. If you tell me that your friend Della from New Orleans loves the Mardi Gras, I will accept and remember that. It is consistent with one schema. But if you also tell me that she hates Southern and creole cooking and suffers in the heat, I may also remember those schema-incongruent facts (Hastie & Kumar, 1979; Hemsley & Marmurek, 1982). In contrast, schema-irrelevant information is easily forgotten. If you tell me that Della prefers purple to orange, I will not especially remember that tangential fact.

One possible explanation for this puzzle (Hastie, 1981) suggests that *schema-discrepant* information receives added attention at input, if task conditions allow it. Given time enough, people elaborate and explain inconsistency, which strengthens the memory trace. For example, if there is time enough, you may think about Della's hatred of creole cooking and hot weather. The more you think about it, the more likely you are to link the two facts, for example, by the notion that both hot food and hot weather make her sweaty and uncomfortable. That link will help you to remember better a fact that was inconsistent with your original ideas (Srull, 1981). Such links can be the product of attentional processes (cf. Hastie, 1980).

Schema-consistent information, on the other hand, is favored by normal retrieval routes. If the schemata stored in memory contain typical information rather than exceptions, then consistent information normally should be favored by retrieval processes. Thus, remembering that the person from New Orleans likes the Mardi Gras is easy because that fact exists as part of prior knowledge about New Orleans. The impact of inconsistency on memory, then, should depend on encoding processes, that is, whether one takes the time to mull over the inconsistency when it is first encountered and to integrate it into memory. This hypothesis is critical because until recently, no one could predict when schemata would guide memory toward consistency and when toward inconsistency. Since memory data provide important evidence for the existence of schemata, predictive accuracy on this point is crucial. Note that much of the data cited so far as evidence for person, self, and role schemata consist of schematic effects on memory, and in particular of schema-consistent memory. Accordingly, it is important to know whether attentional processes can account for the times when schema-consistent memory has an advantage and when schema-inconsistent memory does.

Indeed, there is evidence that attentional processes determine the type of schematic memory. Remembering inconsistent information does seem to depend on whether sufficient study time is allowed (Sentis & Burnstein, 1979). However, this research is only indirect evidence for Hastie's hypothesis. In the most direct test to date, Brewer, Dull, and Lui (1981) found that inconsistent information required longer encoding time than did consistent or irrelevant information. Subsequently, inconsistent information was well remembered, presumably because of the added attention at input (i.e., longer encoding). Consistent information also was well recalled, despite its short initial processing time, presumably because it was already stored as part of the knowledge structure. Irrelevant information neither elicited attention nor was easily remembered (cf. Berman, Read, & Kenny, in press).

Another series of studies suggests exactly what people may be doing if they spend a longer time encoding inconsistent information (Crocker, Hannah, & Weber, 1983; Kulik, 1983). As Hastie hypothesized, people faced with inconsistency are likely to spend time to explain it so that it fits an existing schema-based impression. One way to do that is by attributing the inconsistent behavior to temporary situational causes, which then makes it irrelevant to the existing schema-based impression. If it is irrelevant, it can be quickly forgotten. On the other hand, if one is forced to attribute the inconsistency to the personality of the person (i.e., to dispositional causes), then one must fit it in with the existing schema-based impression of the person's personality. Hence it should not be forgotten. For example, if I tell you about my polite friend who gave up his subway seat to an elderly gentleman, that is congruent with the polite schema and therefore remembered on that basis. If I tell you that my normally polite friend got in line in front of three people at the bank, you may have to devote more attention to this because of its inconsistency. If you decide that it must have been an emergency (i.e., temporary situation), then you can forget about it. But if, after devoting attention to the inconsistency, you come to the conclusion that he does not care what other people think, which is an attribution about his personality (i.e., a dispositional attribution), then you will have to figure out how his uncaring disposition fits with the schema for being polite. Accordingly, you are unlikely to forget his behavior in the bank.

To summarize, inconsistent behavior requires explanation, which takes time when the information is encountered—that is, at encoding. If people can attribute inconsistent behavior to situational causes, they can forget the behavior and presumably maintain their schema-based impression. If forced at encoding to attribute inconsistent behavior to dispositional causes, they remember it. In contrast, consistent behavior may be remembered regardless of the encoding processes. To the extent that consistent information typically is stored as part of a social schema, it will be easily remembered and the schema can be maintained without change. (For other resolutions of schema-based memory for consistent versus inconsistent information, see Bellezza & Bower, 1981; L. F. Clark & Woll, 1981; Srull, 1981; Woll & Graesser, 1982).

Evaluations and inferences   Schemata of all kinds are usually difficult to change, and in some cases this fact has considerable social impact. Role schemata that contain rigid views of in-groups and out-groups are a prime example. In the section on memory, we saw that the content of an out-group schema is "they are all alike, different from us, and bad besides." If so, then it is not surprising that any given "us-category" is liked better than any given "them-category," under most circumstances (Brewer, 1979; Wilder, 1981; cf. Sherif, Harvey, White, Hood, & Sherif, 1961). When a teacher arbitrarily assigns students to teams for course projects, each team soon assumes its own superiority; students quickly forget that they were divided up by the highly selective criterion of preferring to sit in the front right-hand corner of the classroom rather than the front left. Merely telling them that they are now a group leads them to reward their own group more, and to see its members as having better personalities, nicer looks, less responsibility for failing on a task, and more responsibility for succeeding. Even arbitrary in-group members are seen as having greater similarity to oneself (Allen & Wilder, 1975; Billig & Tajfel, 1973; Brewer & Silver, 1978; D. L. Hamilton, 1979; Wilder & Cooper, 1981). Competition and status differences between groups exaggerate in-group favoritism.

What, if anything, moderates in-group effects on evaluation? A major way to reduce them appears to be forcing people to notice the actual dissimilarities within their own group, which would tend to undercut the coherence of the in-group schema. People are most likely to favor the in-group when they have little information other than in-group or out-group status. Given nothing else on which to base assumptions, people assume similarity to self and positive attributes for members of their own group.

Is in-group favoritism undercut when members of the in-group get to know out-group members? Not necessarily. When people know a bit more about people from the out-group, they may overreact to the scant information they do have. For example, white admissions committees who encounter a good application from a black student (i.e., an out-group member) are likely to perceive the application as better than the same application coming from a white student (in-group). But they are also likely to see a weak application from a black student as worse than if it came from a white. The out-group polarization effect, as it is called, cuts both ways. Good outsiders are better and bad outsiders are worse than comparable insiders (Linville, 1982b; Linville & Jones, 1980).

The out-group polarization effect appears to be caused by a lack of complexity in the schema for the out-group. A little information about an out-group member is a dangerous thing, since it allows the perceiver to go overboard in either a positive or negative direction, depending on the drift of the scant information. An out-group schema is less complex than an in-group schema. One knows more about one's own group, so a few items of positive or negative information do not tip the balance so easily. Thus evaluations of credentials from an in-group member are more moderate than when the same credentials come from an out-group member (Linville, 1982b; Linville & Jones, 1980). The effect is consistent across various role schemata: out-group polarization occurs for categories based on age, race, sex, and probably more.

Summary and implications It should be obvious by now that role schemata play a critical role in intergroup perceptions. In particular, they explain much of the way stereotypes operate. Categorizing others leads to exaggerating perceived differences between groups and minimizing perceived differences within each group. Perceivers especially minimize the variability of out-groups. Furthermore, people interpret information in ways that confirm their uniform, general expectations or schemata. Memory selectively favors schema-consistent knowledge much of the time; people often forget the individual but remember the schema. If incongruent information is noticed, it may be attributed to situational causes and forgotten if possible. Otherwise, incongruent information may be noticed and considered in detail, with the result that it becomes highly memorable.

Evaluation is affected by categorization, especially if people are categorized into in-groups and out-groups. Similarity to self and positive attributes are expected of the in-group, if in-group members are given no other information. Given the more complex information about one's own group, evaluations of in-group individuals become more moderate. Given simple information about the out-group, evaluations polarize.

The litany of schematic effects presents a pessimistic picture for the prospect of changing people's schemata in general and their role schemata in particular. If role schemata are so fundamental to the processes of intergroup perception, memory, and evaluation, how does one reduce their effects? One might question whether one can or should try to change people's propensity to stereotype others according to role schemata. If stereotypes are a fundamental part of human cognition, perhaps there is nothing "wrong" with them (McCauley, Stitt, & Segal, 1980). They may be viewed merely as more or less accurate judgments of the probability that a member of a particular group will possess a particular attribute (McCauley & Stitt, 1978).

The view of stereotypes simply as part of a normal cognitive process applied to people has become widespread (D. L. Hamilton, 1981a; A. G. Miller, 1982). It contrasts sharply with the traditional view of stereotypes as an irrational isolated phenomenon (Ashmore & Del Boca, 1980). But viewing stereotypes as a normal part of cognition does not mean they cannot be changed. Indeed, the cognitive view of stereotypes makes novel suggestions about how to change them. The classic prescription for reducing prejudice is intergroup contact, under conditions of equal status, common goals, cooperation, and moderate intimacy (see review by Amir, 1976). Unfortunately, the in-group/out-group literature indicates that these very conditions are difficult to create as soon as people categorize each other into "us" and "them." Out-groups are perceived as inferior, as adversaries, as competitive, and as different from one's own group.

Nevertheless, contact may reduce stereotypic beliefs and prejudice when *alternative schemata* are made salient (Rose, 1981; Wilder, 1981). If researchers and change-agents assume that people are going to categorize each other anyway, they can substitute benign categories for negative ones. For example, suppose a physical education class has been divided into sections for humanities students and for science students. The two groups are likely to stereotype each other on the basis of role schemata for the types of majors. One negative aspect of the stereotypes is likely to be presumed ability, even if there is no actual difference. A possible way to break down such stereotypes would be to substitute alternative benign bases for categorization. For example, the sections might be broken up into teams that cut across majors. The temporary teams then become the implicit bases for categorization, rather than presumed ability levels.

In addition, *individual contact* between in-group and out-group members can undercut categorization. When groups deal with groups, categories are especially salient, but when individuals encounter individuals, that is less true (Locksley, Hepburn, & Ortiz, 1982; Sears, 1983). Moreover, if people are forced to confront schema-discrepant information about another individual, they are more likely to evaluate the person on his or her own merits, especially if they need the person for something (S. T. Fiske, Beattie, & Milberg, 1983; Erber & Fiske, 1983).

Finally, if *interactions are structured* rather than ambiguous, people's preexisting schemata are less likely to rule. The schematic interpretations of stereotyping provide some preliminary ideas for changing the impact of role schemata.

EVENT SCHEMATA

In addition to person, self, and role schemata, there are event schemata or scripts; they are structures that describe appropriate sequences of events in well-known situations (Abelson, 1981; Schank & Abelson, 1977), for example, restaurant visits, sporting events, job interviews, and the like. Event schemata point out the effects of schemata on activity: complex sequences of behavior, typical procedures for getting things done, and so on. Consider the following example: "John was seated in the restaurant. He looked at the menu and decided to order lobster. Later, when he had paid his waiter, he left immediately." This is a standard sequence of events for a restaurant meal. The script is composed of several sequential steps common to eating in most restaurants (sitting down, looking at the menu, ordering, etc.). Scripts contain props (such as the menu), roles (such as waiter), and sequence rules (such as reading the menu before ordering). Event schemata are abstracted from experience with everyday occurrences and applied to the understanding of new experiences.

Perception and memory   Event schemata guide information processing much as do person, self, and role schemata. For example, imagine seeing on television the following actual Eskimo folktale. It includes these events: the hero participates in a battle, is shot with an arrow, feels nothing, returns home, some mysterious black thing comes out of his mouth, and then he suddenly dies at sundown; no explanation for these bizarre events is given. Recounting the story afterwards, non-Eskimo Americans would be likely to distort it in ways that fit their own cultural event schemata. (Or else assume that somebody mixed up the reels and abandon the effort.) Non-Eskimo Americans would be likely to recall the battle because conflict makes a good story in their culture. It is consistent with one type of story schema for them. But they might forget the black thing coming out of the hero's mouth, or spend a lot of time trying to interpret it, because the event does not fit with their story schema expectations (Bartlett, 1932). Native Americans hearing the story might have a story schema that allows them to interpret the black thing coming out of the hero's mouth as his soul departing at sunset. Different cultures supply people with different schemata for a good story, and these event schemata may guide both perception and memory.

Event schemata can also involve visual perspectives. For example, in one study subjects read about a traffic accident between a cab and a motorcycle, but some subjects were asked to visualize the situation from one point of view and others from the other point of view. Although all subjects read the same story, the visual perspective they adopted determined what they recalled. The motorcyclist was on the main road, and the cab driver was emerging from a tunnel. When imagining the situation from the motorcyclist's point of view, people disproportionately recalled details visible only from his perspective (e.g., a boarded-up gas station, a hitchhiker with a knapsack). Similarly, people taking the cab driver's role recalled details uniquely visible from his vantage point (e.g., glistening tiles in the tunnel). Thus the exact way that memory is guided by schemata for an event (e.g., a traffic accident) may depend on physical perspective (S. T. Fiske, Taylor, Etcoff, & Laufer, 1979; Owens, Dafoe, & Bower, 1977).

Inference Without looking back, recall the restaurant story narrated at the start of this section. What happened? What did John do first? What did he eat? In this thought experiment, you should have recalled that John ate lobster. However, the story never stated that John actually ate the lobster, merely that he ordered it and paid for it. The eating step is a perfectly reasonable inference, but it is an inference nonetheless.

The gap-filling function of scripts is similar to that of other schemata that create memory for consistent events that were in fact never presented. However, researchers understand the process in more detail in scripts because scripts are explicitly built around plans and procedures, which are temporally organized sequences of events (Bellezza & Bower, 1982; G. H. Bower, Black, & Turner, 1979). First things come first and enable later events to occur. That is, suppose the telling of a story scrambles the usual sequence of events. For example, a child may get mixed up narrating a doctor visit that somehow starts with the shot and the lollipop scene and manages to end with the waiting room scene. In that case, the listener will tend to rearrange the story into its usual sequence when remembering it. Scripts contain certain norms about proper sequence. They also include shared ideas of where the story is segmented into scenes, and this implies that scripts are organized hierarchically (into acts and scenes) as well as sequentially (scenes follow each other).

One of the interesting insights about scripts is the so-called ghost effect (G. H. Bower et al., 1979). That is, if several variations on the same script are encountered, gap filling is exaggerated, as if the ghost of general case invoked by one script then hovers over related scripts as well. If you happen to see three Westerns in one weekend, you have invoked the general case so often that, in remembering any individual film, you increase your likelihood of misremembering facts from the general case that were never present in any given instance. For example, you might attribute the usual ending (i.e., the cowboy in the white hat won the woman), when in fact it was left ambiguous or omitted every time. The expected sequence of events is reinforced for any one instance by invoking the general case several times.

The sequential aspect of scripts provides one more insight into the workings of schemata. In a script, each event paves the way for the event that follows it, so many events require the preceding event as an "enabling condition." That is, being seated at a restaurant enables the arrival of the waiter. This makes the components of scripts potentially more interdependent than the components of other social schemata. For example, your self-schema for independence may include as evidence the times you have traveled alone and your preference for solitary work, and these may be linked in memory, but there is not any enabling link between them. Traveling alone does not enable working alone or vice versa. The components of many social schemata are relatively independent. In contrast, the components of a script are more interdependent.

Consequently, in a script, deviations can bring the whole process to a halt. This leads to the prediction that although people often recall schema-consistent information, with scripts they may especially remember inconsistent information. Deviations from the restaurant script, for example, might include obstacles (the menu is in Chinese), errors (the waiter gives too much change), and distractions (John forgot his money and has to wash dishes). Each of these is a problem that has to be solved before continuing. Note that irrelevant details (such as the wall being white) are likely to be forgotten, because they are not involved in the procedure of marching through the script. Inconsistencies may be harder to ignore in most scripts than in other social schemata (Graesser, Gordon, & Sawyer, 1979; Graesser, Woll, Kowalski, & Smith, 1980; D. A. Smith & Graesser, 1981).

Summary Scripts or event schemata describe sequences of activity from everyday life. They contain props, roles, and sequence rules. Scripts also may be subdivided into segments (scenes). Like other schemata, scripts guide the perception of ambiguous information and often shape memory toward schema-consistent information. Inferences can be seen as filling in gaps where information was missing, and gap filling appears to be exaggerated by repeated encounters with the script. Most of the functions of scripts echo those of other schemata, in their focus on relevant — and usually on consistent — information in perception, memory, and inference.

A NOTE ON CONTENT-FREE OR PROCEDURAL SOCIAL SCHEMATA

Anyone who reads further in the schema literature will discover that some uses of the term *schema* do not refer to content-specific knowledge structures such as person, self, role, or event schemata (S. E. Taylor & Crocker, 1981), as described in the preceding pages. Instead, they refer to apparently "content-free" schemata, such as balance schemata, linear-ordering schemata, and causal schemata. Such a schema apparently operates like a processing rule or *procedure* that specifies links among items of information but not much of the rich informational content itself.

Such content-free schemata include *balance schemata*, for example, borrowed from the literature on attitudes (Heider, 1958). We will discuss balance theory in more detail later (Chapter 12), but summarize it now to illustrate the point. A balance schema consists of three cognitive elements in what is called a triad: a perceiver (P), another person (O), and an attitude object (X). They may be linked by positive or negative relationships. For example, if you (P) like your roommate (O), that is a positive link. If you both like science fiction (X), the P-X and O-X relationships both are positive, too. Three positive relationships constitute a balanced triad. If both you and your roommate hate science fiction, the P-X and O-X relationships both are negative, and the triad is still balanced. Agreeing friends constitute one type of balanced triad. Conversely, if you dislike each other (P-O is negative) and disagree about science fiction (P-X is positive and O-X is negative or vice versa), the triad is still balanced. In sum, agreeing friends and disagreeing enemies are considered to compose balanced (schema-consistent) triads. The balance schema specifies that disagreeing friends and agreeing enemies provide an imbalanced (schema-inconsistent) triad. As schemata go, a balance schema is relatively impoverished, for it consists solely of three cognitive elements and the links among them.

Despite being relatively content free, balance schemata do have many properties that are similar to informationally rich schemata. For example, under most circumstances, balanced (schema-consistent) information is learned more easily (DeSoto, Henley, & London, 1968; Press, Crockett, & Rosenkrantz, 1969; Zajonc & Burnstein, 1965a), recalled more accurately (Gerard & Fleischer, 1967; Picek, Sherman, & Shiffrin, 1975) and recognized faster (Sentis & Burnstein, 1979).

Nevertheless, balance schemata contrast with informationally rich schemata that specify more than the links among elements. Compare, for example, a relatively content-free balance schema to a relatively content-rich script. A script, like a balance schema, specifies links among elements: for instance, in a doctor visit patients sit in the waiting room before rather than after seeing the doctor. But a script specifies something more than those links, as do most other schemata. The script specifies roles, props, settings, and so on, each of which contains multiple attributes. Thus a script specifies both content and the links among the parts of the content. A balance schema consists almost entirely of its links. The elements are highly constrained: a perceiver, another, and an attitude object. A balance schema, then, is more a set of rules than it is a richly organized knowledge structure.

Other types of schema also emphasize links over content. A *linear-ordering schema* (Tsujimoto, Wilde, & Robertson, 1978) organizes transitive, hierarchical relationships. Size, weight, speed, and other attributes fit into a transitive relationship that may be viewed as a content-free schema. For example, suppose Pam runs faster than Diane, and Diane runs faster than Jill, then Pam runs faster than Jill. The schema is impoverished in that it specifies only a rule (i.e., transitivity) that links the elements. Causal schemata (Kelley, 1972b), discussed in Chapter 2 under attribution theories, are another example of schemata that resemble content-free rules more than rich knowledge structures (S. E. Taylor & Crocker, 1981, discuss others).

Schema Growth and Change

So far, we have considered the effects of social schemata on perception, memory, and inference. Another set of issues concerns the "state" of the schema itself. How easily do schemata change and under what circumstances? How do they develop in the first place? Once developed, how are they cued to go from inactive to active status? Schema growth and change is a major set of unfinished business in social schema research (Crocker, Fiske, & Taylor, in press).

THE PERSEVERANCE EFFECT

Schemata facilitate information processing, for the most part, by allowing the general case to fill in for a specific example. No single example fits the schema perfectly, but most fit well enough. If people changed their schemata to fit every nuance of every new example, the information-processing advantages of schemata would be substantially lost. The *perseverance effect*, as it is called, describes a major feature of schemata: they often persist stubbornly even in the face of evidence to the contrary.

Schemata can be so robust that they persevere even when people are informed that the evidence in support of them is false. In a study designed to demonstrate this point, people were told that a new personality test showed them to be especially socially sensitive; presumably they may have activated or begun to build a self-schema for themselves as socially sensitive and to think of all the reasons why that was true. When then informed that the test was in fact not genuine, they nevertheless continued to believe themselves socially sensitive (L. Ross, Lepper, & Hubbard, 1975). If one assumes that the test originally activated or created a self-schema for social sensitivity, this study shows how hard it is to get people to change a schema once it is put in place. However, the same research could be interpreted as showing how malleable people's schemata are, because the social sensitivity schema was so easily activated or installed in the first place. Presumably, it would not be so easy if they were originally self-schematic on social insensitivity at the start.

Once convinced of their social sensitivity, people remain convinced even when the initial data are disqualified. By that time, only one piece of evidence among many has been withdrawn, because people will have mustered other evidence of their own in support of the socially sensitive self-schema (C. A. Anderson, Lepper, & Ross, 1980). Any time people are asked to imagine an event, to explain how it might occur, or to consider how a judgment might be true, they perceive it as more likely (C. A. Anderson, 1983; Carroll, 1978; Fischhoff, 1975; Gregory, Cialdini, & Carpenter, 1982; L. Ross, Lepper, Strack, & Steinmetz, 1977).

A further variant on perseverance is that people not only ignore many exceptions to the schema, they sometimes perversely interpret the exception as proving the schema. When people with strong prior beliefs encounter mixed or inconclusive evidence, they may reinterpret the evidence as if it were firm support for their schema or belief system, causing their beliefs to persevere or even become more extreme. People who believe in the effectiveness of capital punishment, for example, might read research that shows it has no deterrence effect. If they have a well-established schema on the topic, they are likely to perceive the research as either irrelevant or simply unconvincing: "If this lousy study is the best they can do, all their evidence must be pretty weak, so now I know I'm right." Of course, the research on their own side of the issue seems flawless and of extraordinary relevance by comparison (Lord, Ross, & Lepper, 1979; cf. Ajzen, Dalto, & Blyth, 1979; Darley & Gross, 1983).

The tendency for people's schemata to persevere extends even to times when no new evidence is encountered, but the person simply thinks about the topic. If one has a well-developed schema for some area of knowledge, mere thought of any sort polarizes judgments in whatever direction the judgments already tend (Tesser, 1978). For example, if you initially dislike your lab partner, simply thinking about the person is likely to make matters worse. Conversely, if you rather like the person, thinking about him or her is likely to increase your liking. More thought creates more polarization (Sadler & Tesser, 1973; Tesser & Conlee, 1975). Why might this be true?

Thinking about somebody enables you to muster evidence in favor of your initial view of the person, which makes your schema for the person persevere and polarize, as you think up new justifications that fit your judgment. The schema notion thus comes in to describe the process of fitting new thoughts to an existing organization of knowledge. If a fair amount of pre-existing schematic knowledge did not exist, the polarization effect would not occur. Thus, if most men know little about women's fashions, a man who sits and thinks about women's fashions will not become any more extreme about them; similarly, most women who sit and contemplate men's fashions should not become any more opinionated about them (Tesser & Leone, 1977). Once a person has a well-developed schema on a given topic, however, the person's judgments do become extreme with thought. Moreover, information that fits the polarized judgments is judged more quickly and recalled more easily than is relatively moderate information (Judd & Kulik, 1980).

Is there any hope of making people more responsive to evidence? Telling people that the evidence is in fact mixed and that they should try to be unbiased does not undercut the perseverance effect. However, perseverance does seem to be undercut by telling people to think carefully about *how* they are evaluating the evidence and to watch their biases as they go through the process of interpreting the data (Lord, Lepper, & Thompson, 1980). For example, people strongly favoring capital punishment could be told to pay attention to their own tendency to discount evidence from the other side and bolster evidence from their own side. In effect, when subjects are asked to monitor their own cognitive processes, they are finally able to overcome the tendency to interpret any and all data as justifying more extreme confidence in the validity of the schema. Another strategy to undercut the perseverance effect draws on its presumed causes. That is, as noted earlier, when people explain why their schema should hold true, they believe it even more. The converse should also hold, that when people have to explain why their favorite theory might be wrong, that is, to counterargue it, the perseverance effect is moderated (C. A. Anderson, 1982).

In sum, then, the perseverance effect describes the ways that schemata serve to reinterpret incoming information in support of the existing schema, allowing it to continue unchanged. Mixed or negative evidence can backfire, unless people are told to monitor their own judgment processes or forced to counterargue their own schemata.

SCHEMA DEVELOPMENT

If schemata are so robust once they are formed, it becomes even more critical to know how they develop in the first place. Although social schema development is only beginning to be explored in social cognition research (Crocker, Fiske, & Taylor, in press), a few principles are clear already. Well-developed schemata are likely to be more abstract, more complex, more organized, more moderate, and more conservative.

The more often one encounters schema-relevant examples, the more abstract the schema becomes (Abelson, 1976), other things being equal. This occurs because people generalize schemata from experience with instances of the category in question (J. R. Anderson, 1981; J. R. Anderson, Kline, & Beasley, 1979; N. S. Johnson, 1981). Consider how people learn an abstract driving schema from experience with concrete instances. The first car you try to drive has a certain feel to the clutch, a certain shift pattern, and the headlight switch in a certain place. Your driving schema is likely to be very concretely limited to that car until you have driven several. The more cars you drive, the more abstract and general your conception of clutches, shift patterns, and headlight switches.

The same is true for any sort of schema that evolves from concrete to abstract, whether it is learning the ropes of an organization (Martin, 1982; Martin, Harrod, & Siehl, 1980) or finding out about birthday parties as a child (Nelson, 1980). People abstract schemata from similar events, and the crucial change in levels of abstraction seems to come between one experience and two; moving from one to two similar events creates a bigger jump in abstraction than does moving from two to three or more. Accordingly, abstraction may not prove a useful index of a schema's stage of development, if abstraction is insensitive to specific degrees of experience.

Besides abstraction, other properties of schemata are likely to change with increasing experience. Mature schemata are likely to be more complex than immature ones (Linville, 1982b; Linville & Jones, 1980). The more you drive, the more dimensions of cars become important to you in evaluating them. From merely considering color and comfort, you learn to consider factors ranging from mileage and safety to whether its steering is tight. All other things being equal, greater complexity moderates judgment. The more variety one has encountered, the more complex the issues, the less clear-cut it all seems, and the less extreme one's judgment.

Mature schemata are also more organized than newly formed schemata. Although complexity concerns the number of dimensions that describe schematic content, organization concerns the number and structure of links among schematic contents. The schemata of experts contain more elements than the schemata of novices. This is not surprising, considering that they know more than novices do. Experts' schemata also are organized differently. Specifically, their schemata contain more links among the elements, and possibly a more complex hierarchy (Chase & Simon, 1973; Chi & Koeske, 1983; Larkin, McDermott, Simon, & Simon, 1980; McKeithen, Reitman, Rueter, & Hirtle, 1981). In sum, mature schemata are richer and more organized than newly developed schemata. Thus, compared to a novice, a race car driver would know the proper way to understand the mechanic's comment that his distributor bushings were worn. The diagnosis would fit in compactly with other knowledge about the electrical system, rather than sounding like a bizarre form of insult. Consequently, it would be understood and remembered better and faster by the expert.

One consequence of experts' well-developed schemata is that, despite the greater amount and complexity of their knowledge, its compact and well-organized quality frees processing capacity. Consequently, experts notice, recall, and use schema-discrepant material more than novices do. In contrast, novices' simple, ill-defined schemata limit them to the more obvious schema-consistent material (Fiske, Kinder, & Larter, 1983). In accord with their greater sensitivity to inconsistency, experts moderate their judgments to allow for the ambiguity of the information given. Thus experience creates more organized schemata and allows greater capacity for managing inconsistencies.

Finally, experience may promote conservative processing strategies. That is, the more complex one's knowledge, the more one can—and may wish to—assimilate exceptions without abandoning the schema (S. E. Taylor & Winkler, 1980). However, experts may be less willing than novices to shift schemata appropriately. In some ways, they have more invested, making them resistant to change (cf. Crocker et al., in press).

Mature schemata have other costs that come up when one attempts to learn new information. At some stages, a developing schema can be helpful and at other stages confusing to learning related concepts. Three stages can be identified: a little knowledge may help learning related concepts; moderate knowledge may actually hurt related learning; and a lot of knowledge may become largely irrelevant to related learning (S. T. Fiske & Dyer, 1983; Hayes-Roth, 1977; Thorndyke & Hayes-Roth, 1979).

Consider the overlapping motor schemata of driving a car and driving a motorcycle. A beginning driver, who has just learned that cars have clutches, brakes, and accelerators, can apply this knowledge of the components of driving a car to help learn the slightly different but overlapping components of driving a motorcycle. A little knowledge can be helpful. A moderately new car driver, who had begun to automate the sequence of shifting, accelerating, and braking, would be hopelessly confused by trying to learn motorcycle driving at that point. Moderate levels of car-driving skill could only interfere with acquiring the related motorcycle-driving skills. Once expert, however, car drivers have automated all the processes. At that point, learning to drive a motorcycle should not be hindered or helped by car-driving skills, which have become a self-contained unit and so would not interfere. Once schemata have become fully developed, they may be irrelevant to learning related concepts.

To summarize, schemata change as they develop out of repeated exposures with instances. Schemata become more abstract, more complex, and often more moderate. They also seem to become more organized and compact, which frees up the capacity to notice discrepancies and to assimilate exceptions without altering the schema. Schemata may also become more conservative, that is, resistant to change. Finally, depending on their stage, developing schemata can help, hurt, or be irrelevant to the learning of related skills.

SCHEMA ACTIVATION

Once schemata have developed, they are available for application to new situations. One can think of them as resting in an inactive state, waiting to be cued, that is, changed to active status. What determines which of many relevant schemata will be activated in any given encounter? Upon meeting a new person the first week of school, you might categorize him or her as a New Yorker, an ex-cheerleader, a competitor, or a dormmate. All of these roles may apply, but which will dominate your impression and interactions? Several principles may determine schema activation, but basically only two have received research attention (Higgins & King, 1981; Thorndyke & Yekovich, 1980; Wyer & Srull, 1981).

A schema's activation is determined partly by how recently it has been activated in the past. For example, having used a word in one sentence, a writer is more likely to use it again within a few sentences. A person who has just been mugged is especially likely to interpret people loitering in doorways as lurking with evil intent. The *priming effect*, as it is called, even carries over to irrelevant contexts. In one study (Higgins, Rholes, & Jones, 1977), people were first exposed to positive or negative traits (e.g., adventurous versus reckless). In a seemingly unrelated context, they read about Donald, who shot rapids, drove in a demolition derby, and planned to learn skydiving. People who had earlier been primed with the relevant positive trait *adventurous* evaluated Donald more positively than people who had been primed with *reckless*. The priming effect did not occur when the priming traits were inapplicable to the Donald description (e.g., *neat* or *sly*). The priming effect suggests that, in the selection of a person schema to apply to the interpretation of new information, those recently activated are more accessible (see also Woll & Martinez, 1982). One account of the priming effect holds that activating a schema places it at the top of the mental heap or "storage bin," displacing others downward (Srull & Wyer, 1979; Wyer & Srull, 1980, 1981).

A given schema is also more likely to be activated if it has been applied frequently in the past. If Charles perceives all his professors as antagonistic, it would be harder for him to interpret suggestions as friendly interest rather than as persecution. His persecution schema is more frequently applied than his helpful schema, so it is more available for use in the future. It is as if frequency of activation causes a concept to store up a charge, rather like a battery. It is then ready to discharge that energy wherever applicable (Higgins & King, 1981). A frequently used schema is, in a sense, permanently primed; paranoid Charles is always ready to see persecution. It is possible that frequency and recency of activation are linked in the following way: a frequently activated schema has a higher probability of being recently activated at any given time (Wyer & Srull, 1980).

Besides recency and frequency, schema get activated by other means. Observational purpose determines what schemata are most likely to be activated. Consider Charles's girlfriend, Linda. Suppose she is not paranoid but has the general observational purpose of empathizing with his plight. The nonparanoid Linda may begin to see why Charles should form coalitions with other students, complain to the dean, and cover his trail whenever possible. Empathy promotes a shared focus on the other person's *goals* (see Chapter 8 for more details).

In contrast, if my observational purpose is forming an impression of Charles, whom I have just met, I am less likely to focus on his self-protective goals than on his paranoid traits (Hoffman & Mischel, 1980). Other observational purposes might include memorizing his actions, predicting his future behavior, or recreating his physical (rather than psychological) perspective; each activates different schemata (C. E. Cohen, 1981a; C. E. Cohen & Ebbesen, 1979; S. T. Fiske et al., 1979; Gould & Sigall, 1977; D. L. Hamilton, Katz, & Leirer, 1980b; Jeffery & Mischel, 1979).

Finally, affect and motivation determine schema accessibility. Unmet needs can prime one's interpretations of ambiguous stimuli (F. H. Allport, 1955; Erdelyi, 1974). People out of gas look for gas stations; hungry people notice food; the lovelorn see potential mates everywhere. Furthermore, highly emotional schemata should be more accessible than neutral ones (Klinger, Barta, & Maxeiner, 1980). If you are both low on gas and upset with your date, you are likely to be more preoccupied with the person than with the gas pump, given most people's emotional priorities.

In summary, schemata are triggered easily if they have been recently or frequently activated in the past. Schemata also are guided by observational goals such as empathizing, forming an impression, memorizing actions, predicting behavior, or recreating physical perspective. Affect and motivation also prime schemata.

SCHEMA CHANGE

Most schema research deals with stimuli that completely fit or do not fit a given category. The problem of partial fit is relatively unexplored. Most people do not perfectly fit a certain type. How does this affect social information processing? Do people make schema-based inferences with less certainty when the instance is a partial fit? Do perceivers change their schemata when someone fails to fit the mold? Suppose a young lady meets a young man at a mixer and decides that he is a construction worker. But he does not totally fit her construction worker schema. Hence she will have to resolve the ambiguities of his joint interests in both football and opera. To what extent will she change her impression of him and to what extent will she change her impression of construction workers? The former seems more likely, but we lack careful research to establish the effects of partial fit with any certainty.

One of the clear effects of schemata, as we have seen, is that people tend to make the data fit the schema, rather than vice versa. However, when there is a partial fit, the perceiver may not apply the schema with complete confidence. Our young lady probably will make less stereotyped inferences, say about the fellow's intelligence, than if he were a perfect construction worker type. If her hypothesis is that he is "sort of an artsy construction worker," it is not clear how she will proceed. What is clear is that she will be forced to form a coherent impression of his consistent and discrepant attributes, since they coexist in one person. She may either try to resolve or to ignore the discrepancies in her impression of him as an individual. A salient lack-of-fit is likely to moderate usually-obtained schematic effects (S. T. Fiske, 1982).

Alternatively, the partial fit between data and schema can cause the schema itself to change, under certain specifiable circumstances and in certain probable ways. First, there is some indication that inconsistencies within groups (Rothbart et al., 1979) require less resolution than inconsistencies within individuals (Hastie & Kumar, 1979; cf. Srull, 1981; Wyer & Gordon, 1982). A construction crew that includes one opera buff is still a fairly typical construction crew. An individual construction worker who likes Verdi is not a typical individual construction worker. In all probability, the group stereotype is more likely to persevere in the face of ill-fitting evidence than is a stereotype about an individual. We expect more variation within members of a given social group than within a given individual's behavior.

When schemata for a group do change on the basis of encountering discrepancy, the perceiver's reaction to lack of fit may take one of three forms. The *bookkeeping model* proposes that each discrepant encounter changes the schema gradually, while the *conversion model* proposes that a single concentrated encounter with incongruence can change a schema totally and suddenly (Rothbart, 1981). The *subtyping model* suggests that incongruence causes the perceiver to form subcategories within the overall schema, for example, deciding that there are artsy construction workers as well as the more standard kind, but meanwhile maintaining the schema for the group as a whole (S. E. Taylor, 1981).

Current research has pitted these models against each other (Crocker & Weber, 1983; Weber & Crocker, 1983), by examining the organization of discrepant information. The conversion model predicts the most change when information is concentrated in a few discrepant individuals. The subtyping model predicts the least change when information is concentrated in a few discrepant individuals, because those people can be subtyped as exceptions, leaving the general case intact. The bookkeeping model predicts equal change, regardless of the organization of information. In one study designed to test these models competitively, subjects were exposed to a set of behaviors, one-third of which were discrepant with an occupational stereotype (librarians and lawyers). The discrepant behaviors were either dispersed across individuals within the occupation or concentrated within single individuals. Stereotypes changed the most when discrepant behaviors were dispersed, a result that supports the subtyping model. Thus, to return to the construction worker example, encountering a crew in which one member likes Verdi, another writes sonnets, another cooks gourmet food, and another is earning money for law school will do more to change the perceiver's construction worker stereotype than encountering one construction worker with all those attributes (Weber & Crocker, 1983; cf. Rothbart, Fulero, Jensen, Howard, & Birrell, 1978). The exception that proves the rule can be subtyped and forgotten, leaving the schema in place.

Schemata change under some other specifiable circumstances, in addition to encounters with dispersed discrepancies. Discrepant information is most likely to cause schema change when the lack of fit is undeniable, that is, considerable, unambiguous, memorable, and stable (Crocker, Fiske, & Taylor, in press). If the lack of fit is moderate or ambiguous, the discrepant instance can be assimilated (i.e., distorted to fit) to the schema; similarly, if the discrepant instance can be forgotten or attributed to unstable (i.e., situational) causes, clearly it will have little impact (Crocker, Hannah, & Weber, 1983).

In sum, when people encounter an instance that is a partial fit to the most relevant schema, they may make schema-based inferences less extremely, or with less certainty. Moreover, a series of partially fitting instances may eventually cause the schema to change in various ways, especially if the discrepant instances are dispersed and otherwise undeniable.

The Role of Schemata in Social Cognition Research

The schema concept has proved useful in social cognition research. It has generated an explosion of research. It is intuitively appealing. It grapples with broad and enduring issues. It can be pinned down into precise theoretical frameworks. Generally speaking, it describes the ways that complex, generic, prior knowledge affects people's handling of new information.

How do schemata differ from other social cognitive elements, such as attributions, beliefs about control, and attitudes? The schema concept implies cognitive principles that potentially cut across attributions, attitudes, and other elements of social perception (S. T. Fiske & Linville, 1980). Schemata are concerned with information processing. They suggest how social expectations are represented in memory and how they affect attention to consistent and inconsistent data. Assuming schema-based expectations, psychologists can use attribution theories (Chapters 2-4) to explain what one does with the congruent and incongruent information. For example, attributions suggest how people explain consistency and inconsistency, once they notice it. As we have seen, information inconsistent with a schema may be attributed to transitory causes, and so the inconsistency can be discounted. Moreover, if the inconsistency cannot be discounted, attribution theory supposes that incongruent behavior is particularly informative about an individual's personality dispositions (as apart from his or her social group); whereas congruent behavior is not informative about that individual (E. E. Jones & McGillis, 1976).

Schemata influence other important social cognitive elements. For example, one's feelings of control (Chapter 5) are probably enhanced by having a relevant schema for any given situation. If you meet someone new, you would probably feel more comfortable, the more you could fit the person to some prior schema and the more familiar you were with that person's type. Because a sense of predictability leads to a sense of control, schemata enhance perceived control. Finally, attitudes (Chapter 12) suggest how people feel about and are likely to act toward individuals who fit different schemata. Unlike attitudes, schemata do not necessarily include either affect or behavior, though sometimes they may include both.

To conclude, a schema contains abstract knowledge about types of people and events as a class, not a representation of every instance ever encountered. Other concepts such as attitudes and attributions do not address the issue of cognitive representation (nor are they intended to). The schema concept reflects a search for broadly applicable principles of information processing. Nevertheless, the term *schema* is not itself a well-developed theory any more than the term *attribution* is a theory. As we have seen, schemata are concepts within various detailed theories of information-processing that deal specifically with perception, memory, and inference.

In describing the effects of schemata on the encoding, retrieval, and judgment of new information, we have made the subtle transition from the elements to the processes of social perception. The elements of social cognition are attributions of causality; beliefs about control; and schemata for people, the self, roles, and events. All of these may be considered more or less static structures in one's mind. But by themselves they predict nothing. Once set into the context of social information processes such as attending, remembering, and inferring, their impact becomes dynamic. The next few chapters address each of these processes in turn, and then we address methods for studying them.

Summary

Social schema research is based on the premise that there is no unambiguous reality in the external world—people actively construct social reality. Ideas about schemata can be traced back to three sets of roots. The first is impression formation research on trait stimuli; it predicted impression responses from two competing frameworks—an algebraic model and a configural model. Each failed to win a conclusive victory over the other, however, because of theoretical and methodological gaps. Reacting to the ultimate futility of the controversy, social psychologists began to formulate detailed process models and measures, some of which drew on cognitive schema research. The second root of schema research lies in cognitive psychology's research on memory. The recent revolution in cognitive research provided new tools for describing the active social information processor. Especially noteworthy is the research on general knowledge as a guide to inference and memory. A third line of research also contributed to social schema theories, by showing categorical perception based on family resemblance with fuzzy sets, instead of rigid rules.

Social research demonstrates a range of schematic effects and different types of schemata all show similar effects on perception, memory, and inference. Person schemata include personality traits and goals. Perceiving a person to fit a given trait operates on many of the same principles as does perceiving an object to belong to a given category. Like other schemata, person schemata cause people falsely to remember and infer category-consistent but never-seen attributes. These effects are strongest when the schema is present at both encoding and retrieval.

Self-schemata contain people's knowledge of themselves on dimensions that are important to them. Self-schemata allow people to filter information relevant to the schema efficiently, whether information about themselves or others. Memory for schema-consistent information can be retrieved rapidly, so familiar schematic judgments are made quickly. Novel judgments, however, can be slower for schematics than for aschematics because of the large quantities of relevant information available. Self-schemata appear to be formed for dimensions on which people are distinctive or extreme compared to others.

Role schemata used in stereotyping further add to the catalog of schematic effects. Role schemata are based on age, race, sex, or occupation, and they describe the norms and behaviors that fit a given group in society. Categorization reduces perceived within-group variability and exaggerates perceived between-group variability. People often perceive information in ways that confirm their stereotypes. People recall schema-consistent and schema-discrepant information better than irrelevant information, but which of the former two has the advantage is not clear. Apparently, attention accrues to discrepancy, and normal memory routes favor consistency. Regardless of schema-based memory, evaluations are favorable to the perceiver's in-group and evaluations polarize for out-groups. Although role schemata tend to be resilient, intergroup contact can, under some circumstances, alter them.

Scripts, which are schemata for social events, contain props, roles, scenes, and sequence rules. Like other schemata, they can guide perception, memory, and inference toward consistency with the typical case. However, because of their tightly linked temporal structure, they may be more likely than other schemata to encourage memory for inconsistency.

Content-free schemata are rules for the relationships among elements. A balance schema and a linear ordering schema are examples. They do not contain much content knowledge, but they do show standard schematic effects: preference for schema-consistent information in perception, memory, and inference.

Schemata grow and change in some ways that are well documented. The perseverance effect describes how people reinterpret information to support existing beliefs, despite mixed or negative evidence. Successful debiasing can occur if people monitor their own judgment processes or are forced to counterargue their own schemata.

When schemata do change, research shows that schema development increases abstraction, complexity, and efficiency; it also makes the schema's components more linked. The facilitating or hindering effect of schemata on learning related concepts depends on the degree of schema development. Schema activation comes from frequency and recency of prior activation, although observational purpose and emotions probably guide schema activation, too. Once selected, less than perfect schematic fit is likely to moderate the usually obtained schematic effects.

Generally, the schema concept emphasizes the common features of conceptually driven information processing across a variety of domains, and as such it is of value as a general construct in social cognition research.

part two

processes in
social cognition

Attention and encoding are the first steps in
social information processing. Without them,
nothing else can happen: attributions cannot be
made; control cannot be attempted; schemata
cannot be applied. Before any internal infor-

attention

mation processing can occur, the stimuli outside the person have to be brought
to the mind. The name for this general process is *encoding*. Encoding trans-
forms an external stimulus into an internal representation. The encoding
process involves a tremendous amount of cognitive work. The instant a
stimulus registers on the senses, the process of interpretation begins. Immediately, some details are lost, others altered, and still others are fabricated.
Such inferences are stored along with the raw data and become indistinguishable from them. The process of encoding influences both attention and
memory, which will concern us in this chapter and the next.

Attention is related to the encoding process. Attention often focuses on
what is currently being encoded; whatever occupies consciousness is defined as
the focus of attention. Attention, however, is not limited to the encoding of
external stimuli. Attention also can be occupied by information retrieved from
memory. If you are thinking about something you remember, that memory is
the focus of your attention. Whether attention is directed *outward* toward
encoding external objects or *inward* toward memory, attention is usually seen
as having two components, *direction* (selectivity) and *intensity* (effort). When
you read this book, you are presumably focusing on it rather than on the
radio, the conversation in the hall, or the itch on your leg. Even given your
choice to focus selectively on the book, you can allocate more or less intense
mental effort to it. Attention, then, is the amount of selective cognitive work
you do (Kahneman, 1973; Norman, 1976; Posner, 1982). Thus attention is
occupied by the current contents of the mind (which are termed *active*,
working, or *short-term memory*). One is attending to the internal or external
stimuli that are in conscious focal awareness.

People do not attend evenly to all aspects of their environment. They
watch some things closely and ignore others altogether. In this chapter, we are
concerned with understanding what determines interpersonal attention. To

anticipate what we discuss, let us look at several principles psychologists have advanced to predict people's focus of attention in social settings. One is that people attend to stimuli that are salient or vivid. This is not as circular as it sounds. As the first parts of the chapter will show, salience and vividness are stimulus properties that typically but not necessarily attract attention. A stimulus is *salient* relative to its context. For example, a person who is seven feet tall is salient in most contexts (except on a basketball team), and he will typically attract attention. A stimulus is *vivid* regardless of context, by virtue of its inherent properties. Describing a star basketball center in a colorful case history is inherently a more vivid stimulus than describing the same person merely by vital statistics.

Attention also depends on environmental cues. If someone is pointing a movie camera at the basketball player's friend, who is only six feet tall, you will notice the friend even if he would not otherwise be salient. Similarly, if the movie camera is on you, your attention will not be on the tall fellow, but on yourself instead. A third major determinant of attention thus includes those environmental cues that focus you on yourself or others; in the third section of the chapter we deal with variations in *self-awareness*.

In the chapter's final two sections, we take up various personality factors that determine people's usual focus of attention. We conclude the chapter with the applications of attention to issues in health, anxiety, helping, and transgression. In every case, one's focus of attention turns out to have unexpectedly large effects on judgment, feelings, and behavior. While it might seem trivial, attention has extremely important social consequences.

Salience: A Property of Stimuli in Context

Suppose you, a student, walk into a roomful of octogenarians. Everyone but you has gray hair and wrinkles; everyone is at least 60 years older than you. You will probably feel conspicuous. All eyes will be on you, your every word will be recalled, your every move will seem more important than it is, you will be stereotyped as representing the "young person's point of view," and your performance will be evaluated more strongly than other people's. Whether you are the solo youngster, oldster, male, female, black, white, or whatever in an otherwise homogenous group, the striking experience of being a salient social stimulus is the same.

From an objective perspective, one's salience is logically irrelevant to social judgment. Nevertheless, research on salience supports the uncomfortable experience of the solo as being a center of attention, as looming larger than life, and as the recipient of relatively extreme reactions (S. E. Taylor, 1981; S. E. Taylor, Fiske, Close, Anderson, & Ruderman, 1977). Salience can be brought about in many other ways, as we will see below. But, regardless of the reasons a person is salient, the social consequences are several.

ANTECEDENTS OF SOCIAL SALIENCE

The causes of social salience all depend on the immediate or the larger context (McArthur, 1981; S. E. Taylor & Fiske, 1978). Table 7.1 lists the antecedents of salience. In the case of the solo, attributes of a person that are novel in the immediate context cause the person to be the center of attention. Being 18 years old is not cause for comment in a college classroom, but it will attract attention in a nursing home. Researchers have documented solo status as a function of sex, race, and characteristics such as wearing the only red shirt in a roomful of blues (Kanter, 1977; McArthur & Post, 1977; S. E. Taylor *et al.*, 1977; Wolman & Frank, 1975). These forms of salience draw on perceptual and social novelty.

Another form of salience draws entirely on perceptual features of the stimulus that make it figural in the immediate context. Perceptual principles based on Gestalt psychology predict that stimuli will be salient if they are bright, complex, changing, moving, or otherwise stand out from their drab background (McArthur & Post, 1977). Thus salience effects occur as a function of relative brightness (one person being literally in the spotlight), relative motion (one person sitting in a rocking chair), and relative complexity (one person in a loudly patterned shirt). Such figural people attract longer gazes than do nonfigural people (McArthur & Ginsberg, 1981).

Moving out of the immediate context to the larger social context, a person also can become salient if he or she behaves in ways that do not fit people's prior knowledge about that individual, his or her social category, or people in general (E. E. Jones & McGillis, 1976; see Table 7.1). Say your bookworm roommate suddenly takes up aerobic exercise; behavior that is unusual for a particular person invariably catches and holds attention. Your roommate will be temporarily salient to you. Behavior that is out-of-role or unusual for a social category also catches attention, such as an executive who drives a Jeep to work. Similarly, attributes and behavior that are unusual for people in general attract attention. Thus a person who weighs 300 pounds is a salient stimulus, because most people weigh less than that. Your attention will probably focus on a heavy person, just as it would on any visually novel stimulus such as a physically handicapped person (Langer, Taylor, Fiske, & Chanowitz, 1976) or a bicycle in a tree. All three types of salience are based on expectations (about the person, the social category, or people in general).

The last principle of salience, based on expectations about people in general, has been extended in two ways (S. T. Fiske, 1980). First, extreme stimuli are more salient than moderate stimuli. To give an example, people gaze longer at extremely positive stimuli, such as movie stars, and at extremely negative stimuli, such as traffic accidents. Since both positive and negative extremes are more unusual than moderate stimuli, extreme stimuli are salient. Second, most people expect mildly positive stimuli in general. Most people are optimistic about the outcomes they expect to be dealt by others and by life in general (Parducci, 1968). Hence negative stimuli in general are more salient

TABLE 7.1
The Causes of Social Salience

A person can be salient relative to the perceiver's

Immediate context

By being novel (solo person of that race, sex, hair color, shirt color)
By being figural (bright, complex, moving)

Prior knowledge or expectations

By being unusual for that person (e.g., behaving in unexpected ways)
By being unusual for his or her social category (e.g., behaving in out-of-role ways)
By being unusual for people in general (e.g., behaving negatively or extremely)

Other attentional tasks

By being goal relevant (e.g., being a boss, a date)
By dominating the visual field (e.g., sitting at the head of the table, being on camera more than others)
By the perceiver being instructed to observe the person

than positive ones; because most people are optimists, negative stimuli are unexpected and thus salient.

A rather different principle of salience is that attention depends in part on the perceiver's goals. For example, people attend more to others on whom their outcomes are dependent. If two people are talking and one is your new boss or a prospective date, you will watch that person more closely than the other (Berscheid, Graziano, Monson, & Dermer, 1976; S. E. Taylor, 1975). People attend to significant others.

Salience can also be created by more deliberate interventions into social settings. For example, salience can hinge on seating position in a group; the person directly opposite you should be especially salient because that person dominates your visual field (S. E. Taylor & Fiske, 1975). Thus, if you want to have maximum impact on the leadership of a meeting, sit opposite the chairperson at the head or foot of a long table; if you want to fade into the background, sit on the sidelines. In a videotape, decreasing or increasing the time a person is on camera has some similar effects (Eisen & McArthur, 1979). The most direct manipulation of attention is instructing people to watch one person rather than another (S. E. Taylor & Fiske, 1975).

To review, a person can be salient relative to the immediate context, relative to the perceiver's prior knowledge or expectations, or relative to other attentional tasks. Note that the key word common to all these ways of creating salience is *relative*: stimulus novelty occurs relative to an immediate or broader context, a stimulus is figural relative to other stimuli present, and perceiver perspective is relative to the context. We will come back to the point that salience is relative.

CONSEQUENCES OF SOCIAL SALIENCE

Regardless of the way salience is created, its effects are robust and wide ranging (McArthur, 1981; S. E. Taylor & Fiske, 1978). As suggested by the experience of the solo, salience makes a stimulus larger than life in various judgments. Prominence shows up most in perceptions of causality. Salient people are seen as especially influential in a given group. A solo young person in a roomful of older people, for example, would be seen as having a lot of impact on the group. He or she would probably be credited with setting the tone of a discussion, deciding on topics, and as generally guiding the conversation. Salient behavior is also seen as less under the control of the situation and as particularly indicative of the solo person's underlying disposition. The behavior of the token young person would be interpreted as reflecting the "real person," rather than the constraints of the awkward situation. Generally speaking, then, causal attributions follow the focus of attention. Because people generally see other people as causal agents (Heider, 1958; E. E. Jones & Nisbett, 1972; L. Ross, 1977), attention normally exaggerates this tendency (S. T. Fiske, Kenny, & Taylor, 1982).

However, if a person's passivity is emphasized, attention can exaggerate perceptions of susceptibility to influence as well (Strack, Erber, & Wicklund, 1982). Researchers designed an experiment to show that salience exaggerates causal judgments in the direction implied by prior knowledge. Student subjects read biographies of targets who were described either as socially influential or as susceptible to social influence. One of the targets also appeared on the videotape screen (i.e., he was the more salient), and he was later judged as especially influential or especially susceptible. Thus salience exaggerated judgments in the direction they initially tended. Generally, people are expected to be more active than passive. So if you know nothing about someone, attention will exaggerate his or her perceived influence, rather than perceived susceptibility to influence. Hence the usual effect of attention is to enhance perceived influence. In sum, then, attention exaggerates causal perceptions in whichever direction they are already heading.

This principle extends to noncausal perception as well. Evaluations are exaggerated in whichever direction they initially tend. If a person is unpleasant, being a solo will cause disproportionate condemnation; similarly, a pleasant solo is exaggeratedly praised (S. E. Taylor et al., 1977). Evaluations can be nudged in one direction or another by prior expectations, as well. For example, people observing a defendant on trial are judging the person's criminality (or lack thereof), which can invoke a negative expectation. If a defendant in criminal proceedings is viewed negatively, salience should cause him to be viewed especially negatively. On the other hand, when he is judged as a person (a more positive expectation), salience should cause him to be viewed especially positively (Eisen & McArthur, 1979; see also McArthur & Solomon, 1978). Salience cuts both ways in evaluations.

If salient social stimuli elicit attention, perceived prominence, and extreme evaluations, it would stand to reason that they also should enhance memory.

Unfortunately, the data are strikingly uneven. Some kinds of memory are enhanced and some are not (McArthur, 1981; S. E. Taylor & Fiske, 1978). The unevenness of salience effects on memory is critical, so we will take a closer look at it in a later section.

Salience may not reliably enhance quantity of recall, but it does increase the organization and consistency of memory in several ways. The more attention one pays to another person, to an attitude object, or to one's own behavior, the more coherent the impression becomes. Attention structures impressions, emphasizing features that fit and adjusting those that do not. To return to the solo young person example: in a nursing home, you are likely to be seen as representing the "younger generation's" perspective. You may be stereotyped as a typical young person, with all the relevant young person attributes inferred. Observers may interpret your intelligent remarks as precocious rather than wise and your politics as naive rather than insightful. In short, you may be seen as typical of your category (S. E. Taylor, 1981; S. E. Taylor et al., 1977).

Similarly, with increased attention, the evaluative components of an impression are likely to be brought into consistency with each other, and evaluations become more extreme. Prolonged attention or thought over a period of time creates polarized impressions, but only for people who possess the relevant schema or cognitive structure (Tesser, 1978). Perhaps an example will clarify this phenomenon. The more that sailors think about a particular yacht, the more they see it as an extremely good or bad example of its class and the more they find it appealing or unappealing; as they think about the yacht, its features all are assimilated to their emerging impression. Landlubbers, in contrast, would not gain any additional structure or insight by prolonged attention. Their extended contemplation of the yacht nets no added coherence. In effect, they are not in the same boat. Their view of the same yacht is simpler and less coherent to begin with, and attention will not make it more structured and complex. Thus objects or people about whom one has an initial opinion become more coherent with attention and increase in evaluative extremity, if one knows anything about that class of objects or people.

We have seen that salience and attention have a variety of effects on judgments. Attention exaggerates attributions of causal influence and exaggerates evaluations, in whatever direction they initially tend. Attention sometimes increases memory. Finally, attention encourages stereotypes and polarizes impressions. How robust are these effects of temporary salience on important social judgments? Salience effects are not confined to bland conversations in psychology laboratories. In fact, efforts to increase interest and to enrich stimulus materials turn out to enhance the effect (McArthur, 1981). For example, the attributional effects of salience emerge when people are watching a murder trial, an aggressive encounter, or intimate self-disclosures (Eisen & McArthur, 1979; McArthur & Solomon, 1978; S. E. Taylor, Crocker, Fiske, Sprinzen, & Winkler, 1979). Moreover, the attributional effect also occurs when people are distracted, under time pressure, or making a delayed judgment

(Strack *et al.*, 1982; S. E. Taylor *et al.*, 1979). Salience effects on evaluations and stereotypes also occur in real-world organizations (Kanter, 1977; Wolman & Frank, 1975). There is one possible exception to the generally pervasive effects of social salience. It appears that if stimuli are personally quite significant, involvement may eliminate the impact of salience (Borgida & Howard-Pitney, 1983; but see S. E. Taylor *et al.*, 1979). Notwithstanding that exception, salience and differential attention have robust, pervasive effects on important social perceptions.

Vividness: An Inherent Property of Stimuli

Vividness is a phenomenon that is highly related to salience. Whereas salience is determined by the relation of an object to its context, vividness is inherent in a stimulus itself. Thus, for example, a plane crash is more salient during peacetime than in the context of wartime carnage. But a plane crash is inherently more vivid than a normal flight, a detailed description of a particular accident is more vivid than the statistics about it, and an accident in your local airport is more vivid than an accident elsewhere. A stimulus is vivid, to the extent that it is "(a) emotionally interesting, (b) concrete and imagery-provoking, and (c) proximate in a sensory, temporal or spatial way" (Nisbett & Ross, 1980, p. 45). Do vivid stimuli have similar effects to salient stimuli? As we will see, although theory and common sense would suggest that vivid stimuli are especially impactful, research suggests that they are not.

THE CASE FOR VIVIDNESS EFFECTS

Vividness effects seem commonplace in daily life. Consider two versions of the same sponsor-a-child advertisement. One version describes little Felicia and her 12 brothers and sisters, orphaned and living off the sales of firewood they gather in the countryside and carry by hand into the big city. A photograph depicts her large, innocent eyes with long lashes and her brave upturned face; she is standing in a clean but ragged dress, surrounded by squalor. At this very moment, Felicia is hoping for help. Ten dollars will feed her for a month. Before you write your check, consider another version of the same ad. It merely states the statistics on world malnutrition and child neglect, listing 25 countries in which the program operates. The second appeal is rational, informative, abstract, and distant; your donation seems less likely. Why? In both cases, your conscience gives the same counsel, but the first ad seems more likely to attract your attention initially, to change your attitudes, and to elicit the desired behavior. All this is obvious, and as the idea person in an ad agency, you could have thought up the vivid ad yourself.

Psychological theorists have postulated precisely such vividness effects, on several conceptual grounds. Vivid information is predicted to be more persuasive than pallid information of equal or greater validity, first of all because vivid information should come to mind more easily (Nisbett & Ross, 1980; Tversky & Kahneman, 1973). By this argument, vivid information is processed more fully at encoding, and therefore its memory trace should be stronger. Hence it would be recalled faster or more fully. In this view, judgments and attitudes are based on the information most available in memory. Second, vivid information is by definition highly imageable, that is, likely to provoke internal visual representations. According to this argument, visual codes are especially memorable, so vivid information again would come to the fore in memory-based judgments and attitudes. Finally, vivid information seems to have more emotional impact on the perceiver; affective overtones are hypothesized to enhance its impact on judgments. In short, the impact of vivid information on human judgment, especially persuasion, would seem to be self-evident.

Unfortunately, there is little empirical evidence for vividness effects (see S. E. Taylor & Thompson, 1982, for a review). According to the research, messages that are written in concrete and colorful language are no more likely to change attitudes than are abstract and dry messages. Enlivening the ad copy in the appeal to save Felicia apparently would be to no avail. Research shows that messages accompanied by photographs usually have no greater appeal, so little Felicia as a poignant photograph versus a faceless story might well have equal impact. Similarly, videotaped messages only sometimes have enhanced impact. And finally, direct experience, which would seem the ultimate in vividness, does not necessarily change attitudes more effectively than does second-hand contact. A Peace Corps volunteer who had worked in Felicia's village would not necessarily have different attitudes than his brother who stayed home.[1] In sum, vividness does not work well empirically, although intuitively it seems as if it should.

The major exception to this pattern of negative results is that individual case histories do persuade more effectively than do group statistics. Little Felicia as a heartrending story does carry more impact than do the worldwide hunger statistics. However, it is not clear that this result speaks to the vividness effect. Research that manipulates concrete (versus dull) language, photographs (versus none), and videotapes (versus transcripts) holds most other information constant. Contrasting case history and statistical information is more problematic. They differ in far too many ways to assume that it is differences in vividness that cause any differences in their persuasive impact. For example, a case history communicates one particular scenario by which the existing facts could occur, for example, an underprivileged child might survive by selling firewood. Statistics communicate a different sort of information, such as life expectancy averaged over many instances. Hence information nonequiva-

---

1. Saying that direct experience may not change attitudes is not the same as denying that direct experience may affect the *acquisition* of attitudes or the impact of attitudes on *behavior*; it clearly does both (see Chapters 12 and 13).

lency is confounded with vividness; that is, the effects of the two are not separated. Together with the failure to find effects from other types of vividness, this problem suggests that the information differences and not vividness per se accounts for the fact that case histories are highly persuasive (S. E. Taylor & Thompson, 1982).

So far, we have seen no clear evidence for the effects of vivid information on persuasion and judgments, when information is held constant on other factors. One lingering possibility suggests that vivid information would have its greatest impact after a delay. By this logic, all information is relatively easy to recall immediately after receiving it. After a delay, however, the pallid information's relative weakness allows it to fade, leaving vivid information intact. Although one study has in fact found evidence for this hypothesis (Reyes, Thompson, & Bower, 1980) several others have not, and one (P. Wright & Rip, 1981) found the reverse. Accordingly, vividly presented information does not seem to have an effect after a delay either.

WHY DOES THE VIVIDNESS EFFECT SEEM SO PLAUSIBLE?

It appears that there is, in fact, little evidence for the vividness effect. If so, what would lead people to the intuitive conclusion that there is a vividness effect? One possibility is that vividness has some effect on us that is mistaken for persuasion. Three hypotheses suggest themselves. First, people often remember vividly presented information and may erroneously infer that they were persuaded. By this reasoning, when people report real-world cases of so-called vividness effects, what they are often retrieving is a memorable event, not an example of having been persuaded or otherwise influenced by that event. For example, one frequently televised advertisement in Los Angeles shows an exceptionally attractive and obviously braless young lady sashaying through the corridors of a men's clothing store. No one we know in Los Angeles has missed the ad. Few people, however, remember the name of the clothing store. Indeed, advertising lore is full of accounts of prize-winning ads that were taken off the air for failing to increase sales (Haslett, 1976). Memorability and persuasion need not go hand in hand.

Second, people are entertained by vividly presented information, and they may erroneously assume they were persuaded. Good storytellers are in demand at cocktail parties, while those who provide the latest statistics from their research are shunned. No one would, however, claim that the good storyteller is intrinsically persuasive—merely jolly and good fun. This independence of persuasiveness and vividness was put well by one of Carl Sagan's colleagues in describing Sagan's "gift for vividness": "Carl is very often right and always interesting. That is in contrast to most academics, who are always right and not very interesting" (*Time*, October 20, 1980, p. 68). Vivid communications are frequently perceived as more graphic, more vivid, or more interesting than nonvivid communications in precisely those studies that go on to find no effect on judgments. Thus the entertainment value of vividness does seem to be functionally distinct from its persuasive impact (S. E. Taylor & Wood, 1983).

A third hypothesis about the illusory effect of vividly presented information can be derived from work in advertising. Advertising is often cited as an example of the successful use of vividness, and so it is useful to debunk that myth. Advertisers do not, in fact, rely on vividly presented presentations to sell products (Aaker, 1975; Ogilvy, 1963). Effective ads are typically targeted to and constructed around the needs of a narrowly defined specific population (e.g., lower-middle-class black women, aged 25-35). If a particular ad is both vivid and persuasive, it is thought to achieve its success because the vivid component alerted the target population to a product that would meet an already existing need, rather than because it created a need via the vivid presentation. Vividness does not itself persuade, but it may catch the attention of people who are prime targets for persuasion.

To summarize, the absence of robust empirical evidence for vividness can be reconciled with its apparent effect in the real world by arguing that memorability, entertainment value, or occasional impact under conditions of need mistakenly lead people to believe that vividly presented information uniformly has an impact on judgment and persuasion.

FUTURE DIRECTIONS FOR VIVIDNESS RESEARCH

However, if we assume that our real-world intuitions are correct and that a vividness effect does exist, then it follows that the attempts to examine it experimentally have been flawed in some important way or that it does occur, but only under special circumstances that most experiments have so far failed to duplicate. Several principles define the boundaries of the vividness effect (S. E. Taylor & Thompson, 1982). First, many attempts to operationalize vividness confuse vivid messages with vivid presentations. If the message context is too vivid, the gimmicks may draw people's attention away from the message itself (Eagly & Himmelfarb, 1978). The young lady in the aforementioned clothing store ad is one such example of content being overwhelmed by form (so to speak).

Second, there is some empirical evidence that pallid written material conveys more information but that vivid video or live material helps to catch people's attention, if they are relatively uninvolved (Chaiken & Eagly, 1976). Video ads capture people's attention, but they also prompt people to deal mostly with superficial information, such as whether the speaker is good-looking (Chaiken & Eagly, 1983). Vivid information may work on the attentional stage, especially for uninvolved recipients.

If recipients of a message are already highly involved, vividness is not needed to capture attention. Their attention is already captured. What they need are cogent arguments and time to think about them. Written materials allow involved recipients the time to consider the message arguments in detail, which is crucial to persuading such people (Petty & Cacioppo, 1979; see also

Chapter 12). In this view, then, vivid ads serve mainly to catch the attention of people who are uninvolved, but written information does the persuasion for people who are involved.

Another possibility begins by noting that even a pallid message will be attended to when there is nothing else in the environment. Experimental settings are engineered to minimize competing demands on subjects' attention. Social psychologists who know their craft are skilled at creating barren environments dominated by impactful manipulations. With nothing else to do or notice, subjects attend to the experimental stimuli whether or not the stimuli are relatively vivid. Hence the vividness manipulation cannot increase attention because it already is at fairly high levels and cannot go much higher. Perhaps, then, in the laboratory, there is little variability in absolute levels of attention.

In contrast, the confusion of the real world imposes constant attentional choices on people. Students' selective attention to a classroom lecture varies when the outside hallway is noisy or when the view outside the window is especially entertaining. Either one creates a distraction, a stimulus competing for student attention. In that situation, the flashy or vivid lecturer should have a distinct advantage over the dull one.

Vividness effects may well depend on differential attention among competing stimuli, in which case vivid messages will dominate pallid messages. Conditions in the real world promote differential attention, but the laboratory does not. This difference may account for the discrepancy between the intuitive plausibility of vividness effects and their apparent empirical failure. This conclusion brings vividness quite close conceptually to salience, which was defined specifically in terms of context. Vivid stimuli may have no inherently greater impact; their impact may be differentially great only when they are contrasted with more pallid and dull stimuli that are simultaneously competing for attention.

A Closer Look at Attention, Salience, and Vividness

It is impressive to consider the range of perceptions and behaviors guided by the seemingly trivial factor of what catches the eye (or ear). When people do attend to salient or vivid stimuli, it appears to be the selective component of attention, rather than its effort component, that creates these effects. Recall from the definition we gave at the chapter's outset that attention has two separate components. Differential selective attention rather than attentional intensity seems to be the key factor in a person's attentional choices.

Why should attention have such pervasive effects on social judgment? If a woman at a party is wearing a magenta dress, she will be salient, assuming no one else is wearing loud colors. What exactly happens when you notice a woman dressed in neon-bright magenta and later overattribute causality to her or exaggerate evaluations of her? Psychologists have proposed several processes to connect differential attention and differential judgments; some of these candidates for mediation (i.e., the connection) have been debunked and some supported. The potential mediators include exaggerated recall, perceptual organization, type of processing, and affective involvement.

RECALL AS A MEDIATOR

The female guest in the magenta dress would stand out in most crowds and attract your attention. As you notice her throughout the evening, you take in bits of her behavior and overhear fragments of her conversation. When your roommate afterwards asks you what you thought of her, you may have a larger quantity of raw data about her than about another woman who was dressed in gray. It would seem reasonable to assume that you would have firmer opinions about the woman with the magenta dress because you recall more about her.

Much attention research has tested just such a model of mediation, that is, that salience enhances memory, which in turn influences judgments. However, we noted earlier that salience does not reliably enhance recall. Consequently, if attention does not always increase recall, larger quantities of recall could not cause the standard attentional effects on judgments. Researchers have shown that judgments do not depend on the total amount of salient information people recall (S. E. Taylor & Fiske, 1975; S. T. Fiske et al., 1982). In some cases, enhanced memory and exaggerated judgments are correlated (Harvey, Yarkin, Lightner, & Town, 1980; E. R. Smith & Miller, 1979b), but not always. Hence recall is not a necessary condition for creating the effects of attention on judgments.

A related possibility is that ease or availability of memory, rather than quantity, is facilitated by differential attention. In this view, it is not that more information is recalled about salient stimuli, but instead that information about salient stimuli is recalled more easily. In the party example, instances of the magenta woman's behavior come to mind more rapidly than do instances of nonsalient people's behavior. Consequently, her behavior is overrepresented as evidence in subsequent causal analyses. This availability model of attention effects on attribution has received some support (Pryor & Kriss, 1977).

Another potential reason that attention affects judgments is channel-specific recall. That is, if one's attention is captured by visually salient stimuli, then only visual recall will be overrepresented in memory. Thus memory for the magenta woman's conversation will not be enhanced, but memory for her dress and gestures will be. Similarly, if Randy is salient by virtue of his loud voice, recall of what he said and how he said it should be enhanced, but not recall of his appearance. However, this channel-specific model has little support (S. T. Fiske et al., 1982; McArthur & Ginsberg, 1981; Robinson & McArthur, 1982; S. E. Taylor et al., 1979, Study 1).

Another potential mediator of attentional effects is causally relevant recall. Why should people make their causal inferences from data that have no bearing on causality? In this view, people are not so inefficient as to use useless information. Helpful data such as talking time, an imposing appearance, and dominant behaviors are considered diagnostic; remembering them in particular should predict causality. Moreover, dominant behavior and appearance seem inherently to attract attention in most contexts. Attributes relevant to perceived causality tend to have an impact perceptually as well as inferentially. They tend to be events rather than nonevents ("he talked a lot" versus "he sat silently") and to be vivid rather than pallid ("she gestured excitedly" rather than "she smiled occasionally"). Thus, suppose your attention initially is drawn to someone because of her magenta dress. While looking at her longer than at her gray-dressed colleague, you will especially notice her causally relevant dominant behaviors rather than irrelevant behaviors or submissive behaviors. Accordingly, the judgment is in effect being made at encoding and recall, on the basis of information that is doubly salient—salient because the person is salient and salient because the dominant behavior itself is salient. This view has received some support (S. T. Fiske *et al.*, 1982; Pavelchak, Fiske, & Lau, 1982).

To summarize, psychologists have posited several memory processes that intervene between differential attention and exaggerated causal attributions. Sheer quantity of memory, the ease or availability of memory, and channel-specific memory do not seem to account for the effects of salience on attributions. Causally relevant memory, especially memory for dominant behavior and appearance, does seem to be enhanced by attention. That sort of memory, in turn, leads to exaggerated attributions.

THE GIBSONIAN APPROACH TO SOCIAL PERCEPTION

The idea that interpersonal judgments are based on the retrieval of relevant evidence is part of many explanations of social cognition phenomena, besides the preceding analysis of salience effects on attribution. Cognitive approaches to social situations rely heavily on memory both to explain and to measure the phenomena (see Chapter 8). The major assumption behind this practice is that humans actively operate on external stimuli by organizing them into memory representations, which are then available for later retrieval. In contrast to this view stands some research that emphasizes perceptual selectivity and organization that comes at an earlier stage in the process. The difference between memory organization and perceptual organization is roughly that between rearranging information that is already in your brain and arranging information at the time you take it in. Inspired by J. J. Gibson's work in object perception (1966, 1979), several theorists have suggested that most of the important activity in social understanding occurs at perceptual encoding (Baron, 1980; Lowe & Kassin, 1980; McArthur, 1980; McArthur & Baron, 1983; Weary, Swanson, Harvey, & Yarkin, 1980), rather than as the result of retrieving relevant evidence from memory (cf. Neisser, 1976).

The Gibsonian perspective suggests, for example, that causal attributions result from segmenting the perceptual field and that memory is irrelevant

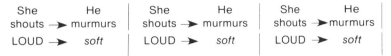

First segmentation of neighbors' quarrel

She		He		She		He		She		He
shouts	→	murmurs		shouts	→	murmurs		shouts	→	murmurs
LOUD	→	soft		LOUD	→	soft		LOUD	→	soft

Second segmentation of neighbors' quarrel

He		She		He		She		He		She
threatens	→	retreats		threatens	→	retreats		threatens	→	retreats
BIG	→	small		BIG	→	small		BIG	→	small

Note: Each vertical rule represents a breakpoint between two perceptual units.

Fig. 7.1 Perceptual segmentation of behavioral sequences resulting in different causal judgments.

(McArthur, 1980). To illustrate, assume you overhear your neighbors quarreling. She screams at him, and he murmurs in reply; this sequence alternates for some minutes. In relating the incident to your roommate, you describe the woman as causing the argument because each segment of the interaction begins with her salient vocal behavior. Each of her loud comments marks a new perceptual unit that finishes with his soft reply. She shouts, and he murmurs. Since causality requires temporal precedence, starting each unit with her irresistably places her in a squarely causal role. (See the top of Fig. 7.1.)

Now replay the fight but assume that you can see what is going on as well as hear it. (Assume further that they both do not turn on you for being a peeping tom, however scientifically disinterested.) The fight actually commences with him walking into the room and gesturing violently at her. She replies and retreats. He threatens her again, speaking in ominously low tones, and she backs off, arguing defensively. He threatens, and she retreats. The causal segments now commence each time with his physical gestures and her retreats. His physical gestures are perceptually big relative to her little retreats, in much the same way her shouts were loud compared to his soft murmurs. Hence the units now begin with him: he makes big physical threats and she makes little movements of retreat. Now the man would be described as causing the argument. Note that this perceptual analysis of causal attribution de-emphasizes memory. The causal judgments are implicit at encoding; differential memory may also result, but the theorists do not see it as determining the effect of attention on judgments (McArthur, 1980).

This analysis is all the more interesting because there is considerable evidence that perceptual segmentation has important effects on social judgments. This has been shown by researchers who measure perceptual segmentation directly. The technique for measuring perceptual segments or units involves subjects watching a film and pushing a button to indicate the end of each given segment and the beginning of a new one; the button push is taken to indicate what is called a breakpoint between segments. Segments are defined in whatever way seems natural to the individual (Newtson & Engquist, 1976; Newtson, Engquist, & Bois, 1977). The unitizing method (as it is called) is reliable and valid and surprisingly comfortable for subjects. People largely agree on the perceptual units in a given scene. For example, if the neighbors' quarrel were shown in a silent film, people would generally agree on the breakpoints indicated in the bottom row of Fig. 7.1.

The unitizing technique has revealed that the breakpoints between perceptual units have special properties. The breakpoint moments of a film, when shown as a series of stills in isolation from the rest of the film, nonetheless coherently convey the story. Nonbreakpoints (at equivalent intervals) do not adequately summarize the story. Recognition memory for breakpoints is also superior to recognition for nonbreakpoints (see Newtson, 1976). The implication is that behavior is segmented at points of maximal information (Newtson, 1980; Newtson, Rindner, Miller, & LaCross, 1978; but for dissent, see C. E. Cohen, 1981a; C. E. Cohen & Ebbesen, 1979; Ebbesen, 1980).

In conclusion, researchers who support the direct perception or Gibsonian view argue that it quite directly contradicts the idea that inferences depend upon cognitive processes and on memory in particular. According to this view, cognitive constructs (such as observational goals or schema-based expectations) enter into the inference process only to the degree that such factors influence the initial perception of an event, as it is directly observed (Engquist, Newtson, & LaCross, 1979; Massad, Hubbard, & Newtson, 1979; see Chapter 6, "Social Schemata," for other references). With respect to causal attribution, the Gibsonian view would argue that attributions result from perceptual organization, such as temporal sequence, or the contrast of large to small stimuli; the Gibsonian view suggests that causal inference occurs automatically during the perception of an event, an idea with which others agree (R. D. Sherman & Titus, 1982; E. R. Smith & Miller, 1979b). Although there is some evidence to the contrary (Vinokur & Ajzen, 1982), the Gibsonian view is a helpful counterpoint to the standard explanations of memory as a basis for social judgments.

Overall, it seems reasonable that considerable complex mental activity occurs upon perception as well as later (cf. Newtson, 1980). Granting that, however, the distinction between perception and cognition begins to evaporate. Perception is constructive encoding, on the one hand, and cognition can entail immediate construction, on the other. In other words, complex structuring clearly occurs very quickly. Whether one always labels such mental activity "cognitive," or sometimes "perceptual" and sometimes "cognitive" depending on its rapidity, is a matter of theoretical preference. The controversy does point out the necessity for focusing on attentional processes. But there is to date no clear evidence that either "perceptual" or "cognitive" activity is wholly dominant.

A NOTE ON ANALYZING ATTENTION

By now, the pervasive effects of attentional focus should be clear. Attention often is captured by salient stimuli, which are perceptually figural or novel in a given context; attention does not seem to be captured by vivid stimuli, which are proximal, emotional, imageable, or concrete. Possibly, it is necessary for vivid stimuli simultaneously to compete for attention with pallid stimuli in order to have a differential effect. In any case, one's focus of attention disproportionately guides interpretation and judgment of salient stimuli. Some of the pervasive effects of attention emerge long after encoding, at the retrieval stage, well after the initial act of attention.

It is difficult empirically to disentangle attentional and retrieval effects. One might, for example, initially attribute differential recall to differential attention, yet, as we have seen, it is entirely possible to pay lots of attention to something and to recall very little of it. Thus recall effects may stem from attentional focus, but they may also stem from cues present at retrieval. As the first step in inference, attentional processes potentially affect everything that follows. Consequently, they are difficult to isolate.

One way to remedy this problem is to locate attentional effects better by using more direct approaches. Psychologists rarely use direct measures of attention, yet many of these direct measures are available, as we will discuss in Chapter 10. Simple techniques include, for example, timing with a stopwatch how long a person looks at one or another person in a conversation. Complex methods include elaborate corneal reflectors that enable precise measurement of the exact spot upon which a person's gaze rests from moment to moment (see S. E. Taylor & Fiske, 1981, for a review of these and other attentional measures). Any efforts to measure attentional processes more directly will pin down their effects better.

Self-Awareness: Attention to Oneself or to the Environment

To this point, we have examined stimulus features—vividness and salience—that can determine social attention. A third line of research focuses on the ways that environmental stimuli can focus one's attention inward or outward. This research examines variations in one's self-awareness or self-focused attention.

ENVIRONMENTAL FOCUS VERSUS SELF-FOCUS

The original theory of objective self-awareness is based on several straightforward assumptions (Duval & Wicklund, 1972). It dichotomizes attention into self-focus and environmental focus. When people are reminded of themselves, they are said to become aware of themselves as social objects. In this state of objective self-awareness, the self is perceived as "me," the object or recipient of reaction. The self then is the focus of attention. For example, when you first get up to give a presentation in front of a class or at a conference, and you are busy wondering what they will think of you, you are objectively self-aware. In contrast, when people are distracted from thinking about themselves, they are more aware of the environment. After you get started in your presentation, you no longer focus on yourself, but on your audience and on your notes. You lose yourself in your talk. The environment, not the self, is the focus of attention.

Later revisions of the theory refined the distinction between environmental and self-focus in several respects (Carver, 1979; Carver & Scheier, 1981a). First, the self-environment dichotomy is imperfect. Attention constantly and rapidly switches back and forth, instead of focusing wholly and for long periods of time on either the self or the environment. Moreover, the dichotomy is paradoxical in that it is external stimuli that focus attention inward. Various environmental factors create self-attention: a mirror, a camera, an audience, and a tape recording of one's voice all can make people aware of themselves (Wicklund, 1975).

The self-environment dichotomy of attention is also misleading because self-attention is not unitary; the self is an incredibly complex stimulus. When you are thinking about yourself, you could be thinking about any of your values (e.g., being considerate) or about any of your feelings (e.g., anger) or any number of self-relevant aspects. Self-focus can make various features of the self salient, depending on the circumstances. For example, males who are self-focused are generally less aggressive toward females, presumably because the considerate part of their ideal selves normally is salient (Scheier, Fenigstein, & Buss, 1974). But the considerate part of their ideal selves may not always be salient. People who are self-focused sometimes are more aggressive than otherwise. This happens when the angry part of themselves is made salient (Scheier, 1976; Scheier & Carver, 1977). Clearly, then, various aspects of people's selves can become salient, including either positive norms or negative emotions. Since the self has many aspects, self-attention per se does not lead to a single outcome. Even though the general distinction between environmental and self-focus is imperfect, it also has many important ramifications.

COMPARING ONESELF TO IDEAL STANDARDS

Imagine going out to dinner at an elegant restaurant with plush carpets, dark wood paneling, and mirrors. You are seated facing your date and also—maddeningly—you are forced to gaze directly into the mirror on the wall behind the person. Try as you might to position yourself, you keep seeing your own face as you drink, nibble, and make conversation. Despite your best efforts, you keep noticing your windblown hair, the awkward way you smile, and the unattractive way you chew. Feeling utterly foolish by the time hors d'oeuvres arrive, you flee to the bathroom to comb your hair and vow to change tables upon your return.

Self-attention causes people to compare themselves to their ideals, and more specifically to whichever ideal standard is salient at the time. For example, if you were seated opposite a mirror at a business meeting, you might focus more on whether you appeared competent than on whether you appeared attractive.

In comparing ourselves to an ideal, we often fall short in our own eyes (Duval & Wicklund, 1972; Wicklund, 1975, 1978, 1979; Wicklund & Frey, 1980). Consequently, according to the original statement of the theory, objective self-awareness is aversive. Later refinements of the theory, however, state that self-attention need not focus on positive ideal standards for the self. Some internal standards are negative, as when eight-year-old Katy remembers her mother saying, "I certainly hope you are not as rude at Jane's house as she is when she visits here." Failing to imitate a negative ideal is obviously cause for pride, not aversion. Hence positive or negative affect can result from one's success or failure to match behavior to standards (Carver, 1979). One may even exceed a positive standard and feel good (Wicklund, 1975). Therefore, self-attention need not be aversive, contrary to the original theory and to what one might think at first.

In those cases where people do compare themselves to an ideal and then (inevitably) fall short, self-attention is indeed aversive. As in the restaurant example, people often attempt to escape when confronted with their own inadequacies (Duval & Wicklund, 1972; Gibbons & Wicklund, 1976). If a speedy and dignified exit is impossible, self-aware people struggle to conform to the salient ideals, which may be their own standards or other people's. In general, self-aware people are likely to be more honest, more helpful, more industrious, and less punitive than others (e.g., Reis & Burns, 1982; see Wicklund & Frey, 1980, for a review). One view of self-awareness is that it civilizes us because it reminds us of our better selves; in that sense, it is a theory of the conscience or superego, according to Wicklund. The notion that self-awareness awakens one's conscience emphasizes motivation as an important link between attentional focus and behavior.

In general, self-focus appears to set in motion an adjustment process. Given a standard, either positive or negative, people automatically compare and accordingly adjust their behavior. They attempt behavioral conformity to standards, compare their adjusted behavior with the ideal standard, and either decide that it matches the standard or does not; this process is called feedback. They continue adjusting and comparing in feedback cycles until they meet the standard or until they give up. A series of feedback loops set in motion by self-attention goes under the name *cybernetic theory of self-regulation* (Carver & Scheier, 1981a). To understand the basic principle of any cybernetic model, think of the parallel with a household furnace thermostat, which monitors the discrepancy between a set standard (e.g., 72 degrees) and the existing situation (e.g., 65 degrees). When the standard and the existing situation are discrepant, the thermostat initiates a chain of events (starting the furnace) that changes the existing situation to fit the standard (warms the house to 72 degrees). When the comparison indicates that the standard and the situation are no longer discrepant, the adjustment process ceases. A similar feedback and adjustment process could operate when you try to match any standard you set for yourself, for example, getting a geometry proof right or impressing your adviser. Psychologists think that self-attention initiates and maintains such an adjustment process within people.

For example, Carver and Scheier (1982) conducted a study, drawing on the idea that people (especially college students) presumably have an internal standard that favors achievement. When self-focused, they attempt behavioral conformity to that standard, and they may succeed or fail. If they fail, their positive or negative expectancy regarding the probable outcome determines the next step. In the study, subjects were exposed to consistent success or failure experiences on a series of printed mazes, in order to induce favorable or unfavorable outcome expectancies on a final maze. They were also made self-focused or not by the strategic placement of a mirror. That is, when they began work on the final maze, some subjects had to sit in front of a mirror, while others did not. The researchers hypothesized that self-focus could initiate behavioral conformity to the achievement standard. In other words, they expected the mirror to make success (on the maze) a more salient goal. Self-focus (mirror) in combination with favorable or unfavorable outcome expectancy (previous success or failure) predicted how far the subjects successfully progressed on the final maze. Given self-focus, previous outcomes determined performance, but without self-focus, that was not the case. Other research supports the effects of attentional self-focus on performance (Carver & Scheier, 1981a).

The critical point is that trying to fit a standard may be a simple result of attending to a discrepancy and not based on a motivational aversion to one's own inadequacy, as the original self-awareness theory would have it (Carver & Scheier, 1981b; Gibbons, Carver, Scheier, & Hormuth, 1979). However, debate over the exact nature of the attentional interpretation continues (Ellis & Holmes, 1982; Hull & Levy, 1979; Wicklund & Hormuth, 1981). All agree, however, that self-focus is importantly attentional and that it sets in motion an adjustment process.

Finally, the self-regulation theory generally posits that adjustment attempts will precede giving up. For example, if you stare at yourself in the restaurant mirror, you may smooth your hair or straighten your collar, to conform better to your ideal standard of attractiveness. If you notice a huge stain down your front, you may be tempted to leave altogether. Thus people do not always try to escape self-focus; self-awareness causes withdrawal only when change is hopeless. When adjustment attempts are doomed to failure, most people may try to escape either mentally or physically. That is, you may ask your date to leave early, or you may stay but feel self-conscious and emotionally withdrawn.

To summarize the model of self-attention, consider an example. Your conservative great-uncle Gregory happens to be firmly opposed to nuclear power plants. If made to focus on himself—as when a family gathering asks for his opinion—Gregory's attention can focus either on his conservative ideals or on his one liberal attitude. Each alternative implies different actions with respect to signing a petition in favor of increased governmental regulation of nuclear power, so it matters which aspect of himself he focuses on. If the setting makes him self-focused, and he is attending to his "no nukes" belief, he will sign it. Alternatively, if he focuses on his conservative ideology, he may not sign it. No motivationally aversive state need be assumed; he simply notes the discrepancy relevant to whichever standard is salient and adjusts his behavior.

A host of research indicates that self-attention enhances attitude-attitude and attitude-behavior consistency in just this way (Gibbons, 1978; Pryor, Gibbons, Wicklund, Fazio, & Hood, 1977; Salancik & Conway, 1975; Scheier & Carver, 1980; see S. E. Taylor & Fiske, 1978, pp. 266-267, for other references). If the environment makes salient a person's private self, that is, attitudes, and if the person concentrates on them (i.e., is self-focused), then consistency is enhanced with regard to whichever attitudes are salient (Carver & Scheier, 1981a). But if the situation makes external norms salient, then self-aware people will conform to those. Uncle Gregory may sign the petition because of a salient family consensus as much as because of his own attitudes. One challenge psychologists face in self-awareness research is to specify a priori *which* internal cues or external standards will be made salient, since the relative salience of these cues and standards determines behavior.

Individual Differences in Attention

The research we have discussed so far has all employed situational manipulations of attentional focus: lights, cameras, action, mirrors, seating position, colored shirts, and the like. You could have the impression that it simply takes a skilled director, costumer, and scene designer to manipulate people's reactions: given the right theatrical setup, every observer will respond in the same way. But the audience is not a faceless mass; they are individuals. Everyone does not respond similarly to attentional contingencies. At this point, we turn to consider the individual predispositions people bring with them to the experimental scene: people's chronic variations in attentional style and focus.

SELF-CONSCIOUSNESS

Here is a chance to know yourself. Complete the scale in Table 7.2, and then read on.

The scale, as a whole, measures self-consciousness, which is the dispositional version of self-awareness. It reflects a general tendency to attend to the self across situations (Fenigstein, Scheier, & Buss, 1975). Note that self-focus and self-attention are general terms, while self-consciousness refers to the disposition, and self-awareness refers to situationally manipulated self-attention.

Table 7.3 describes these distinctions. Your X score from Table 7.2 taps private self-consciousness, your general disposition to be aware of your own thoughts, feelings, and internal states. Your so-called Y score is an index of public self-consciousness, your general disposition to be aware of external aspects of yourself, your behavior, and how you are seen by others. The two subscales are only moderately correlated, so just because you are aware of yourself as a social object (public self), that does not mean that you are necessarily aware of your internal experiences (private self), or vice versa.

The self-consciousness scale does seem to measure what it intends to measure: self-focus. For example, dispositional self-consciousness predicts a high degree of self-relevant answers on a sentence completion task; self-conscious subjects supplied many self-relevant endings to sentence stems. For example, they were more likely to complete the stem "It's fun to daydream about" with answers like "my success" or "being loved" rather than "marrying Tom" or "giving a party for friends," reflecting internal rather than external focus (Carver & Scheier, 1978).

One important implication of the self-consciousness scale is that the public and private dimensions make different predictions under some circumstances. People who are publicly self-conscious are more likely to adjust their (expressed) attitudes if they know they are about to interact with other people

TABLE 7.2
Self-Consciousness Scale
(After A. Fenigstein, M. F. Scheier, & A. H. Buss, Public and private self-consciousness: Assessment and theory, *Journal of Consulting and Clinical Psychology*, 1975, *43*, 522-527. Copyright 1975 by the American Psychological Association. Adapted by permission of the authors.)

Indicate whether you generally agree (A) or disagree (D) with each of the following items.

_____ 1. I'm always trying to figure myself out.

_____ 2. I'm concerned about my style of doing things.

_____ 3. Generally, I'm not very aware of myself.

_____ 4. I reflect about myself a lot.

_____ 5. I'm concerned about the way I present myself.

_____ 6. I'm self-conscious about the way I look.

_____ 7. I never scrutinize myself.

_____ 8. I'm generally attentive to my inner feelings.

_____ 9. I usually worry about making a good impression.

Give yourself a point on Score X for each "agree" answer to items 1, 4, and 8, and for each "disagree" answer to items 3 and 7. Give yourself a point on Score Y for each "agree" answer to items 2, 5, 6, and 9. Note that the entire scale is considerably larger than the excerpt above.

TABLE 7.3
Four Kinds of Self-Focus or Self-Attention

Self-awareness (caused by situations)

Public: Awareness of external aspects of self, e.g., cued by audience, voice recordings, cameras.

Private: Awareness of own internal states, e.g., cued by mirrors.

Self-consciousness (caused by disposition)

Public: Awareness of external aspects of self, cued by personality.

Private: Awareness of own internal states, cued by personality.

who disagree with them. If Valerie acquires a new roommate with drastically different political views, for example, she may publicly go along, just to keep things smooth. On the other hand, people who are high on private self-consciousness (and low on public) are more likely to express attitudes that remain consistent over time (Scheier, 1980).

A second feature of dispositional self-consciousness is that it mimics situational self-awareness. That is, self-focus has similar effects regardless of whether it is caused by one's disposition or one's situation. Just as one can have public and private self-consciousness as a function of disposition, one can have public and private self-awareness as a function of an audience and a mirror, respectively (Froming, Walker, & Lopyan, 1982). Both the dispositional and situational kinds of private self-attention have similar effects. For example, private self-attention of either kind can exaggerate affective reactions; this is presumably because people in both cases are more aware of their internal states (Scheier & Carver, 1977; cf. Fenigstein, 1979). In many cases, the dispositional and the situational dimensions echo each other in exaggerating affect.

Under certain conditions, however, self-awareness of either a dispositional or a situational sort can also *moderate* affective reactions. When environmental cues mislead one about one's feelings, high private self-focus minimizes one's suggestibility (Scheier, Carver, & Gibbons, 1981). If your roommate is privately self-focused for either situational or dispositional reasons, he or she will not respond to persuasive appeals that begin, "Look, I know what you really want . . ." or "Let me tell you what you're feeling . . ." Private self-focus of either a dispositional or situational sort focuses attention on internal reactions and moderates responses to external pressures (Scheier & Carver, 1980).

OTHER INDIVIDUAL DIFFERENCES IN ATTENTION

Attentional focus enters into a variety of other personality factors besides self-consciousness. Locus of control (discussed in Chapter 2, "Attribution Theory"), for example, relates broadly to people's conception of the world as controlled by themselves and therefore as predictable and structured (internals) or as controlled by the environment and therefore perhaps not so predictable and structured (externals). People who think the sun rises and sets at their command (internal locus of control) might find the environment worthy of their careful attention, since they think they can manipulate it. People who feel they are the victims of capricious and unknowable circumstances (external locus of control) would feel there is no use in paying attention to the environment, since they feel they cannot change it.

A variety of evidence indicates that internals indeed are more skilled at directing their attentional focus than are externals; they more actively select and structure incoming stimuli (Wolk & DuCette, 1974). Consequently, internals attend more sensitively to the task at hand (Davis & Phares, 1967; Lefcourt, Lewis, & Silverman, 1968; Lefcourt & Wine, 1969). Externals tend to be distracted by novel, irrelevant cues after internals have grown accustomed to them (Berggren, Ohman, & Fredrikson, 1977). High internal people would concentrate on their work efficiently, even when workers are sandblasting outside the window, while external people would have more trouble. In sum, internals expect the world to be under their control, and they employ sensitive attentional strategies to make it so.

People also use attention to control their contact with unpleasant events. People who differ on the *repression-sensitization* dimension deal with threatening stimuli in one of two ways (Byrne, 1964). A person who approaches threats is a sensitizer; for example, a sensitizer might investigate a scorpion discovered by accident in the closet. A repressor would tend to avoid the threat by getting rid of it as quickly as possible. Similarly, a sensitizer is likely to investigate psychological threats by mulling them over and coming up with intellectual explanations for them. A repressor is more likely to avoid psychological threats by trying not to think about them or by making up excuses to forget about them. Consequently, when repressors and sensitizers encounter information that contradicts their attitudes, they respond differently. Repressors focus on supportive information and avoid counter-attitudinal information (Olson & Zanna, 1979). Repressors also avoid noticing the initial symptoms of an illness (Byrne, Steinberg, & Schwartz, 1968) and avoid critical feedback at least under some circumstances (Mischel, Ebbesen, & Zeiss, 1973; but see Graziano, Brothen, & Berscheid, 1980). Repressors' attentional style makes them perpetually more unwilling than most people to confront the unpleasant side of life.

Another individual difference that bears directly on attentional processes is *need for stimulation* (Sales, 1971). People who seek out complex, interesting, and intense stimuli are *reducers*, whose neural processes dampen incoming stimuli. Reducers metaphorically have cotton in their ears and tinted glasses over their eyes because of the reduced levels at which their brains transmit sensory stimuli. To maintain an optimal level of experienced stimulation, since their senses are permanently muffled, reducers have to increase the volume and illumination in the world outside. Your sensation-seeking friends who skydive, eat spicy food, and listen to loud music may be reducers.

In contrast, *augmenters'* internal processes amplify incoming stimuli; metaphorically, they have on hearing aids with the volume permanently turned up and sight that provides its own high intensity lamp. Consequently, they must surround themselves with less intense stimuli, to maintain the same optimal level of received stimulation. Augmenters, who have a low need for external stimulation, prefer relatively subtle stimuli. They are likely to prefer a nice peaceful sail, to detect nuances of flavor in cooking, and to appreciate softer music. In picking a plaid scarf, an augmenter might choose a simple, as opposed to a complex tartan. On the other hand, reducers attend more closely to complex material than augmenters do, and they pick less subtle patterns. When the environment does not provide the desired level of stimulation, reducers create their own sensory input. In a waiting room, reducers read magazines, search their purses or pockets, and wander about the room. In a group discussion, reducers talk more than augmenters (Sales, 1971).

Self-monitoring, a concept we will discuss more thoroughly in Chapter 13, describes the extent to which people usually attend to social situations as guides for their behavior, in contrast to people who usually attend to their own inner states as guides for their behavior (M. Snyder, 1979). Individual differences in whether people do monitor themselves with respect to the situation (high self-monitors) or do not (low self-monitors) seem at least partially a function of attention. Since high self-monitors are concerned with behaving in a socially appropriate manner, they are more likely to watch the situation than to watch themselves in seeking guides to action. Low self-monitors are more concerned with whether their behavior is consistent with their enduring needs and values, so they are more likely to attend to themselves. One might expect that people who attend to social situations would be relatively socially sensitive and skilled in perceiving other people. High self-monitors indeed are attuned to subtle cues of social context and to other people's attempts to manipulate or deceive them (Ickes & Barnes, 1977; see M. Snyder & Campbell, 1982, for references). Self-monitoring, then, is at least partly an attentional phenomenon.

So far, we have covered self-consciousness, locus of control, repression-sensitization, need for stimulation, and self-monitoring. Other individual differences that relate to attentional style have been researched most often in applied settings, to which we now turn.

Attention in Applied Settings

ATTENTION TO PHYSICAL SYMPTOMS IN TYPE A'S AND IN ATHLETES

There is some truth to the stereotype of the hard-driving business executive who is aiming for a heart attack at age 45. As we noted in Chapter 5, "Psychological Control," research on the Type A coronary-prone behavior pattern indicates that Type A people aggressively struggle against time, constantly pushing themselves to accomplish more and more, faster and faster (Friedman & Rosenman, 1974). Type A's experience time as passing faster than do Type B's; they interrupt other people to complete their sentences for them; they work at top speed even without deadlines; and they become aggressive when frustrated (Glass, 1977). In short, Type A's are impatience personified.

One central attribute of the Type A pattern is attentional style (Matthews, 1982). Type A's focus more on stimuli that are central to the task at hand and less on stimuli that are peripheral (Humphries, Carver, & Neumann, 1983; Matthews & Brunson, 1979). To the extent that this strategy keeps them from being distracted by trivia, it is adaptive. An executive who can write reports on the airplane quite simply accomplishes more. To the extent that the ignored peripheral stimuli include the Type A's own physical ailments, such a relentlessly task-oriented focus is hardly adaptive.

Type A's do in fact report less fatigue and fewer physical symptoms when they are working (Carver, Coleman, & Glass, 1976; Weidner & Matthews, 1978). Consequently, they may delay reporting health problems at the critical early stages, when timely treatment could still prevent a seriously disabling illness. And Type A's may not use symptoms to monitor their later behavior when the doctor has prescribed a treatment such as occasional naps to relieve fatigue. Moreover, the Type A's intensely focused attention is accompanied by chronic levels of arousal that can strain the cardiovascular system (Matthews & Brunson, 1979). In sum, then, Type A's are efficiently hyperalert, but they neglect "minor," task-irrelevant cues such as physical symptoms, which potentially endanger their lives.

It might seem odd that attention would play such an important role in symptom reporting, but there is considerable evidence that under many other circumstances people simply do not notice their physical symptoms. Research indicates that attention in fact is crucial in the awareness of physical symptoms. People who are distracted often feel less pain and fatigue, and consequently they can perform better for the same level of felt discomfort. In one study testing this idea, some people ran on a cross-country course, where the scenery changed constantly; they ran faster than others who ran the same distance on a track, where the externally boring environment presumably left them nothing to notice but how tired they were. Both groups reported feeling equally worn out at the end of the run, but the cross-country course allowed one group to run faster for the same amount of experienced discomfort (Pennebaker & Lightner, 1980). Furthermore, the symptoms people do notice are likely to be determined by their own prior theories about how they should feel (Leventhal, Nerenz, & Straus, 1980; Pennebaker & Skelton, 1981). If people expect to feel tired, they may notice the appropriate fatigue cues, but if they expect to rise above it, they may not notice them. In sum, noticing and interpreting one's physical state is heavily determined by selective attention, whether one is a Type A or not (cf. McCaul & Haugtvedt, 1982; Mullen & Suls, 1982).

Physical sensations can, of course, be sufficiently salient so as over-whelmingly to require one's attention, but it depends on what else is going on. Sitting comfortably in your favorite chair reading this book, you may not be able to imagine ignoring truly severe pain. But consider the many athletes who have played out a crucial game while running about on a broken leg. Differential attention is part of the key. If the external environment is demanding enough, one simply may not notice one's internal state. Given a quieter external environment, one is more likely to notice symptoms.

MANAGING ANXIETY

Inward and outward attentional focus are implicated in other types of performance besides athletics. People who are anxious about exams sometimes sabotage their own performance by thinking more about their own feelings than about the task at hand. Test-anxious people are especially likely to be self-focused and even more so during exams. Since anxiety reduces the range of cues attended to (Easterbrook, 1959), test-anxious people find that their precious attentional resources are even more limited than usual, precisely when they can ill afford to be worrying instead of working. In psychologists' attempts to explain the mechanism of test anxiety, it appears that attention to one's own anxiety—that is, worry—is more debilitating than the arousal produced by the anxiety (e.g., Morris & Liebert, 1970; Wine, 1971).

The thoughts the worried people might be thinking are likely to include how badly they expect to do and how much they are to blame for their failures (Gren, 1977; Sarason & Stoops, 1978). Furthermore, their task-related effort will be a direct function of whether they expect to do well or badly. Since self-attention exaggerates such positive or negative outcome expectancies (Carver, Blaney, & Scheier, 1979), the prognosis is poor for pessimistic and self-preoccupied test-anxious people. Expecting the worst and dwelling on in-adequacies fosters low self-esteem, self-attention, and poor performance in settings other than exams (Brockner, 1979a, 1979b; Brockner & Hulton, 1978). The vicious cycle *can* be arrested by focusing attention away from the derogated self and onto the task. Accordingly, the best short-term advice for a bad case of performance nerves is to ignore them and get to work.

Other dysfunctional behavior also can be cured by attentional strategies, at least in the short term. Consider Mark, a person with a chronic stuttering problem. He feels as if he has no control over his behavior, which makes matters worse. Every time he stammers in public, he may berate himself for being inarticulate, and perhaps he blames it on his own lack of effort or ability to deal constructively with his anxiety. If Mark attributes his stuttering problem to himself, he builds up a negative self-image. Added to that is the fact that it is always the most stressful situations that bring out his stammering in the worst way. Given the stress, loss of control, and self-deprecation, Mark becomes even more anxious, which of course exacerbates his problem (Storms & McCaul, 1976).

The more a person ruminates about some types of dysfunctional behavior, such as stuttering, the worse the behaviors get. Many problems with a physiological outcome—such as stuttering, insomnia, or impotence—are especially likely to be exacerbated by dwelling on them. Addictions such as overeating, alcoholism, and smoking can also occur in such self-defeating cycles. A third class of problems likely to fall into this category are behaviors that require focused attention. As anyone who has ever tried to park a car with an audience knows, driving (as well as test taking) is sabotaged by one's attention directed to one's inadequate performance, especially when attention would be directed more profitably toward the task itself. Shifting one's attention away from the problem is not a permanent cure, of course. It may work well in the short run and keep the problem from getting worse, but long-run solutions may require more permanent methods, such as outside help.

ATTENTION AND TRANSGRESSION

The central point underlying the effects of attention on various forms of behavior seems to be that people act on whatever norms are made salient, especially when forced to reflect on themselves. Children who are reminded of the norm to take only one Halloween candy and who are made to feel self-conscious are less likely to transgress the norm (Beaman, Klentz, Diener, & Svanum, 1979). College students are less likely to cheat on exams when they are self-aware (Diener & Wallbom, 1976), presumably since the salient norm is against cheating. When competitive norms are emphasized, self-aware students cheat more (Vallacher & Solodky, 1979). Similar effects are obtained with aggression. When the salient norms condone aggression, self-aware people are more aggressive, and when the salient norms prohibit aggression, self-aware people are less aggressive (Carver, 1974; Scheier et al., 1974).

As we noted earlier, in any situation it is important to predict ahead of time exactly which norms are to be considered salient. Even an explicit statement of the standards desired by some authority figure does not guarantee what the salient standards will be. A course instructor can give an impromptu lecture on honesty in the classroom, but if the whole school is geared toward intense competition for limited places in prestigious graduate and professional schools, a different standard may prevail.

Summary

Encoding consists of taking in external stimuli and creating internal representations of them. Attention can be occupied by whatever is being encoded or by material retrieved from long-term memory.

Stimuli that typically attract attention have specific features that make them salient relative to the environment. Thus stimuli that are statistically or contextually novel, negative, or extreme, and relatively bright, moving, or complex all are salient. Stimuli that deviate from prior expectations are salient, too. Salience also can be created by direct manipulations of physical perspective or instruction. The effects of salience include concentrated attention, exaggerated ratings of causality, extreme evaluations, stereotyping, and polarized impressions.

Vividness effects are not as accepted as salience effects. Although it is intuitively appealing that emotional, concrete, and proximal stimuli would especially have impact, the research evidence on vividness is incomplete and inconsistent. Case histories do carry more weight than statistics, but probably for reasons other than their vividness. Vivid information may well be memorable and entertaining, and vivid information may catch the attention of people who have an already existing need, increasing the possibility of their thinking they have been persuaded. Possibly vivid information catches attention but does not persuade. Vivid stimuli may have a greater impact when they compete for differential attention with dull stimuli, that is, under conditions that mimic the bustle of everyday life. In both areas of research—salience and vividness—differential attention appears to be the key. Attention to novel stimuli or to emotionally involving stimuli does not operate in absolute terms. Rather, attentional effects operate by selective focus on one stimulus in preference to another.

The mechanisms by which attention affects judgment may be several. Enhanced recall of salient or vivid stimuli is not a necessary condition for attentional effects. Causally prominent features of stimuli are overrepresented in memory and in ratings; that is, dominant behavior captures attention, is memorable, and influences judgments. Some psychologists who offer explanations for salience effects lean more toward cognitive and inferential activity at encoding; others deny the role of such activity and emphasize strictly perceptual processes. One point of consensus, however, is clear: considerable organization occurs at encoding rather than later.

Self-awareness research describes the effects of attention to various aspects of the self and the environment. When people self-attend, they compare themselves to salient standards and adjust their behavior accordingly, if possible. Standards may be positive or negative, and different standards may be salient at different times. If adjustment to the salient standard is not possible, people try to escape the self-focusing situation.

In addition to various situational manipulations of attention, individual differences in attentional style influence inferences and behavior. Self-consciousness refers to the dispositional counterpart of self-awareness; it divides into public self-consciousness (awareness of oneself as a social object) and private self-consciousness (awareness of one's internal experiences). Other individual differences in attentional style include locus of control, repression-sensitization, need for stimulation, and self-monitoring. All influence where people direct their attention and accordingly the stimuli people use to make judgments.

Attentional phenomena provide useful insights into a range of applied situations. In health psychology, Type A (coronary-prone) individuals have been shown to be hyperalert to task cues and remarkably insensitive to peripheral cues, including their own physical symptoms. In achievement settings, attention to one's own test anxiety interferes with attention to the task at hand, which then sabotages performance. As with other acts, cheating is determined by attention to salient standards of morality, competition, and the like. In each case, the problem can be solved partially by teaching people to redirect their attention to the desired stimuli (i.e., their own symptoms, the task itself, positive moral standards).

Locating the pervasive effects of attention depends on closing the gap between internal processes and their observable effects, which continues to be both a methodological and a conceptual challenge.

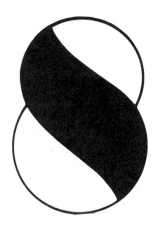

How wonderful, how very wonderful the operations of time, and the changes of the human
mind! . . . If any one faculty of our nature may
be called *more* wonderful than the rest, I do
think it is memory. There seems something
more speakingly incomprehensible in the
powers, the failures, the inequalities of mem-
ory, than in any other of our intelligences. The memory is sometimes so
retentive, so serviceable, so obedient: at others, so bewildered and so
weak; and at others again, so tyrannic, so beyond control. We are, to be
sure, a miracle every way; but our powers of recollecting and of forgetting
do seem peculiarly past finding out. (Austen, 1922, p. 172)

person memory

The human mind indeed is wonderful, but memory is no longer "peculiarly
past finding out." Cognitive psychologists have made considerable progress in
understanding memory. Of all the cognitive exports to social cognition
research, memory ranks as a top theoretical and methodological orientation.
Social cognitive researchers often infer cognitive structures and processes from
retrieval processes. Even attentional processes are sometimes inferred from
retrieval, as we saw in the preceding chapter. But memory storage and retrieval
are not simple processes, as we will see in this chapter.

In this chapter we first examine how people remember complex social
events. An eyewitness to a mugging, for example, has a lot of details to keep
straight. Current models of memory suggest how people succeed and fail.
Second, we address the wide range of content in social memory; different types
of content (e.g., appearance, behavior, traits) may be stored in different ways.
Third, we investigate context: what people remember is influenced by the
contexts in which they initially encode and later retrieve the information.
Important features of the context include the person's current task purpose, the
person's prior psychological context (i.e., other information he or she has been
thinking about), and the organization the person brings to the information.
Finally, we consider the complex relationship of memory to other cognitive
processes (in particular, attention and inference).

Basic Features of Memory

Suppose you are standing at a busy intersection waiting for the light to change. Across the street, you see a young man knock down an elderly woman, grab her purse, and run away. By the time you can get across the street, he is long gone, so you turn your attention to her. Just as you have discovered that she is angry but unhurt, a police officer arrives and takes down your description of what happened. How is this event stored in your memory?

PROPOSITIONAL NETWORKS: THE MOST COMMON MEMORY MODEL

In the last chapter on attention, we noted that encoding is the process of taking in raw data and creating a mental representation of it. The exact format of that representation is called a memory code. A variety of possible codes will be discussed later, but the one most commonly discussed is called a *propositional network*. The most usual propositional accounts agree on some basic points (J. R. Anderson, 1976; Rumelhart, Lindsay, & Norman, 1972; Wickelgren, 1981; see J. R. Anderson, 1980a, or D. A. Norman, 1976, for a more general overview of memory research). There are other theories of memory structure, but the propositional model is the best developed. First, the usual accounts suppose the events can be stored as a series of propositions. For example, "The woman stands on the corner" is one proposition; others are "The woman is elderly," "The man knocks down the woman," and so forth. Each proposition consists of a set of nodes and links, in which each node is an idea (a noun, verb, or adjective), and each link is the relation between ideas. Early versions of this model were described in Chapter 6 ("Social Schemata"), when the simple associationist models were described.

Figure 8.1 shows the propositional model applied to part of the mugging story. Although the notation is complex (see Fig. 8.1 for details), it illustrates three critical features of current memory models. One critical feature of current models of human memory is that they are *associative*; that is, most refer to associations between nodes (the woman) linked to other nodes (elderly). The associative feature of a propositional code has implications for important interpersonal events. Suppose you were called in to give eyewitness testimony on the mugging case. The organization of long-term memory into an associative node-link structure means that you will recall related facts together. That is, if you start out thinking about the woman herself, it may be easier to recall her attributes (e.g., elderly, standing on the corner) than to recall the man's attributes (e.g., young). One practical prediction of associative memory models, then, is that you will tend to recall related events together.

Moreover, the associative links are *directional*; for example, it might be easier to remember all the facts, if you go from the node for the woman to the node representing the corner on which she stood, rather than vice versa. Thus, if someone a year later asked you, "Where was that elderly mugging victim standing?" you could answer more easily than if asked, "Who was standing on that corner last year?" A third important feature of current associative theories

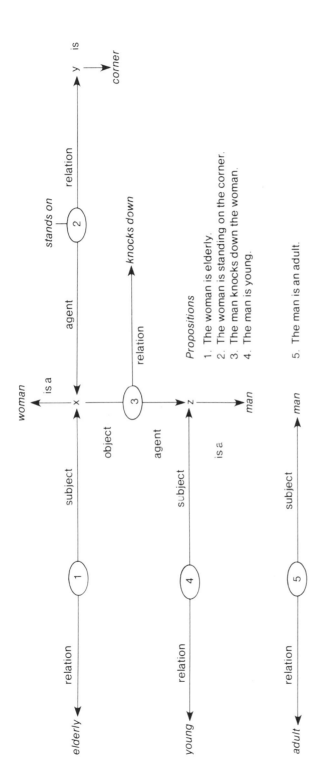

Fig. 8.1 Propositional network model for knowledge that "The elderly woman standing on the corner is knocked down by the young man." (After J. R. Anderson, 1980a) Each separate proposition is indicated by an ellipse. For example, the first proposition ("The woman is elderly") is represented by the nodes and links on the upper left of the figure. The numbered ellipses indicate the other propositions. Starting at ellipse 1, anything connected by arrows moving away from the ellipse is part of that particular proposition. For example, "elderly" and "woman" both are connected to the ellipse by arrows from it and to them. But "stood on" is not part of the first proposition; accordingly, the link from the ellipse labeled "1" to "stood on" is interrupted by an arrow pointing the wrong way. The other notation that needs explaining is the use of x, y, and z. They indicate that x is one particular woman, who is also elderly. If the proposition were "Women are elderly" (i.e., the entire category of women is elderly), the x would be replaced by the word "woman" in the figure. For example, the proposition "The man is an adult" (true of all men) would be denoted differently than "This particular man is young" (see propositions 4 and 5 in the figure). For present purposes, the notation illustrates the precision with which details of meaning can be represented in a propositional network.

is that the links are *labeled*. If asked who (agent) mugged whom (object), you would have the proper relationships stored in memory. Memory can be used to answer the question at hand by using the appropriately labeled links.

A fourth feature of propositional memory models is that the links are strengthened each time they are *activated*. That is, recall proceeds by your starting at one point (e.g., the woman) and activation spreading along links between the nodes. Every time you recall that the woman was elderly, for example, that activates both nodes in memory ("elderly" and "woman"), strengthening the link between them. There are practical implications to the point that the links among ideas are strengthened by their joint activation. If you frequently rehearse (that is, mentally repeat) your testimony, you are less likely to forget any of the practiced details because they have been activated often and the links to them are strong. Note, however, that you are also less likely to remember unrehearsed facts, since the links to those are weak in comparison to the links among the rehearsed events. The lawyer preparing you to be a witness is likely to know that frequent reviews of the testimony ahead of time will strengthen its coherence and avoid awkward surprises, such as your remembering new events on the witness stand. For related reasons, lawyers worry about delayed trials. Witnesses disappear eventually, of course, but equally important, even if available, they forget. Forgetting depends in part on the recency of activating (thinking about) any given idea. Hence a smart lawyer prepares the witness shortly before the trial, as well as at spaced intervals before that, to take advantage of both recent and frequent activation.

To review, propositional models of memory share the assumptions that memory consists of nodes for ideas and associative links among the nodes. The associative links are posited to be directional, labeled, and strengthened by activation.

SHORT-TERM MEMORY AND LONG-TERM MEMORY

Another critical feature of many current memory models is the idea that there is a long-term memory and a short-term (or working) memory. So far, we have been discussing the propositional structure of long-term memory. In many current memory models, the activated portion of long-term memory represents consciousness. That is, the long-term memory nodes that are currently most active make up the contents of focal attention. Memory retrieval consists of activating the appropriate nodes, which brings them to consciousness, if activation is above a certain threshold. Because the most active nodes can change rapidly, the conscious part of long-term memory (that is, what you are thinking about right now) is called the short-term memory. Things move in and out of consciousness or short-term memory as they become activated and deactivated. There appears to be a limited capacity for activation, which means that short-term memory is quite limited in scope. In other words, few things can be held in mind simultaneously.

The consequences of the rather severe limits on short-term memory can be illustrated by a lawyer's questioning a witness on the stand. A witness will be unable to keep lots of details in mind at once, so the person may contradict earlier testimony that is out of his or her current consciousness. Short-term memory is normally assumed to hold about seven items of information. An "item" of information could be as small as a single letter or digit, or it could be a "chunk" of letters (i.e., a word on the mugger's sweatshirt) or a chunk of digits (i.e., the time on your watch). In practical terms, the limits of short-term memory mean that people can pay attention to only a few things at a time. One solution to having too many things to process at once is to attend to them each in turn.

In contrast to the limits of short-term memory, the capacity of the overall network of long-term memory storage seems, practically speaking, to be limitless. A lawyer who urges a witness to struggle to remember crucial details may be banking on this: the information is all there; it is only a question of finding it. For long-term memory, the issue is not capacity (or how much one knows) but retrieval (whether or not one can find it). As we will see, many models of social memory are concerned primarily with how retrieval is influenced by the organization of long-term memory and by the links among items.

EPISODIC AND SEMANTIC MEMORY

Long-term memory sometimes is viewed as containing two types of information: *episodic* and *semantic*. Episodic memory refers to specific events or concrete experiences, and semantic memory refers to the meaning of concepts at a more general level. When memory is viewed as a hierarchy, episodic memory is at the most concrete, lower levels, and semantic memory is at the more general, upper levels. For example, the particular mugging you witnessed would be stored as an episodic memory, while your overall ideas about muggings would be stored as part of semantic memory. Although all cognitive psychologists do not agree on this distinction, social cognition researchers have found it useful, as we will see later. One practical result of memory ranging from single episodes or events to general semantic concepts is that memory for the general concept can intrude on memory for the specific episode. For example, if you generally expect elderly mugging victims to be helpless, you may mistakenly recall that this particular woman made no special effort to resist the mugger, whether or not she actually did. Note that this principle also is supported by much of the research discussed as evidence for schemata (Chapter 6).

Lawyers also seem to know about the continuum of episodic and semantic memory. An unscrupulous or careless attorney may ask subtly leading questions that take advantage of semantic memory intruding on episodic memory. For example, in the mugging case, an attorney might ask if you recall "the woman falling down while she was standing near the parked cars," although in fact there were no parked cars. However, it is a reasonable inference from semantic memory that there must have been parked cars at the corner. Even though the phrase "parked cars" is tangential to the question, and you answer simply by describing her fall, the damage has been done. If later asked whether or not there were cars parked at the corner, the typical witness may confuse the mention of them in prior questioning with their actual presence at the scene of the crime (Loftus, 1979). Similarly, if a witness examines a preliminary lineup, the person may later remember having seen one of the suspects before but not distinguish between the occasion of the lineup and that of the mugging. The (innocent) suspect may be misidentified as the mugger because he is familiar.

SUMMARY

To review, many psychologists think long-term memory consist of networks of ideas, with associative links among related nodes. They assume the links are directional, labeled, and strengthened by activation. The activated nodes enter into consciousness or short-term memory, which has a rather limited capacity. Long-term memory has a quite large capacity, in contrast. It is posited to be organized in hierarchical clusters of related knowledge. Some of the lower levels of the hierarchy are specific episodic memory, and the upper levels are conceptual semantic memory. Conceptual knowledge has a tendency to dominate specific memories. The basic features of memory have specific implications for what is called person memory—that is, what one remembers about other people—as we will see in the remainder of the chapter.

Contents of Person Memory

Human beings are incredibly rich stimuli. To appreciate this, imagine what you have stored in memory about your mother. Where could you begin to describe her? You could start with what she looks like, but even that is difficult. Her appearance depends on whether she is happy or sad, awake or tired, at a formal or informal occasion. And then what is her behavior like? That too depends on the situation. Your memory for her personality, attitudes, and relationships is even harder to characterize. If people, especially those we know well, seem so multifaceted, how does memory do them justice?

Several attempts to catalog the contents of person memory have revealed its richness. People can retrieve from memory quantities of detail about the *appearance, behavior,* and *traits* of other people (S. T. Fiske & Cox, 1979; Ostrom, 1975). In one study of people describing others, people mentioned appearance first and then moved to traits and behaviors (S. T. Fiske & Cox, 1979). People started their descriptions with the most concrete, observable features and moved to abstract, inferable features. It would seem that one useful way to think about the range of person information is to consider a continuum from wholly observables (e.g., appearance) to strictly inferables (e.g., traits). People may be cautious about inferables; they are more willing to report their inferences about the traits of people familiar to them than inferences about the traits of strangers. No such differences exist for appearance. However, even in descriptions of strangers, traits are more common than behaviors. Of course, descriptions do not reflect all that people remember, since they may not be totally candid about what is in their minds (D. J. Schneider, 1977). For example, it could be that people actually do make and store many trait attributions about strangers but are less confident or more reluctant to say so.

Most research on social memory concerns the traits of strangers, largely because those are the most practical stimuli for laboratory research. Because traits are the most common stimuli, we begin the next section with them, then consider behavior, and then appearance. One important possibility that emerges from reviewing the contents of person memory is that the propositional code most commonly assumed by memory researchers may fit trait information better than behavior and appearance information (cf. Hastie & Carlson, 1980).

MEMORY FOR TRAITS: INFORMATION
STORED IN PROPOSITIONAL CODES

Traits are not directly observable; people do not walk around with signs labeling their personalities. Traits are abstract; they may be inferred from appearance and behavior or from other traits. Trait inference is a complex process, and attribution theory (Chapters 2-4) is concerned in a large part with that complex process. Many researchers believe that, once inferred, traits are stored in propositional networks of the sort described above. The proposition, as noted earlier, is the format or code in which trait information is stored. To date, there is no particular reason to assume traits differ from other abstract nonsocial knowledge in the way they are encoded (although no research has addressed this point specifically). We will see that other kinds of social knowledge may be stored in other codes.

The way people organize their trait knowledge in memory seems to have some unique qualities of its own. When people are asked to report which traits generally go together or which imply each other, two main dimensions emerge. Personality attributes fall along one continuum of *social desirability* and another of *competence* (Rosenberg & Sedlak, 1972; D. J. Schneider, 1973; Schneider, Hastorf, & Ellsworth, 1979). Terms like *warm, pleasant,* and *sociable* appear near each other and those like *intelligent, industrious,* and *determined* also appear near each other, in people's mental maps of the personality domain. For many of us, then, the two crucial things that organize our memory for someone else's traits are answers to these questions: Is this person friendly and fun? and What is this person good at? However, there are some exceptions to the general rule that people organize their trait knowledge by sociability and competence; some people may group their trait knowledge instead by its relevance to integrity, attractiveness, maturity, and so on (Kim & Rosenberg, 1980).

MEMORY FOR BEHAVIOR: A TEMPORAL CODE?

Behavioral information may be stored in a propositional code, as is trait information, but some researchers believe behavior instead may be stored another way because of the kind of information it is. Behavior has a built-in temporal feature. That is, to remember behavior requires remembering a series of things in a certain order. As with scripts or event schemata (Chapter 6), there is sequential information, and there are enabling conditions. To return to the mugging example, the behaviors involved are sequential (the man approached the woman, then the man knocked down the woman, etc. See Fig. 8.2). Some of the behaviors also are enabling conditions for the next behavior (he knocked her down in order to take her purse) and some are not (he took her purse, and then he ran away). Because of the sequential and enabling aspects of a series of behaviors, it may be more convenient to think of behavior as stored in a temporal code. A temporal code may represent a second type of memory code, in addition to propositional code, which preserves sequential information (cf. J. R. Anderson, 1982; Schank & Abelson, 1977).

At a minimum, we can safely say that behavioral information and trait information differ in level of abstraction. This difference emerges in two respects. First, as noted earlier, behavior lies toward the concrete, observable end, and traits lie toward the abstract, inferable end of person attributes. There is a second, related difference in the relative abstraction of traits and behaviors. In terms of the distinctions among different sorts of memory, behaviors resemble episodic memory, while traits resemble semantic memory. That is, remembering a behavior is influenced both by its basis in direct observation and by its being a specific, one-time event. For example, remembering that the mugger shouted at the elderly victim is not based on inference but on observation, and it is a single, unique episode in memory. Both features make it a more concrete memory. In contrast, remembering the mugger as hostile is based on inference from his behavior, and it is a piece of general semantic knowledge about people who shout. Both features make the trait a more abstract memory. Because traits are more abstract, they are more economical and general than behaviors (R. B. Allen & Ebbesen, 1981; Carlston, 1980; Ostrom, Lingle, Pryor, & Geva, 1980). Behavior is a less efficient piece of information to store than is a trait, precisely because it is episodic and concrete. Thus it is not surprising that people typically report traits more than behavior in describing others, and that person memory researchers study traits more often than behaviors.

MEMORY FOR APPEARANCE: AN ANALOG CODE?

A third type of content in person memory is appearance. As we will see, most of the standard person memory research mentioned in the remainder of the chapter concerns traits (and to some extent behavior) but neglects appearance. The essential features of memory for appearance are that it is quite basic, extremely accurate under some conditions, and may be stored in yet a third code.

At the most concrete level of person memory, the appearance of another person constitutes a quite basic, crucial set of data that allows us to recognize the person. For example, you may recognize the mugger in a lineup by the odd shape of his beard. Appearance also allows us to make new trait inferences and to cue old ones. For example, if the mugger has muscular legs, you may infer

M = young man
W = elderly woman
P = purse
E = enabling link (see text)

M   approached   W
          ↓ E
M   knocked down   W
          ↓ E
M   took   P
          ↓
M   ran away

Fig. 8.2 A sequential representation of a mugging.

that he is athletic (Secord, 1958). Alternatively, his riotously disheveled hair may remind you of an old friend who was impulsive and undisciplined, and you may transfer that assumption to the new person (Secord, 1958). Appearance also prompts emotional reactions; for example, people assume physically attractive others to be especially sociable and competent, and they often like them as a consequence (Berscheid & Walster, 1978). If the mugger were especially unattractive, you might find him even more repulsive than otherwise. Finally, the importance of appearance in social settings is shown by the impact of individual differences in the ability to process visual information about others. That is, people who tend to form vivid mental images of others can have more accurate memories for other social information than do nonvivid imagers (Swann & Miller, 1982). It seems that being good at imagining people's appearance also enables one to remember their behavior and other characteristics.

The distinctiveness and importance of appearance in the stored impressions we have of others is further illustrated by the resilience of memory for faces. Laboratory studies reveal that people's ability to recognize faces is just short of phenomenal, with close to 100 percent accuracy over long periods of time (T. G. R. Bower, 1970; Freides, 1974; Neisser, 1967). The reasons for the strength of visual memory are not entirely clear, but one possibility is that visual stimuli do not attract attention as automatically as do other stimuli. That is, a bright flash may not draw attention as quickly as a loud noise. Moreover, processing visual information requires that one actively orient one's eyes toward the stimulus, while processing auditory information does not require that one actively orient one's ears. To compensate for these weaknesses in visual information processing, people may bias toward thorough encoding of visual cues, as a general strategy (Posner, Nissen, & Klein, 1976); this bias toward visual cues may enhance memory for faces.

Curiously, the laboratory results on the accuracy of memory for faces are contradicted by real-world research on eyewitness testimony; people often do little better than guess when attempting to identify an alleged criminal in a lineup (Loftus, 1979). To make matters worse, jurors and the witnesses themselves do not seem to be aware of the unreliability of eyewitness reports (Wells, Lindsay, & Tousignant, 1980). What does the contradiction between laboratory studies of recognition memory and real-world studies of eyewitness accuracy imply about memory for appearance? Differences in the two settings may explain the contradiction. In the laboratory, stimuli are not moving, distractions are minimal, emotions and arousal are virtually absent, viewing conditions are unobscured and well lit, no strong prior theories interfere, and so on. In eyewitness research, the volatile and confusing features of actual settings are retained, and memory not surprisingly is garbled. The difference is roughly like that between trying to remember the face of someone who ambushed you in a dark alley and trying to recognize a face you stare at in the library, with full daylight, complete leisure, and no emotional intrusions. Of course, the library face should be easier to remember accurately.

Another factor that sometimes can make eyewitness identification worse than identification in the laboratory is that cross-race accuracy is far worse than own-race accuracy (Malpass & Kravitz, 1969). This difference may be because people react more superficially to those of another race (Chance & Goldstein, 1981). And, indeed, superficial encoding does hurt memory for faces (G. H. Bower & Karlin, 1974); that is, the less thought you give to people when you meet them, the less likely you are to remember their faces accurately. Besides paying closer attention to people of your own race, another factor that affects cross-racial identification is one's experience with members of the other race; cross-race experience improves accuracy (Brigham, Maass, Snyder, & Spaulding, 1982). In all, because crimes against people are often rapid, unexpected, confusing, and sometimes against people of another race, perhaps the low levels of eyewitness accuracy are not surprising. Even when totally wrong, however, people retain some sort of mental images for the appearance of others. How is this visual information represented?

To this point, we have assumed that a propositional code characterizes memory for traits and a sequential code may characterize memory for behaviors. Several theorists have suggested another code, such that memory for visual details is stored in what is called an *analog code* (Kosslyn & Pomerantz, 1977; Paivio, 1971; Shepard & Podgorny, 1978). Analog representations preserve the continuous quantitative relationships of the information depicted. A mercury thermometer is an analog representation of temperature; a longer column of mercury represents a greater amount of heat. A digital thermometer is not an analog representation because it simply provides a symbolic readout (in digits) whose form is unrelated to the thing it represents. Dial-faced watches also are analogs, in that each movement of the hands represents a given quantity of time; a change of 90 degrees represents twice as much time as a change of 45 degrees. Digital watches, in contrast, give a symbolic representation of time in digits. Analog representations of social information such as the mugging would include mental photographs, films, maps, or scale models of the event. Visual information may be stored in the form of such mental images, as opposed to propositions describing all the visual details in words.

Some of the more intriguing research to emerge from the analog approach to visual memory suggests that mental images may mimic reality in odd ways. To illustrate, try the following thought experiment. Form an image of the back of your family's house or apartment building. Make sure you have a clear, complete image in mind. Now count the windows on the top floor of the front of the building. Erase the whole image from your mind. Now imagine your family house again, but focus on the front. Count the windows again. It should seem faster and easier to count the windows if you initially focus on the front rather than if you initially focus on the back (Kosslyn, Pinker, Smith, & Shwartz, 1979). Scanning a mental image apparently takes time, and the time it takes is proportional to the time it would take to scan the thing itself (called the percept). In a sense, when you are "in the back," you have to come around to the front to count the windows, but when you are "in front" already, you can just look up and count them. The longer distance from front to back is longer both actually and mentally than the shorter distance from front to front. Thus the mental representation retains some features of, and so is a direct analog for, the percept.

Despite the empirical and intuitive basis for a separate analog (image-based) memory code, it is not totally clear that it necessarily exists. Propositional and analog models both can be made to account for scanning and other related results (J. R. Anderson, 1978, 1979; Pylyshyn, 1973, 1981); consequently, these intriguing results do not prove the existence of a special code for imagery. One basic problem is that although almost everyone has the experience of having mental images, the experience does not necessarily mean that images are codes for storing and processing information. The imagery notion holds great intuitive appeal, however, and it is often theoretically convenient to consider memory as having at least three codes, one verbal and propositional; one temporal and sequential; one visual and analog (J. R. Anderson, 1982; Hastie & Carlston, 1980).

AFFECT: A FOURTH CODE?

A major aspect of all people's social perception is affective, that is, positive versus negative reactions to social stimuli. This dominant affective factor cuts across traits, behavior, and appearance. Regardless of which other dimensions organize people's descriptions of other people (i.e., sociability, competence, integrity), the overall affective dimension emerges (Kim & Rosenberg, 1980). In their minds, people appear to group affectively positive social stimuli all together and separate from affectively negative social stimuli. The importance of the affective dimension generalizes to a wide range of stimuli (Osgood, Suci, & Tannenbaum, 1957) and to virtually all analyses of people's emotions (Chapter 11). Almost anything one remembers about another person's appearance, behavior, or traits potentially has an affective reaction linked to it. Affect's property of cutting across essentially all domains suggests that it may constitute yet another type of memory code, in addition to propositional, sequential, and image codes (Hastie & Carlston, 1980; Zajonc, Pietromonaco, & Bargh, 1982). There is to date no empirical evidence directly supporting affect as a fourth code, but it seems a likely development.

SUMMARY

The contents of person memory certainly include inferable traits, possibly stored as a propositional network. Observable behaviors also are important and may be stored in a sequential code. Finally, person memory includes appearance, perhaps stored as images in an analog code. Despite these possible differences in memory code, behaviors and traits show similar effects across a wide range of memory tasks, as we will see in the rest of this chapter. Thus it is not clear that the possible distinctions between codes for traits and behavior make a difference to most research on person memory. Finally, information about traits, behaviors, and appearance all may be organized within a framework based on affect, which will be discussed later, in Chapter 11. Besides appearance, behavior, and traits, other attributes of people are important but have received less attention: other people's attitudes, relationships, background, contexts, and more are also stored in memory, but there is no evidence on special codes for these attributes. People obviously remember enormous amounts about others; consequently, the next question is how people encode all that detail and how they retrieve it.

Contexts in Person Memory

The contexts for encoding and retrieving interpersonal information importantly determine what people remember. One sort of context concerns one's task purpose. Consider the difference between forming an impression of a new teaching assistant for the purpose of reporting back to a roommate who is considering joining that section, and trying to empathize with the teaching assistant's problems when you discover that he or she is a friend of the family and needs a shoulder to cry on. Of course, you will focus on different aspects of the person, depending on whether you are empathizing or forming an impression. You also will organize your memory differently in each case. If you are forming an impression, you need to organize your memory in terms of traits: competence, clarity, concern, wit, and the like. If you are empathizing, you need to organize your memory in terms of goals: what is the person trying to accomplish, what does the person feel like, and how can you help the person? As we shall see in the section on task purpose, different processes of comprehending others result in markedly different memories. In addition to one's purpose, prior context—that is, other things recently on one's mind—tends to prime what one remembers and how. Finally, the organization one brings to the information one is trying to remember shapes how one goes about it. We will take up each of these factors in turn: task purpose, prior context, and the material itself.

HOW TASK PURPOSE AFFECTS MEMORY

One's memory for information about other people appears to improve the more psychologically engaging and less superficial the purpose with which one approaches learning about them. As we will see, instructions to recall someone's behavior are not as helpful to memory as instructions to form an impression, which is not as helpful to memory as instructions to empathize. The most psychologically engaging task purposes of all might be comparing the other with oneself or expecting to interact with the other, and both those tasks seem to enhance memory relative to some other tasks.

A major explanation for variations in memory as a function of task is that deeper or more elaborate processing improves memory. Borrowing a concept from cognitive psychology, researchers say shallow depth of processing is typified by what are called *structural* tasks such as deciding if a word is written in capitals or in lower case letters. Medium depth is typified by *phonemic* tasks such as deciding if a word rhymes with another word. Deep processing is typified by *semantic* tasks such as deciding if a word is a synonym of another (Craik & Lockhart, 1972). The deeper the level of initial processing, the better one's subsequent memory, according to the depth of processing model.

An example may clarify this idea. Suppose you are proofreading a poem for a friend. In one instance, she has asked you merely to check the typefaces (a "structural" task), because her fancy typewriter sometimes slips into italics by accident. You could "read" the entire poem without really ever remembering its content. In another instance, she has asked you to check her rhymes and rhythm (a phonemic task), which would enable you to remember more than the structural task would. In still another instance, she asks you to read for her style, to see if it flows and if she picked the right words (a semantic task). You would remember much more of the poem because you would be attending to the meanings of the words, which is in a sense a deeper level of processing (Craik & Lockhart, 1972).

Person memory research suggests other levels of processing that depend on psychological engagement. Suppose your friend tells you the poem is all about her relationship with you; doubtless you would pay close attention and remember it rather well indeed, as you judged whether or not you thought it actually applied to you. As we will see, the more psychologically involving one's purpose in processing information, the more memorable it is likely to be. Depth of processing is one explanation for this phenomenon, although it has some limitations, as we will see later.

Forming impressions versus memorizing One might expect that people best remember others when they are explicitly asked to memorize aspects of the other's behavior. Quite the contrary turns out to be the case. People told to remember details about another person may actually remember *less* than people who are merely forming an impression of that person (D. L. Hamilton, 1981b; D. L. Hamilton, Katz, & Leirer, 1980a, 1980b; Hartwick, 1979; Srull, 1981, 1983; Wyer & Gordon, 1982).

The superiority of an impression task over a memory task is supported by a series of studies in which subjects were given instructions either to memorize or to form an impression of a series of behaviors (D. L. Hamilton *et al.*, 1980b). Subjects read a list that included items such as "had a dinner party for some friends last week," "helped a woman fix her bicycle," "checked some books out of the library," and "wrote an articulate letter to his congressman." Subjects who simply were memorizing by rote recalled fewer items than subjects who were trying to form an impression.

Why should forming an impression enhance memory? Forming an impression of someone requires the perceiver to make sense of many individual items of information; the perceiver typically tries to form a coherent whole. For example, this may involve fitting the individual items of information to a preexisting person schema involving traits or goals (Chapter 6). It turns out that the same coherent organization that helps people to make sense of another person also aids memory. In deciding how someone can be simultaneously brave and deceitful, one is forced to elaborate, explain, and make connections to other things in memory. One creates links among the to-be-remembered items in memory. Such links increase the alternative retrieval routes; that is, the more links one creates to an item in memory, the more likely it is to be recalled (e.g., J. R. Anderson, 1974, 1980a).

A series of studies supports the idea that forming an impression causes people to organize the information by linking it to prior interpersonal knowledge. In one study, subjects forming an impression organized their memories into clusters representing different categories of information, such as abilities, interpersonal characteristics, and interests (D. L. Hamilton, 1981b). In the list above, for example, one might cluster together the behavior that fits with the trait competent (library, congressman). Other research concurs that perceivers forming an impression tend to organize by trait categories (Hoffman, Mischel, & Mazze, 1981; Jeffery & Mischel, 1979). Thus, forming an impression encourages organization in terms of psychologically meaningful categories, and in terms of traits in particular.

Memory instructions have a rather different effect from impression instructions. Research shows that subjects have various different organizational strategies for memorizing social information; in particular, memory task subjects appear to use more variable organizational strategies. For example, in one study, subjects told to memorize the above list did not cluster the behavior in the same way as did impression subjects (D. L. Hamilton, 1981a). It is hard to know what organizational strategy those particular memory subjects used, but sometimes subjects think up arbitrary mnemonic devices. For example, a person might think of a key word in each sentence that matches the first four letters of the alphabet: *articulate, bicycle, checked out, dinner*. Since the mnemonic is arbitrary, it might not work very well, although it is certainly better than nothing.

Alternatively, in other studies, subjects sometimes organize by whatever the stimulus materials make salient, that is, by traits, situations, or goals, depending on what is most available (Hoffman *et al.*, 1981; Jeffery & Mischel, 1979). This can lead memory subjects in some settings to outperform impression subjects, contrary to the more usual effect. One reason for this is that some materials make goals especially salient. Goals can be particularly effective devices for recall because they are specific. Goals create direct links in memory both to a specific situation and within a sequence of behavior. For example, if you organize your memory by the idea that John had the goal to make friends with his neighbor Jane, that creates fairly specific links in memory to his helping repair her bicycle and having a dinner party (assuming she was invited). In contrast, Mischel and his colleagues argue that traits are more general than goals, so they are less distinctive retrieval cues. If you organize your memory by a trait, for example, that someone performed several sociable behaviors, that is not much help because he could be sociable in many different situations and toward many different people. One implication of the superiority of goals over traits as aids to memory is that when memory task subjects are given materials that fit a goal better than a trait, they may outperform impression-oriented subjects because they are flexible enough to use goals when it is more appropriate to the materials.

Thus the impression-set advantage can be reversed (Hoffman *et al.*, 1981) for some people with some stimulus materials. The point, then, is that a memory task creates more variable and flexible organizational strategies, while an impression task encourages organization by traits. Organization by traits is likely to be superior to most arbitrary strategies that subjects think up on their own, but inferior to a goal-based strategy when the to-be-remembered material particularly fits a goal-based organization.

In sum, people forming impressions use psychologically meaningful categories—traits in particular—to organize their memories. Most of the time, this strategy is to their advantage. Relative to psychologically irrelevant mnemonics (e.g., alphabetical order), traits appear effective. Sometimes, however, traits may be relatively ineffective bases for organizing person memory; for example, goals can be more effective bases for organizing memory. Effectiveness depends in part on the nature of the material to be recalled. In the majority of cases, though, the task purpose of forming an impression aids memory. When asked to form an impression, people organize information about others into a single coherent personality portrait (cf. Asch, 1946; D. L. Hamilton, 1981a; Ostrom, Pryor, & Simpson, 1981; Chapter 6, "Social Schemata"). When asked to memorize, they use other strategies that do not necessarily depend on a coherent analysis of personality. On average, people forming impressions remember information about others better than do people memorizing. Table 8.1 summarizes this research and that of the next three sections.

Empathizing   If forming an impression requires more psychological engagement, encourages deeper processing, and is usually more effective than memorizing someone's actions, then empathizing requires even more engagement and deeper processing on the perceiver's part. Consequently, empathizing can be an even more effective memory strategy than forming an impression. Just consider the differences among (1) tracking your new roommate's morning routine, so you can coordinate using the shower conveniently (memorizing); (2) deciding whether your roommate is likable, responsible, and fun (impression); and (3) trying to understand how he or she feels about the death of a parent (empathy). Empathy usually demands far more of the social perceiver than do impressions and memory. Empathy is defined as the ability to share in another's feelings; empathy hence requires some effort. Accordingly, people instructed to empathize remember more about the target than do people who are detached (Harvey, Yarkin, Lightner, & Town, 1980). Empathizers also make many more attributions than do detached subjects; that is, they are more likely to explain why the person behaved as he or she did. Quite probably the additional work that goes into constructing explanations improves memory; attributions provide the additional retrieval routes that increase the chances of recalling the material explained (G. H. Bower & Masling, 1978).

People empathize with another person's perspective when both are in the same mood (G. H. Bower, Gilligan, & Monteiro, 1981), have similar personalities, share cooperative goals (Hornstein, Marton, Rupp, Sole, & Tartell, 1980), or take the role of the other. As an instance of role taking, readers who keep a story character's motives in mind organize their memory on that basis; understanding someone's goals enables readers to build links among the person's various actions (Owens, Bower, & Black, 1979). If you do not know anything about Mark, then his staying up until dawn, phoning a professor, and photocopying 600 pages do not form a particularly coherent sequence. If you are told that he is trying to meet a thesis deadline, the same disconnected actions take on new meaning. Empathy promotes a focus on the other person's goals, and as we have already noted, goals provide a strong memory aid.

Taking another person's emotional perspective is not the only way to empathize. Simply taking the other person's visual perspective provides an imaged vantage point that aids recall (S. T. Fiske, Taylor, Etcoff, & Laufer, 1979). If Jenny tells you about a tennis match from her perspective, you remember the physical setting from her point of view (e.g., what her opponent looked like, the sun in her eyes, etc.). Imaginary perspective can be induced any number of ways, from direct instruction (read this story from Mary's perspective) to stylistic variations well known to novelists. A detail as subtle as "Bill came in the door and brought the newspaper over to Mary" would set up the story from Mary's perspective, in contrast to "Bill went in the door and took the newspaper over to Mary." A single consistent point of view aids recall for

TABLE 8.1
Effects of Various Task Purposes on Person Memory

Task	Effect
Memorizing	Variable memory, organized by whatever is available, including psychologically irrelevant categories
Forming impressions	Good memory, organized by traits
Empathizing	Excellent memory, organized by goals
Self-reference (comparing to oneself)	Excellent memory, organized by psychological categories (traits or goals)
Future interaction	Better memory than memorizing, effect on organization not yet clear

story details (Black, Turner, & Bower, 1979). Just as constructing an empathic perspective enhances recall for the person's motives and psychological vantage point, constructing a vicarious visual perspective enhances recall for the person's physical viewpoint. From the existing data, it is not yet clear whether vicarious visual perspective promotes a focus on the other person's goals, in the same way that taking his or her psychological perspective does.

To summarize, people's memory for other people is enhanced by empathy and role taking, perhaps because they promote a focus on the person's goals, which improves memory. Empathy can be induced by sharing a mood, personality, goal, or visual perspective.

Self-reference: comparisons to oneself Thus far, we have seen that increased levels of psychological engagement (deeper processing) improve memory. In moving along a continuum of task purposes from memorizing to forming an impression to empathizing, memory typically improves at each step (see Table 8.1). One of the most psychologically engaging purposes upon encountering another person might well be self-referent processing, that is, judging interpersonal information with respect to oneself. A self-referent task purpose does improve memory relative to some other task purposes (Rogers, Kuiper, & Kirker, 1977).

Why does self-referent processing improve memory? One argument is that self-reference forges links to a rich self-schema (Markus, 1977; Chapter 6) that later aids memory. Some work shows differences between self- and other-referent encoding that would be consistent with the self-schema explanation (Kuiper & Rogers, 1979). For example, in one study, subjects rated adjectives on one of four tasks: how long? (structural task), how specific? (semantic task), describes experimenter? (other-referent task), and describes self? (self-referent task). Self-referent processing produced superior recall and ratings of greater confidence and ease in making the judgment.

However, other findings challenge the view that self-schemata are necessary to explain self-referent memory advantages (G. H. Bower & Gilligan, 1979; Keenan & Baillet, 1980). Relative to memorizing, any person-oriented task (i.e., self or other referent encoding), especially when the other is familiar, may provoke more psychological engagement, deeper processing, and so improve memory. Various person-oriented tasks show organization by psychological categories, such as traits and goals, none of which necessarily relate to one's self-schema (D. L. Hamilton et al., 1980b). Thus it still remains an open possibility that the self-reference advantage is not unique to the self but would apply to encoding in any person-oriented or psychological terms.

Future interaction   The depth of processing continuum so far has included memorizing, forming an impression, empathizing, and self-reference. Taking the continuum one step further, if people are learning about another person for the purpose of interacting with the person later, that should provoke even more psychological engagement, or so-called deeper processing. Preliminary evidence suggests that expected interaction improves memory relative to the task of memorizing the other person's behavior (Srull & Brand, 1983). It appears that the expected interaction creates a more coherent impression, with many links among the items; this in turn aids memory retrieval. As more data come in, the effects of relatively high levels of psychological engagement should become clearer. The data so far are consistent with a continuum of processing depth.

Comment on depth of processing   Interpretations of task purpose based on the depth of processing idea should be qualified by the fact that depth of processing has been criticized recently (e.g., Baddeley, 1978), for several reasons. First, there may be nothing inherent in any given task that requires its necessarily eliciting shallow or deep processing. That is, one could expect to interact with another person but still process information about that person in a relatively shallow fashion. Similarly, one could memorize information but still process it in a relatively deep fashion. The point is that levels of processing are not absolute for any given task purpose; there are different levels of processing possible within any task such as memorizing, forming an impression, empathizing, self-reference, or expected interaction.

There is a second problem with the depth of processing idea and the related concept of elaborating links among to-be-remembered items: there is no consensus on independent measures of processing depth or of elaboration (Baddeley, 1978). For social cognition research, these caveats suggest that the cognitive underpinnings of task purpose effects on memory need further clarification and should be borrowed cautiously.

Summary   Several types of task purposes shape people's memory for other people. The tasks vary in the implied depth of processing and level of elaboration of links among to-be-remembered items. For instance, forming impressions of people requires more thorough processing and elaboration than does merely memorizing people's behavior; consequently, impression-task memory is typically enhanced. Empathizing involves imagining the other person's goals, and it facilitates memory because the imagined goals provide very specific links among items in memory. Imagining another person's visual perspective facilitates memory for perceptual details apparent from that person's point of view. Self-referent encoding creates memory superior to various nonsocial tasks and sometimes superior to other-referent encoding. Future interaction may create the most detailed memory of all, although there is little evidence on this point. In general, "deeper" processing improves memory, in requiring the elaboration of links to related concepts.

Task purpose effects are important because a basic assumption behind social cognition researchers' use of theories and methods from cognitive psychology's memory research is that social and nonsocial settings will be essentially parallel. The direct borrowing assumes that one remembers information the same way, regardless of whether one is learning a list of words describing a person or simply learning a list of words irrelevant to a person. Thus, for example, the differences between memory under an impression task and under a memorizing task create boundaries for directly translating some of the cognitive research to social settings.

PRIMING: THE EFFECTS OF PRIOR CONTEXT

Suppose you have just emerged from a lunchtime discussion of how relentlessly competitive students at your school can be. Walking across campus, you encounter Cliff, who enthusiastically tells you about the exam on which he just scored 100 percent. How do you interpret Cliff's motive in telling you that he set the class curve? In the context of your prior discussion, you are likely to interpret his behavior as competitive. In contrast, if you had just come from a discussion of commitment to one's work, you might interpret his behavior as justifiable pride in his achievement.

A growing research literature concerns a phenomenon called *priming*: the effects of prior context on the interpretation and retrieval of information. Priming is specifically a name for the fact that recently and frequently activated ideas come to mind more easily than ideas that have not been activated. Priming was addressed initially in Chapter 6 under the topic of schema activation, but it will be addressed in more detail here. As noted earlier, exposing people to positive or negative trait terms (e.g., adventurous versus reckless) causes people at a later time to rate and recall ambiguous behavior (e.g., shooting rapids) as correspondingly positive or negative, because of the meaning that had been primed (Higgins, Rholes, & Jones, 1977; Srull & Wyer, 1979). The prior context effect is stronger when descriptive as well as evaluative meanings are primed. That is, the ambiguous behavior is more likely to be seen as reckless when relevant negative concepts have been primed than when irrelevant negative concepts have been primed. Moreover, priming effects can operate automatically, without one's awareness (Bargh & Pietromonaco, 1982).

Priming effects have long-term as well as short-term consequences. The context of a stimulus can affect its ratings as much as a week later when it is no longer in that context (Higgins & King, 1981; Higgins et al., 1977; Srull & Wyer, 1980). This is an important point. It suggests that a transitory and perhaps arbitrary context can affect the way a stimulus is encoded permanently. If a stimulus potentially can be encoded as one of several alternative categories, short-term context may determine which category is applied in the long term. Important social categories such as race and sex can be primed in this fashion (Higgins & King, 1981). That is, if one encounters someone in the context of hearing her give a militantly feminist speech, one is especially likely to think of her in terms of her gender, rather than her profession or her race. But if she is the only short person in the room, one might think of her in terms of her height. In both cases, context determines which category is used to encode information about her into memory, and the effects of such category priming can be enduring.

Moreover, priming has effects on important social behavior. For example, one classic set of research can be interpreted as consistent with the effects of priming on aggression. When people are angry at someone, the impulse to harm the person is more likely to be carried to action when in the presence of aggressive cues. A gun lying on a nearby table provokes aggressive behavior (Berkowitz, 1974). Priming is one possible explanation of this. Priming can affect problem solving and creativity, too. In one study, subjects attempted to solve the following problem: given a candle, a book of matches, and a box of thumb tacks, how can the candle be attached to the wall so that the candle burns properly and does not drip on the floor? Some subjects, who were primed beforehand into thinking of containers as separate from their contents (e.g., tray and tomatoes versus tray of tomatoes), were able to solve the problem quickly. The configuration (container and contents as separable entities) primed related configurations and facilitated problem solving (Higgins & Chaires, 1980). The solution to the problem, incidentally, is to empty the box of tacks, treating it as a box and tacks, and to tack the box up as a platform for the candle.

Persistent differences in what is primed by one's typical situation may lead to individual differences in what is chronically primed most easily for different people. We all know people who seem to perceive everyone in terms of how smart they are, or how trustworthy, or how good-looking. People for whom a particular personality dimension is an easily and typically accessible construct are more likely to remember and describe others in those terms. For example, Higgins, King, and Mavin (1982) identified people's most typically accessible personality dimensions by observing the first and most frequent dimensions that arose in their descriptions of themselves and their friends (e.g., intelligent, witty, gracious). The dimensions that people spontaneously mention are presumably the ones that usually come to mind most easily, when the environment primes them. Dimensions that are frequently accessed or permanently primed may become central aspects of one's personality.

Priming seems to represent more of an encoding than a retrieval bias. Retrieval consists of later activating the mental representation created by encoding and bringing it to consciousness. Researchers suggest several reasons that priming seems to be more a function of encoding (see Fig. 8.3). One reason is that the priming effect decreases with wider gaps between a prime and a stimulus (row one versus row two of the figure). The wider gap presumably interferes with encoding the stimulus in terms of the prime. In one study subjects worked on a priming task that required them to use hostile words (e.g., *leg, break, arm, his*); they then read a paragraph describing Donald's behavior, which was ambiguous with regard to hostility (e.g., demanding his money back from a store, lying to avoid a blood donation). All subjects rated Donald after the priming task and the paragraph. Half the subjects experienced a delay between the paragraph and the rating (row one of the figure), and half the subjects experienced a delay between the priming task and the paragraph (row two of the figure). Priming effects were biggest in the first case, when there was a delay between the paragraph and the judgment (Srull & Wyer, 1980). This result suggests that it is important that the prime and stimulus occur in close temporal proximity.

Moreover, priming increases with wider gaps between primed stimulus and retrieval. In Fig. 8.3, row one shows larger priming effects than row three. Once having encoded the primed stimulus, the longer it sits in memory linked to that particular prime, the stronger the effect of the prime. Furthermore, primes *after* stimulus presentation have little or no effect (row four). This fact suggests that encoding a stimulus in the context of a prime is more important than retrieving it in the context of the prime (Srull & Wyer, 1980; see Chapter 6, "Social Schemata," for other references).

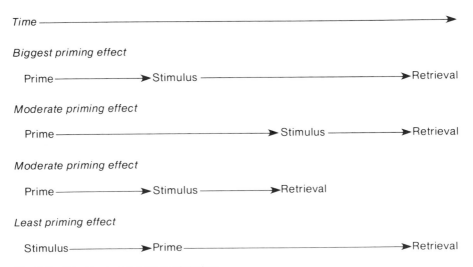

Fig. 8.3 Priming as a function of timing.

In sum, although perceivers may not know it, prior contexts have important effects in priming memory, judgment, creativity, and social behavior, both in the short and long term.

THE ORGANIZATION OF SOCIAL INFORMATION IN MEMORY

So far, we have discussed features surrounding the stimulus that shape how it is remembered. Task purpose and prior context both affect the organization and accessibility of person memory, as we have seen. A related feature of context is the organization perceivers bring to the stimulus. Organization is determined by the nature of the context and the material itself. Information about a person does not come organized in a package; it is encountered over time and interspersed with information about other people. Unfortunately, researchers usually present subjects with a single isolated stimulus person, and in so doing, they are arbitrarily separating out that person as a single unit. Subjects have little choice but to organize their memories on a person-by-person basis, in that case. Ostrom and his colleagues suggest that other forms of organization are possible (Ostrom *et al.*, 1981). For example, you might have mental categories for all the premedical students you know and all the runners you know; single persons might not be the invariable units of organization. Figure 8.4 shows two ways to organize the same information.

When do people organize their social memories by person? One condition appears to be familiarity; a familiar person is more likely to be stored as a separate unit than is an unfamiliar person (Pryor & Ostrom, 1981; Pryor, Simpson, Mitchell, Ostrom, & Lydon, 1982). In one study, subjects tried to remember the facts about a person who was tall, bearded, honest, and a self-taught leader and to remember the facts about another person who was opinionated, religious, black, and a champion athlete. If Abraham Lincoln and Mohammed Ali came to mind, the subjects' job was easy, and their subsequent memory protocols grouped the attributes in two separate clusters on a person-by-person basis. On the other hand, if the same attributes were presented in different combinations not suggesting familiar people (e.g., someone who was a tall, tough, religious, outspoken golfer), no famous people were likely to come to mind. Subjects' memory was not organized by person when recalling information about unfamiliar others.

Other forms of organization also depend on the organization suggested by the context and the material presented. For example, in some cases the situation may be a more important category than the person; that is, some of the people who are in your statistics class may also be in your exercise class, and you may recognize them in each context, but you may not make the connection that the same person is in both classes if you do not know the person well and do not organize the information by person. Alternatively, the time at which one learns information may organize it, depending on the circumstances (e.g., you might group together the people who were your friends freshman year versus your friends senior year). Another factor is the sequence in which one learns the characteristics and the fact that they all refer to the same person (J. R.

Stimulus presented

Jane is a movie buff.
Diane is a runner.
David is a pre-med student.
Jane is a pre-med student.
David is a runner.

Organization by interests

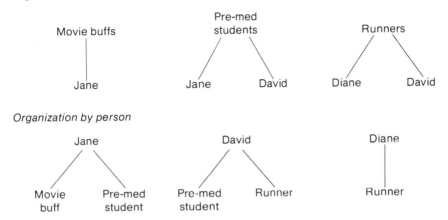

Organization by person

Fig. 8.4 Two different organizations of person memory.

Anderson & Hastie, 1974). If one learns the separate attributes first and only later learns that a single person possesses all of them, one is less likely to organize by person. Finally, anticipated future interaction increases the likelihood of organization by person (Srull & Brand, 1983).

However it is produced, organization by person seems to improve memory over other types of organization. When subjects are presented with information organized by person (as opposed to randomly organized), they recall more (Srull, 1983). In sum, the nature of the context and the material affects the extent to which memory is organized by person, and therefore the likelihood it will be well remembered.

Memory as a Mediator of Other Cognitive Processes

Having discussed some ways that the task, the context, and the material affect person memory, we should consider how memory ties into the rest of the cognitive system. How does the retrieval of relevant material affect subsequent inferences and judgments? It turns out that memory, at least as measured by many traditional tests, is surprisingly independent of many other seemingly relevant cognitive processes. This section considers the relationship between judgments and memory for the data on which they apparently were based.

THE BASIC PROBLEM OF MEMORY, JUDGMENT, AND INFERENCE

One might expect that judgments result from information stored in memory. Attributions, evaluations, and other judgments seemingly ought to draw on the amount and organization of relevant data in memory. For example, suppose a young lady meets a young man who is arrogant, domineering, and a fantastic dancer. Assuming she remembers equal numbers of incidents that represent each of these attributes, her overall impression of the young man should be negative. Yet if someone asks her whether she likes to dance with him at a party, she may well respond positively—even enthusiastically. Why? Because her decision depends on judgment-relevant memory. Her total memory for the fellow is not necessarily relevant to the specific decision. Researchers studying the links between memory and judgment first implicitly assumed that perceivers drew on all memory available about a given person when trying to form a judgment. Not surprisingly, judgments in social cognition often do not correlate with total memory when irrelevant attributes are included (S. T. Fiske, 1981).

Judgment-relevant recall correlates better with judgments than does total memory. Part of the reason for this is that judgment-relevant recall is what people actually use to make the judgment, so of course they are correlated. Another reason that judgment-relevant recall predicts judgments is that it includes both raw data (i.e., directly observed behaviors) and inferences (i.e., inferred traits) mixed together in memory. For example, the aforementioned young lady interpreted raw behavioral data about the young man as relevant to certain inferred traits such as dancing ability, dominance, warmth, intelligence, and the like; the trait inferences then become an integral part of the information remembered. Hence, having seen her prospective date interrupt others, make decisions for the group, and monopolize the discussion, the young lady may well interpret his upright posture as dominant and add that trait to her memory of him. But she could just as easily have interpreted his good posture as consistent with his dancing ability; the same ambiguous attribute can be interpreted different ways. In various settings, raw data is likely to be encoded along with inferences as soon as the data are perceived (S. T. Fiske, Kenny, & Taylor, 1982; Kintsch, 1974; McArthur, 1980; Reder, 1979; E. R. Smith & Miller, 1979, 1983).

Inferences and raw data may be intermingled particularly in social settings. That is, whenever social perception occurs, inferences seem to occur automatically. This might be true for two reasons, which are related to some of the differences between social and nonsocial cognition that we noted in Chapter 1. First, much important social information is perceived only indirectly. The behavior of the young man in the above example might be perceived by one person as dominant, but by someone else as that of an extravert. Traits, which are a central feature of social cognition, must be inferred from behavior.

Second, prediction and control may be more at issue in person perception than in object perception, since the stimulus has a mind of its own. For example, the young man (the stimulus, in this case) may realize that his date's interest in him lies solely in his resemblance to Fred Astaire. He may alter his behavior accordingly, by dancing better (if he simply wants her to like him) or dancing worse (if he wants her to like him for other things). In contrast, perceivers can assume an object does not change when someone judges it. Perhaps, for these reasons, social perceivers are especially likely to go beyond the information given, and mingle inferences with raw data in social memory.

Once inferences are incorporated into social memory, they are likely to dominate raw data. As we have seen throughout this book, preconceptions often influence one's perceptions of people and social situations. Consequently, one cannot study memory for the raw data as given and automatically assume that it is uncontaminated by inferences relevant to it. Memory is composed of inferences combined with raw data. The distinction between inference and data has arisen in several cognitive theories, and, as we will see, they shed some light on the importance of inference in social settings.

REALITY MONITORING: INTERNAL INFERENCES VERSUS EXTERNAL DATA

People cannot always distinguish things they think (inferences) from things they perceive (data). This problem entails distinguishing internally generated ideas (inferences) and externally generated ideas (data). People are not always able to remember whether an idea is their own (inference, internal source) or was communicated to them by someone else (raw data, external source). This problem is called reality monitoring (M. K. Johnson & Raye, 1981), that is, keeping track of things you see or hear versus things you yourself think.

One couple, for example, has problems with monitoring the source of things they hear and, rather comically, they generate rumors in the following way: she infers from economic trends that the price of gas is going to double and tells her friend. After they have both forgotten the conversation, he tells her that he heard that gas prices are about to double. She responds that she heard that somewhere too, and since they had both heard it, it must be true. They are now more convinced than ever.

Perceivers can distinguish between an internal and external source more easily than between two external sources. Generally speaking, the question "Did I think that or did Harold say it?" is easier to answer than the question "Did Stuart or Harold tell me that?" Only the first is a reality monitoring error.

If a person is trying to remember whether something really happened or whether it was an inference, there are several factors that help to avoid such errors, that is, to avoid confusing internally and externally generated memories (M. K. Johnson & Raye, 1981). Each type of memory has its own characteristics, and that fact helps to distinguish them. For example, externally generated information is more fixed and objective. (She definitely heard him say that the price of gas will be double, not triple what it is now.) Internally generated information is more malleable and ambiguous. (She vaguely remembers thinking she should probably buy a smaller car at some point.) Moreover, externally based memory is tied to specific spatial and temporal contexts and is linked to concrete sensory information. (She may remember his expression as he told her about the trends.) Externally generated memory also includes more detailed content, since thought is relatively schematic or skeletal, compared to perception. (There are more facts and figures to remember about the price increases, but fewer concrete "facts" about one's process of making the decision to buy a small car.) Internally generated material, compared to externally generated material, includes more process information, that is, how it got there. (She can remember changing her mind several times before reaching the decision.) Since thought is less automatic than perception, it is more likely to be accompanied by memories of the introspective process.

Inferences, then, are more vague, they are less vulnerable to verification, and they refer back to autobiographical memory (memory for the self and events that have happened to oneself). To the extent that people can rely on the features of inferences (internal source) that typically distinguish them from data (external source), people will be able to separate them in memory. To the extent that people cannot rely on such features, they will confuse inference and data.

SEMANTIC VERSUS EPISODIC MEMORY

People are frequently unable to differentiate between inferences and data in memory. In addition to this difficulty in distinguishing them, the two types of memory differ in ease of retrieval. Inferences seem to be more easily retrieved. Indeed, experimental evidence suggests that memory for inferences may dominate memory for data. The distinction between inference and data parallels an older distinction in cognitive psychology between semantic and episodic memory (Tulving, 1972), which we noted at the beginning of the chapter. To reiterate, semantic memory consists of concepts (which must be inferred), while event memory consists of concrete experiences (which are closer to the raw data).

There are several reasons why semantic memory might be recalled more easily than episodic memory in social cognition (Carlston, 1980). All of them hinge on the idea that semantic memory consists of an elaborate network, while episodic memory consists of relatively isolated single events. First, semantic memory for people consists of traits and trait inferences; these are embedded in a rich multidimensional structure very like other kinds of semantic memory. This structure is sometimes called the perceiver's *implicit personality theory* (D. J. Schneider, 1973). The structure contains the connections among various traits (e.g., "generous" is close to "sociable" but irrelevant to "intelligent" and contradictory to "selfish"). The implicit personality theory network of linkages provides many alternate retrieval routes to any given trait, so the network facilitates the accessibility of any given trait inference. Episodes are not embedded in the same sort of richly interconnected structure and so should be harder to retrieve. For example, an episode in which someone gives you a ride home is not especially well linked to other episodes in memory, compared with a trait inference such as generous.

Second, semantic memory may be more easily retrieved than episodic memory because semantic memory is characterized by deeper levels of processing. As seen in a previous section, more elaborate thought facilitates retrieval (Craik & Lockhart, 1972). When people think about something, they make new links or elaborations between it and their existing knowledge. For example, in thinking about a friend's trait of generosity, one may process it relatively deeply; in thinking about the friend giving one a ride home, one may process it relatively shallowly. Again, the links provided by deeper processing would allow many alternative retrieval routes to the trait inference, which facilitates memory.

Third, making inferences organizes memory for events. The organizing function of traits increases their impact on recall of behavior (cf. Altom & Lingle, 1980; Lingle, Geva, Ostrom, Leippe, & Baumgardner, 1979; Ostrom et al., 1980). For example, if you fit two events (the ride home and a loan of money) under the trait generous, it may help to organize them in memory, and the trait will be more memorable than either behavior. All this suggests that inferences will be easier to remember than the specific events on which they are based. Thus it seems clear that inferences often dominate episodes in memory.

Inferences often dominate episodes in making judgments as well. Again, this seems to be partly because social inferences, especially traits, are embedded in the perceiver's implicit personality theory. For example, when a personality judgment is requested, one's semantic memory—composed of general abstract trait representations—may be searched initially, in order to answer the question about the other person. If a general question is asked, a general answer may be given on the basis of a simple match to general semantic notions stored in memory (cf. Lingle & Ostrom, 1979). For example, someone might ask you to judge if a friend is generous; there are two ways you might draw on general semantic memory to answer the question. Either you may already think of your friend as generous, or you may think your friend is kind and that most kind people are generous, but in both cases you can find the general semantic judgment in memory and answer accordingly.

If the general answer has not been stored already, however, then people may make an exhaustive search of all the relevant episodic information in memory (R. B. Allen & Ebbesen, 1981; Ebbesen & Allen, 1979). That is, you may think back to your friend's various behaviors and decide if they fit the meaning of generous. This is a two-stage model: check semantic memory, then search episodic memory. It saves time for the decision maker, since checking semantic memory simply consists of retrieving the relevant trait if it is there. The initial checking stage is a simple judgment. Searching episodic memory for the relevant information is more complicated because one may have to retrieve several relevant episodes and then decide what general trait applies. The more time-consuming second stage is required only when the easier judgment did not provide an answer.

The advantage of storing one's prior general judgments means that event memory need not be consulted each time a general semantic judgment is requested. Instead, people refer back directly to a prior judgment, as in the example above (Lingle et al., 1979; cf. S. T. Fiske, 1982; S. T. Fiske, Beattie, & Milberg, 1983; Higgins, McCann, & Fondacaro, 1982; Higgins & Rholes, 1978).

One consequence is that once an event contributes to the initial judgment, subsequent memory for that event itself will be independent of its initial impact on the judgment (N. H. Anderson & Hubert, 1963; Dreben, Fiske, & Hastie, 1979; Riskey, 1979). It is as if people isolate the relevant component of each event, combine it with the current judgment, and then remember the judgment. Whether or not they recall the events that contribute to the judgment is another matter.

In summary, the relationship of inferences to events is complicated by the fact that the two are confounded in memory. First, people are not always certain whether something was an externally generated event or an internally generated inference. Second, people typically combine several external events into a single summary judgment. They they access the summary rather than their memory for the individual events in later retrievals. Thus, frequently, internally generated inferences or judgments dominate memory for externally generated event data.

CONCLUSION

Memory is not correlated in any simple way with important social inferences. People do not necessarily base their judgments on everything they remember. People make inferences and forget the data on which they were based. Some psychologists may have overestimated or oversimplified the role of memory in important social settings. Why, then, do psychologists study memory? The contents of people's brains are presumably the major determinants of what they do; certainly the contents of someone else's brain are not the major determinant of what one does. Moreover, the relationships between memory and judgment are often subtle but predictable, as just seen. Judgments often occur in reaction to stimuli not currently present. In that case, the reactions must depend on some form of memory for the stimulus. Furthermore, memory helps define the range of possible responses. Certainly, if something is not in memory, it may well be outside the range of responses the person has available. The importance of memory structure and process is a basic premise of social cognition.

Personality and Memory

Charlotte is always losing keys, particularly when distracted. Gerald regularly misses lunch and drink appointments. In both cases, the forgetfulness appears unintentional, and yet in both cases, it seems to be tied to general levels of anxiety. Some clinical psychologists view what things people forget and when they forget them as valuable evidence for what the people find threatening. Someone who loses only office keys may be feeling ambivalent about work, for example.

Various personality factors correlate with styles of remembering (and forgetting) social information (Kihlstrom, 1981). For example, reinterpretations of classical Freudian repression explore how people's memory processes are biased in ways that keep threatening material out of conscious awareness (Erdelyi & Goldberg, 1979; Mandler, 1975). Threatening material includes anything associated with conflict or anxiety, and people indeed do seem to have difficulty recalling negative events in general (Matlin & Stang, 1978). One example of memory repressing negative or threatening material comes from work on achievement-related memory (Kihlstrom, 1981). People low in achievement motivation are likely to find unfinished tasks threatening and to forget about them. For example, they would not walk out of an unfinished exam mulling over the questions they could not answer. For people high in achievement motivation, on the other hand, unfinished tasks present a challenge and are remembered.

To take another example, sex-role orientation guides memory toward role-congruent words (S. L. Bem, 1981; Markus, Crane, Bernstein, & Siladi, 1982). Men and women who identify themselves as relatively "male-typed" (aggressive and competitive) recall more "masculine" and fewer "feminine" words; people who identify themselves as relatively "female-typed" (sensitive and cooperative) show the opposite pattern. Similarly, the work on self-schemata all can be viewed as evidence of an individual difference that affects memory (Kuiper & Rogers, 1979; Markus & Smith, 1981). One's idiosyncratic self-concept focuses memory toward schema-relevant information about oneself and others. Even autobiographical memory is shaped by self-concept; if you think of yourself as independent, it is easier to remember the time you ran away from home for a day at age ten than it is to remember the time you were traumatized by losing your mother in the grocery store.

In considering the links between personality and memory, it is probably better to think of person and situation in combination as influencing memory, rather than to think of certain people as invariably having certain biases (Mischel, 1968). That is, it is unlikely that competitive people invariably remember their classmates' Graduate Record Exam (GRE) scores, but a competitive situation (e.g., discussing postgraduate plans) might be especially likely to elicit competition-oriented memory from competitive people. Moreover, it is the person's situation as he or she perceives it that shapes recollection. Most people might not perceive a smile from a teacher as indicative of how they are doing in class, but a highly competitive person might; the situation is interpreted as relevant to competition, rather than, say, simple sociability. But it is the individual person's interpretation that determines that the smile will be recalled as evidence of past success (Kihlstrom, 1981).

A Note on Normative Implications

Memory processes, more than attentional processes, for instance, suggest normative criteria; that is, they lend themselves to evaluation against a standard such as efficiency or accuracy. Efficiency in memory is defined as ease of access, the amount of wasted effort, and the degree of focus in retrieval. Accuracy in memory, of course, means whether or not one is correct. These dual standards are more complex than they appear, and they often conflict. Efficiency may interfere with accuracy, as the following quotation illustrates. Dr. Watson writes of Sherlock Holmes, who claimed to know a thing or two about the most efficient memory strategies:

> His ignorance was as remarkable as his knowledge. Of contemporary literature, philosophy and politics he appeared to know next to nothing. Upon my quoting Thomas Carlyle, he inquired in the naivest way who he might be and what he had done. My surprise reached a climax, however, when I found incidentally that he was ignorant of the Copernican Theory and of the composition of the Solar System. That any civilized human being in this nineteenth century should not be aware that the earth travelled round the sun appeared to me to be such an extraordinary fact that I could hardly realize it.
>   "You appear to be astonished," he said, smiling at my expression of surprise. "Now that I do know it I shall do my best to forget it!"
>   "To forget it!"
>   "You see," he explained, "I consider that a man's brain originally is like a little empty attic, and you have to stock it with such furniture as you choose. A fool takes in all the lumber of every sort that he comes across, so that the knowledge which might be useful to him gets crowded out, or at best is jumbled up with a lot of other things, so that he has a difficulty in laying his hands upon it. Now the skillful workman is very careful indeed as to what he takes into his brain-attic. He will have nothing but the tools which may help him in doing his work, but of these he has a large assortment, and all in the most perfect order. It is a mistake to think that little room has elastic walls and can distend to any extent. Depend upon it there comes a time when for every addition of knowledge you forget something that you knew before. It is of the highest importance, therefore, not to have useless facts elbowing out the useful ones."
>   "But the Solar System!" I protested. (Doyle, 1930, pp. 13-14)

As it happens, Holmes was probably wrong in believing that long-term memory is inherently limited in precisely that way. But Holmes was partially right in his worry about interference among various items of information. The more related concepts one knows, the more potential there is for inefficiency. Let us examine the *accuracy* and *efficiency* criteria in turn.

ACCURACY

Accuracy in person memory has a limited meaning, in part because of the difficulty of determining accuracy in memory for people. The general problem of accuracy in social perception has long been a problem for social and personality psychologists. Early person perception researchers were concerned with people's ability correctly to identify the traits and emotions of others (Bruner & Tagiuri, 1954; D. J. Schneider *et al.*, 1979). But it soon became apparent that one cannot assess correctness without having a clear criterion of what makes a perception or memory correct. Given the difficulty psychologists have in establishing what people's traits and emotions actually are, it is difficult to evaluate the ordinary person's accuracy at the task of person perception. (For a more complete discussion, see D. J. Schneider *et al.*, 1979.)

Cronbach (1955) dealt a severe blow to the person perception research on accuracy by pointing out that theoretically there are many different sorts of error, and each one separately contributes to accuracy (or its lack). Although Cronbach was interested in judgment accuracy, his analysis can be applied to memory accuracy just as easily. One's memory can be more or less accurate about people in general, more or less accurate about specific people, more or less accurate about specific attributes, or more or less accurate about specific attributes for specific people. Current research in person memory tends to use as its accuracy criterion the most concrete of these four types—specific attributes remembered about a specific person.

The person memory laboratory is (by necessity) simplified. Subjects in memory experiments do not usually have to judge, only to remember judgments they are given. That is, subjects do not have to figure out who is Republican, who is an artist, or who is boring among a group of stimulus people. Because the people's attributes are presented directly, subjects do not have to worry about the accuracy of inferring the attributes from raw data. Since the stimulus people are created with certain obvious behaviors and traits, the accuracy criterion for initial inferences is not a problem in the laboratory. The subject is accurate if he or she remembers the traits or behaviors that were presented as stimuli. Unfortunately, in real life, things are more complex. You may remember a fellow we both met at a conference as being intellectual and sophisticated, while I may remember him as pompous. Since our original perceptions shape what we recall, accuracy in real-world person memory confounds encoding biases with inferential biases to a greater degree than do less ambiguous stimuli in the laboratory.

EFFICIENCY

Regardless of how one defines accuracy, efficiency can be a conflicting goal. One type of memory efficiency is ease of access, which often means reaction time to retrieval or recognition. There is a tension between speed and accuracy; that is, in general, the faster people are, the more likely they are to be wrong. Efficiency and accuracy can be sacrificed for each other, then.

Another type of efficiency includes the amount of wasted effort, specifically the ratio of inaccurate to accurate memory. In recognition tests that ask, "Have you seen this item before?" efficiency can be captured by comparing hit rates (correct yes answers) to false alarms (incorrect yes answers) in recognition; this ratio is used in what is called a signal detection index (Hartwick, 1979). In free recall tests that ask, "Tell me everything you can remember about this person," the equivalent would be the ratio of intrusions (made-up answers) to accuracies.

A third criterion for efficiency is how focused one's memory search is. For example, can related items be found clustered together? And are they in categories appropriate to the task (cf. D. L. Hamilton, 1981)? If memory organization reflects the problem at hand, then you are halfway to solving it. For most purposes, for example, it is more efficient to cluster in memory all of someone's attributes that relate to social behavior, separately from those related to task performance; it is usually less efficient to cluster attributes by the order in which you learned them (Ostrom *et al.*, 1980). Efficiency then ultimately depends on one's purpose.

Summary

Memory is critical to social cognition research and theory. Many psychologists think memory consists of associative networks of propositions that link related concepts. The links are labeled and directional associations among ideas, and the links are strengthened each time they are activated. People are more likely to retrieve recently and frequently activated concepts than concepts not recently or frequently used. The currently active contents of long-term memory compose consciousness or short-term memory. A distinction often made in social cognition research is that long-term memory has two types: semantic memory, which consists of concepts and ideas, and episodic memory, which consists of concrete events.

The contents of person memory range from inferable traits to observable appearance and behavior. Traits fit well into the most common model of memory, the propositional code. Behavior may instead be represented in a temporal code that preserves information about event sequences. Appearance may be represented in a separate sort of code, an analog imagery code. Also, considering the importance of appearance in person memory, it is worth noting that people's accuracy in real-world settings is surprisingly limited. A fourth possible memory code may be affect, but because of the limited research results we cannot be certain about this.

Much of the research on person memory concerns how one's task purpose affects what is recalled. Impression sets and other psychologically oriented tasks provide more coherence and better memory than does mere memorization. Relative to an impression set, the other psychologically oriented tasks provide equally strong or stronger memory; such tasks include empathizing with people, relating them to the self, or expecting to interact with them. The more psychologically engaging, more elaborated or deeper the processing on any encoding task, the better the memory for task-relevant material.

Besides task purpose, prior context affects person memory. Prior contexts include concepts one has recently had in mind; such concepts can prime related material in memory, increasing its accessibility. Finally, the organization one brings to the material determines how it is remembered; various situational and stimulus features determine the extent to which memory is organized on a person-by-person basis. For example, as familiarity increases, the material is more likely to be recalled by person, rather than, say, simply in the sequence it was learned.

Memory is not linked to other cognitive processes in the most simple or obviously expected ways. Judgments are not correlated with total recall, but instead with judgment-relevant recall. Judgment-relevant recall intermingles both inferences and raw data. People are not especially good at distinguishing between inferences and raw data in memory. For example, people cannot easily distinguish internally generated ideas (inferences) from externally generated ideas (data). Nor can people always distinguish their own summary judgments from the raw events on which they were based. Despite the inability to distinguish them, inferences tend to dominate raw data.

Individual differences in memory are best thought of as interactions between personality and situation. That is, certain types of people disproportionately remember particular information in particular settings.

Given all the determinants of memory, it is useful to consider the normative criteria for accuracy and efficiency of memory. These criteria, however, may be contradictory. Accuracy is difficult to assess, because the true nature of the stimulus person is difficult to establish. Efficiency is a difficult criterion, too, because it can be defined and measured in several ways and because it depends on the task at hand. Nevertheless, people's memories seem to function remarkably well in managing the wealth of information stored about self and others.

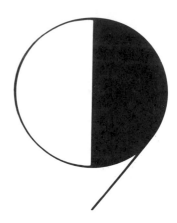

Inference is the central concern of social cognition. It is both a process and a product. As a process, it involves deciding what information to gather to address a given issue or question, collecting that information, and combining it in some form. As a product, it is the outcome of the reasoning process (Nisbett & Ross, 1980).

social inference

In this chapter, we are concerned primarily with the social inference process, that is, how well the social perceiver specifies what information is relevant to a given judgment, how fairly he or she samples information, and whether or not he or she follows appropriate rules in combining information into a judgment. We also consider higher order processes that draw on some of these fundamental relevancy, sampling, and combinational judgments of frequency or probability.

We have already considered the subject of inference in other chapters. Attribution theory (Chapters 2-4) is both a delineation of the methods by which people make causal inferences and an analysis of the causal inference itself. Schemata strongly influence how we process information and what inferences we draw, as we pointed out in Chapter 6. Memory for information about other people is composed of intermingled inferences and raw data, as we noted in Chapter 8. Attitudes are a kind of inference, and in Chapter 12 we will outline the cognitive processes underlying how attitudes are formed and how attitudes affect other judgments. We could draw similar ties to other chapters, for the inference process is basic to all aspects of social cognition.

Unlike some other areas of social psychology, social inference and research on it are dominated by the dictates of normative theory. By normative theories, we mean that there are standard, optimally correct ways of performing each of the steps that a social perceiver must do to form an inference (e.g., gathering and sampling data, combining information), and the social perceiver's methods and conclusions are compared with these normative models for accuracy. Why is normative theory so dominant in social inference? The reason is that research on social inference generally assumes, either implicitly or explicitly, that inference is goal directed (i.e., made to achieve some purpose). For example, one may need to make a decision or choose from several options, or one may need to understand a situation before one can act on it. If goals dominate the inference process, then clearly some ways of reaching a goal are better than others (e.g., faster or less error prone). Accordingly, the social perceiver seemingly ought to use them (Einhorn & Hogarth, 1981). The normative models for making judgments and choices are known collectively as behavioral decision theory, and thus, it is against the principles of behavioral decision theory that social inference may be compared (Einhorn & Hogarth, 1981; Slovic, Fischhoff, & Lichtenstein, 1977).

Accordingly, a confrontation, implicit in attribution research (Chapter 4), emerges explicitly when one attempts to compare the normative model with actual inferences, and it is the conflict between the rational person or naive scientist view of the social perceiver and, for lack of a better term, the cognitive miser perspective. If normative theory provided a good description of the social inference process, this chapter and indeed this book would be a description of formal logic and statistical models of inference. But the human information processor does not typically behave in this idealized fashion. Rather, the capacity to process information on line is very limited, as we noted in the discussion of the limits of short-term memory in Chapter 8. So, at a minimum, the inference process is marked by a willingness to use strategies that move information through the system quickly, rather than thoroughly. The label, "cognitive miser," then, stems from the necessary stinginess with which attention and processing time are allocated to stimuli in the real world (S. E. Taylor, 1981).

Long-term storage in memory, however, is quite cheap (Chapter 8). One of the authors regularly wonders, for example, why her memory should choose to store the lyrics of approximately 2,000 old rock songs and all the books of the Old Testament, when there are so many things that are more important. The advantage of so much storage space is that prior information, beliefs, and inferences can be stored in the form of schemata or other knowledge structures (Chapter 6) where they are accessible when new inferences must be drawn (G. H. Bower, 1977; Klatzky, 1975).

Armed with limited on-line capacity and a large amount of stored knowledge, what else characterizes the social perceiver? As we noted in our discussion of attributions (Chapters 2-4) and schemata (Chapter 6), the inference process is often conservative, straying on the side of accepting preexisting beliefs over new or counterintuitive ones. It is also self-centered, drawing on personal experience and beliefs over information provided from other sources, especially social ones. There is, then, a sharp contrast between what the rational person would do with unlimited cognitive resources (i.e., the normative model) and what the cognitive miser does do with limited ones (the descriptive model). In this chapter we explore the inferential strategies of the cognitive miser more fully.

Following our consideration of the cognitive miser's intuitive inferential strategies, we return to a major question. Since we fall so short of normative inferential strategies, how do we manage at all? Does the social perceiver know something that normative theories of inference do not take into account? Are normative models even appropriate standards against which to compare everyday inference?

But first let us examine how everyday inferences are made. In so doing, we will trace temporally the process whereby the social perceiver gathers data, decides how good they are, and combines them into a judgment. Figure 9.1 presents in a rough temporal fashion the sequence the perceiver goes through in forming an inference.

The Process of Forming Inferences

GATHERING INFORMATION

Every day, the social perceiver makes numerous, apparently complex judgments. When asked by a friend what a mutual acquaintance, Rick, is like, one must decide how much and what kind of information to provide. Is his fanaticism over football or passion for young women relevant or should one only mention his good sense of humor, his quirk of forgetting people's names, and his love of lengthy political debates? Even the smallest inference or judgment begins with the process of deciding what information is relevant and sampling the information that is available.

According to the normative model, the social perceiver should weigh all relevant evidence in arriving at a conclusion, but, as we have already seen in our discussion of schemata (Chapter 6) and memory (Chapter 8), the process of deciding what information is relevant or how one is to interpret the evidence is heavily influenced by preexistent expectations or schemata. Similarly, the information I convey to my friend about Rick will be different if my friend is an attractive 19-year-old undergraduate woman than if she is a 67-year-old Democratic party veteran.

Selecting data according to preexistent expectations or theories is perfectly appropriate under many circumstances (see Nisbett & Ross, 1980). It would be a bad doctor indeed who started from scratch with each new medical case he or she encountered, instead of letting the interpretation of symptoms be guided by the frequency of a particular illness, characteristics of the patient, knowledge of what illnesses are "going around" and the like. A slightly pudgy adolescent girl with occasional fainting spells could have a brain tumor, but it is more likely that she has low blood pressure or that she is dieting and has not eaten enough food.

Nonetheless, there are many circumstances in which characterizing information on the basis of preexistent theories is unwise. Three such conditions are noted by Nisbett and Ross (1980). The first is if the theory itself is faulty or suspect; for example, if the physician concludes that the fainting adolescent is possessed by demons, her parents might at least want a second opinion. Second, if an individual is characterizing data on the basis of a theory but believes his or her inferences are objectively based on raw data, problems can

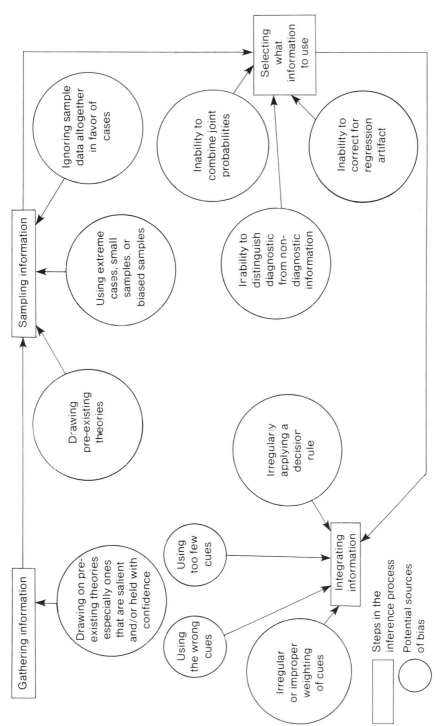

Fig. 9.1 Inferential processes and their potential sources of bias.

result. The physician who sends the girl home after a cursory examination with instructions to eat a big dinner may well have ignored other less likely causes of fainting such as diabetes or epilepsy, but the physician may believe that a thorough examination was conducted. Third, theory-guided inferences create problems when the theory overrules consideration of the data altogether. The doctor who dismisses the adolescent as an overzealous dieter prior to examining her would be guilty of this error, as well as of gross negligence.

Theories are particularly likely to guide the collection of data if the theory is held with great confidence, if it is very salient in the theory holder's mind, and if the available data are sufficiently ambiguous that they do not, in themselves, suggest an alternative theory (Nisbett & Ross, 1980). To take specific examples, suppose the physician's own daughter suffers from anorexia nervosa, a nervous disorder most common among adolescent girls that amounts to self-starvation. The sight of another adolescent, weak perhaps from hunger, might make his overzealous dieting theory so compelling that the physician ignores other possibilities. However, if other symptoms such as a history of insulin shock or seizures were present, virtually all physicians would reject any private theory in favor of one that better fits the data, such as diabetes or epilepsy respectively.

SAMPLING INFORMATION

Once the social perceiver has decided what information is relevant to an inference, a task which can be biased by preexisting theories, the data must be sampled. For example, if you want to know if the students in your class enjoy the course, you must decide whom to ask and how many people to ask. When people are describing already available samples, their accuracy in estimating frequencies, proportions, or averages is quite good, so long as no prior theories or expectations are present to influence such estimates. Thus, for example, if you already had your classmates' course evaluations, you could presumably estimate their average evaluation quite easily. However, when prior theories or expectations do exist, describing data can be as influenced by the theory as deciding what data are relevant (see Nisbett & Ross, 1980; S. E. Taylor & Crocker, 1981, for reviews).

When samples are not already available, the process of sampling and drawing inferences from samples presents another host of pitfalls. To begin with, *sample estimates can be thrown off by extreme examples* within the sample. In one study (Rothbart, Fulero, Jensen, Howard, & Birrell, 1978), subjects were given information about members of two groups, including the fact that some of the members had committed crimes. For one sample, only moderate crimes were listed, whereas in the other sample, a few examples of particular heinous crimes were included. Although the actual frequency of committing crimes was the same in the two groups, subjects misremembered that more individuals committed crimes in the second group, presumably because the extreme examples had prompted a strong association between that group and crime (Tversky & Kahneman, 1974). Frequency estimation, then, a skill crucial to correct use of sample information, can be misled by other, irrelevant characteristics of the sample.

In drawing inferences from samples, *the social perceiver is often inadequately aware of sample size.* Small samples often produce poor estimates of a population's characteristics, whereas larger samples are more reliable. Nonetheless, people will often overgeneralize from a small unrepresentative sample (Nisbett & Ross, 1980; Tversky & Kahneman, 1974). A friend of the authors who had spent virtually all of his early years living in Manhattan revealed that, until he was 25 years old, he believed that Queens was nothing more than a burial ground for New York City. For that entire time, his sole ventures into Queens were to Kennedy or La Guardia airports, trips that afford little more than a view of acres and acres of cemeteries. Presumably, a better sampling of the streets of Queens would have revealed more of its riches.

In addition to size of sample, *people are also insufficiently attentive to biases in samples.* When gathering his or her own sample, an individual will often ask a few friends or acquaintances their opinions, forgetting that a sample of one's friends is scarcely random. Usually, one picks friends or acquaintances precisely because they are similar on at least some dimensions, and hence their opinions are likely to be at least somewhat similar to one's own. Under some circumstances, biased sampling may not matter. If you want to know if a movie is good so you can decide if you want to see it, canvassing friends who are similar is perfectly appropriate. However, if you want to decide whether to take your entire assemblage of visiting relatives to a movie, the bias in the sample of your friends' opinions might matter a lot; if your friends have a penchant for motorcycles and raunchy humor and your grandparents do not, you may wish you had sampled more carefully.

Furthermore, *when given information about a sample's typicality, people will often fail to use it.* In one study (Hamill, Wilson, & Nisbett, 1980), researchers told subjects they would be viewing a videotaped interview with a prison guard who was either typical of most guards or very atypical of most guards, or typicality information was not provided. Subjects then saw the tape in which the guard appeared as a highly compassionate, concerned individual or as an inhumane, macho, cruel one. Subjects were later asked a set of questions about the criminal justice system that included questions about prison guards. Results showed that, regardless of the initial typicality information, subjects exposed to the interview with the humane guard were more favorable in their attitudes toward prison guards than were subjects who saw the interview with the inhumane guard.

Some studies have shown that when people are reassured that sample information is reliable and valid, they make more confident inferences about population characteristics (Kassin, 1979b; Wells & Harvey, 1977). However, it is unlikely that subjects characteristically assume that samples are representative and valid, which would explain their willingness to use small and/or biased samples. Rather, it seems far more likely that questions of sample adequacy rarely arise in a person's mind. For example, people will often make stronger inferences from a small sample than a large sample, even though both samples are available to them, and the sample size problem should be readily apparent (Tversky & Kahneman, 1974). Furthermore, subjects will use biased sample information even when those sources of bias are abundantly clear, as in the "atypical" guard example above. Hence, although people do make better inferences after their attention has been called to such criteria as the representativeness or validity of a sample, these occasions might best be thought of as exceptions rather than the rule.

UNDERUTILIZING BASERATE INFORMATION

If you wanted to know how good a particular school's football team is, what would be your best source of information: going to one particular game or checking their win-loss record of the entire season? The answer, of course, is the season's win-loss record, since it provides a more reliable and valid indicator of a team's ability; a single game can be biased by many temporary factors such as bad weather, injuries, or simply a bad day. Nonetheless, people's impressions are often overwhelmed by a particular example (e.g., a single game), when better assessments (e.g., the season record) are available. To put it more generally, even when sampling has already been done for an individual and he or she is presented with good estimates of population characteristics (such as averages, prior probabilities, or proportions), those estimates may be ignored. Earlier, in Chapter 4, the fact that people underutilize consensus information in making causal attributions was pointed out. This failure to use consensus information can be thought of as part of a larger problem. This problem is the tendency of people to ignore general, broadly based information about population characteristics (i.e., baserate information) in favor of more concrete anecdotal, but usually less valid and reliable information. Vibrant examples simply outweigh more reliable, but abstract baserate information.

In one study, for example (Hamill et al., 1980), subjects read a colorful account of a woman who had been living on welfare with her numerous children for many years and who clearly could not be said to be among the truly needy. This stereotypic case of welfare abuse was set in context either by baserate statistics indicating that welfare recipients often take advantage of the system and stay on welfare a long time, or by statistics suggesting that the average welfare recipient is on the rolls only a short time, implying that the case history provided to subjects was highly atypical. Despite the available baserate information, subjects responded as if the case history were representative of welfare recipients under both conditions, and their judgments were more influenced by it than by the more valid baserate information (Ginosar & Trope, 1980; Hamill et al., 1980; S. E. Taylor & Thompson, 1982).

Perhaps people simply do not understand baserate information or its relationship to judgment tasks. Several studies have debunked this possibility by showing that when baserate information is the only information available, people will draw on it as a basis for their inferences (Hamill et al., 1980; Nisbett

& Borgida, 1975). For example, if you know a team's win-loss record and have never seen a particular game, you will clearly use the win-loss record to characterize the team's ability. Why are people so often swayed by colorful case history examples when better or qualifying baserate information is also available? In the past, researchers have generally assumed that the vivid quality of the more compelling case examples simply overwhelms the more pallid and dull statistical information (Nisbett & Ross, 1980). However, an analysis of the so-called vividness effect suggests that this interpretation may be in error (S. E. Taylor & Thompson, 1982; Chapter 7, "Attention"); rather, there seems to be some quality intrinsic to statistical or baserate information that itself limits its use.

One possibility is that people often do not see the relevance of baserate information to the judgment task (Borgida & Brekke, 1981; Kassin, 1979b; Tversky & Kahneman, 1978; Zuckerman, 1979). A particular building in Los Angeles has been occupied by four different restaurants in less than three years. Each has failed, and that information should give any prospective restaurateur pause for thought. Nonetheless, as each culinary venture folds, an eager new one steps in to fill the breach, only to fail again. Presumably, each idealistic entrepreneur assumes that his or her own concept is the one that will make the place work (an Irish pub, a pasta place, soup and salad). None seemingly can appreciate the baserate information that virtually screams out, "No one comes here!" Hence each loses, so that the next inexperienced capitalist, ignorant of the relevance of baserate information, can seal his or her own financial fate as well.

In support of the possibility that people simply do not see the relevance of baserate information, a number of studies demonstrate that people are more likely to use baserate information if its causal relevance to the judgment task is made salient than if it is not (Ajzen, 1977; Manis, Dovalina, Avis, & Cardoze, 1980; Tversky & Kahneman, 1978). In one study, subjects were told about a late-night auto accident involving a cab that an eyewitness thought might have been blue. Subjects were then informed that in that city, 85 percent of the cabs are green and 15 percent are blue. Although subjects should have concluded that the culprit's cab was probably green on the basis of the baserate information, few did. Instead, most drew on the report of the eyewitness, and decided the cab was probably blue. However, a second group was told that 85 percent of the accidents in the city are caused by blue cabs and 15 percent by green cabs; these subjects did use the baserate information to qualify their inferences. Presumably, people see accident rate statistics as relevant to judgments about accidents, whereas they do not perceive information about the prevalence of particular cabs as relevant to the judgment, though in fact it is. Hence, when people perceive baserate information as relevant to a judgment, they use it in preference to colorful case history information. Interestingly enough, the mirror image of this effect is also true: when researchers manipulate case history information so it is less relevant to the judgment task, people ignore it in favor of baserate information (Ginosar & Trope, 1980).

To summarize, then, people rarely incorporate baserate and other statistical information adequately into an inference task except when it is the only information available. When other, less valid, but more engaging anecdotal evidence is present, people often ignore relevant baserates (Bar-Hillel & Fischhoff, 1981; Manis, Avis, & Cardoze, 1981; Manis et al., 1980). The greater vividness or catchiness of other kinds of information such as case histories does not seem to be the reason why people underutilize baserate information. Rather, it may be that people do not understand the relevance of baserates to typical social judgments, relative to other types of information. These findings have been applied widely in decision making (Hogarth, 1980; Nisbett & Ross, 1980) and stereotyping (Locksley, Borgida, Brekke, & Hepburn, 1980; Locksley, Hepburn, & Ortiz, 1982). The consequences of the failure to use baserate information, as the restaurant example suggests, can be extreme.

UNDERSTANDING PROBABILITY AND REGRESSION

Many of the biases in everyday inference suggest a conservative bent that favors prior beliefs or theories over new and sometimes statistically superior evidence. However, given the task of generating future predictions from simple probabilistic information, the perceiver often looks like an irresponsible radical. These radical tendencies can be explained by people's misunderstanding of at least two phenomena: (1) using *probabilistic information*, particularly combining joint probabilities, and (2) recognizing the predictive limitations of extreme values, that is, *regression*.

We will begin with the use of probabilistic information. Most of us know that a penny has no memory. It does not, for example, remember if it turned up heads the last time it was flipped. Nonetheless, some of us, having seen the penny turn heads up four times in a row, would predict tails very confidently on the fifth trial, feeling it is time that tails came up. The penny, however, is starting from scratch each time, and so the actual probability of tails is .5, just as it always is, assuming the penny has not been tampered with. Most of us, in fact, are aware of this gambler's fallacy, and would consider ourselves fairly sophisticated on the subject of probability.

But most people are not at all skilled at combining probabilities. Consider the following example. Comedians make their living, in part, by sketching out highly recognizable portraits of people that make us laugh. "Consider the Nerd. He's a skinny guy, right? He walks like this? [Comedian minces across the stage.] And he carries an umbrella even when it's not raining?" With each detail, the audience's laugh of recognition grows. Yet the paradox of the well-drawn portrait is that with each detail, recognizability increases, but actual probability of occurrence decreases. One might well find a nerd on the street and he might well be skinny, but the likelihood that he would also be mincing and carrying an umbrella is low. The likelihood that any two or more events will co-occur (i.e., their joint probability) is the product of their probabilities of occurring alone; accordingly, their joint probability cannot exceed the probability of the least probable single event. Under many circumstances, however, people make more extreme predictions for the joint occurrence of events than for any event alone.

In one study (Slovic *et al.*, 1977), researchers gave subjects information about individuals and then asked them to predict the likelihood that particular events would occur in their lives, either jointly or singly. For example, subjects were told that an individual was gregarious and literary. When asked how likely it was that he was an engineering major, they responded that it was very unlikely. However, when asked how likely it was that he would start out as an engineering major and switch to journalism, an event with a far lower likelihood of occurrence than simply majoring in engineering, subjects gave this event a much higher rating. Presumably, they could readily see that a gregarious, literary person would decide journalism was for him and not engineering, and they could not see how such a person would stay an engineer. Obviously, the perceiver's problems in successfully combining joint probabilities stem from the oft-mentioned conflict between data and prior theories. Again, it is the prior theory (gregarious, literary people are not engineers) that wins out, with the consequence of more extreme conclusions than are warranted by the data.

Regression is also a phenomenon related to prediction from probabilistic information, and it is also poorly understood by most people. Regression refers to the fact that extreme events will, on the average, be less extreme when reassessed at a different point in time. To illustrate this elusive phenomenon, consider four people who take a test such as the mathematics section of the Graduate Record Exam (GRE). Suppose the four all have exactly equal mathematical ability and should all get 600 on the test. Will they all get 600? Probably not. Random factors can intrude that will affect performance, some favorably, some adversely. One person (A) may have had trouble sleeping the night before and perform more poorly than he would otherwise. A second person (B) may have coincidentally studied exactly the same examples as appeared on the test and thus do quite well. A third person (C) may be distracted by the gum chewer next to her and lose a few points, and the fourth person (D) may have gotten a good seat in the testing room and do well.

But if all the information one had about these four students was their performance on this one test, one might conclude that two of them (B and D) are quite bright, but that the other two (A and C) are not as good. Asked to predict their future performance, the inclination would be to predict high scores for B and D and lower ones for A and C. What would, in fact, happen? In all likelihood, on a second test, B and D would not look as good as they previously did, whereas A and C would look better. Why? B and D each had random factors working in their favor that, precisely because they are random, would no longer be present at the second session. Likewise, A and C each had random error working against them that would not be present at Time 2. Although random error would still be present at Time 2, it would be equally likely to favor or disfavor each of the four students, rather than consistently favoring B and D and disfavoring A and C. Thus, at the second test, B and D should fare worse and A and C better. Table 9.1 illustrates the phenomenon of regression.

The message of regression, then, is that when one must make an inference based on limited and unreliable information, one will be most accurate if one ventures a prediction that is less extreme than the information on which it is based. A restaurant that is fabulous one night will probably not be quite as good when you drag your friends there, having raved endlessly about its cuisine. Your scathing assessment of a pitcher's potential may make you look very foolish when he pitches a shutout in his next game. Bitter experience notwithstanding, experimental evidence, as well as common observation, consistently shows that when people are provided with extreme values of predictor information, they draw extreme inferences about subsequent behavior (Jennings, Amabile, & Ross, 1982; Kahneman & Tversky, 1973).

There are rare instances in which regression, or at least something very much like it, is appreciated. For example, the response of literary critics to an author's blockbusting first novel is often to hedge their bets. Praise may be glowing, but it is often couched in cautionary language that urges readers to wait for the next product; previous experience dictates that second novels are often less stellar than first ones. However, one might well ask if an appreciation of regression underlies these conservative predictions. Although in rare cases it may, more often some theory, and not random error, is credited with the poor second showing. Authors are said to "burn themselves out" on the first novel or to have "said it all," leaving no material for a second try. Others are thought to be immobilized or blocked by their first success. Although some of these points may, in fact, be true, regression alone is fully capable of accounting for the second-book effect. Yet how often has one read a review of a mediocre second novel in which the critic pointed out that the inferior product could have been predicted by chance?

THE DILUTION EFFECT

Under some circumstances, the social perceiver can be induced to make more conservative inferences. Suppose I tell you I have a friend Judith who is 35, stocky, and has lived with the same female roommate for five years. You may conclude that she is probably a lesbian. However, if I also tell you that she is a paralegal, takes fiction writing courses in night school, drives a blue Toyota, and is very close to her brothers and sisters, you may wonder if she is gay, but not immediately assume that she is. Why? The first three bits of information I mentioned can be thought of as *diagnostic* with respect to whether Judith is gay or not, because unmarried, stocky females with constant female companions are often thought to be gay. However, the extra information about her job, car, and leisure activities diluted that diagnostic information with a lot of nondiagnostic information, that is, information that would not lead you to conclude that she is gay or straight, but which is simply neutral with respect to the inference. In short, I reduced her similarity to the stereotype of gayness by

TABLE 9.1
Regression toward the Mean: Taking the GREs Twice

Time 1

Given four students (A, B, C, D) of equal ability, all should score a 600 on the Graduate Record Examination:	But random factors enter in, raising or lowering their scores:	Actual score at time 1:	Conclusion:
A 600	−10 (slept poorly)	590	B and D look strong; A and C look weaker
B 600	+15 (studied examples similar to test items)	615	
C 600	−17 (gum chewer was a distraction)	583	
D 600	+12 (got a good seat in the test room)	612	

Time 2

Given same four students taking test again:	Different random factors are present, raising or lowering scores:	Actual score at time 2:	Conclusion:
A 600	+12 (had a good breakfast)	612	A and D look strong; B and C look weaker
B 600	−10 (sat near the window)	590	
C 600	− 4 (had a slight cold)	596	
D 600	+ 5 (was "on" that day)	605	

deepening her characterization and making her a person, so your confidence in drawing any extreme inferences about her may thereby be lessened.

A number of studies have now examined this *dilution effect*, and all have shown that when diagnostic information is diluted with nondiagnostic information, inferences are less extreme (Nisbett, Zukier, & Lemley, 1981). It would be encouraging if one could conclude from this evidence that people understand the phenomenon of regression. Unhappily, no such conclusion is warranted. When diagnostic information is highly predictive of some outcome and accordingly justifies extreme inferences, nondiagnostic information still dilutes it, leading to overly conservative predictions (Zukier, 1982). For example, knowing that a student's grade point average (GPA) has been extremely high should lead one to predict continued high performance. However, when the high GPA information is diluted with irrelevant information such as the fact that the student drives a Honda, always wears plaid shirts, and used to work part-time as a draftsman, overly conservative predictions about future GPA are generated.

When the diluting nondiagnostic information turns out to be diagnostic for some other attribute, it loses its diluting capacity for the original information, and extreme inferences again result (Gangestad & Borgida, 1981). For example, the relevance of a high GPA for future academic performance may be diluted if one also learns that the student works out three hours a day; as a consequence, when asked to predict future academic performance, an overly conservative prediction (e.g., "he will do moderately well") will result. However, if one then learns that he is on the basketball team, "working out" becomes diagnostic for playing basketball. As a consequence, it no longer dilutes the GPA information, and a prediction of high future academic performance will result.

The failure to appreciate regression, then, appears to be a robust oversight in the social perceiver's inferential inventory. Usually, regression is not detected, but even when it is, as in the second-novel example discussed earlier, people often assume logical reasons rather than random factors explain the effect. Although extreme inferences due to ignorance of regression can be guarded against by the dilution effect, the dilution effect itself constitutes a misunderstanding of the relevance of diagnostic and nondiagnostic information to the judgment process.

INTEGRATING INFORMATION

The task of bringing information together and combining it into a judgment is also problematic when compared against the normative model. The person's combinatorial shortcomings are particularly well illustrated when he or she is matched against a computer given the same information. The computer always does as well or better. How can one demonstrate this fact? First, it is necessary to find a judgment task in which roughly the same kinds of information are contained in every case; second, there must be a decision rule regarding how that information is to be combined to reach a decision for each case. Such judgment tasks are relatively common. Stock must be reordered after considering likely demand, current inventory, and cash flow. Patients must be diagnosed and treated once clinical observations, presenting symptoms, and test results are known. Students are admitted to or rejected from graduate school on the basis of test scores, grade point average, past work, and letters of recommendation. A normatively appropriate way of completing such a task is to take each case (e.g., student), take each of the bits of information relevant to the judgment (e.g., GPA, letters of recommendation, GRE scores), multiply each bit by its weight (e.g., count GREs twice as much as GPA and GPA half again as much as letters of recommendation), add it up for a total case score, and compare the case's score against other case scores to pick the best ones. This process employs a *linear model*, so called because the total impression is an additive combination of the available information. It is a task that can be efficiently and effectively completed by a properly programmed computer.

It should be noted that a linear combination is not the only way such repeating decisions can be reliably made. Various *nonlinear* combinations may also be reliably utilized to make decisions. The following two decision rules are nonlinear: "Place full order of stock when inventory drops to 35 percent, unless previous order was placed more than six months ago, in which case order only half as much." Or "Weigh GPA twice as heavily as letters of recommendation, unless GPA is lower than 3.0, in which case weigh it evenly with letters." The nonlinear nature of these rules makes them no less readily programmable for a computer, so they can be employed for decision-making purposes as readily as a linear combination. And, more to the point, using either type of rule is more reliable than the human decision maker.

Unfortunately, the human decision maker often has an exaggerated view of his or her ability to accomplish this task, so much so that the idea of letting it fall to a computer meets with strenuous objections. Clinical intuition, it is felt, would be sacrificed to a rigid numerical formula, and unusual instances or special cases would slip through the cracks.

Anyone who has ever sat on an admissions or membership committee and seen "clinical intuition" in operation probably knows already that the process is often random and inconsistent, full of blatant stereotyping, unwarranted favoritism, and irrational dislikes. Dawes (1980) presents a particularly entertaining account of the process at several leading universities. A slang peculiar to the admissions process quickly develops. *Pinnochios* are applicants with high ratings from letter writers on all but one characteristic, such as maturity or independence; hence their profile has a long jag or nose. They are to be avoided, since anyone who attracts enough attention to get that low a rating on some attribute must be really bad. *Jock essays* are essays that are too short; *geos* are students who would add geographic diversity, such as a Hawaiian applying to an East coast school. And everyone seems to be looking for the proverbial "neat small-town kid." Very often, comparisons are made to apparently similar students with whom one has already had experience: "Aha. Another Smedley. He was smart, but a drudge. Not a creative bone in his body" (Abelson, 1976). Frequently, these analogies are drawn on the basis of minimal similarity, such as having a record that excels in everything except physical education.

Despite such problems, this process is loudly defended. Its defenders maintain that generally, decision makers do use the linear model, and that departures from the model are made so as to pick up the "sleeper," the prodigal son returning to the fold, or the late bloomer. Table 9.2 presents a hypothetical account of the process employed for two fictitious graduate school admissions cases given a linear decision rule, a nonlinear decision rule, and an intuitive human decision maker (see Burgess, 1941; L. R. Goldberg, 1968, 1970).

Two extensive analyses of studies have pitted the clinical judge against the computer or other mechanical aids (Meehl, 1954; J. Sawyer, 1966); both yielded the same conclusion: computers or other mechanical aids always do as well or better than clinical judges. What does the computer do, and why does it do it so well? The computer merely does more consistently what human judges believe they do. It uses the criteria established by people, but it uses the criteria consistently, weighs them in a reliable way, combines the information accurately, and makes a judgment. What does the human decision maker do wrong? People usually believe they are using more cues and making more complex judgments than they actually are. One professor, upon reading this research, correlated her own rankings of prospective students with several admissions criteria and found, to her embarrassment and surprise, that GRE scores were virtually the sole basis for her decisions. Not only do people not use as many cues as they think they are using, they also do not weigh those cues the way they believe they do. One may believe one is giving extra weight to prior evidence of research skills when one actually is not. Thus, when it comes to combining multiple sources of information, the social perceiver is again misled by hunches about particular individuals' probable successes or failures or by attention to one, instead of multiple, cues (Dawes, 1976, 1980).

Although support for clinical judgment lingers, it is clear that for decisions that can be made using a constant decision rule, the computer outperforms the person. Clinical judges are, of course, important in picking out what variables need to go into the decision. However, when it comes to integrating the information to reach a decision, the person is best left out of the process.

ASSESSING COVARIATION

Judgments of covariation, that is, how strongly two things are related, are essential to many inference tasks, both formal and informal. Much of our folk wisdom states correlations such as the adage, "Blondes have more fun," or the assumption that all work and no play leads to dullness. Mickey Gilley's observation, "Don't the girls all get prettier at closing time" (Don't the boys, too?) assumes a correlation between time and perceived attractiveness (Penne- baker et al., 1979). Covariation is also the basis of many formal inference tasks. Kelley's covariation model of attribution (see Chapter 2) presupposes that the social perceiver is able to observe the covariation of an outcome across

TABLE 9.2
Comparison of the Linear Model, the Nonlinear Model, and a Human Decision Maker: Will Stinch and Crabble Be Admitted to Graduate School?

	Case A: Gerald Stinch	*Case B: Amanda Crabble*
	GRE: 650 Verbal, 710 Math GPA: 3.8 Letters of recommendation: Hardworking, diligent	GRE: 620 Verbal, 590 Math GPA: 2.9 Letters of recommendation: A bit of a dreamer, hasn't come into her own
Linear model (as applied by computer)	Score = 2 (GREs) + 1 (GPA) + .5 (Letter of recommendation)	
Decision:	Admit Stinch.	Reject Crabble.
Nonlinear model (as applied by computer)	Score = 2 (GREs) + 1 (GPA) + .5 (Letter of recommendation), unless GPA is less than 3.0, in which case score is 3 (GREs) + .5 (GPA) + 1 (Letter of recommendation)	
Decision:	Admit Stinch.	Reject Crabble.
Human decision maker	Aha. Another Smedley. Not a creative bone in his body.	Aha. Another Woodley? She was a great theoretician—got off to a slow start, though.
Decision:	Reject Stinch.	Admit Crabble.
Probable outcome given reliable and valid admissions criteria	Stinch will do well.	Crabble will do less well.

time, modality, persons, and entities with at least reasonable accuracy, so that an attribution can be formulated. Research on perceived control and on helplessness is based on the (in)capacity of the individual to see a relationship between his or her behavior and desirable outcomes (Chapter 5). And schemata (Chapter 6) are believed to be formed through the observation of co-occurring events.

Given the importance of covariation to judgment tasks, the question of how well the perceiver detects covariation is a critical one. The answer seems to be not very well (see Crocker, 1981; Nisbett & Ross, 1980, for reviews), when one compares the naive perceiver's estimates with the normative statistical model for assessing covariation (see Smedslund, 1963; Ward & Jenkins, 1965, for early references). The normative model for calculating covariation consists of several specific steps, and the research evidence to date suggests that the social perceiver is bias prone on most of them. These steps are illustrated in Fig. 9.2.

First, the perceiver must understand what data are relevant to assess covariation. For example, to test the adage, "Blondes have more fun," one needs to know the number of blonde men and women who have fun, the number of blondes who do not, the number of brunettes and redheads who have fun, and the brunettes and redheads who do not. Most people do not realize that all four kinds of evidence are relevant to the covariation task; rather they tend to concentrate primarily on the fun-loving blondes, believing that evidence that supports the adage is most relevant to its truth value. Indeed, this is a general propensity of the social perceiver that has been noted in other contexts: when testing the validity of an idea, people tend to seek instances that confirm the idea, rather than instances on all sides of the issue (e.g., Arkes & Harkness, 1980; G. H. Bower, Black, & Turner, 1979; Franks & Bransford, 1971; see also Fazio, Sherman, & Herr, 1982, for a related point). Yet, by nature, such statements as "Blondes have more fun" are comparative (All blondes or most? More fun than who?), so all four types of information are needed.

The second step in assessing covariation is sampling cases, because, as in the case above, one obviously cannot check out all blonde, brunette, and redheaded men and women. As has been noted, people are very poor samplers. Their own range of acquaintances and contacts, on whom they frequently draw, is certainly biased, but most people seem to be unaware of this fact (Crocker, 1981). Small samples may be overused (Tversky & Kahneman, 1974), and, at times, when sample results disagree with one's own hunches, the sample results are rejected or go unrecognized as contradictory (Arkes & Harkness, 1980; Crocker, 1981).

The third step in the covariation process is classifying instances as to type of evidence. Here again, the social perceiver's expectations often get in the way. Negative instances, that is, cases that contradict the proposed relationship, may be mislabeled as positive if they are ambiguous, or if not, dismissed as being due to error or faulty sampling. Positive instances that fit expectations are more quickly or easily identified and incorporated into the inference task (e.g., Owens, Bower, & Black, 1979; Harris, Teske, & Ginns, 1975).

In the fourth stage, the perceiver must recall the evidence and estimate the frequency of each type of evidence. As was evident in Chapter 8, memory is certainly not infallible; it is particularly good for confirming cases and, under some circumstances, it is also good for strongly disconfirming cases (Hastie & Kumar, 1979; but see Crocker, Hannah, & Weber, 1983). Thus the ecstatic blonde and the deliriously happy raven-haired person may be remembered, while the three happy "mousy browns" may be forgotten.

Finally, and only after the previous four steps have been completed, the social perceiver is ready to combine the evidence in the proper form. How

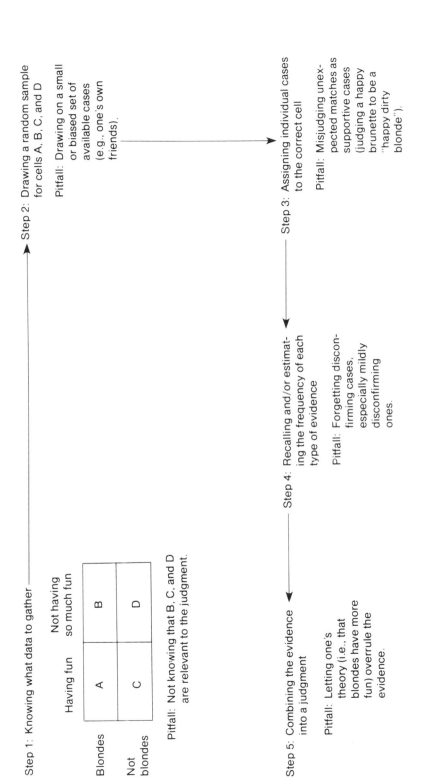

Step 1: Knowing what data to gather

	Having fun	Not having so much fun
Blondes	A	B
Not blondes	C	D

Pitfall: Not knowing that B, C, and D are relevant to the judgment.

Step 2: Drawing a random sample for cells A, B, C, and D

Pitfall: Drawing on a small or biased set of available cases (e.g., one's own friends).

Step 3: Assigning individual cases to the correct cell

Pitfall: Misjudging unexpected matches as supportive cases (judging a happy brunette to be a "happy dirty blonde").

Step 4: Recalling and/or estimating the frequency of each type of evidence

Pitfall: Forgetting disconfirming cases, especially mildly disconfirming ones.

Step 5: Combining the evidence into a judgment

Pitfall: Letting one's theory (i.e., that blondes have more fun) overrule the evidence.

Fig. 9.2 The assessment of covariation and its pitfalls: Do blondes have more fun?

successfully is this task accomplished? In fact, the ability of the social perceiver to estimate degree of covariation, once all the data have been assembled, has been too much impugned. Previous researchers have often confused errors of perceived relevance, sampling, classification, and recall of evidence as errors in computation, thereby underestimating the social perceiver's computational abilities (Crocker, 1981). This is not, however, to suggest either that the perceiver successfully computes correlation coefficients in his or her head or that estimates of covariation, however made, are usually accurate. Perceivers' estimates of covariation generally track, though somewhat underestimate, actual covariation, as long as no strong prior expectation about the degree of relationship between the two variables exists (Jennings, Amabile, & Ross, 1982).

Certain ways of presenting covariation information favor accuracy more than others. People tend to be more accurate in their estimations of covariation when the actual frequencies of cases are low, when all information can be observed simultaneously rather than serially, when the data are summarized, when instructions are clear, when there is repeated exposure to the data (Cordray & Shaw, 1978; Crocker, 1982), and when the concept of non-contingency (i.e., the absence of a relationship between two variables) is understood (see Crocker, 1981, for a review).

The most important factor influencing inaccuracy in covariation estimates is whether or not individuals have a theory or prior expectation about the relationship between the two variables (Nisbett & Ross, 1980). When people have no theory, they may somewhat underestimate or not perceive a co-variation, even when a statistician would consider the relationship to be quite strong (Jennings *et al.*, 1982). However, when a relationship between two variables is expected, subjects greatly overestimate the degree of relationship that exists or impose a relationship when none actually exists. This intriguing phenomenon has been termed *illusory correlation*.

ILLUSORY CORRELATION

In an early example of the illusory correlation phenomenon, Chapman (1967) presented college student subjects with lists of paired words such as *lion–tiger*, *lion–eggs*, and *bacon–eggs*. Subjects were then asked to report how often each word was paired with each other word; in fact, all words were paired with each other an equal number of times. Nonetheless, subjects reported that words that were associated in meaning such as *bacon-eggs* had been paired more frequently than those not associated in meaning. Within the word list, in addition, there had been two items that were longer than the other words in the list, specifically *blossoms* and *notebook*. Subjects also inferred that these two words had more frequently been paired, apparently because they shared the distinctive quality of length. Chapman reasoned, then, that at least two factors can produce an illusory correlation: *associative meaning*, in which two items are seen as belonging together because they "ought" to on the basis of prior expectations (e.g., *bacon-eggs*); and *paired distinctiveness*, in which two items are thought to go together because they share some unusual feature (*blossoms–notebook*).

A second study (Chapman & Chapman, 1967, 1969) pursued the associative meaning basis for illusory correlations in a somewhat unsettling context. As most of us know, clinical psychologists and psychiatrists have a number of tests that are intended to provide them with information on how people think about themselves and the world. For example, one may be asked to draw a person and from that drawing, certain aspects of one's self-concept are inferred. Chapman and Chapman gave college-student subjects a set of drawings from the Draw-a-Person test on which the drawer's psychological symptoms also appeared. After looking over the pictures, subjects were asked what drawing characteristics went with what psychological symptoms. In fact, the drawing characteristic–symptom pairings were established by chance, with no reliable relationship between the two. These students nonetheless "discovered" many of the same relationships on which professionals base their diagnoses, such as the idea that enlarged eyes go with paranoia or that no hands on a drawing indicates psychological withdrawal. Even when subjects were given careful instructions, lots of time, and incentives to be correct, they persisted in "seeing" the nonexistent relationships between symptoms and drawing attributes.

Why are these results so disconcerting? In recent years, these kinds of psychological "projective" tests have come under fire as unreliable and invalid, yet despite negative evidence, many clinicians tenaciously continue to use them. What the Chapmans' study suggests, of course, is that the faith one has in such instruments can be illusory, maintained solely by the expectations one has about their diagnostic value and not on any real value they might have (see also Chapman & Chapman, 1982).

Most recently, the concept of illusory correlation has applied to stereotyping (D. L. Hamilton, 1979). In particular, Hamilton and Gifford (1976) argued that paired distinctiveness can explain some negative stereotyping of minority group members. Specifically, majority-group members have relatively few contacts with minority-group members, and negative behaviors are also relatively infrequent. It may be that members of the majority group make an illusory correlation between the two rare events and infer that minority-group members are more likely to engage in negative behaviors. To test this point, Hamilton and Gifford gave subjects a list of statements about members of group A and group B. Statements about group A were twice as numerous as statements about group B, and positive statements were twice as numerous as negative ones; the relative frequency of positive and negative statements was the same for both groups. Nonetheless, the subjects misrecalled the uncommon, negative behaviors as more frequently paired with the uncommon group, group B. The study was also replicated with positive events as the more infrequent ones, and the results indicated that an illusory correlation between minority status and positive features can occur as well. However, since negative events are perceived to be more rare than positive events (Parducci, 1968), the more likely situation in real life is that minority-group members and negative events will be disproportionately perceived to covary.

Certainly, other factors than paired distinctiveness contribute to the development of negative stereotypes. Majority-group members may have a disproportionately negative sample of minority-group members' behavior, because they usually encounter minority-group members in low status roles and because the news media more frequently highlight minority-group members' negative acts. Furthermore, majority-group members may already hold negative stereotypes about minority groups. Accordingly, an associative meaning basis for seeing a relationship between minority-group members' behavior and negative behavior may also exist. Research by McArthur and Friedman (1980), in fact, confirms that both associative meaning (or prior expectations) and paired distinctiveness contribute to the stereotyping of minority-group members. Overall, their results suggest that associative meaning is the stronger determinant of stereotyping (see also D. L. Hamilton & Rose, 1980, and Chapter 6, "Social Schemata").

The twin topics of covariation estimation and illusory correlation are important for several reasons. First, as a complex operation, the estimation of covariation represents a concatenation of many of the errors and biases in the social perceiver's intuitive strategies, such as detecting what information is relevant, sampling it correctly, and recalling it accurately. Second, because covariation is often an interim inference upon which other, more complex inferences are subsequently based, the flaws that mark covariation estimation may have repercussions farther down the line in terms of the accuracy with which the social perceiver describes and acts on the environment. Finally, errors in the estimation of covariation again highlight how the inference process is biased conservatively toward conclusions that people expect to be true and how the theories people have regarding the functioning of the social environment predominate in guiding the inference process. As we will see in the next section, these theories also predominate in the social perceiver's interpretation of the past.

LEARNING FROM THE PAST

The maxim, "Those who ignore the past are condemned to relive it," implies that, were we scrupulously to turn our attention backward in time, rather than forward, we would learn important lessons. Although this adage may contain an element of truth, research on hindsight questions how seriously we ought to believe it. Everyone is familiar with the Monday morning quarterback who, with the advantage of retrospection, knows what could have and should have been done to win the game. He claims that the opposition's moves could have been anticipated, that the home team ought to have foreseen them, and that a particular strategy (his) clearly would have been successful.

Twenty-twenty hindsight seems to be a robust phenomenon. Work by Fischhoff and his colleagues (Fischhoff, 1975, 1980, 1982b; Fischhoff & Beyth, 1975; Fischhoff, Slovic, & Lichtenstein, 1977) indicates that it is very difficult to ignore knowledge of an actual outcome and to generate unbiased inferences about what could or should have happened. In retrospect, people exaggerate what could have been anticipated. Moreover, when people's predictions about future events are compared with postdictions about events that have already happened, results show that people distort and misremember their own predictions to conform with what really happened (Fischhoff & Beyth, 1975; D. J. Bem & McConnell, 1970).

The ubiquitous role of the social perceiver's theory-generating capacity also should not be underestimated as a basis for reconstructing the past. Even the most random sequence of events can be forced with enough thought into a logical causal chain. Once that causal chain of reasons is firmly in place, it may be hard to see events as other than inevitable. Furthermore, interventions that would presumably have set some other causal sequence into effect may seem particularly compelling because they seem so logical. Chance or situational factors that may have heavily influenced what actually occurred may be overlooked. For example, in a football game, an opponent's series of moves may appear to be part of an overall plan, when in fact it capitalizes on chance events such as an injury or a fumble. Nonetheless, once labeled as a plan, it is likely to be seen as predictable ("They did the same thing in the Tennessee game"), and solutions to it seem obvious ("We should have switched to a running game").

What ought we to learn from the past? Rarely are the lessons of history clear, since inevitably they are inextricably tinged with the advantage of hindsight. Participants in events do not know the full import of those events before they happen ("Dear Diary, The Hundred Years' War started today," Fischer, 1970, cited in Fischhoff, 1980, p. 84). Since it is hard to estimate what should have been foreseen and still harder to assess the role of environmental and chance factors in producing outcomes that have already occurred, what is actually learned from history is unclear.

In short, we are creatures of the present, trapped inferentially by what we already know. As in the case of other inference tasks, our methods of assessment are highly fallible and are often driven by a priori or easily constructed theories, rather than by objective data. Finally, the answers themselves, that is, what it is we should be learning from the past, are indeterminant. Perhaps, then, a better maxim than that which opened this section might be one of Fischhoff's own: "While the past entertains, ennobles, and expands quite readily, it enlightens only with delicate coaxing" (1980, p. 80).

Heuristics: A Rapid Form of Reasoning

Thus far, the discussion of inference has focused on what the perceiver seems not to do well by showing that the methods used to accomplish inferential tasks fall short of the normative models that could be used to accomplish them. This section focuses more heavily on what the social perceiver does do, rather than on what he or she should do, and identifies when these methods succeed and when they fail.

As already seen, the social perceiver often must make complex judgments under conditions that may not be best suited to accuracy or thoroughness. One must figure out the best way to break the news to one's parents that one is dropping out of school and try to guess what their reactions might be. One must decide if a safe and reasonably satisfying romantic relationship should be abandoned for a new, exciting fling whose future is uncertain. One must decide if collaborating on a project with another is better than doing it all oneself. Seemingly unlimited amounts of information could be brought to bear on any one of these decisions, but much of it would be of uncertain value. Furthermore, if thoroughly evaluated, all of these decisions could occupy the better part of a week; but, if so, nothing else would get done. For these reasons—time constraints, complexity and/or volume of the relevant information, and uncertainty about the evidence itself—it is unrealistic for the social perceiver to use exhaustive strategies for making judgments. Thus the social perceiver must, under most circumstances, be a "satisficer" who makes adequate inferences and decisions, rather than an "optimizer" who reaches the best possible inferences and decisions (March & Simon, 1958).

In a ground-breaking, highly influential paper, Tversky and Kahneman (1974) sketched out some processes used by people for making judgments about uncertain events. They argued that people often use *heuristics* or shortcuts that reduce complex problem solving to more simple judgmental operations.

THE REPRESENTATIVENESS HEURISTIC

One such heuristic, termed *representativeness*, is used to make inferences about probability (Kahneman & Tversky, 1973; Tversky & Kahneman, 1982). It can help answer such questions as: How likely is it that person or event A is a member of category B? (e.g., Is George a football player?), or Did event A originate from process B? (e.g., could the sequence of coin tosses H-H-T-T have occurred randomly?). For example, consider the following description: "Steve is very shy and withdrawn, invariably helpful, but with little interest in people, or in the world of reality. A meek and tidy soul, he has a need for order and structure, and a passion for detail" (Tversky & Kahneman, 1974). Suppose you are now asked to guess Steve's occupation. Is he a farmer, a trapeze artist, a librarian, a salvage diver, or a surgeon?

With adequate information about the frequency and personality characteristics of the people in these different occupations, one could conceivably tally up the probability of a meek surgeon, shy trapeze artist, and so on, and actually calculate the likelihood that Steve is in each occupation. This task would, however, take a very long time, and good information on which to base the calculations would undoubtedly be lacking. In such cases, the representativeness heuristic provides a quick solution. One estimates the extent to which Steve is representative of or similar to the average person in each of the other categories and makes one's judgment about his occupation accordingly. In the present case, one is likely to guess that Steve is a librarian, because the description of Steve is representative of attributes stereotypically associated with librarians.

The representativeness heuristic, then, is basically a relevancy judgment that produces a probability estimate, that is, How probable is it that A is an instance of category B? Using this heuristic will usually produce fairly good answers, perhaps as good as those produced by a more exhaustive analysis of the information available for the task, because relevancy is usually a good criterion for making probability judgments. However, when the representativeness heuristic is used by the social perceiver, he or she may be insensitive to other factors, independent of judged relevancy, that affect actual probability of occurrence (Kahneman & Tversky, 1973).

One such factor is *prior probability of outcomes*. If Steve lives in a town with lots of chicken farmers and only a few librarians, one's judgment that he is a librarian should be tempered by this fact; that is, it is simply more likely that he is a chicken farmer than a librarian. Nonetheless, as noted earlier, people often ignore prior probabilities and instead base their judgment solely on similarity, for example, the fact that Steve resembles a librarian.

Another factor that people often ignore in judgments of representativeness is *sample size*. Suppose you are at the state fair running a booth in which you try to guess the occupation of anyone who pays a quarter. Suppose 4 of your first 5 clients are librarians, and you subsequently discover that the librarians' convention is in town. How confident should you be that the next individual in line is also a librarian? Would you be more or less confident than if 12 of the first 20 individuals you saw had turned out to be librarians? Most people making this judgment feel more confident that the next individual in line is a librarian if 4 of the first 5 individuals are librarians than if 12 of the first 20 are. Their confidence is, in fact, misplaced. As already noted, sampling theory dictates that estimates derived from a large sample are more reliable than estimates derived from a small one. Thus, even though 4 out of 5 looks like better odds than 12 out of 20, the 12 out of 20 is the more reliable indicator.

Judgments made on the basis of representativeness may also show an *insensitivity to predictive value*, that is, insensitivity to the relevance or quality of the information as a predictor of some outcome. For example, if the description of Steve as a meek and tidy soul had been written by Steve's kindergarten teacher after a scant few weeks of classes, its relevance to Steve's career choice would be weak indeed, whereas if written by Steve's adviser after four years of college, one might want to give it more weight. Nonetheless, people often behave as though information is to be trusted regardless of its source, and make equally strong or confident inferences, regardless of the information's predictive value. This *illusion of validity* may also be present when the information is a particularly good fit to the judgment. For example, if the description of Steve contained the additional sentence, "He is a bookish sort who peers intently over his wire-rimmed spectacles," our confidence in

Steve's destiny as a librarian might be vastly increased. However, upon learning "he scuba dives in his spare time, and at one time in his life was a heavy cocaine user," we might begin to back off from a strong prediction. Whether the information is accurate and fully reliable or out-of-date, inaccurate, and based on hearsay may, however, matter little. Apparent validity or invalidity is the stronger basis for its acceptance or rejection.

Finally, *misconceptions about chance* can also bias representativeness judgments. People have quite well-developed ideas of what chance events ought to look like. In flipping a coin several times, for example, one expects to see a sequence like H-T-H-T-T-H, not a seemingly orderly one like T-T-T-H-H-H. When asked to judge which sequence is more likely to occur, many people will erroneously pick the first one, because it looks random, whereas the second sequence is, in fact, statistically just as likely to occur.

The representativeness heuristic, then, is a quick, though occasionally fallible, method of estimating probability via judgments of relevancy. It is also perhaps our most basic cognitive heuristic. The act of identifying people as members of categories, or the act of assigning meaning to actions, is fundamental to all social inference and behavior; that is, the question, "What is it?" must be answered before any other cognitive task can be performed.

THE AVAILABILITY HEURISTIC

Availability is a heuristic that is used to evaluate the frequency or likelihood of an event on the basis of how quickly instances or associations come to mind (Tversky & Kahneman, 1973). For example, if I am asked whether a lot of women my age are having babies now, I will likely think over the number of friends and acquaintances I know who have or are about to have babies and respond on the basis of the relative frequency of examples or ease with which examples come to mind. As is the case with the representativeness heuristic, little cognitive work need be conducted to accomplish this task. I can provide a frequency estimate on the basis of how quickly or easily instances or associations can be retrieved. If I have no trouble bringing to mind examples of pregnant friends, I will likely estimate that there is a small baby boom in my age group, whereas if it takes me a while to think of someone who is having a baby, I will scale down my estimate of my cohort's productivity.

Under many circumstances, use of the availability heuristic will produce correct answers. After all, when examples of something can be brought to mind easily, it is usually because there are lots of them. However, there are also biasing factors that can increase or decrease the availability of some class of phenomena or events without altering its actual overall frequency. For example, the fact that I have a newborn baby means not only that I spend time with other mothers more than I normally would, but that I am also probably more likely to notice whether someone has a child or not than I would otherwise. Thus, when I think of examples of new mothers, my available supply of examples is biased, and my estimate of the birth rate is likely to be higher than is warranted. When a class has easily retrieved instances, it will seem more numerous than will an equally frequent category that has less easily retrieved instances.

Search biases, as well as *retrieval biases,* can skew one's frequency estimations by biasing the number of available instances. For example, for some categories of events, it is easier to search for instances than it is for other categories. Estimating the birth rate at a church or temple would, for example, produce a higher estimate than would estimating the birth rate among co-workers; because people frequently take their children to church or temple but rarely bring them to work, the ease with which instances can be brought to mind varies dramatically between the two settings.

Finally, the *ease with which one can imagine* particular events can bias frequency estimates. For example, when people are asked to guess the major causes of death in this country, they often assume more deaths result from such dramatic events as accidents, fires, drownings, or shootings than is actually the case. At the same time, they underestimate death from more common causes such as stroke or heart disease. Newspapers and television programs have created colorful, easily imaged instances of the former events, and hence it is easy to bring images or associations to mind, whereas a death from disease rarely makes it past the obituary page (see Slovic *et al.,* 1976, for a discussion of this research).

Ease of retrieval of instances is one way of estimating frequency via the availability heuristic as just seen; *strength of association* is another. Associative bonds are strengthened by repeated examples (Chapter 8, "Person Memory"); hence the strength of an association between any two things is usually likely to be a fairly good estimate of the frequency of some class of events. As with ease of retrieval of instances, however, associative strength may be biased by factors irrelevant to actual frequency. For example, if I live in a city like Pittsburgh that stresses family values, I may infer that the birthrate is higher than if I lived in a city like Los Angeles, known for its wild singles' life. In the former city, the virtues and accomplishments of children may be extolled, thus creating a belief that there are many children around, whereas in Los Angeles children keep a rather low profile.

The potential biasing effects of the availability heuristic on frequency estimates have been neatly demonstrated in the context of stereotyping by Rothbart and his associates (Rothbart *et al.,* 1978). Subjects were given trait information about members of a hypothetical group under one of two conditions. They either saw the names of several different group members (Ed, Phil, Fred, Joe) paired with a particular trait (lazy) or they saw the same name-trait pairing (Phil is lazy) an equivalent number of times. In addition, some subjects saw a lot of name-trait pairings (high memory load condition), whereas other subjects saw relatively few name-trait pairings (low memory load). After seeing the pairings, subjects were asked to characterize the group as a whole. If people are able to remember accurately which name(s) were paired with which traits, then inferences about the group as a whole should be stronger if several group members have a particular trait than if only one member has the trait. When the total number of name-trait pairings subjects were exposed to was low (low memory load condition), subjects showed this caution in their inferences about the group. However, when the total number of name-trait pairings was high (high memory load condition), it was apparently difficult for subjects to keep straight how many individuals had which traits, and they began to behave as if multiple instances of the same name-trait pairing were as informative as several different names paired with that trait. Under high memory load, the group came to be characterized as lazy even when only a few of its members actually were lazy.

The social world is often overwhelmingly informative, and as such it usually mirrors the high memory load condition more than the low memory load condition. This fact could, then, facilitate the formation of group stereotypes from the behavior of just a few individuals whose behavior shows up a large number of times. Because media are more focused on negative than positive events, these biases could favor the formation of negative group stereotypes, particularly if group membership is salient when mentioned in media coverage.

The availability heuristic has been a highly influential idea within social psychology, and it can provide an explanatory mechanism for a wide range of social phenomena, including stereotyping (D. L. Hamilton & Rose, 1978) and the perseverance of discredited beliefs (L. Ross, Lepper, & Hubbard, 1975; L. Ross, Lepper, Strack, & Steinmetz, 1977; see S. E. Taylor, 1982b, for a review). It has also been offered as an explanation for other phenomena such as salience (S. E. Taylor, 1982b; see Chapter 7), judgments of responsibility (M. Ross & Sicoly, 1979; see Chapter 4), predictions (e.g., Carroll, 1978; Slovic et al., 1976) and causal attributions (Pryor & Kriss, 1977). It may well have been overused. Many tasks do not require even the small amount of work engaged by use of the availability heuristic. The amount of information we already have stored in memory, as in the form of schemata for well known types of social events or people, means that answers to many of the inferences we must form are already available, as long as we can access the correct schema. The implication of this assumption is that, generally, people will draw on the representativeness heuristic to identify what schema or category is appropriate for retrieving information more than they will draw on the availability heuristic for making judgments.

THE SIMULATION HEURISTIC

One use of availability is in the construction of hypothetical scenarios to try to estimate how something will come out. This inferential technique is known as the *simulation* heuristic (Kahneman & Tversky, 1982). Consider, as an example, how you would answer the question, "What is your dad going to think when he finds out you have smashed up the car?" You may think of what you know about your father and his reactions to crises, run through these events in your mind, and generate several possibilities; the ease with which a particular ending comes to mind is used to judge what is likely to happen in real life. Your father could refuse to pay your college tuition next term, or he could ignore the whole thing, but in your judgment, it is easiest to imagine that he will strongly suggest that you find a job so that you can help pay for the car.

The simulation heuristic may be used for a wide variety of tasks including prediction (How will Joan like Tom?) and causality (Is the dog or the kid to blame for the mess on the floor?). It is particularly relevant to situations of near misses. For example, consider the following:

> Mr. Crane and Mr. Tees were scheduled to leave the airport on different flights, at the same time. They traveled from town in the same limousine, were caught in a traffic jam, and arrived at the airport thirty minutes after the scheduled departure time of their flights.
> Mr. Crane is told that his flight left on time.
> Mr. Tees is told that his flight was delayed, and just left five minutes ago.
> Who is more upset?
> Mr. Crane or Mr. Tees. (Kahneman & Tversky, 1982, p. 203)

Virtually everyone says, "Mr. Tees." Why? Presumably, one can imagine no way that Mr. Crane could have made his plane, whereas, were it not for that one long light or the slow baggage man or the illegally parked car or the error in the posted departure gate, Mr. Tees would have made it. Thus the simulation heuristic and its ability to generate *if only* conditions can be used to understand the psychology of near misses and the frustration, regret, grief, or indignation they may produce (cf. Chapter 11).

ANCHORING AND ADJUSTMENT

When making judgments under uncertainty, people will sometimes reduce ambiguity by starting with a beginning reference point or anchor and then adjusting it to reach a final conclusion. If, for example, you are asked to guess how many people attended the USC-UCLA football game, and you have absolutely no idea, it is helpful to know that the previous week's game in the same stadium drew a crowd of 23,000. You may then guess 30,000, assuming that a USC-UCLA contest would draw a bigger crowd. So it is with social judgments as well, which often require anchors for making judgments about others (e.g., Wyer, 1976).

As it happens, the *anchoring and adjustment* heuristic has received less attention from social psychologists than have representativeness and availability. However, we have already discussed phenomena that constitute instances of the anchoring and adjustment heuristic. Recall from Chapter 4 the self-based or false consensus effect in attributions. When asked to estimate how many people would perform some activity (e.g., wear a sandwich board around campus), subjects' estimates are substantially influenced by the decision they would make for themselves. Although we know intellectually that not everyone would behave as we do, our estimates of others' behavior are not adjusted sufficiently from the anchor our own behavior provides. Likewise, our egocentric estimations of responsibility may represent an inability to correct adequately for our own biases in recalling our own contributions. As the two previous examples suggest, it is very possible that the most prominent anchor from which we estimate or judge others' social behavior is ourselves and our social environment (e.g., Fong & Markus, 1982; Markus & Smith, 1981). We may, for example, judge how aggressive or shy another person is as an adjusted inference from our own self-rating on these same qualities.

Judgments may also be anchored by irrelevant details of a situation that nonetheless suggest a beginning reference point. Suppose you are accosted by a religious fanatic who tells you the world is about to end and who shows you data on arms buildup to prove it. You may know to discount what he says because he is untrustworthy, but his communication nonetheless provides an anchor for the topic. Thus, when asked your attitude toward the issue, you may show a shift in the direction of his communication. Similarly, in attributing attitudes to others, you may be aware of constraints on their attitude expression (e.g., a reporter had to write an anti-Castro article, because his editor told him to); nonetheless, with the communication itself as an anchor, you may fail to correct sufficiently for the constraints (and thus infer that the writer is indeed anti-Castro). Quattrone, Finkel, and Andrus (1982) have suggested that these robust findings—failing to discount adequately a low credibility communication and failing to correct for situational constraints in the attribution of attitudes—can be understood as anchoring and insufficient adjustment effects.

Anchors and examples of anchoring and adjustment are ubiquitous in social situations, perhaps precisely because social behavior is so ambiguous and relatively free of objective yardsticks. When we can, we use ourselves as anchors, but when those reference points are ambiguous, we may use the behavior and attributes of others or we may be anchored by irrelevant details of a situation.

HEURISTICS: A POSTSCRIPT

The heuristics discussed by Tversky and Kahneman (1974; Kahneman & Tversky, 1982) are described in Table 9.3. Psychologists have sometimes behaved as if these few—representativeness, availability, anchoring—are the only ones people use. Yet the overall point made by this influential line of work is that the social perceiver is virtually always using heuristics to a greater or lesser extent, including general ones like representativeness that can be applied across a wide variety of situations and idiosyncratic ones that apply only to one's particular job or hobbies. Certainly there are circumstances in which people become more thoughtful and less reliant on heuristics and under such circumstances, better inferences may be reached. But heuristics are fundamental to inference, making rapid information processing possible. Thus an investigation of the abundant heuristics of daily life in addition to those already outlined would be extremely useful for understanding both the wisdom and flaws of everyday thinking (see for example, Kahneman & Tversky, 1982; Nisbett, Krantz, Jepson, & Kunda, 1983).

TABLE 9.3
Some Heuristic Strategies for Making Judgments under Uncertainty
(After Tversky & Kahneman, 1974)

Heuristic	Some types of judgment heuristic is used for	Description	Example
Representativeness	Probability judgment	Representativeness is a judgment of how relevant A is to B; high relevance yields high estimates that A originates from B	Deciding that George (A) must be an engineer because he looks and acts like your stereotype of engineers (B)
Availability	Frequency or probability judgments	Availability is the estimate of how frequently or likely a given instance or occurrence is, based on how easily or quickly an association or examples come to mind	Estimating the divorce rate on the basis of how quickly one can think of examples of divorced friends
Adjustment and anchoring	Estimates of position on a dimension	Anchoring and adjustment is the process of estimating some value by starting with some initial value and then adjusting it to the new instance	Judging another person's productivity based on one's own level of productivity

AWARENESS OF COGNITIVE PROCESSES

Were one to undertake to improve the social perceiver's inferential processes, the effort would likely begin by alerting the perceiver to the problem and instructing him or her to be attentive to inferential errors in the future. Such instructions would presuppose that people have at least some awareness of the inferential processes they are using and that they can draw on that awareness at will.

In a highly controversial paper, Nisbett and Wilson (1977b) maintained that people have little or no access to their cognitive processes. In fact, there is a substantial amount of anecdotal evidence from psychological studies indicating that many, if not most, experimental subjects have no idea of the forces in the experiment influencing their behavior. Taking these observations as their point of departure, Nisbett and Wilson conducted a series of experiments (Nisbett & Wilson, 1977a; T. D. Wilson & Nisbett, 1978) in which they systematically manipulated factors that influenced subjects' behavior and then asked the subjects to report what factors led them to behave as they did. For example, in one study, billed as an investigation of consumer preferences, subjects were asked to inspect four nightgowns, laid out on a table, and indicate which one they would choose. There is, in fact, a strong serial position effect for these kinds of tasks, such that people typically prefer the right most item to those that are to its left. (Why this position preference exists is not fully known.) Subjects in the experiment also showed this serial position effect, but when asked why they made the particular choice they had, they offered explanations that centered on qualities of the chosen garment itself. When it was suggested that serial position might have influenced their decision, subjects expressed considerable skepticism. Such occurrences are well known to most experimenters debriefing subjects after a social psychology experiment.

In another study involving less trivial behaviors (J. A. Weiss & Brown, 1977), college student women kept a record of their daily mood for a two-month period and also reported on factors that might be expected to influence their mood, such as amount of sleep, day of the week, sexual activity, stage of the menstrual cycle, and weather. The women were also asked to indicate what factors they thought had influenced their mood. Statistical procedures were then used to estimate which factors actually had influenced mood, and the results were compared with the women's theories about what factors had been influential. Overall, there was little match between objective and subjective estimates of factors affecting mood. For example, whereas the women themselves believed that amount of sleep was an important influence on mood, day of the week turned out to be a much stronger determinant. (Mood is better later on in the week.) An extensive series of additional studies (Nisbett & Wilson, 1977b) yields essentially the same conclusion: subjects' reports of what factors have influenced their behavior bear little relationship to the statistical profiles of factors indicating what actually influenced their behavior.

If we accept Nisbett and Wilson's interpretation that subjects have little or no access to their own cognitive processes, what are the sources for subjects' explanations for their behavior? Nisbett and Wilson argue that when people state the factors that have influenced their behavior, they are merely reporting their theories about what causes what, theories that any observer might share. For example, when one thinks about a bad or a good mood, a bad or a good night's sleep easily comes to mind as a good explanation of mood, whereas one is less likely to think, "I must be depressed because this is Tuesday." This is because theories about the relationship between sleep and mood are more common than those about the relationship between week day and mood. Hence when subjects are reporting what has influenced their mood, they may be actually reporting their beliefs about what influenced their mood, rather than actual determinants. An observer, such as one's roommate, may well share the same theory and give the same explanation: "Ralph is in a good mood because he slept well last night." When observers' explanations match those of the people involved in the behavior themselves, the possibility that their shared explanations stem from a common theory about what influences what is a strong possibility. As Nisbett and Wilson point out, under such circumstances, there is no reason to believe that the actor has any special access to his or her own cognitive processes (see also T. D. Wilson, Hull, & Johnson, 1981).

One should not infer from the previous discussion that people are always wrong in their theories of what causes their behavior. Indeed, on many, if not most occasions, people are right. If I ask you why you are crying, and you say, "Because my boyfriend left me," you are probably correct in your analysis. The fact that a theory is correct, however, or that it correctly applies to a particular case, does not imply that its holder has special access to his or her cognitive processes (T. D. Wilson *et al.*, 1981). Everyone knows that relationship break-ups can be sad.

Nisbett and Wilson's analysis touched off a heated response (e.g., Kraut & Lewis, 1982; E. R. Smith & Miller, 1978; P. White, 1980). Major criticisms hinged on several points. First, Nisbett and Wilson's argument is hard to falsify. When subjects are wrong about what factors influenced their behavior, Nisbett and Wilson can be viewed as supported; when subjects are right, if the subjects' explanation is shared by another person, it could well be due to a shared theory; hence Nisbett and Wilson's argument can again be construed as supported. Finally, if subjects are right about their explanation and the explanation is not shared by someone else, it may well be because subjects know things about their past behavior that others do not know, not because they have internal access to their cognitive processes.

A second problem is that, with rare exceptions (e.g., J. A. Weiss & Brown, 1977), the studies that support Nisbett and Wilson's position have asked subjects to report on trivial or obscured influences on their behavior, such as the serial position effect described earlier. Realistically, subjects could not be expected to be aware of these types of factors.

Third, it has been argued that Nisbett and Wilson's particular methodological procedures often do not provide a fair test of the accuracy of subjects' reports. For example, subjects are often asked to report on factors that were manipulated experimentally; having been exposed to only one experimental condition and having no knowledge of what the other experimental conditions may have been makes it hard for subjects to infer comparatively what might have influenced their behavior (see, particularly, E. R. Smith & Miller, 1978; Nisbett & Ross, 1980).

There are also statistical problems with the interpretation of some of Nisbett and Wilson's evidence. The average of a whole group of subjects' ratings concerning what factors might have influenced their behavior are sometimes compared against actual influences on the subjects' behavior; the more appropriate statistical comparison would compare individual ratings of perceived influence with actual influence on the same individual's behavior (Kraut & Lewis, 1982).

And finally, critics say that Nisbett and Wilson have maximized the conditions under which subjects would not be able to retrieve their thought processes. When conditions more suitable to such access are created, such as an involving task, high motivation to be accurate, or well-chosen probes to try to get at cognitive processes, evidence for access to internal thought processes may be found (Wright & Rip, 1981).

Nisbett and Ross (1980) rebutted several of these criticisms, but the fact that the position remains hard to falsify has led to a stalemate on the issue (Wright & Rip, 1981). What is the status of their argument? Nisbett and Wilson (1977b) have clearly demonstrated the weak version of their argument: there are many causes of individual behavior of which individuals themselves are not customarily aware. It is still a matter of controversy whether the strong version of the argument is valid, that is, that people have little or no access to their cognitive processes as a rule.

Even the weak version of Nisbett and Wilson's argument has important implications for the inferential process. If we optimistically ask the social perceiver to set prior theories aside and pay attention to the many subtle but normatively important factors that ought to be influencing behavior, our optimism may well be misplaced. It seems unlikely that the task could be accomplished well or thoroughly. Self-insight into cognitive processes is surely limited, if existent at all, and hence the idea that the social perceiver can describe, let alone straighten out, the inference process on his or her own is dubious.

Inference: An Overall Evaluation

Overall, how does the social perceiver fare on tasks of social inference? The evidence reviewed suggests that, like the proverbial adolescent in his first amorous forays, we may be fast, but we aren't very good. Most of our shortcuts such as using judgmental heuristics and relying on prior theories or schemata enable us to accomplish inference tasks quickly, but level of accuracy, as compared against normative models, seems to be quite poor. Indeed, there are few glowing tributes to the inferential abilities of the social perceiver. Reviews of inferential errors uniformly express dismay at our ability to solve problems correctly and wonder at the fact that people muddle through as well as they apparently do (e.g., Einhorn, 1980; Hogarth, 1980; Nisbett & Ross, 1980; Shweder, 1980; Tversky & Kahneman, 1974). Hence there is a puzzle: Why aren't inferential errors more problematic for daily living than they apparently are? Why, if shortcuts and strategies are so fraught with error, does their use persist?

There are at least two approaches one can take to this puzzle. The first maintains that normative models of inference are inappropriate standards for evaluating intuitive inferential strategies because intuitive inferential strategies take into account factors that normative models do not consider, factors that will be described in a moment. Thus this argument maintains that intuitive strategies should persist and not necessarily give way to normative strategies. The second approach maintains that even though intuitive inferential strategies can lead to incorrect answers, the errors and biases may be inconsequential or self-correcting. Both arguments have considerable validity and together seem to resolve the puzzle.

ARE NORMATIVE MODELS POOR STANDARDS FOR EVALUATING INTUITIVE INFERENCE?

A number of researchers who have examined the so-called pitfalls of intuitive inference are now coming to the opinion that normative models are often inappropriate bases for evaluating intuitive inferential strategies (Einhorn & Hogarth, 1981; Hogarth, 1981; Kahneman & Tversky, 1982; Nisbett, Krantz, Jepson, & Fong, 1982; Nisbett *et al.*, 1983). One reason is that conditions that make it possible to use a normative model are rarely present in the real world. Often, information is neither reliable, unbiased, nor complete. Even if it is, it may not be presented in a clear or usable fashion. Sometimes the information may not even be available. And even if it were, use of the normative model might be prohibitively time-consuming. Suppose, for example, you believe that terriers bite. Is it really worth it to you to get a sample of terriers, observe how often they bite, get a sample of other dogs, see how often they bite, and calculate a correlation coefficient? How many dogs would you need? How long should you wait before you decide that any given dog is not going to bite? What breed should your comparison dogs be? Where are you going to find enough terriers? In sum, isn't it just easier to avoid terriers? The conditions that maximize accuracy in inferences appear infrequently in real life. Accordingly, in many situations, one could not apply an ideal, statistical model, even if one were so inclined (see Crocker, 1981; Nisbett *et al.*, 1982).

Another problem with applying the normative model to most daily inferential situations is that normative models ignore the content and thus the context of a decision in favor of its formal structure. Thus, for example, deciding which of three brands of eggs to buy and deciding which of three people to marry could easily be treated as equivalent decisions under the normative model, if the information about the three options varied from each other in the same systematic ways. Yet the intuitive processes used for the two decisions would probably vary, and rightfully so.

The normative model generates inferential standards, given a fixed time and environment (i.e., all other things being equal). But decisions are made and inferences are drawn in dynamic environments, so predictions made for static environments may be inappropriate for changing ones (Hogarth, 1981). For example, if one observes an extremely high unemployment rate in Pennsylvania, knowledge of regression might lead one to expect a less extreme unemployment rate when it is reassessed. But such an estimate would ignore the fact that the steel industry is in deep trouble. Given such contextual knowledge, one might appropriately predict that unemployment in Pennsylvania will be at least as high, if not higher, when it is next calculated. Other so-called biases in intuitive inferential strategies may be similarly understood as efforts to draw appropriate inferences, given changing conditions (Hogarth, 1981).

The normative model also fails to take account of the important role that feedback plays in generating inferences (Einhorn, 1982; Hogarth, 1981); judgments are viewed as discrete events with no history or future. But most people verbalize even their most tentative judgments to others and receive some feedback as to whether they are on the right track. Thus inferences are made in a world filled with consequences. One's commitment to any one inference can be small, because once ventured, personal experience or communication may prove it correct or show it to be wrong, and one can then change one's inferences. Thus intuitive inferences are not choices that, once made, commit one irrevocably to a cognitive or behavioral course. Rather, in many cases, inferences may be tentative forays to be modified on the bases of the responses they evoke.

There are also circumstances when the type of judgment to be made suggests use of a different model than a normative one. Take the example of a fledgling job candidate who at lunch spills his water, sends his lamb chop flying into his neighbor's lap, and rests his elbow in the butter (Nisbett *et al.*, 1982). He is nervous, true, and his nervousness is clearly tied to situational factors, not dispositional ones. Furthermore, this is a very modest sample of his behavior, and it is likely to be a very poor predictor of future behavior. Normatively, one should probably discount these incidents. But consider the alternative, practical model of the person who must make the job hiring decisions. He or she must select a candidate who can consistently perform well and perform well under pressure. Wouldn't you rather have your sales made by someone who puts his butter on his roll, instead of his suit? In short, statistically normative models are only one kind of model that can be applied to social judgments. It may be the case that alternative models held by people directly involved in making those judgments generate valid criteria that inherently conflict with the standards generated by normative models.

Finally, we should note that the judgment situations used in experimental tests are often stacked against intuitive strategies of inference (Fischhoff, 1982a; Kahneman & Tversky, 1982). For example, the tasks may be unfamiliar or unfair (e.g., being set up to calculate a correlation in one's head) or they may be misconstrued by subjects. Or information may be presented in a format conducive to use of the normative model and not contain the kind of contextual detail that would facilitate use of an effective intuitive strategy. This methodological bias in experimental evidence, then, may lead to a more negative portrait of our inferential abilities than we deserve.

The preceding arguments are not intended to imply that normative models are always inappropriate as standards for daily inference, nor should the reader conclude that intuitive reasoning processes are better because they take content, context, and time into account. Indeed, methodological bias notwithstanding, this chapter is peppered with examples of blatantly incorrect inferences made through intuitive reasoning strategies. Why aren't these biases and errors more problematic for daily living?

ARE INFERENTIAL ERRORS INCONSEQUENTIAL OR SELF-CORRECTING?

There are several reasons why our inferential strategies persist despite errors. One is that they produce more right answers than wrong ones. For example, the availability and representativeness heuristics, though vulnerable to certain biases, undoubtedly lead to correct conclusions most of the time. Some strategies are relatively robust against certain errors, and in other cases one shortcoming may cancel out another (Nisbett & Ross, 1980). As noted earlier, the dilution effect (i.e., the finding that extreme predictions can be attenuated by the presence of irrelevant information), for example, can guard against the failure to appreciate regression toward the mean. Furthermore, most of our strategies can be employed very quickly and easily, and hence, even acknowledging some error, they are likely to pay off in time and energy saved by not using the more exhaustive and exhausting normative strategies.

Some of the errors produced by faulty inferential procedures will not matter. For example, if one's biased impressions will not affect one's future behavior, as in forming an incorrect impression of a person one meets only once, then the bias will be trivially important. In fact, little is known about the correspondence between inferences and behavior generally; if the correspondence is low, inferential errors may matter little. Biases may also matter little if they are constant over time. For example, if one regards one's boss as gruff, it may not matter that she is gruff only when she is in the boss role, if that is the only circumstance under which one interacts with her.

Biases may matter little when decisional alternatives are of near equal value. A student choosing between Harvard and Yale may make his final decision based on a biased sample of one friend's experience, but stereotypes and chauvinism aside, he will receive a trivially better education at one place over the other. Finally, our biases may have little impact on our strategies, because the conclusions we can draw from them are so often ambiguous. Consider the graduate admissions process. It is the rare graduate student who turns out to be a hot-shot. If one accepts five students and they have average careers and rejects five students who also have average careers, then one can find little apparent fault with one's decision-making process, even if it was actually made with the worst possible method. If one of the five rejected students goes on to excel, then one might conclude that an error was made in one case, and that that student should have been accepted. Still, one out of ten is not a bad error rate. Obviously, this reasoning is fallacious. However, it serves to underscore the fact that many of our processing errors do not yield blatantly bad results, so the processes may appear perfectly adequate.

Many sources of error will correct themselves. Whenever biases do not persist over time, the process will begin to correct itself with repeated encounters. For example, if several of one's friends have recently been divorced, one's estimate of the divorce rate may be temporarily exaggerated via the availability heuristic, but assuming that one's friends do not continue to have divorces indefinitely, one's estimated divorce rate should eventually come into line with objective data. Finally, and perhaps more important, in many cases, error will be detected through feedback (Hogarth, 1981). For example, normal conversation provides a basis for reality testing one's inferences, and blatantly false conclusions with far-reaching implications are likely to be corrected. This is particularly likely to be true of errors due to self-centered biases; for example, if the assertion that one performs one's share of the housework meets with apoplectic objections from one's spouse, that opinion is likely to be modified.

But erroneous perceptions with severe consequences, under some circumstances, persist. The contribution of inferential errors to the development and maintenance of pejorative stereotypes is one striking example. In short, one cannot trust biases in our strategies to be inconsequential, and accordingly, methods for the detection and correction of biased inferences are needed.

CAN WE IMPROVE THE INFERENCE PROCESS?

Perhaps those cases in which we do strikingly well at inferential tasks could serve as a model for improving the judgment process more generally. We have, after all, constructed a technological world of literally breathtaking proportions. But, as Nisbett and Ross (1980) point out, our triumphs are usually collective enterprises involving the pooling of many different kinds of expertise. They are often accomplished with the help of inferential aids such as calculators or computers. Perhaps most important, these products usually result from the cumulative effort of many years of formal research. In short, when we succeed strikingly, we do so because we use normative models and built-in devices and safeguards to ensure that we adhere to those models and because we make judgments collectively by pooling expertise. Our successes, then, may be successful precisely because we do not use our intuitive inferential strategies.

This point suggests several possible approaches for improving inferential strategies. Perhaps we should try to make the naive perceiver more like the formal scientist. Education in statistics and methodology, buttressed by the use of formal memory aids, is one approach (Einhorn, 1980; Nisbett et al., 1982). Bringing normative models into folk wisdom via catchy maxims that embody normative or statistical principles (Nisbett & Ross, 1980) is another possibility. With formal training or constant reminders of appropriate inferential techniques, formal methods may creep into everyday inference. Another solution is to get people to give up their attachment to hunches, theories, or clinical intuition by more often turning problems over to experts or computers. This is no small task. There is already evidence sufficient to justify such a move in many decision-making domains, but the evidence has been largely ignored. Moreover, none of these recommended methods is foolproof. Collectively made decisions have their own unique types of errors (e.g., Janis, 1972; Shaw, 1971), and trained statisticians and other experts are sometimes just as vulnerable to inferential errors as laypersons (Kahneman & Tversky, 1973; Tversky & Kahneman, 1974). In summary, there seems little that can be done that will drastically alter our inferential capabilities for most common judgment tasks. Rather, we will likely muddle through, as we have in the past, with the hope and expectation that nothing too dire will result from the errors and biases to which we are so curiously oblivious.

Summary

Inference is the process of collecting and combining often diverse and complex information into a judgment. It is a task that must be accomplished by the social perceiver daily, for even the most mundane of social observations is often based on an apparently complex inference. For many of the steps that are involved in making inferences there is a normative model that describes the ideal manner in which the steps could be accomplished and that points to a correct answer. When compared against a normative model, the social perceiver's skills look quite weak.

Deciding what data are relevant to a judgment is often marked by prior expectations or theories; sampling is often biased, and biases in already existing samples are often ignored. Strong inferences are frequently drawn from small and unreliable samples. When good baserate information describing population characteristics is available, it is often overlooked in favor of less reliable, but seemingly more relevant, case history or anecdotal information. People are particularly poor at using and combining probabilistic information, often manifesting great confidence in the truth of unlikely events. Regression—the fact that extreme events will, on the average, be less extreme when observed again—is poorly understood by the social perceiver; instead, extreme events are frequently used to predict future extreme events.

The social perceiver fares little better at combining information into a judgment. Typically, computers do a more reliable job of weighting and combining diverse bits of information than the person; people may think they are combining cues in a complex fashion, but they may actually be using very few cues and combining them unreliably.

Covariation, the estimate of degree of association between two events, is a concatenation of many of the previously described skills (e.g., detecting relevancy, sampling, combining information), so it is subject to many errors. When data are already collected and clearly summarized, instructions are clear, and no a priori theory about degree of covariation exists, the social perceiver does fairly well at estimating covariation. However, in the presence of an a priori theory, the theory usually overrides the data in covariation estimates. Finally, in learning from past behavior or errors, people usually overestimate what could have been foreseen.

Given that the social perceiver does not behave in a normatively appropriate fashion, what does he or she do? One answer is that heuristics and other shortcuts are often used to reduce complex inferential tasks to simple ones. One such heuristic is representativeness; the perceiver decides how likely it is that an object is a member of some category on the basis of whether the object's features are similar to the essential features of the category. Another heuristic is availability, which involves estimating frequency or likelihood by how quickly instances or associations can be brought to mind. The simulation heuristic uses availability to determine what outcome is most likely, given a set of circumstances. The anchoring and adjustment heuristic enables the perceiver to use an already existing anchor or estimate and adjust from that anchor to reach an estimate for some new problem. Heuristics facilitate rapid inferential processing and often produce correct answers; however, they may also be vulnerable to a number of serious errors of which the perceiver is usually unaware.

Since the inference process is marked by such pitfalls, what are the chances of improving it? Unfortunately, recent work suggests that insight into our own cognitive process may be limited. Furthermore, faith in collective decision making and in the education process as a method of improving individual inference may be at least somewhat misplaced. Hence it seems unlikely that we will see radical changes in our inferential capabilities in the future. What is striking about social inference is that we do as well as we do. One reason we do so well is that intuitive inferential strategies take into account content, context, and change, which normative strategies do not; hence our strategies may be particularly suited to the types of daily problems we must solve. Moreover, many errors that an individual makes in social inference may be inconsequential for behavior; others will cancel each other out; and others will be detected through communication. Hence the trade-off that we make of thoroughness for speed may well pay off in most situations.

designing research in social cognition

A snapshot of the social perceiver's mind would show a variety of cognitive elements—attributions, beliefs about control, and schemata. The first section of this book dealt with such cognitions as relatively static entities. But a still photograph tells only part of their story. To see how they function, one needs a movie that shows action, interaction, and change. Social cognitive elements in motion are social cognitive processes. In the last three chapters, we have discussed the processes of attention, memory, and inference. Analysis of process addresses the *how* questions of social cognition. Process analysis reveals how the elements get there in the first place, and once in place how they are used. How does focus of attention influence causal attribution? How do schemata influence memory? How do people infer control or its lack? In this chapter we illustrate some of the methods for analyzing such processes that operate on the elements of social cognition. Process represents the dynamic, rather than static part of social cognition.

More formally, a process model is a statement of the presumed stages through which external stimuli are noticed, taken in, mentally represented, stored in memory, retrieved from memory, and used in judgment or inference. Simple process models have been discussed already without our identifying them as such. For example, Jones and Davis's theory of correspondent inference posits that people first notice and then use socially undesirable information in making attributions. Kelley's covariation model of attribution posits that people gather, retrieve, and combine information across several dimensions. Schema-based process models propose that attention focuses on schema-relevant data, memory emphasizes general abstractions that apply to many specific instances, and inferences fit with the general case. Process models are a standard feature of research on social cognition.

Process models have been present in social psychology for some time. For example, many attitude theories contained explicit or implicit statements about cognitive process (Zajonc, 1968a). The techniques for formally testing cognitive process models, however, did not exist until recently. Consequently, the earlier process models outstripped the available methodology. The models that once were ahead of their time now are being tested with currently available techniques. Chapter 12 illustrates these points further.

WHY IS PROCESS ANALYSIS IMPORTANT?

Process is implicit in everything we have covered so far and has been part of social psychology for some time. It has a central role in the study of social cognition for several reasons. First, theories about process are potentially more general than theories about content; that is, the same procedure may well operate on a wide variety of stimuli, both social and nonsocial. For example, figuring out why your car will not start has analogies to figuring out why a friend is being difficult. One asks similar questions: Is he/she/it always this way on cold mornings? Do other people have this problem with him/her/it? Are most relationships this much trouble? One comes to similar conclusions based on a given pattern of evidence, whether the problem to be solved is social or not. In contrast, theories about any given content area, even within social perception, are historically and culturally bounded (Kruglanski, 1979). I may solve car problems the way my great-great-grandmother solved stubborn horse problems and the way my great-great-granddaughter will solve rocket problems. The content is transitory, but the more enduring problems concern processes psychologists presume hold across many content areas.

Second, theories about process are important because no cognitive or social cognitive element by itself does anything. Attributions, beliefs, and schemata simply exist until they are used in a set of procedures. This insight above all typifies social cognition theories: Exactly what processes explain how people think about people?

Third, process analysis allows methodological precision that has both practical and intellectual benefits. Fine-grained methods for process analysis have been borrowed from cognitive psychology and considerably adapted to the benefit of social psychology. The hallmark of social cognitive methodology is to specify the steps in social information processing.

There are scientific and intellectual advantages to specifying processes carefully. Most important, specifying the sequence of steps creates a more precise model than one would have otherwise. The series of stages provides a theoretical framework for understanding more precisely how people think about others. In science, theorists must state assumptions as explicitly and precisely as possible. Methodological precision challenges scientists' intellectual creativity as well. The satisfaction of finding all the pieces and figuring out how they go together has the appeal of a Chinese puzzle. Being ingenious about the intricacies of a process model is not simple, but it can be entertaining at least and is often a major intellectual accomplishment.

There are practical advantages to process analysis as well. It becomes important and feasible to think about, for example, whether stereotypes have their biggest impact at encoding or retrieval. This may in turn have implications for social change. Suppose you have a stereotype about computer programmers. If you know someone is a computer expert, do you selectively notice certain stereotypic behavior and remember most of what you noticed? Or do you notice a variety of stereotypic and not stereotypic behavior in a relatively unbiased fashion, but selectively retrieve only the stereotypic behavior, once you find out that he is a computer programmer?

This fine distinction may seem unimportant, but it determines whether you can contradict a stereotype by reminding people of discrepancies they already know about or whether you have to present people with fresh contradictory evidence. A stage analysis of the stereotyping process allows people to target their interventions more carefully. Specifying stages also has practical implications for persuasion in advertising, health, and legal settings, for example, as will be seen in Chapter 12.

So far we have argued that theories about process are more enduring than theories about content and that theories about process are necessary to make the content do something. Methods for analyzing process theories are typified by a focus on the sequential steps involved; this precision has practical payoffs as well as intellectual appeal.

WHY IS IT DIFFICULT TO STUDY COGNITIVE PROCESSES?

Studying process is not easy, however, because it contains a logical paradox. The models describe nonobservable cognitive events posited to go on inside the perceiver's mind. Cognition is supposed to mediate between an observable stimulus and an observable response. Because cognitive events themselves are not observable, researchers are left with external traces of the internal processes. To illustrate, suppose a researcher has a simple model that people make decisions by retrieving relevant evidence and reviewing it. The stimulus is the necessity for a decision, the response is the decision, and the internal process is retrieving stored knowledge. This preliminary process model is shown in the top row of Fig. 10.1. The researcher might test the model by asking undergraduates as they choose a major to list everything they can recall about their various alternatives and see if the sheer amount of listed evidence pro and con predicts their decisions. The internal process of retrieval has been given an external trace.

But several questions are unanswered: how exactly do people go about retrieving evidence pro and con? To understand the process fully, one might build a more detailed model of the decision-relevant retrieval process. In this view, people who have to make a decision consider their initial inclinations, and, if these inclinations are positive, people make associations to other positive memories, which results in their retrieving evidence consistent with their preliminary preference. The same process could operate for an initially negative preference. The revised process model is illustrated in the second row of Fig. 10.1. It sets up a new stimulus (retrieve preliminary preference), a new response (retrieve evidence), and a new internal process (associations among

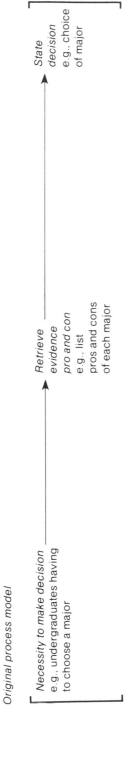
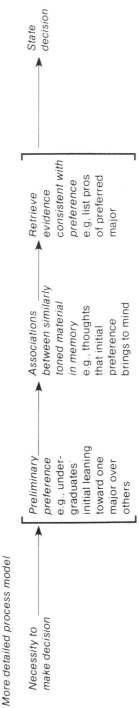

Original process model

Necessity to make decision e.g., undergraduates having to choose a major ⟶ Retrieve evidence pro and con e.g., list pros and cons of each major ⟶ State decision e.g., choice of major

More detailed process model

Necessity to make decision ⟶ Preliminary preference e.g., under-graduates' initial leaning toward one major over others ⟶ Associations between similarly toned material in memory e.g., thoughts that initial preference brings to mind ⟶ Retrieve evidence consistent with preference e.g., list pros of preferred major ⟶ State decision

Fig. 10.1 Process models at different levels of detail.

similarly toned material). If one were to apply this revised model to picking a major, the researcher would no longer simply ask undergraduates to pick a major and see what they recalled about it, but might ask them about their initial preference and what it brought to mind. The revised model details the original model more thoroughly.

Inside every process model is another process model, as the example of picking a major and Fig. 10.1 indicate. Like a metaphorical onion, every external layer peels back to reveal what becomes another external layer. You can never observe the ultimate inside, because every inside turns into an outside when you examine it. This is the paradox of process analysis. The infinite regress stops when the individual scientist decides to get out and turn the matter over to someone who habitually works at a more minute level. For social cognition researchers, the next level is cognitive psychologists. For cognitive psychologists, the next level is physiological experts. Social psychologists typically stop at the level that isolates the individual from other people. Because the goal is to predict people's reactions in interpersonal settings, going down to the level of physiology, for example, is too far removed from the level of interest to most social psychologists. The level at which one chooses to study process is largely a matter of scientific priorities and intellectual taste.

Having picked a level for a process model and having specified the cognitive steps, the researcher has to locate methods that tap those steps as directly as possible. The whole process involves considerable detective work, and this stage resembles the point at which the inspector has developed a theory of how the crime might have been accomplished (or here, a model of how the process could possibly operate). Now the detective must decide which tools will reveal the most from the available evidence. Having only the evidence and not being able to observe the crime itself, the inspector's choice of method matters enormously. Someone who looks for bloodstains when finger-print analysis is required simply will not get very far. Methodological precision gets answers, in social cognition as in crime detection.

Traditional Methods for Studying Process

MULTIPLE STUDIES, EACH FOR DIFFERENT PARTS OF THE SAME MODEL

Social psychologists have traditionally tackled the problem of measuring process by conducting a series of studies, each of which addresses a piece of an overall model. For example, suppose a series of black job applicants performs poorly compared to whites in a job interview conducted by a white. One possible model of this performance problem fingers the interviewer as the culprit; that is, if the white interviewer has negative expectations about the performance of blacks, the person may communicate those expectancies non-verbally, which in turn makes the applicant uncomfortable and unlikely to perform optimally (Word, Zanna, & Cooper, 1974).

To test this model in which race and performance are linked by the interviewer's nonverbal behavior, Word, Zanna, and Cooper (1974) did a pair of studies (see Fig. 10.2). In the first, black and white job applicants were interviewed, and the nonverbal behavior of the white interviewers was measured. The applicants were confederates of the experimenter, all trained to act the same way, in order to minimize any difference in their actual performance in the interview. As predicted, the real subjects, that is, the white interviewers, were less friendly and personal when interviewing blacks: the typical inter-

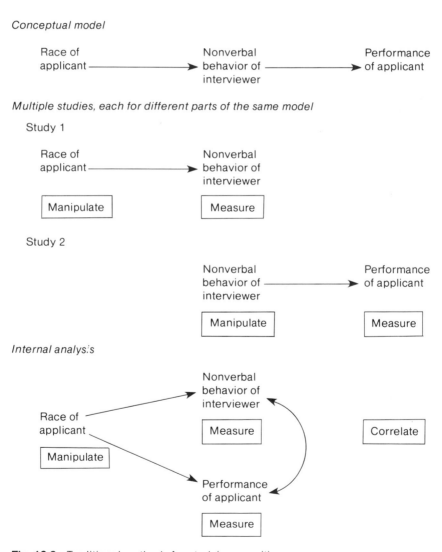

Fig. 10.2 Traditional methods for studying cognitive processes.

viewer sat farther away, terminated the interview sooner, tended to lean away from the candidate, and did not speak as smoothly.

In a second study—and here is where the methodological elegance and pitfalls both come in—the researchers trained interviewers to behave nonverbally in precisely the two different ways the original interviewers had treated black and white applicants. The new interviewers thus were confederates of the experimenter. In the impersonal (i.e., "black") treatment, white students were interviewed by white confederates who sat farther away, took less time on the interview, and so on. In the personal (i.e., "white") treatment, the students were treated in the friendly manner normally reserved for whites. As predicted, the students treated impersonally performed less well, reciprocated the impersonal nonverbal style of the interviewer, and thought the interviewer unfriendly and inadequate. Thus the pair of studies supports the model that race affects an interviewer's nonverbal behavior, which in turn affects applicants' performance.

Despite the convincing case this particular study makes (and we picked it as a fine example of this technique), it has the methodological problem shared by other research of this paradigm. Because the hypothesized mediator is measured in the first study and manipulated as a treatment in the second, one can never know with certainty that it is indeed the same variable in the two studies. Suppose, for example, that the interviewer's distance, brevity, and speech errors reflected discomfort rather than hostility. The nonverbal behavior emitted spontaneously in Study 1 could differ considerably from that deliberately acted out in Study 2. Perhaps the second set of interviewers acted hostile, while the first set of interviewers merely had been uncomfortable. Cutting short an interview in a condescending manner differs from cutting it short out of discomfort, and perhaps the two sets of nonverbal behavior differed in that respect.

The technique thus involves two studies with two different versions of the same variable. This is a problem that can come up in many other research paradigms, including the nontraditional ones that follow. But it is integral to the technique of breaking a multistage process model into pieces and testing the pieces separately. The many-studies, one-model technique hence can be quite convincing, as is the case here. But it is not above criticism. Few techniques are, of course, yet this particular issue poses a problem for arguing process models from this technique.[1]

---

1. The criticisms of the multiple-studies technique have the status of alternative explanations for the results. Such alternative explanations typically are handled by conducting new studies with non-overlapping weaknesses. Conducting several studies illustrates the advantage of triangulating on a problem, that is, viewing it from more than one (methodological) perspective to gain a more complete perception of it. Triangulation and converging methods are recommended ways to compensate for the shortcomings of all the methods we discuss in this chapter.

INTERNAL ANALYSIS

There is an alternative traditional strategy for analyzing a process model. One can try to capture the entire process within a single study and then analyze the links among the stages. It is called internal analysis because the links are inferred from correlations all internal to one study, and typically internal to each single experimental condition of the study.

As an example, again consider whether links between an applicant's race and performance can be mediated by the nonverbal behavior of the white interviewer. The same people could be measured on all three variables at once, instead of in two separate studies. That is, white interviewers could interact with black and white applicants, as in the original Study 1, and the nonverbal behavior of the white interviewers could be assessed. But instead of using confederate applicants all trained to act the same way, the performance of naive applicants could be measured too. Correlations between applicant performance and interviewer nonverbal behavior could be assessed to support the model (see curved line near the bottom of Fig. 10.2). Internal analysis takes care of the many-studies, one-model problem of translating a measured variable (Study 1) into a manipulated variable (Study 2). This useful technique has been used to great advantage in many psychological experiments.

Unfortunately, internal analysis does not demonstrate direction of causality, nor does it isolate variables properly. On the first point, if two variables both are affected by race and if they correlate with each other, several patterns of causality are possible, not just the one advanced by the researcher. One variable may indeed cause the other, as hypothesized. That is, interviewer nonverbal behavior may cause applicant performance, as the expectancy idea would predict. However, variations in the applicant's performance also may cause nonverbal reactions from the interviewer. Moreover, applicant performance and interviewer nonverbal behavior may be correlated because some other variable (e.g., interviewer warmth) causes both of them. The moral, then, is that correlation does not imply causation. Nor does it imply direction of causality, if causality exists.

Second, with regard to isolating variables, internal analysis does not allow researchers to be confident that they have identified the correct variable. That is, internal analysis examines the relationships among measured variables, which may not be isolated from other unmeasured variables. For example, in Study 2, performance of the applicant is a measured variable that correlates with interviewer nonverbal behavior. Quite possibly, interviewer nonverbal behavior is even more highly correlated with the applicant nonverbal behavior. The researcher might therefore be measuring the wrong variable and never know it. Such problems in isolating variables are an integral part of any correlational analysis, problems which can only be solved by using experimental manipulations. In the next section, we will discuss some manipulations that are particularly relevant to social cognition research.

In sum, then, traditional experimental methods have some strengths and some limits in their ability to help us detect processes, both cognitive and interpersonal.

Particular Manipulations for Particular Hypotheses

Some experimental manipulations are particularly well suited to studying process. A *process manipulation* is specially designed to reveal cognitions by interfering with, augmenting, or interrupting some stage in a process model. The assumptions underlying a process manipulation are that its content (what) is held constant, but, for example, its timing (when) or modality (how) changes. Each of the most frequently used process manipulations is designed to answer certain specific questions. Different methods are used for different purposes.

To illustrate, suppose one were interested in answering a question about racial stereotypes that was different from the Word *et al.* study. Suppose one wanted again to study the effects of racial stereotypes on performance, but this time to focus on perceptions of performance, and the specific question of interest was to locate the effect as primarily occurring at encoding or retrieval. Instead of simply manipulating a target person's race, one could manipulate *when* subjects discover the target person's race. If subjects overhear someone in a job interview, and only afterward learn that the applicant is black or white, does that have as much impact as discovering the applicant's race at the outset? The timing of a manipulation before or after encountering the stimulus would help the researcher to pinpoint the manipulation's effects as occurring at the encoding or retrieval stage. In Chapter 6, "Social Schemata," we discussed this technique with regard to locating the effects of schemata on encoding and retrieval; in Chapter 8, "Person Memory," we discussed this technique with regard to the timing of priming effects.

This technique could test a relatively specific process model in the following way (see Fig. 10.3). Hearing the interview first and the race after means that race could only have its effect on selective retrieval and reinterpretation after the fact. Hearing the race *before* the interview means that its effects could occur either as selective encoding or as selective retrieval and reinterpretation. If the impact of the race-before condition (encoding plus retrieval) is stronger than the race-after condition (retrieval only), then encoding effects probably make an important difference. What this result would mean is that one's assumptions about blacks and whites influence one's inferences about a particular person only or primarily when one knows the person's race from the

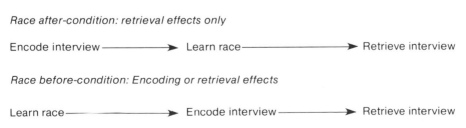

Race after-condition: retrieval effects only

Encode interview ⎯⎯⎯⎯⎯➤ Learn race⎯⎯⎯⎯⎯⎯➤ Retrieve interview

Race before-condition: Encoding or retrieval effects

Learn race⎯⎯⎯⎯⎯➤ Encode interview⎯⎯⎯⎯⎯➤ Retrieve interview

Fig. 10.3 An example of a process manipulation.

outset. Whatever information one has learned before learning the person's race would be less influenced by racial assumptions, if encoding effects were stronger than retrieval effects. If there is no difference between the two conditions, one cannot be certain of their relative impact. This method is difficult to follow on first encounter perhaps, but advantageous in the inferences it allows researchers to make. As it happens, encoding usually has a stronger effect than does retrieval alone, as we have noted in previous chapters (Rothbart, Evans, & Fulero, 1979; Zadny & Gerard, 1974). This fact suggests that stereotypes have substantial impact on people's initial interpretation of information.

However, the encoding-retrieval manipulation is not foolproof. For one thing, the effects of encoding and retrieval biases are similar, even if retrieval biases turn out to be weaker. If both encoding and retrieval affect knowledge the same way, then the distinction may matter less because the final product is the same in either case. For another thing, the encoding-retrieval manipulation is confounded with time. That is, stage of intervention is not all that varies between the before and after conditions; the length of time subjects have to mull over the stereotype also varies. Hence perhaps time matters more than stage, and one cannot draw any firm conclusions from that process manipulation by itself. Furthermore, encoding and retrieval may well not be totally independent; how we encode things often affects how we retrieve them. Both might be important, and their combined effect might be more complex than one would suppose at first. These criticisms show that process manipulations are not watertight, although they are useful if one knows their limitations. They are standard designs for tapping into cognitive models of process (see S. E. Taylor & Fiske, 1981, for more detail).

For another example of a process manipulation designed to answer a specific question, consider techniques for pinpointing the channel of an effect, that is, whether it operates in verbal or auditory mode. One way to do this is presenting the same information two ways. If one thought that an interviewer's tone of voice (auditory mode) communicated biased expectancies more effectively than did his or her particular word choice (verbal mode), one could have some applicants interviewed by telephone and some by exchanging questions and answers over a computer terminal linkup. That would help isolate some information (question content) from others (content plus tone of voice). The manipulation might begin crudely to tease apart the impact of the two modalities.

The channel-specific manipulation has its problems, primarily because you cannot convey precisely the same information in video and audio channels. Thus, if you get a difference, you do not know if it is due to the information conveyed or to the channel's inherent impact.

For the moment, these illustrations of standard process manipulations will suffice, though there are many others. Finding just the right process manipulation can have the same satisfaction as successfully diagnosing a sporadic problem with your car. But using the wrong one is just plain silly or misguided.

If you know precisely what a particular manipulation is designed to do, you know how it should be applied, why it breaks down, and what its reasonable limits are.

Measuring the Traces of Cognitive Processes

As an adjunct to experimental manipulations of the stimuli and the context that confront the social perceiver, researchers sometimes use measures that are particularly sensitive to the traces of cognitive processes. The cognitive processes we have discussed in the last three chapters (attention, memory, and inference) are not observable directly, but their traces are. For example, a person's direction of attention (process) has an observable trace or record (where the person is looking). Researchers then attempt to measure the process trace. This section is concerned with such measures.

A variety of standard measurement methods has evolved from cognitive psychology, and a sample of them illustrates the most common solutions to the problem of getting inside the head (S. E. Taylor & Fiske, 1981). Again, we cannot cover the area entirely, but the sampling may provide insight into how social cognition data are generated from the traces of attention, memory, and inference processes.

MEASURING THE TRACES OF ATTENTION

Measuring attention (or, more accurately, measuring the traces of attention) helps to inform the researcher about what is currently active in the subject's mind. As discussed in Chapters 7 and 8 ("Attention" and "Person Memory"), subjects attend to stimuli that are in conscious focal awareness. That is, attention consists of what is currently being encoded into memory or what is currently retrieved from memory. Thus one aspect of attention can include external stimuli that are being encoded at the current moment, that is, transformed from sensations to memory representations. We defined attention as having a directional (selectivity) component and an intensity (effort) component. Some of the process measures focus more on the directional component and some more on the effort component.

Measuring the direction of attention can be illustrated by the following progression from coarser to finer grained levels. Suppose one wanted to test the hypothesis that people pay attention to other people who shape their fates. It seems reasonable to suppose that, when someone is in a meeting and one of the other people present is a boss, boyfriend, or girlfriend, the person's attention is most likely to rest on that significant other. This sensible hypothesis is not easily tested, however, in part because it is not easy to measure attention. A sloppy way to go about it would be to measure what subjects recall about each person present at such a meeting. But attention does not always result in recall (as we saw in Chapter 7, "Attention"), so that is not very satisfactory.

A more precise method would be to force subjects to choose whom they watched. Multiple videotapes of the meeting could be made, in which each camera focused on only one person. Subjects could then observe the group members on the separate videotapes but be forced to choose to watch only one person at any given time. A record of which person they watched and for how long would be an elegantly simple measure of attention (Berscheid, Graziano, Monson, & Dermer, 1976). Moreover, subjects would not even know their attention was being monitored. This matters because if people thought their selective attention to their boss or romantic partner were being measured, they might modify their behavior and the researcher would not get valid results.

Other attentional measures focus on the direction of attention in a fairly fine-grained manner. For example, one can videotape people's eye movements (Olson & Zanna, 1979), and one can use a machine that records gaze direction by reflecting light off the subject's cornea (Just & Carpenter, 1976; McArthur & Ginsberg, 1981).

Measures that focus relatively more on the intensity component of attention include ways to measure the duration of the subject's attention. For example, one technique includes presenting all one's stimuli on slides and letting subjects control the slide changer switch. This would give one a measure of how long they look at each slide (S. T. Fiske, 1980). Another procedure is letting people gaze at a stack of information or at a bulletin board and timing them with a stopwatch as they look at each thing in turn (Langer, Taylor, Fiske, & Chanowitz, 1976; Mischel, Ebbesen, & Zeiss, 1973; S. E. Taylor, 1975).

These are all useful measures of the traces of a cognitive process, namely attention. However, these techniques have potential problems that stem from the gap between the trace of the process (gaze direction or duration) and the process itself (attention). Each technique assumes that people are thinking about whatever they are observing. Hence there is little allowance for daydreamers. These measures also do not tell *what* the subject is thinking as the person gazes upon boss or romantic partner. Finally, even if the person is thinking about the object observed, these measures do not reveal how much effort the person is putting into those thoughts. Nonetheless, the attentional measures do come close to directly tapping the object of people's current thoughts as they think them, which of course is the point.

MEASURES OF THE TRACES OF MEMORY PROCESSES

What could be easier than testing someone's memory? Ask any professor who has to give an exam to measure student memory. As it happens, it is not so easy to tell what is in there. Recognition and recall are two general classes of memory measures used alike by professors and by cognitive social psychologists (see Hastie *et al.*, 1980, for examples). Memory generally is thought to involve two types of process—search and discrimination. Recognition and recall measures focus differentially on these two processes, as we shall see.

Recognition tests are like multiple choice or true-false exams; they focus on the discrimination process. Their object is to determine whether the pupils or subjects can distinguish things they have seen before from things that merely resemble what they learned but are not indeed old facts. Students generally prefer multiple choice to essay exams because multiple choice exams seem easier. The right answer is provided; they only have to recognize it. Thus the test examines only part of the normal retrieval process, that is, only the discrimination (is the item old or new) but not the search. Recognition tests can be quite difficult, if the alternatives are close and easily confused, as any student knows. Thus recognition measures can be sensitive to subtle nuances and lapses, depending on how picky the decision has to be.

An alternative memory measure involves *recall*, which includes both search and discrimination. In this sense, recall is like an essay exam. One has both to search for the idea and to decide if it is the right one. Thus it is more work than recognition, which simply involves deciding. This, of course, is what bothers and challenges students about essay exams; essays require un-aided retrieval of information. Recall measures and essay exams require careful coding or grading on the researcher's or professor's part. Since the answers are not constrained, they can be highly idiosyncratic and difficult to quantify.

To summarize, then, recognition or true-false tests are easy to grade, but difficult to make up. The professor or researcher has to make up wrong answers that correspond to the exact ways that people will misunderstand the material, which requires having a detailed understanding of how people are thinking in the first place. Recall and essay exams allow more breadth in responses, so they can help the professor or researcher to discover what is in the minds of the students or subjects, if the tester has no clear idea beforehand. However, they are harder to grade or code.

What are the practical differences between recall and recognition measures in social cognition? As we just suggested, simple recall measures may be more likely to be useful at the early stages of research, when one does not have a clear model of exactly how people are thinking about a problem. Free recall lets people tell it in their own words, which can help the researcher to discover the initial outlines of the processes people are using. As an illustration, suppose you want to find out what informal categories people have for thinking about the people in their lives. Some categories might include "those young female psychology faculty" or "those middle-aged male administrators" or "those athletes in the back row." To find out what those categories are, one could ask people to recall characteristics of people they know and observe which category labels come up. That could be a useful first step for exploring the range of categories people use.

But if one wanted to find out exactly how people *use* the informal categories, a more fine-grained analysis would be in order. Suppose you had a model stating that people initially categorize others and then remember the person's category better than the specific person. This model would suggest that people trying to recognize someone might mix up two people who both fall into the category. A professor might mix up two students who both fall into the category "back-row athletes."

A recognition test might be better suited to testing the fine-grained model than a free recall test would be. So, for example, one could see whether people can correctly recognize names of people in certain categories. The model would predict that people would be more likely to confuse the names of two people within the athlete category than to confuse the names of one person from the athlete category and another from the administrator category. Recognition can allow a relatively precise test of some models. But free recall might allow one to develop the model in the first place. The point is that no one method is superior; one simply has to work with whichever is most appropriate to one's specific question.

Memory measures are the most popular methods for deriving cognitive elements and processes. But they have their limits. First, people tend to assume that more memory means subjects are performing better. But more is not necessarily better. Irrelevant facts may get in the way. If you ask me how to get to the airport and I reminisce about the great meal I once had at a restaurant on the road to the airport, the extra details I have recalled are almost certainly no help to you. Thus what probably matters is the specific relevance and utility of recall with regard to the task at hand, not sheer quantity of free associations to a given topic.

Another problem typical of memory measures is that people may not use what they remember. Memory is not always related in a simple way to the most apparently obvious other reactions it should predict, as we saw in Chapter 8, "Person Memory." Decisions, beliefs, and attributions, for example, may be predictable by only a subset of people's total memory—the part that they view as relevant or sufficient for the judgment (S. T. Fiske, Kenny, & Taylor, 1982; Love & Greenwald, 1978; Lingle & Ostrom, 1979). If you ask me what I recall about my great-uncle, I could go on for hours about his intelligence, energy, generosity, conservative politics, and old-fashioned notions of morality. I could also describe his living room furniture and favorite breakfast in some detail. But if you ask me whether or not I intend to visit him, the sole deciding factors might be his quick wit and my family loyalty. The point is that people use a fraction of what they can remember upon request. Memory measures, like other measures, have to be precise in order to predict the subjects' other reactions.

MEASURING THE TRACES OF THE INFERENCE PROCESS

Researchers often index inference processes by how long it takes people to make the inference. Decision times, as they are sometimes called, are second in popularity only to memory measures. Ordinary people also use decision times to gauge how much processing someone else does, and the logic of social cognition researchers is similar. If I ask you who sang "The Copacabana" and when, and you immediately answer Barry Manilow in 1978, I would judge that you had the answer stored in an easily accessible fashion and that you did not need to go through a lot of intervening steps to get there. If you pause, struggle, and finally give a hesitant answer, it would be clear that you had had to think harder. Perhaps you sang the first few bars of the song to yourself (assuming you know it), thought about where you were when you first heard it, and then calculated the year from that. The difference between an oldies expert and an ordinary person is partly a matter of cognitive strategy, and decision time is one index of that.

Decision time has been used, for example, as a gauge of people's cognitive strategies for retrieving information about themselves; this usage came up under the topic of self-schemata (Markus, 1977). If Sandy knows she is athletic and that is important to her, then her athletic self-schema allows her quickly to answer questions about her physical abilities. On the other hand, if Jane has not thought much about her ability to catch a pass, or which way to run in a game of touch football, and furthermore she could hardly care less, then her lack of an athletic self-schema should make her answer questions about her sports ability more slowly.[2]

Decision times can be broken down into more detail, if one has in mind a model of the sequence people go through in making a given inference. Suppose you wanted to test two competing models of how people answer survey questions such as "How many magazine subscriptions do you have?" According to one model, people have to remember each magazine they get and keep a running total as they recall each one in turn. Under this model, people who subscribe to many magazines will take more time to answer the question than will people who subscribe to few. According to another model, people carry the number of their subscriptions around in their heads all the time; if this were true, the number of magazines people get will not affect their time to answer the question. Examining the relationship between response time and number of subscriptions would shed some light on the plausibility of each model.

The response times could be broken down into still more detail, if you discovered that people take (for example) five seconds per subscription for retrieval and summing. You could also measure how long it takes people to answer a separate memory question ("Name all the magazines you get"), and see if it could be a component of the other process. If people took seven seconds per magazine merely to recall them, your model is less plausible than if they took three seconds (see Fig. 10.4). This, of course, is a crude caricature of a rather more complex and delicate process, but it illustrates the basic logic (McClelland, 1979; D. A. Taylor, 1976).

Cognitive psychologists have identified several problems with decision-time techniques. One is that each information-processing stage may be performed entirely differently in isolation (e.g., retrieval only) than when it is part of a sequence (e.g., retrieval plus summing) (Pachella, 1974; Sternberg, 1969a, 1969b). Other specific criticisms of decision time as a measure include problems basic to most current cognitive models (S. E. Taylor & Fiske, 1981). For

---

2. Remember that the actual results are more complex than the summary idea that self-schemata shorten decision time; under some circumstances, self-schemata lengthen decision time (see Chapter 6, "Social Schemata").

Question: How many magazine subscriptions do you have?

Hypothesized process to answer question

Retrieve each magazine name $\rightarrow$ add it to total number retrieved so far (repeat until finished).

Hypothesized process supported if	*Hypothesized process not supported if*
a) Time for answering is proportional to number of subscriptions	a) Time for answering is independent of number of subscriptions
b) Time for each retrieval (e.g., 3 seconds) + Time for each summation (unknown)	b) Time for each retrieval (e.g., 7 seconds) + Time for each summation (unknown)
could = Time for each retrieval and summation (5 seconds)	= Time for each retrieval and summation (5 seconds)

Fig. 10.4   One analysis of decision time.

example, are the processes in question truly serial in nature? That is, what if they happened all at once, in parallel? (Suppose people remember several magazines all at the same time, rather than recalling first one, then the next.) If two processes overlap in time, one cannot assume that their combined time is the sum of their two separate times. One must specify such assumptions in one's model.

Other issues hinge on translating cognitive psychologists' techniques to realistic social stimuli, which are relatively complex. Decision times are extraordinarily sensitive to details of the stimulus. For example, frequently used and shorter words are processed faster, so one must control for these factors in social (as in nonsocial) research. Other extraneous factors so far unknown may influence social stimuli in particular. For example, certain affect-laden words might be processed faster than neutral words. If so, one would have to control for this feature or else risk noisy and imprecise data. As a rule, social stimuli are likely to be less tractable to precise control than are nonsocial stimuli, for some of the reasons noted at the end of Chapter 1.

A related issue is that social cognition models are rarely well enough specified to warrant fine-grained decision-time measures. In all, decision time is useful at the relatively well-defined end of social cognition. But it is somewhat limited in its application to highly generalizable social phenomena.

A COMMENT ON PROCESS-TRACING MEASURES

Some of the new process measures may strike a neophyte as obscure at best and bizarre at worst. Why do social cognition researchers use such seemingly peculiar techniques when it might seem that it could be so much simpler?

Without understanding the reasons behind the measures, one might suppose that it would be easier simply to ask people how they think. It indeed would save scientists a lot of grief if people could report accurately on what influenced them and how. Unfortunately people may be unmotivated or even unable to do so, as we saw in Chapter 9, "Social Inference." If you ask an interviewer why he chose a white job candidate over a black one, his answer may be uninformative (because he preferred her), self-serving (because he was certain the white one was smarter), or simply wrong (because he thinks people always pick the first one they see). Given that we will not get far by directly confronting people, the standard process-tracing techniques are reasonable and helpful tools.

Putting It All Together

So far, we have discussed process-oriented manipulations and cognitive measures of the traces left by the processes of attention, memory, and inference. Now it is time to assemble them into a single overall model. Analyzing the individual stages of process models, as described so far, constitutes the most common method in social cognition. But the enterprise is like ordering a pizza. If the delivery boy arrived with a ball of dough, a container of tomato sauce, a chunk of cheese, and a can of anchovies, you would say a bit more than "You forgot the mushrooms." Studying attention, memory, and inference in isolation is a bit like this. It would be silly to make claims about the cheese by itself and then be surprised to see that it melts into the tomato sauce when it is put into its proper context. Ultimately, if you want pizza, you have got to put the ingredients together and see how they cook up. If you are just interested in anchovies, on the other hand, it is a mistake to order the whole pizza. All metaphor aside, the point is this: any scientist has to choose a level of analysis. When the components of a process combine, they inevitably are altered. Few social cognition researchers tackle more than one component at a time, but a couple of techniques have evolved to get at the whole process from attention to memory to inference: computer simulation and structural modeling.

COMPUTER SIMULATION

The basic premise of *computer simulation* of psychological processes (Abelson, 1968; Huesmann, 1980; Simon, 1979) is that if one truly understands a process, one can program it. Computers force the modeler to specify every detail, leaving nothing to chance or guesswork. If one's ideas about the processes are complete, the program will work; that is, it will take the same input that the person does and produce the same output. The program forces one to be explicit about everything, but it also allows one to be complex about many things at once. Because the computer keeps track of all the details, a subprocess such as attention can be combined with another subprocess such as retrieval without confusion.

A simulation can help the researcher to discover distinctions that might not have been apparent otherwise. Suppose one has a hypothesis that people have scripts for common social events (see Chapter 6, "Social Schemata"). Suppose further that one thinks people handle departures from the normal script by trying again until the normal procedure works. For example: "John went to a restaurant. He sat down and signaled the waitress. She did not come." What does John do next? According to the initial model, John signals her again. Assuming she simply failed to notice him the first time, this strategy might work.

If the model were programmed into a computer simulation, the machine would cycle through the blocked step of signaling the waitress until it proved successful (i.e., until the waitress came over so John could order). However, suppose John is signaling the wrong person, perhaps another customer. No amount of repetition would overcome the obstacle, and the computer would doggedly keep trying the same thing again and again. One's computer account might be exhausted rather quickly. The simulation reveals that only some departures from the script can be solved through repetition. Others will have to be solved by trying a different procedure. One discovers such unexpected outcomes because of the precision the computer requires. No one would simulate as simpleminded a process as that described here, but as the model becomes more complex, one is even more likely to discover logical flaws and unexpected outcomes through simulation. In explaining a process model to the computer, one explains it to oneself.

Simulation above all forces one fully to detail one's process model. What does a restaurant script *do* and how does it do it? Describing the contents of the restaurant script does not explain how it works in action. Simulating how it takes in new information, fits it to normal expectations, and spits out a response is an attempt to tackle the whole process, not just a part of it.

The advantages and disadvantages of simulation for social cognition research are complex (S. E. Taylor & Fiske, 1981), but chief among the disadvantages is the difficulty of knowing when a simulation has it right. One classic technique, the Turing test (1950), pits a computer against a person, with a judge in a separate room trying to distinguish the human from nonhuman responses. The more trouble the judge has in differentiating between computer and human, the better the simulation. This intriguing procedure is not now in much use, however.

A fundamental problem in computer simulation is how psychologically realistic to be. Most researchers give computers the same inputs they give humans and attempt to produce the same outputs that humans do; the researchers may or may not be concerned with making the computer plod through the same intervening steps the human does. To build a complete process model, one should not just work with inputs ("John went into the restaurant," etc.) and outputs ("Try signaling the waitress again."). One should try to get at the same intervening steps that humans do, for example, "If the waitress does not come over, decide why. If the failure is due to her not noticing the signal, try again." The goal of psychological realism should extend to *all* the intervening steps of the process that the researcher has specified.

Computer simulation has yet to have much impact in social cognition. Nevertheless, its indirect impact is enormous, in that, for example, schemata were imported from work in computer-based simulations of cognitive processes. Its future impact remains an open but promising question.

STRUCTURAL MODELS

A *structural model* is another technique that researchers can use to test several steps in a process model all at once. It is a statistical method that refines the technique of internal analysis, which was described earlier under the heading of traditional methods. Structural models entail a lot of statistics beyond the scope of this book (Bentler, 1980; Kenny, 1979). But the logic of structural models is important. Just as computer simulations tackle the whole process, structural models encourage one to measure each piece of the process and see how the pieces all fit together. So, for example, one might have a model that a job applicant's race causes warm or cold interviewer nonverbal behavior, which in turn affects applicant performance. As noted earlier, internal analysis could be based on a correlation between the two measured variables of interviewer behavior and applicant performance (see the curved line on the top half of Fig. 10.5). If the two variables correlate, it unfortunately might be because each is affected similarly by the manipulation. Applicant race might affect interviewer nonverbal behavior, and applicant race might affect applicant performance, but the two measured variables might not be causally related.

Structural modeling allows one to test directly whether interviewer nonverbal behavior affects applicant performance. Knowing that they correlate because the same thing causes both is not as useful as knowing that one causes the other, regardless of their common antecedent. The bottom of Fig. 10.5 depicts a structural model. The usual statistical techniques do not test the link from a presumed mediator (e.g., interviewer nonverbals) to the variable of interest (e.g., applicant performance).

One drawback to structural modeling is that correlations never imply causality; only randomized experimental manipulations can do that. But because researchers often use correlational analysis to supplement experiments, it would be useful if they did so in more precise structural models, as is beginning to be common practice (e.g., S. T. Fiske *et al.*, 1982; Moreland & Zajonc, 1979).

Remaining Issues in Process Analysis

Using cognitive methods in social settings is a bit like guerrillas in a jungle using sensitive electronic weapons designed for use in modern conventional warfare. Many of the assumptions underlying the design of your arsenal are simply inapplicable when you are waist-deep in a swamp. Anyone intending to

Model tested by internal analysis

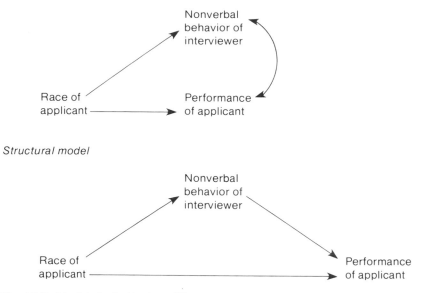

Fig. 10.5 Models tested by two different techniques.

attack social problems with cognitive technology should read the instruction manuals and think hard about the design specifications. One set of traps for the unwary is methodological and the other set is conceptual.

METHODOLOGICAL PITFALLS

Cognitive process measures vary considerably in their practical utility and technical precision. First, the results obtained by a standard cognitive measure may be highly ambiguous. Decision time, for example, does not reveal what exactly people are thinking, only that they take longer or shorter times over their choices. Time is only time, and a prolonged gaze, for example, may reflect curiosity or confusion or daydreaming. In selecting the materials for use with attentional measures, one has to control for novelty and ambiguity. Similarly, recall is only recall, and it says nothing about whether people actually use what they remember or are merely generating it for mental exercise. The notion that people might take cognitive excursions merely for their enter-tainment value simply does not occur to most serious scientists. And yet the ambiguity of many decision time, gaze time, or recall measures does not preclude the possibility.

A second methodological issue is that some techniques limit the use of other techniques. Imagine the poor fellow in a psychology experiment where the overzealous researchers are simultaneously trying to measure his looking time, his decision time, his recall, and his recognition. The subject is likely to resemble a one-man band, switching off the slide projector with a foot pedal, writing down what he remembers with his right hand, making a choice with his left hand, and gazing up at the stimulus set with whatever attention he can still manage. Of course, this is exaggerated, but the practical problem is real. Subjects cannot do everything at once, and in choosing an attentional measure over a memory measure, researchers inevitably limit the questions they can answer.

Another problem related to this is that many cognitive techniques create a trade-off between precision of measurement (reliability and internal validity) and generalizability of results (external validity). This problem has arisen in other contexts, and the same answer applies exactly: one often has to choose between technical precision and socially realistic research settings.

The final methodological point is wholly practical. In pursuing internal validity, social cognition researchers cannot afford to become paradigm bound. That is, they cannot afford to invest all their efforts in a single measure that focuses on only one thing. Flexibility and variety in methods allow convergence on a phenomenon. Usually this means that social cognition research cannot afford to be too narrowly confined to one technique, especially if it involves an extravagant use of time or money, assuming the same insights could be gained another way.

The methodological problems touched on here do not exhaust the possibilities, although they may have threatened to exhaust the reader. Nor are the problems unique to cognitive measures. Nevertheless, borrowed tools are often abused. Social cognition methods are indeed easy to use—badly. This chapter serves as a reminder to those intending to do such research: do your homework and read up on the techniques you choose (see S. E. Taylor & Fiske, 1981, for references on all these points).

CONCEPTUAL PITFALLS

The assumptions behind cognitive methods are sometimes well specified and sometimes not, but it is the researcher's responsibility to know what they are. The fundamental assumption, of course, is that cognitions intervene between stimulus and response. Consequently, one taps those intangible cognitions as carefully as possible. But not all social responses are cognitively mediated; as we noted in Chapter 1, perhaps some are perceptual or behavioral. Thus some attempts to measure cognitive process models can be misguided from the very beginning.

Furthermore, most methods used in social cognition assume that the processes are linear: A leads to B leads to C. But what about feedback? What if B and C cause each other? For example, your memory of another person's behavior doubtless can cause your attributions about her friendliness. But your attributions, once made, can also reshape your memory. Thus they each cause each other. Such feedback violates the linear assumption of one-way causality. Other forms of nonlinearity are possible, limited only by the imagination (or hallucinations) of the researcher. Linearity is a conceptual pitfall that limits many current cognitive methods (E. R. Smith, 1982).

While we are muddying the conceptual waters, a related point is that divisions among stages of process or types of cognitions invariably are wrong. Simplifications are evils necessary to science. But it is wise to remember that all simplifications are fundamentally wrong: attributions have elements of control in them, attention involves inference, memory includes both judgments and raw data, and so on. Life is not a series of boxes connected by arrows. Although the boxes are a convenient fiction, as one researcher put it, you would not want to live in them.

Summary

Process analysis takes cognitive elements (attributions, beliefs about control, schemata) and sets them in motion, creating development, change, and interaction. Cognitive processes include attention, retrieval, and inference: methodological precision allows one to begin defining the processes in detail. The challenge is to find observable traces of the nonobservable processes.

Traditional methods for examining process include combining several studies that tackle each step separately. While this method can be powerful, the links among the separate studies must be carefully designed. For example, one study's dependent variable (measure) may be another study's independent variable (experimental treatment), and the two variables are not always comparable. A second traditional method is to supplement experiments with internal analyses of the relationships among various measures in a given study. If the measures correlate, this fact increases the chances that one causes the other, but it is no guarantee, because various patterns of causality can underlie any given correlation.

Experimental manipulations have evolved to test process models in particular ways. Process manipulations, as they are called, provide standard solutions to standard problems. For example, to learn whether a schema has its effect at initial encoding or at retrieval from memory, one can manipulate whether people receive the schema label before or after encountering the stimulus. Similarly, the effects of visual and auditory presentation modes sometimes can be pinpointed by presenting information in one channel or the other.

Different processes have their own associated measures. For example, attention can be examined by measuring how long people look at stimuli that vary in specified ways. Attentional measures tend to assume that people are thinking about whatever they are observing, but this assumption may not always be justified. Moreover, attentional measures do not reveal the content or effort of people's thoughts. Memory can be examined by recognition measures that focus on the discrimination process or by recall measures that tap both search and discrimination processes. Each is suited to different issues. Memory measures tend to assume more recall is better, and that people use what they remember, although neither of these assumptions is certain. Inference processes are often measured by decision time, longer times reflecting more complex processing. Decision times sometimes can be divided up into stages, and sometimes analyzed by interfering at different stages and gauging the overall effect on the duration of the process. Although social stimuli are often too complex for precise decision time analyses, the technique is useful given extremely well-specified models.

Two techniques exist for looking at process models in their entirety. The stages of information processing can be assembled into a single operating computer simulation that allows the researcher to see if the hypothesized processes actually work. If they do, the process model demonstrates a sufficient way to get the job done, if not necessarily a realistically human way. Structural models provide another way to put it all together, analyzing complex patterns of correlations for their compatibility with a proposed model.

Process measures vary in the ambiguity of their results, the extent to which they preclude the use of other measures, their interference with the social validity of the study, and their expense. Furthermore, some responses may not be cognitively mediated, or if mediated, not linear. Other standard assumptions such as limitations in cognitive capacity also require close examination in careful process analysis.

part three

beyond cognition

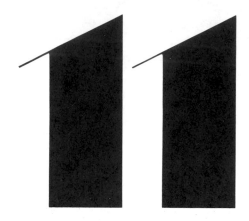

Social cognition can be rather like a desert at dawn: dry and cold, but fascinating, if you know something about it. One might react, as did one psychology professor, "If you're going to have all that sand, why not have a beach?" If a desert is a beach minus the ocean, social cognition until recently has been thought minus feelings. However, cold cognition ultimately comes up short, especially in the realm of thinking about people. After roughly ten years of intensive work on social cognition, researchers are coming to the conclusion that the rather arid field could use some irrigation by affect.

affect

Fundamental questions arise when one attempts to integrate affect and cognition. The history of research on emotion reveals long struggles over the role of cognitive processes in affect. (For a review of cognitive and other theories of emotion, see Strongman, 1978.) Two questions in particular concern us here. First, how do thought processes shape what people feel? Are cognitions a necessary antecedent to affect? Second, how do feelings shape what people think? What is the role of affect in memory and inference? One possible answer to both sets of questions is that affect and cognition are rather separate systems that operate independently. At the end of the chapter, we consider the provocative separate systems view.

As we shall see, most of the social cognition work on affect is quite recent and draws heavily on current theories of memory architecture and cognitive processes. Earlier work on cognition and affect preceded the recent advances in cognitive psychology. In this respect, the new wave of research on affect and cognition is unique. We restrict our discussion here to those analyses most tied to current work in cognitive psychology. (For a collection of such work, see M. S. Clark & Fiske, 1982.)

DIFFERENTIATING AFFECTS, FEELINGS, EMOTIONS, EVALUATIONS, AND MOODS

First, we should define our terms. *Affect* is a generic term for a whole range of feelings and emotions. *Feelings* include relatively mild subjective reactions that are essentially either pleasant or unpleasant. The feelings most frequently studied by social psychologists are *evaluations*: that is, simple positive and negative reactions to others, such as attraction, liking, prejudice, and so forth. Such positive and negative evaluations have obvious importance in social interaction. Evaluations may be distinguished from feelings that have a less specific target, that is, *moods*. One can have an evaluative reaction toward another person, but one typically does not have a mood reaction toward another person. Moods affect a wide range of social cognitions and behaviors, as we shall see. Like evaluation, mood is primarily considered as simply positive or negative.

But feelings—simple positive and negative reactions—do not capture the intensity and complexity of affect. Think how limited our worlds would be if all we could say was, "I feel good (bad) today" or "I feel good (bad) about you." More differentiated terms are needed to capture the distinctions between being elated and being contented, between being sad and being angry. *Emotion* refers to a more complex assortment of affects than simply good feelings and bad feelings, such as sadness, anger, delight, and serenity. Emotion also can imply intense feelings with physical manifestations, including physiological arousal.

Two major dimensions of affect recur in empirical analyses: pleasantness and arousal (J. A. Russell, 1978, 1980). As Fig. 11.1 shows, a wide range of emotion fits sensibly into this framework. Subjects were asked to group together a large number of emotion terms, according to their similarity. Statistical analyses (multidimensional scaling) identified two underlying dimensions. For example, according to the subjects, being distressed feels about as negative as being gloomy, but being distressed involves higher levels of arousal and being gloomy involves lower levels. In the figure, *gloomy* lies between *miserable* (more negative, more aroused) and *bored* (less negative, less aroused). More importantly, converging evidence from various sources confirms this framework. Other taxonomies have been suggested (Davitz, 1970; Plutchik, 1970; Schlosberg, 1954; Wundt, 1897), and, like horoscopes, they all have the eerie quality of seeming reasonable when you read them but not necessarily having much empirical support. Also, the taxonomies all involve judgments of the semantics or conceptual meaning of emotion, rather than some more direct examination of actual affective states.

Moving to actual affect reveals a curious feature not evident from the above semantic taxonomies. Researchers usually have assumed that the evaluative component of affect is bipolar, which means that positive and negative feelings are negatively correlated, that is, endpoints of a single continuum (J. A. Russell, 1979). The more you feel happy, the less you feel miserable, right? This is not always true. Over time, the same person can make you feel delighted and depressed, frustrated and satisfied. Looking at any real reactions over time, positive and negative feelings can easily co-occur. People's reactions to presidential candidates (Abelson, Kinder, Peters, & Fiske, 1982) and to their lives in general (Bradburn & Caplovitz, 1965; Warr, Barter, & Brownbridge, 1983) can be characterized by ambivalence. People's reactions to specific relationships and situations over time are likely to yield contradictory feelings.

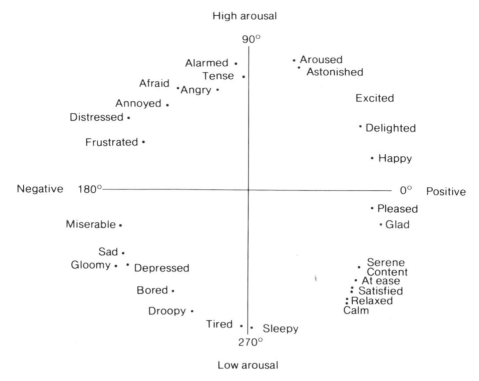

Fig. 11.1 A circumplex model of affect: Direct circular scaling coordinates for twenty-eight affect words. (Adapted from J. A. Russell, A circumplex model of affect, *Journal of Personality and Social Psychology*, 1980, *39*, 1151-1178. Copyright 1980 by the American Psychological Association. Adapted by permission of the author.)

If one characterizes affect as ranging along a continuum from positive to negative, one cannot distinguish between indifference and ambivalence. Both would fall at the middle of the continuum, yet they are quite different. Positive and negative affect can be independent of each other in real life, and not polar opposites as psychologists have sometimes assumed.

Preliminary issues aside, the main business of this chapter is to look at how cognition and affect influence each other. Throughout the book, affect has surfaced periodically: attributional analyses of emotional lability, depression, attraction, and prejudice (Chapters 2 and 3); defensive attribution (Chapter 4); evaluative implications of schemata (Chapter 6); affect and involvement in attention (Chapter 7); and affect as a possible fourth code in person memory (Chapter 8). Affect has played various supporting roles but mainly two: either as the result of cognitive analysis, or as a basis for cognitive analysis. In most of this chapter we examine research directly confronting these two issues. But first, a brief bit of historical context helps put perspective on the long-standing question of the relationship between affect and cognition.

Early Theories

A century ago, William James (1884/1968) proposed that the feeling of autonomic feedback (heart rate, stomach tension) and muscular feedback (posture, facial expressions) constitutes emotion. In this view, the physiological patterns unique to each emotion reveal to us what we are feeling. To understand this better, think about how you feel when you have just been to the dentist and the novocaine has not yet worn off; it is difficult to feel wholly cheerful or wholly angry. The anesthetic only numbs a few mouth muscles, yet somehow it seems to numb your emotions as well. This hints at the importance of physiology in the experience of emotion. The James-Lange theory of emotion—so called because Conrad Lange invented a similar theory at the same time as James (Lange, 1885/1922)—downplayed the role of cognition or mental activity as a sole basis for emotion.

Decades after James, this theory was devastated by Walter Cannon's dual argument that (1) visceral sensations are too diffuse to account for all the different emotions, and (2) the autonomic system responds too slowly to account for the speed of emotional responses (1927). Following this critique, many psychologists assumed that physiological contributions to emotion were limited to diffuse arousal and did not include specific patterns of bodily sensation. (For modern dissent on this point, see G. E. Schwartz, Weinberger, & Singer, 1981.) A basic problem thus remained: if arousal is not differentiated, but simply ranges from high to low, how can one account for the rich texture of emotional experience?

Physiological Theories of Emotion

Researchers have proposed that physiology provides the richness of emotional experience, either through facial feedback or through intensifying existing emotions.

FACIAL FEEDBACK THEORY

The facial feedback hypothesis holds that emotional events directly trigger certain innate configurations of muscles, and that we become aware of feelings only upon feedback from the face (Tomkins, 1962). The locus of emotional complexity is solely in the face. According to the facial feedback theory, development and upbringing constrain the range of expressions people adopt and so also the range of emotions they can feel (Izard, 1972, 1977). Thus, over time, people build up a repertoire of emotions, on the basis of innate facial reactions and on the basis of the facial muscles they are allowed to use in expressing their feelings. Arousal can be integrated into the facial feedback viewpoint by arguing that the face is sensitive enough to provide the separate qualities of different emotional expressions, while arousal provides the intensity (Laird, 1974).

There is clear evidence for the fundamental idea that facial expressions exert a direct effect on mood, on emotion, and on affect-laden judgments such as attitudes. One typical experiment involved manipulating people's facial expressions (Laird, 1974). Subjects were induced to smile or frown without labeling their expressions as such. The experimenter did this by attaching electrodes to subjects' faces, supposedly to monitor the minute electrical activity of facial muscles. Subjects were then told to contract and relax various specific muscles, until they had assumed a smile or a frown. Hence the experimenter had created a plausible excuse so the subjects would not consciously think of their facial contortions as smiles or frowns. People then held the pose and observed various stimuli; their emotional reactions were moderated by their posed facial expressions. For example, they rated various cartoons as not so funny when they had to "frown" compared to when they had to "smile." Other researchers have obtained similar effects (e.g., Duncan & Laird, 1977; Lanzetta, Cartwright-Smith, & Kleck, 1976; Rhodewalt & Comer, 1979).

Nevertheless, there is some disagreement about the effect of facial expressions on affect. Some researchers do not replicate the finding that manipulated facial expressions change emotion (Buck, 1980; Ellsworth & Tourangeau, 1981; Tourangeau & Ellsworth, 1979; versus Hager & Ekman, 1981; Izard, 1981; Tomkins, 1981b). One likely explanation for some of the contradictory findings is that telling people simply to *exaggerate* their spontaneous facial expressions produces changes in emotion, while rigidly *posed* expressions sometimes change emotions and sometimes do not (Laird, 1974; Zuckerman, Klorman, Larrance, & Spiegel, 1981). Indeed, this makes some sense because the physiology of spontaneous expressions may differ from posed ones (G. E. Schwartz, Fair, Salt, Mandel, & Klerman, 1976). In the end, the simplest version of the facial feedback idea is not supported unequivocally (cf. Leventhal, 1980).

The issues related to facial feedback theory are complex and beyond our current task of examining the role of cognition in affect. Nevertheless, facial expressions are clearly one important element in the experience of emotion. They suggest also that cognition is at most only one part of affect. The facial feedback researchers make that point by positing a direct effect of muscular feedback on affect, unmediated by cognition. Recent attempts to integrate muscular feedback into theories of emotion underline the shift toward combining cognitive and physiological factors in theories of affect (M. S. Clark, 1982; Leventhal, 1980, 1982; Zajonc, Pietromonaco, & Bargh, 1982). In part, this effort was inspired by facial feedback research. In part, it came about as a result of social psychological research on arousal and affect, to which we now turn.

AROUSAL THEORIES

One line of affect research has centered specifically on the role of arousal. Remember that one conclusion of the James-Cannon controversy was that arousal was diffuse and not patterned differently for the different emotions. If arousal is experienced as nonspecific, that is, as not patterned to specific emotions (as many now believe), being excited by anger or by elation should not strongly differ physiologically. The social cognition arousal theorists argue precisely that: arousal patterns do not differentiate among the emotions. Rather, they argue that arousal intensifies emotional responses triggered by other mechanisms. The theorists then ask: What are the origins of arousal, how does it intensify emotion, and does its interpretation require deliberate cognitive activity?

Zillmann's theory of excitation transfer (1978), first covered in Chapter 3, "Applications of Attribution Theory," describes arousal as one of the major features in emotional responses. As an example, assume that Ralph is sitting in his room alone, when the door opens with a crash. Ralph jumps up in surprise. In stomps his friend, angry and upset. She explains that she just had a most frustrating meeting with a faculty member they both know. As she explains how unfair the professor is, Ralph becomes upset, too. Together they decide to go see an older student they both know, who may provide some new perspectives on the situation. As they walk out, Ralph lapses into silence, thinking about how angry he now is. In this example, Ralph responds in three major ways (Zillmann, 1978). He shows an arousal response to two separate stimuli, the door crashing open and his friend who is upset. Clearly, his arousal from the crashing sound is an automatic, unconditioned response, while his arousal on his friend's behalf is a learned, empathic response. Thus, as Zillmann has argued, arousal has two potential origins: automatic and learned. Similarly, Ralph's behavioral responses are of two sorts. The startle reaction is automatic, and going to see the older student is a learned response. Finally, his experience of feeling angry hinges on his being aware of his arousal and his behavior. Of these three components in emotional reactions, the experience is the most cognitive aspect.

The three components of emotion operate somewhat independently. For example, Ralph could be angrily aroused, and take action, but not stop to think about the experience of feeling angry. Cognitive theories typically do not allow for emotional responses in which people act or feel without thinking, as we will see. Behaviorist theories, in contrast, are explicitly concerned with behavior rather than conscious thought related to emotion. The behaviorist theories account rather well for instantaneous emotional reactions (as in the above example), which the purely cognitive theories do not (e.g., Hebb, 1949; Hull, 1943, 1952; Spence, 1960). Some attempt to integrate the behaviorist and cognitive approaches would appear to be in order, especially if cognitive theories are to deal successfully with behavior (Zillmann, 1978).

Arousal intensifies a wide range of responses, both cognitive and behavioral. And arousal that comes from seemingly innocent sources can intensify affect toward seemingly irrelevant people and objects that step into view. For example, people who had just exercised responded more angrily to provocation by a confederate than did people not physiologically aroused (Zillmann, 1978; Zillmann & Bryant, 1974; see also Chapter 3). Their excitation may have transferred from its source to an irrelevant response. Even if unable to take immediate action, people may commit themselves to future actions (e.g., revenge) while excited, so that the effects of excitation transfer can last long after the actual arousal dissipates (Bryant & Zillmann, 1979). Arousal can enhance positive responses as well as negative ones. In another study, people who exercised and then received pleasant feedback about their performance responded more positively to a series of irrelevant attitude questions (How much do you like your school?") than did subjects who received the same feedback but who had not exercised (M. S. Clark, 1982). Arousal also enhances affectively positive attributions (Gollwitzer, Earle, & Stephan, 1982). In sum, arousal intensifies both positive and negative affective responses.

There is evidence that people can be aroused by an affect-laden stimulus without even being fully aware of the stimulus (Corteen & Wood, 1972). Moreover, arousal can intensify responses even when people are unaware of being aroused. People in such situations may think they are no longer aroused by the exercise, yet physiological measures would show that they are. An intriguing line of research supports this view (Cacioppo, 1979). Heart patients wearing implanted pacemakers participated in an attitude change study. When their heart rate was slightly (and safely) accelerated by an adjustment to the pacemaker, they more vigorously counterargued a persuasive communication. What is especially intriguing is that people's cognitive responses were increased by actual but unperceived changes in arousal. Note that this contrasts with the misattribution research stemming from Schachter's work and covered in Chapter 2, "Attribution Theory" (e.g., Valins, 1966); in that work, people were sometimes led to think they were aroused when they actually were not, and then their interpretations were manipulated. Hence the misattribution research deals with perceived but not necessarily actual arousal, while the arousal and emotion work deals with actual but not necessarily perceived arousal.

SUMMARY

To review, early theories of emotion set the stage for a continuing debate over the role of cognition and physiology in affective responses. James hypothesized that unique physiological patterns occur in direct response to emotional stimuli, essentially without cognitive mediation. His view was undermined by Cannon, who argued that visceral responses are too slow and too diffuse to differentiate the many separate emotions. Facial feedback theorists argue, as James did, that the different emotions come directly from physiological sensations. But instead of relying on the diffuse arousal system, the theorists suggest that the sensitive facial musculature provides the different patterns for various emotions. The newer arousal theorists do not argue that different patterns of arousal create different emotions, rather that arousal intensifies emotional responses that originate from automatic or learned responses. Both facial feedback theorists and arousal theorists downplay the importance of cognition in emotional responses, compared to the theories to be covered next.

Social Cognitive Foundations of Affect

A wide range of social psychological research addresses emotionally laden interpersonal phenomena: aggression, attraction, stereotyping, guilt, embarrassment, self-esteem, and more (Kiesler, 1982). Much of this existing work implicitly assumes that thought precedes feeling. For example, in most stereotyping research, researchers assume the cognition-affect sequence: people apply a (cognitive) generalization to a person on the basis of category membership, and (affective) prejudice results (Brigham, 1971). In attitude research, the broad outlines of the analysis are similar. For example, cognitive consistency theories such as dissonance theory posit that cognitive discrepancies precede the affective discomfort that leads to attitude change (Abelson et al., 1968). In regard to attribution theories (Chapters 2-4) and balance theory (Chapters 6 and 12), some of Heider's unpublished writings provide strong evidence for a cognition-affect link (Benesh & Weiner, 1982). Many social psychologists have assumed that cognition is a major basis for affective reactions (for an exception, see behaviorist theories of attitudes and attraction: Clore & Byrne, 1974; Lott & Lott, 1974; Staats & Staats, 1958).

SCHACHTER'S THEORY

Schachter's theory of emotional lability nicely solved the continuing problem of how arousal can be so diffuse but emotion can be so specific. Recall from Chapter 2, "Attribution Theory," where Schachter's theory was first introduced, that he suggested a two-component view of emotion. Diffuse physiological arousal gives rise to cognitive interpretation, often based on the social context; cognitive activity serves to differentiate emotions. In this view and those that follow from it, emotions are viewed as mediated by cognitive interpretation. Note that this differs from some of the views just discussed that focus more directly on unmediated physiological responses. However, Schachter's cognitive theory has had considerable impact on social psychology's research on emotion, as we saw in Chapter 2-4, and as we will see next.

Most social psychological research on affect-laden phenomena, especially Schachter's work and its offshoots, has viewed cognitive processes as integral to emotion. Several theories have evolved that take Schachter's theory a few steps further or that more generally extend cognitive analyses of affect to a relatively fine-grained level.[1]

---

1. Other theories of emotion, besides those derived from Schachter, also rely on cognition as causing affect. These theories emphasize the way people appraise the value of a stimulus with respect to its impact on themselves (Arnold, 1970; Lazarus, Averill, & Opton, 1970). These cognitive theories of emotion predate the recent cognitive revolution, so they lack detailed models of cognitive process. They also have had less impact on social cognition research, so they will not be discussed here. See Shaver and Klinnert (1982) for an optimistic view of their potential.

MANDLER'S MIND AND EMOTION

The basic features of Mandler's theory are similar to Schachter's: environmental inputs generate arousal, and cognitive interpretation labels that arousal (Mandler, 1975; Strongman, 1978). Fig. 11.2 depicts the model as it can be applied to social cognition (S. T. Fiske, 1981). Physiological arousal is produced by "interrupts" or unexpected events that alert the organism to cope with an environmental contingency. Arousal comes from two related kinds of interrupts. One kind is the disconfirmation of a perceptual schema, as when you encounter a song that stops in the middle or includes discordant notes. Another kind of interrupt comes from interfering with complex sequences of intended behavior, that is, goals. For example, if you drop your keys while trying to get in the door, that interrupts a relatively minor goal, so it should cause a small amount of arousal. If you drop your keys while trying to impress the date of your dreams, that interrupts a potentially more complex goal, so it should cause more arousal. Physiological arousal gives emotion its intensity. The more complex the interrupted goal or schema, the more intense the arousal.

Arousal also sets off cognitive interpretation. The interruption may be interpreted positively or negatively, which specifies the exact quality of the emotion you feel. If your interpretation is that you are clumsy, you may feel foolish and irritated. But if your interpretation is that you were distracted by your date's green eyes, you may feel in love. Whatever the cognitive interpretation, it shapes not only the quality of one's affect, but also one's memory and inferences about the event.

For some types of judgment, primarily those involving perceptual schemata rather than goals, the degree of interruption and arousal determines the

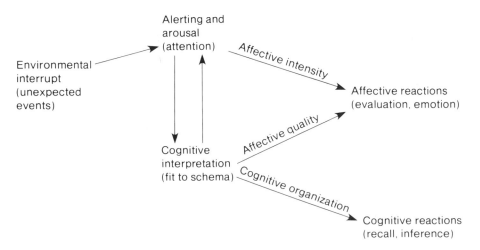

Fig. 11.2 An embellished version of Mandler's model. (After S. T. Fiske, 1981)

positivity of the response (Mandler, 1982). Mandler suggests that in these realms, disconfirmations of perceptual schemata range from zero (total familiarity) to extreme (total discord). On the whole, Mandler suggests, familiarity is good, a little novelty is better, but total discord is unpleasant (cf. Berlyne, 1970; D. W. Fiske & Maddi, 1961; Leventhal, 1974). Mandler mainly analyzes what he calls judgments of value, pertaining to one's taste in music, art, food, beauty, and the like. Other types of judgment not analyzed by Mandler are more directly relevant to social settings. These include affective judgments about oneself in relationship to others, to which we now turn.

BERSCHEID'S ANALYSIS OF EMOTION IN CLOSE RELATIONSHIPS

Berscheid has presented a compelling case for the application of Mandler's framework to emotions in close relationships (Berscheid, 1982). Consider the normal course of a long-term intimate relationship. At first, emotions run high (and low) as two people get to know each other's similarities and idiosyncrasies. As they become better acquainted, there are fewer surprises of both the pleasant and unpleasant sort. As the novelty wears off, emotions run to fewer extremes, and either complacency or boredom may settle in. When the initial intensity wears off, does that mean less potential for emotion? No. Quite the contrary. If the relationship broke up, emotional intensity would run to extremes. It is only when the relationship functions smoothly that emotions seem flat and calm. The irony is that one can best gauge the intensity of a long-term relationship when it is terminated—or interrupted.

Berscheid's analysis goes as follows: the more intimate the relationship, the more two people's goals depend on each other. Their complex behavioral sequences are intermeshed, and the more intermeshed they are, the more seriously each person can interrupt the other (see Fig. 11.3). Interdependent goals can range from simple behavior sequences, such as doing the laundry jointly, to complex behavior sequences, such as collaborating on work. The greater the interdependence, then, the greater the potential for intense negative emotion, if one partner leaves or dies. Positive emotions, in this analysis, result when the other person unexpectedly facilitates one's goals. Unexpected help causes more pleasure than help that one already expected or took for granted. If the intermeshed sequences run off smoothly, on the other hand, there will be no interruptions and little emotion. Hence, Berscheid notes, there is the paradox that the most intimate or interdependent relationships may show as little emotion as a distant relationship, simply because the intimate one is working well. An intimate relationship, thus, is defined by the potential for emotional intensity, which results from highly interdependent goals.

One implication of this perspective is that one can measure the intimacy of a relationship by its interdependency—that is, by the frequency, strength, and diversity of two people's intermeshed goals; it is not useful to measure the intimacy of a relationship by the level of day-to-day emotion the two people experience. Furthermore, this analysis explains why obstacles to a relationship often heighten its passion, since emotion stems from interruptions. For exam-

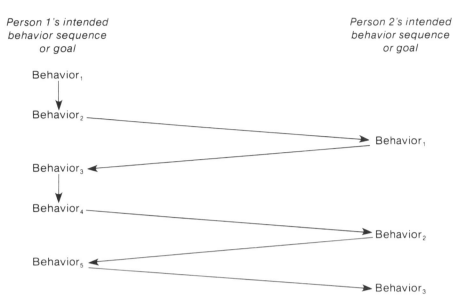

Person 1's intended behavior sequence or goal

Person 2's intended behavior sequence or goal

Fig. 11.3 Model of two people with an interdependent behavior sequence, creating a precondition for each to interrupt the other and experience emotion. (After Berscheid, 1982)

ple, parental interference can interrupt a romantic relationship and make it more intense. Other puzzles are also resolved, such as the possibility of liking people but not feeling strongly emotional about them because they do not have the power to interrupt one's life. Finally, there is the devilish case in which one emphatically dislikes a person who nonetheless causes one great emotion, even positive emotion, because the person has the power to facilitate or to interrupt one's goals. You may dislike an obnoxious acquaintance, but if she does you an unexpected favor, you may have positive feelings as a result, although you still dislike her.

To summarize, both Mandler and Berscheid analyze emotion as resulting from interruptions. Interrupted expectations, whether in a symphony or in a close relationship, create arousal and cognitive interpretations. The nature of the interpretation determines the quality of affect, while the extent of the interruption and subsequent arousal determine the intensity of affect. While extensive research has not yet resulted directly from these frameworks, the theoretical perspectives are promising indeed because they are specific enough to be tested and because they provide a coherent theoretical account of a diverse range of phenomena.

Mandler's and Berscheid's models focus primarily on the interruption of one's goals or schemata as a cause for emotion. Thus, because both goals and schemata are cognitive structures, the models assume that cognition is a necessary antecedent for emotion.

SOCIAL SCHEMATA AND AFFECT

Three independent lines of research have investigated the role of schemata or generic knowledge structures in affect. These researchers assume, as do Mandler and Berscheid, that cognitive processes precede affect. Unlike that work, their emphasis is on the successful application of a knowledge structure, rather than on the interrupted application of a knowledge structure. Moreover, the knowledge structures in this case are social schemata, whereas in the previous work they were goals or perceptual schemata. The following work on schemata and affect supports the idea that the complexity, organization, and fit of prior knowledge can create affective reactions.

Linville's work (1982a, 1982b), reviewed in Chapter 6, "Social Schemata," focuses on the affective consequences of informational complexity. Recall that people tend to evaluate out-group members (low complexity) more extremely than in-group members (high complexity). Thus, the greater the complexity of a knowledge structure, the more moderate the affect it elicits. For example, you may know a dozen dimensions that determine whether a given football team is any good, but I can think of only two or three offhand; if your set of football knowledge is more complex than mine, your evaluations of any random team's attributes will be more mixed. Because I am integrating fewer attributes, any random piece of new information is likely to have considerable impact on my judgment, making it more extreme. Thus, the more attributes considered, the more mixed the information is likely to be, and the more moderate the overall evaluation will be. People differ considerably in how complexly they perceive a given domain of knowledge. You may be complex about football, but I am complex about murder mysteries.

Individual differences in one's general complexity about other people support a similar perspective on the relationship between knowledge and affect. For example, people who are more cognitively complex about other people in general also give more varied emotional responses to other people's situations (Sommers, 1981). Thus one can be complex about a specific domain (football, murder mysteries) or about people in general; cognitive complexity of both sorts influences affective responses.

Another view of the link between knowledge structures and affect is that thought polarizes feelings because it leads to a tighter organization of the attributes of a given stimulus, for those who possess a schema for thinking about it (Tesser, 1978). The more you consider your team's chances for the league championship (holding constant the amount of knowledge you have), the more you will force all of your team's attributes to fall into place as consistently pro or consistently con. Over time, people can make an instance fit most any schema they choose, so evaluation becomes more extreme as the attributes become more organized. No amount of thought on my part about your team will polarize my evaluations of it, since I have insufficient prior information to rearrange. Note that this differs a great deal from Linville's theory, as just described. Linville predicts that affect is polarized when stimulus complexity is initially low. Tesser predicts that affect becomes polarized over time as a result of complexity that is reduced as one organizes an instance to fit a schema.

A third view of the link between schemata and affect emphasizes the fit of new information to prior knowledge. In this view, some schemata include affect. When an instance is fit to an affect-laden schema, the appropriate affect is cued (S. T. Fiske, 1981, 1982). Thus, deciding that someone is a good example of a rich snob or a shallow playboy has clear affective consequences. To the extent people fit a stereotypic mold, they receive the affect triggered by the stereotype. If they are a poor fit to a negative stereotype, they may be given benefit of the doubt, and the affective reaction moderates. Affect-laden social knowledge structures range from the cultural prejudice against the prototypic slimy politician to prejudice against local campus stereotypes of preppies, athletes, computer science majors, and artists; affective schemata also include one's own particular ideal mate or standard date. If a person fits an existing schema, one does not have to proceed piecemeal to total up the pros and cons of each individual attribute; the affective reaction may have been calculated previously or otherwise already linked to the category. Thus schema-triggered affect is an efficient affective processing device: one can say, "I know that type, and I know how I feel about him or her."

A variety of research, then, supports the idea that cognitive factors such as complexity, organization, and fit of prior knowledge shape affective reactions to new stimuli.

OBTAINED OUTCOMES AND AFFECT

Two final sets of theories also suggest that cognitions are a necessary antecedent to emotions. Cognitions (attributions) about one's obtained outcomes, and cognitions (thoughts) about one's alternative outcomes both contribute to emotion.

In an earlier discussion of applied attribution theories (Chapter 3), we described Weiner's dimensions of causality: internal-external, stable-unstable, and controllable-uncontrollable (Weiner, 1980a, 1982; Weiner, Russell, & Lerman, 1973). Each is relevant to attributions for achievement outcomes and subsequent emotional reactions to them. Locus and controllability determine the specific nature of the emotional reaction to one's own or another's outcomes, whereas high stability intensifies it. For example, suppose you feel gratitude toward another person who chose to help you. The cause is external (the other person) and controllable (choosing to help). If the person had been forced to help you (external locus but not controllable), you would not feel grateful. The stability dimension usually exaggerates affective responses.

To illustrate Weiner's taxonomy, suppose you get an A on an exam, and that it was one for which you studied hard. What do you feel? Chances are, given a positive outcome for which you are responsible, you feel pride. Now suppose you fail an exam, and you know it is your own fault for not studying hard enough. What do you feel? Probably you feel guilt over a negative outcome that you brought on yourself. Now suppose you ask someone out, and the person rejects you with only a flimsy excuse. How do you feel toward the person? Probably angry and sad. Finally, suppose the same person turns you down for a night on the town because the person's apartment building just burned down. Now you probably feel pity. Several lines of work support the idea that emotions are contingent on one's outcomes and their perceived causes. It is not just whether you win or lose but how you interpret the game.

Although Weiner's taxonomy does not produce any surprises, it serves to systematize people's intuitions about the ways that outcomes produce emotion (cf. Roseman, 1979). It is a naive psychology model (cf. Chapter 1) and so should agree with most people's experience. But it relies on more than intuition for support. The evidence for the attributional antecedents of emotion comes, for example, from studies in which subjects read a story. The dimensions of causality are varied, and then subjects are asked what the protagonist would feel (Weiner *et al.*, 1978). In one study, subjects read the following:

> Francis studied intensely for a test he took. It was very important for Francis to record a high score on this exam. Francis received an extremely high score on the test. Francis felt that he received this high score because he studied so intensely [his ability in this subject; he was lucky in which questions were selected; etc.] How do you think Francis felt upon receiving this score? (Weiner *et al.*, 1978, p. 70)

In this example, most people think Francis would feel pride.

In other studies, people think about emotional incidents in their own lives and the reasons for those incidents (Weiner, Russell, & Lerman, 1979); some of these studies focus on achievement, others on affiliation, and others on help giving. Despite this range of tests, they all come to the same conclusion that attributions can cause emotion in the manner described.

However, all the research is limited to verbal reports of hypothetical or past emotion. This is also true of other research discussed here (e.g., Abelson *et al.*, 1982; J. A. Russell, 1979, 1980). What if people's reports about what they feel differ from what they actually do feel? What about feelings that people cannot articulate for one reason or another? What about real, active feelings in the present rather than already past or potential feelings? At a minimum, the studies do reflect people's reported interpretations of what they think they have felt or would feel. Given the importance of language in emotion, relying on self-reports is one useful approach. Moreover, these studies are supported by work that finds that attributions are a major determinant of affective reactions (McFarland & Ross, 1982).

Understanding the attributional basis of emotion already has proven useful to other research. The attribution-emotion link has helped cognitive psychologists to build emotion into memory models: in working toward a computer simulation that will "understand" emotions, Weiner's attribution work provides a systematic set of rules for emotional interpretations of personal outcomes (G. H. Bower & Cohen, 1982). Outside the lab, the attribution-emotion results also have been applied to people's emotional reactions to major life outcomes such as their financial situations (E. R. Smith & Kluegel, 1982).

ALTERNATIVE OUTCOMES AND AFFECT

In addition to Weiner's work on cognitions (attributions) about one's obtained outcomes, other psychologists have focused on cognitions (beliefs) about one's alternative outcomes. These theories describe the effects on emotion of what-could-be and what-might-have-been. Work by Abelson and by Kahneman and Tversky focuses on cognitions about emotions as "alternative worlds." Abelson's framework (1981a, 1983) examines the emotional effects of alternative future outcomes that are incompatible with each other, for example, that are either good or bad and not both possible at once. Incompatibility can occur at any of several stages in a sequence of events, as follows (see Fig. 11.4). Suppose two friends have decided spontaneously to go away for the weekend (goal). They decide to go camping (planned action), so they make reservations at their favorite campground (causal instrumentality). If the actual outcome is as expected (i.e., their campsite is waiting for them), there is little cause for emotion (except perhaps low-key contentment).

Now suppose that they arrive and verify their reservations with the park ranger, but they hear that the campsite may be flooded. What do they feel as they drive toward it? Probably suspense. There is a potential gap in the link between instrumentality and outcome (see Fig. 11.4). Now suppose the uncertainty occurs at an earlier stage. Suppose they arrive at the park entrance and their alleged reservation draws nothing but a blank look from the ranger. There is a potential gap in the link between planned action and causal instrumentality. As the ranger double checks the files, what do the would-be campers feel? Probably hope and fear. If the uncertainty occurs at a still earlier stage, perhaps between goal and action, they would again feel differently. That is, if it is clear that they want to go away for the weekend (goal) but they cannot decide whether they can go camping or whether they will have to visit boring relatives (two action alternatives), they may agonize over which action to plan. Or, to take the incompatibility back still further to earlier in the sequence, if their uncertainty encompasses the initial goal of going away at all, they will feel conflict. Other combinations of alternative outcomes produce various other emotions (Abelson, 1981a, 1983). Although there is as yet no research stemming from this framework, it illustrates another way to systematize the relationship between people's outcomes and their feelings.

A second example of alternative outcomes that determine emotions also deals with mental simulations of outcomes. This one does not focus on what might yet be but rather on what might have been. Consider how you feel when you just miss meeting a friend by moments versus how you feel when you miss the person by a couple of hours. Which circumstance is more frustrating?

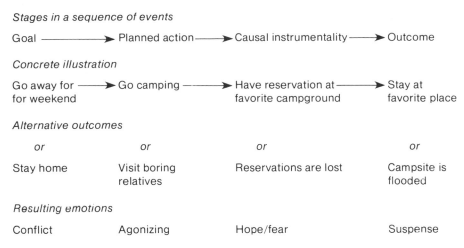

Fig. 11.4 Alternative future outcomes as a basis for emotion. (After Abelson 1981a)

Recall the simulation heuristic from Chapter 9, "Social Inference"; in one study of this phenomenon, Kahneman and Tversky (1982) gave subjects two missed-plane scenarios, that is, the plane was delayed and just now left versus the plane left on time and long ago; 96 percent of their subjects agreed that the former would be more upsetting. The ease of imagining alternative outcomes influences the emotional impact of the obtained outcome. The more easily the event might have been otherwise, the more upset one gets.

In another investigation of the same phenomenon, subjects read the story of someone dying in a traffic accident either while taking an unusual route home from work or while leaving at an unusual time. Subjects agreed that the person's relatives would be more likely to regret the one departure from his habitual routine (e.g., either time or route) than to regret normal events (e.g., that he had always commuted to work). As people imagine undoing the event, they are more likely to imagine changing things toward normal than changing things away from normal. Mental undoing operates by the easiest or so-called "downhill" changes rather than more difficult or "uphill" changes. Grieving relatives focus on what was unusual in that fatal day's events, not on what was routine.

There are other accounts that relate goals and outcomes to emotions (Clore & Kerber, 1980; deRivera, 1977; Ortony & Collins, 1982). The basic point is common, even when some features differ: the quality and intensity of emotions can depend on perceived outcomes. To review, Weiner's work focuses on obtained outcomes and their perceived causes. In his view, attributions shape one's emotional responses to success and failure. Two other theories emphasize the impact of imagined outcomes or alternative worlds. Abelson's theory proposes that emotions can be based on what might be—

alternative future outcomes, actions, goals. Kahneman and Tversky's research supports the idea that emotions can be based on what might have been—alternative past outcomes. All three sets of ideas endorse the general proposition that cognitions can be an important cause of affective responses. And all three remain to be examined empirically in the context of actual emotion.

Affective Foundations of Cognition

This section focuses on the consequences of affect for cognitions and cognitive processes. In particular, mood influences memory and judgment, and in general, emotions influence cognitive processes.

MOOD EFFECTS ON MEMORY AND JUDGMENT

We have a friend who recently fell in love. He is delightful but difficult to be around for long. It is not that he continually talks about his newfound love, although she is a frequent topic of conversation. Rather, he has developed the disconcerting habit of finding everything uniformly wonderful. If your car breaks down, he extols the virtues of walking. If it rains, he points out how much the city needs water. If someone insults you, he explains it as a temporary aberration. While it is nice to be around someone so cheerful, he is a little relentless. We also have a friend (in fact, several) who recently fell out of love—or more accurately, recently divorced. These people all tend to see the world through mud-colored glasses. Their cars never work right; it seems to rain selectively on them; and most people they encounter strike them as dreadful bores. Aware that their gloom darkens everything, they do struggle not to complain all the time, but their initial reactions to most situations are negative.

Research shows that people in good moods are more helpful, more open to conversations with strangers, like others more, and are more satisfied even with their cars and other possessions, compared with people in neutral moods (see M. S. Clark & Isen, 1982). Mood has been manipulated in a wide range of ways in this research, from receiving an unexpected gift to being congratulated on success at a task. For example, in one study, people in a shopping mall were given a free sample (a note pad or a nail clipper) by a female confederate. The experimenter then separately approached the people, who presumably were in a good mood, and gave them a seemingly unrelated consumer survey. People who had received a gift rated their cars and television sets more positively than people who did not (Isen, Shalker, Clark, & Karp, 1978).

The pervasive effects of mood on behavior and judgment seem to be caused by the availability of mood-congruent thoughts. That is, being in a good mood leads to positive associations in memory, and being in a bad mood tends to lead to negatively toned cognitions (Bartlett & Santrock, 1977; M. S. Clark & Waddell, 1983; Wright & Mischel, 1982). Researchers posit the basic process to be this: if similarly toned material tends to be linked in memory,

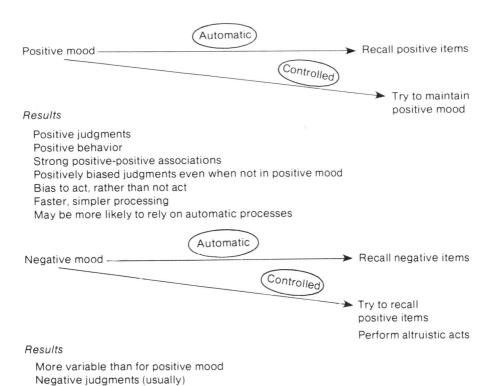

Fig. 11.5 Effects of positive and negative mood on cognition and cognitive processing.

then activating one positive or negative item automatically primes other positive or negative items.[2] Figure 11.5 summarizes the effects of positive and negative moods.

Moods prime similarly toned material in memory, but the effect of negative mood is more variable than that of positive mood. This may be because they often operate in different ways. First, the priming process usually seems to operate automatically (M. S. Clark & Isen, 1982); that is, mood primes similarly toned material without one's awareness, effort, or intent. These features in part define an automatic process (W. Schneider & Shiffrin, 1977; Shiffrin &

2. This effect may be related to the category priming effect discussed in Chapter 6, "Social Schemata," and Chapter 8, "Person Memory." In both cases, something previously activated seems to make accessible material that is conceptually or affectively similar. The "something" in the earlier priming research was a conceptual category, while the "something" in this research seems to be simply positivity or negativity, which is not limited to one specific category of information.

Schneider, 1977). However, priming can also be a controlled process. Controlled processes are deliberate, conscious strategies that require some effort. People in bad moods may be more likely to switch from automatic to controlled processes (M. S. Clark & Isen, 1982), in order to escape the bad mood. Consequently, people often take charge of their mind's propensity to jump from gloomy thought to gloomy thought. Controlled processes for short-circuiting negative associations include such old devices as counting your blessings, looking for the silver lining, and trying to remember your favorite things (S. E. Taylor, Lichtman, & Wood, in press). People in a bad mood also may pull themselves out of it by being helpful to others (Cialdini & Kenrick, 1976; Kenrick, Baumann, & Cialdini, 1979), especially if the cost of helping is low (Weyant, 1978) and if helping would not destroy the good mood (Isen & Levin, 1972). Thus, although both good and bad moods can elicit controlled processes, negative moods seem more likely to do so.

The priming of negative associations differs from positive ones in another way, as a result of invoking controlled strategies. If people are more likely to resist automatic associations to negatively toned material, the negative-negative associations are likely to be weaker and fewer than the associations among positively toned material (M. S. Clark & Isen, 1982). These possibilities may help to account for the so-called Pollyanna effect (Matlin & Stang, 1978), the finding that positive material has a persistent advantage over negative material in information processing and judgments. People typically remember positive material more easily and make positively biased judgments. All other things being equal, most people seem to be moderately optimistic. The Pollyanna effect would stand to reason if positive material is linked to more things, and if therefore positive material is more accessible to memory than is negative. Since positive material is more likely to come to mind when one is making a judgment, presumably that would bias the judgment in a more positive direction.

Another distinction between positive and negative moods is that the former are more likely to facilitate many types of behavior. A good mood makes one think of all the good consequences of a given act, so one is more likely to follow through on the behavior. For example, when considering helping someone, people in a positive mood may think of their own pride in a good deed and of the other person's gratitude, rather than of the hassle involved. A bad mood, of course, makes one think of all the negative consequences of the act, which accentuates the costs of helping, making it less likely (M. S. Clark & Isen, 1982).

A final difference between the effects of positive and negative moods is a change in the decision processes likely to result from each. Mood affects the content of inferences, as we have seen, and it may affect whether processing is automatic or controlled. Furthermore, mood affects one's style of decision making. That is, being in a good (as opposed to neutral) mood speeds processing of material relevant to the decision, facilitates the flow of ideas, makes things come to mind effortlessly, and simplifies the perceived complexity of the decision (Isen, Means, Patrick, & Nowicki, 1982; Masters, Barden, & Ford, 1979). For example, cheerful subjects were more likely to fall prey to the availability heuristic (Chapter 9, "Social Inference"); that is, they were more likely to make frequency estimates by relying on ease of retrieval, rather than to use the normatively correct, more complex strategy in a frequency estimation task (Isen et al., 1982). Specifically, subjects were asked to estimate the proportion of famous people on a list in which the famous people actually were outnumbered; most subjects relied on the ease of retrieving names to estimate the proportions. That is, the famous names were easier to remember, so their frequency was overestimated. Happy subjects, however, were especially likely to base their estimates on fewer names and to make more mistakes in recall.

What does this research imply about the behavior of happy people? In general, happy subjects make faster decisions, based on less information, than do neutral controls. Sometimes happy subjects are more biased, as a result of overlooking important details, but sometimes they are more efficient, as a result of skipping redundant details. Happy subjects sometimes take more risks, as a result of being especially optimistic, and sometimes they take fewer risks, as a result of trying to maintain their current good mood. Although behavioral responses depend on the circumstances, happy subjects seem to behave more extremely than neutral subjects in any case (Isen et al., 1982). Fig. 11.5 presents a summary of these lines of research.

NETWORK MODELS OF THE EFFECTS OF MOOD ON MEMORY

Another research program studying the effects of mood on memory differs from the research we just discussed in three major ways: it uses different manipulations of mood, it focuses on constructing relatively more detailed process models, and it does not emphasize behavior as much as the social psychological research does. Bower's program of research (G. H. Bower, 1981; G. H. Bower & Cohen, 1982) has found that mood-congruent stimuli are more salient and better learned at encoding (cf. Nasby & Yando, 1982). For example, happy or sad subjects might read a story about a happy character and a sad character and then be asked with whom they identified. Or they might watch a videotape of themselves and another person, noting instances of positive and negative behavior. In both cases, subjects focus their attention on the character or the behaviors that are mood congruent (G. H. Bower & Cohen, 1982). Further, moods serve as retrieval cues; it is easier to remember things learned in a given mood when the same mood is reinstated at recall. Finally, moods influence judgments of friends, self, possessions, and the future (cf. M. Snyder & White, 1982).

The paradigm cognitive psychologist Bower uses differs from that of social psychologists Clark and Isen, in that Bower and his associates use hypnosis to induce moods. This distinction is important because they get similar results with a totally different method. Bower's method requires highly suggestible subjects, who are then hypnotized, and then instructed to replay an appropriately emotion-laden scene from their past. When the subjects have made themselves moderately happy or sad, they are asked to maintain the feeling as they undertake the experimental tasks. Other researchers' manipulations of mood include talking about happy or sad experiences (Bartlett, Burleson, & Santrock, 1982), reading emotionally evocative sentences (Teasdale & Fogarty, 1979), or manipulating people's facial expressions (Laird, Wagener, Halal, & Szegda, 1982). Moreover, the mood-congruent memory effect holds whether mood is positive or negative, as noted above, and whether the mood is high or low on physiological arousal (M. S. Clark, Milberg, & Ross, in press).

Across a wide range of manipulations and measures, emotionally consistent material is easier to recall than is inconsistent material. That is, material that matches one's mood at encoding or retrieval is easier to learn than material that does not. The theory created to account for these results posits that emotion is simply a retrieval cue like any other. This means that memories or events that come to mind at the same time as a given emotion are linked to that emotion, and hence (indirectly) to other emotion-congruent memories or events (see Fig. 11.6). Mood-congruent learning may operate through subjects' elaborations, that is, elaborations create more links in memory for congruent material. Or it may operate because mood-congruent material is self-relevant, and the self is a rich source of retrieval cues. Or it may be that the intensity of emotional reactions creates stronger links to memory. In any case, if material relevant to a given mood all is linked in memory then reinstating that mood should help people remember that material. Greater memory for mood-congruent events seems to fit well into a network theory of memory (G. H. Bower, 1981; M. S. Clark & Isen, 1982).

Most network models would predict that memory is organized in clusters of conceptually related items. This implies that not only emotion but also conceptual similarity should determine the effects of mood on memory and judgment. However, research does not support the prediction that conceptual similarity enhances mood-priming effects (E. J. Johnson & Tversky, 1983). It turns out that reading a disturbing account of someone's gory death causes people to make more pessimistic predictions in *general*, about risks not even remotely related to the case history. This contradicts a simple network model of emotional memory, which would suggest affect generalization decreasing from more to less related items. To the extent that affect simply links similarly toned material, without regard for conceptual similarity, a network model may be an incomplete account.

To summarize, a number of studies demonstrate that people generally make mood-congruent judgments, remember mood-congruent material, and behave in mood-congruent ways. The effects are typically clearest for positive moods; negative moods have more variable effects. The effects of mood on memory and judgment have been obtained under many research paradigms, with considerable consistency. Network models of memory have been proposed to account for these pervasive influences of affect on cognitions.

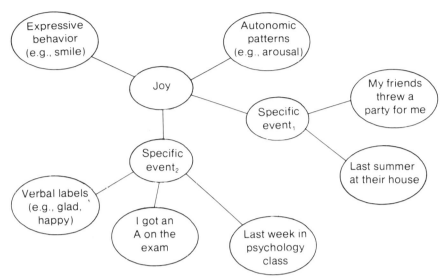

Fig. 11.6 A network model of emotion. (After G. H. Bower, 1981)

INFLUENCE OF AFFECT ON COGNITIVE PROCESSING

Thus far, we have considered the effects of feelings on specific cognitive variables: learning, memory, decisions, and judgments. Consider a possible effect of emotions on cognitive processes in general. Emotions can interrupt any ongoing cognitive process. Note that this is a different statement from Mandler's and Berscheid's theories, in which emotions are caused by interruptions. Here, emotions create interruptions. This happens to people in everyday situations. Recently a group including some very attractive men walked into a restaurant. As the waitress described the day's specials, she focused her attention in turn on each member of the party. By the time she had made eye contact with each, she had totally lost her routine and could not remember a thing. One interpretation was that her feelings of attraction had her completely flustered. (This was actually borne out later by her sending over a carafe of wine.) In effect, her feelings interrupted her cognitive activity. One need not be a bored waitress for this to happen; a student trying to write a term paper may be interrupted often as thoughts of the fight he had with his girlfriend intrude on his concentration. The idea that emotions have just such a disruptive quality enters into two cognitively oriented theories of affect.

One theory describes emotional controls on cognition. In that theory, people's emotions act to alert them to important goals; emotions are alarm signals that divert people from pursuing one goal and point them toward pursuing another goal that has meanwhile increased in importance (Simon 1967, 1982). This view follows from the premise that people are capacity-limited information processors. That is, they can pursue basically only one goal at a time, whether it is reciting a menu, writing a term paper, or thinking about the opposite sex. An information processor potentially could handle multiple goals by ranking their relative importance and completing each in turn, at leisure. Unfortunately, such an obsessive android might get run over by a truck if it was attending only to the goal of locomoting to work and not attending to the goal of staying in one piece. That is, survival demands that the organism be able to interrupt the currently active goal sequence before completion, if other environmental contingencies demand it (Simon, 1967, 1982). Emotions, such as fear of an onrushing moving van, can function to draw prompt attention to urgent goals. Examples of such high priority items include environmental stimuli that warn of potential danger (producing fear), physiological stimuli that demand refueling of one kind or another (hunger), and cognitive associations that trigger unmet emotional needs (attraction, loneliness). In this view, the physiological arousal that accompanies emotion comes from the interruptive feature of emotional stimuli. Note that the interrupting effect of emotion on behavior is to alter goals, rather than to create disorganized responses.

This promising notion remains to be tested directly. However, existing research supports the basic premise that intense emotion interrupts information processing. For example, emotionally salient material presented outside one's conscious awareness quickly captures one's conscious attention (Nielsen & Sarason, 1981). Emotionally charged events are especially memorable (Brown & Kulik, 1977) and occupy much of people's daily thoughts (Klinger, Barta, & Maxeiner, 1980). Thus emotion interrupts both attention and memory. Earlier, we noted that interruptions of one's activities or expectations can produce emotional reactions (Mandler, 1975). Here we note that emotions themselves can interrupt ongoing activities.

A related concept of emotion as interruption emerges from the cybernetic theory of self-attention (Carver & Scheier, 1982; see Chapter 7, "Attention"). Recall that the theory describes self-focused people as noticing discrepancies between their current state and the achievement of some goal or standard. When people notice the discrepancy, they attempt to adjust their behavior in order to reduce the discrepancy. The person may succeed and move on to another goal. If the person fails, the theory states that the person will keep trying. The person may repeatedly try and fail. Thus there has to be a provision in the theory for the person to give up. Otherwise, the theory portrays an organism that marches onward into a corner, without knowing when it is beaten (Scheier & Carver, 1982).

In one example of emotion research under this general framework, snake phobics were given the goal of handling a three-foot boa constrictor. When the subjects were self-focused, emotions apparently provided an interrupt, and they ceased their attempt sooner than those who were not self-focused (Scheier, Carver, & Gibbons, 1981; cf. Carver, Blaney, & Scheier, 1979). Fear and anxiety in particular interrupt ongoing behavior, causing a reassessment of one's probability of success at the current goal. If one expects to succeed, fear and anxiety instigate greater effort. If one expects to fail, emotions can interrupt the current goal sequence to institute a potentially more successful goal or cause the person to withdraw from the attempt.

To summarize, emotion sometimes affects cognitive processing by interrupting ongoing activity and initiating activity on a more urgent or potentially fruitful front. Life-threatening events, unmet emotional needs, and performance failure all can disrupt one's focus of current processing and encourage a new effort. Emotions can alter one's goals and consequently one's processing priorities.

The Separate Systems View

In this chapter we have examined research investigating, first, the cognitive bases of some emotional responses and, second, the emotional bases for some cognitive responses. In this final section we examine the possibility that affect and cognition are largely independent. The separate systems view suggests that affective and cognitive processes may proceed in parallel without influencing each other much, under some circumstances. Moreover, affective reactions may occur faster and at a more basic level than cognitive processes.

THE ARGUMENT FOR AFFECT INDEPENDENT OF COGNITION

Despite the scientific and commonplace idea that we think about things in order to decide how we feel, there is a case for affect preceding cognition, rather than vice versa (Zajonc, 1980b). As an example, consider how you make major life decisions, such as where to go to college or who to pick for a long-term close relationship. At least one person talked about her decision process this way: "I kept thinking about what a good mate he would make. He is reliable, sensitive, caring, successful, and everything you could want. So why don't I love him?" Another person choosing between two jobs went through the exercise of listing all the pros and cons of each. But somehow it kept not coming out right. The one with more pros and fewer cons was not the one she wanted. A third person finally picked a college on the amazing ability of its student tour guide to walk backwards over curbs and cobblestones without tripping. How often do we make important decisions on the basis of rational cognitive analysis and how often on the basis of emotional preferences guided by no apparently relevant cognitive data? Affective processes may operate rather independently of cognitive processes, according to this view. The conceptual argument raised by Zajonc has generated a fair amount of theoretical controversy (Lazarus, 1982), so it is useful to understand his argument in some detail.

First, Zajonc suggests, affective reactions are primary. Evaluations are made and then justified; decisions are based on preference rather than computation. When one is picking a college, sometimes one's reasons simply do not add up rationally; one fundamentally knows one's preferred choice, but not necessarily the exact cognitive list that would justify it.

Second, affect is basic. Evaluation is a major and universal component of virtually all perception and meaning. Whether you visit the campus or talk to a student or read the brochure—that is, across a wide range of experiences—you are constantly having positive and negative reactions. It is difficult to understand something without evaluating it.

Third, affective reactions are inescapable. While you may or may not notice the details of the college buildings, you cannot easily avoid your feelings about the place. A growing sense of belonging there (or not) is more difficult to ignore than is the specific geography of the campus.

Fourth, affective judgments tend to be irrevocable, in contrast to cognitive judgments. One cannot be wrong about how one feels, but one can be wrong about what one believes: hence, affect is less vulnerable to persuasion than is cognition. Once having decided that you feel good (or bad) about a school, that feeling is more difficult to change than is your belief that it has a large library.

Fifth, affect implicates the self. While cognitive judgments rest on features inherent in the object, affective judgments describe our own reactions to the object. Your feelings about a college have to do with you yourself being a student in it. In contrast, your knowledge about the place (e.g., its reputation) can be independent of your own role in it.

Sixth, affective judgments are difficult to verbalize. Much emotional response is communicated nonverbally; words for affective reactions always seem to fall short of the experience. Chances are, you can talk more easily about the college's features than you can about exactly how it makes you feel.

Seventh, affective reactions may not depend on cognition. The features that people use to discriminate a stimulus may not be the same features that people use to decide whether or not they like it. Totaling up the pros and cons of two choices, but deciding that the totals did not come out right, is a prime example of this. Since there is evidence on this point, we will come back to this surprising idea.

Finally, affective reactions may become separated from content. One sometimes can know how one feels about a person but cannot remember where and how the person was previously encountered. Think of the last time you passed someone vaguely familiar on the street. Chances are, you could more easily report how you felt about the person than how exactly you know each other. With regard to colleges, the point is that you may forget exactly which place had squash courts and which place had Chinese language classes, but you are unlikely to forget your feelings about the different places.

MERE EXPOSURE RESEARCH

The last pair of arguments about the nature of affect formed the basis for a research program demonstrating that people can know how they feel about an object before they know how to recognize it. The opening bars of a classic old song on the radio may be enough to let most of us know whether or not this is a golden oldie we like, but many of us cannot identify it until hearing the words (and some of us not even then without the help of a resident expert).

Several studies document precisely this phenomenon of feeling a warm familiar glow that is accompanied by a total lack of recognition. People grow to like an initially unobjectionable stimulus the more frequently it is encountered; this is called the *mere exposure effect* (Zajonc, 1968a).

In mere exposure studies, people see a series of nonsense words, Chinese characters, or yearbook photographs, either many times or few times. The more often people are exposed to the stimulus, the more they favor it. This effect has been thoroughly replicated across many specific circumstances (see Chapter 12, "Attitudes"). The relevant idea here is the golden oldies point: the mere exposure effect does not depend on being able to recognize the stimulus as familiar. In other words, people preferred frequent stimuli to nonfrequent stimuli, even when they could only recognize them both at levels approximating chance guessing.

One study showed that mere exposure to Japanese ideographs influenced affect, independent of recognition for them (Moreland & Zajonc, 1977). These particular results are controversial (Birnbaum & Mellers, 1979a, 1979b; Moreland & Zajonc, 1979); nevertheless, other research comes to the same conclusion using different paradigms. Liking for frequently heard tone sequences was found consistently, even though the tones were only recognized as familiar at approximately chance levels (W. R. Wilson, 1979). Further evidence came from a study using a dichotic listening task, in which one presents the tones in one ear but focuses subjects' attention on a literary passage presented to the other ear. Using this task, one can virtually eliminate recognition for the tone sequences, leaving affective reactions intact. Similar results have been obtained with stimuli more engaging than tone sequences and nonsense words, such as the photographs and interests of fellow students (Moreland & Zajonc, 1982). Thus it appears that affective processes more than cognitive ones underlie the mere exposure effect in person perception and attitude research.

PERSON PERCEPTION AND ATTRIBUTION RESEARCH

A wide range of affective variables are independent of seemingly relevant cognitive variables. For example, evaluative impressions (one kind of affect) can be independent of memory for the details on which they were based (one kind of relevant cognition). Suppose you learn about a new acquaintance who buys groceries for an ailing elderly neighbor. This fact may influence whether you like him, and you may or may not remember his good deed, but the feeling and the memory can be separate (N. H. Anderson & Hubert, 1963; Dreben, Fiske, & Hastie, 1979; Riskey, 1979). Evaluations and recall can be uncorrelated for any given attribute. Similarly, people's affect-laden attributions can be independent of seemingly relevant memory (S. T. Fiske, Taylor, Etcoff, & Laufer, 1979). All this research is consistent with the idea that affect-laden judgments (evaluations, defensive attributions) are not dependent on recalled cognitions.

If affective judgments are not necessarily based on recalled cognitions, then it seems likely that affect is based on reactions to the stimulus at the time it is presented. That is, affect may occur directly upon encoding and categorizing a stimulus (S. T. Fiske, 1982). For example, your evaluation of your neighbor may occur at the time you meet him, based on your perception of his attributes, not afterward, based on your memory of his attributes. Person perception research supports this proposition. The importance of an attribute in an evaluation is not dependent on recall, as noted above, yet weight or importance is dependent on attention at the initial encounter. The longer people gaze at one of a person's attributes, the more weight the attribute carries in an overall evaluation of the person (S. T. Fiske, 1980).

There is an interesting implication of the idea that affect occurs at encoding and can be independent of memory-based cognitive processing. People sometimes may not consult their memories for past affective reactions to the same stimulus. For example, your neighbor may make you angry one day and pleased the next. If you do not remember and think about your past anger on the day he was pleasant to you, the two apparently conflicting emotional reactions you have to him may not be integrated. When people do not recall their previous affective reaction, there is no pressure to bring the separate affective responses into line with each other; it is perfectly reasonable to respond differently on different occasions. In this sense, affect is episodic (based on events) rather than semantic (based on overall consistency of meaning). People's cognitions about other people's traits, in contrast, seem to be more subject to semantic consistency pressures (Abelson et al., 1982). Another manner in which affect and cognition can be relatively separate systems, then, comes from the independence of emotional reactions over time, which contrasts with the apparent dependence of more cognitive reactions over time.

To summarize, Zajonc has suggested that affective and cognitive processes can operate independently of each other. Moreover, affect can precede cognition, in his view. Mere exposure research supports this perspective by showing that liking a frequently seen stimulus is independent of remembering that one has seen it before. Person perception research supports a similar view by showing that affective reactions to others can be independent of memory for details about them. Affect may be based instead on the way the stimulus is encoded initially, rather than on memory.

A NOTE ON COMPARING COGNITION AND AFFECT

Implicit in our discussion so far has been the idea that affect and cognition are somehow comparable. Judgments representing affect so far have included evaluation, preference, differentiated emotions, and defensive attribution, while reactions representing cognition so far have included attention, inference, and memory. The question that arises is, How does one decide what are the relevant cognitions and what are the comparable affective responses?

One illustrative study argues for the separation of comparable affect and cognition. In one of the mere exposure experiments, subjects rated their recognition and liking for random polygons that had been presented at varying frequencies. Although recognition accuracy was only at chance levels, subjects liked the familiar polygons better than the unfamiliar ones, confirming the standard mere exposure effect. These results certainly show, as do others cited, that liking need not depend on accurate memory (Kunst-Wilson, & Zajonc, 1980). But in what sense is recognition accuracy comparable to liking? The study assessed two other variables that help answer this question. Confidence ratings indicated that affective judgments were made with more confidence than recognition judgments, and reaction time measures suggested that affective judgments also may be made faster. Thus affective reactions may be made faster and more confidently than recognition judgments. How does one decide if they are comparable?

There are at least a couple of problems in trying to equate affect and cognition. First, one can question whether these are fair tests, because one can be wrong about a recognition judgment but not about an affective judgment. One can also argue that recognition judgments are more complex than affective judgments, so they are not comparable. But that is precisely the point. The two types of judgment differ in quality, and attempting to make them more similar would destroy them as realistic judgments of their type. Affective judgments are by nature subjective, simple, and direct. Trying to specify a cognitive response that is truly equivalent to a given affective response may be a losing proposition. Nevertheless, it is worthwhile to try specifying which cognitive responses are relevant to any given affective responses.

There is a second problem specific to the argument for separate systems of affect and cognition. To the extent that one argues that they are independent, one is trying to support the absence of a relationship. This is a thankless task, as any statistics professor will insist if you try to prove the null hypothesis of no effect. The more sensible task, though, is to show on what each (cognition and affect) is based, if not entirely on each other (Zajonc, Pietromonaco, & Bargh, 1982). And because the separation cannot be complete, another task is to show the ways in which they do relate. The work covered in this chapter represents several attempts to do just that.

Summary

Defining a role for affect in social cognition requires defining some initial terminology: affect is a general term that includes feelings and emotions. Feelings include evaluations of particular things as good or bad, and feelings include moods, which are not targeted at anything in particular. Emotions are affective reactions differentiated beyond merely positive and negative. The most usual dimensions for differentiating emotions are positive-negative and aroused-unaroused. The positive and negative aspects of emotion often can co-occur in response to the same target; they are not necessarily endpoints of a single continuum but may be two different dimensions.

The history of research on emotion shows a long-standing controversy over the possible roles for physiology and cognition in affect. Facial feedback is an important physiological factor, although its role is still not well under-stood. Arousal is part of most theories, and it is usually characterized as diffuse, rather than specific to particular emotions. Generally, arousal in-tensifies affect. Both the arousal theories and facial feedback theories are examples of approaches that downplay the importance of cognition in affect.

Research on the cognitive bases of affect suggests that the combination of arousal and cognitive interpretation causes emotion. In this view, interruption of complex goal sequences causes arousal and emotion. The amount of cog-nitive interruption guides the intensity and direction of affective reaction. People are said generally to dislike drastic interrupts and prefer small ones. Extending this model to close relationships, two people who are intimate have a greater chance of interrupting each other's plans and expectations. The more intermeshed two people's lives, the more intense the emotion given a disruption. However, if the intermeshed sequences are running smoothly, there may be few interruptions and therefore little day-to-day emotion, although the relation-ship is intimate.

Other cognitive bases of affect include fitting new information to old emotion-laden schemata or knowledge structures. The extremity of an affective response to something can be based on the complexity of one's knowledge about it; complexity encourages moderation of affect. Affective responses can become more organized over time, and simpler organization leads to extremity of affect. Finally, affect may be determined by degree of fit. People who fit negative stereotypes are disliked more than people who do not fit them. When people do not fit one's prior categories, then affective reactions may become more moderate.

The perception of one's actual and potential outcomes also determines affect. The locus and controllability of one's already obtained success and failure determine emotional responses. Imagined future alternatives also gen-erate affect, as one accomplishes various goals, planned actions, and outcomes. Finally, the ease of imagining past alternatives also creates affect. Overall, the quality and intensity of affect can depend on the interpretation of one's outcomes.

Affect influences cognition, as well as vice versa. Mood influences learning, memory, and judgment, such that people in a good mood perceive the world in a positive light. Links among positively toned items in memory make happy people remember happy things. The picture is not necessarily so simple for negative moods, since people more often enlist conscious strategies for escaping them. Hence the links among negatively toned items may be weaker. In contrast, good moods facilitate behavior, speed cognitive processing, and simplify problem solving. Mood-congruent memory may hinge on affect as a retrieval cue, and a network model of memory has been proposed to account for this.

Affect not only influences various specific judgments, but also has an impact on cognitive processes in general. Affect interrupts ongoing activity, causing a reassessment of the activity in question, and sometimes the setting of new goal priorities.

Analyzing the relationship of affect and cognition starts from an assumption often made but not often verified: that cognition precedes affect. It may be that affective and cognitive processes operate separately. A wide range of affective reactions are independent of seemingly relevant cognitive variables. People have affective reactions to stimuli they cannot recognize with certainty, and affective impact can be independent of how memorable information is. All this suggests that many affective reactions occur at encoding, rather than being based on retrieval of relevant evidence. Of course, it is difficult to compare affect and cognition, since the judgments are rarely comparable. The relationships between affect and cognition are complex, difficult, and just beginning to be understood.

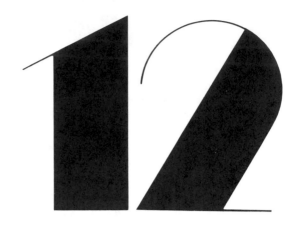

attitudes: cognition and persuasion

Suppose you have a friend from high school coming to visit you at college for the weekend. Your friend happens to be gay, and, although this has never particularly mattered to you, you wonder how your roommate will react. You have known your roommate for only a few months, and the topic of homosexuality has never come up. To avoid any potential awkwardness, it might be better to know beforehand what your roommate's attitude is. You could ask directly, but you might not get an honest answer because your roommate might be trying to conceal antigay prejudices.

Inferring other people's attitudes is a common problem. Attitudes cannot be observed directly, yet we all take them for granted as good predictors of important behavior, ranging from whether two friends will get along well to whether a race riot will occur. Because an attitude must be inferred from an individual's response to a stimulus, it is considered a hypothetical mediating variable. An observer cannot see an attitude. Psychologists assume that an attitude intervenes between an observable stimulus and an observable response, providing the necessary link. Even when behaviorism dominated psychology, the attitude concept remained vital; it continued to be indispensable to almost every social psychological study. As we mentioned in Chapter 1, social psychology has always been cognitive in this respect: it has always posited attitudes as a nonobservable link between an observable stimulus and an observable response.

Attitudes have been defined many different ways by different researchers (e.g., Bagozzi & Burnkrant, 1979; Fishbein, 1967; Himmelfarb & Eagly, 1974). For the purposes of this chapter, the critical point is that attitudes are important elements in social cognition that are affect-laden and that include or are linked to cognitions (beliefs). In part of the next chapter, we will consider the links of attitudes to behavior. Researchers on attitudes point out the separate but interlocking status of affect, cognition, and behaviorial tendencies. Note that all three must be inferred from actual behavior, both verbal and nonverbal, because attitudes cannot be observed directly, any more than any other cognitive element can be. Nevertheless, it is evidence of the importance of attitudes that scientists and ordinary people try to infer them, despite the difficulty of doing so.

BACKGROUND

Attitudes have always been accorded star status in social explanations of human behavior by lay people and professionals alike. By now, it is a textbook cliché to point out that attitudes are the cornerstone of social psychology. Nearly 50 years ago, Gordon Allport declared attitudes to be "the most distinctive and indispensable concept in contemporary American social psychology" (G. W. Allport, 1935, p. 798). The entire field blossomed through the attitude research motivated by World War II. Early social psychology included work on attitudes influenced by propaganda and persuasion (Hovland, Janis, & Kelley, 1953; Hovland, Lumsdaine, & Sheffield, 1949); work on anti-Semitic and antidemocratic prejudice (Adorno, Frenkel-Brunswick, Levinson, & Sanford, 1950); and work on satisfaction and deprivation in the military (Stouffer, Suchman, DeVinney, Star, & Williams, 1949). These early efforts leaned heavily on attitudes both as measures and as important theoretical variables. That is, much of the effort in the first few decades of social psychology was oriented toward learning how to measure attitudes and how to define the attitude concept. This chapter cannot cover the entire field of attitude formation and change. (For longer reviews, see Ajzen & Fishbein, 1980; Cialdini, Petty, & Cacioppo, 1981; Himmelfarb & Eagly, 1974; Kiesler, Collins, & Miller, 1969; Petty & Cacioppo, 1981; Rajecki, 1982; Zimbardo, Ebbesen, & Maslach, 1977.) Instead, this chapter will focus on a subset of attitude research that has been heavily influenced by social cognition approaches.

Social cognition's main contribution to the field of attitude research has been a fine-grained analysis of the mediating processes involved in attitude formation and change. Traditional variables such as characteristics of the communicator, attributes of the message, characteristics of the audience, and the persistence of attitude change are being examined in new ways, adding to the insights developed by earlier theorists. The application of social cognition theories and methods to a well-researched area like attitudes illustrates the merits of the cognitive approach; one could as easily walk through the same exercise for small group research, for example. Focusing on such a central area as attitude research particularly illustrates what is unique about the social cognition approaches. In addition, attitude research supplements social cognition perspectives because it emphasizes the importance of affect and behavior, which is why we have placed this chapter between the chapters on these two topics.

While social cognition research enriches current attitude research, this does not imply that cognition was absent from earlier theories. Without doubt, the most influential approaches to attitudes have been the cognitive consistency theories (Abelson *et al.*, 1968). Dominating social psychology journals in the

1960s, the fundamental model holds that inconsistencies—among cognitions, among affects, or between cognitions and affects—cause attitude change. Cognitive dissonance theory (Festinger, 1957) and balance theory (Heider, 1958) are eminent examples of this. Other major theories of attitudes also can be interpreted as reserving an important role for cognition or beliefs (Fishbein, 1963; Insko & Cialdini, 1969; Kiesler, 1971; M. J. Rosenberg, 1956, 1960). Although we can only allude to the vast literature on attitudes, the critical point is this: cognition has been accorded a major role in practically every attitude theory, with the sole exception of the most narrowly construed applications of classical conditioning to attitudes (Staats & Staats, 1958). However, until recently, work on the role of cognition in attitude theory could not draw on the important advances in cognitive psychology and in social cognition research.

One early theory of attitude change especially foreshadows the current cognitive approaches. The theory is expressly a sequential model of information processing. Remember that Chapter 1 described information-processing models as breaking down mental operations into sequential stages. McGuire's chain of cognitive responses (1969, 1976) outlines the necessary conditions for a persuasive communication to result in behavior; the steps include exposure, attention, comprehension, yielding, retention, retrieval, decision, and behavior.

Consider, as an example, political campaign literature. In order to be effective, campaign managers must *expose* voters to the literature, say, by distributing a leaflet under people's windshield wipers. Next, the voters must *attend* to the communication, which they will not if it is raining that day and they merely use it to scrape mud off their feet upon reaching the car. If they do read the leaflet, they must *comprehend* the message; it must not be written in opaque jargon. Next, voters must *yield* to the message, that is, be persuaded by its contents (which is no mean feat for the campaign manager, of course). They must *retain* the changed attitude, in the face of competing literature, ennui, and disagreeing friends. Upon reaching the voting booth, they have to *retrieve* their attitude; the voters must remember they preferred Smedley rather than Smiley for dogcatcher. They have to *decide* to act on their attitudes despite situational forces to the contrary (perhaps the city's political machine has just offered the voter a bribe to vote for Smiley). And finally, the voter must *behave*, write the X or pull the voting lever, thus securing the effect desired by Smedley's campaign. The entire sequence is described as a series of eight carefully specified cognitive steps resulting in behavior. As such, the theory anticipates more recent cognitively oriented work in attitudes. Moreover, several of the stages specified by McGuire continue to be important in current work.

COMPARING OLDER AND NEWER APPROACHES TO ATTITUDES

The newer cognitive approaches we will discuss in this chapter build on the older attitude theories in several crucial respects. Many of the critical variables are the same. Some of the methodological procedures were established long ago and continue to form the basis of research paradigms. For example, as we will see, current researchers sometimes reuse old experimental designs, adding mainly a more detailed analysis of intervening processes. Another carry-over from older research is that many of the current theoretical issues are variants on earlier problems, as will become clearer. Finally, many of the older approaches were heavily cognitive, in the ways described above.

But there are also differences between older approaches to attitudes and the newer approaches. First, there are what might be called metatheoretical differences between the two; that is, there are major conceptual differences between the overarching framework common to various consistency theories and the overarching framework behind social cognition's approach to attitude research. The "cognitive" consistency theories rested on a strong motivational basis: the metatheory behind consistency theories was that there is a drive to reduce internal discrepancies. The consistency theories were not explicitly designed to be theories about the cognitive system operating on its own nonmotivational principles. In contrast, cognitive approaches are based on current understandings of the cognitive system. For example, to deal with inconsistencies, a current cognitive approach might posit that people resolve discrepancies mainly for reasons of efficiency in memory storage. In contrast, a traditional consistency theory might posit that people resolve discrepancies to avoid the uncomfortable feeling of believing two conflicting things.

Second, there are specific theoretical differences between the older and newer approaches. The newer approaches explicitly draw on cognitive theories unavailable earlier. These theories provide precise frameworks that detail the organization and processing of information in persuasion. These permit a more careful analysis of cognitive processes related to attitude change.

Third, the methods for studying attitude change have evolved in new directions borrowed from cognitive psychology. Attitude theories have long posited internal structures (Zajonc, 1968b), but more fine-grained analysis of cognitive organization and dynamics (typical of cognitive psychology) has become possible in attitude research, with recent advances in measurement techniques. Over the 1970s, then, information-processing research on attitudes expanded in several directions, based on metatheoretical, theoretical, and methodological developments.

In reviewing the directions of newer research, we draw on a framework for persuasion research described by Laswell (1948) and elaborated by Hovland, Janis, and Kelley (1953): who says what to whom with what effect. Thus the sections focus on characteristics of the communicator, the message, the audience, and the effects of attitude change. Although Hovland *et al.*'s program of research did not explicitly represent an information-processing viewpoint, it did anticipate McGuire's chain of persuasion and other theories that emphasize internal processes such as attention and comprehension. Moreover, much of the current cognitive research is an effort to explain effects originally uncovered by the classic Hovland *et al.* research. In the first section of the chapter we discuss attributional approaches to communicator effects. In the second, we discuss a theory called cognitive response analysis, as it applies to communicator, message, and audience variables. In the third and fourth sections we discuss the lasting effects of attitude change on groups and on individuals.

Attributional Approaches to Communicator Effects

Producers of television ads are well aware that their messages have maximum impact if delivered by a gorgeous model, a respected newscaster, or a well-known millionaire; an alternative way to increase message impact is using a communicator blatantly similar to the ordinary person, as is done in "hidden camera" testimonials. The importance of communicator attractiveness, credibility, power, and similarity were first demonstrated by Hovland *et al.* (1953), and these variables have generated research ever since.

One of the early manifestations of social cognition research influencing attitude research came from attribution theories. Attributional perspectives have helped attitude theorists approach the problem of communicator credibility (Eagly, Chaiken, & Wood, 1981). For example, persuasion depends in part on the recipient's analysis of why a communicator advocates a particular position. Recipients attempt to determine the validity of a persuasive message. People come to messages knowing something of the communicator's dispositional and situational constraints (see Fig. 12.1). This understanding generates assessments of the validity of message content. When you hear Ralph Nader speaking to the local Sierra Club chapter, you know that both his own opinion (a dispositional factor) and that of his audience (a situational factor) predispose him to advocate the environmental advantages of strict auto emission controls. If this is, in fact, the message, it simply is less valid and less persuasive than if it were completely independent of such dispositional and situational pressures. Messages constrained by the situation or the communicator may not validly represent the truth, so they are not impactful. It is too easy to attribute Nader's harangue to biases in trying to please his audience (environmentalists) or to his own biases—either in what he knows (knowledge bias) or in what he is willing to say in public (reporting bias). In contrast, if the president of General Motors makes the same environmentalist point to fellow industry chiefs, then he is indeed believable and persuasive.

These predictions about communicator credibility derive from Kelley's (1967, 1972a) analysis of multiple sufficient causes, which states that if several plausible causes exist, the weaker ones are discounted (see Chapter 2, "Attribution Theory"). In this case, if both disposition (he is a crusader) and circumstances (Sierra Club audience) conspire to produce Nader's speech, then the alternative cause, the facts, need not support the speech. A careful step-by-step test of this model demonstrates that subjects' perceptions of communicator background (e.g., he has strong opinions) cause the predicted attributions (e.g., he is biased). Attributions that cast credibility into doubt then decrease opinion change (Wood & Eagly, 1981).

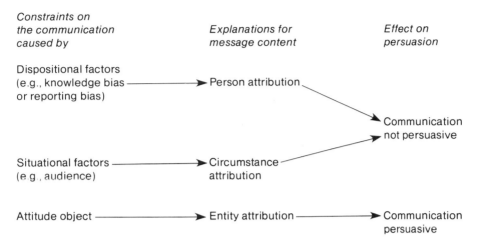

Fig. 12.1 An attributional analysis of communicator effects in persuasion.

Communicator attractiveness can also be analyzed from an attributional perspective. In one study, Eagly and Chaiken (1975) explored the idea that attractive communicators are not only more persuasive in general (a well-established finding) but are especially persuasive if they advocate an undesirable position. Because attractive people are expected to advocate attractive positions, an attractive person advocating an undesirable position must be doing so because the position is valid. To test this, Eagly and Chaiken presented subjects with a communicator who either liked or disliked undergraduates and who made either optimistic or pessimistic statements, for example, about college graduates' employment opportunities or about the future spread of venereal disease. Attractive communicators were considerably more persuasive than unattractive communicators when advocating undesirable (pessimistic) positions (cf. Wachtler & Counselman, 1981).

Attribution theory also offers an explanation for the effects of communicator similarity and agreement. Attribution theories of communicator effects rely on the premise that messages are persuasive when perceived as caused by the external reality of the attitude object, that is, when they are perceived to be valid. Messages are not persuasive when perceived to be caused by the personal perspective of the communicator (such as by biases in attitude or knowledge), by personality factors, or by the motivation to gain something from a particular audience. Messages that are unexpected, given the communicator's dispositions and the communication setting, are more persuasive than are messages wholly predictable on the basis of who is saying them (Eagly et al., 1981; Goethals, 1976).

One specific attributional explanation of communicator similarity and agreement posits that those who agree with us are seen as objective and as responding to the facts of the matter, while those who disagree with us are seen as biased by their own values. Both tendencies are exaggerated by other kinds of dissimilarity between self and other (Goethals, 1976). The attributional explanation for these effects draws on Kelley's covariation model of attribution (Chapter 2) as follows.

Consider two people who are discussing nonsmokers' rights. Agreement would provide support or consensus information, and high consensus can encourage an entity attribution, that is, to the attitude object (i.e., the topic being discussed). In our example, the agreeing pair attribute their shared attitude to the justice of the nonsmokers' rights. However, agreement by a dissimilar other is a particularly informative kind of consensus information; the clearer the consensus, the more likely that the opinion is caused by the entity (the topic) in question, rather than by peculiar people or situations. Consequently, if one of the pair is a smoker and the other a nonsmoker, and if they could actually agree, each would be especially persuaded that the cause was just.

In contrast, low consensus, or a disagreement by another, paves the way for person or situation attributions. When the two people disagree, each thinks the other is not an objective judge of the facts but is letting emotional prejudices get in the way. Given that the situation is usually the same for both parties, the remaining cause has to be the other person's dispositions. However, the arguers are even more likely to believe each other biased (i.e., make a dispositional attribution) if one is a beleaguered smoker and the other an angry nonsmoker, rather than two similar individuals. Thus a dissimilar other exaggerates the effect of disagreement as well as agreement.

To summarize, attribution theories of communicator effects can explain when a communication will be seen as invalid and therefore not persuasive — that is, when a communication is attributed to the dispositional biases of the communicator or the pressures of the situation, it will not be seen as valid. Conversely, attributional analyses can also explain when the communication will be perceived as valid and persuasive — that is, when it can be attributed neither to the communicator nor to the situation. When the attribution for a communication is an entity attribution (i.e., to the attitude object), the communicator is seen as presenting the objective facts, and the communication is maximally persuasive. In sum, attributional analyses have clarified the effects of various communicator variables. Attributional analysis has not addressed other variables related to attitude change, but it is probably more suited to be applied to communicator variables than to be applied to characteristics of the message and audience.

Cognitive Response Analysis

Cognitive response analysis (CRA) represents a major new approach to attitudes. The effects of communicator credibility, message repetition, message comprehensibility, and audience involvement all depend on the amount and kind of thought they provoke, as we will see. CRA provides both a theory and a method for studying this premise. Theoretically, cognitive response analysis argues that attitude change is mainly a function of one's own personal elaborations of external stimuli such as persuasive messages. That is, the theory holds that attitude change often results from active thinking: *elaborating* or personally translating and supplementing the message content and its context. CRA contrasts with models that propose that persuasion depends on learning a message by passively rehearsing it. According to CRA theory, active personal elaborations can either support or disagree with the message. The results of such cognitive activity pro and con presumably cause attitude change. Thus the relative number of counterarguments and supporting arguments in the perceiver's mind cause attitude change, according to the theoretical model. Fig. 12.2 depicts the model as applied to the variables we will discuss here.

Methodologically, cognitive response analysis documents its theoretical model by directly measuring the counterarguments and supporting arguments that presumably cause attitude change. As we mentioned in Chapter 10, "Designing Research," cognitive mediation means that some stimulus causes a cognitive effect, which in turn causes a response. In this case, low or high communicator credibility (stimulus) causes low or high counterarguing (cognitive mediator), which in turn causes attitude change (response). In cognitive response research, subjects not only give an opinion on the topic at hand but also list their thoughts during or just after receiving the communication. The cognitive responses, as they are called, are scored as reactions pro and con, and

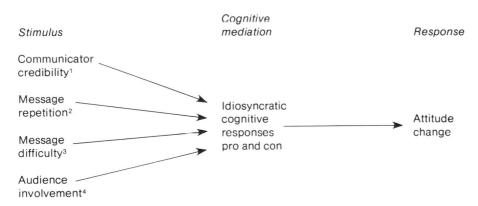

| Stimulus | Cognitive mediation | Response |

Communicator credibility[1]

Message repetition[2]

Idiosyncratic cognitive responses pro and con

Message difficulty[3]

Attitude change

Audience involvement[4]

[1] Credibility effects depend on subjects' involvement and initial opinions (see text for summary).

[2] For linguistic stimuli, if the arguments are cogent, message repetition initially increases agreement, then decreases it; cognitive responses follow the same pattern.

[3] Comprehensible messages with good arguments generate more favorable cognitive responses and are more persuasive.

[4] Involvement stimulates thought, which can lead to favorable or unfavorable cognitive responses and to increased or decreased persuasion, depending on the message and the communicator.

Fig. 12.2 Cognitive response analysis model of persuasion.

presumably mediate attitude change. The CRA technique itself is a simple and elegant way to measure cognitive mediation. As a technique, CRA is compatible with various attitude theories (as described by Petty, Ostrom, & Brock, 1981), and as a methodological technique, it does not guarantee theoretical advances in and of itself. When researchers used the method in concert with the explicit cognitive response theory, however, they can show that attitude change often is caused by one's personal responses to a message. The technique and theory of cognitive response analysis have been applied to communicator, message, and audience variables (Brock, 1967; Greenwald, 1968; Petty, Ostrom, & Brock, 1981). As we will see, one of the major points made by CRA researchers is that many standard attitude change effects depend on how involved the audience (i.e., the subject) is with a particular persuasive message.

COMMUNICATOR CREDIBILITY

Proponents of one model of communicator credibility that draws on the theory of cognitive response analysis maintain that persuasion is a joint function of the involvement of the recipient and the credibility of the communicator (Hass, 1981). Specifically, the theorists propose that uninvolved recipients think more negative thoughts in response to a low credibility communicator than to a high credibility communicator. Involved recipients, in contrast, think more negative thoughts in response to a high credibility communicator. Thus the model draws on the CRA notion that a recipient's own thoughts (pro and con) determine attitude change, although it focuses in particular on the mediating role of counterarguments.

For example, suppose you had little concern about a new federal subsidy to cattle farmers. According to the theory, a high school sophomore's assertion that the program would hurt our economy will produce more vigorous counterargument than will the same assertion made by a Nobel Prize–winning economist. You are willing to take the expert's word for it, while it seems all too easy to mount a counterattack against the high school student. In contrast, if you as a student care about the federal student loan program and you have written to Congress about it (i.e., you are highly involved), then a high school student's assertion that the loan program will damage the economy elicits less counterargument than does the same opinion from a famous economist. In the second case, you actively counterargue and resist the expert's opinion because it is so important to you. Involvement combines with credibility to produce cognitive responses (in this case, counterarguments) that in turn lead to attitude change.

Communicator credibility may have more effect in general on people who are relatively uninvolved. People who are involved pay more attention to message content than to the communicator, so they generate more cognitive responses, which in turn cause attitude change, if the pros outweigh the cons (Petty & Cacioppo, 1981). Thus cognitive response analysis allows a fine-grained understanding of exactly how and for whom a standard variable such as communicator credibility works.

Another example of CRA's application to communicator credibility shows that credibility effects are not just strongest for uninvolved recipients; communicator credibility also matters especially to people in favor of a stand. Proponents of a particular viewpoint may feel it is at best weakly represented if the communicator is only moderately credible. The CRA explanation for this phenomenon combines communicator credibility with the recipient's initial opinion on an issue. In one study testing initial opinion and credibility (Sternthal, Dholakia, & Leavitt, 1978), people who initially favored the Consumer Protection Agency heard a high or moderate credibility source argue for the agency. They then indicated their opinions and listed all the thoughts pro and con that had come to mind in response to the message. The moderately credible communicator surprisingly was more persuasive than the one with high credibility. Furthermore, subjects wrote more supporting arguments and fewer counterarguments for the moderate credibility source. Thus subjects' cognitive responses mediated the effect of moderate credibility. In another study, subjects with initially negative attitudes were more persuaded by the high credibility source. On the assumption that people in favor of a stand are more likely to feel it has been inadequately presented by a moderately low credibility communicator, it makes sense that people would generate more supporting arguments than they would if it were presented by a highly expert communicator. Again, we see that CRA explains exactly how and for whom communicator credibility works.

Thus, to summarize, cognitive response analysis shows that communicator credibility effects on attitude change may depend critically on the recipient's initial opinion and involvement with regard to the issue (see Petty & Cacioppo, 1981, for a longer review). CRA shows that many thoughts pro or con on an issue are generated under specific circumstances. The greatest threat to one's opinion comes from a high credibility source on the other side of an issue with which one is involved. Much cognitive activity is generated on behalf of one's views in that case, and one is consequently relatively unpersuaded. CRA allows a detailed methodological analysis and theoretical specification of classic communicator effects.

MESSAGE REPETITION

Advertisers who air the same television commercial several times during the late late show are both right and wrong to do so. People indeed are more persuaded by a message when they hear it several times, but only up to a point. When the message is repeated ad nauseum, it may have an effect opposite to the one intended. The research on message repetition is best understood as differing with two different kinds of stimuli: nonlinguistic (e.g., the Coca-Cola logo) and linguistic (e.g., the persuasive message). Cognitive response analysis suggests that the differences are due to the amount and valence (direction pro or con) of thoughts generated in each case (A. Sawyer, 1981).

We will begin with nonlinguistic stimuli. Researchers have long known that repeated exposures typically enhance liking (Stang, 1974; Zajonc, 1968a), in what is called the mere exposure effect. Two major qualifications on the mere exposure effect are that the stimulus be initially unfamiliar and that people's initial reaction to the stimulus be neutral or positive (Grush, 1976; Harrison, 1977). When the stimulus is initially evaluated negatively, the exposure effect can evaporate or reverse.

Contrary to the ideas behind cognitive response analysis, the mere exposure effect on nonlinguistic stimuli operates most clearly when recipients are essentially unthinking; that is, they cannot be generating personal responses (pro or con) to the stimulus. Hence, the more you see the Coca-Cola logo, the more you like it, assuming you do not think about it much; the logo has become as familiar as the American flag. Even animals, who presumably do not think at all, show the effect of exposure on preference. Thus people show the effect of repetition quite plainly under circumstances of minimal cognitive processing, or as McGuire (1968) would say, when they are behaving as lazy organisms. Accordingly, cognitive response analysis cannot shed any light on message repetition effects with nonlinguistic stimuli.

Given nonlinguistic stimuli, there is a strong case for a noncognitive (i.e., unmediated) mere exposure effect on preference, and it is worth noting because it provides a stark contrast to CRA. We reviewed some mere exposure research supporting noncognitive mediation in Chapter 11, when we discussed Zajonc's separate systems view of affect and cognition (Moreland & Zajonc, 1977, 1979; W. R. Wilson, 1979). Recall that subjects who do not even recognize stimuli as familiar still show exposure effects on liking (Zajonc, 1980b). Consequently, it is hard to argue that the simple mere exposure effect for nonlinguistic stimuli is cognitively mediated. People show the effect without recognizing the stimulus, without awareness, and without thought. Thus CRA cannot be applied to message repetition effects on nonlinguistic stimuli because they do not appear to be cognitively mediated.

The second kind of stimulus that has been used in research on message repetition is linguistic material, that is, the persuasive message itself. This kind of material does elicit thought, and amount of thought pro and con appears to determine whether or not the mere exposure effect occurs (Petty & Cacioppo, 1981; A. Sawyer, 1981). This point is illustrated by the difference between early work on message repetition and the work inspired by CRA. In a study predating CRA, W. Wilson and Miller (1968) originally found repetition effects on persuasion with prose passages; in this case the prose concerned a lawsuit for damages. Students role played being jury members and were exposed to an attorney's arguments either one time or three times. More exposure led to more agreement. Repetition also markedly increased retention of the arguments after a week's delay. Since retention and attitude change were moderately correlated, Wilson and Miller concluded that at least some of the repetition effect was due to enhanced recall.

A decade after that effort, Cacioppo and Petty (1979) also tackled the question of what mediates message repetition effects. Armed now with cognitive response analysis, they tapped subjects' idiosyncratic responses to the communication immediately after hearing it. Subjects retrospectively listed the thoughts they had had while listening to the communication and indicated whether each thought was pro $(+)$, con $(-)$, or neutral (0). In a separate measure, they were asked to recall the message's arguments. Agreement with the message was completely uncorrelated with recall, and highly correlated with both favorable thoughts positively and unfavorable thoughts negatively. Number of irrelevant thoughts did not correlate with agreement. Thus cognitive responses pro and con, not recall, were shown empirically to mediate the effects of repetition on persuasion.

One important point from this line of research is that the CRA technique of thought listing can support a different sort of cognitive process model than does a model stressing recall as the mediating process. CRA looks at the individual's own idiosyncratic reactions to the argument, rather than at the person's ability simply to remember the argument as given. The advantage of this is that CRA successfully elucidates the processes intervening between exposure and agreement.

As CRA work on message repetition effects has continued, the exact nature of the mediating cognitive process has been specified further. People's cognitive responses to repeated messages support a two-factor model, in which uncertainty reduction and tedium counterbalance each other (Berlyne, 1970; Cacioppo & Petty, 1979; A. Sawyer, 1981). In other words, the first few times your friend explains his thesis to you, repetition aids understanding and convinces you the paper is right, assuming the arguments are cogent. But, after that, it is a bore, and you may begin to counterargue it out of sheer perversity. In the Cacioppo and Petty study mentioned above, for example, agreement first increased with exposure, as subjects comprehended the message and thought about it. Then agreement decreased, presumably as tedium set in. Cognitive responses pro and con followed the same pattern as did agreement, that is, positive at first and then negative, which lends support to the two-factor model. Of course, this model assumes that subjects bother to think about the message, which presupposes at least some involvement; uninvolved subjects do not always show the pattern of initial agreement then disagreement (A. Sawyer, 1981).

The effects of message repetition may seem a dry topic, with application only to that ad jingle you cannot get out of your head because you heard it five times during the late movie last night. But message repetition is important for several reasons. Nonlinguistic stimuli such as the melody from a jingle or the logo from a product show clear effects of repeated exposure. Assuming the stimulus is initially unfamiliar and not aversive, mere exposure to nonlinguistic stimuli reliably increases liking; this is an obvious advantage for advertisers making simple appeals. However, CRA cannot really elucidate the effect because it does not appear to be cognitively mediated.

On the other hand, linguistic stimuli, such as the actual contents of ads, show favorable effects of repetition if the arguments are cogent and the recipient bothers to think about them (see Fig. 12.2). CRA provides the theory that accounts quite nicely for repetition effects on linguistic stimuli. Moreover, the difference between linguistic and nonlinguistic materials is a caveat for ad copywriters. Conceptually, message repetition effects illustrate several crucial points about CRA: the importance of whether or not the recipient is actively thinking, and if thinking, whether those thoughts are pro or con; the possibilities for noncognitive mediation as a contrast to the cognitive mediation proposed by CRA; and the role of CRA as a highly specific theory that solves puzzles in new ways.

MESSAGE DIFFICULTY

As with repetition, cognitive response analysis has revealed that the effects of message difficulty also are influenced by involvement. The number of supporting arguments and counterarguments people generate is a function of involvement, if the message is difficult. Consider trying to understand a difficult statistics lecture. A student who hates the course and has already given up working on it will probably ignore the lecture and daydream. When acting as an uninvolved, lazy organism, one does not make an effort to absorb message content, regardless of its comprehensibility. At intermediate levels of involvement, message difficulty should have maximum impact, since a little added difficulty can make the critical difference between at least some processing and giving up. The majority of the statistics professor's students presumably are at this intermediate level, and they would be very sensitive to message difficulty. That is, message difficulty makes more difference to them than to the totally uninvolved students. At high levels of involvement, message difficulty again makes little difference to comprehension, because people will be motivated to overcome message difficulty no matter what. A new teaching assistant who has never heard the material before will make every effort to understand the lectures regardless of difficulty.

How then does message difficulty cause attitude change? Again, an analysis that draws on the CRA method reveals that the mediating factors may well be the amount and valence of people's cognitive responses. Comprehension not surprisingly encourages persuasion, if the arguments are good (e.g., Eagly, 1974; see Eagly & Himmelfarb, 1978, for others). If you do not understand a message, you cannot easily repeat it to yourself, nor can you muster supporting arguments. Again, people's own idiosyncratic supportive cognitive responses can strengthen the argued viewpoint, but only if people comprehend the message in the first place. The more comprehensible the message, the more the professor's audience can think positively about what he or she has said (assuming the arguments are good). Consequently, the more they comprehend the lecture's good arguments the more they will agree with the professor (Wood & Eagly, 1981).

Eagly also proposes an alternative to the CRA account of message difficulty effects. Message difficulty effects might not be mediated entirely by the buildup of supportive cognitions, as CRA theorists suggest. Instead, an incomprehensible argument might elicit negative affect, simply because it is frustrating not to understand something. The negative affect may then become associated with the attitude object and the persuasive attempt backfires. The frustration, in effect, spills over to discourage persuasion (Chaiken & Eagly, 1976; Eagly, 1974). In this case, message difficulty effects would be at least partially mediated by affect, without cognitive mediation. At this point, this intriguing alternative has yet to receive any firm empirical support.

Cognitive response analysis has been applied to many other features of messages besides difficulty and repetition (Petty & Cacioppo, 1981; Petty, Ostrom, & Brock, 1981). The use of rhetorical questions (Petty, Cacioppo, & Heesacker, 1981), the sheer number of arguments (Chaiken, 1980), and environmental distractions (Petty, Wells, & Brock, 1976) all have been analyzed from this perspective. CRA theory suggests and CRA methodology supports the conclusion that, in every case, the factor critical to persuasion is the amount of active cognitive elaboration pro and con done by the recipient. To generate favorable cognitive responses and to be maximally persuasive, a message should have good arguments, should be repeated a few times but not too many, should be comprehensible, and should be delivered in an atmosphere free of distraction. On the other hand, if the message has *weak* arguments (and so could produce many counterarguments), distraction and a single exposure will inhibit those negative cognitive responses and accordingly enhance persuasion.

AUDIENCE INVOLVEMENT

A summary of the cognitive response research shows that, at every step of the persuasion process, the respondent's amount and valence of cognitive response determines the type of effect that occurs. Because cognitive responses demand an actively thinking recipient, audience involvement has influenced each of the effects discussed so far. Different levels of involvement lead to different types of processing, which lead to greater or lesser reliance on superficial characteristics of the communication. Researchers hypothesize that highly involved subjects employ thoughtful, "systematic" strategies that rely on message content, while uninvolved subjects are particularly likely to use superficial, "heuristic" or shortcut strategies that depend on simple, possibly irrelevant cues such as communicator characteristics (Chaiken, 1980) rather than message content.

We will review the impact of audience involvement on communicator and message effects in a moment, but first it is helpful to define the term. Unfortunately for involvement research, there is limited consensus on how to define *involvement*. Personal importance seems to capture its conceptual meaning (Greenwald, 1981; Greenwald & Leavitt, in press). Researchers have identified different types of involvement. Ego involvement (Sherif & Hovland, 1961) and issue involvement (Kiesler, Collins, & Miller, 1969) imply that an issue has intrinsic importance for beliefs central to a person's identity. These terms can be contrasted with task involvement (Sherif & Hovland, 1961), in which the individual is concerned only with the consequences of a particular response. If a person is interested in maximizing the rewards in a given situation, that is response involvement (Zimbardo, 1960). The different definitions of involvement illustrate the range of factors that might make a person respond more or less thoughtfully to a persuasion attempt that is personally important.

Involvement is operationalized in various ways, again without strong consensus. For example, students might be given a message advocating a change in dormitory visitation hours at their own school versus another school (Petty & Cacioppo, 1979). Or they might be told that a change in university policy is to take place in one year versus in ten years (Petty, Ostrom, & Brock, 1981). Thus the most usual manipulations include some form of personal relevance and future consequences. Regardless of the manipulation, involvement stimulates thought, which can lead to increased or decreased persuasion, depending on the cognitive responses, which in turn depend on the strength of the arguments and on the subject's preexisting attitudes.

One overall way to think about the effects of involvement on cognitive responses and on persuasion is that less involved people operate "on automatic," with little conscious thought (Chaiken, 1980; Petty & Cacioppo, 1979). Highly involved people operate in a controlled mode, with much cognitive activity (LaBerge, 1975; Langer, 1978; W. Schneider & Shiffrin, 1977; Shiffrin & Schneider, 1977). Thus people who are involved generate cognitive responses that are sensitive to the message they encounter: the involved listener will differentiate carefully between strong and weak arguments, and between pro- and counterattitudinal arguments (Petty & Cacioppo, 1979; Petty, Cacioppo, & Goldman, 1981). Given an airtight or a proattitudinal message, he or she will not bother to counterargue, but the involved would counterargue weak or counterattitudinal communications. Someone less involved probably would generate few cognitions, regardless of the message, since this uninvolved person is attending only superficially. Thus people who are involved use systematic, content-based processing strategies that are responsive to the quality of arguments. The less involved rely on heuristic strategies, such as the likability of the source.

Researchers have shown that audience involvement moderates the effects of communicator and message variables, as well as the persistence of attitude change. For example, as we have already seen, communicator credibility effects are strongest for uninvolved recipients. Similarly, communicator attractiveness has the biggest effect on an uninvolved audience. That is, few people would argue that physical attractiveness is a deep or thoughtful basis for believing another person. Similarly, uninvolved recipients are most likely to respond to superficial indications of expertise. Of course, alleged expertise is not a totally reliable reason for agreeing with someone's arguments, but it is convenient. Much of the research on communicator cues may represent only those recipients who are listening to communications at fairly shallow levels. In support of this, highly involved subjects express more message-oriented thoughts (Chaiken, 1980). Cognitive response analysis distinguishes between people who are responding superficially and those who are thinking hard in response to a message. Thus CRA allows one to distinguish between involved and uninvolved subjects' use of communicator cues.

Similarly, message repetition effects depend on involvement. To review, for the linguistic part of an advertisement (as opposed to the logo), repetition cannot easily persuade people unless they bother to think about the sales pitch; the uninvolved person does not always notice even repeated messages. The same is true of message difficulty; subtle changes in comprehensibility will most affect those who are moderately involved. The totally uninvolved will not notice message difficulty because they are paying no attention (e.g., student daydreamers). The highly involved will put in the effort necessary to understand the message regardless of difficulty (e.g., the motivated teaching assistant). Nuances of the message content then should affect the vast middle more than the extremes of the involvement continuum. Thus involvement increases cognitive activity and subsequent attitude change, for moderately repeated and comprehensible messages, if the arguments are cogent.

Finally, involvement also increases the persistence of attitude change beyond the specific experimental setting. To the extent that an attitude is personally relevant and generates active information processing, the attitude persists (Cook & Flay, 1978). Remembering the details of the message itself appears to be less important than self-generated cognitive activity. In studies in which the subjects were likely to focus their cognitive activity on the message, attitudes persisted longer than in studies in which subjects were less likely to generate message-relevant thoughts (Hennigan, Cook, & Gruder, 1982).

To summarize, involvement influences the impact of communicator and message variables as well as the persistence of attitude change. Cognitive response analysis suggests that a thinking recipient is one precondition for cognitively mediated attitude change. An unthinking, uninvolved recipient may generate fewer cognitive responses (pro and con), so any attitude change is more likely to result from relatively superficial responses.

INDIVIDUAL DIFFERENCES IN COGNITIVE RESPONSES AND PERSUASION

In the section on CRA so far we have examined various situational factors that determine the amount of thought people give to persuasive communications. There appears also to be a dispositional factor that determines amount of cognitive response given. Table 12.1 shows some of the items on the scale. Need for cognition (Cacioppo & Petty, 1982) refers to people's chronic level of thoughtfulness in response to external stimuli such as persuasive messages. People high on the need for cognition generate more cognitive responses, both pro and con, to persuasive communications, and are consequently likely to be more or less persuaded depending on the message. The need for cognition is an individual difference variable that specifically addresses the process (cognitive responses) presumed to mediate between external stimulus and attitude change.

The need for cognition is especially promising when considered in contrast to other individual differences that are at best indirectly related to attitude change. That is, there is no simple relationship between persuasibility and

TABLE 12.1
Subset of the Need for Cognition Scale
(From J. T. Cacioppo & R. E. Petty, The need for cognition, *Journal of Personality and Social Psychology*, 1982, *42*, 116-131. Copyright 1982 by the American Psychological Association. Reprinted by permission of the authors.)

1. I really enjoy a task that involves coming up with new solutions to problems.
2. I would prefer a task that is intellectual, difficult, and important to one that is somewhat important but does not require much thought.
3. Learning new ways to think doesn't excite me very much.*
4. The idea of relying on thought to make my way to the top does not appeal to me.*
5. I only think as hard as I have to.*
6. I like tasks that require little thought once I've learned them.*
7. I prefer to think about small, daily projects rather than long-term ones.*
8. I would rather do something that requires little thought than something that is sure to challenge my thinking abilities.*
9. I find little satisfaction in deliberating hard and for long hours.*
10. I don't like to have the responsibility of handling a situation that requires a lot of thinking.*

* Reverse scoring was used on this item.

intelligence, gender, or self-esteem (Eagly, 1978; 1981); these characteristics' impact depends on the specific stage in the chain of persuasion. For example, intelligence and self-esteem are likely to be positively related to attending to new information but negatively related to agreeing with it (McGuire, 1969). That is, smart people might be more persuaded because they read the message carefully, but they might be less persuaded because they evaluate it more critically. To take another example, each gender may be most easily persuaded about topics that are incongruent with its perceived sex role, presumably because people lack information on such topics. That is, many women are easily persuaded by their boyfriends about the causes of engine failure, and many men are easily persuaded by their girlfriends about the causes of a social gaffe. In any case, one cannot make blanket statements such as X's are more easily influenced than Y's. It depends on the topic, on the person, and on the stage of persuasion.

SUMMARY AND COMMENT

Having spent considerable time on cognitive response analysis, we should note its limitations (Eagly & Himmelfarb, 1978; Petty & Cacioppo, 1981). First, although it proposes that people's thoughts mediate attitude change, it does not explain why people support or counterargue what they encounter. In that sense, it is a partial theory and leans on other theories of why people agree or disagree with communications, to provide a complete explanation of attitude change.

Second, it paints a view of people as more thoughtful and thorough than they perhaps are much of the time. People sometimes change their attitudes without the benefit of careful thought. Several theorists (as noted above) have suggested that there are two routes to persuasion, one that is systematic, thoughtful, and relatively slow, and one that is heuristic, superficial, and rapid (Chaiken, 1980; Petty & Cacioppo, 1981). People's use of each route (i.e., their level of cognitive response) is likely to depend on various factors. Involvement is one of the major determinants of which route people take, and others remain to be developed.

Third, some have questioned whether cognitive responses actually cause attitude change or are merely correlated with it (Romer, 1979). That is, if attitudes change for other reasons such as reinforcement contingencies, people may justify the change with cognitive responses pro and con but only after the fact. In this view, cognitive responses do not cause attitude change; they merely accompany it.

Finally, CRA is not well suited to the analysis of noncognitive attitude change. For example, CRA does not account for persuasion based on mere exposure to nonlinguistic stimuli or based on negative affect spillover from a frustratingly difficult message.

Despite these limitations, cognitive response analysis is a powerful theoretical and methodological tool. Theoretically, it proposes that the amount and direction of people's idiosyncratic responses determine attitude change. Methodologically, it supplies the technique of having people list their thoughts pro and con as or just after they encounter a persuasive communication. Such cognitive responses presumably mediate the effects of traditional communicator, message, and audience variables on attitude change. Figure 12.2 (p. 347) presented the summarized effects of communicator credibility, message repetition and difficulty, and audience involvement on cognitive responses and on persuasion. In addition to these situational variables, individual differences in the need for cognition influence how much thought people devote to persuasive communications. Overall, cognitive response analysis has had a major impact on the fine-grained understanding of long-standing issues in attitude research.

Attitude Polarization in Groups

Cognitive response analysis and the attributional approaches to attitude change both focus on the isolated individual who is (more thoroughly or less thoroughly) thinking about the validity of incoming information. But attitudes often change in groups, too. A social cognition analysis of group-level attitude change focuses on the information provided by interaction with others. As do the approaches just covered, it illustrates the flavor and the utility of cognitive approaches for traditional problems in attitude research.

The background for group-level attitude research comes from work in the early 1960s on group decision making. Many people think that groups represent the voice of reason and compromise; decisions made by committee are supposed to be safer than decisions made by individuals. A closer look at group decisions reveals that this is not at all the case. One research area in particular focused on the comparative riskiness of group and individual decisions (Stoner, 1961; Wallach, Kogan, & Bem, 1962). Graduate students were asked to make decisions in and out of groups on items such as the following: "A college senior planning graduate work in chemistry may enter University X where, because of rigorous standards, only a fraction of the graduate students receive the Ph.D., or may enter University Y, which has a poorer reputation but where almost every graduate student receives the Ph.D." In most cases, students who discussed this case (and others like it) emerged from the group discussion favoring a riskier alternative than when they went into the discussion. Thus the group decision was riskier than the average of the individual decisions.

Quantities of research were generated by this counterintuitive result (Rajecki, 1982). Some of the explanations relied on traditional variables such as norms and values, but one relied on a cognitive interpretation of the group interaction. As an example of the more traditional explanations, consider the possible influences of group norms. Researchers proposed that people in cohesive groups feel protected from the consequences of their decision; they can hide behind the group, in effect. This "diffusion of responsibility" hypothesis fell into disfavor when it was discovered that group attitudes do not change simply when a group feels cohesive; rather, some relevant discussion appears to be necessary (D. G. Pruitt & Teger, 1969).

Another traditional explanation researchers proposed was that people value risk more than caution. When people assemble in a group and compare their opinions, most of them discover that at least some others are taking riskier stands than they are. Because risk is valued, so the argument goes, the group gravitates toward the riskier extreme. This explanation in terms of social comparison and "risk as a value" faltered when researchers discovered that many groups shift toward a more cautious extreme after discussion (McCauley, Stitt, Woods, & Lipton, 1973). The shift toward caution also undercut the diffusion of responsibility hypothesis. Why should a group need to diffuse responsibility for more cautious decisions?

These traditional theories and others contrast with one possible cognitive explanation, for which there is some evidence. The *persuasive arguments theory* was advanced by Burnstein and Vinokur (1973, 1975, 1977; Burnstein, Vinokur, & Trope, 1973). In this more cognitive viewpoint, they proposed that attitudes in groups polarize toward relatively extreme (cautious or risky) alternatives when people are exposed to new information. Assume that there is a pool of possible arguments for any given attitude. When group members argue their positions, they may be exposed to other people's arguments that had not yet occurred to them as individuals. Group attitude change depends on whether everyone already has similar arguments, in which case the group members are not exposed to much new information. Change also depends on how many arguments potentially could support a given position. An attitude with many good arguments supporting it has a higher probability of those arguments coming to light than does an attitude with fewer supporting arguments.

One critical test of the persuasive arguments theory comes from a study in which students were (1) exposed to the opinions of others and given time to think about those opinions, (2) exposed to the opinions of others and not given time to think about the opinions, or (3) not exposed to the opinions of others but given time to think about the topic (Burnstein & Vinokur, 1975). Only some students' attitudes changed: those who knew the opinions of others and who had time to generate supporting arguments for them. Support for persuasive arguments theory also comes from studies in which information is exchanged in an actual discussion (Burnstein & Sentis, 1981; Rajecki, 1982).

The theory provides an informational basis for attitude change in groups as a function of exposure to persuasive arguments. It is only one possible explanation for attitude change in groups. Moreover, it describes only one type of attitude change in groups. Nevertheless, it is especially compatible with social cognition theories' reliance on cognitive mediation of attitude change. In all these cases, one's own cognitions or the cognitions of others muster the support and counterargument that create attitude change.

Persisting Cognitive Effects of Attitude Change

So far, we have reviewed three analyses of attitude change that have been heavily influenced by social cognition viewpoints: attributional analyses of communicator effects; cognitive response analyses of communicator, message, and audience variables; and persuasive arguments theory of group attitude change. Once an attitude changes, by whatever route, it affects future cognitive processes. Among them are perception and memory related to attitude-consistent and attitude-discrepant information. Because perception and memory are cognitive processes influenced by attitude change, it is not surprising that social cognition research has had considerable impact on recent work in this area. The consistency theories of attitudes proposed in the late 1950s provide the basis for predicting the effects of attitudes on later cognitive processes, so each of the following sections begins by briefly reviewing the most relevant consistency theory as background and then describes current cognitive interpretations of its effects. In the next four sections we focus on (1) dissonance theory and selective perception, (2) dissonance theory and selective learning, (3) balance theory and selective recall of information about others, and (4) self-perception theory and selective recall of information about the self (cf. Zajonc, 1968b).

DISSONANCE THEORY AND SELECTIVE PERCEPTION

Dissonance theory (Festinger, 1957) is an account of how beliefs and behavior change attitudes; it focuses on the effects of inconsistency among cognitions. Inconsistency is explicitly viewed as causing a motivational state called dissonance. If you believe that smoking causes cancer (a cognition) and you know you smoke anyway (a conflicting cognition about behavior), you leave yourself open to cognitive dissonance. Researchers hypothesized dissonance to cause an aversive state of arousal, and recent work has shown that to be the case (Zanna & Cooper, 1976); if you think about the inconsistency between smoking and knowing that it causes cancer, you become uncomfortable and tense. There is a drive to reduce the arousal (or discomfort) and, consequently, you rearrange your cognitions in order to reduce dissonance. Although theoretically one could change one's behavior to reduce the inconsistency, most dissonance researchers have focused on circumstances in which the inconsistent cognitions are more likely to change. This was partly an experimental strategy designed to focus on cognitive changes. But, in addition, behavior is more responsive to the constraints of reality (i.e., more public), so it is often harder to change than are one's cognitions or attitudes.

Most ways to increase consistency are cognitive. Suppose that you smoke and that you have several cognitions relevant to that behavior. You may have a couple of cognitions consonant with smoking (it tastes good; it is relaxing) and several dissonant with smoking (it causes cancer; it is expensive; it is smelly; other people dislike it). Because the number of dissonant cognitions outweighs the consonant ones, there is cognitive inconsistency, and you may experience dissonance. To reduce the dissonance, there are several changes you can make in your cognitions: for example, you can add or subtract cognitions to increase the ratio of consonant to dissonant ones (e.g., add in the idea that smoking keeps weight down and subtract the smell and the expense); or you can reduce the importance of dissonant conditions (e.g., I'll die of something anyway, so why worry about cancer). This by no means exhausts the possibilities, which are beyond our scope here (see Kiesler et al., 1969, or Zimbardo et al., 1977). To summarize, inconsistent cognitions cause arousal; there is a drive to reduce the arousal; hence inconsistency often leads to a change in one's attitude-relevant cognitions. Consequently, as we will see, people often avoid cognitions that are inconsistent with an attitude they hold or a behavior they have performed.

Consistency theorists in general (Abelson et al., 1968) have had much to say about selective perception as a function of consistency with prior attitudes. People tend to seek out, to notice, and to interpret data in ways that reinforce their attitudes. Dissonance theory in particular predicts that people will avoid information that increases dissonance; that is, that people favor information consistent with their attitudes and behavior. For present purposes, the work on selective perception can be divided into *selective exposure* (seeking consistent information not already present), *selective attention* (looking at consistent information once it is there), and *selective interpretation* (translating ambiguous information to be consistent). Recent work informed by social cognition research represents a continuing interest in old problems, but with the contribution of new ideas and methods.

Selective exposure is a principle that deserves to be true (McGuire, 1969), but much of the initial evidence was unfortunately mixed (Brehm & Cohen, 1962; Freedman & Sears, 1965; Mills, 1968; Wicklund & Brehm, 1976). Various evidence suggests specific qualifications to dissonance theory's predictions about exposure. Notions of intellectual honesty and fairness sometimes prompt people to seek out information that is inconsistent with their attitudes (Sears, 1965). Information's utility and novelty often override dissonance in determining exposure (Brock, Albert, & Becker, 1970). Moreover, there is strong support for de facto selective exposure; that is, most of us inhabit an environment that is biased in favor of positions with which we already agree (Sears, 1968; but see Katz, 1968). People tend to pick friends, magazines, and television shows that reinforce their own attitudes, and their attitudes in turn are reinforced by those agreeing others. Also, people's contacts shape their attitudes in the first place, so of course, people tend to agree with the information that surrounds them. Thus there is little support for selective exposure as a result of one's attitude, except de facto selective exposure. This aspect of selective perception was essentially resolved without the need for social cognition theories and techniques. But it is useful to know this work as background to the other two aspects of selective perception: attention and interpretation.

Attention to consistent and discrepant information is considerably subject to consistency pressures (Brock & Balloun, 1967; A. R. Cohen, Brehm, & Latane, 1959; Jecker, 1964). People spend more time looking at consistent than inconsistent evidence under certain circumstances. Recent work informed by social cognition research has further clarified the understanding of selective attention. For example, in one study (Olson & Zanna, 1979), subjects were divided up into repressors (people who typically avoid threatening stimuli) and sensitizers (people who typically investigate threatening stimuli). Both groups reported their attitudes toward a set of paintings. The experimenter then allowed them to choose two of them to keep. The pairs they could choose all included one painting they liked and one they disliked.

After the decision, subjects looked at the pair they had chosen. Dissonance theory predicts that they would focus on the positive aspects of their choice, that is, the preferred painting within the chosen pair. Repressors, and not sensitizers, behaved as predicted; their looking times at the choice-consistent painting were relatively high compared to control subjects, and they avoided looking at the painting inconsistent with their expressed choice. Thus consistent information elicited the selective attention of repressors only. Selective attention operates for some of the people some of the time. Other research on selective attention similarly takes the fine-grained approach typical of research influenced by work on social cognition (Kleinhesselink & Edwards, 1975).

People also protect their attitudes by selective interpretation (as apart from exposure and attention). Recent work makes a complementary point to some of the work on social schemata (Chapter 6), showing that people's attitudes can change their interpretations of what they see. For example, viewers of the television show "All in the Family" interpret Archie Bunker differently depending on their racial attitudes. Prejudiced viewers interpret Archie Bunker's ethnic slurs as accurate depictions of reality, while unprejudiced viewers interpret them as a satire on bigotry (Vidmar & Rokeach, 1974). Similarly, people's attitudes toward other people can cause selective interpretation of those other people. For example, most people interpret close friends and favored political candidates as sharing their attitudes more closely than is true (Berscheid & Walster, 1978; Kinder, 1978).

To summarize, dissonance theory predicts that people are motivated to avoid information that is inconsistent with their attitudes or choices. The evidence for selective exposure is mixed, but the evidence for selective attention and interpretation is stronger. Thus from the outset people are biased by attention and misperception to gather data that reinforce their beliefs. This early insight from the consistency framework was developed by recent work influenced by social cognition research. It is not that recent developments represent a dramatic shift to social cognition approaches. Rather, the recent work results from steady improvement in theory and method over the last few decades. Some of that improvement shows the influence of cognitive psychology and social cognition research.

DISSONANCE THEORY AND SELECTIVE LEARNING

Proponents of dissonance and other consistency theories predict selective learning and memory for attitudinally consistent information. Thus they would predict that if a couple are quarreling over whether to spend Christmas in the Caribbean or in Vermont, the ski addict will never learn the details of bargain snorkeling tours, while the sun worshipper will never learn the details of the ski packages. Unfortunately, evidence for selective learning is "unambiguously inconclusive" (Greaves, 1972). One reviewer concluded that the published studies yielding evidence for selective learning all must be flukes because there were so many other studies that failed to find such evidence (Greenwald, 1975). Moreover, the evidence that exists often is flawed, and recent research suggests exactly how, based in part on insights from cognitive psychology. For example, many studies have confounded the familiarity and agreeability of arguments (Zanna & Olson, 1982). It is not surprising that the ski enthusiast would recall pro-ski arguments better than pro-sun arguments, since the person has thought about the pro-ski arguments more often. Familiar arguments would be easier to recall, without having to assume any dissonance-based motivation to forget the disagreeable arguments.

Selective learning and retention of attitudinally favorable information do seem to occur under special conditions, defined in part by the contingencies of information-processing. *Incidental learning*, rather than intentional learning, provides clearer support for selective learning effects. That is, people are more likely to be selective when they do not know they will be tested on the material later. A travel agent who frequently has to present the details of cruises and ski packages will remember both kinds of arguments, regardless of how he or she personally feels about them. Being sufficiently motivated also will overwhelm selective learning effects. Other conditions that encourage selective learning all depend on the kind of person one is. People with high self-esteem are more biased by their attitudes, as are people with an internal locus of control. To return to our example, suppose one member of the couple is more self-confident and generally thinks she can influence events around her; she is precisely the one who will forget the other person's discrepant arguments. Finally, people who generally tend to repress unpleasant facts similarly tend to forget attitude-discrepant information (Zanna & Olson, 1982). Thus dissonance theory's prediction of the selective learning of agreeable arguments does seem to be supported under the right circumstances. Although more research is clearly needed, work on cognition and social cognition suggest some contributing factors, such as familiarity of arguments, type of learning, and locus of control. Again, dissonance theorists' early insights have been developed by recent work.

BALANCE THEORY AND SELECTIVE RECALL
OF INFORMATION ABOUT OTHERS

Another consistency theory, *balance theory* (Heider, 1958), also provoked research on learning and retention as a function of consistency (Cottrell, Ingraham, & Monfort, 1971; Picek, Sherman, & Shiffrin, 1975; Zajonc & Burnstein, 1965a, 1965b). Balance theory has influenced social cognition research on schemata (Chapter 6), and recently it has been influenced by social cognition research on mental structure and processing. Balance theory is an early model of cognitive and attitudinal organization. Structures in the perceiver's mind represent the perceiver (P), another person (O), and the mutual attitude object (X) (see Fig. 12.3). You (P) may have an attitude toward your roommate (O) and toward his car (X), and you may perceive him as having a certain attitude toward his car. Your perceptions of the relations among you two and the old clunker may be of two sorts, either positive or negative. Liking, owning, or belonging with something is a positive relationship (+), while disliking or not belonging together is a negative relationship (−).

The combination of relationships among the three of you may be either balanced or imbalanced. For example, if you like your roommate (P-O is +) and he likes his car (O-X is +), then the three of you are a "balanced" trio if you develop an affection for the old car (P-X is +). It is also balanced if your roommate likes his car (O-X is +), you dislike his car (P-X is −), and on reflection you decide he is not your type either ((P-O is −). Both of these relationships are shown in Fig. 12.3. There are several other balanced possibilities besides the two shown. The basic principle is that if the three positive and negative signs multiply out to positive, the structure is balanced.

Now consider the possibility that you like your roommate (+), he adores his car (+), and you cannot stand it (−). There is trouble in store for an imbalanced relationship such as this. Similarly, it would be imbalanced if your roommate adores his car (+), and so do you (+), but you think he is an

Basic cognitive structure

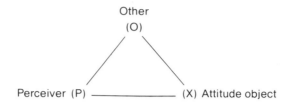

Balanced structures

Imbalanced structures

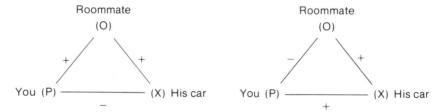

Fig. 12.3 Balance theory triads.

unbearable bore (−). Imbalanced relationships are under some pressure to change toward balance, and that is how the theory predicts attitude change. Your perception of any of the three relationships is likely to change in order to create balance.

The theory has been influenced specifically by both older and recent work on mental structure and representation: balance research shows how cognitive constraints shape learning and memory relevant to attitudes. For example, other people hearing about you, your roommate, and his car will learn and remember the story better if it is balanced. The prediction that balanced relationships are easier to recall is derived in part from consistency theories and in part from recent schematic theories (Chapter 6). Traditional balance research shows, for example, that people can learn and generate balanced social structures more easily than imbalanced ones (Feather, 1969; Zajonc & Burnstein, 1965a). Social schema research suggests that balanced relationships are stored in memory as a single unit. It is easier to remember that two friends agree or that two enemies disagree; this can be a compact item of memory. It is harder to recall that one of two friends likes chocolate and the other hates it and which feels which.

Recent balance researchers suggest cognitive mechanisms that explain why this might be the case (Picek *et al*, 1975; Sentis & Burnstein, 1979). Balanced and imbalanced relationships are stored differently. That is, people appear to store balanced relationships as a single cognitive unit, while imbalanced ones are stored less efficiently, in pieces. That is, within an imbalanced triad, the time it takes to retrieve a single relationship depends on the number of relationships (P-O, O-X, X-P) the experimenter uses as a recall cue; the more pieces of the three-way relationship that are supplied, the faster the triad of relationships can be retrieved. However, with balanced relationships, the number of pieces supplied does not matter; the time to retrieve the entire triad is the same regardless of the number of recall cues. This implies, then, that a balanced triad is a single cognitive unit that must be retrieved all at once (Sentis & Burnstein, 1979).

In sum, balance theorists predict that people will learn and recall balanced sets of information more easily than imbalanced ones. Such bits of information as agreeing friends and disagreeing enemies appear to form a single compact cognitive unit in memory, as opposed to imbalanced combinations.

SELF-PERCEPTION THEORY AND SELECTIVE RECALL
OF INFORMATION ABOUT THE SELF

Besides being terrible at remembering the arguments of those who disagree with them, people show selective memory for their own beliefs. After successful persuasion, people conveniently perceive their attitudes as never having changed at all (D. J. Bem & McConnell, 1970). This prediction follows from *self-perception theory*, one of the earliest attitude theories to bridge the gap between consistency theories and social cognition theories (Chapter 2, "Attribution Theory"). If a person's prepersuasion attitudes are not salient, the person infers new attitudes from his or her own behavior, as self-perception theory would predict (D. J. Bem, 1972). In both dissonance and self-perception theories, then, there is a tendency to recall one's attitudes to bring them in line with one's previous behavior (cf. Fazio, Zanna, & Cooper, 1977; Wixon & Laird, 1976).

Recent evidence from social cognition indicates a complementary process, however. People also misrecall their own behavior in ways that fit their current attitudes. Attitudes exert a directive influence on recall of personal history (M. Ross, McFarland, & Fletcher, 1981). If you ask a military conservative to recall his political activities in 1968, he will recall signing a hawkish petition on Vietnam but not recall helping his best friend secure a draft deferment. People may actually reconstruct their prior actions from their current attitudes, or they may simply more easily remember attitude-consistent material. In either case, even information as concrete as behavior is influenced by consistency pressures, and an analysis based on cognitive principles suggests that the organization of memory can account for the effects of attitudes on memory.

In short, self-perception theory predicts that people infer their attitudes by remembering their behavior. Conversely, recent evidence suggests that people reconstruct their behavior by referring to their attitudes.

A COMMENT ON CONSISTENCY THEORIES AND MEMORY

A general principle emerges from the research inspired originally by consistency theories. Attitudes serve to organize memory (Lingle & Ostrom, 1981; Ostrom, Lingle, Pryor, & Geva, 1980). In particular, making an attitudinal judgment improves recall of attitudinally relevant evidence and creates attitudinally consistent inferences. Hence, if you judge a person's suitability as a pilot, you will remember his eyesight and infer that he has good spatial ability. If you judge his suitability as a comedian, on the other hand, you will recall his infectious laugh and infer that he has stage presence (Lingle, Geva, Ostrom Leippe, & Baumgardner, 1979). The effect seems to be mediated by people's recalling the attitude itself, once it is formed, rather than retrieving and resynthesizing all the individual bits of evidence. Once you have formed an attitude about somebody as a pilot instead of a comedian, that attitude organizes all subsequent judgments, including recall of the data on which the judgment was based. The attitude is easier to recall than is the evidence that supports it (Lingle & Ostrom, 1979).

Summary

An attitude is a hypothetical mediating variable assumed to intervene between stimulus and response. Attitudes involve cognition, affect, and behavior. Social cognition's contribution to the field has been a fine-grained theoretical analysis of the processes involved in attitude formation and change; social cognition approaches also have provided new methodologies. One early theory in particular foreshadowed information-processing approaches: McGuire's eight-step chain of persuasion included exposure, attention, comprehension, yielding, retention, retrieval, decision, and behavior.

Armed with new theories and new methods, cognitive approaches to attitude change focus on old variables in new ways. For example, attributional approaches to communicator credibility indicate that messages are persuasive when they are perceived as valid. When a message is perceived to be caused by external constraints on the communicator or by personal attributes of the communicator, it is less persuasive than when it is perceived to be caused by the objective reality of the attitude entity.

Cognitive response analysis is a major new approach to attitudes, based on social cognition principles. In this view, attitude change is predicated on people's individual thoughts about persuasive information. Aspects of the communicator, the message, and the audience all enhance persuasion to the extent that people elaborate external stimuli in positive ways. To the extent that they counterargue or elaborate in negative ways, people are unpersuaded. Attitude change, then, depends on the amount and type of idiosyncratic responses generated in response to persuasive communications. One implication of CRA is that audience involvement will be critical. That is, uninvolved audiences will generate few cognitive responses of any kind.

Audience involvement is in some respects the foundation of cognitive response analysis. Involvement determines whether people are responding to superficial aspects of the situation, such as the communicator's credibility or the sheer number of arguments, or whether people are responding to the content and quality of the message itself. Involvement increases thoughtful, message-based attitude change.

For instance, communicator credibility effects depend on people's amount of thought. Uninvolved recipients appear to think more in response to a low credibility communicator than a high credibility one. Involved recipients show fewer effects of communicator credibility, but they may think more in response to a high credibility communicator than to a low credibility one. Attitude change in both cases depends on the amount and type of cognitive responses generated.

In contrast, message repetition effects do not appear to depend on thought when the stimuli are nonlinguistic. Mere exposure to nonlinguistic stimuli enhances liking without any particular cognitive activity. However, message repetition with linguistic stimuli does elicit thought. For a repeated persuasive communication, initial repetitions enhance comprehension, positive cognitive response, and agreement, if the arguments are good. Prolonged repetitions create tedium, counterarguments, and disagreement. This model of repetition effects presupposes subjects who are at least minimally involved.

Message difficulty inhibits persuasion, to the extent that recipients cannot comprehend the arguments. The better people understand the arguments (if they are good ones), the more people respond (positively) and the more they are persuaded. Again, involvement combines with message factors to determine cognitive responses, and message difficulty has little influence on the totally uninvolved or the totally involved; it most influences those of intermediate involvement.

Cognitive response analysis relies on personal features of the recipient as well as the external factors just described. People may vary in their need for cognition and so chronically employ more thoughtful strategies or less thoughtful ones for dealing with incoming information.

Attitudes are formed in groups as well as by individuals in isolation. A cognitive approach to the polarization of attitudes in groups proposes that people acquire new information about other group members' attitudes as well as the reasons for those attitudes. The greater the number of unique persuasive arguments brought out in a group, the more likely the group members' attitudes are to change in that direction. This informational theory contrasts with theories of attitude polarization in groups that stress social norms as explanations of attitude shifts.

The effects of attitudes on cognitive processes are numerous. Research inspired by consistency theories of attitudes predicted the effects of attitudes on selective perception, learning, and memory. Social cognition approaches have extended and elaborated those ideas. Beginning with perception, attitudes sometimes cause people to attend to information that is consistent with their attitudes, as predicted by dissonance theory. People also interpret information in ways that support their attitudes, also as predicted by dissonance theory. There is less support for dissonance theory's predictions of initial selective exposure to information not already present.

Dissonance theory also predicts that recall of other people's agreeing arguments will be better than recall of their disagreeing arguments. Under certain conditions suggested by recent research on cognition and social cognition (i.e., incidental learning, low motivation, high self-esteem, and high internal locus of control), people are especially likely to conform to dissonance theory's predictions of selective recall for attitudinally consistent material.

Balance theory predicts that people will learn and remember balanced triads, which are composed of internally consistent information, better than imbalanced triads. There is some evidence that balanced triads are stored as a single cognitive unit. Thus balance theory predicts selective recall of attitude-consistent information that concerns people's relationships with each other.

People also show selective recall of information about themselves. They misremember their own prior attitudes as being the same as their current (new) attitudes. And they misrecall their own prior behavior as consistent with their current (new) attitudes. Thus, in general, attitudes serve to organize memory for attitude-relevant information, and recent social cognition research suggests the mechanisms by which this can occur. More generally, social cognition approaches have provided new theories, new methodologies, and examined some old insights in a relatively fine-grained fashion.

Behavior is the silent and elusive partner of social cognition research. Although cognitions themselves are intrinsically interesting objects of study, people do not think within a vacuum. Daily behaviors and interactions with others

behavior

provide a constant source of information, some redundant and much new, that must be incorporated into cognitive representations. Hence behavior gives rise to cognitions. Behavior is also itself an outgrowth of cognition. In our discussion of social cognition, we have assumed that cognitive interpretations of events are not made for entertainment value, but so social perceivers can understand and predict both their own and others' behavior.

In this chapter, we explore in detail three types of relationships between cognitions and behavior. First, we consider whether cognitions predict behavior directly. Much research in social cognition assumes that cognitions are made about events so that people will know how to behave. For example, if an acquaintance is short with a co-worker, one tries to infer if the acquaintance is a disagreeable person, it has been a bad day, or the co-worker has done a poor job. Through causal analysis, one infers whether one should stay out of the acquaintance's way or not. The inference thus guides one's behavior. In the first section, then, we ask, How direct is the relationship between cognitions and behavior?

Behavior may also be calculated to create particular cognitions in other people's heads. One could presumably tell another person how smart, attractive, popular, or desirable one is, but generally it is considered more socially acceptable to let one's behavior convey such a message. Actions, after all, speak louder than words. Thus behavior has an important self-presentational quality that will be examined in the second section.

Behavior may also be used to test hypotheses. The cognitive analysis of people and events is fraught with ambiguity and uncertainty, as we indicated in Chapter 9 ("Social Inference"). Cognitive interpretations may, then, be held in mind as hypotheses, rather than as certainties, requiring further tests before they can be validated. Behavior can be a good way of testing hypotheses about both the self and others. For example, one may try a new sport, suspect that one is doing better than average at it, and create more challenging conditions to see if one's inference is true. Or a man may have one date with a woman, decide that he thinks he likes her, and quickly plan another date to see if she is indeed the woman for him. People frequently use their behavior to test hypotheses, so, in the third section, we examine how this process occurs.

The Cognition-Behavior Relationship

The question, How direct is the relationship between cognitions and behavior? is not an easy one to answer, at least not simply. First, in the social cognition arena, there has been relatively little research that includes behavioral dependent measures, so opportunities to examine the relationship are relatively few. When the cognition-behavior relationship is examined, sometimes the two parallel each other (e.g., Yarkin, Harvey, & Bloxom, 1981), and sometimes not (see, for example, Nisbett & Valins, 1972; Nisbett & Wilson, 1977a).

To address the cognition-behavior relationship generally, it is necessary to turn to related literatures where similar problems exist. For example, those with an awareness of social psychological history should find the cognition-behavior problem all too familiar. Attitude change research of the 1950s and 1960s produced a similar situation: researchers initially failed to examine the attitude-behavior relationship, and when it was examined, the evidence was highly inconsistent (e.g., Calder & Ross, 1973; Schuman & Johnson, 1976; Wicker, 1969). The literature on the correspondence between personality traits and behavior, though not cognitive in its origins, is also a useful source of hypotheses, in that the relationship between personality traits and behaviors that would theoretically be expected often proved to be weak and unreliable (Mischel, 1968).

Drawing on these literatures, the attempt to clarify when cognitions and behavior go together can take several routes: specifying which behaviors are most likely to be related to particular cognitions; improving measurement procedures so that cognitions and behaviors are more comparable; determining what features of cognitions are most likely to lead to behavioral consequences; understanding situational factors that might moderate the cognition-behavior relationship; and looking for individual differences in cognition-behavior consistency.

WHICH BEHAVIORS ARE RELATED TO COGNITION?

One problem that arises in examining the cognition-behavior relationship is that we may expect too many and too varied behaviors to be related to any given cognition. Consider self-perceptions of friendliness as an example. Some people think of themselves as friendly, others do not. Let us look only at the people who consider themselves friendly (cf. D. J. Bem & Allen, 1974). Should we expect them to be friendly in *all* situations? Certainly, we would expect them to be more friendly than people who consider themselves unfriendly, but there is no reason to expect that they will be friendly every minute of the day.

After all, people have to work, sleep, eat, and do many other nonsocial tasks. What, then, makes a friendly person friendly? It may well be that some people are considered friendly, not because they are friendly a lot, but because they are friendly in those critical situations most relevant to friendliness. In other words, they show consistent friendliness for situations that are prototypic for friendliness.

Recall from the discussion of schemata (Chapter 6) that prototypic persons or activities are those that are most representative of their particular category. Thus, for example, prototypic activities for friendliness might be saying hello to people on campus or welcoming new people enthusiastically. To consider oneself a friendly person, then, perhaps one need only show a high degree of consistency in these prototypic behaviors, and not on behaviors less centrally related to friendliness.

In fact, research supports this contention (Mischel & Peake, 1982). In an examination of self-rated conscientiousness, undergraduates who considered themselves conscientious (or not) were studied in a wide variety of situations that might tap conscientiousness. An independent group of raters judged each of the situations for how central or prototypic it was for conscientiousness. The investigators then calculated cross-situational consistency. Individuals who rated themselves high and low in conscientiousness did not behave differently in situations that were low in prototypicality for conscientiousness. However, when prototypic conscientious situations were examined, the highly conscientious individuals showed significantly greater consistency in their behavior as compared with the individuals who were low in conscientiousness (Mischel & Peake, 1982).

What are the implications of these points for the cognition-behavior relationship generally? They suggest that consistency will be highest when one examines behaviors that are prototypically related to particular cognitions, but that cognition-behavior consistency will be lower when one examines behaviors that are less centrally related to the cognitions in question.

MEASURING COGNITIONS AND BEHAVIORS

Another problem with studying the cognition-behavior relationship concerns how cognitions and behaviors are measured and whether or not they are measured at the same level of specificity. As this issue has been addressed substantially in the attitude-behavior literature, we will examine it in that context.

If you are asked whether you feel needy people should be helped through charity, you may well answer yes. If you are then accosted by a persistent beggar asking for a dollar, you may well decline. Although your attitudes and behavior would appear to be inconsistent, should one consider you to have violated your attitudes? Not necessarily. You may, for example, feel that charity should be managed by institutions, not individuals, or that begging should be discouraged. The apparent inconsistency of your attitude and behavior is caused by the fact that your attitude was assessed very generally, but your behavior was measured in a very specific situation. When attitudes and behaviors are assessed at different levels of specificity, low correspondence may be found. How, then, can attitude and behavior assessment be made more comparable?

One solution is to measure behavior through general behavioral tendencies, employing a multiple-act criterion (e.g., Epstein, 1979). That is, instead of examining the relationship between a general attitude (i.e., toward charity in the abstract) and a single act (i.e., giving money to a specific beggar), one would measure a number of specific acts to get a general behavioral measure. For example, one might measure money given to various causes, time volunteered to help the needy, and so on. The general attitude should, then, predict the general behavioral tendency. Thus, although your general belief about charity may not predict your specific response to a particular panhandler, it should predict your charitable behavior more generally, if we examine how much money, time, or effort you volunteer to each of several causes.

It is unclear why the multiple-act criterion succeeds in demonstrating attitude-behavior consistency. It may succeed because (1) multiple actions provide a better estimate of the individual's typical behavior, (2) employing multiple actions succeeds in including at least one situation that can be highly predicted by attitudes (cf. Monson, Hesley, & Chernick, 1982), or (3) multiple actions include at least two situations which the individual sees as relevant to the attitude and similar to each other, thus warranting similar behavior (cf. Lord, 1982). For whichever reason, correspondence is higher when multiple-act measures of behavior are compared against global attitudes.

A second solution is to measure attitudes more specifically. For example, if you had been asked how you feel about giving money to beggars, instead of how you feel about charity generally, high correspondence between your attitude and behavior might well have been found. Many efforts to examine the attitude-behavior relationship have adopted this approach by assessing attitudes as intentions to behave in specific ways (Ajzen & Fishbein, 1977; Fishbein & Ajzen, 1974, 1975). Specific behavioral intentions predict specific behaviors very well (see Bagozzi, 1981; Saltzer, 1981, for qualifications to this finding).

To summarize, the relationship between attitudes and behavior is strongest when both are assessed at the same level of generality. General attitudes predict general behavioral intentions fairly well, and specific attitudes predict specific behaviors. The lessons for exploring the cognition-behavior link should be quite straightforward. One can expect a low relationship between inferences and behavior if the inference is general and the behavior is specific, whereas if both inference and behavior are measured generally or specifically, the relationship should be stronger.

WHICH COGNITIONS PREDICT BEHAVIOR?

A third approach to the cognition-behavior relationship maintains that some cognitions will show a strong relationship to behavior, whereas others may not. What are the characteristics of cognitions that show a relationship to behavior? To elucidate this issue, we again turn to the attitude-behavior literature.

Ask a person what his or her attitude on a certain topic is, and the person will likely have one. It may be an issue the person has never thought about before and will never think of again, but for that brief moment, he or she may well have an attitude, even a strong one. Clearly, if the attitude is a temporary whim, it will not predict behavior very reliably. This problem—the ubiquity of attitudes—has plagued research on attitude-behavior consistency. Attitudes seem to be everywhere, but several factors influence which attitudes matter to a person and consequently which predict behavior. Which attitudes are really there and which are not?

One factor that determines whether or not attitudes will predict behavior is how they are formed. Attitudes formed from direct experience predict behavior better than do attitudes based on indirect experience (Fazio & Zanna, 1981). In one study, for example, college students were asked their attitudes regarding their university's housing shortage and were later asked to sign a petition concerning the housing shortage. Only those subjects whose attitudes had been formed through direct experience (i.e., sleeping on cots in dorm lounges for several weeks because there were no rooms) showed strong attitude-behavior relationships. Overall, attitudes that are formed through direct experience are more specific; they are held more confidently; they are more stable; and they resist counterargument better than do attitudes not based on direct experience (Fazio & Zanna, 1978; Zanna & Fazio, 1982).

Why are attitudes formed through direct experience more predictive of behavior? There are several possible reasons. First, direct experiences provide a great deal of information, so the attitudes that develop as a consequence may be better informed and more robust. Second, because behavior provided an initial basis for forming the attitude, the behavioral implications of the attitude may be more clear. Third, the links between the attitude and actual experience may make the attitude more accessible in memory, and thus it may be more likely to come to mind when one must act (Fazio & Zanna, 1981). Finally, the fact that attitudes formed through direct experience are often very specific may make specific behavioral implications clear, which may not be true for more vague general attitudes (Borgida, Swann, & Campbell, 1977).

A second feature of an attitude that influences attitude-behavior consistency is vested interest. To the extent that a person's attitude involves self-interest, the person is more likely to act on it. Thus, for example, 18-year-olds are more likely to canvass against a referendum that would raise the drinking age to 21 than are 22-year-olds (Sivacek & Crano, 1982). Similarly, people who believed that the 1974 energy crisis had a strong impact on their lives were more likely to comply with governmental regulations to control energy than were those who estimated the crisis had little personal impact (Sears, Tyler, Citrin, & Kinder, 1978).

Overall, attitudes that matter to a person—those that are based on personal experience, that are held with confidence, and that have implications for one's future—show a stronger relationship to behavior than those that matter little (cf. Kelman, 1974). The implication for the cognition-behavior relationship more generally is that cognitions that emerge from personal rather than indirect experience, and cognitions that have implications for one's future outcomes, may predict behavior better than cognitions that develop merely from mild curiosity or passing interest.

SITUATIONAL FACTORS MEDIATE
COGNITION-BEHAVIOR CONSISTENCY

Situational factors may also influence the cognition-behavior relationship by making particular cognitions salient as guides for behavior. Suppose you are approached by a friend who asks you to help him collect signatures on a petition that allows freshmen and sophomores to have cars on campus. What will you do? If the friend tells you he is desperate because he promised to have one hundred signatures by noon, and has only sixty at ten in the morning, you might help him out of friendship. On the other hand, if a classmate walks by muttering that there are too few parking spaces for the cars already on campus, you might reconsider, not wishing to alienate your own group. Similarly, if the parking petition is billed as a question of individual rights, you might be inclined to favor it, but if you have just read a newspaper editorial decrying the recent rise in air pollution in your community, you might not help out.

This example illustrates that, in trying to examine the consistency question, one must ask, Consistency with what? Social norms? Attitudes? Which set of attitudes? Behavior is strongly influenced by situational factors that may make salient one set of cognitions over others, and one must know what concerns are salient before one can predict the nature of consistency (see Scheier & Carver, 1982).

Social norms can be strong situational determinants of behavior that overwhelm seemingly relevant attitudes (e.g., Bentler & Speckart, 1981; LaPiere, 1934; S. H. Schwartz & Tessler, 1972). For example, asked if you would allow Sleazy Sam into your home, you may respond with some indignation that you would not, but if he shows up at your party as the date of one of your guests, it is unlikely that you will turn him away. Your behavior, then, will be consistent with the norms surrounding the host or hostess role, though it will not be consistent with your attitudes about Sam. Social norms are likely to be especially salient when an audience is present or when one's attention is directed outward toward the situation (rather than oneself); accordingly, behavior is likely to be strongly affected by self-presentational concerns (Cialdini, Levy, Herman, & Evenbeck, 1973; Duval, 1976; Newtson & Czerlinsky, 1974; M. Snyder & Swann, 1976).

Other situational factors favor the use of prior attitudes as a basis for behavior. For example, when attention is focused inward, a person may be more likely to base his or her behavior on enduring attitudes (Wicklund, 1975): Attention to the self minimizes external influences and makes one's prior attitudes more salient (see S. E. Taylor & Fiske, 1978). When people's past behaviors that suggest a particular attitude are made salient, subsequent consistency between attitudes and behavioral intentions is high. In one study, subjects were asked to think of all the negative experiences they had had that were associated with exercise (e.g., being picked last for a team or failing to score a crucial goal). Sometime later when subjects were given a chance to participate in exercise classes, they volunteered for fewer classes than did subjects who had not reconstructed their past negative exercise-related experiences (M. Ross, McFarland, Conway, & Zanna, 1983; see also Borgida & Campbell, 1982).

Why should seemingly trivial aspects of a situation have such a clear impact on people's behavior? Why should it matter what you temporarily recall about your past behaviors or beliefs? Situationally induced salience can put relevant attitudes or norms in the mental foreground, making them more available as guides to action (Borgida & Campbell, 1982; Kiesler, Nisbett, & Zanna, 1969; M. Snyder, 1977). What is salient defines the situation for the individual, reducing ambiguity and inconsistency (R. Norman, 1975); it tells you what should be relevant to your behavior if you are uncertain of what to do. Finally, when global attitudes or values are made salient, responsibility for behaving consistently with one's attitude will loom large (Kiesler, 1971; S. H. Schwartz, 1978). Thus, if cognition behavior linkages are made salient, cognitions and behaviors may typically cohere, but when situational norms are salient, behavior may be consistent with those norms. To predict what cognitions will cohere with behavior, then, one must know what factors in a situation are salient. Self-presentational concerns may dominate behavior or prior beliefs, attributions, expectations, or other influences may, depending on what is salient.

INDIVIDUAL DIFFERENCES MEDIATE CONSISTENCY

The question, Consistent with what? becomes even more appropriate when we examine the role of individual differences in cognition-behavior consistency. Some people show high consistency with social norms, whereas others behave consistently with their attitudes. Some people have an overriding social goal that is manifested chronically in their behavior, whereas others show more behavioral flexibility. We now turn to these individual difference factors.

Self-monitoring We all know people who blend into social situations easily. They seem to know exactly what to do or say. We also know people who are themselves, regardless of what situation they are in, who rarely bend to the norms of the social setting. Such different patterns are termed high and low self-monitoring, respectively (M. Snyder, 1979). Those who act as the situation demands are monitoring themselves with respect to the situation. Those who act on their own internal demands are not monitoring themselves with respect to the situation; they are low self-monitors (M. Snyder, 1974; M. Snyder & Campbell, 1982; M. Snyder & Monson, 1975; M. Snyder & Tanke, 1976).

What, exactly, is self-monitoring? Self-monitoring refers to the ways in which individuals plan, act out, and regulate behavioral decisions in social situations (M. Snyder & Cantor, 1980). Behavioral choices involve utilizing a wide range of information, including knowledge of the characteristics of particular social settings and knowledge of one's own abilities, resources, and stable qualities. M. Snyder (1974) hypothesized that high self-monitors are particularly sensitive to social norms, to situations, and to interpersonal cues regarding how to behave. Low self-monitors, in contrast, are less responsive to these environmental cues and instead draw on salient information from their internal selves to decide how to behave. In essence, then, when faced with a new situation, high self-monitors ask, "What is the ideal person for this situation and how can I be it?" whereas low self-monitors ask, "How can I best be me in this situation?" (M. Snyder, 1979).

Self-monitoring is assessed by a scale (M. Snyder, 1972, 1974), some items of which appear in Table 13.1. First, answer the items in the table. If you answered "false" to items 1, 3, and 5, and "true" to items 2, 4, and 6, you would tend toward the high self-monitoring side. On the other hand, if the reverse pattern characterizes your answers, you tend to be a low self-monitor.

High self-monitors are, in many ways, more socially skilled than low self-monitors (e.g., Ickes & Barnes, 1977). They can communicate a wider range of emotional states, they learn how to behave in new situations faster, they are more likely to initiate conversations, and they have good self-control (see M. Snyder, 1979). When asked to adopt the behavior of another type of person, for example, a reserved, withdrawn, introverted type, high self-monitors are better at it than low self-monitors (Lippa, 1976), and they also appear to be better at discerning the meaning of nonverbal behavior than low self-monitors (see M. Snyder, 1979). When their social outcomes depend on another person, such as a potential date, high self-monitors remember more about the other person and make more confident and extreme inferences about the other (Berscheid, Graziano, Monson, & Dermer, 1976). To the observer, the high self-monitor appears more friendly and less anxious than the low self-monitor (Lippa, 1976).

TABLE 13.1
Sample Items Measuring Self-Monitoring
(After M. Snyder, The self-monitoring of expressive behavior, *Journal of Personality and Social Psychology*, 1974, *30*, 526-537. Copyright 1974 by the American Psychological Association. Adapted by permission of the author.)

Answer the following items, true or false.

1. I find it hard to imitate the behavior of other people.	T	F
2. I would probably make a good actor.	T	F
3. In a group of people, I am rarely the center of attention.	T	F
4. I may deceive people by being friendly when I really dislike them.	T	F
5. I can only argue for ideas which I already believe.	T	F
6. I can make impromptu speeches even on topics about which I have almost no information.	T	F

As might be expected, high self-monitors have great interest in social information, apparently because it is useful to them. They are more likely to seek out information that is relevant to norms for self-presentation in a situation, and they spend more time looking at it. They remember information about another person with whom they will interact better than do low self-monitors (see M. Snyder, 1974); high self-monitors are more responsive to task instructions indicating what the typical behavior is in a given situation than are low self-monitors (M. Snyder & Monson, 1975). High self-monitors are particularly able to construct images of prototypic individuals in particular domains (e.g., the classic extravert or the perfect princess) than are low self-monitors, and are more likely to enter into a social situation when norms are clear; low self-monitors, on the other hand, are more skilled at constructing images of themselves in particular situations (e.g., how they would behave in situations calling for extravertedness), and they are more likely to enter a social situation if it fits their self-conception (M. Snyder & Gangestad, 1981).

Given these differences in the styles and informational preferences of high and low self-monitors, it should not be surprising that their behavior is under the control of different standards and forces. High self-monitors describe themselves as flexible, adaptable, shrewd individuals; when asked to explain the causes of their own behavior, they are likely to point to situational factors. Low self-monitors, in contrast, see themselves as more consistent and principled than highs do, and they offer dispositional explanations for their behavior (e.g., M. Snyder, 1976). Low self-monitors are more likely to show the effects of temporary mood states or fatigue on their behavior than high self-monitors, who are better able to mask these sources of internal interference (Ajzen, Timko, & White, 1982; M. Snyder, 1979; see also Zanna, Olson, & Fazio, 1980).

These differences in self-perceptions are also reflected behaviorally, and as such, the self-monitoring dimension helps to unravel the attitude-behavior consistency problem. High self-monitors show high cross-situational variability in their behavior. Because they behave consistently with social norms that vary from situation to situation, high self-monitors show little consistency across situations. Low self-monitors, on the other hand, show less situational variability in their behavior than high self-monitors, and their future behavior can be better predicted from knowledge of their relevant attitudes (M. Snyder & Swann, 1976). After being induced to perform counterattitudinal behavior, high self-monitors are less likely to infer new attitudes from the counterattitudinal behavior than are low self-monitors. However, there is one situation in which high self-monitors do show attitude-behavior consistency: when the relevance of personal attitudes to behavior is made salient, they are consistent presumably because it is socially desirable to act on one's attitudes (M. Snyder & Kendzierski, 1982; cf. M. Snyder, 1982).

The self-monitoring scale has come under some criticism (Briggs, Cheek, & Buss, 1980), but it does appear to be a multifaceted disposition that predicts social behavior (M. Snyder & Gangestad, 1982; M. Snyder & Kendzierski, 1982). To summarize, then, some apparent cognition-behavior discrepancies result from stable long-term differences in the goals people have for social situations. In the case of self-monitoring, the cross-situational inconsistencies of the high self-monitor express an ability and willingness to become what is necessary to be successful in a given social setting, that is, a desire to be consistent with social norms. In contrast, the high cross-situational consistency of the low self-monitor reflects a commitment to enduring principles and beliefs and a desire to act in accord with them.

Self-consciousness   Theories of self-focused attention (Carver & Scheier, 1981a; Duval & Wicklund, 1972; Wicklund, 1975) suggest that people's behavior follows their attentional focus. Recall from Chapter 7 ("Attention") that people who focus on themselves as a social object are high in public self-consciousness (Fenigstein, Scheier, & Buss, 1975). Such people are concerned with appearances and impressions. In contrast, people high in private self-consciousness focus narrowly on their own internal states. People who are high on public self-consciousness or low on private self-consciousness are unlikely to act on their attitudes, either because appearances matter to them or because they are relatively unaware of their own attitudes. For example, people high on public self-consciousness are relatively discrepant in their privately held versus publicly expressed beliefs about physical punishment (Scheier, 1980). In contrast, people who are low on public self-consciousness and/or high on private self-consciousness do show somewhat greater responsiveness to their internal states including their behavioral tendencies and their attitudes (Froming & Carver, 1981; Scheier, 1980; Scheier & Carver, 1983).

Having learned about both self-monitoring and self-consciousness, the reader may wonder how they differ. In fact, they seem to be different measures of a somewhat similar underlying construct: the propensity to draw on one's enduring, private reactions versus the propensity to utilize social norms and the desires of a social group as standards for behavior. The two constructs seem to measure different aspects of the concept: self-monitoring emphasizes self-presentational skills (or the lack of them) and self-consciousness emphasizes focus of attention. However, self-monitoring and self-consciousness are only weakly related (Carver & Scheier, 1981a; Turner, Scheier, Carver, & Ickes, 1978), and it may be premature from an empirical standpoint to try to integrate them (Schneiderman, Webb, & Davis, 1981; M. Snyder, 1979, in press).

In this section, we have considered two individual difference variables — self-monitoring and self-consciousness — that moderate the cognition-behavior relationship. This limited coverage should not be taken to imply that only these two individual difference variables are determinants of consistency. Rather, they are two in which the cognition-behavior relationship has been extensively explored. In reality, all individual difference variables can be interpreted as moderators of the cognition-behavior relationship in that they predict what chronic goals people have cross-situationally, what kinds of situations they prefer, and what they do when they get to those situations.

To summarize, the cognition-behavior relationship has, to date, received insufficient attention. When it is examined more systematically, prior experience with similar problem areas suggests that the relationship will be variable. Our understanding of that variability can be potentially enlightened by looking at behaviors that are prototypic for particular cognitions, measuring cognitions and behavior at the same level of specificity, identifying those cognitions most likely to have behavioral consequences, examining the situational context for factors that may make particular cognitions salient, and identifying individual difference factors that may moderate the cognition-behavior relationship.

Behavior as Impression Management

As we have just seen, there are many reasons why the relationship between cognitions and behavior can be less than direct. Under at least one set of conditions, however, the relationship between intention and behavior may be very direct: when people have a clear idea of the image they wish to present and conscientiously go about creating it. The image may be temporary, such as trying to fit a prospective employer's idea of what the new sales director should be like, or it can be permanent, such as wanting to convey to others that one is successful, attractive, and fun loving. Impression management is ubiquitous; it is hard to think of a social situation in which some effort to influence how others think of oneself is not going on. In Southern California, even the license plate is used to create an impression regarding occupation (ISUEM4U), friendliness (HI LA), sexual prowess (ALWAZ UP), or even how much the car cost (40 GEES).

Behavior is the vehicle through which impressions are usually enacted, and as such, impression management is much like acting. One cannot simply stand up and do it, at least not well. To create a successful impression requires the right setting, correct props (e.g., style of dress), a good deal of skill, and often some rehearsal—the same ingredients that go into any dramatic production (cf. Goffman, 1959, 1963). It requires the ability to "take the role of the other" (Cooley, 1902; Mead, 1934); that is, to be successful, one must be able to step into the shoes of the target person, see how the impression looks from his or her vantage point, and adjust one's behavior accordingly.

Usually, people strive to make a good impression. However, there are also circumstances under which an ambiguous or poor impression may be one's goal.

MAKING A POSITIVE IMPRESSION

There are many reasons for wanting to create a good impression, such as increasing one's own power, obtaining desired results like a job or promotion, gaining approval from others, and the intrinsic satisfaction of projecting a positive image in both one's own and others' eyes (Schlenker, 1980; M. Snyder, 1977).

How are positive impressions created? One strategy for so doing is *behavioral matching*. If the target other is behaving modestly, usually the impression manager will too, and if the target is behaving in a self-promoting manner, so will the impression manager (e.g., Gergen & Wishnov, 1965; Newtson & Czerlinsky, 1974). However, when the target of one's impression management efforts gives no clear standard of how to behave, people generally attempt to *convey the most positive image* of the self they can (see M. Snyder, 1977; Schlenker, 1980).

Another basic technique of impression management is *conforming to situational norms*. As Alexander and Knight (1971) have noted, for every social setting, there is a pattern of social interaction that conveys the best identity for that setting, which is what they term a "situated identity." For example, at a funeral, the best self-presentation involves wearing dark colors, conveying an appearance of sadness, expressing condolences in a low voice, and mentioning only the positive qualities of the deceased person, regardless of how much of a rogue he or she may have been. People use their knowledge of these situated identities to construct patterns of behavior for themselves (see, e.g., Gergen & Taylor, 1969; E. E. Jones, Gergen, & Davis, 1962).

In addition to behavioral matching, self-promotion, and conformity, people seek to create positive impressions by *appreciating or flattering others*. The sincere appreciation of others' abilities or accomplishments usually has its intended effect of increasing the appreciator's power in the relationship and the target's regard for him or her. However, the effects of flattery are more mixed. Flattery is, by definition, a misrepresentation of one's beliefs about another, and when it is perceived as such by the target, it can backfire. Flattery that is believed to serve the flatterer's ulterior motives is one such condition (e.g., E. E. Jones & Wortman, 1973; Mettee & Aronson, 1974). For example, when a student in a course blatantly and indiscriminately praises the instructor's lectures, the student often succeeds only in arousing the contempt of instructor and peers alike.

Flattery is most successful when given on attributes that the target values but on which he or she questions his or her own standing. For example, telling a prize-winning scientist that he is smart will likely have little effect—he already knows it—but telling him that he is charming may have its intended effect, if he values but doubts his own social skills (see, for example, E. E. Jones & Wortman, 1973; S. C. Jones & Schneider, 1968; J. W. Regan, 1976). Flattery is also successful if it is given with discretion. Those who flatter everyone succeed in impressing few, and those who flatter frequently will have less impact than those who flatter at particular appropriate moments (e.g., E. E. Jones & Wortman, 1973; Mettee & Aronson, 1974). Indirect flattery may be one of the more successful forms of flattery, since it is less vulnerable to detection than are other forms: imitating others, talking about their favorite topics, or even simply paying attention to them and using their names can produce the intended effect of flattery (e.g., Carnegie, 1936; E. E. Jones & Pittman, 1982;

E. E. Jones & Wortman, 1973; Kleinke, Staneski, & Weaver, 1972; see Schlenker, 1980, for a review).

An appearance of *consistency among beliefs or between beliefs and behavior* is another attribute of successful impression management. Generally, it is regarded as a sign of weakness to show or to admit to inconsistency, and people will often go to great lengths to justify apparent inconsistencies. Consider, for example, how the White House must continually cover up disagreements among foreign policy advisers by claiming that diametrically opposite statements merely reflect two components of the same internally consistent policy. The foot-in-the-door technique (Freedman & Fraser, 1966), described earlier in Chapter 2 ("Attribution Theory"), can also be viewed as an example of the need to appear consistent. This technique involves making a small request of someone (e.g., "Please place this small card in your window indicating that you have given to our charity") which then escalates some time later into a larger request (e.g., "We'd like you to place this large placard on your lawn advocating auto safety"). Frequently, those who have already complied with the smaller request will also agree to the larger one, and one possible explanation is that they wish to appear consistent in their own minds and to others.

In any successful self-presentational effort, *verbal and nonverbal behavior should match.* That is, efforts to convey a friendly impression should be accompanied by a forward lean, low interpersonal distance (e.g., sitting close to the person), smiling, and a high level of eye contact. Efforts to discourage the company of another should feature low eye contact, high interpersonal distance, a postural orientation away from the person to whom one is speaking, and little smiling (Exline, 1972; Kleinke, 1975; Mehrabian, 1972). When people are sincere in their message and feel toward the speaker as they are behaving, then verbal and nonverbal cues are usually consistent. However, when a false impression is being conveyed, frequently the nonverbal channel will "leak," giving away the speaker's true feelings (e.g., DePaulo & Rosenthal, 1979; Weitz, 1974). Sometimes, such leakage does not go unnoticed by a target (e.g., Word, Zanna, & Cooper, 1974), and hence the effort at a positive impression may be undermined.

Finally, self-presentation efforts vary, depending on how public they are. When people believe that an audience will find out how good they are at some skill, they will modify their self-presentation efforts in a modest direction, but when others are not expected to find out, self-enhancement is the rule. One of the authors attended a party years ago at which the subject of pool came up. Someone asked her if she played, and she responded that she did, implying that she had gotten rather proficient at it. "Good," replied her companion, "there's a table downstairs. Let's go shoot a few games." There ensued one of the more embarrassing public displays of incompetence within her memory, aggravated no doubt by the additional pressure that her own immodest assessment had placed on her performance.

Overall, then, the goal of creating a positive impression is very common. A variety of impression management techniques have been identified for so doing, but their generalizability has been called into question. Many studies of impression management have been conducted with college students who apparently believe that the way to make a successful self-presentation is to be self-promoting (M. Snyder, 1977). Were similar studies conducted with older adults, the strategies used might be quite different. They might include those advocated by Dale Carnegie (1936) such as being a good listener or talking about the other's interests (cf. M. Snyder, 1977). Only an investigation of impression management with a variety of populations can determine if this is so.

MUDDYING THE WATERS: ATTRIBUTE AMBIGUITY

So far we have considered ways in which people try to induce a positive impression of themselves in others. Sometimes, however, people may wish to obscure the impression others form of them (M. L. Snyder, Kleck, Strenta, & Mentzer, 1979; M. L. Snyder & Wicklund, 1981). No one likes to be categorized. Consider the statements "You can always count on George to do more than his share" and "Linda's always happy." Although positive, they suggest a limit on the target person's behavior or abilities. People like to feel they possess a wide range of abilities and personality attributes. Being typed as one sort of person or another can reduce one's sense of control over one's outcomes, in that it implies that one is no longer free to do the opposite. Being typed also creates expectations in others' minds that one may not be able or may not want to live up to, that is, that constrain one's future behavior. Thus, although Linda may be pleased that others think of her as cheerful, and although George may take satisfaction from the fact that others notice his unselfishness, both may feel a bit robbed of the choice to be grumpy or piggish, respectively. Moreover, Linda may come to feel obligated to be cheerful, and George may feel that he cannot possibly be as unselfish as others now expect.

Accordingly, just as others are coming to form a stable impression of a target, the target may muddy the waters (M. L. Snyder & Wicklund, 1981). There are several ways of making one's attributes ambiguous. One can *engage in an inconsistent behavior*. Linda might choose to be publicly despondent, and George might make a token selfish gesture. One can *provide additional reasons* for the behavior, so that others will discount the importance of stable personality factors. Linda might note that her work and social life are going well, thus making her more cheerful than usual, while George might mention that he has extra time right now to do more than his share. One might *muster consensus* for his or her attributes, maintaining that one is no more happy or unselfish than anyone else. Failing these techniques, one might choose to *leave the situation* altogether or otherwise *avoid evaluating the self*.

Not all attributes constrain one's freedom. Being typed as "resourceful" or "independent" leaves one fairly unconstrained, for example. However, many attributes, both positive and negative, can constrain one's freedom, and when the potentially constraining aspects of an attribute are especially salient, one will likely make an effort to create attribute ambiguity (M. L. Snyder & Wicklund, 1981).

MANAGING A POOR IMPRESSION

Making one's attributes ambiguous becomes especially important under conditions of potential or real failure, because low ability is a possible attribution for such failure. It is virtually always desirable to have others think of one as highly able. High ability is unconstraining—one can do a wide range of things—whereas low ability is very constraining. Thus a person will usually go to great lengths to keep both the self and others from making low ability attributions (cf. Darley & Goethals, 1980). Under these circumstances, then, attribute ambiguity is motivated not only by the need to maintain control over one's outcomes but also by the needs to save face and to maintain self-esteem.

Rendering attributions for failure or potential failure ambiguous involves many of the same strategies as described earlier: doing something inconsistent (e.g., highlighting a success), mustering consensus (e.g., everyone did poorly), or providing additional reasons, so that others will discount the role of ability (M. L. Snyder & Wicklund, 1981). For example, when people anticipate that they will fail in front of others, they will often exaggerate the impediments they will face to provide an advance explanation of their failure (Wortman, Costanzo, & Witt, 1973). One may attribute a failure to low effort or actually engage in low effort, so as to assure an effort-related failure. One may make attributions to a short-term and/or unstable factor such as loss of sleep, but only if there will be no public scrutiny on future similar tasks. Making one's attributes successfully ambiguous, then, is more than just offering an excuse: it involves a careful consideration of what constitutes a plausible, not too damaging, nondiscomfirmable reason for a poor performance (see Darley & Goethals, 1980).

A second way to manage a poor impression is through self-handicapping. In a particularly intriguing analysis, E. E. Jones and Berglas (1978) suggested that the excessive and/or continual use of alcohol or drugs may be motivated by the fact that the abuser needs an excuse for failure. Presumably, attributing failure to being drunk or stoned is less threatening in both one's own eyes and the eyes of others than is attributing failure to incompetence (Kolditz & Arkin, 1982). Other factors than substance abuse may also constitute self-handicapping strategies. T. W. Smith, Snyder, and Handelsman (1982), for example, suggest that attributing performance to test anxiety is less threatening than attributing it to lack of ability, and thereby may be used by some individuals as an explanation for poor test performance. Attributing one's poor performance to low effort (T. W. Smith *et al.*, 1982) or procrastination or overcommitment may serve similar functions.

In support of these conjectures, T. W. Smith, Snyder, and Handelsman had subjects high or low in chronic test anxiety take an intelligence test. Some subjects were told that anxiety hurt performance on the task, others were told that anxiety had no effect on the task, a third group was given no information about the effects of anxiety on the task, and the fourth group was told the test was innocuous. As predicted, highly test-anxious subjects reported particularly high levels of anxiety when they were given no information about anxiety and when they were told anxiety hurts performance. When they believed anxiety did not affect test performance, reported anxiety was somewhat lower; moreover, under these circumstances, the highly test-anxious subjects attributed their performance to (lack of) effort. These results are consistent with an impression management interpretation of self-handicapping because they suggest that the highly test-anxious subjects attributed their performance to whatever was an acceptable excuse for failure.

But, ultimately, how acceptable are these excuses? One of the consequences of self-handicapping or some of the other forms of attribute ambiguity is a poor self-presentation. Although one may avoid a low ability attribution, the price of the exchange can be high: one may look lazy, anxious, drunk, or stoned instead. A further risk of the poor self-presentation is that, often, impression management efforts are internalized. People come to believe that they are the way they act (Gergen, 1968; E. E. Jones et al., 1962; E. E. Jones, Rhodewalt, Berglas, & Skelton, 1981). Although positive impression management efforts can bolster self-esteem, when one has intentionally created a poor self-presentation in others' eyes, the result can be a loss of self-esteem (E. E. Jones et al., 1981).

The preceding discussion is an admittedly brief introduction to the large topic of impression management (see, for example, Schlenker, 1980, for a more extended coverage). The points covered are summarized in Table 13.2. Despite its brevity, the discussion illustrates several important points about behavior and about the cognition-behavior relationship. It is clear from the impression management literature that there is no single causal relationship between cognitions and behavior. Behavior can act in the service of cognition, but cognitions about the self can also change as one successfully enacts a particular self-presentation. Behavior and cognition need not go together at all; one may have one's self-concept firmly rooted in reality, yet successfully role play a very different sort of person (e.g., Schlenker, 1980). Behavior itself may be internally inconsistent, as when the verbal channel conveys one message but the non-verbal channel "leaks" another. However, what all these points also suggest is that social pressures favor cognition-behavior consistency: inconsistencies are often detected and are actively interpreted, usually negatively, when they are. Cognitions often come into line with behavior. People want to see their cognitions and behavior as consistent and strive to create this impression. Overall, impression management is one of the more intriguing topics within behavior, because it demonstrates the variety of ways in which behavior can be used to achieve impressions for the benefit of both the self and others.

TABLE 13.2
Strategies of Self-Presentation

Type of impression effort	Possible motives	Representative strategies
Creating a positive impression	Increase one's power; obtain resources; obtain approval; validate a positive self-image; be liked	Match target's behavior; convey most positive image possible; conform to norms; appreciate or flatter target; appear to be consistent
Creating an ambiguous impression	Avoid stereotyping by others; maintain behavioral freedom; maintain self-esteem; save face	Engage in inconsistent behavior; provide multiple reasons for behavior; proclaim that everyone does it (i.e., muster consensus); leave the field; avoid evaluations
Controlling a negative impression	Control one's own and others' attributions for failure; avoid low-ability attributions; avoid own or others' disappointment over future anticipated failure	Exaggerate impediments to success; exert little effort; self-handicap (i.e., engage in self-destructive behavior, such using drugs or drinking); proclaim one's failure to be due to external and/or unstable factors; make one's attributes ambiguous

Using Behavior to Test Hypotheses about Others

We learn about other people in many different ways. Sometimes we hear about them from others before meeting them or we may have hints about them based on the situations in which we encounter them. At other times one must start from scratch, assembling an impression from the information that is gathered from observing and talking with the person. Regardless of how an impression of another is formed, one may quickly develop hypotheses concerning what the person is like. As one is interacting with the person, how will the hypotheses influence one's behavior? Considerable research suggests that people behave toward others in ways that would tend to confirm the hypotheses they hold about those others. Perceivers employ behavioral strategies for eliciting information from others that preferentially support their hypotheses.

How might this process work? Suppose you learn that Ed has just returned from Tahiti and you quickly form an image of him as a carefree adventurer who seeks exotic places. In your subsequent interactions with him, you may inquire as to other trips he has taken or hobbies he has and learn that he once sailed the Virgin Islands with friends and fed sharks at Marineland as a summer job after high school. All this may seem fairly exotic, but note that you preferentially solicited information that confirmed this image. All of us have at least a few little things about us that make us quasi-exotic, and when those bits are elicited from us in their entirety, we look much more exciting than we really are. After dating Exotic Ed for several weeks, it may emerge that his company flew him to Tahiti for a conference, his uncle is the manager of Marineland and got him the summer job, and the "friends" with whom he sailed the Virgin Islands were his grandparents. The point is that people have a large repertoire of behaviors and experiences and, when they are preferentially sampled by selective questioning, they may fit whatever hypothesis that selective questioning is designed to test.

To demonstrate this point, M. Snyder and Swann (1978a) told college student subjects they would be interviewing another student; half were told to find out if the other was an extravert (e.g., outgoing, sociable), and half were told to find out if the other was an introvert (e.g., shy and retiring). All subjects were then given a set of questions measuring introversion and extraversion, and the students were told to pick a subset of questions they would ask. Subjects who were told to assess extraversion preferentially selected a disproportionate number of extraversion questions (e.g., "What would you do if you wanted to liven things up at a party?"), and those told to assess introversion picked a disproportionate number of introversion questions (e.g., "What factors make it really hard for you to open up to people?"). These questions, in turn, made the target other appear particularly extraverted or introverted respectively, because he or she was providing only the sample of behavior relevant to the questions. This confirmatory hypothesis testing bias has been demonstrated many times (e.g., M. Snyder, Campbell, & Preston, 1982). The bias exists whether the hypothesis concerns an individual's personality traits or characteristics based on group membership such as race, sex, or sexual preference. It occurs regardless of how the hypothesis originated, how likely it is to be true, and whether incentives for accuracy are offered to the hypothesis tester (see M. Snyder & Gangestad, 1981, for a review).

Perhaps even more surprising is the fact that, even when people have fairly balanced information about another person, they may selectively draw on it to support a particular hypothesis. Imagine you are at a party and someone who is clearly infatuated with your roommate inquires selectively about all his or her desirable qualities. As you respond to these questions, you may find your own impression of your roommate improving, in that you have highlighted for the questioner all positive attributes and none of the negative ones. M. Snyder and Cantor (1979) examined this phenomenon by giving subjects a detailed description of a woman and later asking them to assess her suitability for a particular job, either that of a real estate salesperson, which requires extraverted qualities, or that of librarian, which requires more introverted qualities. Although the initial description contained a balanced set of both extraverted and introverted behaviors, subjects selectively recalled behaviors appropriate to the particular job they were supposed to consider. When later asked to rate the woman's suitability for both jobs, each group saw her as more suited to the one for which they had mustered past evidence (see also Lingle, Geva, Ostrom, Leippe, & Baumgardner, 1979; L. Ross, Lepper, & Hubbard, 1975).

The implications of confirmatory hypothesis testing are not confined solely to the impressions individuals form about each other in casual social settings, as the job interview format of Snyder and Cantor's research implies. Another study demonstrated the potential relevance of confirmatory hypothesis testing to courtroom situations, using the example of asking witnesses leading questions (Swann, Giuliano, & Wegner, 1982). Suppose, for example, that a lawyer asks you: "Tell the jury about the last time you got into a fight." The question itself may lead people to conclude that you have a history of aggressive behavior, whether or not you do. In fact, Swann, Giuliano, and Wegner found that the conjectures embodied in such leading questions can themselves be interpreted as evidence for the behavior in question. Furthermore, being put in the position of answering such a leading question forces you to provide information that further confirms the behavior. Assuming you were in at least one fight in your life, you must now tell the jury about the details of the fight. Hence, leading questions are doubly biasing: the question itself is taken as evidence for the behavior, and the answer provides further such evidence. When will the evidence of leading questions be ignored? In a second study, Swann, Giuliano, and Wegner (1982) made it clear that the leading questions were selected at random (drawn from a fish bowl); under these circumstances, the leading questions themselves were not taken as evidence for the existence of the behavior, but the behavioral evidence provided by the answers to those questions still was considered to be relevant. Hence even random conjectures can create misperceptions via confirmatory hypothesis testing.

In sum, confirmatory hypothesis testing has been demonstrated under a fairly broad range of circumstances. It is important to note, however, that methodological factors may contribute to the demonstration of the confirmatory bias. First, the to-be-tested hypothesis is often made particularly salient to subjects through a vivid description of the personality type under question, for example, extraversion (see Trope & Bassok, 1982). Second, in some studies, the list of questions given to subjects to test the hypothesis (e.g., extraversion) includes a heavy proportion of questions that assume that the to-be-tested hypothesis is true. Thus, instead of questions like, "Do you like parties?" (a question to which extraverts might respond yes and introverts no), the list includes questions like, "What would you do to liven up a party?" (a question to which both introverts or extraverts would be virtually forced to give information relevant only to extraversion). When subjects are allowed to create their own questions to test a hypothesis, they rarely choose such biased questions; rather, their questions may feature a behavior characteristic of the to-be-tested hypothesis, but the question itself is unbiased. That is, people will ask "Do you like parties?" if testing extraversion, or "Do you like to be alone?" if testing introversion (L. F. Clark & Taylor, 1983; Trope & Alon, 1980).

In fact, Trope and Bassok (1982) found that subjects testing hypotheses about others preferred diagnostic information (i.e., information most likely to indicate whether or not the hypothesis was true), rather than confirmatory information. There seems little doubt that confirmatory hypothesis testing occurs, but how robust it is remains at issue. It seems most likely to occur if people have a clear hypothesis in mind and choose leading questions to test their hypothesis. When people actually select leading questions, however, remains unknown.

An additional concern regarding the generalizability of the confirmatory bias in hypothesis testing is that rarely are conversations one-way, with one individual asking all the questions and the other merely answering. If true communication occurred, how would a target react to hypothesis testing efforts in a conversation? Would a target person recognize that he or she is being miscast or distorted by the perceiver? Under what circumstances might a target person not only confirm the perceiver's hypothesis but actually come to believe it is true of the self, and under what circumstances will the target seek to disconfirm the hypothesis?

SELF-FULFILLING PROPHECIES: WHEN BEHAVIOR CREATES REALITY

As just noted, confirmatory hypothesis testing can create misperceptions of a target person in the social perceiver's mind through highlighting information that selectively favors the presentation of particular attributes. When this hypothesis-testing process also succeeds in altering the target person's behavior in the direction of the hypothesis, a self-fulfilling prophecy is said to occur. An initially false definition of a situation, then, evokes behaviors which subsequently make the false belief true (Merton, 1957).

A classic demonstration of the self-fulfilling prophecy was done in a classroom situation (Rosenthal & Jacobson, 1968). Teachers were told at the beginning of a school year that certain of their students were potential late bloomers who, with the proper nurturance and guidance, could be expected to excel. In fact, there was nothing to distinguish these students from their peers: they were randomly selected. However, several months later, when the so-called late bloomers' performance was examined, not only had their schoolwork improved, but their IQs had actually increased. Numerous similar investigations, many conducted in classroom settings, testify to the robustness of this effect (see Rosenthal, 1974, for a review). It holds for many different types of expectations, target persons, and situations; both positive and negative expectations can create self-fulfilling prophecies (see, for example, Andersen & Bem, 1981; Fazio, Effrein, & Falender, 1981; S. C. Jones & Panitch, 1971; Sherman, Skov, Hervitz, & Stock, 1981; M. Snyder & Swann, 1978a; Zanna & Pack, 1975).

How do self-fulfilling prophecies come about? There are a variety of contributing factors that can produce them. One factor is the opportunity for the target and the person holding the expectation to interact in ways relevant to the expectation. In the classroom study, for example, teachers undoubtedly gave more encouragement, feedback, and aid to students they expected would profit from the attention; hence the students about whom teachers had positive expectations had the chance to learn more. An expectation is also more likely to lead to a self-fulfilling prophecy if the expectation is held by a high status person (e.g., an authority figure or older, male individual) than if the target is of relatively lower status (Darley & Fazio, 1980). For example, if a researcher tells the student sitting next to you in class that you are a potential late bloomer, that information will probably influence your behavior less than if the researcher tells your teacher the same thing.

Perhaps the most intriguing way in which an expectation can be transmitted from perceiver to target person is through nonverbal behaviors such as eye contact, posture, smiling, nodding, and body angle. For example, in a study described earlier (Chapter 10, "Designing Research"), Word, Zanna, and Cooper (1974) demonstrated that negative expectations communicated nonverbally by an interviewer to an interviewee actually caused the interviewee to perform more poorly.

Self-fulfilling prophecies can even occur over the telephone. M. Snyder, Tanke, and Berscheid (1977) gave college males a folder of information about a female partner that included a bogus picture, representing the woman as either highly attractive or as unattractive. Each male student was then asked to call up the woman whose folder he had received and chat for ten minutes. Tape recordings were made of the conversations. Not only did the men who believed they had attractive partners behave more warmly toward them, but the women who were miscast as highly attractive were perceived by judges to be more friendly, likable, and sociable in their interactions with the men than those miscast as unattractive.

The substantial amount of research on self-fulfilling prophecies implies that such effects are common (see Darley & Fazio, 1980, for a review). In fact, though, several critical steps are required for the effect to occur. As Fig. 13.1 indicates, the perceiver must (1) hold an expectation about a target and (2) behave in a manner consistent with it. The target then (3) interprets the behavior and (4) responds to the perceiver with actions that are (5) subsequently interpreted by the perceiver as consistent with the original expectation (Darley & Fazio, 1980).

It would seem that checks at each step could potentially erase any self-fulfilling prophecy. However, consider, for example, the links among steps 2, 3 and 4. If the perceiver forms a positive expectation about the target and behaves accordingly, the target is likely to assume either that the perceiver especially likes him or her and has good taste or that the perceiver is a likable person; in either case, the target is likely to reciprocate the perceiver's behavior which will set up the self-fulfilling prophecy. Suppose now that the perceiver holds a negative expectation about the target and behaves in a cold, aloof, or even hostile manner. The target may decide that the perceiver is an unpleasant person, and reciprocate the negative behaviors, thus again establishing a self-fulfilling prophecy. Alternatively, either the perceiver or the target may decide to have nothing further to do with the other, terminate the interaction, and leave the interaction. Still, the self-fulfilling prophecy will remain intact.

Under what conditions can a self-fulfilling prophecy be undermined? There appear to be two main conditions: one is when a perceiver "compensates" for the expectation he or she holds about a target; the other is when a target

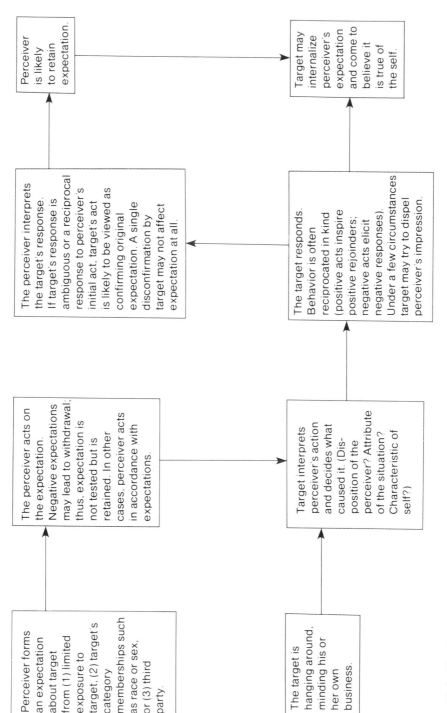

Fig. 13.1 The development of a self-fulfilling prophecy. (After Darley and Fazio, 1980)

Perceiver forms an expectation about target from (1) limited exposure to target, (2) target's category memberships such as race or sex, or (3) third party.

The perceiver acts on the expectation. Negative expectations may lead to withdrawal; thus, expectation is not tested but is retained. In other cases, perceiver acts in accordance with expectations.

The perceiver interprets the target's response. If target's response is ambiguous or a reciprocal response to perceiver's initial act, target's act is likely to be viewed as confirming original expectation. A single disconfirmation by target may not affect expectation at all.

Perceiver is likely to retain expectation.

The target is hanging around, minding his or her own business.

Target interprets perceiver's action and decides what caused it. (Disposition of the perceiver? Attribute of the situation? Characteristic of self?)

The target responds. Behavior is often reciprocated in kind (positive acts inspire positive rejoinders; negative acts elicit negative responses). Under a few circumstances target may try to dispel perceiver's impression.

Target may internalize perceiver's expectation and come to believe it is true of the self.

actively tries to dispel the perceiver's expectations. We will consider each in turn. When a perceiver holds a negative expectation about a target, such as the belief that the target is hostile or cold, the perceiver may compensate for, rather than reciprocate, the expected behavior. Thus, for example, if you expect that another person is hostile, rather than being hostile yourself (reciprocating behavior), you may decide to be extra nice (compensatory behavior), hoping that, in so doing, you can minimize the other's unpleasant behavior (see Bond, 1972; Ickes, Patterson, Rajecki, & Tanford, 1982; Swann & Snyder, 1980).

A study that adopted this format found that subjects who were forewarned that their partner in a study was cold behaved in a warmer fashion toward that individual than subjects who were forewarned their partner was warm; apparently, the warmer style of the subjects expecting a cold partner was intended to minimize the unpleasantness they anticipated in the interaction. The result of the compensatory strategy, not surprisingly, was to elicit behaviors that contradicted the a priori expectation; target individuals who were initially labeled as cold but who were the recipients of those compensatory warm efforts, in fact, behaved more warmly toward their partners than target persons initially labeled as warm, thus canceling any possible self-fulfilling prophecy. However, even compensatory behavioral strategies may not undermine self-fulfilling prophecies. Despite the warm behavior of targets labeled as cold, perceivers clung to their original hypotheses: targets labeled as cold were perceived as more cold than targets labeled as warm (Ickes *et al.*, 1982).

Why might this happen? As is well known from other work on schemata or theory-guided inferences and on hypothesis testing (see Chapters 6 and 9), behavior that is consistent with, irrelevant to, or even mildly inconsistent with prior expectations is often nonetheless interpreted as being consistent with prior expectations. Hence a self-fulfilling prophecy can exist in a social perceiver's mind without it being true in fact (see, for example, Ickes *et al.*, 1982). Nonetheless, compensatory behavioral strategies generally are one important check on the development of self-fulfilling prophecies. When perceivers make an effort to avoid conflict, hostility, or other negative encounters, the unpleasantness they anticipate may well not occur, even though they may not always be aware of that fact.

Target individuals themselves can also prevent the enactment of a self-fulfilling prophecy by refusing to be miscast into some role they feel does not fit. Each of us has no doubt had the experience of finding someone typing us in a way that does not feel correct, and although one may play along temporarily, after a while one is inclined to disabuse him or her. For example, if I find some acquaintance typing me as a workaholic who rarely has any fun, I will quickly do my best to counteract that impression.

To date, the circumstances under which targets will be actively motivated to undo perceivers' erroneous or unflattering expectations have yet to be thoroughly investigated. Researchers have suggested some possibilities (Darley & Fazio, 1980). When the target believes that the perceiver's false impression is based on something the target did, rather than on the perceiver's own personality or on forces in the situation, then the target may be more likely to attempt to correct the misimpression.

Three other factors also appear to be critical in determining whether or not a target will attempt to dispel a perceiver's false impression: (1) how important the perceiver's impression is of the target (false impressions, especially negative ones, held by others important to the target are likely to prompt some dispelling action by the target); (2) how discrepant the perceiver's impression is from the target's own self-impression (more discrepancy should prompt more effort to undo the impression) (see, for example, Baumeister & Jones, 1978; Farina, Allen, & Saul, 1968; Gurwitz & Topol, 1978; Swann, Read, & Hill, 1981); and (3) how certain the target is of the self-relevant attribute in question (more self-certainty prompts greater efforts to dispel the misconception) (Swann, 1983). Of course, under some circumstances, the target may find the perceiver's false impression to be so desirable that the target will attempt to fit it and come to see the self as the perceiver does. This is perhaps the most extreme case of the self-fulfilling prophecy, that is, when not only the target's behavior, but his or her own self-impression comes to fit the perceiver's initially false impression (Fazio et al., 1981; M. Snyder & Swann, 1978b).

In short, then, self-fulfilling prophecies can be created from initially false definitions of situations through a combination of factors: inferential errors, misperceptions, and/or reciprocal or complementary behaviors on the part of the perceiver and the target. Self-fulfilling prophecies occur for both positive and negative impressions and across a wide variety of situations. Although there are some circumstances that counter their occurrence, on the whole, biases in both the perceiver's and the target's interpretations of the meaning of behavior and social norms for reciprocating behavior would seem to favor their development.

BEHAVIOR AS HYPOTHESIS TESTING ABOUT THE SELF

Behavior is often used by the self to try out new roles or styles. The college freshman may leave his nickname Johnny back in high school in favor of the more dignified John for his college professors and classmates. A young woman may use a party at which she knows very few people to try out a new, more sophisticated style of behavior. After a junior year abroad in Paris, a young man may affect a Francophile image, adopting a European style of dress, punctuating his speech with French phrases, and going only to foreign films, to see how others will respond to him. Major life transitions or nonoverlapping sets of activities give a person the chance to develop a new image, because the people in the new situation have no knowledge of what one was like before. Sometimes, these new transitions are successful, so much so that when an individual is put back into an old setting, perhaps a high school reunion or a visit home to see family, the occasion feels peculiar because people are responding to the self in a way that no longer seems appropriate or valid. At other times the transitions are unsuccessful. For example, the pseudosophisticate at the party may discover she is attracting men she does not like and so may return to the more familiar image she had before.

The fact that people need behavior as feedback for hypotheses about the self suggests at least two important things about self-knowledge. First, it suggests that self-knowledge has limits, and one cannot always get a sense of what one will be like in a situation without actually trying out the situation. Second, it makes clear the fact that self-knowledge and how one feels about one's self-presentation can be heavily determined by the social context in which the self behaves and how others react to the self, what G. H. Mead (1934) called the "looking glass self."

Typically individuals seek out people, situations, and feedback that will confirm their beliefs about themselves, rather than those that will disconfirm them (Swann, 1983). If I am at a party and want to feel like and project the image of a fun-loving, happy-go-lucky person, I will likely avoid my colleague who makes me feel like a boring old academician in favor of the company of other fun-loving types. At the end of the party, assuming it has been successful, I will have one more occasion to draw on to bolster my fun-loving self-image. A series of studies by Swann and Read (1981b) suggests that this tendency is fairly widespread. In one study, subjects were led to believe that others' evaluations of them would be either consistent or inconsistent with their own self-image. When given a chance to see these evaluations, subjects spent more time perusing the consistent than the inconsistent feedback. Surprisingly, this was true even when the others' evaluations were negative, such as a belief that one is basically disliked by others.

In their second study, Swann and Read found that when interacting with others, people tend to use behavioral strategies that confirm their self-conceptions rather than those that disconfirm them, and that this tendency is especially strong when one believes others have incorrect beliefs about the self. To take a hypothetical example, suppose you learn that a professor considers you to be an *idiot savant* who knows a lot about psychology but almost nothing about any other topic; you may, if you believe yourself to be a well-informed person, go out of your way in the next meeting to demonstrate your widely diverse interests and abilities so as to change your professor's opinion and bolster your own self-conception (see also Swann & Read, 1981a).

If all else fails in this self-verification effort, you can, of course, preferentially recall the things you did that are consistent with your self-conception, ignoring those that were inconsistent. In Swann and Read's third study, they found that this, too, is an effective way of bolstering self-conceptions. The quest for confirming self-relevant information is so insistent that people will even pay more money for consistent than inconsistent feedback (Swann & Read, 1981a). That is, subjects were given one dollar and told they could spend a dime for each piece of feedback they wanted. They could keep any unspent money. Subjects spent more when the feedback confirmed their self-impressions.

So far, then, it would appear that people use the same confirmatory search processes in testing hypotheses about themselves that they use in testing hypotheses about others. However, we have seen one important difference: the nature of the to-be-tested hypotheses is fixed by prior self-conceptions. When people are induced to assess hypotheses about themselves that are discrepant with their prior self-conceptions, will they also use hypothesis-testing confirmatory strategies? Or will they use strategies that confirm their prior self-conception? For example, if you think of yourself as an extravert, but are induced to reflect upon your introverted qualities, will your hypothesis-testing preferentially examine introversion? The answer appears to be yes.

For example, in one study by M. Snyder & Skrypnek (1981) subjects were first tested on a sex-role inventory (S. L. Bem, 1981) to see if they were primarily masculine, primarily feminine, or androgynous (balanced in masculine and feminine attributes) in their personal attributes. The subjects were then asked to assess their suitability for a job that demanded either typically masculine attributes or typically feminine ones. Regardless of their actual sex-role identity, subjects selectively reported self-relevant information consistent with the requirements of the job, leading them to see themselves as qualified for the position. Not only was evidence supporting the hypothesis preferentially recalled but only supportive evidence predicted final perceptions of the job's suitability for the self. Thus, even when recalled, self-relevant evidence that conflicted with the hypothesis being tested did not affect judgments. Apparently, we can behave ourselves into believing even contradictory hypotheses about ourselves (see also Swann, 1983).

M. Snyder and Skrypnek's study (1981) as well as others (Gergen, 1977; McGuire & Padawer-Singer, 1976; Tedeschi & Lindskold, 1976; see Swann & Hill, 1982, for a discussion) imply that the self-concept is an infinitely malleable entity, subject to whatever hypothesis is being assessed at the moment. Although people may be induced to assess or entertain hypotheses about themselves that conflict with self-conceptions, both experience and extensive research on self-concept (e.g., Block, 1981; Schein, 1956; Wylie, 1979) tell us that such changes may not last for long. When do discrepant hypotheses last and when are they rejected? One condition may be whether or not one has the opportunity to refute inconsistent feedback. Having been miscast by another person, the opportunity to turn him or her around by using behavioral strategies that reverse the other's impressions can undo the false conception in both the other's mind and one's own mind. When allowed to go unchallenged, however, discrepant hypotheses may eventually be accepted by both the evaluator and the self (Swann & Hill, 1982).

When people do not have a chance to undo these misconceptions, how permanent are the alterations in their own self-concept? The answer seems to be, not very permanent. After a few days, any influence of miscasting effects on self-perceptions seems to disappear (Swann & Hill, 1982). Very possibly, people see themselves behaving as they always have, and fall back into their old self-evaluative ways, as the implications of miscasting fade with time. Apparently, then, even when one has effectively convinced oneself of the appropriateness of some new self-conception (as in M. Snyder and Skrypnek's 1981 study described earlier), those alterations in self-conception have little long-term impact (see also L. Ross et al., 1975).

Another factor that favors consistency in self-image is the fact that people have access to their own past history and to internal physiological states that can, at least on some occasions, give them direct feedback about their reactions to some situation. In one study (Valins & Ray, 1967), for example, snake phobics were given false physiological feedback suggesting that they were no longer afraid of snakes. When given the chance to approach, touch, and pick up the snake, many were able to do so, compared with snake phobics who had not received the false feedback. To an observer, the snake phobics would have appeared by their behavior to have accepted the implications of the false feedback and concluded they were no longer afraid of snakes. However, when asked to rate their own fear, the phobics indicated that they were as fearful of snakes as ever. One possible explanation for the discrepancy is that the acts of touching and picking up the snake had yielded a very unambiguous physiological reaction of fear that could not be overriden by false feedback (see Nisbett & Valins, 1972). In fact, a series of similar studies showed the same pattern; subjects who had been given false feedback suggesting a new attitude tried out the implications of the feedback behaviorally, discovered that no change in their initial attitude was necessary, and thus maintained their initial position on the issue (see Nisbett & Valins, 1972).

Finally, consistency in self-image is maintained by the fact that in life, just as in some experiments (Swann & Read, 1981a, 1981b), people select and interpret their own situations and may do so, in part, to gain self-confirming feedback (Swann, 1983). For example, consider the choice of dress for a party. The woman who chooses boots and jeans is trying to convey a different image than the woman in the flower print shirtwaist. Moreover, which of these women will attract the bearded man in the leather vest and which will attract the clean-cut fellow in the alligator shirt? Which pair will end up talking about the marijuana crop in Humboldt County and which pair will evaluate the area's tennis clubs? Blatant stereotyping aside, people clearly choose signs and symbols in their clothes that say a lot about who they are. They then attract and/or gravitate to the people who are consistent with their image, and engage in conversations that confirm their image and values.

Moreover, even when feedback is disconfirming, it may be interpreted as confirming. For example, suppose Alligator Shirt tells Print Shirtwaist that she seems independent. She may not think so. What factors favor her ignoring or treating this information as consistent? First, the norms of polite conversation suggest that the point will receive little attention: Print Shirtwaist will act surprised, and Alligator Shirt, realizing that she is not entirely pleased by his observation, will probably drop it. Second, Print Shirtwaist may well forget the remark, since it is inconsistent information, and she has little prior information to assimilate it to; hence it may get lost in the conversational shuffle.

Finally, Print Shirtwaist may reinterpret the remark ("He was probably referring to the fact that I came to this party by myself") and thereby dismiss the significance of the remark.

To summarize, then, although people can be induced to test hypotheses about the self that disconfirm the self-image, typically the self-image strays in the direction of consistency with past impressions of the self. Consistency is maintained via signs and symbols that are intended to convey a particular image, by association with individuals and situations that are consistent with one's self-image, by strategies of social interaction that seek to confirm the self-image, and by selective recall, dismissal, and/or interpretation of self-relevant information (see Swann, 1983).

HYPOTHESIS TESTING ONE'S ABILITY: ATTRIBUTE UNCERTAINTY AND TASK DIAGNOSTICITY

So far, we have considered hypothesis testing about the self primarily in terms of how one assesses one's own social and personality attributes. In this section, we consider how people assess their abilities using the feedback of their own behavior.

Trope (1975, 1979, 1980, 1983) maintains that in order to make future outcomes predictable and controllable, people need to assess their abilities accurately. Achievement situations provide people with an opportunity to gain ability information. Trope predicts that, in the absence of extrinsic social or material factors that might induce people to save face or strive to succeed, people pick tasks that give them the most information about their abilities. Tasks on which differences in abilities lead to large performance differences are termed *diagnostic;* they are especially likely to be selected by a person because they will provide a lot of ability-related information (Trope, 1979). For example, if a particular individual wanted to know how good he was at spatial abilities, he would probably not pick a child's puzzle or Rubik's Cube to solve: anyone can do the first task; few people can do the second task, and those who can do it may solve it for reasons other than spatial ability. Accordingly, the kind of task this individual would pick might be a set of embedded figures graded in difficulty (e.g., triangles hiding amidst an ever more complex forest of geometric shapes). Seeing how many he can solve would then provide some information about his ability.

Other things being equal, people are most likely to pick highly diagnostic tasks on attributes about which they are most uncertain (Trope, 1979; Trope & Ben-Yair, 1982). For example, an accountant with a dubious romantic reputation is likely to choose a diagnostic social skills task over an arithmetic test, whereas the social butterfly who is trying to decide whether or not to fill out a tax form without assistance will choose the arithmetic test over the social skills test. People will also choose tasks that are maximally diagnostic at the point on which they are most uncertain (Trope, 1979). Thus, for example, if you know you are moderately good on some ability (e.g., pistol shooting), you are unlikely to choose a task that is highly diagnostic at low levels of that ability (e.g., shooting at a standing target at close range); rather, you should pick a task that is diagnostic within the moderate range (e.g., shooting at a slowly moving target at moderate range).

The need to assess one's abilities extends to situations of success and failure. When subjects expect to succeed, they select tasks on which their successful performance will also be informative; likewise, when subjects expect to fail, they select tasks on which failure is diagnostic (Trope, 1979). Uncertainty and task diagnosticity also predict performance; more effort is expended when both uncertainty and task diagnosticity are high than when they are low. Consistent success or consistent failure on a diagnostic task prompts people to stop working on a task sooner (Trope & Ben-Yair, 1982). In sum, Trope's work demonstrates that self-assessment is an important determinant of task selection, especially when knowledge of an ability is uncertain. Presumably, accurate self-assessment enables people to anticipate and control their future performance (see also Buckert, Meyer, & Schmalt, 1979; Trope & Bassok, 1982).

Trope's findings might seem to be at odds with the research discussed in other portions of this chapter. Most notably, M. L. Snyder and his colleagues maintain that we often strive to present our abilities in ambiguous terms in order to enhance impressions others have of us. In contrast, M. Snyder, Swann, and their colleagues have stressed the consistency-seeking aspects of behavioral hypothesis testing. In fact, there may be no contradictions. Different conditions are likely to favor accuracy, self-enhancement, and consistency. For example, public scrutiny of one's actions or an outcome that has strong implications of success or failure may make self-enhancement needs salient. Highlighting one's past behavior may increase pressures toward consistency. But if people are truly to predict and control their environment, then accuracy is important too, and it is to such needs that Trope's work speaks.

Summary

The relationship between cognitions and behavior is complex and elusive. A number of factors influence when and how cognitions and behavior will cohere. Cognitions may be more consistent with behaviors that are prototypic for those cognitions. Measuring cognitions and behavior at a comparable level of specificity is another approach to making the relationship clearer. Attitudes formed from direct experience and/or attitudes that reflect self-interest predict behavior well, and these facts may have implications for the cognition-behavior relationship more generally. Situational factors moderate cognition-behavior consistency by making such factors as social norms or prior attitudes salient. And finally, individual differences in how people approach a situation (e.g., self-monitoring and self-consciousness) influence what cognitions will be salient and guide behavior.

Under some circumstances, the relationship between cognitions and behavior can be strong, as when people use behavior to convey particular impressions to others. Most commonly, people wish to communicate a positive impression. They do so by matching another's behavior with similar behavior, conforming to situational norms, speaking well of themselves, maintaining an appearance of consistency between their attitudes and behavior, and complimenting the other. Efforts at successful self-presentation can also backfire, for example, when an individual flatters another for obvious ulterior motives or "leaks" negative feelings nonverbally.

Under some circumstances, individuals will deliberately present themselves in a more ambiguous or less favorable manner. Being identified as a particular type of person can constrain one's behavioral freedom, and so one may adopt strategies for making one's attributes ambiguous to preserve behavioral flexibility. Alternatively, one may present an unfavorable assessment of one's self to provide an advance excuse for an anticipated failure or substitute a less negative reason for a failure than is actually the case.

Behavior can be used to test hypotheses about both the self and others. In such cases people are apparently biased preferentially to seek out information that confirms the hypothesis. This bias has the effect of making even conjectural or tentative hypotheses look more true than they really are. In the case of hypothesis testing about the self, most hypotheses individuals seek to confirm are those that are consistent with self-image. However, when individuals are induced to consider a hypothesis about the self that runs counter to their existing self-image, they show a preference for hypothesis-confirming information, leading to support for the discrepant self-image. Overall, though, changes in self-concept induced by testing erroneous hypotheses appear to be short-lived; some hypotheses can be rejected on the basis of past history or internal cues, whereas the erroneous quality of other hypotheses may be apparent when one observes one's self behaving as one always has, and not as a new hypothesis suggests.

Under some circumstances, testing a hypothesis about a target can lead the target to behave in ways that confirm the hypothesis; such alterations in reality are termed self-fulfilling prophecies. A self-fulfilling prophecy is most likely to occur if a high status person holds some false positive impression toward a lower status target and behaves toward him or her with warm verbal and nonverbal behavior; under most circumstances, the target is likely to reciprocate the behavior, thus confirming the hypothesis. Negative expectations can also produce self-fulfilling prophecies, as when one individual expects another to be unpleasant, behaves unpleasantly in turn, and so elicits the very behavior from the target he or she anticipated.

Potential self-fulfilling prophecies can also be undermined. When individuals hold negative expectations about another, instead of behaving reciprocally (i.e., negatively), they may compensate and act positively, thus eliciting the opposite behavior of what they expected. Nonetheless, perceivers may continue to perceive the target negatively, despite having elicited disconfirming behavior. Self-fulfilling prophecies can be undermined by targets themselves when they are aware that they are being miscast and wish to undo the impression.

Finally, behavior may be used for diagnostic purposes to gain accurate information about one's own abilities. When people are uncertain about their attributes, they may choose tasks on which differences in performance provide feedback about their own standing.

Overall, then, the relationship between cognition and behavior is a complex one, moderated by situational factors, individual differences, biases in cognitive processes, and variations in social goals. In some cases behavior is used to improve the accuracy of one's cognitions; in other cases, self-enhancement is the goal; and in other cases, the desire to be consistent with prior cognitions is predominant.

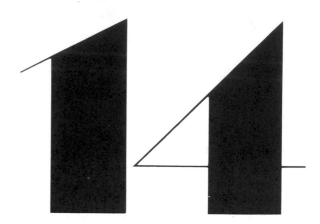

14

Taking the long view on the field of social cognition, one may find it useful to look at where the field has been and where it is going. What questions does the research answer, and what questions does it not

conclusion

even ask? Both sets of questions are determined by the characteristics of the field itself. Research on social cognition is guided by no single theoretical framework. Of course, the same is true of other subfields of social psychology, such as attitudes, small groups, interpersonal attraction, and more. Instead, the research consists of relatively autonomous topics, linked by some shared assumptions and a common interest.

The shared assumptions in social cognition research are those described in the opening chapter. Looking back to the beginning of the book, recall that social cognition research shares these basic features: a concentration on mentalistic explanations, a commitment to process analysis, and cross-fertilization between cognitive and social psychology. Within these broad outlines lies a rich variety of (sometimes isolated) theories and approaches.

Nevertheless, all research on social cognition is concerned with how people make sense of other people and themselves. As such, it is a fearfully complex enterprise, and researchers must exploit every useful approach. A fascinating array of insights has been gained even in the short run, and perhaps the best way to review them is to work through an example of one person trying to understand another person. In reviewing the insights of social cognition, we will see how the social perceiver typically simplifies the world, aiming more for sufficient, rapid understanding rather than accurate, slower understanding. After that, we will critique the field and point to some possible directions for the future.

Review of the Material Covered

As a continuing example through this chapter, suppose you are trying to make sense of a new roommate. Part One of this book concerned the elements that your understanding would comprise, and Part Two concerned the processes you would use to reach this understanding. Part Three concerned the links of your understanding to your emotional reaction to your roommate (affect), to your roommate's influence on your attitudes, and to your behavior toward your roommate.

ELEMENTS OF SOCIAL COGNITION:
ATTRIBUTIONS, CONTROL, AND SCHEMATA

Attributions   First among the elements of understanding your new roommate would be translating the person's behavior into an overall impression. To do this, you have to decide what causes the person's behavior, for example, which behaviors result from stable underlying personality traits and which from situational constraints. Attribution researchers focus on people's causal explanations for behavior (Chapter 2). Their most basic assumptions are these: first, people are motivated to predict and control their social environment; and second, to do this, they have to understand the constants in the environment. Attribution theories are concerned with how people infer constants in the social environment.

For example, most attribution theorists would posit that you want to understand your roommate in part so you can predict your shared environment, for example, whether late-night noise or early-morning clatter (or both or neither) is going to be the rule. If you understand the causes of a particular racket (e.g., an emergency call from home or an early doctor's appointment), you have some sense of whether the noise will reoccur. In single, externally caused instances, you can predict low probability of their reoccurrence. However, a roommate with an 8 a.m. class or a regular metabolic high point at 4 a.m. is likely to be noisy every morning on a fairly predictable basis. Prediction can be based on an analysis of the causes of behavior.

In addition to assuming that causal analysis is catalyzed by a need for prediction and control, attribution researchers at first assumed that the analysis itself is fairly rational and complete. Attribution researchers originally were guided by the naive scientist viewpoint. That is, your attribution about commotion at 4 a.m. will be based on finding out the relevant facts and combining them in a logical manner, at least in the clear light of day, if not when you're tossing and turning. According to early attribution theories, if you fail to analyze rationally, it may be for motivational reasons such as thinking the racket was deliberately targeted at you.

Researchers also presume that causal attributions are important and influence other cognitions, feelings, and behavior. Indeed, the application of attribution research to a wide range of social phenomena suggests that this indeed is the case (Chapter 3). Achievement attributions are a prime example. Analyzing the causes of your roommate's failure to pass a midterm exam will determine how you feel about the failure, what you expect for the future, and whether you volunteer tutoring help or not. Research on sex-role stereotypes suggests that your roommate's gender and the task characteristics may well influence your attributing the failure to ability (if the failed task is gender incongruent) or to effort, luck, or task (if congruent). Other applied research suggests that attributions also are important in understanding the impact of rewards, helping, depression, therapy, and romantic attraction. A major strength of this research has been an enhanced understanding of the dimensions of causality (locus, controllability, and stability) and their impact on cognitions, affect, and behavior. That is, several attributional dimensions affect your responses to your roommate: whether a particular failure was precipitated by internal or external causes that were controllable or not and that were stable or not. Analyses of these dimensions were presumed to proceed in a fairly rational, quasi-scientific manner.

Attribution researchers recently have discovered the limits of the naive scientist view of the social perceiver (Chapter 4). Your analysis of your roommate's behavior is likely to be imperfect not only for motivational reasons but also for purely cognitive reasons. For example, the actor-observer effect strongly suggests that you will be biased to attribute your roommate's nocturnal noise (or morning irritability, for that matter) to dispositional rather than situational causes, but your own noise to temporary frustrations. Also, you will underestimate the importance of consensus information: if your roommate claims that nine out of ten undergraduates are irritable before breakfast, you may be disinclined to let that carry any weight in your judgment that your roommate has an irritable streak. Another attributional tendency includes the self-serving bias, which leads you to believe that success is due to your own efforts, not to situational factors. And the self-centered bias suggests that people overestimate their contribution to shared tasks (you think you do more of the dorm chores than your roommate thinks you do). Taken together, the biases all suggest that your perceptions of anyone, including your roommate, are likely to be somewhat self-centered and difficult to change. This conclusion, of course, conflicts with the rational, naive scientist view of people. It also foreshadows the cognitive miser view that reflects people's focus on efficient rather than accurate understanding.

Researchers on attribution exposed other limitations of the original formulations besides these theoretical differences. For example, methodological and empirical problems arise as well. The simplest version of the internal-external (person-situation) dimension fails to capture much empirical support. And attributions do not yet link clearly enough to other variables. In part, these problems occur because the models are lacking, and in part because the methods often do not track the complexity of the models that do exist.

Despite such theoretical and empirical shortcomings, attribution theories and research have had a mammoth impact on social psychology. Although naive psychology is not a coherent framework that can tie together the somewhat disparate attribution theories, it has been a tremendously useful approach for generating research and understanding. And, more important, attributions themselves are a theoretically necessary link in understanding social cognition. You directly observe your roommate's behavior; you do not directly observe traits. Yet, traits are a primary tool that you and people in general use to think about people. It is necessary, then, to know how people make the inferences that take them from the behavior to the traits. Attribution theories tackle precisely that crucial issue.

Control The social perceiver attempts to identify the internal causes (of which traits are one) or the external causes of other people's behavior. One reason for this effort is the attempt to control or at least to predict one's environment, as we have said. Psychological control thus motivates the attribution process.

The importance of control becomes particularly clear when it is threatened (Chapter 5). People engage in a variety of reactions to a loss of control. They often seek information in an attempt to regain control. They react poorly to stress when control is lost, and they may show reactance and anger or helplessness and possibly depression. Only under rare circumstances do people voluntarily give up control, as when they engage in overlearned (mindless) behavior.

Given the importance of control as an element of social cognition, it is not surprising that research has focused on various means by which people attempt to regain control. Consider, for example, what might happen if your roommate acquired an especially talkative parrot. Assuming that the bird was uncontrollably noisy all the time, how might you react to the loss of control over your audio environment? Six types of control have been identified. Behavior control might consist of putting a cloth over its cage. Cognitive control might consist of trying to think differently about the bird's chatter, say, as a source of entertainment. Decision control might consist of making the conscious choice not to report your roommate's illegal pet to the dorm council. Information control might consist of reading up on the talking habits of parrots, so you would have some sense of when the bird was most likely to be chatty. Retrospective control might consist of understanding after the fact why your roommate bought the foolish bird, and what you might do to prevent the development of an entire aviary in your living quarters. And finally, you would be exerting secondary control if you simply decided not to let the bird aggravate you and ignored it. The methods of restoring control all rely on cognitive and behavioral changes designed to reduce stress.

The settings in which researchers have demonstrated control to be beneficial include the stresses of urban crowding and of medical problems. However, a sense of control can be harmful, too, as research also has shown. For example, one can have an illusion of control over events for which no control, in fact, exists. That is, your roommate's beating you at poker may be determined in a large part by chance, but you are unlikely to give up the notion that you have more control than you do. Alternatively, one can have too much control and become overloaded. For example, your roommate might ask you to make all the decisions for your joint activities, which would be not only disconcerting but also too much to manage. One can also have the wrong kind of control or ineffective control. That is, you might think you can control your roommate's annoying clutter by nagging, cleaning up, or negotiating, but in fact, there may be nothing you can do about it. You might feel temporarily in control and satisfied if your roommate says that polite reminders will cure the clutter, but if they do not work, you will be more irritated than if you were not promised the possibility of control. Individual differences in one's chronic expectations about control qualify the impact of most of these variables. In sum, control is a key element of social cognition.

Schemata   People's attributions and their efforts to control their environment are influenced heavily by a third cognitive element, social schemata. In the effort to make attributions and maintain control, people gather information and, over time, form general expectations about the content and operations of the social world. A schema is a cognitive structure that contains the attributes of a concept and the relationships among those attributes. Social perceivers use schemata to simplify their understanding of the social world. Knowing what to expect from other people, oneself, social roles, and social events, one can focus one's energies on the most relevant features of the situation. That is, schemata often guide perception, memory, and inference toward consistency with prior expectations. This is another example of rapid, efficient understanding at the price of maximal accuracy. However, under some circumstances, schema-driven processing allows one to notice the ways that the data contradict one's expectations.

For example, if your roommate fits the extravert prototype, your schema for that kind of *person* will facilitate your ability to remember all the times people were invited over or the occasions on which you two talked all night. Person schemata include not only traits such as extraversion but also goals, such as trying to make friends. Just as you have schemata for your roommate's traits and goals, you have schemata for your own personality; your *self-schema* is a complex, easily accessible verbal self-portrait that speeds relevant memory and inferences. Self-schemata appear to develop along those dimensions of one's personality that are distinctive.

In a fashion similar to person and self-schemata, *role* schemata describe the appropriate norms and behavior for broad social categories, based on age, race, sex, and occupation. For example, your role schema for students will help you to notice and remember your roommate's cramming for exams and propensity for long intellectual debates. People tend to perceive, interpret, and remember information in ways that confirm their schemata, particularly for groups of which they are not members. Disconfirming or incongruent information requires more effort to process; if that effort is made, it may be well remembered. That is, if you explain or otherwise elaborate the fact that you know a student who never wears blue jeans, you will remember that discrepancy.

Finally, *event* schemata contain people's prior knowledge of the typical sequence of events on standard social occasions such as parties or final exams; event schemata, like other schemata, help people to understand ambiguous information, to remember relevant information, and to infer consistent information where it is missing. A rather different kind of social schema consists entirely of rules for linking content but not much content. This type of *content-free* or procedural schema, like the other four, largely guides perception, inference, and memory toward schema-consistent information.

Schemata grow and change in fairly predictable ways. The perseverance effect describes how schemata resist change by reinterpreting even mixed or contradictory information to fit the schema, unless people monitor themselves closely or try counterarguing their own schemata. Schemata are created in the first place by exposure to relevant instances. As schemata develop they become more abstract, more complex, more organized, more compact, and often more moderate. Your well-developed schema for students is likely to have such features.

In any given instance, schemata are most likely to be activated or cued if they have been used recently or frequently. Observational purpose, as well as affect and motivation, may cue some schemata rather than others. If you think about athletics frequently, or if you are trying to form an impression of your roommate's suitability for the intramural team, your athlete schema is likely to be cued.

Often an instance is only a partial fit to a schema; in such cases, typical schematic effects may be moderated or the schema may change. If your lean muscular roommate also has two left feet, he or she is not exactly a perfect fit to the athlete schema, so you may be less certain that your roommate possesses other stereotypically athletic attributes. Alternatively, schemata can change upon encounters with incongruent information. People may subtype others as special cases of their category, as when you create a new "clumsy athlete" subcategory for your roommate, leaving the overall athlete schema intact. When schemata do change, it appears to be through a gradual bookkeeping type of process, rather than a sudden conversion. If you meet several somewhat clumsy athletes, you may gradually change your schema for athletes as coordinated. If you meet one incredibly clumsy athlete, you probably will not be converted to a new athlete schema.

Overall, the schema concept implies principles that potentially cut across attributions, beliefs about control, and other elements of social cognition. The schema concept is useful only when integrated with specific theories of social information processing. Nevertheless, it is clear that schemata usually operate in the interest of efficiency, if not accuracy.

PROCESSES OF SOCIAL COGNITION

None of the elements of social understanding—attributions, control, or schemata—by themselves do anything. Only when incorporated into the processes of attending, remembering, and inferring does any action occur.

Attention   Some level of attention is a prerequisite for storing external information in long-term memory (Chapter 7). What stimuli, then, typically capture attention? What aspects of your roommate are likely to be the focus of your social cognitive processes?

Salient features of other people include the ways they are figural or stand-outs relative to the environment. Attention will focus on statistical novelties, such as riding a unicycle or having red hair, and on contextual novelties, such as wearing a cowboy hat (outside the Southwest) or a leotard (except at an art school). Attention also focuses on negative or extreme behavior. Most people do not kick their dogs, or overreact to the joys and sorrows of daily life; people who do such negative or extreme things draw attention and comment. In these ways, attention is drawn to stimuli that deviate from prior expectations. Attention is also drawn to social stimuli that are perceptually figural: bright, moving, or complex. Your roommate's sitting under the lamp, constantly jiggling foot, or paisley shirt are most likely to draw attention, compared to more perceptually subtle aspects of your roommate's attributes.

Having captured your attention, these salient features will draw relatively extreme opinions. Your causal attributions also will overrely on the salient features. Thus, not only will the interesting shirt or the novel unicycle elicit extreme evaluations, but they will also seem peculiarly important in your understanding of your roommate. You also may especially remember your roommate's salient attributes, and most likely they will help to organize your impression.

A conception related to salience is vividness. Whereas salience is a feature of stimuli in context, vividness is defined as an inherent feature of the stimulus itself. Unlike salience, vividness does not seem to exert a disproportionate effect on judgment. Of the various examples of vividness that have been tested, only case histories (in contrast to statistics) appear to have disproportionate impact on judgments. For example, if you are considering an exotic vacation spot, your roommate's anecdotes may be more persuasive than the most relevant quotations from the encyclopedia. In any event, the emotional and colorful features of your roommate's stories are likely to be memorable and entertaining, if not ultimately persuasive on any given point.

In interactions with roommates or anyone else, your attention is not always directed outward. Your attention may be self-focused, in which case you are likely to be thinking about various aspects of your own goals or internal standards. If you are not meeting those goals or standards, you may try to correct the situation. For example, if your roommate wants to photograph you, you may think about how fat you are and how soon you can start dieting. Or, more generally, if your roommate is the kind of person who periodically encourages you to contemplate yourself, you may reflect on how you could be more honest, kind, tidy, or hard working. Adjusting your behavior to your ideals may operate through a cycle of adjustment and comparison, set in motion by self-focused attention. If expectations for success are low or if repeated attempts create no progress, you may give up on the goal, whether it is being more honest or starting to lose weight.

Individual differences in people's propensity to focus on themselves or on the situation influence various attentional phenomena in interpersonal settings. Moreover, many of these situations are important: physical symptom reporting, test anxiety, and cheating all are affected by attentional factors.

Attention has a wide range of effects on memory, judgment, affect, and behavior. Again, it serves to focus the social perceiver mainly on that information that tends to be most useful in reaching a fairly rapid, sufficient understanding of the environment. Attention focuses on the unexpected and on the discrepant, which is a fairly effective strategy compared to focusing on what one already knows.

Memory Memory for people includes a wide range of information, which may be stored in different ways (Chapter 8). Traits may be stored in propositional networks, behavior may be stored in a sequential code, and appearance may be stored in image form.

The richness and organization of person memory is affected by one's task purpose. For example, suppose you are watching your roommate at a party. If your purpose is to empathize with your roommate, or to consider how your roommate relates to you personally, you will remember a great deal. If you are forming an impression, you also will remember a fair amount. Any psychologically engaging purpose is likely to create many links among items in memory, organized by the other person's traits, goals, or other psychological attributes. In contrast, sheer memorization does not work as well as creating alternative memory cues. Thus it should be easier to remember that your roommate typically showers at 7:45 a.m. if you consider the behavior in light of your impression of a trait of ambition or a goal of being on time for an 8:30 a.m. class, rather than if you consider the behavior as an isolated fact to memorize.

Context also determines what people remember about others and how they organize it. Dimensions that one has used frequently or recently are especially memorable. You may think of your roommate along dimensions of politeness, if you have recently been lectured on it at home, or along dimensions of liveliness, if you have just been to a party. Moreover, if either of these events is frequent, politeness or liveliness may be primed most of the time in your repertoire of personality concepts.

In real-world contexts, people encounter others across several occasions. Hence memory may be organized by person or by occasions. Frequently encountered individuals are likely to become entities in memory in and of themselves, whereas unfamiliar individuals may not be. That is, you probably think of your roommate as an individual who has various attributes (politeness, liveliness). Other people may not be so individualized in your memory; in effect they are instead organized by situations or other attributes (the lively crowd, the people in your statistics class, your friends from freshman year).

As a general rule, memory for raw data is dominated by memory for the organizing theme and the inferences that resulted from it. You are more likely on the whole to remember your judgments about your roommate than the behaviors that gave rise to them.

In short, a great deal is becoming known about the contents, organization, and processes of person memory. As with research on attributions, control, schemata, and attention, it appears that memory processes often operate in the service of efficiency more than accuracy.

Inference   The third process examined here, social inference, reinforces this last point (Chapter 9). People fall short of thorough normative models for reaching inferences. Social perceivers often select relevant data on the basis of a prior theory. They are usually insensitive to sampling biases. People frequently estimate probabilities inaccurately, but often with great confidence. People often combine information badly, and they are relatively poor at judging covariation.

To take an example, suppose you have to estimate the probability that your roommate will become class president. To make that judgment, you need to decide whether your roommate is organized and outgoing enough to be a successful candidate. Suppose you think about your roommate's behavior around you and your friends and decide, yes, your roommate is both organized and outgoing. In effect, however, you have drawn a biased sample. Your roommate may not be organized and outgoing around other groups of people. Like most people, you would tend to underestimate biases in the sampling of information.

Furthermore, you may overestimate the likelihood of winning the election (a low-probability event) on the grounds of your prior theories about your roommate's charismatic personality. When you try to combine your observations from several settings, you may think you are weighting them all appropriately and carefully, but in fact, you are likely to rely on only a few observations or to be thrown off by your hunches.

Next, suppose you have a covariation judgment about your roommate's outgoing behavior. Obviously, if being outgoing is confined to situations in which quantities of alcohol are consumed, then your roommate may be too shy and withdrawn at other times to be a good candidate. Unfortunately, you are unlikely to be a good judge of the covariation between your roommate's outgoing behavior and amount of alcohol consumed, even if you believe that alcohol makes people extraverted. Your general belief will make you overestimate the specific link between alcohol and extraversion in your roommate's case. Prior theories (or schemata) bias many kinds of inference. One of the ways people are efficient at the cost of accuracy is by relying on their existing theories and not examining the data carefully. Finally, after the election returns are in, you are likely to overestimate the predictability of the outcome.

The social perceiver conserves scarce resources by taking shortcuts; heuristics reduce complex inferential processes to simpler ones. Representativeness, for example, entails estimating probabilities by categorizing an object and then making the judgment on the basis of the category rather than the individual involved. If you decide that your roommate is a good example of a southerner, you may decide about friendliness and warmth on that basis rather than by carefully observing your roommate.

Another heuristic is availability. You may judge your roommate's extraversion by the ease with which examples come to mind. If extraverted behavior is more memorable than introverted behavior, then the availability heuristic will lead you astray. A third heuristic is anchoring and adjustment; if you think most people at your school are fairly introverted, that may bias your initial estimates of your roommate's personality. A fourth heuristic is called the simulation heuristic. It involves imagining the actual outcome in comparison to the possible alternatives. If your roommate lost the election by one vote, it is easy to imagine how the outcome might have been otherwise; therefore it is very frustrating.

By now, you may be wondering about your ability to form an accurate impression of your roommate—or you may be thinking that none of these biases apply to you. Unfortunately, your insight into your own cognitive processes is likely to be limited as well. Even taking a course in social cognition may not improve your accuracy or your insight a great deal. Nevertheless, as is true of most people, you manage to muddle along. The intuitive strategies you have developed probably work fairly accurately in ordinary life.

Designing research Formal procedures for studying cognitive processes have developed in recent years (Chapter 10). Process analysis consists of specifying the steps in a detailed model (A $\rightarrow$ B $\rightarrow$ C) that includes nonobservable processes such as attention, retrieval, and inference. Process measurement consists of finding observable traces of the nonobservable processes.

Traditionally, process models have been studied piecemeal, step by step, in separate investigations, which sometimes produced errors of inference. Short-comings in the early approaches led to a search for other methods to supplement them. First, new *manipulations* provide consensual solutions to some standard types of process analyses. Some manipulations focus on locating the stage of a particular effect (e.g., attention or retrieval), and others emphasize the channel of an effect (e.g., audio or visual). New process *measures* focus in turn on tracing the processes of attention, memory, and inference by fine-grained techniques. Finally, new *methodologies* allow the examination of an entire model at once: computer simulation and structural modeling are beginning to be used in social cognition research.

The new manipulations, measures, and methods vary in their utility. Some provide ambiguous results, others are intrusive, and others are overly confining with regard to other methods. In addition to these methodological pitfalls, the conceptual assumptions are not always entirely valid. Some processes may not be cognitively mediated, for example. Some assumptions about capacity limitation may be unwarranted. We will return to these issues in a moment, as they contribute to more general points about the study of social cognition.

BEYOND COGNITION

In Parts One and Two we examined the elements of social cognition and the processes whereby the elements develop, change, and interact, as well as some tools for studying some of them. At this point, we turned to connecting research on cognitions with other factors important in social settings: affect, attitudes, and behavior. The links are not simple, but some intriguing progress has been made in understanding them.

Affect   Cognition has several possible roles in affective responses (Chapter 11). In some views, cognition is less important in determining affect than are physiological factors such as autonomic arousal and facial feedback. But several viewpoints emphasize the interface between cognition and affect, and researchers have only just begun to address them.

Some researchers hold the view that cognition creates affect. Specifically, arousal combines with a cognitive interpretation to yield affect. If you are feeling upset and you cognitively interpret it as caused by your roommate rather than an exam, your affective response may be anger, rather than anxiety. In some views, arousal is created initially by the interruption of behavior directed toward one's goals. How one cognitively interprets that arousal determines one's affective responses. To return to the roommate example, you may need your roommate's help to accomplish a certain vital goal (such as passing the chemistry exam or driving South at spring break); if you do depend on your roommate, he or she has the power to help you or hurt you. Your roommate can facilitate or interrupt your goal-directed activity, which causes emotional responses, both positive and negative.

Related cognitive views hold that affective responses are a function of fitting new information to affect-laden knowledge structures. The complexity of a knowledge structure influences the extremity of affective responses, with simplicity creating extremity. An example of this simplicity-extremity link would be your evaluations of the unfamiliar crowd at another dorm or school. Because you know little about them, you are likely to see them as all good or all bad. In contrast, a group with which you are very familiar (e.g., the people on your own floor) may be evaluated in less extreme terms. A second view of affect as related to knowledge structures suggests that tighter organization of knowledge over time also creates more extreme responses. This effect of time operates as follows: the more you think about something, the more organized and extreme your evaluations. The more you mull over the virtues and flaws of a particular professor, for example, the more you will like or dislike him or her. Finally, a third view suggests that good fit between prior knowledge structures and new information creates affective responses. If you admire professors in general, and you encounter a professor who is a perfect fit to your stereotype of academics, you will respond quite favorably. If you encounter a professor who is not such a good fit, you may respond more moderately.

Another set of cognitive theories suggests that perceptions of one's outcomes create affective responses. Interpretations of actual past outcomes, imagined alternative past outcomes, and imagined alternative future outcomes all generate affect. Suppose you are judging your roommate's chances of getting into medical school on the basis of his or her academic skills. You decide that a distinguished record in science courses is due mainly to effort; in that case, you will feel more proud of your roommate than if the good record were due to easy exams. Alternative outcomes that might have been can cause emotional reactions, too. If you realize that your roommate missed an A by one point, at least one of you will be more frustrated than if the A was missed by a wide margin. And alternative outcomes that might yet be create affect, such as the suspense before medical school decisions are mailed out or the conflict over where to go, if admitted to more than one. Research on all these possible cognitive bases of affect is sparse to date, but there is some initial progress.

Affect influences cognition, too. Suppose your roommate gets into medical school and your own graduate future looks promising, too: you may be in a cheerful or even euphoric mood. In that case, you are likely to think of all the positive aspects of your life, to remember positive material, to be helpful to others, to solve problems quickly and easily, and generally to be a Pollyanna. Negative feelings can have similar effects, except that people may try to escape them.

If your affective responses become sufficiently strong, they may interrupt ongoing cognitive activity. Particularly if your responses are negative, it is difficult to concentrate on the goal at hand. Urgent emotional demands or a sense of anxiety can cause a reassessment and change in direction.

In contrast to the preceding views that link affect and cognition, it is also possible that affect can be autonomous of cognition under some circumstances. For example, you may not be able cognitively to identify the title of your roommate's favorite record, but you may like its familiar feel nonetheless. Similarly, you may not remember all the reasons you are fond of your roommate, but you may still feel that way. In sum, the relationships between affect and cognition are multiple and complex, but progress is being made toward understanding them.

Attitudes Attitudes incorporate affect, cognition, and behavioral tendencies. As such, they are an interesting domain for exploring the relationships among the three (Chapter 12). The subset of recent attitude research that focuses on the cognitive mediation of persuasion shows some of the utility of cognitive approaches applied to a well established field of inquiry. Cognitive approaches focus on traditional variables, such as communicator credibility, message characteristics, and audience factors. As a running example of attitudes and cognition in action, suppose your busy and versatile roommate is trying to persuade you that your poster collection is tacky. Attributional approaches to this persuasion attempt hinge on your perception of the message's validity. If you think the arguments are not really due to your roommate's refined artistic taste, but instead are motivated by your roommate's pushy personality, or by an impending parental visit, you might decide that the posters are fine. To the extent that your roommate is a cultivated person who haunts art galleries, you might believe the argument. Also, if everyone else you know also suggests hanging the posters in your closet, you might accept the hint.

Cognitive responses to persuasion can reveal the fine-grained processes that underlie attitude change. For example, researchers suggest that if your roommate is a credible communicator about art and if you do not care about the posters, you may not think much about the various arguments and simply accept them without a fight. To the extent your roommate is not credible, you may counterargue the criticisms, either privately or publicly. In any case, your attitude will follow on the cognitive responses generated by your evaluation of the communicator.

Message repetition and message difficulty effects also are illuminated by cognitive response analysis. Repetition of a complex message initially enhances comprehension and persuasion; for example, as your roommate tries to explain the more subtle design flaws in your poster, you may understand and start to be convinced. However, repetition can become tedious nagging. If so, it will backfire, both in the counterarguments you muster and in its intended persuasive effect.

Involvement is a key factor in most cognitive responses to persuasion. The more people care, the more they think and the more they respond to the quality and content of the message, rather than to superficial factors such as communicator attractiveness. Thus, if your poster collection was the cumulative effort of an enjoyable trip in Europe, you may evaluate your roommate's arguments more carefully than if you purchased them all together at the campus bookstore after fifteen minutes of thought.

Attitudes formed in groups are amenable to cognitive analysis, as well. People acquire information from others, and that information can persuade them, to the extent the information is new. Attitudes, whether changed by individuals or by groups, organize people's processing of attitude-relevant information. There is some evidence that people attend to consistent information or interpret information to make it consistent with their attitudes. Under some circumstances, people also remember attitude-consistent information better than inconsistent information. And people tend to recall their prior attitudes as consistent with their current attitudes.

Behavior The relationship of social cognition to behavior has been addressed on several fronts. Extrapolations from personality research suggest that cognitions are likely to predict behaviors that are prototypically related to them, but not behaviors that are less central to them. Lessons from research on attitudes and behavior suggest that cognitions will predict behavior under several conditions. The first condition is when both cognitions and behavior are measured at the same level of specificity. For example, if you want to know whether your roommate will participate in extracurricular activities (general behavior), you should inquire about your roommate's attitudes and other cognitions about clubs in general. Alternatively, if you want to predict your roommate's participating in a specific student theater production, ask about that. Attitude-behavior consistency also depends on the nature of attitude, the situation, and the person. If your roommate's attitude was formed on the basis of direct experience with extracurricular activities, it is more likely to predict behavior. Second, if the situation minimizes pressures to conform to conflicting group norms, your roommate is more likely to act on his or her attitude. Third, if your roommate is a particular kind of person (for example, a low self-monitor or high on private self-consciousness and low on public self-consciousness), he or she will attend to inner thoughts and feelings as guides to action; consequently, his or her attitude is likely to predict behavior. Other cognition-behavior relationships may show the same patterns as the research on attitudes and personality, but researchers have yet to demonstrate that the principles do in fact generalize to social cognitions. The principles serve to suggest conditions under which the cognition-behavior relationship is likely to be strong.

The cognition-behavior relationship is also fairly strong when people are concerned with self-presentation, that is, with communicating a particular set of cognitions. Thus, if you want to make a good impression on your new roommate when you first meet, you may match his or her behavior, conform to the situation, talk about your own good points, or behave in strict accord with your attitudes. You may also compliment your roommate, but flattery will not be successful if it seems insincere. Alternatively, you may choose to make an ambiguous impression (to keep your behavioral options open) or even to make a negative impression (to avoid a worse impression or to create an excuse for potential negative events). All of these are deliberate attempts to behave consistently with particular cognitions (your own intentions), in order to create particular cognitions in another person (your roommate's impression).

Finally, behavior may be related to cognition when people are testing hypotheses about themselves and others. People typically seek information that confirms their hypotheses. For example, if you think your roommate may be an extravert, you probably will ask about his or her behavior at parties (likely to yield confirmatory data) rather than in the library (likely to yield disconfirmatory data). Similarly, if you think of yourself as extraverted, you will seek evidence from others that confirms that self-concept. The confirmatory bias can lead to a self-fulfilling prophecy. That is, if you treat your roommate as extraverted, you may communicate your expectations non-verbally, and your roommate may become more extraverted as a result. However, if your roommate feels you are forming a negative or erroneous impression, he or she may deliberately behave in ways that contradict your hypothesis. Under some circumstances, people do test hypotheses in less biased ways, intentionally choosing diagnostic information rather than favorable or confirmatory information. For example, if you are uncertain about your ability to be extraverted, you may pick situations that would be informative, perhaps trying to meet new people or to see if you can give a good party. In sum, behavior can operate in the service of cognition, or vice versa, but their relationship is not simple.

SUMMARY

To summarize the summary, we have seen that some elements of social cognition include attributions, control, and schemata. Attribution theories describe how people go from observing behavior in a situation to analyzing its causes. The process is far from logical and thorough, but attributions serve the important function of granting people some sense of prediction and control over their lives. Psychological control is central to people's ability to function effectively, as is evident from their efforts to maintain control and from the effects of lost control. Schemata are one element that may provide a sense of prediction and control. They are abstract expectations about how the world generally operates, built up from past experience with specific examples. Schemata generally guide cognitive processes toward information relevant to prior knowledge. People seem to be conservative animals, by and large, with an emphasis on safeguarding their limited capacities. Efficiency, predictability, and generalization sometimes win out over accuracy about specific situations.

Various cognitive processes operate along these principles, although there are some checks and balances. Attention is captured by stimuli that are unexpected. Attention to discrepancies can set in motion an adjustment of expectations or behavior to close the gap. Memory is organized in terms of prior knowledge, although certainly it is not relentlessly fixed that way. Depending on the situation, memory can favor the retrieval of information discrepant with one's expectations. And, depending on one's goals and one's context, memory is flexible enough to be organized around different types of prior knowledge. Inferences also are heavily influenced by prior theories and shortcuts, but inferences are responsive to some forms of feedback. In short, cognitive processes tend to be conservative, but they have some built-in quality controls.

Cognitions carry over to affect, attitudes, and behavior, in many respects. Cognitions can give rise to emotional responses, to attitude change, and to behavioral strategies. But cognitions, affect, and behavior also are fairly autonomous and often do not predict each other terribly well, at least in any simple way. Each is a complex system in its own right, with some spillover to the other three. These linkages are becoming better understood all the time.

What Is Missing and How to Fill the Gaps

Having reviewed the insights gained by the last decade of research on social cognition, it is useful to see what questions remain unanswered and what questions remain unasked. Where does the field fall short of its aims, and what is likely to be done about it? The view concerning people that more or less dominates the field, as we have said, is the cognitive miser perspective. That is, the social perceiver often compromises the thorough, logical, normatively correct procedures that the naive scientist would use. Sometimes people are smart to do this; many of the shortcuts people develop work well most of the time. As a result of these important discoveries, however, research in social cognition sometimes depicts the social perceiver rather narrowly, in several respects (cf. Manis, 1977; S. E. Taylor, 1981).

First, the social perceiver is viewed primarily as a thinker, motivated to understand and predict the environment fairly efficiently, where possible. Other motives and goals are ignored. But people have other goals that differ from sheer understanding for its own sake. For example, what about the moral person? Sometimes people are motivated to think about the just, proper, or fair judgment to make, rather than the most efficient first approximation. Besides the moral person, there is the public person, who worries about saving face. There is also the amusing person, whose goal is to entertain the self or others, merely to make life more pleasant. This person thinks quirky thoughts, plays mental games, and passes the time in search of sheer delight or novelty. Similarly, there is the altruistic person, who thinks about others in order to help them, not to understand, predict, or control them. And there is the antisocial person, who thinks about others in order to hurt them.

The list could go on, but an exhaustive taxonomy of possible goals simply is not useful. The more important point is that cognition serves many masters, and efficient or accurate understanding is only one of them. The solution to this neglect of other motives and goals already is on the horizon in several places. Psychologists have recently urged research on the moral person (naive judge or naive lawyer) (Fincham & Jaspars, 1980). The public person is becoming integrated into research on social cognition by the work on impression management (Chapter 13). Person memory researchers showing the effects of goals on recall also begin to address these issues (Chapter 8).

In all fairness, the task of the field of social cognition is to help us understand how people think about other people, not to understand how they soothe their nagging consciences or protect their fragile egos. Nonetheless, the effects of various processing goals, other than simple efficient understanding, likely will continue to grow in importance.

A related point is how efficient the thinker really is. Neglecting accuracy in the interest of enhancing efficiency is one thing, but maximizing efficiency is another. Just as certainly as people are not optimally precise naive scientists, neither are they optimally efficient information processors. A whiz-kid view of the social perceiver would be just as misguided as the naive scientist view. People's understanding processes doubtless can be highly redundant, laborious, circuitous, time-consuming, and anything but efficient. Thus it is important not to overdo the role of efficiency as the main goal, nor is it appropriate to assume that efficiency is maximized even when it is a major goal.

In addition to being viewed primarily as a thinker, the social perceiver is often viewed as having a somewhat lunatic disregard for external reality. This fantasizer seems to operate solely on whatever convenient fictions are in his or her own head. While there is no doubt that social perceivers actively construct interpretations of the world around them, it is also true that reality imposes constraints on the process. Essentially this complaint has been raised by the Gibsonians, who argue for careful analyses of objective stimulus properties and of possible perceiver-stimulus interactions (Chapter 7). Perception is not all in the head; at least some of it is out in the world. The solution to this focus on the thinker as fantasizer is a thorough analysis of the actual stimuli confronting the perceiver.

The social perceiver also has been viewed as somewhat of a hermit, isolated from the social environment. Missing from much research on social cognition have been other people in a status other than that of stimulus. Other people are not simply targets; they reinforce, disagree, initiate, and otherwise actively inform the perceiver. Perception often is modified through social interaction. When people want to understand themselves and others, they may ask someone else. Problem solving often occurs not simply cognitively but also socially. Some solutions are emerging to counteract the omission of social interaction from social cognition research. One solution appears, for example, in the work on cognitive bases of attitude change in groups (Chapter 12). Elsewhere, too, social cognition research will likely begin to recognize the importance of real interaction contexts, minds in contact with other minds.

Social perception also has been viewed more or less statically. People do not take snapshots of their world; perception is not frozen in time. Perceptions are transformed as the perceiver and the environment grow and change. When the perceiver is depicted as isolated in time, he or she inevitably ends up contemplating old events, as does an archivist, because any photograph of the present immediately becomes the past. The perceiver as archivist does not contemplate the future. Yet real people constantly speculate about the future. People often run through mental simulations to predict, control, or understand their possible futures. Researchers studying plans and goals recognize this, as do those who research affect and alternative future worlds (Chapter 11).

In addition, the social perceiver often has been observed in rather impersonal, superficial, inconsequential settings, as if perceivers were dilettantes. Social perception concerning important life events and intimate relationships may differ considerably from social perception in the lab experiment. For one thing, people dedicate more effort to social understanding when the stakes are higher. They think more, if not more accurately. Applied work on social cognition recognizes this fact explicitly (Chapters 3 and 5).

Finally, people are not blank slates; they apply world knowledge specific to whatever domain they are contemplating. People draw on the resources available, and they vary in their levels of knowledge when it comes to real-world phenomena, ranging from health to politics. People may use different information-processing strategies, depending on how much or how little they know. For example, people who are moderately knowledgeable about an idea may be more sensitive to variations in a routine than are novices, who might skip over them. In addition, regardless of knowledge level, some domains may elicit different strategies than others. For example, concerns about health are more likely to implicate issues of personal control than are concerns about international politics. Similarly, understanding a specific person on your doorstep is more likely to implicate stimulus-based attentional processes, while understanding one's high school sweetheart in retrospect is more likely to implicate memory processes. Many models of social cognition are developed as if they can be independent of the particular domain of judgment, and this is clearly too narrow a view.

To summarize, social cognition research has developed models of people as thinkers, shortchanging other possible goals; as whiz kids, who are impossibly efficient; as fantasizers, ignoring objective reality; as hermits, isolated from the social environment; as archivists, forever looking backward; as dilettantes, outside of consequential social settings; and as blank slates with little domain-specific knowledge. In these senses, work on social cognition has been overly narrow.

In another sense, work on social cognition has not been narrow enough or, rather, precise enough. Theoretical coherence and methodological specificity are the twin goals of science. Refining both in social cognition work is an ongoing effort. Besides the perennial adaption of cognitive methodology that is a hallmark of this work, movements toward physiological measures, toward computer simulation, and toward more sophisticated statistical techniques represent efforts to work toward methodological precision. A lot has been learned already; the understanding of people's social thoughts has become far deeper and more complex than it was ten years ago. The fine-grained methodological approach clearly has paid off, and it will continue to do so.

Theoretical coherence is a more nebulous challenge. No area of social psychology—be it attitudes, attraction, groups, stereotyping, aggression, or altruism—profits from being totally tied down to a single theoretical perspective. Attribution theories emerged in part as a reaction to the great overarching framework formerly provided by consistency theories. Following that, an assortment of loosely linked social cognition theories of information processing has emerged. The assortment gives the field a rich range of perspectives on which to draw, but it may give the newcomer a dizzying sense of excess. And it gives the field a certain lack of cohesion. Nevertheless, the areas of consensus are important. There is a strong shared commitment to understanding the mental processes that occur when people try to understand themselves and others. And there is a message that people muddle along sufficiently well, trying to be efficient, but sometimes at a cost to accuracy and complexity.

The Future of Social Cognition Research

In a decade of concentrated research, considerable progress has been made. An exciting and fast-growing area of research came into being, and already it has created major academic enterprises (articles, books, journals) and major insightful applications (into education, health, law, politics, marketing). The applied side of social cognition research is a critical measure of its success, for two reasons. First, it provides a check on the necessarily constraining assumptions of the lab. Second, it provides a test of the usefulness of the theories. Both these points are critical to the future.

Social cognition researchers have developed elaborate models of how people make inferences when asked to do so in laboratory experiments. In the next several years researchers will probably study people's spontaneous cognitive processes when no one is asking them to think. How do people think in natural settings, when other demands are placed on them? For example, do they make as many attributions as often as social cognition researchers assume they do? When something needs explaining, it is rare that ordinary people are as thoughtful even as many social cognition models suggest. Rather, people often attend to whatever intrudes on them, remember whatever comes to mind most easily, and make inferences using very simple rules. People simplify the real world in order to get by. Stepping outside the laboratory will continue to remind researchers of these aspects of much ordinary thought.

Applications to naturalistic settings also will test the usefulness of social cognition approaches. A theory is of little use if it does not explain something of real concern. The characteristics of real-world situations in which social cognitions appear to have the most impact is important ground for future research. Where and when interventions based on social cognition research seem to work the best will continue to be a proving ground for the field of social cognition.

In a field that has witnessed an explosion of research and theory in the past ten years, consolidation of theory and research is the next likely order of business. With it, there is likely to be increasing emphasis of the roles of social cognition in affectively and behaviorally significant areas. Applied research simultaneously provides continued tests of ideas about social cognition and opportunities for impact in important social settings.

references

Aaker, D. A. *Advertising management.* Englewood Cliffs, N.J.: Prentice-Hall, 1975.

Abelson, R. P. Simulation of social behavior. In G. Lindzey & E. Aronson (Eds.), *The handbook of social psychology* (Vol. 2, 2nd ed.). Reading, Mass.: Addison-Wesley, 1968.

Abelson, R. P. Script processing in attitude formation and decision making. In J. S. Carroll & J. W. Payne (Eds.), *Cognition and social behavior.* Hillsdale, N.J.: Erlbaum, 1976.

Abelson, R. P. Constraint, construal, and cognitive science. Proceedings of the Third Annual Cognitive Science Society Conference, Berkeley, 1981. (a)

Abelson, R. P. The psychological status of the script concept. *American Psychologist,* 1981, *36,* 715-729. (b)

Abelson, R. P. Whatever became of consistency theory? *Personality and Social Psychology Bulletin,* 1983, *9,* 37-54.

Abelson, R. P., Aronson, E., McGuire, W. J., Newcomb, T. M., Rosenberg, M. J., & Tannenbaum, P. H. (Eds.). *Theories of cognitive consistency: A sourcebook.* Chicago: Rand McNally, 1968.

Abelson, R. P., Kinder, D. R., Peters, M. D., & Fiske, S. T. Affective and semantic components in political person perception. *Journal of Personality and Social Psychology,* 1982, *42,* 619-630.

Abrams, R. D., & Finesinger, J. E. Guilt reactions in patients with cancer. *Cancer,* 1953, *6,* 474-482.

Abramson, L. Y., & Alloy, L. B. Judgment of contingency: Errors and their implications. In A. Baum & J. Singer (Eds.), *Advances in environmental psychology* (Vol. 2). Hillsdale, N.J.: Erlbaum, 1980.

Abramson, L. Y., Seligman, M. E. P., & Teasdale, J. D. Learned helplessness in humans: Critique and reformulation. *Journal of Abnormal Psychology,* 1978, *87,* 49-74.

Adorno, T. W., Frenkel-Brunswik, E., Levinson, D. J., & Sanford, R. N. *The authoritarian personality.* New York: Harper, 1950.

Ajzen, I. Intuitive theories of events and the effects of baserate information on prediction. *Journal of Personality and Social Psychology,* 1977, *35,* 303-314.

Ajzen, I., Dalto, C. A., & Blyth, D. P. Consistency and bias in the attribution of attitudes. *Journal of Personality and Social Psychology,* 1979, *37,* 1871-1876.

Ajzen, I., & Fishbein, M. Attitude-behavior relations: A theoretical analysis and review of empirical research. *Psychological Bulletin,* 1977, *84,* 888-918.

419

Ajzen, I., & Fishbein, M. *Understanding attitudes and predicting social behavior.* Englewood Cliffs, N.J.: Prentice-Hall, 1980.

Ajzen, I., & Holmes, W. H. Uniqueness of behavioral effects in causal attribution. *Journal of Personality,* 1976, *44,* 98-108.

Ajzen, I., Timko, C., & White, J. B. Self-monitoring and the attitude-behavior relation. *Journal of Personality and Social Psychology,* 1982, *42,* 426-435.

Alba, J. W., & Hasher, L. Is memory schematic? *Psychological Bulletin,* 1983, *93,* 203-231.

Alexander, C. N., Jr., & Knight, G. W. Situated identities and social psychological experimentation. *Sociometry,* 1971, *34,* 65-82.

Allen, R. B., & Ebbesen, E. B. Cognitive processes in person perception: Retrieval of personality trait and behavioral information. *Journal of Experimental Social Psychology,* 1981, *17,* 119-141.

Allen, V. L., & Wilder, D. A. Categorization, belief similarity, and intergroup discrimination. *Journal of Personality and Social Psychology,* 1975, *32,* 971-977.

Allport, F. H. *Theories of perception and the concept of structure.* New York: Wiley, 1955.

Allport, G. W. Attitudes. In C. Murchison (Ed.), *Handbook of social psychology.* Worcester, Mass.: Clark University Press, 1935.

Allport, G. W. *The nature of prejudice.* Reading, Mass.: Addison-Wesley, 1954.

Altom, M. W., & Lingle, J. H. Episodic and categorical processes in impression change. Paper presented at symposium at the meeting of the American Psychological Association, Montreal, September, 1980.

Amir, Y. The role of intergroup contact in change of prejudice and ethnic relations. In P. A. Katz (Ed.), *Towards the elimination of racism.* New York: Pergamon Press, 1976.

Andersen, S. M., & Bem, S. L. Sex typing and androgyny in dyadic interaction: Individual differences in responsiveness to physical attractiveness. *Journal of Personality and Social Psychology,* 1981, *41,* 74-86.

Anderson, C. A. Inoculation and counter-explanation: Debiasing techniques in the perseverance of social theories. *Social Cognition,* 1982, *1,* 126-139.

Anderson, C. A. Abstract and concrete data in the perseverance of social theories: When weak data lead to unshakeable beliefs. *Journal of Experimental Social Psychology,* 1983, *19,* 93-108.

Anderson, C. A., Horowitz, L. M., & French, R. D. Attributional style of lonely and depressed people. *Journal of Personality and Social Psychology,* 1983, *45,* 127-136.

Anderson, C. A., Lepper, M. R., & Ross, L. Perseverance of social theories: The role of explanation in the persistence of discredited information. *Journal of Personality and Social Psychology,* 1980, *39,* 1037-1049.

Anderson, J. R. Retrieval of propositional information from long-term memory. *Cognitive Psychology,* 1974, *6,* 451-474.

Anderson, J. R. *Language, memory, and thought.* Hillsdale, N. J.: Erlbaum, 1976.

Anderson, J. R. Arguments concerning representations for mental imagery. *Psychological Review,* 1978, *85,* 249-277.

Anderson, J. R. Further arguments concerning representations for mental imagery: A reply to Hayes-Roth and Pylyshyn. *Psychological Review,* 1979, *86,* 395-406.

Anderson, J. R. *Cognitive psychology and its implications.* San Francisco: Freeman, 1980. (a)

Anderson, J. R. Concepts, propositions, and schemata: What are the cognitive units?

Nebraska Symposium on Motivation (Vol. 28). Lincoln: University of Nebraska Press, 1980. (b)

Anderson, J. R. (Ed.) *Cognitive skills and their acquisition.* Hillsdale, N.J.: Erlbaum, 1981.

Anderson, J. R. *The architecture of cognition.* Cambridge, Mass.: Harvard University Press, 1982.

Anderson, J. R., & Bower, G. H. *Human associative memory.* Washington, D.C.: Winston & Sons, 1973.

Anderson, J. R., & Hastie, R. Individuation and reference in memory, proper names and definite descriptions. *Cognitive Psychology,* 1974, *6,* 495-514.

Anderson, J. R., Kline, P. J., & Beasley, C. M., Jr. A general learning theory and its application to schema abstraction. In G. H. Bower (Ed.), *The psychology of learning and motivation.* New York: Academic Press, 1979.

Anderson, N. H. Component ratings in impression formation. *Psychonomic Science,* 1966, *6,* 179-180.

Anderson, N. H. Information integration: A brief survey. In D. H. Krantz, R. C. Atkinson, R. D. Luce, & P. Suppes (Eds.), *Contemporary developments in mathematical psychology.* San Francisco: Freeman, 1974.

Anderson, N. H. Integration theory applied to cognitive responses and attitudes. In R. E. Petty, T. M. Ostrom, & T. C. Brock (Eds.), *Cognitive responses in persuasion.* Hillsdale, N.J.: Erlbaum, 1981.

Anderson, N. H., & Hubert, S. Effects of concomitant verbal recall on order effects in personality impression formation. *Journal of Verbal Learning and Verbal Behavior,* 1963, *2,* 379-391.

Anderson, N. H., & Lampel, A. K. Effect of context on ratings of personality traits. *Psychonomic Science,* 1965, *3,* 433-434.

Anderson, R. C., & Pichert, J. W. Recall of previously unrecallable information following a shift in perspective. *Journal of Verbal Learning and Verbal Behavior,* 1978, *17,* 1-12.

Aristotle. On memory and recollection. In W. D. Ross (Ed.), J. I. Beare, (trans.), *The works of Aristotle.* Oxford: Clarendon Press, 1931.

Arkes, H. R., & Harkness, A. R. Effect of making a diagnosis on subsequent recognition of symptoms. *Journal of Experimental Psychology: Human Learning and Memory,* 1980, *6,* 568-575.

Arkin, R. M., Appelman, A. J., & Burger, J. M. Social anxiety, self-presentation, and the self-serving bias in causal attribution. *Journal of Personality and Social Psychology,* 1980, *38,* 23-35.

Arnold, M. B. Perennial problems in the field of emotion. In M. B. Arnold (Ed.), *Feelings and emotions: The Loyola Symposium.* New York: Academic Press, 1970.

Aronson, E., & Mills, J. The effect of severity of initiation on liking for a group. *Journal of Abnormal and Social Psychology,* 1959, *59,* 177-182.

Asch, S. E. Forming impressions of personality. *Journal of Abnormal and Social Psychology,* 1946, *41,* 258-290.

Ashmore, R. D., & Del Boca, F. K. Conceptual approaches to stereotypes and stereotyping. In D. L. Hamilton (Ed.), *Cognitive processes in stereotyping and intergroup behavior.* Hillsdale, N.J.: Erlbaum, 1980.

Austen, J. *Mansfield Park.* New York: Dutton, 1922.

Averill, J. R. Personal control over aversive stimuli and its relationship to stress. *Psychological Bulletin,* 1973, *80,* 286-303.

Averill, J. R., O'Brien, L., & DeWitt, G. The influence of response effectiveness on the preference for warning and on psychophysiological stress reaction. *Journal of Personality*, 1977, *45*, 395-418.

Ayeroff, F., & Abelson, R. P. E.S.P. & E.S.B.: Belief in personal success at mental telepathy. *Journal of Personality and Social Psychology*, 1976, *34*, 240-247.

Baddeley, A. D. The trouble with levels: A reexamination of Craik and Lockhart's framework for memory research. *Psychological Review*, 1978, *85*, 139-152.

Baer, R., Hinkle, S., Smith, K., & Fenton, M. Reactance as a function of actual versus projected autonomy. *Journal of Personality and Social Psychology*, 1980, *38*, 416-422.

Bagozzi, R. P. Attitudes, intentions, and behavior: A test of some key hypotheses. *Journal of Personality and Social Psychology*, 1981, *41*, 607-627.

Bagozzi, R. P., & Burnkrant, R. E. Attitude organization and the attitude-behavior relationship. *Journal of Personality and Social Psychology*, 1979, *37*, 913-929.

Bandura, A. Toward a unifying theory of behavioral change. *Psychological Review*, 1977, *84*, 191-215.

Barclay, A. M. The effect of female aggressiveness on aggressive and sexual fantasies. *Journal of Projective Techniques and Personality Assessment*, 1970, *34*, 19-26.

Barclay, A. M., & Haber, R. N. The relation of aggressive to sexual motivation. *Journal of Psychology*, 1970, *33*, 462-475.

Bargh, J. A. Attention and automacity in the processing of self-relevant information. *Journal of Personality and Social Psychology*, 1982, *43*, 425-436.

Bargh, J. A., & Pietromonaco, P. Automatic information processing and social perception: The influence of trait information presented outside of conscious awareness on impression formation. *Journal of Personality and Social Psychology*, 1982, *43*, 437-449.

Bar-Hillel, M., & Fischhoff, B. When do base rates affect predictions? *Journal of Personality and Social Psychology*, 1981, *41*, 671-680.

Baron, R. M. Contrasting approaches to social knowing: An ecological perspective. *Personality and Social Psychology Bulletin*, 1980, *4*, 591-600.

Bartlett, F. *A study in experimental and social psychology.* New York: Cambridge University Press, 1932.

Bartlett, J. C., Burleson, G., & Santrock, J. W. Emotional mood and memory in young children. *Journal of Experimental Child Psychology*, 1982, *34*, 59-76.

Bartlett, J. C., & Santrock, J. W. Affect-dependent episodic memory in young children. *Child Development*, 1977, *50*, 513-518.

Baum, A., Aiello, J. R., & Calesnick, L. E. Crowding and personal control: Social density and the development of learned helplessness. *Journal of Personality and Social Psychology*, 1978, *36*, 1000-1011.

Baum, A., Calesnick, L. E., Davis, G. E., & Gatchel, R. J. Individual differences in coping with crowding: Stimulus screening and social overload. *Journal of Personality and Social Psychology*, 1982, *43*, 821-830.

Baum, A., Fisher, J. D., & Solomon, S. K. Type of information, familiarity, and the reduction of crowding stress. *Journal of Personality and Social Psychology*, 1980, *40*, 11-23.

Baum, A., & Gatchel, R. J. Cognitive determinants of reaction to uncontrollable events: Development of reactance and learned helplessness. *Journal of Personality and Social Psychology*, 1981, *40*, 1078-1089.

Baumeister, R. F., & Jones, E. E. When self-presentation is constrained by the target's knowledge. *Journal of Personality and Social Psychology*, 1978, *36*, 608-618.

Beaman, A. L., Klentz, B., Diener, E., & Svanum, S. Self-awareness and transgression in children: Two field studies. *Journal of Personality and Social Psychology*, 1979, *37*, 1835-1846.

Beck, A. T. The development of depression: A cognitive model. In R. M. Friedman & M. M. Katz (Eds.), *The psychology of depression: Contemporary theory and research*. New York: Wiley, 1974.

Beck, A. T. *Cognitive therapy and the emotional disorders*. New York: International Universities Press, 1976.

Bellezza, F. S., & Bower, G. H. Person stereotypes and memory for people. *Journal of Personality and Social Psychology*, 1981, *41*, 856-865.

Bellezza, F. S., & Bower, G. H. Remembering script-based text. *Poetics*, 1982, *11*, 1-23.

Bem, D. J. Self-perception: An alternative interpretation of cognitive dissonance phenomena. *Psychological Review*, 1967, *74*, 183-200.

Bem, D. J. Self-perception theory. In L. Berkowitz (Ed.), *Advances in experimental social psychology* (Vol. 6). New York: Academic Press, 1972.

Bem, D. J., & Allen, A. On predicting some of the people some of the time: The search for cross-situational consistencies in behavior. *Psychological Review*, 1974, *81*, 506-520.

Bem, D. J., & Funder, D. C. Predicting more of the people more of the time: Assessing the personality of situations. *Psychological Review*, 1974, *85*, 485-501.

Bem, D. J., & McConnell, H. K. Testing the self-perception explanation of dissonance phenomena: On the salience of premanipulation attitudes. *Journal of Personality and Social Psychology*, 1970, *14*, 23-31.

Bem, S. L. Gender schema theory: A cognitive account of sex typing. *Psychological Review*, 1981, *88*, 354-364.

Benesh, M., & Weiner, B. On emotion and motivation: From the notebooks of Fritz Heider. *American Psychologist*, 1982, *37*, 887-895.

Bentler, P. M. Multivariate analysis with latent variables: Causal modeling. *Annual Review of Psychology*, 1980, *31*, 419-456.

Bentler, P. M., & Speckart, G. Attitudes cause behaviors: A structural equation analysis. *Journal of Personality and Social Psychology*, 1981, *40*, 226-238.

Berger, S. M., & Lambert, W. W. Stimulus-response theory in contemporary social psychology. In G. Lindzey & E. Aronson (Eds.), *The handbook of social psychology* (Vol. 1, 2nd ed.). Reading, Mass.: Addison-Wesley, 1968.

Berggren, T., Ohman, A., & Fredrikson, M. Locus of control and habituation of the electrodermal orienting response to nonsignal and signal stimuli. *Journal of Personality and Social Psychology*, 1977, *35*, 708-716.

Berkowitz, L. *Roots of aggression: A reexamination of the frustration-aggression hypothesis*. New York: Atherton, 1969.

Berkowitz, L. Some determinants of impulsive aggression: Role of mediated associations with reinforcements for aggression. *Psychological Review*, 1974, *81*, 165-176.

Berlyne, D. E. Novelty, complexity, and hedonic value. *Perception and Psychophysics*, 1970, *8*, 279-286.

Berman, J. S., Read, S. J., & Kenny, D. A. Processing inconsistent social information. *Journal of Personality and Social Psychology*, in press.

Berscheid, E. Attraction and emotional in interpersonal relationships. In M. S. Clark & S. T. Fiske (Eds.), *Affect and cognition: The 17th Annual Carnegie Symposium on Cognition.* Hillsdale, N.J.: Erlbaum, 1982.

Berscheid, E. Emotion. In H. H. Kelley, E. Berscheid, A. Christensen, J. Harvey, T. Huston, G. Levinger, E. McClintock, A. Peplau, & D. R. Peterson (Eds.), *Close relationships.* San Francisco: Freeman, 1983.

Berscheid, E., Graziano, W., Monson, T., & Dermer, M. Outcome dependency: Attention, attribution, and attraction. *Journal of Personality and Social Psychology,* 1976, *34,* 978-989.

Berscheid, E., & Walster, E. H. *Interpersonal attraction.* Reading, Mass.: Addison-Wesley, 1978.

Billig, M., & Tajfel, H. Social categorization and similarity in intergroup behavior. *European Journal of Social Psychology,* 1973, *3,* 27-52.

Birnbaum, M. H., & Mellers, B. A. One-mediator model of exposure effects is still viable. *Journal of Personality and Social Psychology,* 1979, *37,* 1090-1096. (a)

Birnbaum, M. H., & Mellers, B. A. Stimulus recognition may mediate exposure effects. *Journal of Personality and Social Psychology,* 1979, *37,* 391-394. (b)

Black, J. B., Turner, T. J., & Bower, G. H. Point of view in narrative comprehension, memory, and production. *Journal of Verbal Learning and Verbal Behavior,* 1979, *18,* 187-198.

Block, J. Some enduring and consequential structures of personality. In A. I. Rubin *et al.* (Eds.), *Further explorations in personality.* New York: Wiley, 1981.

Bobrow, D. G., & Norman, D. A. Some principles of memory schemata. In A. Collins & D. G. Bobrow (Eds.), *Representation and understanding: Studies in cognitive science.* New York: Academic Press, 1975.

Boggiano, A. K., & Ruble, D. N. Competence and the overjustification effect: A developmental study. *Journal of Personality and Social Psychology,* 1979, *37,* 1462-1468.

Bond, M. H. Effect of an impression set on subsequent behavior. *Journal of Personality and Social Psychology,* 1972, *24,* 301-305.

Borgida, E., & Brekke, N. The base-rate fallacy in attribution and prediction. In J. H. Harvey, W. J. Ickes, & R. F. Kidd (Eds.), *New directions in attribution research* (Vol. 3). Hillsdale, N.J.: Erlbaum, 1981.

Borgida, E., & Campbell, B. Attitude-behavior consistency: The moderating role of personal experience. *Journal of Personality and Social Psychology,* 1982, *42,* 239-247.

Borgida, E., & Howard-Pitney, B. Personal involvement and the robustness of perceptual salience effects. *Journal of Personality and Social Psychology,* 1983, *45,* 560-570.

Borgida, E., Swann, W. B., Jr., & Campbell, B. Attitudes and behavior: The specificity hypothesis revisited. Paper presented at the meeting of the American Psychological Association, San Francisco, August, 1977.

Boring, E. G. *A history of experimental psychology.* Englewood Cliffs, N.J.: Prentice-Hall, 1950.

Bower, G. H. *Human memory.* New York: Academic Press, 1977.

Bower, G. H. Emotional mood and memory. *American Psychologist,* 1981, *36,* 129-148.

Bower, G. H., Black, J. B., & Turner, T. J. Scripts in memory for text. *Cognitive Psychology,* 1979, *11,* 177-220.

Bower, G. H., & Cohen, P. R. Emotional influences in memory and thinking: Data and theory. In M. S. Clark & S. T. Fiske (Eds.), *Affect and cognition: The 17th Annual Carnegie Symposium on Cognition.* Hillsdale, N.J.: Erlbaum, 1982.

Bower, G. H., & Gilligan, S. G. Remembering information related to one's self. *Journal of Research in Personality*, 1979, *13*, 404-419.

Bower, G. H., Gilligan, S. G., & Monteiro, K. P. Selectivity of learning caused by affective states. *Journal of Experimental Psychology: General*, 1981, *110*, 451-473.

Bower, G. H., & Karlin, M. B. Depth of processing pictures of faces and recognition memory. *Journal of Experimental Psychology*, 1974, *4*, 751-757.

Bower, G. H., & Masling, M. Causal explanations as mediators for remembering correlations. Unpublished manuscript, Stanford University, 1978.

Bower, T. G. R. Analysis of a mnemonic device. *American Scientist*, 1970, *58*, 496-510.

Bowers, K. Pain, anxiety, and perceived control. *Journal of Consulting and Clinical Psychology*, 1968, *32*, 596-602.

Bradburn, N. M., & Caplovitz, D. *Reports on happiness.* Chicago: Aldine, 1965.

Bradley, G. W. Self-serving biases in the attribution process: A reexamination of the fact or fiction question. *Journal of Personality and Social Psychology*, 1978, *36*, 56-71.

Bransford, J. D. *Human cognition: Learning, understanding and remembering.* Belmont, Calif.: Wadsworth, 1979.

Bransford, J. D., & Franks, J. J. The abstraction of linguistic ideas. *Cognitive Psychology*, 1971, *2*, 331-350.

Bransford, J. D., & Johnson, M. K. Contextual prerequisites for understanding: Some investigations of comprehension and recall. *Journal of Verbal Learning and Verbal Behavior*, 1972, *11*, 717-726.

Brehm, J. W. *Response to loss of freedom: A theory of psychological reactance.* New York: Academic Press, 1966.

Brehm, J. W., & Cohen, A. R. *Explorations in cognitive dissonance.* New York: Wiley, 1962.

Brehm, S. S., & Brehm, J. W. *Psychological reactance: A theory of freedom and control.* New York: Academic Press, 1981.

Brewer, M. B. An information-processing approach to attribution of responsibility. *Journal of Experimental Social Psychology*, 1977, *13*, 58-69.

Brewer, M. B. In-group bias in the minimal intergroup situation: A cognitive-motivational analysis. *Psychological Bulletin*, 1979, *86*, 307-324.

Brewer, M. B., Dull, V., & Lui, L. Perceptions of the elderly: Stereotypes as prototypes. *Journal of Personality and Social Psychology*, 1981, *41*, 656-670.

Brewer, M. B., & Silver, M. Ingroup bias as a function of task characteristics. *European Journal of Social Psychology*, 1978, *8*, 393-400.

Brickman, P., Rabinowitz, V. C., Karuza, J., Jr., Coates, D., Cohn, E., & Kidder, L. Models of helping and coping. *American Psychologist*, 1982, *37*, 368-384.

Brickman, P., Rabinowitz, V. C., Karuza, J., Jr., Coates, D., Cohn, E., & Kidder, L. An attributional analysis of helping behavior. In L. Berkowitz (Ed.), *Advances in experimental social psychology.* New York: Academic Press, in press.

Brickman, P., Ryan, K., & Wortman, C. B. Causal chains: Attribution of responsibility as a function of immediate and prior causes. *Journal of Personality and Social Psychology*, 1975, *32*, 1060-1067.

Briggs, S., Cheek, J., & Buss, A. H. An analysis of the self-monitoring scale. *Journal of Personality and Social Psychology*, 1980, *38*, 679-686.

Brigham, J. C. Ethnic stereotypes. *Psychological Bulletin*, 1971, *76*, 15-38.

Brigham, J. C., Maass, A., Snyder, L. D., & Spaulding, K. Accuracy of eyewitness identifications in a field setting. *Journal of Personality and Social Psychology*, 1982, *42*, 673-681.

Broadbent, D. E. *Perception and communication*. London: Pergamon Press, 1958.

Brock, T. C. Communication discrepancy and intent to persuade as determinants of counterargument production. *Journal of Experimental Social Psychology*, 1967, *3*, 296-309.

Brock, T. C., Albert, S. M., & Becker, L. A. Familiarity, utility, and supportiveness as determinants of information receptivity. *Journal of Personality and Social Psychology*, 1970, *14*, 292-301.

Brock, T. C., & Balloun, J. L. Behavioral receptivity to dissonant information. *Journal of Personality and Social Psychology*, 1967, *6*, 413-428.

Brockner, J. The effects of self-esteem, success-failure, and self-consciousness on task performance. *Journal of Personality and Social Psychology*, 1979, *37*, 1732-1741. (a)

Brockner, J. Self-esteem, self-consciousness, and task performance: Replications, extensions and possible explanations. *Journal of Personality and Social Psychology*, 1979, *37*, 447-461. (b)

Brockner, J., & Hulton, A. J. B. How to reverse the vicious cycle of low self-esteem: The importance of attentional focus. *Journal of Experimental Social Psychology*, 1978, *14*, 564-578.

Brodt, S. E., & Zimbardo, P. G. Modifying shyness-related social behavior through symptom misattribution. *Journal of Personality and Social Psychology*, 1981, *41*, 437-449.

Bronfenbrenner, U. Lewinian space and ecological substance. *Journal of Social Issues*, 1977, *33*, 199-212.

Brophy, J. E., & Rohrkemper, M. M. The influence of problem ownership on teachers' perceptions of and strategies for coping with problem students. *Journal of Educational Psychology*, 1981, *73*, 295-311.

Broverman, I. K., Broverman, D. M., Clarkson, F. E., Rosenkrantz, P. S., & Vogel, S. R. Sex-role stereotypes and clinical judgments of mental health. *Journal of Consulting Psychology*, 1972, *34*, 1-7.

Broverman, I. K., Vogel, S. R., Broverman, D. M., Clarkson, F. E., & Rosenkrantz, P. S. Sex-role stereotypes: A current appraisal. *Journal of Social Issues*, 1972, *28*, 59-79.

Brown, R., & Kulik, J. Flashbulb memories. *Cognition*, 1977, *5*, 73-99.

Bruner, J. S. Going beyond the information given. In H. Gruber, G. Terrell, & M. Wertheimer (Eds.), *Contemporary approaches to cognition*. Cambridge, Mass.: Harvard University Press, 1957.

Bruner, J. S., & Tagiuri, R. The perception of people. In G. Lindzey (Ed.), *Handbook of social psychology* (Vol. 2). Reading, Mass.: Addison-Wesley, 1954.

Brunswik, E. *Perception and the representative design of psychological experiments.* (2nd ed.). Berkeley and Los Angeles: University of California Press, 1956.

Bryant, J., & Zillmann, D. Effect of intensification of annoyance through unrelated residual excitation on substantially delayed hostile behavior. *Journal of Experimental Social Psychology*, 1979, *15*, 470-480.

Buck, R. Nonverbal behavior and the theory of emotion: The facial feedback hypothesis. *Journal of Personality and Social Psychology*, 1980, *38*, 811-824.

Buckert, U., Meyer, W. U., & Schmalt, H. D. Effects of difficulty and diagnosticity on choice among tasks in relation to achievement motivation and perceived ability. *Journal of Personality and Social Psychology*, 1979, *37*, 1172-1178.

Bulman, R. J., & Wortman, C. B. Attributions of blame and coping in the "real world": Severe accident victims react to their lot. *Journal of Personality and Social Psychology,* 1977, *35,* 351-363.

Burger, J. M. Motivational biases in the attribution of responsibility for an accident: A meta-analysis of the defensive-attribution hypothesis. *Psychological Bulletin,* 1981, *90,* 496-512.

Burger, J. M., & Arkin, R. M. Prediction, control, and learned helplessness. *Journal of Personality and Social Psychology,* 1980, *38,* 482-491.

Burgess, E. W. An experiment in the standardization of the case-study method. *Sociometry,* 1941, *4,* 329-348.

Burnstein, E., & Sentis, K. Attitude polarization in groups. In R. E. Petty, T. M. Ostrom, & T. C. Brock (Eds.), *Cognitive responses in persuasion.* Hillsdale, N.J.: Erlbaum, 1981.

Burnstein, E., & Vinokur, A. Testing two classes of theories about group-induced shifts in individual choice. *Journal of Experimental Social Psychology,* 1973, *9,* 123-137.

Burnstein, E., & Vinokur, A. What a person thinks upon learning he has chosen differently from others: Nice evidence for the persuasive-arguments explanation of choice shifts. *Journal of Experimental Social Psychology,* 1975, *11,* 412-426.

Burnstein, E., & Vinokur, A. Persuasive argumentation and social comparison as determinants of attitude polarization. *Journal of Experimental Social Psychology,* 1977, *13,* 315-332.

Burnstein, E., Vinokur, A., & Trope, Y. Interpersonal comparison versus persuasive argumentation: A more direct test of alternative explanations for group induced shifts in individual choice. *Journal of Experimental Social Psychology,* 1973, *9,* 236-245.

Buss, A. H. *Self-consciousness and social anxiety.* San Francisco: Freeman, 1980.

Buss, A. R. Causes and reasons in attribution theory: A conceptual critique. *Journal of Personality and Social Psychology,* 1978, *36,* 1311-1321.

Buss, A. R. On the relationship between causes and reasons. *Journal of Personality and Social Psychology,* 1979, *37,* 1458-1461.

Byrne, D. Repression-sensitization as a dimension of personality. In B. A. Maher (Ed.), *Progress in experimental personality research.* New York: Academic Press, 1964.

Byrne, D., Steinberg, M. A., & Schwartz, M. S. Relationship between repression-sensitization and physical illness. *Journal of Abnormal Psychology,* 1968, *73,* 154-155.

Cacioppo, J. T. Effects of exogenous changes in heart rate on facilitation of thought and resistance to persuasion. *Journal of Personality and Social Psychology,* 1979, *37,* 489-498.

Cacioppo, J. T., & Petty, R. E. Effects of message repetition and position on cognitive response, recall, and persuasion. *Journal of Personality and Social Psychology,* 1979, *37,* 97-109.

Cacioppo, J. T., & Petty, R. E. The need for cognition. *Journal of Personality and Social Psychology,* 1982, *42,* 116-131.

Cacioppo, J. T., Petty, R. E., & Sidera, J. A. The effects of a salient self-schema on the evaluation of proattitudinal editorials: Top-down versus bottom-up message processing. *Journal of Experimental Social Psychology,* 1982, *18,* 324-338.

Calder, B. J. Endogenous-exogenous versus internal-external attributions: Implications for the development of attribution theory. *Personality and Social Psychology Bulletin,* 1977, *3,* 400-406.

Calder, B. J., Insko, C. A., & Yandell, B. The relation of cognitive and memorial processes to persuasion in a simulated jury trial. *Journal of Applied Social Psychology,* 1974, *4,* 62-93.

Calder, B. J., & Ross, M. *Attitudes and behavior.* Morristown, N.J.: General Learning Press, 1973.

Calder, B. J., Ross, M., & Insko, C. A. Attitude change and attitude attribution: Effects of incentive choice and consequences. *Journal of Personality and Social Psychology,* 1973, *25,* 84-99.

Calder, B. J., & Staw, B. M. Self-perception of intrinsic and extrinsic motivation. *Journal of Personality and Social Psychology,* 1975, *31,* 599-605.

Cannon, W. B. The James-Lange theory of emotions: A critical examination and an alternative theory. *American Journal of Psychology,* 1927, *39,* 106-124.

Cantor, J. R., Bryant, J., & Zillmann, D. Enhancement of humor appreciation by transferred excitation. *Journal of Personality and Social Psychology,* 1974, *30,* 812-821.

Cantor, J. R., & Zillmann, D. The effect of affective state and emotional arousal on music appreciation. *Journal of General Psychology,* 1973, *89,* 97-108.

Cantor, N. Perceptions of situations: Situation prototypes and person-situation prototypes. In D. Magnusson (Ed.), *The situation: An interactional perspective.* Hillsdale, N.J.: Erlbaum, 1980.

Cantor, N., & Mischel, W. Traits as prototypes: Effects on recognition memory. *Journal of Personality and Social Psychology,* 1977, *35,* 38-48.

Cantor, N., & Mischel, W. Prototypes in person perception. In L. Berkowitz (Ed.), *Advances in experimental social psychology* (Vol. 12). New York: Academic Press, 1979.

Cantor, N., Mischel, W., & Schwartz, J. Social knowledge: Structure, content, use, and abuse. In A. Hastorf & A. Isen (Eds.), *Cognitive social psychology.* New York: Elsevier North-Holland, 1982.

Carlston, D. E. The recall and use of traits and events in social inference processes. *Journal of Experimental Social Psychology,* 1980, *16,* 303-328.

Carnegie, D. *How to win friends and influence people.* New York: Simon & Schuster, 1936.

Carroll, J. S. The effect of imagining an event on expectations for the event: An interpretation in terms of the availability heuristic. *Journal of Experimental Social Psychology,* 1978, *14,* 88-96.

Carroll, J. S., & Payne, J. W. *Cognition and social behavior.* Hillsdale, N.J.: Erlbaum, 1976. (a)

Carroll, J. S., & Payne, J. W. The psychology of the parole decision-making process: A joint application of attribution theory and information-processing psychology. In J. S. Carroll & J. W. Payne (Eds.), *Cognition and social behavior.* Hillsdale, N.J.: Erlbaum, 1976. (b)

Carver, C. S. Facilitation of physical aggression through objective self-awareness. *Journal of Experimental Social Psychology,* 1974, *10,* 365-370.

Carver, C. S. A cybernetic model of self-attention processes. *Journal of Personality and Social Psychology,* 1979, *37,* 1251-1281.

Carver, C. S., Blaney, P. H., & Scheier, M. F. Focus of attention, chronic expectancy, and responses to a feared stimulus. *Journal of Personality and Social Psychology,* 1979, *37,* 1186-1195.

Carver, C. S., Coleman, A. E., & Glass, D. C. The coronary-prone behavior pattern and the suppression of fatigue on a treadmill test. *Journal of Personality and Social Psychology,* 1976, *33,* 460-466.

Carver, C. S., & Glass, D. C. The coronary-prone behavior pattern and interpersonal aggression. *Journal of Personality and Social Psychology*, 1978, *36*, 361-366.

Carver, C. S., & Scheier, M. F. Self-focusing effects of dispositional self-consciousness, mirror presence, and audience presence. *Journal of Personality and Social Psychology*, 1978, *36*, 324-332.

Carver, C. S., & Scheier, M. F. *Attention and self-regulation: A control-theory approach to human behavior*. New York: Springer-Verlag, 1981. (a)

Carver, C. S., & Scheier, M. F. The self-attention-induced feedback loop and social facilitation. *Journal of Experimental Social Psychology*, 1981, *17*, 545-568. (b)

Carver, C. S., & Scheier, M. F. Outcome expectancy, locus of attribution for expectancy, and self-directed attention as determinants of evaluations and performance. *Journal of Experimental Social Psychology*, 1982, *18*, 184-200.

Chaiken, S. Communicator physical attractiveness and persuasion. *Journal of Personality and Social Psychology*, 1979, *37*, 1387-1397.

Chaiken, S. Heuristic versus systematic information processing and the use of source versus message cues in persuasion. *Journal of Personality and Social Psychology*, 1980, *39*, 752-766.

Chaiken, S., & Baldwin, M. W. Affective-cognitive consistency and the effect of salient behavioral information on the self-perception of attitudes. *Journal of Personality and Social Psychology*, 1981, *41*, 1-12.

Chaiken, S., & Eagly, A. H. Communication modality as a determinant of message persuasiveness and message comprehensibility. *Journal of Personality and Social Psychology*, 1976, *34*, 605-614.

Chaiken, S., & Eagly, A. H. Communication modality as a determinant of persuasion: The role of communicator salience. *Journal of Personality and Social Psychology*, 1983, *45*, 241-256.

Chance, J. E., & Goldstein, A. G. Depth of processing in response to own- and other-race faces. *Personality and Social Psychology Bulletin*, 1981, *7*, 475-480.

Chanowitz, B., & Langer, E. J. Premature cognitive commitment. *Journal of Personality and Social Psychology*, 1981, *41*, 1051-1063.

Chapman, L. J. Illusory correlation in observational report. *Journal of Verbal Learning and Verbal Behavior*, 1967, *6*, 151-155.

Chapman, L. J., & Chapman, J. P. Genesis of popular but erroneous diagnostic observations. *Journal of Abnormal Psychology*, 1967, *72*, 193-204.

Chapman, L. J., & Chapman, J. P. Illusory correlation as an obstacle to the use of valid psychodiagnostic signs. *Journal of Abnormal Psychology*, 1969, *14*, 271-280.

Chapman, L. J., & Chapman, J. P. Test results are what you think they are. In D. Kahneman, P. Slovic, & A. Tversky (Eds.), *Judgment under uncertainty: Heuristics and biases*. New York: Cambridge University Press, 1982.

Chase, W. G., & Simon, H. A. The mind's eye in chess. In W. G. Chase (Ed.), *Visual information processing*. New York: Academic Press, 1973.

Chaves, J. R., & Barber, T. X. Cognitive strategies, experimenter modeling, and expectation in the attenuation of pain. *Journal of Abnormal Psychology*, 1974, *83*, 356-363.

Chi, M. T. H., & Koeske, R. Network representations of a child's dinosaur knowledge. *Developmental Psychology*, 1983, *19*, 29-39.

Chodoff, P., Friedman, S. B., & Hamburg, D. A. Stress, defenses, and coping behavior: Observations in parents of children with malignant disease. *American Journal of Psychiatry*, 1964, *120*, 743-749.

Chomsky, N. Verbal behavior [Review of Skinner's book]. *Language*, 1959, *35*, 26-58.

Cialdini, R. B., & Kenrick, D. T. Altruism as hedonism: A social development perspective on the relationship of negative mood state and helping. *Journal of Personality and Social Psychology*, 1976, *34*, 907-914.

Cialdini, R. B., Levy, A., Herman, C. P., & Evenbeck, S. Attitudinal politics: The strategy of moderation. *Journal of Personality and Social Psychology*, 1973, *25*, 100-108.

Cialdini, R. B., Petty, R. E., & Cacioppo, J. T. Attitude and attitude change. *Annual Review of Psychology*, 1981, *32*, 357-404.

Clark, L. F., & Taylor, S. E. Hypothesis-testing under different interaction conditions: The questions people ask. Paper presented at the meeting of the American Psychological Association, Anaheim, Calif., August, 1983.

Clark, L. F., & Woll, S. B. Stereotype biases: A reconstructive analysis of their role in reconstructive memory. *Journal of Personality and Social Psychology*, 1981, *41*, 1064-1072.

Clark, M. S. A role for arousal in the link between feeling states, judgments, and behavior. In M. S. Clark & S. T. Fiske (Eds.), *Affect and cognition: The 17th Annual Carnegie Symposium on Cognition*. Hillsdale, N.J.: Erlbaum, 1982.

Clark, M. S., & Fiske, S. T. (Eds.), *Affect and cognition: The 17th Annual Carnegie Symposium on Cognition*. Hillsdale, N.J.: Erlbaum, 1982.

Clark, M. S., & Isen, A. M. Toward understanding the relationship between feeling states and social behavior. In A. Hastorf & A. Isen (Eds.), *Cognitive social psychology*. New York: Elsevier North-Holland, 1982.

Clark, M. S., Milberg, S., & Ross, J. Arousal cues arousal-related material in memory: Implications for understanding effects of mood on memory. *Journal of Verbal Learning and Verbal Behavior*, in press.

Clark, M. S., & Waddell, B. A. Effects of moods on thoughts about helping, attraction and information acquisition. *Social Psychology Quarterly*, 1983, *46*, 31-35.

Clore, G. L., & Byrne, D. A reinforcement-affect model of attraction. In T. L. Huston (Ed.), *Foundations of interpersonal attraction*. New York: Academic Press, 1974.

Clore, G. L., & Kerber, K. Affective schemata in the person perception cycle. Unpublished manuscript, University of Illinois, 1980.

Cohen, A. R., Brehm, J. W., & Latané, B. Choice of strategy and voluntary exposure to information under public and private conditions. *Journal of Personality*, 1959, *27*, 63-73.

Cohen, C. E. Goals and schemas in person perception: Making sense out of the stream of behavior. In N. Cantor & J. Kihlstrom (Eds.), *Personality, cognition, and social behavior*. Hillsdale, N.J.: Erlbaum, 1981. (a)

Cohen, C. E. Person categories and social perception: Testing some boundaries of the processing effects of prior knowledge. *Journal of Personality and Social Psychology*, 1981, *40*, 441-452. (b)

Cohen, C. E., & Ebbesen, E. B. Observational goals and schema activation: A theoretical framework for behavior perception. *Journal of Experimental Social Psychology*, 1979, *15*, 305-329.

Cohen, F., & Lazarus, R. S. Active coping processes, coping dispositions, and recovery from surgery. *Psychosomatic Medicine*, 1973, *35*, 375-389.

Cohen, S. Environmental load and the allocation of attention. In A. Baum & S. Valins (Eds.), *Advances in environmental psychology* (Vol. 1). Hillsdale, N.J.: Erlbaum, 1978.

Collins, A. M., & Quillian, M. R. Experiments on semantic memory and language comprehension. In L. W. Gregg (Ed.), *Cognition and learning.* New York: Wiley, 1972.

Collins, B. E. Four separate components of the Rotter I-E scale: Belief in a difficult world, a just world, a predictable world and a politically responsive world. *Journal of Personality and Social Psychology,* 1974, *29*, 381-391.

Condry, J. Enemies of exploration: Self-initiated versus other-initiated learning. *Journal of Personality and Social Psychology,* 1977, *35*, 459-477.

Conger, J. C., Conger, A. J., & Brehm, S. Fear level as a moderator of false feedback effects in snake phobics. *Journal of Consulting and Clinical Psychology,* 1976, *44*, 135-141.

Cook, T. D., & Flay, B. R. The persistence of experimentally induced attitude change. In L. Berkowitz (Ed.), *Advances in experimental social psychology* (Vol. 11). New York: Academic Press, 1978.

Cooley, C. H. *Human nature and the social order.* New York: Scribner's, 1902.

Corah, N. L., & Boffa, J. Perceived control, self-observation, and response to aversive stimulation. *Journal of Personality and Social Psychology,* 1970, *16*, 1-4.

Cordray, D. S., & Shaw, J. I. An empirical test of the covariation analysis in causal attribution. *Journal of Experimental Social Psychology,* 1978, *14*, 280-290.

Corteen, R. S., & Wood, B. Automatic responses to shock-associated words in an unattended channel. *Journal of Experimental Psychology,* 1972, *94*, 308-313.

Costrich, N., Feinstein, J., Kidder, L., Marecek, J., & Pascale, L. When stereotypes hurt: Three studies of penalties for sex-role reversals. *Journal of Experimental Social Psychology,* 1975, *11*, 520-530.

Cottrell, N. B., Ingraham, L. A., & Monfort, F. W. The retention of balanced and unbalanced cognitive structures. *Journal of Personality,* 1971, *39*, 112-131.

Covington, M. V., & Omelich, C. L. Are causal attributions causal? A path analysis of the cognitive model of achievement motivation. *Journal of Personality and Social Psychology,* 1979, *37*, 1487-1504.

Craik, F. I. M., & Lockhart, R. S. Levels of processing: A framework for memory research. *Journal of Verbal Learning and Verbal Behavior,* 1972, *11*, 671-676.

Crandall, V. C. Sex differences in expectancy of intellectual and achievement reinforcement. In C. P. Smith (Ed.), *Achievement-related motives in children.* New York: Russell Sage Foundation, 1969.

Crandall, V. C., Katkovsky, W., & Crandall, V. J. Children's beliefs in their own control of reinforcement in intellectual-academic situations. *Child Development,* 1965, *36*, 91-109.

Crano, W. D., & Sivacek, J. Hedonic motivation as a determinant of attitude-behavior consistency. *Journal of Personality and Social Psychology,* in press.

Crocker, J. Judgment of covariation by social perceivers. *Psychological Bulletin,* 1981, *90*, 272-292.

Crocker, J. Biased questions in judgment of covariation studies. *Personality and Social Psychology Bulletin,* 1982, *8*, 214-220.

Crocker, J., Fiske, S. T., & Taylor, S. E. Schematic bases of belief change. In R. Eiser (Ed.), *Attitudinal judgment.* New York: Springer-Verlag, in press.

Crocker, J., Hannah, D. B., & Weber, R. Person memory and causal attributions. *Journal of Personality and Social Psychology,* 1983, *44*, 55-66.

Crocker, J., & Weber, R. Cognitive structure and stereotype change. In R. P. Bagozzi & A. M. Tybout (Eds.), *Advances in consumer research* (Vol. 10). Ann Arbor: Association for Consumer Research, 1983.

Cromwell, R. L., Butterfield, E. C., Brayfield, F. M., & Curry, J. J. *Acute myocardial infarction: Reaction and recovery.* St Louis: Mosby, 1977.

Cronbach, L. J. Processes affecting scores on "understanding of others" and "assumed similarity." *Psychological Bulletin,* 1955, *52,* 177-193.

Crosby, F., Bromley, S., & Saxe, L. Recent unobtrusive studies of black and white discrimination and prejudice: A literature review. *Psychological Bulletin,* 1980, *87,* 546-563.

Cunningham, J. D., & Kelley, H. H. Causal attributions for interpersonal events of varying magnitudes. *Journal of Personality,* 1975, *43,* 74-93.

Darley, J. M., & Fazio, R. H. Expectancy confirmation processes arising in the social interaction sequence. *American Psychologist,* 1980, *35,* 867-881.

Darley, J. M., & Goethals, G. R. People's analyses of the causes of ability-linked performances. In L. Berkowitz (Ed.), *Advances in experimental social psychology* (Vol. 13). New York: Academic Press, 1980.

Darley, J. M., & Gross, P. H. A hypothesis-confirming bias in labeling effects. *Journal of Personality and Social Psychology,* 1983, *44,* 20-33.

Davidson, A., & Steiner, I. D. Reinforcement schedules and attributed freedom. *Journal of Personality and Social Psychology,* 1971, *19,* 357-366.

Davis, W. L., & Phares, E. J. Internal-external control as a determinant of information seeking in a social influence situation. *Journal of Personality,* 1967, *35,* 547-561.

Davis, W. L., & Phares, E. J. Parental antecedents of internal-external control of reinforcement. *Psychological Reports,* 1969, *24,* 427-436.

Davison, G. C., Tsujimoto, R. N., & Glaros, A. G. Attribution and the maintenance of behavior change in falling asleep. *Journal of Abnormal Psychology,* 1973, *82,* 124-133.

Davison, G. C., & Valins, S. Maintenance of self-attributed and drug-attributed behavior change. *Journal of Personality and Social Psychology,* 1969, *11,* 25-33.

Davitz, J. R. A dictionary and grammar of emotion. In M. B. Arnold (Ed.), *Feelings and emotion: The Loyola Symposium.* New York: Academic Press, 1970.

Dawes, R. M. Shallow psychology. In J. Carroll & J. Payne (Eds.), *Cognition and social behavior.* Hillsdale, N.J.: Erlbaum, 1976.

Dawes, R. M. You can't systematize human judgment: Dyslexia. In R. A. Shweder (Ed.), *New directions for methodology of social and behavioral science* (Vol. 4). San Francisco: Jossey-Bass, 1980.

Deaux, K. *The behavior of women and men.* Monterey, Calif.: Brooks/Cole, 1976. (a)

Deaux, K. Sex: A perspective on the attribution process. In J. H. Harvey, W. J. Ickes, & R. F. Kidd (Eds.), *New directions in attribution research* (Vol. 1). Hillsdale, N.J.: Erlbaum, 1976. (b)

Deaux, K. Self-evaluations of male and female managers. *Sex Roles,* 1979, *5,* 571-580.

Deaux, K., & Emswiller, T. Explanations of successful performance on sex-linked tasks: What is skill for the male is luck for the female. *Journal of Personality and Social Psychology,* 1974, *29,* 80-85.

Deaux, K., & Farris, E. Attributing causes for one's own performance: The effects of sex, norms, and outcome. *Journal of Research in Personality,* 1977, *11,* 59-72.

de Charms, R. *Personal causation.* New York: Academic Press, 1968.

Deci, E. L. The effects of externally mediated rewards on intrinsic motivation. *Journal of Personality and Social Psychology,* 1971, *18,* 105-115.

Deci, E. L. Intrinsic motivation, extrinsic reinforcement, and inequity. *Journal of Personality and Social Psychology*, 1972, *22*, 113-120.

Deci, E. L. *Intrinsic motivation: Research and theory.* New York: Plenum, 1975.

DePaulo, B. M., & Rosenthal, R. Telling lies. *Journal of Personality and Social Psychology*, 1979, *37*, 1713-1721.

deRivera, J. A structural theory of the emotions. *Psychological Issues*, 1977, *10* (4, Monograph 40).

DeSoto, C. B., Henley, N. M., & London, M. Balance and the grouping schema. *Journal of Personality and Social Psychology*, 1968, *8*, 1-7.

Deutsch, M. Field theory in social psychology. In G. Lindzey & E. Aronson (Eds.), *The handbook of social psychology* (Vol. 1, 2nd ed.). Reading, Mass.: Addison-Wesley, 1968.

Deutsch, M., & Krauss, R. M. *Theories in social psychology.* New York: Basic Books, 1965.

Diener, E., & Wallbom, M. Effects of self-awareness on antinormative behavior. *Journal of Research in Personality*, 1976, *10*, 107-111.

DiVitto, B., & McArthur, L. Z. Developmental differences in the use of distinctiveness, consensus and consistency information for making causal attributions. *Developmental Psychology*, 1978, *5*, 474-482.

Doyle, A. C. *The complete Sherlock Holmes.* Garden City, N.Y.: Doubleday, Doran, 1930.

Dreben, E. K., Fiske, S. T., & Hastie, R. The independence of item and evaluative information: Impression and recall order effects in behavior-based impression formation. *Journal of Personality and Social Psychology*, 1979, *37*, 1758-1768.

Duncan, J. W., & Laird, J. D. Cross-modality consistencies in individual differences in self-attribution. *Journal of Personality*, 1977, *45*, 191-196.

Duncan, J. W., & Laird, J. D. Positive and reverse placebo effects as a function of differences in cues used in self-perception. *Journal of Personality and Social Psychology*, 1980, *39*, 1024-1036.

Duncan, S. L. Differential social perception and attribution of intergroup violence: Testing the lower limits of stereotyping of blacks. *Journal of Personality and Social Psychology*, 1976, *34*, 590-598.

Dutta, S., Kanungo, R. N., & Freibergs, V. Retention of affective material: Effects of intensity of affect on retrieval. *Journal of Personality and Social Psychology*, 1972, *23*, 64-80.

Dutton, D. G., & Aron, A. P. Some evidence for heightened sexual attraction under conditions of high anxiety. *Journal of Personality and Social Psychology*, 1974, *30*, 510-517.

Duval, S. Conformity on a visual task as a function of personal novelty on attitudinal dimensions and being reminded of the object status of self. *Journal of Experimental Social Psychology*, 1976, *12*, 87-98.

Duval, S., & Wicklund, R. A. *A theory of objective self-awareness.* New York: Academic Press, 1972.

Dweck, C. S. The role of expectations and attributions in the alleviation of learned helplessness. *Journal of Personality and Social Psychology*, 1975, *31*, 674-685.

Dweck, C. S., Davidson, W., Nelson, S., & Enna, B. Sex differences in learned helplessness: II. The contingencies of evaluative feedback in the classroom and III. An experimental analysis. *Developmental Psychology*, 1978, *14*, 268-276.

Dweck, C. S., & Goetz, T. E. Attributions and learned helplessness. In J. H. Harvey, W. J.

Ickes, & R. F. Kidd (Eds.), *New directions in attribution research* (Vol. 2). Hillsdale, N.J.: Erlbaum, 1978.

Dweck, C. S., & Reppucci, N. D. Learned helplessness and reinforcement responsibility in children. *Journal of Personality and Social Psychology*, 1973, *25*, 109-116.

Eagly, A. H. Comprehensibility of persuasive arguments as a determinant of opinion change. *Journal of Personality and Social Psychology*, 1974, *29*, 758-773.

Eagly, A. H. Sex differences in influenceability. *Psychological Bulletin*, 1978, *85*, 86-116.

Eagly, A. H. Recipient characteristics as determinants of responses to persuasion. In R. E. Petty, T. M. Ostrom, & T. C. Brock (Eds.), *Cognitive responses in persuasion*. Hillsdale, N.J.: Erlbaum, 1981.

Eagly, A. H., & Chaiken, S. An attribution analysis of the effect of communication characteristics on opinion change: The case of communicator attractiveness. *Journal of Personality and Social Psychology*, 1975, *32*, 136-144.

Eagly, A. H., Chaiken, S., & Wood, W. An attribution analysis of persuasion. In J. H. Harvey, W. J. Ickes, & R. F. Kidd (Eds.), *New directions in attribution research* (Vol. 3). Hillsdale, N.J.: Erlbaum, 1981.

Eagly, A. H., & Himmelfarb, S. Attitudes and opinions. *Annual Review of Psychology*, 1978, *29*, 517-554.

Easterbrook, J. A. The effect of emotion on cue utilization and the organization of behavior. *Psychological Review*, 1959, *66*, 183-200.

Ebbesen, E. B. Cognitive processes in understanding ongoing behavior. In R. Hastie, T. M. Ostrom, E. B. Ebbesen, R. S. Wyer, D. L. Hamilton, & D. E. Carlston (Eds.), *Person memory: The cognitive basis of social perception*. Hillsdale, N.J.: Erlbaum, 1980.

Ebbesen, E. B., & Allen, R. B. Cognitive processes in implicit personality trait inferences. *Journal of Personality and Social Psychology*, 1979, *37*, 471-488.

Ebbinghaus, H. [*Memory: A contribution to experimental psychology.*] (H. A. Ruger and C. E. Bussenius, trans.) New York: Dover, 1964. (Originally published, 1885.)

Egbert, L. D., Batitt, E., Welch, C. E., & Bartlett, M. K. Reduction of postoperative pain by encouragement and instruction of patients. *New England Journal of Medicine*, 1964, *270*, 825-827.

Einhorn, H. J. Overconfidence in judgment. In R. A. Shweder (Ed.), *New directions for methodology of social and behavioral science* (Vol. 4). San Francisco: Jossey-Bass, 1980.

Einhorn, H. J. Learning from experience and suboptimal rules in decision making. In D. Kahneman, P. Slovic, & A. Tversky (Eds.), *Judgment under uncertainty: Heuristics and biases*. New York: Cambridge University Press, 1982.

Einhorn, H. J., & Hogarth, R. M. Behavioral decision theory: Processes of judgment and choice. *Annual Review of Psychology*, 1981, *32*, 53-88.

Eisen, S. V. Actor-observer differences in information inference and causal attribution. *Journal of Personality and Social Psychology*, 1979, *37*, 261-272.

Eisen, S. V., & McArthur, L. Z. Evaluating and sentencing a defendant as a function of his salience and the observer's set. *Personality and Social Psychology Bulletin*, 1979, *5*, 48-52.

Elig, T. W., & Frieze, I. H. A multi-dimensional coding scheme of causal attributes in social and academic situations. *Personality and Social Psychology Bulletin*, 1974, *1*, 94-96.

Elig, T. W., & Frieze, I. H. Measuring causal attributions for success and failure. *Journal of Personality and Social Psychology*, 1979, *37*, 621-634.

Elio, R., & Anderson, J. R. The effects of category generalizations and instance similarity on schema abstraction. *Journal of Experimental Psychology: Human Learning and Memory*, 1981, 7, 397-417.

Ellis, R. J., & Holmes, J. G. Focus of attention and self-evaluation in social interaction. *Journal of Personality and Social Psychology*, 1982, 43, 67-77.

Ellsworth, P. C., & Tourangeau, R. On our failure to disconfirm what nobody ever said. *Journal of Personality and Social Psychology*, 1981, 40, 363-369.

Engel, G. L. A life setting conducive to illness: The giving-up-given-up complex. *Annals of Internal Medicine*, 1968, 69, 293-300.

Enquist, G., Newtson, D., & LaCross, K. Prior expectations and the perceptual segmentation of ongoing behavior. Unpublished manuscript, University of Virginia, 1979.

Enzle, M. E., & Ross, J. M. Increasing and decreasing intrinsic interest with contingent rewards: A test of cognitive evaluation theory. *Journal of Experimental Social Psychology*, 1978, 14, 588-597.

Epstein, S. The stability of behavior: I. On predicting most of the people much of the time. *Journal of Personality and Social Psychology*, 1979, 7, 1097-1126.

Epstein, S. The stability of behavior: II. Implications for psychological research. *American Psychologist*, 1980, 35, 790-806.

Erber, R., & Fiske, S. T. Outcome dependency and attention to inconsistent information. Unpublished manuscript, Carnegie-Mellon University, 1983.

Erdelyi, M. H. A new look at the new look: Perceptual defense and vigilance. *Psychological Review*, 1974, 81, 1-25.

Erdelyi, M. H., & Goldberg, B. Let's not sweep repression under the rug: Towards a cognitive psychology of repression. In J. F. Kihlstrom & F. J. Evans (Eds.), *Functional disorders of memory*. Hillsdale, N.J.: Erlbaum, 1979.

Etaugh, L., & Brown, B. Perceiving the causes of success and failure of male and female performers. *Developmental Psychology*, 1975, 11, 103.

Exline, R. V. Visual interaction: The glances of power and preference. In J. Cole (Ed.), *Nebraska Symposium on Motivation* (Vol. 19). Lincoln: University of Nebraska Press, 1972.

Farina, A., Allen, J. G., & Saul, B. B. The role of the stigmatized person in affecting social relationships. *Journal of Personality*, 1968, 36, 169-182.

Fazio, R. H. On the self-perception explanation of the overjustification effect: The role of the salience of initial attitude. *Journal of Experimental Social Psychology*, 1981, 17, 417-426.

Fazio, R. H., Effrein, E. A., & Falender, V. J. Self-perceptions following social interaction. *Journal of Personality and Social Psychology*, 1981, 41, 232-242.

Fazio, R. H., Sherman, S. J., & Herr, P. M. The feature-positive effect in the self-perception process: Does not doing matter as much as doing? *Journal of Personality and Social Psychology*, 1982, 42, 404-411.

Fazio, R. H., & Zanna, M. P. Attitudinal qualities relating to the strength of the attitude-behavior relationship. *Journal of Experimental Social Psychology*, 1978, 14, 398-408.

Fazio, R. H., & Zanna, M. P. Direct experience and attitude-behavior consistency. In L. Berkowitz (Ed.), *Advances in experimental social psychology* (Vol. 14). New York: Academic Press, 1981.

Fazio, R. H., Zanna, M. P., & Cooper, J. Dissonance and self-perception: An integrative view of each theory's proper domain of application. *Journal of Experimental Social Psychology*, 1977, 13, 464-479.

Feather, N. T. Attitude and selective recall. *Journal of Personality and Social Psychology*, 1969, *12*, 310-319.

Feather, N. T., & Simon, J. G. Reactions to male and female success and failure in sex-linked occupations: Impressions of personality, causal attributions, and perceived likelihood of different consequences. *Journal of Personality and Social Psychology*, 1975, *31*, 20-31.

Federoff, N. A., & Harvey, J. H. Focus of attention, self-esteem, and attribution of causality. *Journal of Research in Personality*, 1976, *10*, 336-345.

Feldman-Summers, S., & Kiesler, S. B. Those who are number two try harder: The effect of sex on attributions of causality. *Journal of Personality and Social Psychology*, 1974, *30*, 846-854.

Fenichel, O. *The psychoanalytic theory of neurosis.* New York: Norton, 1945.

Fenigstein, A. Self-consciousness, self-attention, and social interaction. *Journal of Personality and Social Psychology*, 1979, *37*, 75-86.

Fenigstein, A., Scheier, M. F., & Buss, A. H. Public and private self-consciousness: Assessment and theory. *Journal of Consulting and Clinical Psychology*, 1975, *43*, 522-527.

Ferguson, T. J., Rule, B. G., & Carlson, D. Memory for personally relevant information. *Journal of Personality and Social Psychology*, 1983, *44*, 251-261.

Ferguson, T. J., & Wells, G. L. Priming of mediators in causal attribution. *Journal of Personality and Social Psychology*, 1980, *38*, 461-470.

Festinger, L. A theory of social comparison processes. *Human Relations*, 1954, *40*, 427-448.

Festinger, L. *A theory of cognitive dissonance.* Stanford, Calif.: Stanford University Press, 1957.

Festinger, L., & Maccoby, N. On resistance to persuasive communications. *Journal of Abnormal and Social Psychology*, 1964, *68*, 359-366.

Fiedler, K. Causal schemata: Review and criticism of research on a popular construct. *Journal of Personality and Social Psychology*, 1982, *42*, 1001-1013.

Fields, J. M., & Schuman, H. Public beliefs and the beliefs of the public. *Public Opinion Quarterly*, 1976, *40*, 427-448.

Fincham, F. D., & Jaspars, J. M. Attribution of responsibility: From man the scientist to man as lawyer. In L. Berkowitz (Ed.), *Advances in experimental social psychology* (Vol. 13). New York: Academic Press, 1980.

Fischer, D. H. *Historian's fallacies.* New York: Harper & Row, 1970.

Fischhoff, B. Hindsight ≠ foresight: The effects of outcome knowledge on judgment under uncertainty. *Journal of Experimental Psychology: Human Perception and Performance*, 1975, *1*, 288-299.

Fischhoff, B. For those condemned to study the past: Reflections on historical judgment. In R. A. Shweder (Ed.), *New directions for methodology of social and behavioral science* (Vol. 4). San Francisco: Jossey-Bass, 1980.

Fischhoff, B. Debiasing. In D. Kahneman, P. Slovic, & A. Tversky (Eds.), *Judgment under uncertainty: Heuristics and biases.* New York: Cambridge University Press, 1982. (a)

Fischhoff, B. For those condemned to study the past: Heuristics and biases in hindsight. In D. Kahneman, P. Slovic, & A. Tversky (Eds.), *Judgment under uncertainty: Heuristics and biases.* New York: Cambridge University Press, 1982. (b)

Fischhoff, B., & Beyth, R. "I knew it would happen"—Remembered probabilities of once-future things. *Organizational Behavior and Human Performance*, 1975, *13*, 1-16.

Fischhoff, B., Slovic, P., & Lichtenstein, S. Knowing with certainty: The appropriateness of extreme confidence. *Journal of Experimental Psychology: Human Perception and Performance*, 1977, *3*, 552-564.

Fishbein, M. An investigation of the relationships between beliefs about an object and the attitude toward that object. *Human Relations*, 1963, *16*, 233-240.

Fishbein, M. A consideration of beliefs and their role in attitude measurement. In M. Fishbein (Ed.), *Readings in attitude theory and measurement*. New York: Wiley, 1967.

Fishbein, M., & Ajzen, I. Attitudes toward objects as predictors of single and multiple behavioral criteria. *Psychological Review*, 1974, *81*, 59-74.

Fishbein, M., & Ajzen, I. *Belief, attitude, intention, and behavior: An introduction to theory and research*. Reading, Mass.: Addison-Wesley, 1975.

Fiske, D. W., & Maddi, S. R. *Functions of varied experience*. Homewood, Ill.: Dorsey, 1961.

Fiske, S. T. Attention and weight in person perception: The impact of negative and extreme behavior. *Journal of Personality and Social Psychology*, 1980, *38*, 889-906.

Fiske, S. T. Social cognition and affect. In J. Harvey (Ed.), *Cognition, social behavior, and the environment*. Hillsdale, N.J.: Erlbaum, 1981.

Fiske, S. T. Schema-triggered affect: Applications to social perception. In M. S. Clark & S. T. Fiske (Eds.), *Affect and cognition: The 17th Annual Carnegie Symposium on Cognition*. Hillsdale, N.J.: Erlbaum, 1982.

Fiske, S. T., Beattie, A. E., & Milberg, S. J. A stereotype-piecemeal model of social cognition and social affect. Unpublished manuscript, Carnegie-Mellon University, 1983.

Fiske, S. T., & Cox, M. G. Person concepts: The effects of target familiarity and descriptive purpose on the process of describing others. *Journal of Personality*, 1979, *47*, 136-161.

Fiske, S. T., & Dyer, L. M. The development of social knowledge structures: Positive and negative transfer. Unpublished manuscript, Carnegie-Mellon University, 1983.

Fiske, S. T., Kenny, D. A., & Taylor, S. E. Structural models for the mediation of salience effects on attribution. *Journal of Experimental Social Psychology*, 1982, *18*, 105-127.

Fiske, S. T., & Kinder, D. R. Involvement, expertise, and schema use: Evidence from political cognition. In N. Cantor & J. Kihlstrom (Eds.), *Personality, cognition, and social interaction*. Hillsdale, N.J.: Erlbaum, 1981.

Fiske, S. T., Kinder, D. R., & Larter, W. M. The novice and the expert: Knowledge-based strategies in political cognition. *Journal of Experimental Social Psychology*, 1983, *19*, 381-400.

Fiske, S. T., & Linville, P. W. What does the schema concept buy us? *Personality and Social Psychology Bulletin*, 1980, *6*, 543-557.

Fiske, S. T., Taylor, S. E., Etcoff, N. L., & Laufer, J. K. Imaging, empathy, and causal attribution. *Journal of Experimental Social Psychology*, 1979, *15*, 356-377.

Fong, G. T., & Markus, H. Self-schemas and judgments about others. *Social Cognition*, 1982, *1*, 191-205.

Franks, J. J., & Bransford, J. D. Abstraction of visual patterns. *Journal of Experimental Social Psychology*, 1971, *90*, 65-74.

Freedman, J. L., & Fraser, S. C. Compliance without pressure: The foot-in-the-door technique. *Journal of Personality and Social Psychology*, 1966, *4*, 195-202.

Freedman, J. L., & Sears, D. Selective exposure. In L. Berkowitz (Ed.), *Advances in experimental social psychology* (Vol. 2). New York: Academic Press, 1965.

Freides, D. Human information processing and sensory modality: Cross-modal functions, information complexity, memory, and deficit. *Psychological Bulletin*, 1974, *81*, 284-310.

Friedman, M., & Rosenman, R. H. *Type A behavior and your heart*. New York: Knopf, 1974.

Frieze, I. H., Bar-Tal, D., & Carroll, J. S. *New approaches to social problems*. San Francisco: Jossey-Bass, 1979.

Frieze, I. H., Whitley, B. E., Jr., Hanusa, B. H., & McHugh, M. C. Assessing the theoretical models for sex differences in causal attributions for success and failure. *Sex Roles*, 1982, *8*, 333-343.

Froming, W. J., & Carver, C. S. Divergent influences of private and public self-consciousness in a compliance paradigm. *Journal of Research in Psychology*, 1981, *15*, 159-171.

Froming, W. J., Walker, G. R., & Lopyan, K. J. Public and private self-awareness: When personal attitudes conflict with societal expectations. *Journal of Experimental Social Psychology*, 1982, *18*, 476-487.

Galper, R. E. Turning observers into actors: Differential causal attributions as a function of "empathy." *Journal of Research in Personality*, 1976, *10*, 328-335.

Gangestad, S., & Borgida, E. Intuitive prediction and intuitive regression: Accounting for predictor information. Unpublished manuscript, University of Minnesota, 1981.

Gara, M. A., & Rosenberg, S. The identification of persons as supersets and subsets in free-response personality descriptions. *Journal of Personality and Social Psychology*, 1979, *37*, 2161-2170.

Garber, J., & Seligman, M. E. P. *Human helplessness: Theory and applications*. New York: Academic Press, 1980.

Garland, H., Hardy, A., & Stephenson, L. Information search as affected by attribution type and response category. *Personality and Social Psychology Bulletin*, 1975, *1*, 612-615.

Gatchel, R. J., & Proctor, J. D. Physiological correlates of learned helplessness in man. *Journal of Abnormal Psychology*, 1976, *85*, 27-34.

Geer, J. H., Davison, G. C., & Gatchel, R. I. Reduction of stress in humans through nonveridical perceived control of aversive stimulation. *Journal of Personality and Social Psychology*, 1970, *16*, 731-738.

Geer, J. H., & Maisel, E. Evaluating the effects of the prediction-control confound. *Journal of Personality and Social Psychology*, 1972, *23*, 314-319.

Geidt, F. H. Comparison of visual, content, and auditory cues in interviewing. *Journal of Consulting Psychology*, 1955, *19*, 407-416.

Gerard, H. B., & Fleischer, L. Recall and pleasantness of balanced and imbalanced cognitive structures. *Journal of Personality and Social Psychology*, 1967, *7*, 332-337.

Gerard, H. B., & Hoyt, M. F. Distinctiveness of social categorization and attitude toward ingroup members. *Journal of Personality and Social Psychology*, 1974, *29*, 836-842.

Gergen, K. J. Personal consistency and the presentation of self. In C. Gordon & K. J. Gergen (Eds.), *The self in social interaction* (Vol. 1). New York: Wiley, 1968.

Gergen, K. J. The social construction of self-knowledge. In T. Mischel (Ed.), *The self: Psychological and biological issues*. Totowa, N.J.: Rowman & Littlefield, 1977.

Gergen, K. J., & Taylor, M. G. Social expectancy and self-presentation in a status hierarchy. *Journal of Experimental Social Psychology*, 1969, *5*, 79-92.

Gergen, K. J., & Wishnov, B. Others' self-evaluation and interaction anticipation as determinants of self-presentation. *Journal of Personality and Social Psychology*, 1965, 2, 348-358.

Gibbons, F. X. Sexual standards and reactions to pornography: Enhancing behavioral consistency through self-focused attention. *Journal of Research in Personality*, 1978, 36, 976-987.

Gibbons, F. X., Carver, C. S., Scheier, M. F., & Hormuth, S. E. Self-focused attention and the placebo effect: Fooling some of the people some of the time. *Journal of Experimental Social Psychology*, 1979, 15, 263-274.

Gibbons, F. X., & Wicklund, R. A. Selective exposure to self. *Journal of Research in Personality*, 1976, 10, 98-106.

Gibson, J. J. *The senses considered as perceptual systems.* Boston: Houghton Mifflin, 1966.

Gibson, J. J. *The ecological approach to visual perception.* Boston: Houghton Mifflin, 1979.

Gilbert, G. M. Stereotype persistence and change among college students. *Journal of Abnormal and Social Psychology*, 1951, 46, 245-254.

Gilmor, T. M., & Minton, H. L. Internal versus external attribution of task performance as a function of locus of control, initial confidence, and success-failure outcome. *Journal of Personality*, 1974, 42, 159-174.

Gilovich, T. Seeing the past in the present: The effect of associations to familiar events on judgments and decisions. *Journal of Personality and Social Psychology*, 1981, 40, 797-808.

Ginosar, Z., & Trope, Y. The effects of base rates and individuating information on judgments about another person. *Journal of Experimental Social Psychology*, 1980, 16, 228-242.

Girodo, M. Film-induced arousal, information search, and the attribution process. *Journal of Personality and Social Psychology*, 1973, 25, 357-360.

Girodo, M., & Wood, D. Talking yourself out of pain: The importance of believing that you can. *Cognitive Therapy and Research*, 1979, 3, 21-33.

Glass, D. C. *Behavioral patterns, stress, and coronary disease.* Hillsdale, N.J.: Erlbaum, 1977.

Glass, D. C., Reim, B., & Singer, J. E. Behavioral consequences of adaptation to controllable and uncontrollable noise. *Journal of Experimental Social Psychology*, 1971, 7, 244-257.

Glass, D. C., & Singer, J. E. *Urban stress.* New York: Academic Press, 1972.

Glass, D. C., Singer, J. E., & Friedman, L. N. Psychic cost of adaptation to an environmental stressor. *Journal of Personality and Social Psychology*, 1969, 12, 200-210.

Goethals, G. R. An attributional analysis of some social influence phenomena. In J. H. Harvey, W. J. Ickes, & R. F. Kidd (Eds.), *New directions in attribution research* (Vol. 1). Hillsdale, N.J.: Erlbaum, 1976.

Goethals, G. R., Allison, S. J., & Frost, M. Perceptions of the magnitude and diversity of social support. *Journal of Experimental Social Psychology*, 1979, 15, 570-581.

Goffman, E. *The presentation of self in everyday life.* Garden City, N.Y.: Doubleday, Anchor Books, 1959.

Goffman, E. *Stigma: Notes on the management of spoiled identity.* Englewood Cliffs, N.J.: Prentice-Hall, 1963.

Goldberg, L. R. Simple models or simple processes? Some research on clinical judgments. *American Psychologist*, 1968, 23, 483-496.

Goldberg, L. R. Man versus model of man: A rationale, plus some evidence, for a method of improving on clinical inferences. *Psychological Bulletin*, 1970, *73*, 422-432.

Goldberg, L. R. Differential attribution of trait-descriptive terms to oneself as compared to well-liked, neutral, and disliked others: A psychometric analysis. *Journal of Personality and Social Psychology*, 1978, *36*, 1012-1028.

Goldberg, L. R. Unconfounding situational attributions from uncertain, neutral, and ambiguous ones: A psychometric analysis of descriptions of oneself and various types of others. *Journal of Personality and Social Psychology*, 1981, *41*, 517-552.

Goldberg, P. A. Are women prejudiced against women? *Transaction*, 1968, *4*, 28-30.

Gollwitzer, P. M., Earle, W. B., & Stephan, W. G. Affect as a determinant of egotism: Residual excitation and performance attributions. *Journal of Personality and Social Psychology*, 1982, *43*, 702-709.

Gould, R., & Sigall, H. The effects of empathy and outcome on attribution: An examination of the divergent-perspectives hypothesis. *Journal of Experimental Social Psychology*, 1977, *13*, 480-491.

Graesser, A. C., Gordon, S. E., & Sawyer, J. D. Recognition memory for typical and atypical actions in scripted activities: Tests of a script pointer and tag hypothesis. *Journal of Verbal Learning and Verbal Behavior*, 1979, *18*, 319-332.

Graesser, A. C., Woll, S. B., Kowalski, D. J., & Smith, D. A. Memory for typical and atypical actions in scripted activities. *Journal of Experimental Psychology: Human Learning and Memory*, 1980, *6*, 503-515.

Graziano, W. G., Brothen, T., & Berscheid, E. Attention, attraction, and individual differences in reaction to criticism. *Journal of Personality and Social Psychology*, 1980, *38*, 193-202.

Greaves, G. Conceptual system functioning and selective recall of information. *Journal of Personality and Social Psychology*, 1972, *21*, 327-332.

Greenwald, A. G. Cognitive learning, cognitive response to persuasion, and attitude change. In A. G. Greenwald, T. C. Brock, & T. M. Ostrom (Eds.), *Psychological foundations of attitudes*. New York: Academic Press, 1968.

Greenwald, A. G. Does the Good Samaritan parable increase helping? A comment on Darley and Batson's no-effect conclusion. *Journal of Personality and Social Psychology*, 1975, *32*, 578-583.

Greenwald, A. G. Environmental structure and cognitive structure. In J. Harvey (Ed.), *Cognition, social behavior, and the environment*. Hillsdale, N.J.: Erlbaum, 1980. (a)

Greenwald, A. G. The totalitarian ego: Fabrication and revision of personal history. *American Psychologist*, 1980, *35*, 603-618. (b)

Greenwald, A. G. Self and memory. In G. H. Bower (Ed.), *The psychology of learning and motivation*. New York: Academic Press, 1981.

Greenwald, A. G. Ego task analysis: An integration of research on ego-involvement and self-awareness. In A. Hastorf & A. M. Isen (Eds.), *Cognitive social psychology*. New York: Elsevier North-Holland, 1982.

Greenwald, A. G., & Leavitt, C. Audience involvement in advertising: Four levels. *Journal of Consumer Research*, in press.

Greenwald, A. G., & Pratkanis, A. R. The self. In R. S. Wyer & T. K. Srull (Eds.), *Handbook of social cognition*. Hillsdale, N.J.: Erlbaum, in press.

Gregory, W. L., Cialdini, R. B., & Carpenter, K. M. Self-relevant scenarios as mediators of likelihood estimates and compliance: Does imagining make it so? *Journal of Personality and Social Psychology*, 1982, *43*, 89-99.

Gren, R. Effects of anticipation of positive and negative outcomes on audience anxiety. *Journal of Consulting and Clinical Psychology*, 1977, *46*, 32-39.

Gross, C. F. Intrajudge consistency in ratings of heterogenous persons. *Journal of Abnormal and Social Psychology*, 1961, *62*, 605-610.

Grush, J. E. Attitude formation and mere exposure phenomena: A nonartificial explanation of empirical findings. *Journal of Personality and Social Psychology*, 1976, *33*, 281-290.

Gurin, P., Gurin, G., Lao, R. C., & Beattie, M. Internal-external control in the motivational dynamics of Negro youth. *Journal of Social Issues*, 1969, *25*, 29-53.

Gurwitz, S. B., & Dodge, K. A. Adults' evaluations of a child as a function of sex of adult and sex of child. *Journal of Personality and Social Psychology*, 1975, *32*, 822-828.

Gurwitz, S. B., & Dodge, K. A. Effects of confirmations and disconfirmations on stereotype-based attributions. *Journal of Personality and Social Psychology*, 1977, *35*, 495-500.

Gurwitz, S. B., & Topol, B. Determinants of confirming and disconfirming responses to negative social labels. *Journal of Experimental Social Psychology*, 1978, *14*, 31-42.

Hager, J. C., & Ekman, P. Methodological problems in Tourangeau and Ellsworth's study of facial expression and experience of emotion. *Journal of Personality and Social Psychology*, 1981, *40*, 358-362.

Hall, J. A., & Taylor, S. E. When love is blind: Maintaining idealized images of one's spouse. *Human Relations*, 1976, *29*, 751-761.

Hamill, R. Self-schemas and face recognition: Effects of cognitive structures on social perception and memory. Unpublished doctoral dissertation, University of Michigan, 1980.

Hamill, R., Wilson, T. D., & Nisbett, R. E. Insensitivity to sample bias: Generalizing from atypical cases. *Journal of Personality and Social Psychology*, 1980, *39*, 578-589.

Hamilton, D. L. A cognitive-attributional analysis of stereotyping. In L. Berkowitz (Ed.), *Advances in experimental social psychology* (Vol. 12). New York: Academic Press, 1979.

Hamilton, D. L. *Cognitive processes in stereotyping and intergroup behavior*. Hillsdale, N.J.: Erlbaum, 1981. (a)

Hamilton, D. L. Organizational processes in impression formation. In E. T. Higgins, C. P. Herman, & M. P. Zanna (Eds.), *Social cognition: The Ontario Symposium* (Vol. 1). Hillsdale, N.J.: Erlbaum, 1981. (b)

Hamilton, D. L., & Gifford, R. K. Illusory correlation in interpersonal perception: A cognitive basis of stereotypic judgments. *Journal of Experimental Social Psychology*, 1976, *12*, 392-407.

Hamilton, D. L., & Katz, L. B. A process-oriented approach to the study of impressions. Paper presented at the meeting of the American Psychological Association, Chicago, August, 1975.

Hamilton, D. L., Katz, L. B., & Leirer, V. O. Cognitive representation of personality impressions: Organizational processes in first impression formation. *Journal of Personality and Social Psychology*, 1980, *39*, 1050-1063. (a)

Hamilton, D. L., Katz, L. B., & Leirer, V. O. Organizational processes in impression formation. In R. Hastie, T. M. Ostrom, E. B. Ebbesen, R. S. Wyer, D. L. Hamilton, & D. E. Carlston (Eds.), *Person memory: The cognitive basis of social perception*. Hillsdale, N.J.: Erlbaum, 1980. (b)

Hamilton, D. L., & Rose, T. L. Illusory correlation and the maintenance of stereotypic beliefs. *Journal of Personality and Social Psychology*, 1980, *39*, 832-845.

Hamilton, D. L., & Zanna, M. P. Context effects in impression formation: Changes in connotative meaning. *Journal of Personality and Social Psychology*, 1974, *29*, 649-654.

Hamilton, V. L. Intuitive psychologist or intuitive lawyer? Alternative models of the attribution process. *Journal of Personality and Social Psychology*, 1980, *39*, 767-772.

Hammen, C. On depression: Attributional models. Paper presented at the meeting of the American Psychological Association, Los Angeles, August, 1981.

Hansen, R. D. Commonsense attribution. *Journal of Personality and Social Psychology*, 1980, *39*, 996-1009.

Hansen, R. D., & Donoghue, J. M. The power of consensus: Information derived from one's own and others' behavior. *Journal of Personality and Social Psychology*, 1977, *35*, 294-302.

Hansen, R. D., & O'Leary, V. E. Actresses and actors: The effects of sex on causal attributions. *Basic and Applied Social Psychology*, 1983, *4*, 209-230.

Hanusa, B. H., & Schulz, R. Attributional mediators of learned helplessness. *Journal of Personality and Social Psychology*, 1977, *35*, 602-611.

Harackiewicz, J. M. The effects of reward contingency and performance feedback on intrinsic motivation. *Journal of Personality and Social Psychology*, 1979, *37*, 1352-1363.

Harris, R. J., Teske, R. R., & Ginns, M. J. Memory for pragmatic implications from courtroom testimony. *Bulletin of the Psychonomic Society*, 1975, *6*, 494-496.

Harrison, A. A. Mere exposure. In L. Berkowitz (Ed.), *Advances in experimental social psychology* (Vol. 10). New York: Academic Press, 1977.

Hartley, D. *Observations on man, his frame, his duty, and his expectations.* Delmar, New York: Scholastic Facsimiles, 1966. (Originally published, 1749.)

Hartwick, J. Memory for trait information: A signal detection analysis. *Journal of Experimental Social Psychology*, 1979, *15*, 533-552.

Harvey, J. H. Attribution of freedom. In J. H. Harvey, W. J. Ickes, & R. F. Kidd (Eds.), *New directions in attribution research* (Vol. 1). Hillsdale, N.J.: Erlbaum, 1976.

Harvey, J. H., & Harris, B. Determinants of perceived choice and the relationship between perceived choice and the expectancy about feelings of internal control. *Journal of Personality and Social Psychology*, 1975, *31*, 101-106.

Harvey, J. H., Harris, B., & Barnes, R. D. Actor-observer differences in the perceptions of responsibility and freedom. *Journal of Personality and Social Psychology*, 1975, *32*, 22-28.

Harvey, J. H., Harris, B., & Lightner, J. M. Perceived freedom as a central concept in psychological theory and research. In L. C. Perlmuter & R. A. Monty (Eds.), *Choice and perceived control.* Hillsdale, N.J.: Erlbaum, 1979.

Harvey, J. H., Ickes, W. J., & Kidd, R. F. *New directions in attribution research* (Vol. 1). Hillsdale, N.J.: Erlbaum, 1976.

Harvey, J. H., Ickes, W. J., & Kidd, R. F. *New directions in attribution research* (Vol. 2). Hillsdale, N.J.: Erlbaum, 1978.

Harvey, J. H., Ickes, W. J., & Kidd, R. F. *New directions in attributions research* (Vol. 3). Hillsdale, N.J.: Erlbaum, 1981.

Harvey, J. H., & Jellison, J. M. Determinants of perceived choice, number of options, and perceived time in making a selection. *Memory and Cognition*, 1974, *2*, 539-544.

Harvey, J. H., & Johnston, S. Determinants of the perception of choice. *Journal of Experimental Social Psychology*, 1973, *9*, 164-179.

Harvey, J. H., & McGlynn, R. P. Matching words to phenomena: The case of the fundamental attribution error. *Journal of Personality and Social Psychology*, 1982, *43*, 345-346.

Harvey, J. H., Town, J. P., & Yarkin, K. L. How fundamental is "The fundamental attribution error"? *Journal of Personality and Social Psychology*, 1981, *40*, 346-349.

Harvey, J. H., & Tucker, J. A. On problems with the cause-reason distinction in attribution theory. *Journal of Personality and Social Psychology*, 1979, *37*, 1441-1446.

Harvey, J. H., & Weary, G. *Perspectives on attributional processes*. Dubuque, Iowa: W. C. Brown, 1981.

Harvey, J. H., Wells, G. L., & Alvarez, M. D. Attribution in the context of conflict and separation in close relationships. In J. H. Harvey, W. Ickes, & R. F. Kidd (Eds.), *New directions in attribution research* (Vol. 2). Hillsdale, N.J.: Erlbaum, 1978.

Harvey, J. H., Yarkin, K. I., Lightner, J. M., & Town, J. P. Unsolicited interpretation and recall of interpersonal events. *Journal of Personality and Social Psychology*, 1980, *38*, 551-568.

Haslett, D. M. Distracting stimuli: Do they elicit or inhibit counterargumentation and attitude shift? *European Journal of Social Psychology*, 1976, *6*, 81-94.

Hass, R. G. Effects of source characteristics on cognitive responses and persuasion. In R. E. Petty, T. M. Ostrom, & T. C. Brock (Eds.), *Cognitive responses in persuasion*. Hillsdale, N.J.: Erlbaum, 1981.

Hastie, R. Memory for behavioral information that confirms or contradicts a personality impression. In R. Hastie, T. M. Ostrom, E. B. Ebbesen, R. S. Wyer, D. L. Hamilton, & D. E. Carlston (Eds.), *Person memory: The cognitive basis of social perception*. Hillsdale, N.J.: Erlbaum, 1980.

Hastie, R. Schematic principles in human memory. In E. T. Higgins, C. P. Herman, & M. P. Zanna (Eds.), *Social cognition: The Ontario Symposium* (Vol. 1). Hillsdale, N.J.: Erlbaum, 1981.

Hastie, R., & Carlston, D. Theoretical issues in person memory. In R. Hastie, T. M. Ostrom, E. B. Ebbesen, R. S. Wyer, D. L. Hamilton, & D. E. Carlston (Eds.), *Person memory: The cognitive basis of social perception*. Hillsdale, N.J.: Erlbaum, 1980.

Hastie, R., & Kumar, P. A. Person memory: Personality traits as organizing principles in memory for behavior. *Journal of Personality and Social Psychology*, 1979, *37*, 25-38.

Hastie, R., Ostrom, T. M., Ebbesen, E. B., Wyer, R. S., Hamilton, D. L., & Carlston, D. E. *Person memory: The cognitive basis of social perception*. Hillsdale, N.J.: Erlbaum, 1980.

Hayes-Roth, B. Evolution of cognitive structure and processes. *Psychological Review*, 1977, *84*, 260-278.

Hayes-Roth, B., & Hayes-Roth, F. Concept learning and the recognition and classification of exemplars. *Journal of Verbal Learning and Verbal Behavior*, 1977, *16*, 321-338.

Hebb, D. O. *The organization of behavior: A neuropsychological theory*. New York: Wiley, 1949.

Heider, F. Social perception and phenomenal causality. *Psychological Review*, 1944, *51*, 358-374.

Heider, F. *The psychology of interpersonal relations*. New York: Wiley, 1958.

Hemsley, G. D., & Marmurek, H. H. C. Person memory: The processing of consistent and inconsistent person information. *Personality and Social Psychology Bulletin*, 1982, *8*, 433-438.

Hendrick, I. Instinct and the ego during infancy. *Psychoanalytic Quarterly*, 1942, *11*, 33-58.

Henker, B., & Whalen, C. K. The many messages of medication: Hyperactive children's perceptions and attributions. In S. Salzinger, J. Antrobus, & J. Glick (Eds.), *The ecosystem of the "sick" child.* New York: Academic Press, 1980.

Hennigan, K. M., Cook, T. D., & Gruder, C. L. Cognitive tuning set, source credibility, and the temporal persistence of attitude change. *Journal of Personality and Social Psychology,* 1982, *42,* 412-425.

Higgins, E. T. The 'communication game': Implications for social cognition. In E. T. Higgins, C. P. Herman, & M. P. Zanna (Eds.), *Social cognition: The Ontario Symposium* (Vol. 1). Hillsdale, N.J.: Erlbaum, 1981.

Higgins, E. T., & Chaires, W. M. Accessibility of interrelational constructs: Implications for stimulus encoding and creativity. *Journal of Experimental Social Psychology,* 1980, *16,* 348-361.

Higgins, E. T., Herman, C. P., & Zanna, M. P. *Social cognition: The Ontario Symposium* (Vol. 1). Hillsdale, N.J.: Erlbaum, 1981.

Higgins, E. T., & King, G. A. Accessibility of social constructs: Information-processing consequences of individual and contextual variability. In N. Cantor & J. F. Kihlstrom (Eds.), *Personality, cognition, and social interaction.* Hillsdale, N.J.: Erlbaum, 1981.

Higgins, E. T., King, G. A., & Mavin, G. H. Individual construct accessibility and subjective impressions and recall. *Journal of Personality and Social Psychology,* 1982, *43,* 35-47.

Higgins, E. T., Kuiper, N. A., & Olson, J. M. Social cognition: A need to get personal. In E. T. Higgins, C. P. Herman, & M. P. Zanna (Eds.), *Social cognition: The Ontario Symposium* (Vol. 1). Hillsdale, N.J.: Erlbaum, 1981.

Higgins, E. T., McCann, C. D., & Fondacaro, R. The "communication game": Goal-directed encoding and cognitive consequences. *Social Cognition,* 1982, *1,* 21-37.

Higgins, E. T., & Rholes, W. S. "Saying is believing": Effects of message modification on memory and liking for the person described. *Journal of Experimental Social Psychology,* 1978, *14,* 363-378.

Higgins, E. T., Rholes, W. S., & Jones, C. R. Category accessibility and impression formation. *Journal of Experimental Social Psychology,* 1977, *13,* 141-154.

Himmelfarb, S., & Eagly, A. H. *Readings in attitude change.* New York: Wiley, 1974.

Hiroto, D. S., & Seligman, M. E. P. Generality of learned helplessness in man. *Journal of Personality and Social Psychology,* 1975, *31,* 311-327.

Hoffman, C., & Mischel, W. Objectives and strategies in the lay person's categorization of behavior. Paper presented at the meeting of the American Psychological Association, Montreal, September 1980.

Hoffman, C., Mischel, W., & Mazze, K. The role of purpose in the organization of information about behavior: Trait-based versus goal-based categories in person cognition. *Journal of Personality and Social Psychology,* 1981, *40,* 211-225.

Hogarth, R. M. *Judgment and choice: The psychology of decision.* New York: Wiley, 1980.

Hogarth, R. M. Beyond discrete biases: Functional and dysfunctional aspects of judgmental heuristics. *Psychological Bulletin,* 1981, *90,* 197-217.

Holmes, D. S. Dimensions of projection. *Psychological Bulletin,* 1968, *69,* 248-268.

Holmes, D. S., & Houston, B. K. Effectiveness of situation redefinition and affective isolation in coping with stress. *Journal of Personality and Social Psychology,* 1974, *29,* 212-218.

Hornstein, H. A., Martin, J., Rup, A. H., Sole, K., & Tartell, R. The propensity to recall another's completed and uncompleted tasks as a consequence of varying social relationships. *Journal of Experimental Social Psychology*, 1980, *16*, 362-375.

Houston, B. K. Dispositional anxiety and the effectiveness of cognitive strategies in stressful laboratory and classroom situations. In C. D. Spielberger & I. G. Sarason (Eds.), *Stress and anxiety* (Vol. 4). New York: Wiley, 1977.

Hovland, C. I., Janis, I. L., & Kelley, H. H. *Communication and persuasion*. New Haven, Conn.: Yale University Press, 1953.

Hovland, C. I., Lumsdaine, A. A., & Sheffield, F. D. *Experiments on mass communication*. Princeton, N.J.: Princeton University Press, 1949.

Howard, J. W., & Rothbart, M. Social categorization and memory for ingroup and outgroup behavior. *Journal of Personality and Social Psychology*, 1980, *38*, 301-310.

Huesmann, L. R. Process models of social behavior. In N. Hirschberg (Ed.), *Multivariate methods in the social sciences: Application*. Hillsdale, N.J.: Erlbaum, 1980.

Hull, C. L. *Principles of behavior*. New York: Appleton-Century-Crofts, 1943.

Hull, C. L. *A behavior system: An introduction to behavior theory concerning the individual organism*. New Haven, Conn.: Yale University Press, 1952.

Hull, J. G., & Levy, A. S. The organizational functions of the self: An alternative to the Duval and Wicklund model of self-awareness. *Journal of Personality and Social Psychology*, 1979, *37*, 756-768.

Hume, D. *A treatise on human nature being an attempt to introduce the experimental method of reasoning into moral subjects*. Fair Lawn, N.J.: Oxford University Press, 1978. (Originally published, 1739.)

Humphries, C., Carver, C. S., & Neumann, P. G. Cognitive characteristics of the Type A coronary-prone behavior pattern. *Journal of Personality and Social Psychology*, 1983, *44*, 177-187.

Huston-Stein, A., Pohly, S. R., & Mueller, E. The influence of masculine, feminine, and neutral tasks on children's achievement behavior, expectancies of success, and attainment values. *Child Development*, 1971, *42*, 195-207.

Ickes, W. J., & Barnes, R. D. The role of sex and self-monitoring in unstructured dyadic interactions. *Journal of Personality and Social Psychology*, 1977, *35*, 315-330.

Ickes, W. J., & Kidd, R. F. Attributional analysis of helping behavior. In J. H. Harvey, W. J. Ickes, & R. F. Kidd (Eds.), *New directions in attribution research* (Vol. 1). Hillsdale, N.J.: Erlbaum, 1976.

Ickes, W. J., Patterson, M. L., Rajecki, D. W., & Tanford, S. Behavioral and cognitive consequences of reciprocal versus compensatory responses to preinteraction expectances. *Social Cognition*, 1982, *1*, 160-190.

Insko, C. A., & Cialdini, R. B. A test of three interpretations of attitudinal verbal reinforcement. *Journal of Personality and Social Psychology*, 1969, *12*, 333-341.

Isen, A. M., & Levin, P. F. The effect of feeling good on helping: Cookies and kindness. *Journal of Personality and Social Psychology*, 1972, *21*, 384-388.

Isen, A. M., Means, B., Patrick, R., & Nowicki, G. Some factors influencing decision-making strategy and risk taking. In M. S. Clark & S. T. Fiske (Eds.), *Affect and cognition: The 17th Annual Carnegie Symposium on Cognition*. Hillsdale, N.J.: Erlbaum, 1982.

Isen, A. M., Shalker, T. E., Clark, M. S., & Karp, L. Affect, accessibility of material in memory, and behavior: A cognitive loop? *Journal of Personality and Social Psychology*, 1978, *36*, 1-12.

Izard, C. E. *The face of emotion.* New York: Appleton-Century-Crofts, 1972.

Izard, C. E. *Human emotions.* New York: Plenum, 1977.

Izard, C. E. Differential emotions theory and the facial feedback hypothesis of emotion activation: Comments on Tourangeau and Ellsworth's "The role of facial response in the experience of emotion." *Journal of Personality and Social Psychology*, 1981, *40*, 350-354.

Jacobs, L., Berscheid, E., & Walster, E. Self-esteem and attraction. *Journal of Personality and Social Psychology*, 1971, *17*, 84-91.

James, W. What is an emotion? In M. Arnold (Ed.), *The nature of emotion.* Baltimore: Penguin, 1968. (Originally published, 1884.)

Janis, I. L. *Psychological stress.* New York: Wiley, 1958.

Janis, I. L. *Victims of groupthink.* Boston: Houghton Mifflin, 1972.

Janis, I. L., & Mann, L. *Decision making: A psychological analysis of conflict, choice, and commitment.* New York: Free Press, 1977.

Janoff-Bulman, R. Characterological versus behavioral self-blame: Inquiries into depression and rape. *Journal of Personality and Social Psychology*, 1979, *37*, 1789-1809.

Jecker, J. D. The cognitive effects of conflict and dissonance. In L. Festinger (Ed.), *Conflict, decision, and dissonance.* Stanford, Calif.: Stanford University Press, 1964.

Jeffery, K. M., & Mischel, W. Effects of purpose on organization and recall of information in person perception. *Journal of Personality*, 1979, *47*, 397-419.

Jellison, J. M., & Green, J. A self-presentation approach to the fundamental attribution error: The norm of internality. *Journal of Personality and Social Psychology*, 1981, *40*, 643-649.

Jenkins, C. D., Rosenman, R. H., & Friedman, M. Replicability of rating the coronary-prone behavior pattern. *British Journal of Preventive and Social Medicine*, 1968, *22*, 16-22.

Jenkins, H. M., & Ward, W. C. Judgments of contingency between responses and outcomes. *Psychological Monographs*, 1965, *79* (1, Whole No. 594).

Jennings, D., Amabile, T. M., & Ross, L. Informal covariation assessment: Data-based vs. theory-based judgments. In A. Tversky, D. Kahneman, & P. Slovic (Eds.), *Judgment under uncertainty: Heuristics and biases.* New York: Cambridge University Press, 1982.

Johnson, E. J., & Tversky, A. Affect generalization and the perception of risk. *Journal of Personality and Social Psychology*, 1983, *45*, 20-31.

Johnson, J. E. The effects of accurate expectations about sensations on the sensory and distress components of pain. *Journal of Personality and Social Psychology*, 1973, *27*, 261-275.

Johnson, J. E. Stress reduction through sensation information. In I. G. Sarason & C. D. Spielberger (Eds.), *Stress and anxiety.* Washington, D.C.: Hemisphere, 1975.

Johnson, J. E. Psychological interventions and coping with surgery. In A. Baum, S. E. Taylor, & J. E. Singer (Eds.), *The handbook of health psychology: Social aspects of health.* Hillsdale, N.J.: Erlbaum, in press.

Johnson, J. E., & Leventhal, H. Effects of accurate expectations and behavioral instructions on reactions during a noxious medical examination. *Journal of Personality and Social Psychology*, 1974, *29*, 710-718.

Johnson, J. E., Morissey, J. F., & Leventhal, H. Psychological preparation for an endoscopic examination. *Gastrointestinal Endoscopy*, 1973, *19*, 180-182.

Johnson, M. K., & Raye, C. L. Reality monitoring. *Psychological Review*, 1981, *88*, 67-85.

Johnson, N. S. The role of schemata in comprehension and memory: A developmental perspective. Paper presented at the meeting of the American Psychological Association, Los Angeles, August 1981.

Jones, E. E. How do people perceive the causes of behavior? *American Scientist*, 1976, *64*, 300-305.

Jones, E. E., & Berglas, S. Control of attributions about the self through self-handicapping strategies: The appeal of alcohol and the role of underachievement. *Personality and Social Psychology Bulletin*, 1978, *4*, 200-206.

Jones, E. E., & Davis, K. E. From acts to dispositions: The attribution process in person perception. In L. Berkowitz (Ed.), *Advances in experimental social psychology* (Vol. 2). New York: Academic Press, 1965.

Jones, E. E., Davis, K. E., & Gergen, K. J. Role playing variations and their informational value for person perception. *Journal of Abnormal and Social Psychology*, 1961, *63*, 302-310.

Jones, E. E., Gergen, K. J., & Davis, K. E. Some determinants of reactions to being approved or disapproved as a person. *Psychological Monographs*, 1962, *76* (Whole No. 521).

Jones, E. E., & Harris, V. A. The attribution of attitudes. *Journal of Experimental Social Psychology*, 1967, *3*, 1-24.

Jones, E. E., Kanouse, D. E., Kelley, H. H., Nisbett, R. E., Valins, S., & Weiner, B. (Eds.). *Attribution: Perceiving the causes of behavior.* Morristown, N.J.: General Learning Press, 1972.

Jones, E. E., & McGillis, D. Correspondent inferences and the attribution cube: A comparative reappraisal. In J. H. Harvey, W. J. Ickes, & R. F. Kidd (Eds.), *New directions in attribution research* (Vol. 1). Hillsdale, N.J.: Erlbaum, 1976.

Jones, E. E., & Nisbett, R. E. The actor and the observer: Divergent perceptions of the causes of behavior. In E. E. Jones, D. E. Kanouse, H. H. Kelley, R. E. Nisbett, S. Valins, & B. Weiner (Eds.), *Attribution: Perceiving the causes of behavior.* morristown, N.J.: General Learning Press, 1972.

Jones, E. E., & Pittman, T. S. Toward a general theory of strategic self-presentation. In J. Suls (Ed.), *Psychological perspectives on the self.* Hillsdale, N.J.: Erlbaum, 1982.

Jones, E. E., Rhodewalt, F., Berglas, S., & Skelton, J. A. Effects of strategic self-presentation on subsequent self-esteem. *Journal of Personality and Social Psychology*, 1981, *41*, 407-421.

Jones, E. E., & Thibaut, J. W. Interaction goals as bases of human inference in interpersonal perception. In R. Tagiuri & L. Petrullo (Eds.), *Person perception and interpersonal behavior.* Stanford, Calif.: Stanford University Press, 1958.

Jones, E. E., Worchel, S., Goethals, G. R., & Grumet, J. F. Prior expectancy and behavioral extremity as determinants of attitude attribution. *Journal of Experimental Social Psychology*, 1971, *7*, 59-80.

Jones, E. E., & Wortman, C. *Ingratiation: An attributional approach.* Morristown, N.J.: General Learning Press, 1973.

Jones, J. M. *Prejudice and racism.* Reading, Mass.: Addison-Wesley, 1972.

Jones, S. C., & Panitch, D. The self-fulfilling prophecy and interpersonal attraction. *Journal of Experimental Social Psychology*, 1971, *7*, 356-366.

Jones, S. C., & Schneider, D. J. Certainty of self-appraisal and reactions to evaluations from others. *Sociometry*, 1968, *31*, 395-403.

Judd, C. M., & Johnson, J. T. Attitudes, polarization, and diagnosticity: Exploring the effect of affect. *Journal of Personality and Social Psychology*, 1981, *41*, 26-36.

Judd, C. M., & Krosnick, J. A. Attitude centrality, organization, and measurement. *Journal of Personality and Social Psychology*, 1982, *42*, 436-447.

Judd, C. M., & Kulik, J. A. Schematic effects of social attitudes on information processing and recall. *Journal of Personality and Social Psychology*, 1980, *38*, 569-578.

Just, M. A., & Carpenter, P. A. Eye fixations and cognitive processes. *Cognitive Psychology*, 1976, *8*, 441-480.

Kahneman, D. *Attention and effort.* Englewood Cliffs, N.J.: Prentice-Hall, 1973.

Kahneman, D., & Tversky, A. On the psychology of prediction. *Psychological Review*, 1973, *80*, 237-251.

Kahneman, D., & Tversky, A. The simulation heuristic. In D. Kahneman, P. Slovic, & A. Tversky (Eds.), *Judgment under uncertainty: Heuristics and biases.* New York: Cambridge University Press, 1982.

Kanfer, F. H., & Goldfoot, D. A. Self-control and tolerance of noxious stimulation. *Psychological Reports*, 1966, *18*, 79-85.

Kanfer, F. H., & Seidner, M. L. Self-control: Factors enhancing tolerance of noxious stimulation. *Journal of Personality and Social Psychology*, 1973, *25*, 381-389.

Kant, I. *Critique of pure reason.* New York: St. Martin's Press, 1969. (Originally published, 1781.)

Kanter, R. *Men and women of the corporation.* New York: Basic Books, 1977.

Kanungo, R. N., & Dutta, S. Retention of affective material: Frame of reference or intensity? *Journal of Personality and Social Psychology*, 1966, *4*, 27-35.

Kaplan, M. F. Context effects in impression formation: The weighted average versus the meaning-change formulation. *Journal of Personality and Social Psychology*, 1971, *19*, 92-99.

Kaplan, M. F. Evaluative judgments are based on evaluative information: The weighted average versus the meaning-change formulation. *Memory and Cognition*, 1975, *3*, 375-380.

Karniol, R., & Ross, M. The development of causal attributions in social perception. *Journal of Personality and Social Psychology*, 1976, *34*, 455-464.

Karniol, R., & Ross, M. The effect of performance-relevant and performance-irrelevant rewards on children's intrinsic motivations. *Child Development*, 1977, *48*, 482-487.

Kassin, S. M. Base rates and prediction: The role of sample size. *Personality and Social Psychology Bulletin*, 1979, *5*, 210-213. (a)

Kassin, S. M. Consensus information, prediction, and causal attribution: A review of the literature and issues. *Journal of Personality and Social Psychology*, 1979, *37*, 1966-1981. (b)

Katz, E. On reopening the question of selectivity in exposure to mass media. In R. Abelson *et al.* (Eds.), *Theories of cognitive consistency: A sourcebook.* Chicago: Rand-McNally, 1968.

Kazdin, A. E., & Bootzin, R. R. The token economy: An evaluative review. *Journal of Applied Behavioral Analysis*, 1972, *5*, 343-372.

Keenan, J. M., & Baillet, S. D. Memory for personally and socially relevant events. In R. S. Nickerson (Ed.), *Attention and performance VIII.* Hillsdale, N.J.: Erlbaum, 1980.

Kelley, H. H. Attribution theory in social psychology. In D. Levine (Ed.), *Nebraska Symposium on Motivation* (Vol. 15). Lincoln: University of Nebraska Press, 1967.

Kelley, H. H. Attribution in social interaction. In E. E. Jones, D. E. Kanouse, H. H.

Kelley, R. E. Nisbett, S. Valins, & B. Weiner (Eds.), *Attribution: Perceiving the causes of behavior.* Morristown, N.J.: General Learning Press, 1972. (a)

Kelley, H. H. Causal schemata and the attribution process. In E. E. Jones, D. E. Kanouse, H. H. Kelley, R. E. Nisbett, S. Valins, & B. Weiner (Eds.), *Attribution: Perceiving the causes of behavior.* Morristown, N.J.: General Learning Press, 1972. (b)

Kelley, H. H., & Michela, J. L. Attribution theory and research. *Annual Review of Psychology,* 1980, *31,* 457-501.

Kellogg, R., & Baron, R. S. Attribution theory, insomnia, and the reverse placebo effect: A reversal of Storms and Nisbett's findings. *Journal of Personality and Social Psychology,* 1975, *32,* 231-236.

Kelman, H. C. Attitudes are alive and well and gainfully employed in the sphere of action. *American Psychologist,* 1974, *29,* 310-324.

Kendall, P., & Hollon, S. *Cognitive-behavioral intentions: Theory, research, and procedures.* New York: Academic Press, 1979.

Kendzierski, D. Self-schemata and scripts: The recall of self-referent and scriptal information. *Personality and Social Psychology Bulletin,* 1980, *6,* 23-29.

Kenny, D. A. *Correlation and causality.* New York: Wiley-Interscience, 1979.

Kenrick, D. T., Baumann, D. J., & Cialdini, R. B. A step in the socialization of altruism as hedonism: Effects of negative mood on children's generosity under public and private conditions. *Journal of Personality and Social Psychology,* 1979, *37,* 747-755.

Kenrick, D. T., & Cialdini, R. B. Romantic attraction: Misattribution versus reinforcement explanations. *Journal of Personality and Social Psychology,* 1977, *35,* 381-391.

Kiesler, C. A. *The psychology of commitment: Experiments linking behavior to belief.* New York: Academic Press, 1971.

Kiesler, C. A. Comments. In M. S. Clark & S. T. Fiske (Eds.), *Affect and cognition: The 17th Annual Carnegie Symposium on Cognition.* Hillsdale, N.J.: Erlbaum, 1982.

Kiesler, C. A., Collins, B. E., & Miller, N. *Attitude change: A critical analysis of theoretical approaches.* New York: Wiley, 1969.

Kiesler, C. A., Nisbett, R. E., & Zanna, M. P. On inferring one's beliefs from one's behavior. *Journal of Personality and Social Psychology,* 1969, *11,* 321-327.

Kihlstrom, J. F. On personality and memory. In N. Cantor & J. F. Kihlstrom (Eds.), *Personality, cognition, and social interaction.* Hillsdale, N.J.: Erlbaum, 1981.

Kim, M. P., & Rosenberg, S. Comparison of two structural models of implicit personality theory. *Journal of Personality and Social Psychology,* 1980, *38,* 375-389.

Kimmel, H. D. Instrumental factors in classical conditioning. In W. Prokasy (Ed.), *Classical conditioning.* New York: Appleton-Century-Crofts, 1965.

Kinder, D. R. Political person perception: The asymmetrical influence of sentiment on perceptions of presidential candidates. *Journal of Personality and Social Psychology,* 1978, *36,* 859-871.

Kinder, D. R., Peters, M. D., Abelson, R. P., & Fiske, S. T. Presidential prototypes. *Political Behavior,* 1980, *2,* 315-337.

Kintsch, W. *The representation of meaning in memory.* Hillsdale, N.J.: Erlbaum, 1974.

Kintsch, W., & van Dijk, T. A. Toward a model of text comprehension and production. *Psychological Review,* 1978, *85,* 363-394.

Klagsbrun, S. C. Communications in the treatment of cancer. *American Journal of Nursing,* 1971, *71,* 944-948.

Klatzky, R. L. *Human memory: Structures and processes.* San Francisco: Freeman, 1975.

Klatzky, R. L., Martin, G. L., & Kane, R. A. Influence of social-category activation on processing of visual information. *Social Cognition*, 1982, *1*, 95-109.

Klein, D. C., Fencil-Morse, E., & Seligman, M. E. P. Learned helplessness, depression, and the attribution of failure. *Journal of Personality and Social Psychology*, 1976, *33*, 508-516.

Kleinhesselink, R. R., & Edwards, R. E. Seeking and avoiding belief-discrepant information as a function of its perceived refutability. *Journal of Personality and Social Psychology*, 1975, *31*, 787-790.

Kleinke, C. L. *First impressions: The psychology of encountering others.* Englewood Cliffs, N.J.: Prentice-Hall, 1975.

Kleinke, C. L., Staneski, R. A., & Weaver, P. Evaluation of a person who uses another's name in ingratiating or noningratiating situations. *Journal of Experimental Social Psychology*, 1972, *8*, 457-466.

Klinger, E., Barta, S. G., & Maxeiner, M. E. Motivational correlates of thought content frequency and commitment. *Journal of Personality and Social Psychology*, 1980, *39*, 1222-1237.

Knight, J. A., & Vallacher, R. R. Interpersonal engagement in social perception: The consequence of getting into the action. *Journal of Personality and Social Psychology*, 1981, *40*, 990-999.

Koffka, K. *Principles of Gestalt psychology.* New York: Harcourt, Brace, & World, 1935.

Kohler, W. *The place of value in a world of facts.* New York: Likeright, 1976. (Originally published, 1938.)

Kolditz, T. A., & Arkin, R. M. An impression management interpretation of the self-handicapping strategy. *Journal of Personality and Social Psychology*, 1982, *43*, 492-502.

Koller, P. S., & Kaplan, R. M. A two-process theory of learned helplessness. *Journal of Personality and Social Psychology*, 1978, *36*, 1177-1183.

Kosslyn, S. M., Pinker, S., Smith, G. E., & Shwartz, S. P. On the demystification of mental imagery. *The Behavioral and Brain Sciences*, 1979, *2*, 535-581.

Kosslyn, S. M., & Pomerantz, J. R. Imagery, propositions, and the form of internal representations. *Cognitive Psychology*, 1977, *9*, 52-76.

Krantz, D. S., Baum, A., & Wideman, M. V. Assessment of preferences for self-treatment and information in health care. *Journal of Personality and Social Psychology*, 1980, *39*, 977-990.

Krauss, R. M. Impression formation, impression management, and nonverbal behaviors. In E. T. Higgins, C. P. Herman, & M. P. Zanna (Eds.), *Social cognition: The Ontario Symposium* (Vol. 1). Hillsdale, N.J.: Erlbaum, 1981.

Kraut, R. E., & Lewis, S. H. Person perception and self-awareness: Knowledge of one's influences on one's own judgments. *Journal of Personality and Social Psychology*, 1982, *42*, 448-460.

Kruglanski, A. W. The endogenous-exogenous partition in attribution theory. *Psychological Review*, 1975, *82*, 387-406.

Kruglanski, A. W. The place of naive contents in a theory of attribution: Reflections on Calder's and Zuckerman's critiques of the endogenous-exogenous partition. *Personality and Social Psychology Bulletin*, 1977, *3*, 592-605.

Kruglanski, A. W. Causal explanation, teleological expansion: On radical particularism in attribution theory. *Journal of Personality and Social Psychology*, 1979, *37*, 1447-1457.

Kruglanski, A. W., Hamel, I. Z., Maides, S. A., & Schwartz, J. M. Attribution theory as a special case of lay epistemology. In J. H. Harvey, W. Ickes, & R. F. Kidd (Eds.), *New directions in attribution research* (Vol. 2). Hillsdale, N.J.: Erlbaum, 1978.

Kuiper, N. A. Depression and causal attributions for success and failure. *Journal of Personality and Social Psychology*, 1978, *36*, 236-246.

Kuiper, N. A. Convergent evidence for the self as a prototype. *Personality and Social Psychology Bulletin*, 1981, *7*, 438-443.

Kuiper, N. A., & Derry, P. A. The self as a cognitive prototype: An application to person perception and to psychopathology. In N. Cantor & J. F. Kihlstrom (Eds.), *Personality, cognition, and social interaction*. Hillsdale, N.J.: Erlbaum, 1981.

Kuiper, N. A., MacDonald, M. R., & Derry, P. A. Parameters of a depressive self-schema. In J. Suls & A. G. Greenwald (Eds.), *Psychological perspectives on the self* (Vol. 2). Hillsdale, N.J.: Erlbaum, 1983.

Kuiper, N. A., & Rogers, T. B. Encoding of personal information: Self-other differences. *Journal of Personality and Social Psychology*, 1979, *37*, 499-514.

Kulik, J. A. Confirmatory attribution and the perpetuation of social beliefs. *Journal of Personality and Social Psychology*, 1983, *44*, 1171-1181.

Kulik, J. A., & Taylor, S. E. Premature consensus on consensus? Effects of sample-based versus self-based consensus information. *Journal of Personality and Social Psychology*, 1980, *38*, 871-878.

Kun, A., & Weiner, B. Necessary versus sufficient causal schemata for success and failure. *Journal of Research in Personality*, 1973, *7*, 197-207.

Kunst-Wilson, W. R., & Zajonc, R. B. Affective discrimination of stimuli that cannot be recognized. *Science*, 1980, *207*, 557-558.

LaBerge, D. Acquisition of automatic processing in perceptual and associative learning. In P. M. A. Rabbit & S. Dornic (Eds.), *Attention and performance* (Vol. 5). New York: Academic Press, 1975.

Laird, J. D. Self-attribution of emotion: The effects of expressive behavior on the quality of emotional experience. *Journal of Personality and Social Psychology*, 1974, *29*, 475-486.

Laird, J. D., Wagener, J., Halal, M., & Szegda, M. Remembering what you feel: Effects of emotion on memory. *Journal of Personality and Social Psychology*, 1982, *42*, 646-657.

Lange, C. G. *The emotions*. Baltimore: Williams & Wilkins, 1922. (Originally published, 1885.)

Langer, E. J. The illusion of control. *Journal of Personality and Social Psychology*, 1975, *32*, 311-328.

Langer, E. J. Rethinking the role of thought in social interaction. In J. H. Harvey, W. I. Ickes, & R. F. Kidd (Eds.), *New directions in attribution research* (Vol. 2). Hillsdale, N.J.: Erlbaum, 1978.

Langer, E. J., & Abelson, R. P. A patient by any other name . . . : Clinician group difference in labeling bias. *Journal of Consulting and Clinical Psychology*, 1974, *42*, 4-9.

Langer, E. J., & Benevento, A. Self-induced dependence. *Journal of Personality and Social Psychology*, 1978, *36*, 886-893.

Langer, E. J., Blank, A., & Chanowitz, B. The mindlessness of ostensibly thoughtful action: The role of "placebic" information in interpersonal interaction. *Journal of Personality and Social Psychology*, 1978, *36*, 635-642.

Langer, E. J., & Imber, L. When practice makes imperfect: Debilitating effects of over-learning. *Journal of Personality and Social Psychology*, 1979, *37*, 2014-2024.

Langer, E. J., Janis, I. L., & Wolfer, J. Effects of a cognitive coping device and preparatory information on psychological stress in surgical patients. *Journal of Experimental Social Psychology*, 1975, *11*, 155-165.

Langer, E. J., & Rodin, J. The effects of choice and enhanced personal responsibility for the aged: A field experiment in an institutional setting. *Journal of Personality and Social Psychology*, 1976, *34*, 191-198.

Langer, E. J., & Roth, J. Heads I win, tails it's chance: The illusion of control as a function of the sequence of outcomes in a purely chance task. *Journal of Personality and Social Psychology*, 1975, *32*, 951-955.

Langer, E. J., & Saegert, S. Crowding and cognitive control. *Journal of Personality and Social Psychology*, 1977, *35*, 175-182.

Langer, E. J., Taylor, S. E., Fiske, S. T., & Chanowitz, B. Stigma, staring, and discomfort: A novel stimulus hypothesis. *Journal of Experimental Social Psychology*, 1976, *12*, 451-463.

Lanzetta, J. T., Cartwright-Smith, J., & Kleck, R. E. Effects of nonverbal dissimilation on emotional experience and autonomic arousal. *Journal of Personality and Social Psychology*, 1976, *33*, 354-370.

LaPiere, R. T. Attitudes versus actions. *Social Forces*, 1934, *13*, 230-237.

Larkin, J. H., McDermott, J., Simon, D. P., & Simon, H. A. Models of competence in solving physics problems. *Science*, 1980, *200*, 1335-1342.

Laswell, H. D. The structure and function of communication in society. In L. Byron (Ed.), *Communication of ideas*. New York: Harper, 1948.

Lau, R. R. The origins of health locus of control beliefs. *Journal of Personality and Social Psychology*, 1982, *42*, 322-334.

Lau, R. R., & Russell, D. Attributions in the sports pages. *Journal of Personality and Social Psychology*, 1980, *39*, 29-38.

Lau, R. R., & Ware, J. E. Refinements in the measurement of health-specific locus of control dimensions. Working paper (WD-232-HHS). Santa Monica, Calif.: Rand Corporation, December 1980.

Lazarus, R. S. Thoughts on the relations between emotion and cognition. *American Psychologist*, 1982, *37*, 1019-1024.

Lazarus, R. S., Averill, J. R., & Opton, E. M., Jr. Towards a cognitive theory of emotion. In M. B. Arnold (Ed.), *Feelings and emotions: The Loyola Symposium*. New York: Academic Press, 1970.

Lefcourt, H. M. *Locus of control: Current trends in theory and research*. Hillsdale, N.J.: Erlbaum, 1976.

Lefcourt, H. M., Lewis, L., & Silverman, I. W. Internal vs. external control of reinforcement and attention in a decision making task. *Journal of Personality*, 1968, *36*, 663-682.

Lefcourt, H. M., & Wine, J. Internal versus external control of reinforcement and the deployment of attention in experimental situations. *Canadian Journal of Behavioural Sciences*, 1969.

Lepper, M. R., & Greene, D. *The hidden costs of reward*. Hillsdale, N.J.: Erlbaum, 1978.

Lepper, M. R., Greene, D., & Nisbett, R. E. Undermining children's intrinsic interest with extrinsic rewards: A test of the "overjustification" hypothesis. *Journal of Personality and Social Psychology*, 1973, *28*, 129-137.

Lepper, M. R., Sagotsky, G., Dafoe, J. L., & Greene, D. Consequences of superfluous social constraints: Effects on young children's social inferences and subsequent intrinsic interest. *Journal of Personality and Social Psychology*, 1982, *42*, 51-64.

Lerner, M. J. The effect of responsibility and choice on a partner's attractiveness following failure. *Journal of Personality*, 1965, *33*, 178-187.

Lerner, M. J. The desire for justice and reactions to victims. In J. McCauley & L. Berkowitz (Eds.), *Altruism and helping behavior*. New York: Academic Press, 1970.

Lerner, M. J., & Matthews, G. Reactions to suffering of others under conditions of indirect responsibility. *Journal of Personality and Social Psychology*, 1967, *5*, 319-325.

Leventhal, H. Emotions: A basic problem for social psychology. In C. Nemeth (Ed.), *Social psychology: Classic and contemporary integrations*. Chicago: Rand-McNally, 1974.

Leventhal, H. Toward a comprehensive theory of emotion. In L. Berkowitz (Ed.), *Advances in experimental social psychology* (Vol. 13). New York: Academic Press, 1980.

Leventhal, H. The integration of emotion and cognition: A view from the perceptual-motor theory of emotion. In M. S. Clark & S. T. Fiske (Eds.), *Affect and cognition: The 17th Annual Carnegie Symposium on Cognition*. Hillsdale, N.J.: Erlbaum, 1982.

Leventhal, H., Brown, D., Shacham, S., & Engquist, G. Effects of preparatory information about sensations, threat of pain, and attention on cold pressor distress. *Journal of Personality and Social Psychology*, 1979, *37*, 688-714.

Leventhal, H., & Everhart, D. Emotion, pain, and physical illness. In C. E. Izard (Ed.), *Emotion and psychopathology*. New York: Plenum, 1979.

Leventhal, H., Nerenz, D., & Straus, A. Self-regulation and the mechanisms for symptom appraisal. In D. Mechanic (Ed.), *Psychological epidemiology*. New York: Watson, 1980.

Lewicki, P. Social psychology as viewed by its practitioners: Survey of SESP members' opinions. *Personality and Social Psychology Bulletin*, 1982, *8*, 409-416.

Lewin, K. *Field theory in social science*. New York: Harper, 1951.

Lingle, J. H., Dukerich, J. M., & Ostrom, T. M. Accessing information in memory-based impression judgments: Incongruity *vs.* negativity in retrieval selectivity. *Journal of Personality and Social Psychology*, 1983, *44*, 262-272.

Lingle, J. H., Geva, N., & Ostrom, T. M. Cognitive processes in person perception. Paper presented at the meeting of the American Psychological Association, Chicago, September 1975.

Lingle, J. H., Geva, N., Ostrom, T. M., Leippe, M. R., & Baumgardner, M. H. Thematic effects of person judgments on impression organization. *Journal of Personality and Social Psychology*, 1979, *37*, 674-687.

Lingle, J. H., & Ostrom, T. M. Retrieval selectivity in memory-based impression judgments. *Journal of Personality and Social Psychology*, 1979, *37*, 180-194.

Lingle, J. H., & Ostrom, T. M. Principles of memory and cognition in attitude formation. In R. E. Petty, T. M. Ostrom, & T. C. Brock (Eds.), *Cognitive responses in persuasive communications*. New York: McGraw-Hill, 1981.

Linville, P. W. Affective consequences of complexity regarding the self and others. In M. S. Clark & S. T. Fiske (Eds.), *Affect and cognition: The 17th Annual Carnegie Symposium on Cognition*. Hillsdale, N.J.: Erlbaum, 1982. (a)

Linville, P. W. The complexity-extremity effect and age-based stereotyping. *Journal of Personality and Social Psychology*, 1982, *42*, 193-211. (b)

Linville, P. W., & Jones, E. E. Polarized appraisals of outgroup members. *Journal of Personality and Social Psychology*, 1980, *38*, 689-703.

Lippa, R. Expressive control and the leakage of dispositional introversion-extraversion during role-playing teaching. *Journal of Personality*, 1976, *44*, 541-559.

Locke, D., & Pennington, D. Reasons and other causes: Their role in attribution processes. *Journal of Personality and Social Psychology*, 1982, *42*, 212-223.

Locke, J. *Essay concerning human understanding.* New York: Oxford University Press, 1979. (Originally published, 1690.)

Locksley, A., Borgida, E., Brekke, N., & Hepburn, C. Sex stereotypes and social judgment. *Journal of Personality and Social Psychology,* 1980, *39,* 821-831.

Locksley, A., Hepburn, C., & Ortiz, V. Social stereotypes and judgments of individuals: An instance of the base rate fallacy. *Journal of Experimental Social Psychology,* 1982, *18,* 23-42.

Loftus, E. F. *Eyewitness testimony.* Cambridge, Mass.: Harvard University Press, 1979.

London, H. *Psychology of the persuader.* Morristown, N.J.: General Learning Press, 1973.

Lorber, J. Good patients and problem patients: Conformity and deviance in a general hospital. *Journal of Health and Social Behavior,* 1975, *16,* 213-225.

Lord, C. G. Schemas and images as memory aids: Two modes of processing social information. *Journal of Personality and Social Psychology,* 1980, *38,* 257-269.

Lord, C. G. Predicting behavioral consistency from an individual's perception of situational similarities. *Journal of Personality and Social Psychology,* 1982, *42,* 1076-1088.

Lord, C. G., Lepper, M. R., & Thompson, W. C. Inhibiting biased assimilation in the consideration of new evidence on social policy issues. Paper presented at the meeting of the American Psychological Association, Montreal, September 1980.

Lord, C. G., Ross, L., & Lepper, M. R. Biased assimilation and attitude polarization: The effects of prior theories on subsequently considered evidence. *Journal of Personality and Social Psychology,* 1979, *37,* 2098-2109.

Lott, A. J., & Lott, B. E. The role of reward in the formation of positive interpersonal attraction. In T. L. Huston (Ed.), *Foundations of interpersonal attraction.* New York: Academic Press, 1974.

Love, R. E., & Greenwald, A. G. Cognitive responses to persuasion as mediators of opinion change. *Journal of Social Psychology,* 1978, *104,* 231-241.

Lowe, C. A., & Kassin, S. M. A perceptual view of attribution: Theoretical and methodological implications. *Personality and Social Psychology,* 1980, *6,* 532-542.

Maccoby, E. E., & Jacklin, C. N. *The psychology of sex differences.* Stanford, Calif.: Stanford University Press, 1974.

Mahoney, M. *Cognition and behavior modification.* Cambridge, Mass.: Ballinger, 1974.

Maier, S. F., & Seligman, M. E. P. Learned helplessness: Theory and evidence. *Journal of Experimental Psychology: General,* 1976, *105,* 3-46.

Major, B. Information acquisition and attribution processes. *Journal of Personality and Social Psychology,* 1980, *39,* 1010-1024.

Malpass, R. S., & Kravitz, J. Recognition for faces of own and other race. *Journal of Personality and Social Psychology,* 1969, *13,* 330-334.

Malpass, R. S., Lavigueur, H., & Weldon, D. E. Verbal and visual training in face recognition. *Perception and Psychophysics,* 1973, *14,* 285-292.

Mandler, G. *Mind and emotion.* New York: Wiley, 1975.

Mandler, G. The structure of value: Accounting for taste. In M. S. Clark & S. T. Fiske (Eds.), *Affect and cognition: The 17th Annual Carnegie Symposium on Cognition.* Hillsdale, N.J.: Erlbaum, 1982.

Mandler, G., & Watson, D. L. Anxiety and the interruption of behavior. In C. D. Spielberger (Ed.), *Anxiety and behavior.* New York: Academic Press, 1966.

Mandler, J. Categorical and schematic organization in memory. In C. R. Puff (Ed.), *Memory organization and structure.* New York: Academic Press, 1979.

Manis, M. Cognitive social psychology. *Personality and Social Psychology Bulletin*, 1977, *3*, 550-566.

Manis, M., Avis, N. E., & Cardoze, S. Reply to Bar-Hillel and Fischhoff. *Journal of Personality and Social Psychology*, 1981, *41*, 681-683.

Manis, M., Dovalina, I., Avis, N. E., & Cardoze, S. Base rates can affect individual predictions. *Journal of Personality and Social Psychology*, 1980, *38*, 231-248.

March, J. G., & Simon, H. A. *Organizations*. New York: Wiley, 1958.

Markus, H. Self-schemata and processing information about the self. *Journal of Personality and Social Psychology*, 1977, *35*, 63-78.

Markus, H., Crane, M., Bernstein, S., & Siladi, M. Self-schemas and gender. *Journal of Personality and Social Psychology*, 1982, *42*, 38-50.

Markus, H., & Fong, G. The role of the self in other perception. Unpublished manuscript, University of Michigan, 1979.

Markus, H., Hamill, R., & Sentis, K. P. Thinking fat: Self-schemas for body weight and the processing of weight relevant information. Unpublished manuscript, University of Michigan, 1979.

Markus, H., & Sentis, K. P. The self in social information processing. In J. Suls (Ed.), *Psychological perspectives on the self* (Vol. 1). Hillsdale, N.J.: Erlbaum, 1982.

Markus, H., & Smith, J. The influence of self-schemata on the perception of others. In N. Cantor & J. Kihlstrom (Eds.), *Personality, cognition, and social interaction*. Hillsdale, N.J.: Erlbaum, 1981.

Markus, H., Smith, J., & Moreland, R. L. The role of the self in social perception: A cognitive analysis. *Psychological Review*, in press.

Marshall, G. D., & Zimbardo, P. G. Affective consequences of inadequately explained physiological arousal. *Journal of Personality and Social Psychology*, 1979, *37*, 970-988.

Martin, J. Stories and scripts in organizational settings. In A. M. Hastorf & A. M. Isen (Eds.), *Cognitive social psychology*. New York: Elsevier North-Holland, 1982.

Martin, J., Harrod, W., & Siehl, C. The development of knowledge structures. Paper presented at the meeting of the American Psychological Association, Montreal, September 1980.

Maslach, C. Negative emotional biasing of unexplained arousal. *Journal of Personality and Social Psychology*, 1979, *37*, 953-969.

Massad, C. M., Hubbard, M., & Newtson, D. Selective perception of events. *Journal of Experimental Social Psychology*, 1979, *15*, 513-532.

Masters, J. C., Barden, R. D., & Ford, M. E. Affective states, expressive behavior, and learning in children. *Journal of Personality and Social Psychology*, 1979, *37*, 380-390.

Matlin, M., & Stang, D. *The Pollyanna principle*. Cambridge, Mass.: Schenkman, 1978.

Matthews, K. A. Psychological perspectives on the Type A behavior pattern. *Psychological Bulletin*, 1982, *91*, 293-323.

Matthews, K. A., & Brunson, B. I. Allocation of attention and the Type A coronary-prone behavior pattern. *Journal of Personality and Social Psychology*, 1979, *37*, 2081-2090.

Matthews, K. A., & Glass, D. C. Stressful life events and their contexts. In B. P. Dohrenwend & B. S. Dohrenwend (Eds.), *Life stress and illness*. New York: Watson, 1981.

Matthews, K. A., Scheier, M. F., Brunson, B. I., & Carducci, B. Attention, unpredictability, and reports of physical symptoms: Eliminating the benefits of predictability. *Journal of Personality and Social Psychology*, 1980, *38*, 525-537.

Mayer, F. S., Duval, S., & Duval, V. H. An attributional analysis of commitment. *Journal of Personality and Social Psychology*, 1980, *39*, 1072-1080.

McArthur, L. Z. The how and what of why: Some determinants and consequences of causal attribution. *Journal of Personality and Social Psychology*, 1972, *22*, 171-193.

McArthur, L. Z. Illusory causation and illusory correlation: Two epistemological accounts. *Personality and Social Psychology Bulletin*, 1980, *6*, 507-519.

McArthur, L. Z. What grabs you? The role of attention in impression formation and causal attribution. In E. T. Higgins, C. P. Herman, & M. P. Zanna (Eds.), *Social cognition: The Ontario Symposium* (Vol. 1). Hillsdale, N.J.: Erlbaum, 1981.

McArthur, L. Z. Judging a book by its cover: A cognitive analysis of the relationship between physical appearance and stereotyping. In A. Hastorf & A. Isen (Eds.), *Cognitive social psychology*. New York: Elsevier North-Holland, 1982.

McArthur, L. Z., & Baron, R. Toward an ecological theory of social perception. *Psychological Review*, 1983, *90*, 215-238.

McArthur, L. Z., & Friedman, S. A. Illusory correlation in impression formation: Variations in the shared distinctiveness effect as a function of the distinctive person's age, race, and sex. *Journal of Personality and Social Psychology*, 1980, *39*, 615-624.

McArthur, L. Z., & Ginsberg, E. Causal attribution to salient stimuli: An investigation of visual fixation mediators. *Personality and Social Psychology Bulletin*, 1981, *7*, 547-553.

McArthur, L. Z., & Post, D. L. Figural emphasis and person perception. *Journal of Experimental Social Psychology*, 1977, *13*, 520-535.

McArthur, L. Z., & Solomon, L. K. Perceptions of an aggressive encounter as a function of the victim's salience and the perceiver's arousal. *Journal of Personality and Social Psychology*, 1978, *36*, 1278-1290.

McCauley, C., & Stitt, C. L. An individual and quantitative measure of stereotypes. *Journal of Personality and Social Psychology*, 1978, *36*, 929-940.

McCauley, C., Stitt, C. L., & Segal, M. Stereotyping: From prejudice to prediction. *Psychological Bulletin*, 1980, *87*, 195-208.

McCauley, C., Stitt, C. L., Woods, K., & Lipton, D. Group shift to caution at the race track. *Journal of Experimental Social Psychology*, 1973, *9*, 80-86.

McCaul, K. D., & Haugtvedt, C. Attention, distraction, and cold-pressor pain. *Journal of Personality and Social Psychology*, 1982, *43*, 154-162.

McClelland, J. L. On the time relations of mental processes: An examination of systems of process in cascade. *Psychological Review*, 1979, *86*, 287-330.

McCloskey, M. E., & Glucksberg, S. Natural categories: Well-defined or fuzzy sets. *Memory and Cognition*, 1978, *6*, 462-472.

McFarland, C., & Ross, M. Impact of causal attributions on affective reactions to success and failure. *Journal of Personality and Social Psychology*, 1982, *43*, 937-946.

McGeoch, J. A. *The psychology of learning*. New York: McKay, 1942.

McGuire, W. J. Personality and susceptibility to social influence. In E. F. Borgatta & W. W. Lambert (Eds.), *Handbook of personality theory and research*. Chicago: Rand McNally, 1968.

McGuire, W. J. Nature of attitudes and attitude change. In G. Lindzey & E. Aronson (Eds.), *The handbook of social psychology* (Vol. 3, 2nd ed.). Reading, Mass.: Addison-Wesley, 1969.

McGuire, W. J. Some internal psychological factors influencing consumer choice. *Journal of Consumer Research*, 1976, *2*, 302-309.

McGuire, W. J., McGuire, C. V., Child, P., & Fujioka, T. Salience of ethnicity in the spontaneous self-concept as a function of one's ethnic distinctiveness in the social environment. *Journal of Personality and Social Psychology*, 1978, *36*, 511-520.

McGuire, W. J., & Padawer-Singer, A. Trait salience in the spontaneous self-concept. *Journal of Personality and Social Psychology*, 1976, *33*, 743-754.

McHugh, M. C., Frieze, I. H., & Hanusa, B. H. Attributions and sex differences in achievement: Problems and new perspectives. *Sex Roles*, 1982, *8*, 467-479.

McIntosh, J. Processes of communication, information seeking, and control associated with cancer: A selective review of the literature. *Social Science and Medicine*, 1974, *8*, 167-187.

McKiethen, K. B., Reitman, J. S., Rueter, H. H., & Hirtle, S. C. Knowledge organization and skill differences in computer programmers. *Cognitive Psychology*, 1981, *13*, 307-325.

Mead, G. H. *Mind, self, and society*. Chicago: University of Chicago Press, 1934.

Meehl, P. E. *Clinical versus statistical prediction: A theoretical analysis and review of the literature*. Minneapolis: University of Minnesota Press, 1954.

Mehrabian, A. Nonverbal communication. In J. Cole (Ed.), *Nebraska Symposium on Motivation* (Vol. 19). Lincoln: University of Nebraska Press, 1972.

Meichenbaum, D. *Cognitive-behavior modification: An integrative approach*. New York: Plenum, 1977.

Merton, R. K. *Social theory and social structure*. New York: Free Press, 1957.

Metalsky, G. I., & Abramson, L. Y. Attributional styles: Toward a framework for conceptualization and assessment. In P. C. Kendall & S. D. Hollon (Eds.), *Cognitive-behavioral intentions: Assessment methods*. New York: Academic Press, 1981.

Metalsky, G. I., Abramson, L. Y., Seligman, M. E. P., Semmel, A., & Peterson, C. Attributional styles and life events in the classroom: Vulnerability and invulnerability to depressive mood reactions. *Journal of Personality and Social Psychology*, 1982, *43*, 612-617.

Mettee, D. R., & Aronson, E. Affective reactions to appraisal from others. In T. L. Huston (Ed.), *Foundations of interpersonal attraction*. New York: Academic Press, 1974.

Meyer, J.P. Dimensions of causal attribution for success and failure: A multivariate investigation. Unpublished doctoral dissertation, University of Western Ontario, Canada, 1978.

Meyer, J. P. Causal attribution for success and failure: A multivariate investigation of dimensionality, formation, and consequences. *Journal of Personality and Social Psychology*, 1980, *38*, 704-718.

Meyer, J. P., & Mulherin, A. From attribution to helping: An analysis of the mediating effects of affect and expectancy. *Journal of Personality and Social Psychology*, 1980, *39*, 201-210.

Michela, J. L., Peplau, L. A., & Weeks, D. G. Perceived dimensions of attributions for loneliness. *Journal of Personality and Social Psychology*, 1983, *43*, 929-936.

Mill, J. *The analysis of the phenomena of the human mind*. New York: Kelley, no date. (Originally published, 1869.)

Mill, J. S. *System of logic, ratiocinative and inductive*. Toronto: University of Toronto Press, 1974. (Originally published, 1843.)

Miller, A. G. (Ed.). *In the eye of the beholder: Contemporary issues in stereotyping*. New York: Praeger, 1982.

Miller, A. G., Jones, E. E., & Hinkle, S. A robust attribution error in the personality domain. *Journal of Experimental Social Psychology*, 1981, *17*, 587-600.

Miller, D. T. Ego involvement and attributions for success and failure. *Journal of Personality and Social Psychology*, 1976, *34*, 901-906.

Miller, D. T. What constitutes a self-serving attributional bias? A reply to Bradley. *Journal of Personality and Social Psychology*, 1978, *36*, 1221-1223.

Miller, D. T., & Norman, S. A. Actor-observer differences in perceptions of effective control. *Journal of Personality and Social Psychology*, 1975, *31*, 503-515.

Miller, D. T., Norman, S. A., & Wright, E. Distortion in person perception as a consequence of the need for effective control. *Journal of Personality and Social Psychology*, 1978, *36*, 598-602.

Miller, D. T., & Ross, M. Self-serving biases in attribution of causality: Fact or fiction? *Psychological Bulletin*, 1975, *82*, 213-225.

Miller, F. D., Smith, E. R., & Uleman, J. Measurement and interpretation of situational and dispositional attributions. *Journal of Experimental Social Psychology*, 1981, *17*, 80-95.

Miller, N. M., Maruyama, G., Beaber, R. J., & Valone, K. Speed of speech and persuasion. *Journal of Personality and Social Psychology*, 1976, *34*, 615-624.

Miller, R. L., Brickman, P., & Bolen, D. Attribution versus persuasion as a means for modifying behavior. *Journal of Personality and Social Psychology*, 1975, *31*, 430-441.

Miller, S. M. Controllability and human stress: Method, evidence, and theory. *Behavior Research and Therapy*, 1979, *17*, 287-306.

Mills, J. Interest in supporting and discrepant information. In R. P. Abelson, E. Aronson, W. J. McGuire, T. M. Newcomb, M. J. Rosenberg, & P. H. Tannenbaum (Eds.), *Theories of cognitive consistency: A sourcebook*. Chicago: Rand McNally, 1968.

Mills, R. T., & Krantz, D. S. Information, choice, and reactions to stress: A field experiment in a blood bank with laboratory analogue. *Journal of Personality and Social Psychology*, 1979, *37*, 608-620.

Mischel, W. *Personality and assessment*. New York: Wiley, 1968.

Mischel, W., Ebbesen, E. B., & Zeiss, A. M. Selective attention to the self: Situational and dispositional determinants. *Journal of Personality and Social Psychology*, 1973, *27*, 129-142.

Mischel, W., & Peake, P. K. Beyond déjà vu in the search for cross-situational consistency. *Psychological Review*, 1982, *89*, 730-755.

Monat, A., Averill, J. R., & Lazarus, R. S. Anticipatory stress and coping reactions under various conditions of uncertainty. *Journal of Personality and Social Psychology*, 1972, *24*, 237-253.

Monson, T. C., & Hesley, J. W. Causal attributions for behavior consistent or inconsistent with an actor's personality traits: Differences between those offered by actors and observers. *Journal of Experimental Social Psychology*, 1982, *18*, 46-432.

Monson, T. C., Hesley, J. W., & Chernick, L. Specifying when personality traits can and cannot predict behavior: An alternative to abandoning the attempt to predict single-act criteria. *Journal of Personality and Social Psychology*, 1982, *43*, 385-399.

Monson, T. C., & Snyder, M. Actors, observers, and the attribution process: Toward a reconceptualization. *Journal of Experimental Social Psychology*, 1977, *13*, 89-111.

Moreland, R. L., & Zajonc, R. B. Is stimulus recognition a necessary condition for the occurrence of exposure effects? *Journal of Personality and Social Psychology*, 1977, *35*, 191-199.

Moreland, R. L., & Zajonc, R. B. Exposure effects may not depend on stimulus recognition. *Journal of Personality and Social Psychology*, 1979, *37*, 1085-1089.

Moreland, R. L., & Zajonc, R. B. Exposure effects in person perception: Familiarity, similarity, and attraction. *Journal of Experimental Social Psychology*, 1982, *18*, 395-415.

Morgan, M. The overjustification effect: A developmental test of self-perception interpretations. *Journal of Personality and Social Psychology*, 1981, *40*, 809-821.

Morris, L. W., & Liebert, R. M. Relationship of cognitive and emotional components of test anxiety to physiological arousal and academic performance. *Journal of Consulting and Clinical Psychology*, 1970, *35*, 332-337.

Mullen, B., & Suls, J. "Know thyself": Stressful life changes and the ameliorative effect of private self-consciousness. *Journal of Experimental Social Psychology*, 1982, *18*, 43-55.

Nasby, W., & Yando, R. Selective encoding and retrieval of affectively-valent information: Two cognitive consequences of mood. *Journal of Personality and Social Psychology*, 1982, *43*, 1244-1253.

Neisser, U. *Cognitive psychology*. Englewood Cliffs, N.J.: Prentice-Hall, 1967.

Neisser, U. *Cognition and reality*. San Francisco: Freeman, 1976.

Nelson, K. Characteristics of children's scripts for familiar events. Paper presented at the meeting of the American Psychological Association, Montreal, September 1980.

Newell, A., & Simon, H. A. *Human problem solving*. Englewood Cliffs, N.J.: Prentice-Hall, 1972.

Newtson, D. Foundations of attribution: The perception of ongoing behavior. In J. H. Harvey, W. J. Ickes, & R. F. Kidd (Eds.), *New directions in attribution research* (Vol. 1). Hillsdale, N.J.: Erlbaum, 1976.

Newtson, D. An interactionist perspective on social knowing. *Personality and Social Psychology Bulletin*, 1980, *6*, 520-531.

Newtson, D., & Czerlinsky, T. Adjustment of attitude communications for contrasts by extreme audiences. *Journal of Personality and Social Psychology*, 1974, *30*, 829-837.

Newtson, D., & Engquist, G. The perceptual organization of ongoing behavior. *Journal of Experimental Social Psychology*, 1976, *12*, 436-450

Newtson, D., Engquist, G., & Bois, J. The objective basis of behavior units. *Journal of Personality and Social Psychology*, 1977, *35*, 847-862

Newtson, D., Rindner, R., Miller, R., & LaCross, K. Effects of availability of feature changes on behavior segmentation. *Journal of Experimental Social Psychology*, 1978, *14*, 379-388.

Nielsen, S. L., & Sarason, S. G. Emotion, personality, and selective attention. *Journal of Personality and Social Psychology*, 1981, *41*, 945-960.

Nisbett, R. E., & Borgida, E. Attribution and the psychology of prediction. *Journal of Personality and Social Psychology*, 1975, *32*, 932-943.

Nisbett, R. E., Borgida, E., Crandall, R., & Reed, H. Popular induction: Information is not necessarily informative. In J. S. Carroll & J. W. Payne (Eds.), *Social cognition*. Hillsdale, N.J.: Erlbaum, 1976.

Nisbett, R. E., Caputo, C., Legant, P., & Maracek, J. Behavior as seen by the actor and as seen by the observer. *Journal of Personality and Social Psychology*, 1973, *27*, 154-164.

Nisbett, R. E., Krantz, D. H., Jepson, C., & Fong, G. T. Improving inductive inference. In D. Kahneman, P. Slovic, & A. Tversky (Eds.), *Judgment under uncertainty: Heuristics and biases*. New York: Cambridge University Press, 1982.

Nisbett, R. E., Krantz, D. H., Jepson, C., & Kunda, Z. The use of statistical heuristics in everyday inductive reasoning. *Psychological Review*, 1983, *90*, 339-363.

Nisbett, R. E., & Ross, L. *Human inference: Strategies and shortcomings of social judgment.* Englewood Cliffs, N.J.: Prentice-Hall, 1980.

Nisbett, R. E., & Schachter, S. Cognitive manipulation of pain. *Journal of Experimental Social Psychology,* 1966, *2,* 227-236.

Nisbett, R. E., & Valins, S. Perceiving the causes of one's own behavior. In E. E. Jones, E. E. Kanouse, H. H. Kelley, R. E. Nisbett, S. Valins, & B. Weiner (Eds.), *Attribution: Perceiving the causes of behavior.* Morristown, N.J.: General Learning Press, 1972.

Nisbett, R. E., & Wilson, T. D. The halo effect: Evidence for unconscious alteration of judgments. *Journal of Personality and Social Psychology,* 1977, *35,* 250-256. (a)

Nisbett, R. E., & Wilson, T. D. Telling more than we can know: Verbal reports on mental processes. *Psychological Review,* 1977, *84,* 231-259. (b)

Nisbett, R. E., Zukier, H., & Lemley, R. E. The dilution effect: Non-diagnostic information weakens the implications of diagnostic information. *Cognitive Psychology,* 1981, *13,* 248-277.

Norman, D. A. *Memory and attention: An introduction to human information processing.* New York: Wiley, 1976.

Norman, R. Affective-cognitive consistency, attitudes, conformity, and behavior. *Journal of Personality and Social Psychology,* 1975, *32,* 83-91.

Ogilvy, D. *Confessions of an advertising man.* London: Quality Book Club, 1963.

Olson, J. M., & Zanna, M. P. A new look at selective exposure. *Journal of Experimental Social Psychology,* 1979, *15,* 1-15.

Ortony, A., & Collins, A. M. Principia pathematica. Unpublished manuscript, University of Illinois, 1982.

Orvis, B. R., Cunningham, J. D., & Kelley, H. H. A closer examination of causal inference: The roles of consensus, distinctiveness, and consistency information. *Journal of Personality and Social Psychology,* 1975, *32,* 605-616.

Osgood, C. E., Suci, G. J., & Tannenbaum, P. H. *The measurement of meaning.* Urbana: University of Illinois Press, 1957.

Osterhouse, R. A., & Brock, T. C. Distraction increases yielding to propaganda by inhibiting counterarguing. *Journal of Personality and Social Psychology,* 1970, *15,* 344-358.

Ostrom, T. M. Cognitive representation of impressions. Paper presented at the meeting of the American Psychological Association, Chicago, August 1975.

Ostrom, T. M. Between-theory and within-theory conflict in explaining context effects in impression formation. *Journal of Experimental Social Psychology,* 1977, *13,* 492-503.

Ostrom, T. M., Lingle, J. H., Pryor, J. B., & Geva, N. Cognitive organization of person impressions. In R. Hastie, T. M. Ostrom, E. B. Ebbesen, R. S. Wyer, Jr., D. Hamilton, & D. E. Carlston (Eds.), *Person memory: The cognitive basis of social perception.* Hillsdale, N.J.: Erlbaum, 1980.

Ostrom, T. M., Pryor, J. B., & Simpson, D. D. The organization of social information. In E. T. Higgins, C. P. Herman, & M. P. Zanna (Eds.), *Social cognition: The Ontario Symposium* (Vol. 1). Hillsdale, N.J.: Erlbaum, 1981.

Owens, J., Bower, G. H., & Black, J. B. The "soap-opera" effect in story recall. *Memory and Cognition,* 1979, *7,* 185-191.

Owens, J., Dafoe, J., & Bower, G. Taking a point of view: Character identification and attributional processes in story comprehension and memory. Paper presented at the meeting of the American Psychological Association, San Francisco, August 1977.

Pachella, R. G. The interpretation of reaction time in information-processing research. In B. Kantowitz (Ed.), *Human information processing*. Hillsdale, N.J.: Erlbaum, 1974.

Paivio, A. *Imagery and verbal processes*. New York: Holt, Rinehart and Winston, 1971.

Parducci, A. The relativism of absolute judgments. *Scientific American*, 1968, *219*, 84-90.

Park, B., & Rothbart, M. Perception of out–group homogeneity and levels of social categorization: Memory for the subordinate attributes of in–group and out–group members. *Journal of Personality and Social Psychology*, 1982, *42*, 1051-1068.

Passer, M. W. Perceiving the causes of success and failure revisited: A multi-dimensional scaling approach. Unpublished doctoral dissertation, University of California, Los Angeles, 1977.

Pavelchak, M. A., Fiske, S. T., & Lau, R. R. The bias toward positive evidence for causality in attention, memory, and attribution. Unpublished manuscript, Carnegie-Mellon University, 1982.

Pennebaker, J. W., Burnam, M. A., Schaeffer, M. A., & Harper, D. C. Lack of control as a determinant of perceived physical symptoms. *Journal of Personality and Social Psychology*, 1977, *35*, 167-174.

Pennebaker, J. W., Dyer, M. A., Caulkins, R. S., Litowitz, D. L., Ackreman, P. L., Anderson, D. B., & McGraw, K. M. Don't the girls get prettier at closing time: A country and western application to psychology. *Personality and Social Psychology Bulletin*, 1979, *5*, 122-125.

Pennebaker, J. W., & Lightner, J. M. Competition of internal and external information in an exercise setting. *Journal of Personality and Social Psychology*, 1980, *39*, 165-174.

Pennebaker, J. W., & Skelton, J. A. Selective monitoring of physical sensations. *Journal of Personality and Social Psychology*, 1981, *41*, 213-223.

Pervin, L. A. The need to predict and control under conditions of threat. *Journal of Personality*, 1963, *31*, 570-587.

Peterson, C., Schwartz, S. M., & Seligman, M. E. P. Self-blame and depressive symptoms. *Journal of Personality and Social Psychology*, 1981, *41*, 253-259.

Peterson, L. R., & Peterson, M. Short-term retention of individual items. *Journal of Experimental Psychology*, 1959, *58*, 193-198.

Pettigrew, T. F. Social evaluation theory: Convergences and applications. In D. Levine (Ed.), *Nebraska Symposium on Motivation* (Vol. 15). Lincoln: University of Nebraska Press, 1967.

Pettigrew, T. F. The ultimate attribution error: Extending Allport's cognitive analysis of prejudice. *Personality and Social Psychology Bulletin*, 1979, *5*, 461-476.

Petty, R. E., & Brock, T. C. Thought disruption and persuasion: Assessing the validity of attitude change experiments. In R. E. Petty, T. M. Ostrom, & T. C. Brock (Eds.), *Cognitive responses in persuasion*. Hillsdale, N.J.: Erlbaum, 1981.

Petty, R. E., & Cacioppo, J. T. The importance of cognitive and physiological processes in persuasion. Paper presented at the meeting of the American Psychological Association, San Francisco, August 1977.

Petty, R. E., & Cacioppo, J. T. Issue involvement can increase or decrease persuasion by enhancing message-relevant cognitive responses. *Journal of Personality and Social Psychology*, 1979, *37*, 1915-1926.

Petty, R. E., & Cacioppo, J. T. *Attitudes and persuasion: Classic and contemporary approaches*. Dubuque, Iowa: W. C. Brown, 1981.

Petty, R. E., Cacioppo, J. T., & Goldman, R. Personal involvement as a determinant of argument-based persuasion. *Journal of Personality and Social Psychology*, 1981, *41*, 847-855.

Petty, R. E., Cacioppo, J. T., & Heesacker, M. Effects of rhetorical questions on persuasion: A cognitive response analysis. *Journal of Personality and Social Psychology*, 1981, *40*, 432-440.

Petty, R. E., Ostrom, T. M., & Brock, T. C. *Cognitive responses in persuasive communications: A text in attitude change.* Hillsdale, N.J.: Erlbaum, 1981.

Petty, R. E., Wells, G. L., & Brock, T. C. Distraction can enhance or reduce yielding to propaganda: Thought disruption versus effort justification. *Journal of Personality and Social Psychology*, 1976, *34*, 874-884.

Phares, E. J. *Locus of control in personality.* Morristown, N.J.: General Learning Press, 1976.

Phares, E. J., & Wilson, D. G. Responsibility attribution: Role of outcome severity, situational ambiguity, and internal-external control. *Journal of Personality*, 1972, *40*, 392-406.

Phares, E. J., Wilson, K. G., & Klyver, N. W. Internal-external control and attribution of blame under neutral and distractive conditions. *Journal of Personality and Social Psychology*, 1971, *18*, 285-288.

Pheterson, G. I., Kiesler, S. B., & Goldberg, P. A. Evaluation of the performance of women as a function of their sex, achievement, and personal history. *Journal of Personality and Social Psychology*, 1971, *19*, 114-118.

Picek, J. S., Sherman, S. J., & Shiffrin, R. M. Cognitive organization and coding of social structures. *Journal of Personality and Social Psychology*, 1975, *31*, 758-768.

Piliavin, I. M., Rodin, J., & Piliavin, J. A. Good samaritanism: An underground phenomenon. *Journal of Personality and Social Psychology*, 1969, *13*, 289-299.

Pittman, N. L., & Pittman, T. S. Effects of amount of helplessness training and internal-external locus of control on mood and performance. *Journal of Personality and Social Psychology*, 1979, *37*, 39-47.

Pittman, T. S., Emery, J., & Boggiano, A. K. Intrinsic and extrinsic motivational orientations: Reward-induced changes in preference for complexity. *Journal of Personality and Social Psychology*, 1982, *42*, 789-797.

Pittman, T. S., & Pittman, N. L. Deprivation of control and the attribution process. *Journal of Personality and Social Psychology*, 1980, *39*, 377-389.

Plutchik, R. Emotions, evolution, and adaptive processes. In M. B. Arnold (Ed.), *Feelings and emotions: The Loyola Symposium.* New York: Academic Press, 1970.

Plutchik, R., & Ax, A. F. A critique of determinants of emotional state by Schachter and Singer (1962). *Psychophysiology*, 1967, *4*, 79-82.

Posner, M. I. Cumulative development of attentional theory. *American Psychologist*, 1982, *37*, 168-179.

Posner, M. I., & Keele, S. W. On the genesis of abstract ideas. *Journal of Experimental Psychology*, 1968, *77*, 353-363.

Posner, M. I., & Keele, S. W. Retention of abstract ideas. *Journal of Experimental Psychology*, 1970, *83*, 304-308.

Posner, M. I., Nissen, M. J., & Klein, R. M. Visual dominance: An information processing account of its origins and significance. *Psychological Review*, 1976, *83*, 157-171.

Press, A. N., Crockett, W. H., & Rosenkrantz, P. S. Cognitive complexity and the learning of balanced and unbalanced social structures. *Journal of Personality*, 1969, *37*, 541-553.

Pruitt, D. G., & Teger, A. I. The risky shift in group betting. *Journal of Experimental Social Psychology*, 1969, *5*, 115-126.

Pruitt, D. J., & Insko, C. A. Extension of the Kelley attribution model: The role of comparison-object consensus, target-object consensus, distinctiveness and consistency. *Journal of Personality and Social Psychology*, 1980, *39*, 39-58.

Pryor, J. B., Gibbons, F. X., Wicklund, R. A., Fazio, R. H., & Hood, R. Self-focused attention and self-report. *Journal of Personality*, 1977, *45*, 514-527.

Pryor, J. B., & Kriss, N. The cognitive dynamics of salience in the attribution process. *Journal of Personality and Social Psychology*, 1977, *35*, 49-55.

Pryor, J. B., & Ostrom, T. M. The cognitive organization of social information: A converging-operations approach. *Journal of Personality and Social Psychology*, 1981, *41*, 628-641.

Pryor, J. B., Simpson, D. D., Mitchell, M., Ostrom, T. M., & Lydon, J. Structural selectivity in the retrieval of social information. *Social Cognition*, 1982, *1*, 336-357.

Pylyshyn, Z. W. What the mind's eye tells the mind's brain: A critique of mental imagery. *Psychological Bulletin*, 1973, *80*, 1-24.

Pylyshyn, Z. W. The imagery debate: Analogue media versus tacit knowledge. *Psychological Review*, 1981, *88*, 16-45.

Pyszczynski, T. A., & Greenberg, J. Role of disconfirmed expectations in the instigation of attributional processing. *Journal of Personality and Social Psychology*, 1981, *40*, 31-38.

Quattrone, G. A. Overattribution and unit formation: When behavior engulfs the person. *Journal of Personality and Social Psychology*, 1982, *42*, 593-607.

Quattrone, G. A., Finkel, S. E., & Andrus, D. C. Anchors away! On overcoming the anchoring bias across a number of domains. Unpublished manuscript, Stanford University, 1982.

Quattrone, G. A., & Jones, E. E. The perception of variability within ingroups and outgroups: Implications for the Law of Small Numbers. *Journal of Personality and Social Psychology*, 1980, *38*, 141-152.

Rajecki, D. W. *Attitudes: Themes and advances.* Sunderland, Mass.: Sinauer, 1982.

Reder, L. M. The role of elaborations in memory for prose. *Cognitive Psychology*, 1979, *11*, 221-234.

Reder, L. M. The role of elaboration in the comprehension and retention of prose: A critical review. *Review of Educational Research*, 1980, *50*, 5-53.

Reder, L. M., & Anderson, J. R. A partial resolution of the paradox of interference: The role of integrating knowledge. *Cognitive Psychology*, 1980, *12*, 447-472.

Reed, S. K. Pattern recognition and categorization. *Cognitive Psychology*, 1972, *3*, 382-407.

Reeder, G. D., & Brewer, M. B. A schematic model of dispositional attribution in interpersonal perception. *Psychological Review*, 1979, *86*, 61-79.

Regan, D. T., & Fazio, R. On the consistency between attitudes and behavior: Look to the method of attitude formation. *Journal of Experimental Social Psychology*, 1977, *13*, 28-45.

Regan, D. T., & Totten, J. Empathy and attribution: Turning observers into actors. *Journal of Personality and Social Psychology*, 1975, *32*, 850-856.

Regan, J. W. Liking for evaluators: Consistency and self-esteem theories. *Journal of Experimental Social Psychology*, 1976, *12*, 156-169.

Rehm, L. P. A self-control model of depression. *Behavior Therapy*, 1977, *8*, 787-804.

Rehm, L. P., & O'Hara, M. W. Understanding depression. In I. H. Frieze, D. Bar-Tal, & J. S. Carroll (Eds.), *New approaches to social problems.* San Francisco: Jossey-Bass, 1979.

Reis, H. T., & Burns, L. B. The salience of the self in responses to inequity. *Journal of Experimental Social Psychology,* 1982, *18,* 464-475.

Reisenzein, R. The Schachter theory of emotion: Two decades later. *Psychological Bulletin,* 1983, *94,* 239-264.

Reiss, M., Rosenfeld, P., Melburg, V., & Tedeschi, J. T. Self-serving attributions: Biased private perceptions and distorted public descriptions. *Journal of Personality and Social Psychology,* 1981, *41,* 224-251.

Reyes, R. M., Thompson, W. C., & Bower, G. H. Judgmental biases resulting from differing availabilities of arguments. *Journal of Personality and Social Psychology,* 1980, *39,* 2-12.

Rhodewalt, F., & Comer, R. Induced-compliance attitude change: Once more with feeling. *Journal of Experimental Social Psychology,* 1979, *15,* 35-47.

Riskey, D. R. Verbal memory processes in impression formation. *Journal of Experimental Psychology: Human Learning and Memory,* 1979, *5,* 271-281.

Robinson, J., & McArthur, L. Z. The impact of salient vocal qualities on causal attributions for a speaker's behavior. *Journal of Personality and Social Psychology,* 1982, *43,* 236-247.

Rodin, J. Density, perceived choice and response to controllable and uncontrollable outcomes. *Journal of Experimental Social Psychology,* 1976, *12,* 564-578.

Rodin, J., & Langer, E. J. Long-term effects of a control-relevant intervention with the institutionalized aged. *Journal of Personality and Social Psychology,* 1977, *35,* 897-902.

Rodin, J., Solomon, S. K., & Metcalf, J. Role of control in mediating perceptions of density. *Journal of Personality and Social Psychology,* 1978, *36,* 988-999.

Rogers, T. B. A model of the self as an aspect of human information processing. In N. Cantor & J. Kihlstrom (Eds.), *Personality, cognition, and social interaction.* Hillsdale, N.J.: Erlbaum, 1981.

Rogers, T. B., Kuiper, N. A., & Kirker, W. S. Self-reference and the encoding of personal information. *Journal of Personality and Social Psychology,* 1977, *35,* 677-688.

Romer, D. Distraction, counterarguing, and the internalization of attitude change. *European Journal of Social Psychology,* 1979, *9,* 1-17.

Rosch, E. Principles of categorization. In E. Rosch & B. B. Lloyd (Eds.), *Cognition and categorization.* Hillsdale, N.J.: Erlbaum, 1978.

Rosch, E., & Mervis, C. B. Family resemblances: Studies in the internal structure of categories. *Cognitive Psychology,* 1975, *7,* 573-605.

Rosch, E., Mervis, C. B., Gray, W., Johnson, D., & Boyes-Braem, P. Basic objects in natural categories. *Cognitive Psychology,* 1976, *8,* 382-439.

Rose, T. L. Cognitive and dyadic processes in intergroup contact. In D. L. Hamilton (Ed.), *Cognitive processes in stereotyping and intergroup behavior.* Hillsdale, N.J.: Erlbaum, 1981.

Roseman, I. Cognitive aspects of emotion and emotional behavior. Paper presented at the meeting of the American Psychological Association, New York, September 1979.

Rosenbaum, R. M. A dimensional analysis of the perceived causes of success and failure. Unpublished doctoral dissertation, University of California, Los Angeles, 1972.

Rosenberg, M. J. Cognitive structure and attitudinal affect. *Journal of Abnormal and Social Psychology,* 1956, *53,* 367-372.

Rosenberg, M. J. An analysis of affective-cognitive consistency. In C. I. Hovland & M. J. Rosenberg (Eds.), *Attitude organization and change*. New Haven, Conn.: Yale University Press, 1960.

Rosenberg, S., Nelson, C., & Vivekanathan, P. S. A multidimensional approach to the structure of personality impressions. *Journal of Personality and Social Psychology*, 1968, *9*, 283-294.

Rosenberg, S., & Olshan, K. Evaluative and descriptive aspects in personality perception. *Journal of Personality and Social Psychology*, 1970, *16*, 619-626.

Rosenberg, S., & Sedlak, A. Structural representations of implicit personality theory. In L. Berkowitz (Ed.), *Advances in experimental social psychology* (Vol. 6). New York: Academic Press, 1972.

Rosenfield, D., Folger, R., & Adelman, H. F. When rewards reflect competence: A qualification of the overjustification effect. *Journal of Personality and Social Psychology*, 1980, *39*, 368-376.

Rosenman, R. H., Friedman, M., Straus, R., Wurm, M., Kositchek, R., Hahn, W., & Werthessen, N. T. A predictive study of coronary heart disease. *Journal of the American Heart Association*, 1964, *189*, 103-110.

Rosenthal, R. *On the social psychology of the self-fulfilling prophecy: Further evidence for Pygmalion effects and their mediating mechanisms*. New York: MSS Modular Publications, 1974. (Module 53.)

Rosenthal, R., & Jacobson, L. F. *Pygmalion in the classroom*. New York: Holt, Rinehart and Winston, 1968.

Ross, L. The intuitive psychologist and his shortcomings: Distortions in the attribution process. In L. Berkowitz (Ed.), *Advances in experimental social psychology* (Vol. 10). New York: Academic Press, 1977.

Ross, L., Amabile, T. M., & Steinmetz, J. L. Social roles, social control, and biases in social-perception processes. *Journal of Personality and Social Psychology*, 1977, *35*, 485-494.

Ross, L., Greene, D., & House, P. The "false consensus effect": An egocentric bias in social perception and attribution processes. *Journal of Experimental Social Psychology*, 1977, *13*, 279-301.

Ross, L., Lepper, M. R., & Hubbard, M. Perseverance in self-perception and social perception: Biased attribution processes in the debriefing paradigm. *Journal of Personality and Social Psychology*, 1975, *32*, 880-892.

Ross, L., Lepper, M. R., Strack, F., & Steinmetz, J. Social explanation and social expectation: Effects of real and hypothetical explanations on subjective likelihood. *Journal of Personality and Social Psychology*, 1977, *35*, 817-829.

Ross, L., Rodin, J., & Zimbardo, P. G. Toward an attribution therapy: The reduction of fear through induced cognitive-emotional misattribution. *Journal of Personality and Social Psychology*, 1969, *12*, 279-288.

Ross, M. Salience of reward and intrinsic motivation. *Journal of Personality and Social Psychology*, 1975, *32*, 245-254.

Ross, M. The self-perception of intrinsic motivation. In J. H. Harvey, W. J. Ickes, & R. F. Kidd (Eds.), *New directions in attribution research* (Vol. 1). Hillsdale, N.J.: Erlbaum, 1976.

Ross, M., & Fletcher, G. Attribution and social perception. In G. Lindzey & A. Aronson (Eds.), *The handbook of social psychology* (3rd ed.). Reading, Mass.: Addison-Wesley, in press.

Ross, M., McFarland, C., Conway, M., & Zanna, M. P. The reciprocal relation between attitudes and behavior recall: Committing people to newly formed attitudes. *Journal of Personality and Social Psychology*, 1983, *45*, 257-267.

Ross, M., McFarland, C., & Fletcher, G. J. O. The effect of attitude on the recall of personal histories. *Journal of Personality and Social Psychology*, 1981, *40*, 627-634.

Ross, M., & Olson, J. M. An expectancy-attribution model of the effects of placebos. *Psychological Review*, 1981, *88*, 408-437.

Ross, M., & Sicoly, F. Egocentric biases in availability and attribution. *Journal of Personality and Social Psychology*, 1979, *37*, 322-337.

Rothbart, M. Memory processes and social beliefs. In D. Hamilton (Ed.), *Cognitive processes in stereotyping and intergroup behavior*. Hillsdale, N.J.: Erlbaum, 1981.

Rothbart, M., Evans, M., & Fulero, S. Recall for confirming events: Memory processes and the maintenance of social stereotyping. *Journal of Experimental Social Psychology*, 1979, *15*, 343-355.

Rothbart, M., Fulero, S., Jensen, C., Howard, J., & Birrell, B. From individual to group impressions: Availability heuristics in stereotype formation. *Journal of Experimental Social Psychology*, 1978, *14*, 237-255.

Rothbaum, F., Weisz, J. R., & Snyder, S. S. Changing the world and changing the self: A two-process model of perceived control. *Journal of Personality and Social Psychology*, 1982, *42*, 5-37.

Rotter, J. B. Generalized expectancies for internal versus external control of reinforcement. *Psychological Monographs*, 1966, *80* (1, Whole No. 609).

Rotter, J. B. External control and internal control. *Psychology Today*, 1971, *5*, 37-42, 58-59.

Rubovits, P. C., & Maehr, M. L. Pygmalion in black and white. *Journal of Personality and Social Psychology*, 1973, *25*, 210-218.

Rumelhart, D. E., Lindsay, P. H., & Norman, D. A. A process model for long-term memory. In E. Tulving & W. Donaldson (Eds.), *Organization of memory*. New York: Academic Press, 1972.

Rumelhart, D. E., & Ortony, A. The representation of knowledge in memory. In R. C. Anderson, R. J. Spiro, & W. E. Montague (Eds.), *Schooling and the acquisition of knowledge*. Hillsdale, N.J.: Erlbaum, 1977.

Russell, D. The causal dimension scale: A measure of how individuals perceive causes. *Journal of Personality and Social Psychology*, 1982, *42*, 1137-1145.

Russell, J. A. Evidence of convergent validity on the dimensions of affect. *Journal of Personality and Social Psychology*, 1978, *36*, 1152-1168.

Russell, J. A. Affective space is bipolar. *Journal of Personality and Social Psychology*, 1979, *37*, 345-356.

Russell, J. A. A circumplex model of affect. *Journal of Personality and Social Psychology*, 1980, *39*, 1161-1178.

Ryan, R. M. Control and information in the intrapersonal sphere: An extension of cognitive evaluation theory. *Journal of Personality and Social Psychology*, 1982, *43*, 450-461.

Ryan, W. *Blaming the victim*. New York: Random House, Vintage, 1971.

Sadler, O., & Tesser, A. Some effects of salience and time upon interpersonal hostility and attraction during social isolation. *Sociometry*, 1973, *36*, 99-112.

Saegert, S. Crowding: Cognitive overload and behavioral constraint. In W. Preiser (Ed.), *Environmental design research* (Vol. 2). Stroudsburg, Pa.: Dowden, Hutchinson, & Ross, 1973.

Saegert, S., Mackintosh, E., & West, S. Two studies of crowding in urban public spaces. *Environment and Behavior*, 1975, 7, 159-184.

Sagar, H. A., & Schofield, J. W. Racial and behavioral cues in black and white children's perceptions of ambiguously aggressive acts. *Journal of Personality and Social Psychology*, 1980, 39, 590-598.

Salancik, G. R., & Conway, M. Attitude inference from salient and relevant cognitive content about behavior. *Journal of Personality and Social Psychology*, 1975, 32, 829-840.

Sales, S. M. Need for stimulation as a factor in social behavior. *Journal of Personality and Social Psychology*, 1971, 19, 124-134.

Saltzer, E. B. Cognitive moderators of the relationship between behavioral intentions and behavior. *Journal of Personality and Social Psychology*, 1981, 41, 260-275.

Sarason, I. G., & Stoops, R. Test anxiety and the passage of time. *Journal of Consulting and Clinical Psychology*, 1978, 46, 102-109.

Sawyer, A. Repetition, cognitive responses, and persuasion. In R. E. Petty, T. M. Ostrom, & T. C. Brock (Eds.), *Cognitive responses in persuasion*. Hillsdale, N.J.: Erlbaum, 1981.

Sawyer, J. Measurement and prediction, clinical and statistical. *Psychological Bulletin*, 1966, 66, 178-200.

Schachter, S. *The psychology of affiliation*. Stanford, Calif.: Stanford University Press, 1959.

Schachter, S. The interaction of cognitive and physiological determinants of emotional state. In L. Berkowitz (Ed.), *Advances in experimental social psychology* (Vol. 1). New York: Academic Press, 1964.

Schachter, S. *Emotion, obesity and crime*. New York: Academic Press, 1971.

Schachter, S., & Singer, J. E. Cognitive, social, and physiological determinants of emotional state. *Psychological Review*, 1962, 69, 379-399.

Schachter, S., & Singer, J. E. Comments on the Maslach and Marshall-Zimbardo experiments. *Journal of Personality and Social Psychology*, 1979, 37, 989-995.

Schank, R. C., & Abelson, R. P. *Scripts, plans, goals, and understanding: An inquiry into human knowledge structures*. Hillsdale, N.J.: Erlbaum, 1977.

Scheier, M. F. Self-awareness, self-consciousness, and angry aggression. *Journal of Personality*, 1976, 44, 627-644.

Scheier, M. F. The effects of public and private self-consciousness on the public expression of personal beliefs. *Journal of Personality and Social Psychology*, 1980, 39, 514-521.

Scheier, M. F., Buss, A. H., & Buss, D. M. Self-consciousness, self-report of aggressiveness, and aggression. *Journal of Research in Personality*, 1978, 12, 133-140.

Scheier, M. F., & Carver, C. S. Self-focused attention and the experience of emotion: Attraction, repulsion, elation, and depression. *Journal of Personality and Social Psychology*, 1977, 35, 625-636.

Scheier, M. F., & Carver, C. S. Private and public self-attention, resistance to change, and dissonance reduction. *Journal of Personality and Social Psychology*, 1980, 39, 390-405.

Scheier, M. F., & Carver, C. S. Cognition, affect, and self-regulation. In M. S. Clark & S. T. Fiske (Eds.), *Affect and cognition: The 17th Annual Carnegie Symposium on Cognition*. Hillsdale, N.J.: Erlbaum, 1982.

Scheier, M. F., Carver, C. S., & Gibbons, F. X. Self-focused attention and reactions to fear. *Journal of Research in Personality*, 1981, *15*, 1-15.

Scheier, M. F., & Carver, C. S. Two sides of the self: One for you and one for me. In J. Suls & A. G. Greenwald (Eds.), *Psychological perspectives on the self* (Vol. 2). Hillsdale, N.J.: Erlbaum, 1983.

Scheier, M. F., Fenigstein, A., & Buss, A. H. Self-awareness and physical aggression. *Journal of Experimental Psychology*, 1974, *10*, 264-273.

Schein, E. H. The Chinese indoctrination program for prisoners of war: A study of attempted "brainwashing." *Psychiatry*, 1956, *19*, 149-172.

Schlenker, B. R. *Impression management: The self-concept, social identity, and interpersonal relations.* Monterey, Calif.: Brooks/Cole, 1980.

Schlenker, B. R., & Miller, R. S. Egocentrism in groups: Self-serving biases or logical information processing? *Journal of Personality and Social Psychology*, 1977, *35*, 755-764.

Schlosberg, H. Three dimensions of emotion. *Psychological Review*, 1954, *61*, 81-88.

Schneider, D. J. Implicit personality theory: A review. *Psychological Bulletin*, 1973, *79*, 294-309.

Schneider, D. J. Situational and stimulus factors in free descriptions of people. Paper presented at the meeting of the American Psychological Association, San Francisco, August 1977.

Schneider, D. J., & Blankmeyer, B. L. Prototype salience and implicit personality theories. *Journal of Personality and Social Psychology*, 1983, *44*, 712-722.

Schneider, D. J., Hastorf, A. H., & Ellsworth, P. C. *Person perception.* Reading, Mass.: Addison-Wesley, 1979.

Schneider, W., & Shiffrin, R. M. Controlled and automatic human information processing: I. Detection, search, and attention. *Psychological Review*, 1977, *84*, 1-66.

Schneiderman, W., Webb, W., & Davis, B. Self-monitoring and states of awareness. Unpublished manuscript, Marshall University, 1981.

Schulz, R. Effects of control and predictability on the physical and psychological well-being of the institutionalized aged. *Journal of Personality and Social Psychology*, 1976, *33*, 563-573.

Schulz, R., & Brenner, G. Relocation of the aged: A review and theoretical analysis. *Journal of Gerontology*, 1977, *32*, 323-333.

Schulz, R., & Hanusa, B. H. Long-term effects of control and predictability-enhancing interventions: Findings and ethical issues. *Journal of Personality and Social Psychology*, 1978, *36*, 1194-1201.

Schuman, H., & Johnson, M. P. Attitudes and behavior. *Annual Review of Sociology*, 1976, *2*, 161-207.

Schumer, R. Context effects in impression formation as a function of the ambiguity of test traits. *European Journal of Social Psychology*, 1973, *3*, 333-338.

Schur, E. M. *Labeling deviant behavior: Its sociological implications.* New York: Harper & Row, 1971.

Schwartz, G. E., Fair, P. L., Salt, P., Mandel, M. R., & Klerman, G. L. Facial muscle patterning to affective imagery in depressed and nondepressed subjects. *Science*, 1976, *192*, 489-491.

Schwartz, G. E., Weinberger, D. A., & Singer, J. A. Cardiovascular differentiation of happiness, sadness, anger, and fear following imagery and exercise. *Psychomatic Medicine*, 1981, *43*, 343-364.

Schwartz, S. H. Normative explanations of helping behavior: A critique, proposal, and empirical test. *Journal of Experimental Social Psychology*, 1973, *9*, 349-364.

Schwartz, S. H. Temporal instability as a moderator of the attitude-behavior relationship. *Journal of Personality and Social Psychology*, 1978, *36*, 715-724.

Schwartz, S. H., & Tessler, R. C. A test of a model for reducing measured attitude-behavior discrepancies. *Journal of Personality and Social Psychology*, 1972, *24*, 225-236.

Sears, D. O. Biased indoctrination and selectivity of exposure to new information. *Sociometry*, 1965, *28*, 363-376.

Sears, D. O. The paradox of de facto selective exposure. In R. P. Abelson *et al.* (Eds.), *Theories of cognitive consistency: A sourcebook*. Chicago: Rand McNally, 1968.

Sears, D. O. The person-positivity bias. *Journal of Personality and Social Psychology*, 1983, *44*, 233-250.

Sears, D. O., Tyler, T. R., Citrin, J., & Kinder, D. R. Political system support and public response to the energy crisis. *American Journal of Political Science*, 1978, *22*, 56-82.

Secord, P. F. Facial features and inference processes in interpersonal perception. In R. Tagiuri & L. Petrullo (Eds.), *Person perception and interpersonal behavior*. Stanford, Calif.: Stanford University Press, 1958.

Secord, P. F. Stereotyping and favorableness in the perception of Negro faces. *Journal of Abnormal and Social Psychology*, 1959, *59*, 309-321.

Secord, P. F., Bevan, W., & Katz, B. Perceptual accentuation and the Negro stereotype. *Journal of Abnormal and Social Psychology*, 1956, *53*, 78-83.

Seeman, M., & Evans, J. W. Alienation and learning in a hospital setting. *American Sociological Review*, 1962, *27*, 772-782.

Seligman, M. E. P. *Helplessness*. San Francisco: Freeman, 1975.

Seligman, M. E.P., Abramson, L. Y., Semmel, A., & Von Baeyer, C. Depressive attributional style. *Journal of Abnormal Psychology*, 1979, *88*, 242-247.

Semin, G. R., & Rosch, E. Activation of bipolar prototypes in attribute inferences. *Journal of Experimental Social Psychology*, 1981, *17*, 172-484.

Sentis, K. P., & Burnstein, E. Remembering schema consistent information: Effects of a balance schema on recognition memory. *Journal of Personality and Social Psychology*, 1979, *37*, 2200-2211.

Sentis, K. P., & Markus, H. Self-schemas and recognition memory. Unpublished manuscript, University of Michigan, 1979.

Shaver, K. G. Defensive attribution: Effects of severity and relevance on the responsibility assigned for an accident. *Journal of Personality and Social Psychology*, 1970, *14*, 101-113. (a)

Shaver, K. G. Redress and conscientiousness in the attribution of responsibility for accidents. *Journal of Experimental Social Psychology*, 1970, *6*, 100-110. (b)

Shaver, K. G. *An introduction to attribution processes*. Cambridge, Mass.: Winthrop, 1975.

Shaver, P., & Klinnert, M. Schachter's theories of affiliation and emotion: Implications of developmental research. In L. Wheeler (Ed.), *Review of Personality and Social Psychology* (Vol. 3). Beverly Hills: Sage, 1982.

Shaw, M. E. *Group dynamics*. New York: McGraw-Hill, 1971.

Shepard, R. N., & Podgorny, P. Cognitive processes that resemble perceptual processes. In E. Rosch & B. Lloyd (Eds.), *Cognition and categorization*. Hillsdale, N.J.: Erlbaum, 1978.

Sherif, M., Harvey, O. J., White, B. J., Hood, W. R., & Sherif, C. W. *Intergroup conflict and cooperation: The robbers' cave experiment.* Norman: University of Oklahoma Press, 1961.

Sherif, M., & Hovland, C. I. *Social judgment: Assimilation and contrast effects in communication and attitude change.* New Haven, Conn.: Yale University Press, 1961.

Sherman, R. D., & Titus, W. Covariation information and cognitive processing: Effects of causal implications on memory. *Journal of Personality and Social Psychology*, 1982, *42*, 989-1000.

Sherman, S. J., Skov, R. B., Hervitz, E. F., & Stock, C. B. The effects of explaining hypothetical future events: From possibility to probability to actuality and beyond. *Journal of Experimental Social Psychology*, 1981, *17*, 142-158.

Sherrod, D. R., Hage, J. N., Halpern, P. L., & Moore, B. S. Effects of personal causation and perceived control on responses to an aversive environment: The more control the better. *Journal of Experimental Social Psychology*, 1977, *13*, 14-27.

Shiffrin, R. M., & Schneider, W. Controlled and automatic human information processing: II. Perceptual learning, automatic attending, and general theory. *Psychological Review*, 1977, *84*, 127-190.

Shweder, R. A. (Ed.). Fallible judgment in behavioral research. In *New directions for methodology of social and behavioral science* (Vol. 4). San Francisco: Jossey-Bass, 1980.

Sicoly, F., & Ross, M. Facilitation of ego-biased attributions by means of self-serving observer feedback. *Journal of Personality and Social Psychology*, 1977, *35*, 734-741.

Simmons, C. H., & Lerner, M. J. Altruism as a search for justice. *Journal of Personality and Social Psychology*, 1968, *9*, 216-225.

Simon, H. A. Motivational and emotional controls of cognition. *Psychological Review*, 1967, *74*, 29-39.

Simon, H. A. Information processing models of cognition. *Annual Review of Psychology*, 1979, *30*, 363-396.

Simon, H. A. Comments. In M. S. Clark & S. T. Fiske (Eds.), *Affect and cognition: The 18th Annual Carnegie Symposium on Cognition.* Hillsdale, N.J.: Erlbaum, 1982.

Singerman, K. G., Borkovec, T. D., & Baron, R. S. Failure of a misattribution therapy manipulation with a clinically relevant target behavior. *Behavior Therapy*, 1976, *7*, 306-313.

Sivacek, J., & Crano, W. D. Vested interest as a moderator of attitude-behavior consistency. *Journal of Personality and Social Psychology*, 1982, *43*, 210-221.

Skinner, B. F. *Verbal behavior.* New York; Appleton-Century-Crofts, 1957.

Skinner, B. F. Operant behavior. *American Psychologist*, 1963, *18*, 503-515.

Skipper, J. K., Tagliacozzo, D. L., & Mauksch, H. O. Some possible consequences of limited communication between patients and hospital functionaries. *Journal of Health and Social Behavior*, 1964, *5*, 34-39.

Slovic, P., Fischhoff, B., & Lichtenstein, S. Cognitive processes and societal risk taking. In J. S. Carroll & J. W. Payne (Eds.), *Cognition and social behavior.* Hillsdale, N.J.: Erlbaum, 1976.

Slovic, P., Fischhoff, B., & Lichtenstein, S. Behavioral decision theory. *Annual Review of Psychology*, 1977, *28*, 1-39.

Smedslund, J. The concept of correlation in adults. *Scandinavian Journal of Psychology*, 1963, *4*, 165-173.

Smith, D. A., & Graesser, A. C. Memory for actions in scripted activities as a function of typicality, retention interval, and retrieval task. *Memory and Cognition*, 1981, *9*, 550-559.

Smith, E. E., Adams, N., & Schorr, D. Fact retrieval and the paradox of interference. *Cognitive Psychology*, 1978, *10*, 438-464.

Smith, E. R. Beliefs, attributions, and evaluations: Nonhierarchical models of mediation in social cognition. *Journal of Personality and Social Psychology*, 1982, *43*, 248-259.

Smith, E. R., & Kluegel, J. R. Cognitive and social bases of emotional experience: Outcome, attribution, and affect in data from a national survey. *Journal of Personality and Social Psychology*, 1982, *43*, 1129-1141.

Smith, E. R., & Miller, F. D. Limits on perception of cognitive processes: A reply to Nisbett and Wilson. *Psychological Review*, 1978, *85*, 355-362.

Smith, E. R., & Miller, F. D. Attributional information processing: A reaction time model of causal subtraction. *Journal of Personality and Social Psychology*, 1979, *37*, 1723-1731. (a)

Smith, E. R., & Miller, F. D. Salience and the cognitive mediation of attribution. *Journal of Personality and Social Psychology*, 1979, *37*, 2240-2252 (b)

Smith, E. R., & Miller, F. D. Mediation among attributional inferences and comprehension processes: Initial findings and a general method. *Journal of Personality and Social Psychology*, 1983, *44*, 492-505.

Smith, M. C. Children's use of the multiple sufficient cause schema in social perception. *Journal of Personality and Social Psychology*, 1975, *32*, 737-747.

Smith, T. W., & Pittman, T. S. Reward, distraction, and the overjustification effect. *Journal of Personality and Social Psychology*, 1978, *36*, 565-572.

Smith, T. W., Snyder, C. R., & Handelsman, M. M. On the self-serving function of an academic wooden leg: Test anxiety as a self-handicapping strategy. *Journal of Personality and Social Psychology*, 1982, *42*, 314-321.

Snyder, M. Individual differences and the self-control of expressive behavior (Doctoral dissertation, Stanford University, 1972). *Dissertation Abstracts International*, 1972, *33*, 4533A-4534A.

Snyder, M. The self-monitoring of expressive behavior. *Journal of Personality and Social Psychology*, 1974, *30*, 526-537.

Snyder, M. Attribution and behavior: Social perception and social causation. In J. H. Harvey, W. J. Ickes, & R. F. Kidd (Eds.), *New directions in attribution research* (Vol. 1). Hillsdale, N.J.: Erlbaum, 1976.

Snyder, M. Impression management. In L. S. Wrightsman (Ed.), *Social psychology in the seventies*. New York: Wiley, 1977.

Snyder, M. Self-monitoring processes. In L. Berkowitz (Ed.), *Advances in experimental social psychology* (Vol. 12). New York: Academic Press, 1979.

Snyder, M. On the influence of individuals on situations. In N. Cantor & J. Kihlstrom (Eds.), *Personality, cognition and social interaction*. Hillsdale, N.J.: Erlbaum, 1981.

Snyder, M. Personality and social behavior. In G. Lindzey & E. Aronson (Eds.), *The handbook of social psychology* (3rd ed.). Reading, Mass.: Addison-Wesley, in press.

Snyder, M. When believing means doing: Creating links between attitudes and behavior. In M. P. Zanna, E. T. Higgins, & C. P. Herman (Eds.), *Consistency in social behavior: The Ontario Symposium* (Vol. 2). Hillsdale, N.J.: Erlbaum, 1982.

Snyder, M., & Campbell, B. H. Self-monitoring: The self in action. In J. Suls (Ed.), *Psychological perspectives on the self* (Vol. 1). Hillsdale, N.J.: Erlbaum, 1982.

Snyder, M., Campbell, B. H., & Preston, E. Testing hypothesis about human nature: Assessing the accuracy of social stereotypes. *Social Cognition*, 1982, *1*, 256-272.

Snyder, M., & Cantor, N. Testing hypotheses about other people: The use of historical knowledge. *Journal of Experimental Social Psychology*, 1979, *15*, 330-342.

Snyder, M., & Cantor, N. Thinking about ourselves and others: Self-monitoring and social knowledge. *Journal of Personality and Social Psychology*, 1980, *39*, 222-234.

Snyder, M., & Gangestad, S. Hypothesis-testing processes. In J. H. Harvey, W. Ickes, & R. F. Kidd (Eds.), *New directions in attribution research* (Vol. 3). Hillsdale, N.J.: Erlbaum, 1981.

Snyder, M., & Gangestad, S. Choosing social situations: Two investigations of self-monitoring processes. *Journal of Personality and Social Psychology*, 1982, *43*, 123-135.

Snyder, M., & Kendzierski, D. Acting on one's attitudes: Procedures for linking attitude and behavior. *Journal of Experimental Social Psychology*, 1982, *18*, 165-183.

Snyder, M., & Monson, T. C. Persons, situations, and the control of social behavior. *Journal of Personality and Social Psychology*, 1975, *32*, 637-644.

Snyder, M., & Skrypnek, B. J. Testing hypotheses about the self: Assessments of job suitability. *Journal of Personality*, 1981, *49*, 193-211.

Snyder, M., & Swann, W. B., Jr. When actions reflect attitudes: The politics of impression management. *Journal of Personality and Social Psychology*, 1976, *34*, 1034-1042.

Snyder, M., & Swann, W. B., Jr. Behavioral confirmation in social interaction: From social perception to social reality. *Journal of Experimental Social Psychology*, 1978, *14*, 148-162. (a)

Snyder, M., & Swann, W. B., Jr. Hypothesis testing processes in social interaction. *Journal of Personality and Social Psychology*, 1978, *36*, 1202-1212. (b)

Snyder, M., & Tanke, E. D. Behavior and attitude: Some people are more consistent than others. *Journal of Personality*, 1976, *44*, 501-517.

Snyder, M., Tanke, E. D., & Berscheid, E. Social perception and interpersonal behavior: On the self-fulfilling nature of social stereotypes. *Journal of Personality and Social Psychology*, 1977, *35*, 656-666.

Snyder, M., & Uranowitz, S. W. Reconstructing the past: Some cognitive consequences of person perception. *Journal of Personality and Social Psychology*, 1978, *36*, 941-950.

Snyder, M., & White, P. Moods and memories: Elation, depression, and the remembering of events of one's life. *Journal of Personality*, 1982, *50*, 149-167.

Snyder, M. L., & Jones, E. E. Attitude attribution when behavior is constrained. *Journal of Experimental Social Psychology*, 1974, *10*, 585-600.

Snyder, M. L., Kleck, R. E., Strenta, A., & Mentzer, S. J. Avoidance of the handicapped: An attributional ambiguity analysis. *Journal of Personality and Social Psychology*, 1979, *37*, 2297-2306.

Snyder, M. L., Smoller, B., Strenta, A., & Frankel, A. A comparison of egotism, negativity, and learned helplessness as explanations for poor performance after unsolvable problems. *Journal of Personality and Social Psychology*, 1981, *40*, 24-30.

Snyder, M. L., Stephan, W. G., & Rosenfield, D. Egotism and attribution. *Journal of Personality and Social Psychology*, 1976, *33*, 435-441.

Snyder, M. L., Stephan, W. G., & Rosenfield, D. Attributional egotism. In J. H. Harvey, W. Ickes, & R. F. Kidd (Eds.), *New directions in attribution research* (Vol. 2). Hillsdale, N.J.: Erlbaum, 1978.

Snyder, M. L., & Wicklund, R. A. Attribute ambiguity. In J. H. Harvey, W. Ickes, & R. F. Kidd (Eds.), *New directions in attribution research* (Vol. 3). Hillsdale, N.J.: Erlbaum, 1981.

Solomon, S., Holmes, D. S., & McCaul, K. D. Behavioral control over aversive events: Does control that requires effort reduce anxiety and physiological arousal? *Journal of Personality and Social Psychology*, 1980, *39*, 729-736.

Sommers, S. Emotionality reconsidered: The role of cognition in emotional responsiveness. *Journal of Personality and Social Psychology*, 1981, *41*, 553-561.

Spanos, N. P., Horton, C., & Chaves, J. F. The effects of two cognitive strategies on pain threshold. *Journal of Abnormal Psychology*, 1975, *84*, 677-681.

Spence, K. W. *Behavior theory and conditioning*. New Haven, Conn.: Yale University Press, 1960.

Srull, T. K. Person memory: Some tests of associative storage and retrieval models. *Journal of Experimental Psychology*, 1981, *7*, 440-462.

Srull, T. K. Organizational and retrieval processes in person memory: An examination of processing objectives, presentation format, and the possible role of self-generated retrieval cues. *Journal of Personality and Social Psychology*, 1983, *44*, 1157-1170.

Srull, T. K., & Brand, J. F. Memory for information about persons: The effect of encoding operations on subsequent retrieval. *Journal of Verbal Learning and Verbal Behavior*, 1983, *22*, 219-230.

Srull, T. K., & Wyer, R. S., Jr. The role of category accessibility in the interpretation of information about persons: Some determinants and implications. *Journal of Personality and Social Psychology*, 1979, *37*, 1660-1672.

Srull, T. K., & Wyer, R. S., Jr. Category accessibility and social perception: Some implications for the study of person memory and interpersonal judgments. *Journal of Personality and Social Psychology*, 1980, *38*, 841-856.

Staats, A. W., & Staats, C. K. Attitudes established by classical conditioning. *Journal of Abnormal and Social Psychology*, 1958, *57*, 37-40.

Stang, D. J. Methodological factors in mere exposure research. *Psychological Bulletin*, 1974, *81*, 1014-1025.

Staub, E., & Kellet, D. S. Increasing pain tolerance by information about aversive stimuli. *Journal of Personality and Social Psychology*, 1972, *21*, 198-203.

Staub, E., Tursky, B., & Schwartz, G. E. Self-control and predictability: Their effects on reactions to aversive stimulation. *Journal of Personality and Social Psychology*, 1971, *18*, 157-162.

Steiner, I. D. Perceived freedom. In L. Berkowitz (Ed.), *Advances in experimental social psychology* (Vol. 5). New York: Academic Press, 1970.

Steiner, I. D. Three kinds of reported choice. In L. C. Perlmuter & R. A. Monty (Eds.), *Choice and perceived control*. Hillsdale, N.J.: Erlbaum, 1979.

Stephan, W. G., Berscheid, E., & Walster, E. Sexual arousal and heterosexual perception. *Journal of Personality and Social Psychology*, 1971, *20*, 93-101.

Stephan, W. G., Rosenfield, D., & Stephan, C. Egotism in males and females. *Journal of Personality and Social Psychology*, 1976, *34*, 1161-1167.

Sternberg, S. The discovery of processing stages: Extension of Donders method. In W. G. Koster (Ed.), *Attention and performance II*. Amsterdam: North-Holland, 1969. (a)

Sternberg, S. Memory scanning: Mental processes revealed by reaction-time experiments. *American Scientist*, 1969, *57*, 421-457. (b)

Sternthal, B., Dholakia, R., & Leavitt, C. The persuasive effect of source credibility: Tests of cognitive response. *Journal of Consumer Research, 1978, 4,* 252-260.

Stevens, L., & Jones, E. E. Defensive attribution and the Kelley cube. *Journal of Personality and Social Psychology,* 1976, *34,* 809-820.

Stoner, J. A. F. A comparison of individual and group decisions involving risk. Unpublished master's thesis, School of Industrial Management, MIT, 1961.

Storms, M. D. Videotape and the attribution process: Reversing actors' and observers' points of view. *Journal of Personality and Social Psychology,* 1973, *27,* 165-175.

Storms, M. D., & McCaul, K. D. Attribution processes and emotional exacerbation of dysfunctional behavior. In J. H. Harvey, W. J. Ickes, & R. F. Kidd (Eds.), *New directions in attribution research* (Vol. 1). Hillsdale, N.J.: Erlbaum, 1976.

Storms, M. D., & Nisbett, R. E. Insomnia and the attribution process. *Journal of Personality and Social Psychology,* 1970, *16,* 319-328.

Stotland, E., & Blumenthal, A. L. The reduction of anxiety as a result of the expectation of making a choice. *Canadian Journal of Psychology,* 1964, *18,* 139-145.

Stouffer, S. A., Suchman, E. A., DeVinney, L. C., Star, S. A., & Williams, R. M., Jr. *The American soldier: Vol. 1. Adjustment during army life.* Princeton, N.J.: Princeton University Press, 1949.

Strack, F., Erber, R., & Wicklund, R. A. Effects of salience and time pressure on ratings of social causality. *Journal of Experimental Social Psychology,* 1982, *18,* 581-594.

Strongman, K. T. *The psychology of emotion.* New York: Wiley, 1978.

Surber, C. F. Effects of information reliability in predicting task performance using ability and effort. *Journal of Personality and Social Psychology,* 1981, *40,* 977-989.

Swann, W. B., Jr., & Hill, C. A. When our identities are mistaken: Reaffirming self-conceptions through social interaction. *Journal of Personality and Social Psychology,* 1982, *43,* 59-66.

Swann, W. B., Jr. Self-verification: Bringing social reality into harmony with the self. In J. Suls & A. G. Greenwald (Eds.), *Psychological perspectives on the self* (Vol. 2). Hillsdale, N.J.: Erlbaum, 1983.

Swann, W. B., Jr., Giulano, T., & Wegner, D. M. Where leading questions can lead: The power of conjecture in social interaction. *Journal of Personality and Social Psychology,* 1982, *42,* 1025-1035.

Swann, W. B., Jr., & Hill, C. A. When our identities are mistaken: Reaffirming self-conceptions through social interaction. *Journal of Personality and Social Psychology,* 1982, *43,* 59-66.

Swann, W. B., Jr., & Miller, L. C. Why never forgetting a face matters: Visual imagery and social memory. *Journal of Personality and Social Psychology,* 1982, *43,* 475-480.

Swann, W. B., Jr., & Read, S. J. Acquiring self-knowledge: The search for feedback that fits. *Journal of Personality and Social Psychology,* 1981, *41,* 1119-1128. (a)

Swann, W. B., Jr., & Read, S. J. Self-verification processes: How we sustain our self-conceptions. *Journal of Experimental Social Psychology,* 1981, *17,* 351-372. (b)

Swann, W. B., Jr., & Snyder, M. On translating beliefs into action: Theories of ability and their application in an instructional setting. *Journal of Personality and Social Psychology,* 1980, *38,* 879-888.

Swann, W. B., Jr., Stephenson, B., & Pittman, T. S. Curiosity and control: On the determinants of the search for social knowledge. *Journal of Personality and Social Psychology,* 1981, *40,* 635-642.

Sweeney, P., & Moreland, R. L. Self-schemas and the perseverance of beliefs about the self. Paper presented at the meeting of the American Psychological Association, Montreal, September 1980.

Szpiler, F. A., & Epstein, S. Availability of an avoidance response as related to automatic arousal. *Journal of Abnormal Psychology*, 1976, *85*, 73-82.

Tagiuri, R., & Petrullo, L. (Eds.). *Person perception and interpersonal behavior*. Stanford, Calif.: Stanford University Press, 1958.

Tagliacozzo, D. L., & Mauksch, H. O. The patient's view of the patient's role. In E. G. Jaco (Ed.), *Patients, physicians, and illness* (2nd ed.). New York: Free Press, 1972.

Tajfel, H., Sheikh, A. A., & Gardner, R. C. Content of stereotypes and the inference of similarity between members of stereotyped groups. *Acta Psychologica*, 1964, *22*, 191-201.

Tajfel, H., & Wilkes, A. L. Classification and qualitative judgment. *British Journal of Psychology*, 1963, *54*, 101-114.

Tavris, C., & Offir, C. *The longest war*. New York: Harcourt Brace Jovanovich, 1977.

Taylor, D. A. Stage analysis of reaction time. *Psychological Bulletin*, 1976, *83*, 161-191.

Taylor, S. E. On inferring one's own attitudes from one's behavior: Some delimiting conditions. *Journal of Personality and Social Psychology*, 1975, *31*, 126-131.

Taylor, S. E. Hospital patient behavior: Reactance, helplessness, or control? *Journal of Social Issues*, 1979, *35*, 156-184.

Taylor, S. E. The interface of cognitive and social psychology. In J. Harvey (Ed.), *Cognition, social behavior, and the environment*. Hillsdale, N.J.: Erlbaum, 1981.

Taylor, S. E. The availability bias in social perception and interaction. In D. Kahneman, P. Slovic, & A. Tversky (Eds.), *Judgment under uncertainty: Heuristics and biases*. New York: Cambridge University Press, 1982. (a)

Taylor, S. E. Social cognition and health. *Personality and Social Psychology Bulletin*, 1982, *8*, 549-562. (b)

Taylor, S. E., & Crocker, J. Schematic bases of social information processing. In E. T. Higgins, C. P. Herman, & M. P. Zanna (Eds.), *Social cognition: The Ontario Symposium* (Vol. 1). Hillsdale, N.J.: Erlbaum, 1981.

Taylor, S. E., Crocker, J., & D'Agostino, J. Schematic bases of social problem-solving. *Personality and Social Psychology Bulletin*, 1978, *4*, 447-451.

Taylor, S. E., Crocker, J., Fiske, S. T., Sprinzen, M., & Winkler, J. D. The generalizability of salience effects. *Journal of Personality and Social Psychology*, 1979, *37*, 357-368.

Taylor, S. E., & Fiske, S. T. Point-of-view and perceptions of causality. *Journal of Personality and Social Psychology*, 1975, *32*, 439-445.

Taylor, S. E., & Fiske, S. T. Salience, attention, and attribution: Top of the head phenomena. In L. Berkowitz (Ed.), *Advances in experimental social psychology* (Vol. 11). New York: Academic Press, 1978.

Taylor, S. E., & Fiske, S. T. Getting inside the head: Methodologies for process analysis. In J. Harvey, W. Ickes, & R. Kidd (Eds.), *New directions in attribution research* (Vol. 3). Hillsdale, N.J.: Erlbaum, 1981.

Taylor, S. E., Fiske, S. T., Close, M., Anderson, C., & Ruderman, A. Solo status as a psychological variable: The power of being distinctive. Unpublished manuscript, Harvard University, 1977.

Taylor, S. E., Fiske, S. T., Etcoff, N. L., & Ruderman, A. J. Categorical bases of person memory and stereotyping. *Journal of Personality and Social Psychology*, 1978, *36*, 778-793.

Taylor, S. E., & Koivumaki, J. H. The perception of self and others: Acquaintanceship, affect, and actor-observer differences. *Journal of Personality and Social Psychology*, 1976, *33*, 403-408.

Taylor, S. E., Lichtman, R. R., & Wood, J. V. Adjustment to breast cancer: Physical, socio-demographic, and psychological predictors. Unpublished manuscript, University of California, Los Angeles, 1982.

Taylor, S. E., Lichtman, R. R., & Wood, J. V. Attributions, beliefs about control, and adjustment to breast cancer. *Journal of Personality and Social Psychology*, in press.

Taylor, S. E., & Thompson, S. C. Stalking the elusive "vividness" effect. *Psychological Review*, 1982, *89*, 155-181.

Taylor, S. E., & Winkler, J. D. Development of schemas. Paper presented at the meeting of the American Psychological Association, Montreal, September 1980.

Taylor, S. E., & Wood, J. V. The vividness effect: Making a mountain out of a molehill? In R. P. Bagozzi & A. M. Tybout (Eds.), *Advances in consumer research*. Ann Arbor: Association for Consumer Research, 1983.

Teasdale, J. D., & Fogarty, S. J. Differential effort of induced mood on retrieval of pleasant and unplesant events from episodic memory. *Journal of Abnormal Psychology*, 1979, *88*, 248-257.

Tedeschi, J. T., & Lindskold, S. *Social psychology: Interdependence, interaction, and influence*. New York: Wiley, 1976.

Tennen, H., & Eller, S. J. Attributional components of learned helplessness and facilitation. *Journal of Personality and Social Psychology*, 1977, *35*, 265-271.

Tesser, A. Self-generated attitude change. In L. Berkowitz (Ed.), *Advances in experimental social psychology* (Vol. 11). New York: Academic Press, 1978.

Tesser, A., & Conlee, M. C. Some effects of time and thought on attitude polarization. *Journal of Personality and Social Psychology*, 1975, *31*, 262-270.

Tesser, A., & Leone, C. Cognitive schemas and thought as determinants of attitude change. *Journal of Experimental Social Psychology*, 1977, *13*, 340-356.

Tetlock, P. E., & Levi, A. Attribution bias: On the inconclusiveness of the cognition-motivation debate. *Journal of Experimental Social Psychology*, 1982, *18*, 68-88.

Thibaut, J. W., & Kelley, H. H. *The social psychology of groups*. New York: Wiley, 1959.

Thompson, S. C. Will it hurt less if I can control it? A complex answer to a simple question. *Psychological Bulletin*, 1981, *90*, 89-101.

Thompson, S. C., & Kelley, J. J. Judgments of responsibility for activities in close relationships. *Journal of Personality and Social Psychology*, 1981, *41*, 469-477.

Thorndike, E. L. *Human nature and the social order*. New York: Macmillan, 1940.

Thorndyke, P. W., & Hayes-Roth, B. The use of schemata in the acquisition and transfer of knowledge. *Cognitive Psychology*, 1979, *11*, 82-106.

Thorndyke, P. W., & Yekovich, F. R. A critique of schema-based theories of human story memory. *Poetics*, 1980, *9*, 23-49.

Tillman, W. S., & Carver, C. S. Actors' and observers' attributions for success and failure: A comparative test of predictions from Kelley's cube, self-serving bias, and positivity bias formulations. *Journal of Experimental Social Psychology*, 1980, *16*, 18-32.

Tomkins, S. S. *Affect, imagery, and consciousness* (Vol. 1). New York: Springer, 1962.

Tomkins, S. S. Script theory: Differential magnification of affects. In H. E. Howe, Jr., & R. A. Dienstbier (Eds.), *Nebraska Symposium on Motivation* (Vol. 26). Lincoln: University of Nebraska Press, 1980.

Tomkins, S. S. The quest for primary motives: Biography and autobiography of an idea. *Journal of Personality and Social Psychology*, 1981, *41*, 306-329. (a)

Tomkins, S. S. The role of facial response in the experience of emotion: A reply to Tourangeau and Ellsworth. *Journal of Personality and Social Psychology*, 1981, *40*, 355-357. (b)

Tourangeau, R., & Ellsworth, P. C. The role of facial response in the experience of emotion. *Journal of Personality and Social Psychology*, 1979, *37*, 1519-1531.

Trope, Y. Seeking information about one's own ability as a determinant of choice among tasks. *Journal of Personality and Social Psychology*, 1975, *32*, 1004-1013.

Trope, Y. Uncertainty-reducing properties of achievement tasks. *Journal of Personality and Social Psychology*, 1979, *37*, 1505-1518.

Trope, Y. Self-assessment, self-enhancement, and taste preference. *Journal of Experimental Social Psychology*, 1980, *16*, 116-129.

Trope, Y. Self-assessment in achievement behavior. In J. M. Suls & A. G. Greenwald (Eds.), *Psychological perspectives on the self* (Vol. 2). Hillsdale, N.J.: Erlbaum, 1983.

Trope, Y., & Alon, E. Testing hypotheses about the personality of another person. Unpublished manuscript, University of Toronto, 1980.

Trope, Y., & Bassok, M. Confirmatory and diagnosing strategies in social information gathering. *Journal of Personality and Social Psychology*, 1982, *43*, 22-34.

Trope, Y., & Ben-Yair, E. Task construction and persistence as means for self-assessment of abilities. *Journal of Personality and Social Psychology*, 1982, *42*, 637-645.

Trope, Y., & Burnstein, E. A disposition-behavior congruity model of perceived freedom. *Journal of Experimental Social Psychology*, 1977, *13*, 357-368.

Tsujimoto, R. N. Memory bias toward normative and novel trait prototypes. *Journal of Personality and Social Psychology*, 1978, *36*, 1391-1401.

Tsujimoto, R. N., Wilde, J., & Robertson, D. R. Distorted memory for exemplars of a social structure: Evidence for schematic memory processes. *Journal of Personality and Social Psychology*, 1978, *36*, 1402-1414.

Tulving, E. Episodic and semantic memory. In E. Tulving & W. Donaldson (Eds.), *Organization of memory*. New York: Academic Press, 1972.

Tunnell, G. Sex role and cognitive schemata: Person perception in feminine and androgynous women. *Journal of Personality and Social Psychology*, 1981, *40*, 1126-1136.

Turing, A. M. Computing machinery and intelligence. *Mind*, 1950, *59*, 433-460.

Turner, R. G., Scheier, M. F., Carver, C. S., & Ickes, W. Correlates of self-consciousness. *Journal of Personality Assessment*, 1978, *42*, 285-289.

Tversky, A., & Kahneman, D. Availability: A heuristic for judging frequency and probability. *Cognitive Psychology*, 1973, *5*, 207-232.

Tversky, A., & Kahneman, D. Judgment under uncertainty: Heuristics and biases. *Science*, 1974, *185*, 1124-1131.

Tversky, A., & Kahneman, D. Causal schemata in judgments under uncertainty. In M. Fishbein (Ed.), *Progress in social psychology*. Hillsdale, N.J.: Erlbaum, 1978.

Tversky, A., & Kahneman, D. Judgments of and by representativeness. In D. Kahneman, P. Slovic, & A. Tversky (Eds.), *Judgment under uncertainty: Heuristics and biases*. New York: Cambridge University Press, 1982.

Tybout, A. M., & Scott, C. A. Availability of well-defined internal knowledge and the attitude formation process: Information aggregation versus self-perception. *Journal of Personality and Social Psychology*, 1983, *44*, 474-491.

Tyler, T., & Devinitz, V. Self-serving bias in the attribution of responsibility: Cognitive versus motivational explanations. *Journal of Experimental Social Psychology*, 1981, *17*, 408-416.

Valins, S. Cognitive effects of false heart-rate feedback. *Journal of Personality and Social Psychology*, 1966, *4*, 400-408.

Valins, S., & Nisbett, R. E. Attribution processes in the development and treatment of emotional disorders. In E. E. Jones, D. E. Kanouse, H. H. Kelley, R. E. Nisbett, S. Valins, & B. Weiner (Eds.), *Attribution: Perceiving the causes of behavior.* Morristown, N.J.: General Learning Press, 1972.

Valins, S., & Ray, A. Effects of cognitive desensitization on avoidance behavior. *Journal of Personality and Social Psychology*, 1967, *20*, 239-250.

Vallacher, R. R., & Solodky, M. Objective self-awareness, standards of evaluation, and moral behavior. *Journal of Experimental Social Psychology*, 1979, *15*, 254-262.

Vidmar, N., & Rokeach, M. Archie Bunker's bigotry: A study in selective perception and exposure. *Journal of Communication*, 1974, *24*, 36-47.

Vinokur, A., & Ajzen, I. Relative importance of prior and immediate events: A causal primacy effect. *Journal of Personality and Social Psychology*, 1982, *42*, 820-829.

Wachtler, J., & Counselman, E. When increasing liking for a communicator decreases opinion change: An attributional analysis of attractiveness. *Journal of Experimental Social Psychology*, 1981, *17*, 386-395.

Wallach, M. A., Kogan, N., & Bem, D. J. Group influence on individual risk taking. *Journal of Abnormal and Social Psychology*, 1962, *65*, 75-86.

Wallston, B. S., & Wallston, K. A. Locus of control and health: A review of the literature. *Health Education Monographs*, 1978, *6*, 107-117.

Walster, E. Assignment of responsibility for an accident. *Journal of Personality and Social Psychology*, 1966, *3*, 73-79.

Walster, E. Passionate love. In B. I. Murstein (Ed.), *Theories of attraction and love.* New York: Springer, 1971.

Ward, W. D., & Jenkins, H. M. The display of information and the judgment of contingency. *Canadian Journal of Psychology*, 1965, *19*, 231-241.

Warr, P., Barter, J., & Brownbridge, G. On the independence of positive and negative affect. *Journal of Personality and Social Psychology*, 1983, *44*, 644-651.

Watson, J. *Behaviorism.* New York: Norton, 1930.

Weary, G. Examination of affect and egotism as mediators of bias in causal attributions. *Journal of Personality and Social Psychology*, 1980, *38*, 348-357.

Weary, G., Harvey, J. H., Schweiger, P., Olson, C. T., Perloff, R., & Pritchard, S. Self-presentation and the moderation of the self-serving bias. *Social Cognition*, 1982, *1*, 140-159.

Weary, G., Swanson, H., Harvey, J. H., & Yarkin, K. L. A molar approach to social knowing. *Personality and Social Psychology Bulletin*, 1980, *6*, 574-581.

Weber, R., & Crocker, J. Cognitive processes in the revision of stereotypic beliefs. *Journal of Personality and Social Psychology*, 1983, *45*, 961-977.

Wegner, D. M., & Finstuen, K. Observers' focus of attention in the simulation of self-perception. *Journal of Personality and Social Psychology*, 1977, *35*, 56-62.

Wegner, D. M., & Vallacher, R. R. Common-sense psychology. In J. Forgas (Ed.), *Social cognition: Perspectives on everyday understanding*. New York: Academic Press, 1981.

Weidner, G., & Matthews, K. A. Reported physical symptoms elicited by unpredictable events and the Type A coronary-prone behavior pattern. *Journal of Personality and Social Psychology*, 1978, *77*, 1213-1220.

Weiner, B. A theory of motivation for some classroom experiences. *Journal of Educational Psychology*, 1979, *71*, 3-25.

Weiner, B. A cognitive (attribution)-emotion-action model of motivated behavior: An analysis of judgment of help-giving. *Journal of Personality and Social Psychology*, 1980, *39*, 186-200. (a)

Weiner, B. *Human motivation*. New York: Holt, Rinehart and Winston, 1980. (b)

Weiner, B. The emotional consequences of causal attributions. In M. S. Clark & S. T. Fiske (Eds.), *Affect and cognition: The 17th Annual Carnegie Symposium on Cognition*. Hillsdale, N.J.: Erlbaum, 1982.

Weiner, B., Frieze, I., Kukla, A., Reed, L., Rest, S., & Rosenbaum, R. M. Perceiving the causes of success and failure. In E. E. Jones, D. E. Kanouse, H. H. Kelley, R. E. Nisbett, S. Valins, & B. Weiner (Eds.), *Attribution: Perceiving the causes of behavior*. Morristown, N.J.: General Learning Press, 1972.

Weiner, B., & Litman-Adizes, T. An attributional, expectancy-value analysis of learned helplessness and depression. In J. Garber & M. E. P. Seligman (Eds.), *Human helplessness: Theory and applications*. New York: Plenum, 1980.

Weiner, B., Russell, D., & Lerman, D. Affective consequences of causal ascriptions. In J. H. Harvey, W. J. Ickes, & R. F. Kidd (Eds.), *New directions in attribution research* (Vol. 2). Hillsdale, N.J.: Erlbaum, 1978.

Weiner, B., Russell, D., & Lerman, D. The cognition-emotion process in achievement-related contexts. *Journal of Personality and Social Psychology*, 1979, *37*, 1211-1220.

Weiss, J. A., & Brown, P. Self-insight error in the explanation of mood. Unpublished manuscript, Harvard University, 1977.

Weiss, J. M. Effects of coping behavior in different warning signal conditions on stress pathology in rats. *Journal of Comparative and Physiological Psychology*, 1971, *77*, 1-30.

Weiss, J. M., Glazer, H. I., & Pohorecky, L. A. Neurotransmitters and helplessness: A chemical bridge to depression. *Psychology Today*, 1974, *8*, 58-62.

Weiss, J. M., Glazer, H. I., & Pohorecky, L. A. Coping behavior and neurochemical changes: An alternative explanation for the original "learned helplessness" experiments. In G. Serban & A. Kling (Eds.), *Animal models in human psychobiology*. New York: Plenum, 1976.

Weiss, J. M., Stone, E. A., & Harrell, N. Coping behavior and brain norepinephrine level in rats. *Journal of Comparative and Physiological Psychology*, 1970, *72*, 153-160.

Weitz, S. (Ed.). *Nonverbal communication*. New York: Oxford University Press, 1974.

Wells, G. L., & Harvey, J. H. Do people use consensus information in making causal attributions? *Journal of Personality and Social Psychology*, 1977, *35*, 279-293.

Wells, G. L., Lindsay, R. C. L., & Tousignant, J. P. Effects of expert psychological advice on human performance in judging the validity of eyewitness testimony. *Law and Human Behavior*, 1980, *4*, 275-285.

Wetzel, C. G. Self-serving biases in attribution: A Bayesian analysis. *Journal of Personality and Social Psychology*, 1982, *43*, 197-209.

Weyant, J. M. Effects of mood states, costs, and benefits of helping. *Journal of Personality and Social Psychology*, 1978, *36*, 1169-1176.

White, G. L., Fishbein, S., & Rutstein, J. Passionate love and the misattribution of arousal. *Journal of Personality and Social Psychology*, 1981, *41*, 56-62.

White, P. Limitation on verbal reports of internal events: A refutation of Nisbett and Wilson and of Bem. *Psychological Review*, 1980, *87*, 105-112.

White, R. W. Motivation reconsidered: The concept of competence. *Psychological Review*, 1959, *66*, 297-333.

Wickelgren, W. A. Human learning and memory. *Annual Review of Psychology*, 1981, *32*, 21-52.

Wicker, A. W. Attitudes vs. actions: The relationship of verbal and overt behavioral responses to attitude objects. *Journal of Social Issues*, 1969, *41*, 41-78.

Wicklund, R. A. *Freedom and reactance*. Hillsdale, N.J.: Erlbaum, 1974.

Wicklund, R. A. Objective self-awareness. In L. Berkowitz (Ed.), *Advances in experimental social psychology* (Vol. 8). New York: Academic Press, 1975.

Wicklund, R. A. Three years later. In L. Berkowitz (Ed.), *Cognitive theories in social psychology*. New York: Academic Press, 1978.

Wicklund, R. A. The influence of self-awareness on human behavior. *American Scientist*, 1979, *67*, 187-193.

Wicklund, R. A., & Brehm, J. W. *Perspectives on cognitive dissonance*. Hillsdale, N.J.: Erlbaum, 1976.

Wicklund, R. A., & Duval, S. Opinion change and performance facilitation as a result of objective self-awareness. *Journal of Experimental Social Psychology*, 1971, *7*, 319-342.

Wicklund, R. A., & Frey, D. Self-awareness theory: When the self makes a difference. In D. M. Wegner & R. R. Vallacher (Eds.), *The self in social psychology*. New York: Oxford University Press, 1980.

Wicklund, R. A., & Hormuth, S. E. On the functions of the self: A reply to Hull and Levy. *Journal of Personality and Social Psychology*, 1981, *40*, 1029-1037.

Wilder, D. A. Perceiving persons as a group: Categorization and intergroup relations. In D. L. Hamilton (Ed.), *Cognitive processes in stereotyping and intergroup behavior*. Hillsdale, N.J.: Erlbaum, 1981.

Wilder, D. A., & Allen, V. L. Group membership and preference for information about others. *Personality and Social Psychology Bulletin*, 1978, *4*, 106-110.

Wilder, D. A., & Cooper, W. E. Categorization into groups: Consequences for social perception and attribution. In J. Harvey, W. Ickes, & R. Kidd (Ed.), *New directions in attribution research* (Vol. 3). Hillsdale, N.J.: Erlbaum, 1981.

Wilder, D. A., & Thompson, J. E. Intergroup contact with independent manipulations of ingroup and outgroup interaction. *Journal of Personality and Social Psychology*, 1980, *38*, 589-603.

Wills, T. A. Downward comparison principles in social psychology. *Psychological Bulletin*, 1981, *90*, 245-271.

Wilson, T. D., Hull, J. G., & Johnson, J. Awareness and self-perception: Verbal reports on internal states. *Journal of Personality and Social Psychology*, 1981, *40*, 53-70.

Wilson, T. D., & Lassiter, G. D. Increasing intrinsic interest with superfluous extrinsic constraints. *Journal of Personality and Social Psychology*, 1982, *42*, 811-819.

Wilson, T. D., & Linville, P. W. Improving the academic performance of college freshmen: Attribution therapy revisited. *Journal of Personality and Social Psychology*, 1982, *42*, 367-376.

Wilson, T. D., & Nisbett, R. E. The accuracy of verbal reports about the effects of stimuli on evaluations and behavior. *Social Psychology*, 1978, *41*, 118-131.

Wilson, W., & Miller, H. Repetition, order of presentation, and timing of arguments and measures as determinants of opinion change. *Journal of Personality and Social Psychology*, 1968, *9*, 184-188.

Wilson, W. R. Feeling more than we can know: Exposure effects without learning. *Journal of Personality and Social Psychology*, 1979, *37*, 811-821.

Wine, J. Test anxiety and direction of attention. *Psychological Bulletin*, 1971, *76*, 92-104.

Winkler, J., & Taylor, S. E. Preference, expectations, and attributional bias: Two field studies. *Journal of Applied Social Psychology*, 1979, *2*, 183-197.

Wittgenstein, L. *Philosophical investigations*. New York: Macmillan, 1953.

Wixon, D. R., & Laird, J. D. Awareness and attitude change in the forced-compliance paradigm: The importance of when. *Journal of Personality and Social Psychology*, 1976, *34*, 376-384.

Wolfson, M. R., & Salancik, G. R. Observer orientation and actor-observer differences in attributions for failure. *Journal of Experimental Social Psychology*, 1977, *5*, 441-451.

Wolk, S., & DuCette, J. Intentional performance and incidental learning as a function of personality and task dimension. *Journal of Personality and Social Psychology*, 1974, *29*, 90-101.

Woll, S. B., & Graesser, A. C. Memory discrimination for information typical or atypical of person schemata. *Social Cognition*, 1982, *1*, 287-310.

Woll, S. B., & Martinez, J. M. The effects of biasing labels on recognition of facial expressions of emotion. *Social Cognition*, 1982, *1*, 70-82.

Woll, S. B., Weeks, D. G., Fraps, C. L., Pendergrass, J., & Vanderplas, M. A. Role of sentence context in the encoding of trait descriptors. *Journal of Personality and Social Psychology*, 1980, *39*, 59-68.

Wolman, C., & Frank, H. The solo woman in a professional peer group. *American Journal of Orthopsychiatry*, 1975, *45*, 164-171.

Wong, P., & Weiner, B. When people ask "why" questions, and the heuristics of attributional search. *Journal of Personality and Social Psychology*, 1981, *40*, 650-663.

Wood, W. Retrieval of attitude-relevant information from memory: Effects on susceptibility to persuasion and on intrinsic motivation. *Journal of Personality and Social Psychology*, 1982, *42*, 798-810.

Wood, W., & Eagly, A. H. Stages in the analysis of persuasive messages: The role of causal attributions and message comprehension. *Journal of Personality and Social Psychology*, 1981, *40*, 246-259.

Word, C. O., Zanna, M. P., & Cooper, J. The nonverbal mediation of self-fulfilling prophecies in interracial interaction. *Journal of Experimental Social Psychology*, 1974, *10*, 109-120.

Wortman, C. B. Some determinants of perceived control. *Journal of Personality and Social Psychology*, 1975, *31*, 282-294.

Wortman, C. B. Causal attributions and personal control. In J. H. Harvey, W. Ickes, & R. F. Kidd (Eds.), *New directions in attribution research* (Vol. 1). Hillsdale, N.J.: Erlbaum, 1976.

Wortman, C. B., & Brehm, J. W. Responses to uncontrollable outcomes: An integration of reactance theory and the learned helplessness model. In L. Berkowitz (Ed.), *Advances in experimental social psychology* (Vol. 8). New York: Academic Press, 1975.

Wortman, C. B., Costanzo, P. R., & Witt, T. R. Effect of anticipated performance on the attributions of causality to self and others. *Journal of Personality and Social Psychology,* 1973, *27,* 372-381.

Wortman, C. B., & Dintzer, L. Is an attributional analysis of the learned helplessness phenomenon viable? A critique of the Abramson-Seligman-Teasdale reformulation. *Journal of Abnormal Psychology,* 1978, *87,* 75-90.

Wortman, C. B., & Dunkel-Schetter, C. Interpersonal relationships and cancer: A theoretical analysis. *Journal of Social Issues,* 1979, *35,* 120-155.

Wright, J., & Mischel, W. Influence of affect on cognitive social learning person variables. *Journal of Personality and Social Psychology,* 1982, *43,* 901-914.

Wright, P. Cognitive responses to mass media advocacy. In R. E. Petty, T. M. Ostrom, & T. C. Brock (Eds.), *Cognitive responses in persuasion.* Hillsdale, N.J.: Erlbaum, 1981.

Wright, P., & Rip, P. D. Retrospective reports on the causes of decisions. *Journal of Personality and Social Psychology,* 1981, *40,* 601-614.

Wright, R. A., & Brehm, S. S. Reactance as impression management: A critical review. *Journal of Personality and Social Psychology,* 1982, *42,* 608-618.

Wundt, W. *Outlines of psychology.* New York: Stechert, 1897. (Translated 1907).

Wyer, R. S., Jr. Changes in meaning and halo effects in personality impression formation. *Journal of Personality and Social Psychology,* 1974, *29,* 829-835.

Wyer, R. S., Jr. An investigation of relations among probability estimates. *Organizational Behavior and Human Performance,* 1976, *15,* 1-18.

Wyer, R. S., Jr., & Gordon, S. E. The recall of information about persons and groups. *Journal of Experimental Social Psychology,* 1982, *18,* 128-164.

Wyer, R. S., Jr., Henninger, M., & Hinkle, R. An information analysis of actors' and observers' belief attributions in a role-playing situation. *Journal of Experimental Social Psychology,* 1977, *13,* 199-217.

Wyer, R. S., Jr., & Srull, T. K. The processing of social stimulus information: A conceptual integration. In R. Hastie, T. M. Ostrom, E. B. Ebbesen, R. S. Wyer, D. Hamilton, & D. E. Carlston (Eds.), *Person memory: The cognitive basis of social perception.* Hillsdale, N.J.: Erlbaum, 1980.

Wyer, R. S., Jr., & Srull, T. K. Category accessibility: Some theoretical and empirical issues concerning the processing of social stimulus information. In E. T. Higgins, C. P. Herman, & M. P. Zanna (Eds.), *Social cognition: The Ontario Symposium* (Vol. 1). Hillsdale, N.J.: Erlbaum, 1981.

Wyer, R. S., Jr., Srull, T. K., Gordon, S. E., & Hartwick, J. Effects of processing objectives on the recall of prose material. *Journal of Personality and Social Psychology,* 1982, *43,* 674-688.

Wyer, R. S., Jr., & Watson, S. F. Context effects in impression formation. *Journal of Personality and Social Psychology,* 1969, *12,* 22-33.

Wylie, R. *The self concept.* Lincoln: University of Nebraska Press, 1979.

Yandrell, B., & Insko, C. A. Attribution of attitudes to speakers and listeners under assigned-behavior conditions: Does behavior engulf the field? *Journal of Experimental Social Psychology,* 1977, *3,* 269-278.

Yarkin, K. L., Harvey, J. H., & Bloxom, B. M. Cognitive sets, attribution, and social interaction. *Journal of Personality and Social Psychology,* 1981, *41,* 243-252.

Yarkin, K. L., Town, J. P., & Wallston, B. S. Blacks and women must try harder: Stimulus persons' race and sex attributions of causality. *Personality and Social Psychology Bulletin,* 1982, *8,* 21-24.

Zadny, J., & Gerard, H. B. Attributed intentions and informational selectivity. *Journal of Experimental Social Psychology*, 1974, *10*, 34-52.

Zajonc, R. B. Attitudinal effects of mere exposure. *Journal of Personality and Social Psychology, Monograph Supplement*, 1968, *9*, 1-27. (a)

Zajonc, R. B. Cognitive theories in social psychology. In G. Lindzey & E. Aronson (Eds.), *The handbook of social psychology* (Vol. 1, 2nd ed.). Reading, Mass.: Addison-Wesley, 1968. (b)

Zajonc, R. B. Cognition and social cognition: A historical perspective. In L. Festinger (Ed.), *Four decades of social psychology*. New York: Oxford University Press, 1980. (a)

Zajonc, R. B. Feeling and thinking: Preferences need no inferences. *American Psychologist*, 1980, *35*, 151-175. (b)

Zajonc, R. B., & Burnstein, E. The learning of balanced and unbalanced social structures. *Journal of Personality*, 1965, *33*, 153-163. (a)

Zajonc, R. B., & Burnstein, E. Structural balance, reciprocity, and positivity as sources of cognitive bias. *Journal of Personality*, 1965, *33*, 570-583. (b)

Zajonc, R. B., Pietromonaco, P., & Bargh, J. Independence and interaction of affect and cognition. In M. S. Clark & S. T. Fiske (Eds.), *Affect and cognition: The 17th Annual Carnegie Symposium on Cognition*. Hillsdale, N.J.: Erlbaum, 1982.

Zanna, M. P., & Cooper, J. Dissonance and the attribution process. In J. H. Harvey, W. J. Ickes, & R. F. Kidd (Eds.), *New directions in attribution research* (Vol. 1). Hillsdale, N.J.: Erlbaum, 1976.

Zanna, M. P., & Fazio, R. H. The attitude-behavior relation: Moving toward a third generation of research. In M. P. Zanna, E. T. Higgins, & C. P. Herman (Eds.), *Consistency in social behavior: The Ontario Symposium* (Vol. 2). Hillsdale, N.J.: Erlbaum, 1982.

Zanna, M. P., & Hamilton, D. L. Further evidence for meaning change in impression formation. *Journal of Experimental Social Psychology*, 1977, *13*, 224-238.

Zanna, M. P., & Olson, J. M. Individual differences in attitudinal relations. In M. P. Zanna, E. T. Higgins, & C. P. Herman (Eds.), *Consistency in social behavior: The Ontario Symposium* (Vol. 2). Hillsdale, N.J.: Erlbaum, 1982.

Zanna, M. P., Olson, J. M., & Fazio, R. H. Attitude-behavior consistency: An individual difference perspective. *Journal of Personality and Social Psychology*, 1980, *38*, 432-440.

Zanna, M. P., Olson, J. M., & Fazio, R. H. Self-perception and attitude-behavior consistency. *Personality and Social Psychology Bulletin*, 1981, *7*, 252-256.

Zanna, M. P., & Pack, S. J. On the self-fulfilling nature of apparent sex differences in behavior. *Journal of Experimental Social Psychology*, 1975, *11*, 583-591.

Zillmann, D. Excitation transfer in communication-mediated aggressive behavior. *Journal of Experimental Social Psychology*, 1971, *7*, 419-434.

Zillmann, D. Attribution and misattribution of excitatory reactions. In J. H. Harvey, W. Ickes, & R. F. Kidd (Eds.), *New directions in attribution research* (Vol. 2). New York: Wiley, 1978.

Zillmann, D., & Bryant, J. Effect of residual excitation on the emotional response to provocation and delayed aggressive behavior. *Journal of Personality and Social Psychology*, 1974, *30*, 782-791.

Zillmann, D., Katcher, A. H., & Milavsky, B. Excitation transfer from physical exercise to subsequent aggressive behavior. *Journal of Experimental Social Psychology*, 1972, *8*, 247-259.

Zimbardo, P. G. Involvement and communication discrepancy as determinants of opinion conformity. *Journal of Abnormal and Social Psychology*, 1960, *60*, 86-94.

Zimbardo, P. G. *The cognitive control of motivation: The consequence of choice and dissonance.* Glenview, Ill.: Scott, Foresman, 1969.

Zimbardo, P. G., Ebbesen, E. B., & Maslach, C. *Influencing attitudes and changing behavior.* Reading, Mass.: Addison-Wesley, 1977.

Zuckerman, M. On the endogenous-exogenous partition in attribution theory. *Personality and Social Psychology Bulletin,* 1977, *3,* 389-399.

Zuckerman, M. Actions and occurrences in Kelley's cube. *Journal of Personality and Social Psychology,* 1978, *36,* 647-656.

Zuckerman, M. Attribution of success and failure revisited, or: The motivational bias is alive and well in attribution theory. *Journal of Personality,* 1979, *47,* 245-287.

Zuckerman, M., Klorman, R., Larrance, D. T., & Spiegel, N. H. Facial, autonomic, and subjective components of emotion: The facial feedback hypothesis versus the externalizer-internalizer distinction. *Journal of Personality and Social Psychology,* 1981, *41,* 929-944.

Zuckerman, M., & Mann, R. W. The other way around: Effects of causal attributions on estimates of consensus, distinctiveness, and consistency. *Journal of Experimental Social Psychology,* 1979, *15,* 582-597.

Zuckerman, M., Mann, R. W., & Bernieri, F. J. Determinants of consensus estimates: Attribution, salience, and representativeness. *Journal of Personality and Social Psychology,* 1982, *42,* 839-852.

Zukier, H. The role of the correlation and the dispersion of predictor variables in the use of nondiagnostic information. *Journal of Personality and Social Psychology,* 1982, *43,* 1163-1175.

author index

Achievement attribution model, 47, 49-53
    affect in, 50-53, 56
    applications of, 52-53
        to helping behavior, 51
        to sex stereotyping, 53-55
    critiques of, 52-53
Actor-observer effect, 76-80, 98
    informational explanation of, 77-78
    limitations of, 79-80, 98
    perceptual explanation of, 76
Affect, 414
    and alternative outcomes, 324-326, 338
    ambivalence of, 311-312
    arousal theories of, 313-316, 337-338
    attributional theories of, 322-324, 338
    characteristics of, 333-334
    cognitive theories of, 317-333, 337, 338
        behaviorist theories versus, 315
        emotional lability, 317
    complexity of, 310-311
    definition of, 310
    determinants of, 410-411
    dimensions of, 311, 312
    effect of individual differences on, 321
    effect of schemata on, 321-322, 338
    encoding as basis of, 335-336
    and facial feedback theory, 313-314,
        337-338
    impact of, 326-333, 338-339
        on behavior, 328, 329
        on inference, 328-329
        on memory, 326-330, 338
    as interrupting effect, 331-333, 338-339
    interruption and arousal theories of,
        318-319
    and intimate relationships, 319-321
    and mere exposure effect, 335, 337
    methodological problems in study of,
        336-337
    network models of, 330-331

subject index

    relationship of to cognition, 333-337,
        339, 410, 411
    methodological issues in, 336-337
Anchoring and adjustment heuristic, 273-
    274, 275, 284, 408-409
    as false consensus effect, 273
Anxiety, effect of attention on, 209-210,
    212
Arousal
    attributional analyses of, 36-39, 68-70
    impact of on affect, 313-316, 337-338
    interrupts as cause of, 318-319, 338
    in social cognition theory, 315, 316
Attention, 184-212, 414
    components of, 184, 194
    definition of, 184
    effects of consistency on, 360, 361, 368
    and exaggerated attributions, 194-196
    and extreme evaluations, 188, 189-190
    focus of, 405-406, 407
    impact of, 199, 407
        on anxiety, 209-210, 212
        on behavior, 210, 212
        on causal attributions, 188, 189-190,
            406
        on memory, 188-189
    individual differences in, 203-207, 211,
        406
        locus of control, 205-206
        need for stimulation, 206-207
        repression-sensitization dimension,
            206
        self-consciousness, 203-205
        self-monitoring, 207